Macmillan/McGraw-Hill Edition

McGRAW-HILL READING

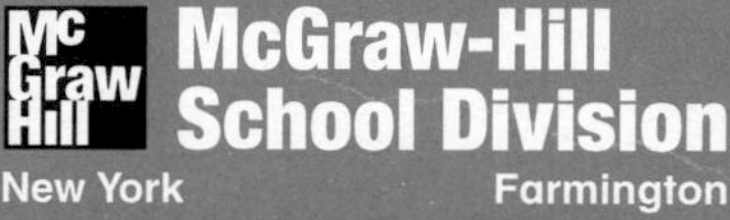

McGraw-Hill School Division
New York Farmington

Contributors

The Princeton Review, Time Magazine, Accelerated Reader

The Princeton Review is not affiliated with Princeton University or ETS.

McGraw-Hill School Division

A Division of The ***McGraw-Hill*** *Companies*

McGraw-Hill School Division
Two Penn Plaza
New York, New York 10121

Printed in the United States of America

ISBN 0-02-184760-6/3, Bk.1, U.2
5 6 7 8 9 043/073 04 03 02 01

McGRAW-HILL READING

McGraw-Hill
School Division
New York
Farmington

Selected Quizzes Prepared by
Accelerated Reader

McGraw-Hill Reading Authors Make the Difference...

Dr. James Flood

Ms. Angela Shelf Medearis

Dr. Jan E. Hasbrouck

Dr. Scott Paris

Dr. James V. Hoffman

Dr. Steven Stahl

Dr. Diane Lapp

Dr. Josefina Villamil Tinajero

Dr. Karen D. Wood

Contributing Authors

Dr. Barbara Coulter

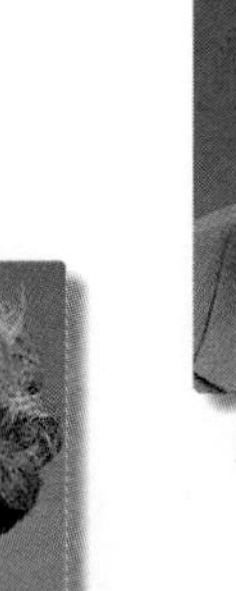
Ms. Frankie Dungan

Dr. Joseph B. Rubin

Dr. Carl B. Smith

Dr. Shirley Wright

Part 1

START TOGETHER

Focus on Reading and Skills

All students start with the SAME:

- Read Aloud
- Pretaught Skills
  - Phonics
  - Comprehension
- Build Background
- Selection Vocabulary

...Never hold a child back. Never leave a child behind.

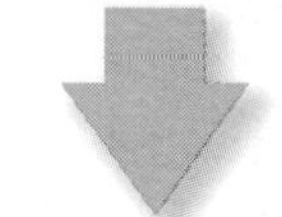

Part 2

MEET INDIVIDUAL NEEDS

Read the Literature

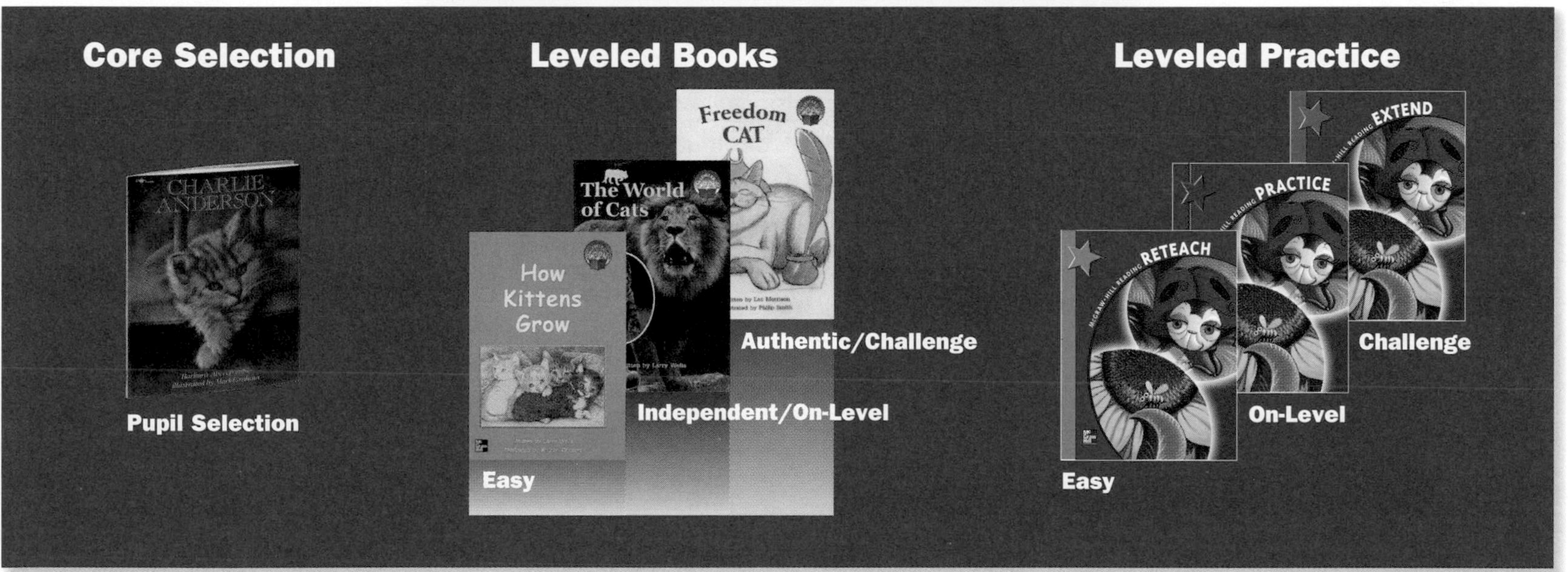

Examples Taken From Grade 2

Part 3

FINISH TOGETHER

Build Skills

All students finish with the SAME:

- Phonics
- Comprehension
- Vocabulary
- Study Skills
- Assessment

McGraw-Hill Reading Applying the Research

Phonological Awareness

Phonological awareness is the ability to hear the sounds in spoken language. It includes the ability to separate spoken words into discrete sounds as well as the ability to blend sounds together to make words. A child with good phonological awareness can identify rhyming words, hear the separate syllables in a word, separate the first sound in a word (onset) from the rest of the word (rime), and blend sounds together to make words.

Recent research findings have strongly concluded that children with good phonological awareness skills are more likely to learn to read well. These skills can be improved through systematic, explicit instruction involving auditory practice. McGraw-Hill Reading develops these key skills by providing an explicit Phonological Awareness lesson in every selection at grades K-2. Motivating activities such as blending, segmenting, and rhyming help to develop children's awareness of the sounds in our language.

Guided Instruction/ Guided Reading

Research on reading shows that guided instruction enables students to develop as independent, strategic readers. The *reciprocal-teaching model* of Anne-Marie Palincsar encourages teachers to model strategic-thinking, questioning, clarifying, and problem-solving strategies for students as students read together with the teacher. In McGraw-Hill Reading, guided instruction for all Pupil Edition selections incorporates the Palincsar model by providing interactive questioning prompts. The *guided-reading model* of Gay Su Pinnell is also incorporated into the McGraw-Hill Reading program. Through the guided-reading lessons provided for the leveled books offered with the program, teachers can work with small groups of students of different ability levels, closely observing them as they read and providing support specific to their needs.

By adapting instruction to include successful models of teaching and the appropriate materials to deliver instruction, McGraw-Hill Reading enables teachers to offer the appropriate type of instruction for all students in the classroom.

Phonics

Our language system uses an alphabetic code to communicate meaning from writing. Phonics involves learning the phonemes or sounds that letters make and the symbols or letters that represent those sounds. Children learn to blend the sounds of letters to decode unknown or unfamiliar words. The goal of good phonics instruction is to enable students to read words accurately and automatically.

Research has clearly identified the critical role of phonics in the ability of readers to read fluently and with good understanding, as well as to write and spell. Effective phonics instruction requires carefully sequenced lessons that teach the sounds of letters and how to use these sounds to read words. The McGraw-Hill program provides daily explicit and systematic phonics instruction to teach the letter sounds and blending. There are three explicit Phonics and Decoding lessons for every selection. Daily Phonics Routines are provided for quick reinforcement, in addition to activities in the Phonics/Phonemic Awareness Practice Book and technology components. This combination of direct skills instruction and applied practice leads to reading success.

Curriculum Connections

As in the child's real-world environment, boundaries between disciplines must be dissolved. Recent research emphasizes the need to make connections between and across subject areas. McGraw-Hill Reading is committed to this approach. Each reading selection offers activities that tie in with social studies, language arts, geography, science, mathematics, art, music, health, and physical education. The program threads numerous research and inquiry activities that encourage the child to use the library and the Internet to seek out information. Reading and language skills are applied to a variety of genres, balancing fiction and nonfiction.

Integrated Language Arts

Success in developing communication skills is greatly enhanced by integrating the language arts in connected and purposeful ways. This allows students to understand the need for proper writing, grammar, and spelling. McGraw-Hill Reading sets the stage for meaningful learning. Each week a full writing-process lesson is provided. This lesson is supported by a 5-day spelling plan, emphasizing spelling patterns and spelling rules, and a 5-day grammar plan, focusing on proper grammar, mechanics, and usage.

Meeting Individual Needs

Every classroom is a microcosm of a world composed of diverse individuals with unique needs and abilities. Research points out that such needs must be addressed with frequent intensive opportunities to learn with engaging materials. McGraw-Hill Reading makes reading a successful experience for every child by providing a rich collection of leveled books for easy, independent, and challenging reading. Leveled practice is provided in Reteach, Practice, and Extend skills books. To address various learning styles and language needs, the program offers alternative teaching strategies, prevention/intervention techniques, language support activities, and ESL teaching suggestions.

Assessment

Frequent assessment in the classroom makes it easier for teachers to identify problems and to find remedies for them. McGraw-Hill Reading makes assessment an important component of instruction. Formal and informal opportunities are a part of each lesson. Minilessons, prevention/intervention strategies, and informal checklists, as well as student self-assessments, provide many informal assessment opportunities. Formal assessments, such as weekly selection tests and criterion-referenced unit tests, help to monitor students' knowledge of important skills and concepts. McGraw-Hill Reading also addresses how to adapt instruction based on student performance with resources such as the Alternate Teaching Strategies. Weekly lessons on test preparation, including test preparation practice books, help students to transfer skills to new contexts and to become better test takers.

For information on research that supports this program, visit ***www.mhschool.com/reading***

McGraw-Hill Reading

Theme Chart

GRADE LEVEL	Experience Experiences can tell us about ourselves and our world.	Connections Making connections develops new understandings.
Kindergarten	**My World** We learn a lot from all the things we see and do at home and in school.	**All Kinds of Friends** When we work and play together, we learn more about ourselves.
Subtheme 1	At Home	Working Together
Subtheme 2	School Days	Playing Together
1	**Day by Day** Each day brings new experiences.	**Together Is Better** We like to share ideas and experiences with others.
2	**What's New?** With each day, we learn something new.	**Just Between Us** Family and friends help us see the world in new ways.
3	**Great Adventures** Life is made up of big and small experiences.	**Nature Links** Nature can give us new ideas.
4	**Reflections** Stories let us share the experiences of others.	**Something in Common** Sharing ideas can lead to meaningful cooperation.
5	**Time of My Life** We sometimes find memorable experiences in unexpected places.	**Building Bridges** Knowing what we have in common helps us appreciate our differences.
6	**Pathways** Reflecting on life's experiences can lead to new understandings.	**A Common Thread** A look beneath the surface may uncover hidden connections.

MULTI-AGE Classroom

Using the same global themes at each grade level facilitates the use of materials in multi-age classrooms.

Themes: Kindergarten – Grade 6

Expression	Inquiry	Problem Solving	Making Decisions
There are many styles and forms for expressing ourselves.	By exploring and asking questions, we make discoveries.	Analyzing information can help us solve problems.	Using what we know helps us evaluate situations.
Time to Shine We can use our ideas and our imagination to do many wonderful things.	**I Wonder** We can make discoveries about the wonders of nature in our own backyard.	**Let's Work It Out** Working as part of a team can help me find a way to solve problems.	**Choices** We can make many good choices and decisions every day.
Great Ideas	**In My Backyard**	**Try and Try Again**	**Good Choices**
Let's Pretend	**Wonders of Nature**	**Teamwork**	**Let's Decide**
Stories to Tell Each one of us has a different story to tell.	**Let's Find Out!** Looking for answers is an adventure.	**Think About It!** It takes time to solve problems.	**Many Paths** Each decision opens the door to a new path.
Express Yourself We share our ideas in many ways.	**Look Around** There are surprises all around us.	**Figure It Out** We can solve problems by working together.	**Starting Now** Unexpected events can lead to new decisions.
Be Creative! We can all express ourselves in creative, wonderful ways.	**Tell Me More** Looking and listening closely will help us find out the facts.	**Think It Through** Solutions come in many shapes and sizes.	**Turning Points** We make new judgments based on our experiences.
Our Voices We can each use our talents to communicate ideas.	**Just Curious** We can find answers in surprising places.	**Make a Plan** Often we have to think carefully about a problem in order to solve it.	**Sorting It Out** We make decisions that can lead to new ideas and discoveries.
Imagine That The way we express our thoughts and feelings can take different forms.	**Investigate!** We never know where the search for answers might lead us.	**Bright Ideas** Some problems require unusual approaches.	**Crossroads** Decisions cause changes that can enrich our lives.
With Flying Colors Creative people help us see the world from different perspectives.	**Seek and Discover** To make new discoveries, we must observe and explore.	**Brainstorms** We can meet any challenge with determination and ingenuity.	**All Things Considered** Encountering new places and people can help us make decisions.

UNIT 2

Contents

Nature Links

Nature can give us new ideas.

REALISTIC FICTION

SKILLS			
Study Skill	**Comprehension**	**Vocabulary**	**Phonics**
• Using Reference Sources: Telephone Directory	• **Introduce** Cause and Effect • **Review** Cause and Effect • **Introduce** Draw Conclusions	• **Introduce** Context Clues	• Syllable Patterns

INFORMATIONAL STORY

SKILLS			
Study Skill	**Comprehension**	**Vocabulary**	**Phonics**
• Using Reference Sources: Dictionary	• **Introduce** Compare and Contrast • **Review** Compare and Contrast • **Review** Draw Conclusions	• **Introduce** Antonyms and Synonyms	• Consonant Clusters

DREAM WOLF 204A

written and illustrated by ***Paul Goble***

SKILLS			
Study Skill	**Comprehension**	**Vocabulary**	**Phonics**
• Using Reference Sources: Encyclopedia	• **Review** Cause and Effect • **Review** Compare and Contrast	• **Review** Context Clues	• Consonant Clusters

PLAINS INDIAN LEGEND

SPIDERS AT WORK 226A

written by ***Diane Hoyt-Goldsmith***

SKILLS			
Study Skill	**Comprehension**	**Vocabulary**	**Phonics**
• Using Reference Sources: Dictionary	• **Introduce** Important Information • **Review** Important Information • **Review** Draw Conclusions	• **Review** Antonyms and Synonyms	• Consonant Clusters

SCIENCE NONFICTION

WEB WONDERS 244A

Special Report

SKILLS			
Study Skill	**Comprehension**	**Vocabulary**	
• Using Reference Sources: Use a Resource	• **Review** Compare and Contrast • **Review** Important Information	• **Review** Context Clues • **Review** Antonyms and Synonyms	

SCIENCE ARTICLE

Unit Planner

	WEEK 1 City Green	WEEK 2 The Sun, the Wind and the Rain
Leveled Books	**Easy:** *Simon Says, "Go for It!"* **Independent:** *Save the Sea Turtles!* **Challenge:** *Potlatch for Kwiskwis*	**Easy:** *Winter in the Arctic* **Independent:** *Pompeii: A Doomed City* **Challenge:** *Dinosaurs Lived Here*
Tested Skills	**Comprehension** Cause and Effect, 144A–144B, 171E–171F; Draw Conclusions, 171G–171H **Vocabulary** Context Clues, 171I–171J **Study Skills** Reference Sources, 170	**Comprehension** Compare and Contrast, 174A–174B, 203E–203F; Draw Conclusions, 203G–203H **Vocabulary** Antonyms and Synonyms, 203I–203J **Study Skills** Reference Sources, 202
Minilessons	**Phonics and Decoding: Syllable Patterns,** 151 **Prefixes,** 147 **Character,** 149 **Main Idea,** 153 **Setting,** 159 **Make Predictions,** 161 **Fact and Opinion,** 165	**Phonics and Decoding: Consonant Clusters,** 189 **Cause and Effect,** 183 **Suffixes,** 185 **Make Inferences,** 187 **Sequence of Events,** 193 **Summarize,** 197
Language Arts	**Writing:** Explanatory Writing, 171K **Grammar:** Common and Proper Nouns, 171M–171N **Spelling:** Syllable Patterns, 171O–171P	**Writing:** Explanatory Writing, 203K **Grammar:** Singular and Plural Nouns, 203M–203N **Spelling:** Words with Consonant Clusters, 203O–203P
Activities		
	Read Aloud: "A Garden," 142E	**Read Aloud:** "The Hurricane," 172E
	Stories in Art: *Together Protect the Community,* 142/143	**Stories in Art:** *Naples: Vesuvius Erupting,* 172/173
Curriculum Connections	**Social Studies:** Map Skills, 146	**Social Studies:** Mountain Facts, 182
	Science: Weather, 148	**Music:** Weather Dances, 186
	Drama: Fables, 154	**Science:** Magical Volcanoes, 190
	Math: Garden Plot, 156	**Math:** Making Graphs, 192
CULTURAL PERSPECTIVES	Japanese Gardens, 150	Sun Hats, 178

WEEK 3 Dream Wolf	WEEK 4 Spiders at Work	WEEK 5 Web Wonders	WEEK 6 Review, Writing Process, Assessment
Easy: *Lost at Sea* **Independent:** *The Clever Jackal* **Challenge:** *The Boy and the Water Buffalo*	**Easy:** *Perry Mantis, Private Eye* **Independent:** *Listen for the Rattle!* **Challenge:** *Life on the Great Barrier Reef*	Self-Selected Reading of Leveled Books	Self-Selected Reading
☑ **Comprehension** Cause and Effect, 206A–206B, 225E–225F Compare and Contrast, 225G–225H ☑ **Vocabulary** Context Clues, 225I–225J ☑ **Study Skills** Reference Sources, 224	☑ **Comprehension** Important and Unimportant Information, 228A–228B, 243E–243F Draw Conclusions, 243G–243H ☑ **Vocabulary** Antonyms and Synonyms, 243I–243J ☑ **Study Skills** Reference Sources, 242	☑ **Comprehension** Compare and Contrast, 246A–246B Important and Unimportant Information, 253E–253F ☑ **Vocabulary** Antonyms and Synonyms, 253G–253H Context Clues, 253I–253J ☑ **Study Skills** Reference Sources, 252	☑ **Assess Skills** Cause and Effect Draw Conclusions Compare and Contrast Important and Unimportant Information Context Clues Antonyms and Synonyms Reference Sources ☑ **Assess Grammar and Spelling** Review Nouns, 255G Review Spelling Patterns, 255H ☑ **Unit Progress Assessment** ☑ **Standardized Test Preparation**
Phonics and Decoding: Consonant Clusters, 209 **Make Inferences,** 213 **Sequence of Events,** 215 **Suffixes,** 217 **Summarize,** 219	**Phonics and Decoding: Consonant Clusters,** 237 **Context Clues,** 231 **Make Generalizations,** 233 **Main Idea,** 235		
Writing: Explanatory Writing, 225K **Grammar:** Irregular Plural Nouns, 225M–225N **Spelling:** Words with Consonant Clusters, 225O–225P	**Writing:** Explanatory Writing, 243K **Grammar:** Possessive Nouns, 243M–243N **Spelling:** Plurals, 243O–243P	**Writing:** Explanatory Writing, 253K **Grammar:** Sentence Combining with Nouns, 253M–253N **Spelling:** Words from Science, 253O–253P	**Unit Writing Process:** Explanatory Writing, 255A–255F
Read Aloud: "Seeing the Animals," 204E **Stories in Art:** *Family Going Shopping*, 204/205 **Math:** Group Numbers to 10, 208 **Science:** The Wolves Return, 210 **Social Studies:** Plains Horses, 218	**Read Aloud:** "Spider on the Floor," 226E **Stories in Art:** *Ruby-Throat & Columbine*, 226/227 **Social Studies:** Spider Maps, 230 **Math:** Graphs, 232 **Science:** Silk, 234	**Read Aloud:** "Arachne the Spinner," 244E **Stories in Art:** *Unusual Hopi Coiled Basket with Spider Design*, 244/245	GROUP **Cooperative Theme Project Research and Inquiry:** Community as Ecosystem, 141
Plains Traditions, 216	Spider Stories, 236		

UNIT 2

Unit Resources

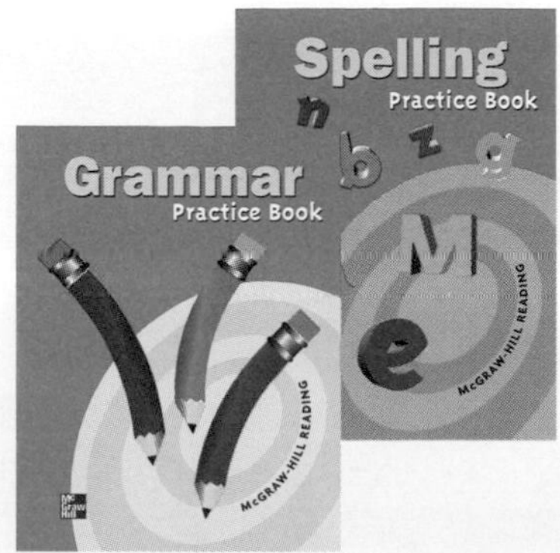

LITERATURE

LEVELED BOOKS

Easy

- ***Simon Says, "Go for It!"***
- ***Winter in the Arctic***
- ***Lost at Sea***
- ***Perry Mantis, Private Eye***

Independent

- ***Save the Sea Turtles!***
- ***Pompeii: A Doomed City***
- ***The Clever Jackal***
- ***Listen for the Rattle!***

Challenge

- ***Potlatch for Kwiskwis***
- ***Dinosaurs Lived Here***
- ***The Boy and the Water Buffalo***
- ***Life on the Great Barrier Reef***

THEME BIG BOOK Share *This is Our Earth* to set the unit theme and make content-area connections.

LISTENING LIBRARY AUDIOCASSETTE Recordings of the student book selections and poetry

SKILLS

LEVELED PRACTICE

Practice Book: Student practice for comprehension, vocabulary, and study skills; plus practice for instructional vocabulary and story comprehension. Take-Home Story included for each lesson.

Reteach: Reteaching opportunities for students who need more help with assessed skills.

Extend: Extension activities for vocabulary, comprehension, story, and study skills.

TEACHING CHARTS Instructional charts for modeling vocabulary and tested skills. Also available as transparencies.

WORD BUILDING MANIPULATIVE CARDS Cards with words and structural elements for word building and practicing vocabulary.

LANGUAGE SUPPORT BOOK

ESL Parallel teaching lessons and appropriate practice activities for students needing language support.

PHONICS/PHONEMIC AWARENESS PRACTICE BOOK Additional practice focusing on vowel sounds, phonograms, blends, digraphs, and key phonetic elements.

LANGUAGE ARTS

GRAMMAR PRACTICE BOOK Provides practice for grammar and mechanics lessons.

SPELLING PRACTICE BOOK Provides practice with the word list and spelling patterns. Includes home involvement activities.

DAILY LANGUAGE ACTIVITIES Sentence activities that provide brief, regular practice and reinforcement of grammar, mechanics, and usage skills. Available as blackline masters and transparencies.

McGraw-Hill School **TECHNOLOGY**

Phonics **CD-ROM** provides extra phonics support.

***inter*NET CONNECTION** extends lesson activities through Research and Inquiry ideas.

Visit ***www.mhschool.com/reading.***

Resources for
Meeting Individual Needs

UNIT 2	EASY	ON-LEVEL	CHALLENGE	LANGUAGE SUPPORT
City Green	**Leveled Book:** *Simon Says, "Go for It!"* **Reteach,** 38–44 **Alternate Teaching Strategies,** T60–T66 **Writing:** Give Directions, 171L Phonics CD-ROM	**Leveled Book:** *Save the Sea Turtles!* **Practice,** 38–44 **Alternate Teaching Strategies,** T60–T66 **Writing:** How-To Pamphlet, 171L Phonics CD-ROM	**Leveled Book:** *Potlatch for Kwiskwis* **Extend,** 38–44 **Writing:** Interview, 171L	**Teaching Strategies,** 144C, 145, 149, 151, 155, 171L **Language Support,** 41–48 **Alternate Teaching Strategies,** T60–T66 **Writing:** Write a Plan, 171K–171L Phonics CD-ROM
The Sun, the Wind and the Rain	**Leveled Book:** *Winter in the Arctic* **Reteach,** 45–51 **Alternate Teaching Strategies,** T60–T66 **Writing:** Postcard, 203L Phonics CD-ROM	**Leveled Book:** *Pompeii: A Doomed City* **Practice,** 45–51 **Alternate Teaching Strategies,** T60–T66 **Writing:** Journal Entry, 203L Phonics CD-ROM	**Leveled Book:** *Dinosaurs Lived Here* **Extend,** 45–51 **Writing:** Paragraph, 203L	**Teaching Strategies,** 174C, 175, 183, 189, 203L **Language Support,** 49–56 **Alternate Teaching Strategies,** T60–T66 **Writing:** Write an Essay, 203K–203L Phonics CD-ROM
Dream Wolf	**Leveled Book:** *Lost at Sea* **Reteach,** 52–58 **Alternate Teaching Strategies,** T60–T66 **Writing:** Invitation, 225L Phonics CD-ROM	**Leveled Book:** *The Clever Jackal* **Practice,** 52–58 **Alternate Teaching Strategies,** T60–T66 **Writing:** Write a Diary, 225L Phonics CD-ROM	**Leveled Book:** *The Boy and the Water Buffalo* **Extend,** 52–58 **Writing:** News Article, 225L	**Teaching Strategies,** 206C, 207, 211, 225L **Language Support,** 57–64 **Alternate Teaching Strategies,** T60–T66 **Writing:** Write Directions, 225K–225L Phonics CD-ROM
Spiders at Work	**Leveled Book:** *Perry Mantis, Private Eye* **Reteach,** 59–65 **Alternate Teaching Strategies,** T60–T66 **Writing:** Spider Poster, 243L Phonics CD-ROM	**Leveled Book:** *Listen for the Rattle!* **Practice,** 59–65 **Alternate Teaching Strategies,** T60–T66 **Writing:** Keep a Diary, 243L Phonics CD-ROM	**Leveled Book:** *Life on the Great Barrier Reef* **Extend,** 59–65 **Writing:** Life as a Spider, 243L	**Teaching Strategies,** 228C, 229, 231, 237, 243L **Language Support,** 65–72 **Alternate Teaching Strategies,** T60–T66 **Writing:** Write a Report, 243K–243L Phonics CD-ROM
 Web Wonders	**Review** **Reteach,** 66–72 **Alternate Teaching Strategies,** T60–T66 **Writing:** Web Sight, 253L	**Review** **Practice,** 66–72 **Alternate Teaching Strategies,** T60–T66 **Writing:** Spinning a Story, 253L	**Review** **Extend,** 66–72 **Writing:** Letter to the Editor, 253L	**Teaching Strategies,** 246C, 247, 253L **Language Support,** 73–80 **Alternate Teaching Strategies,** T60–T66 **Writing:** Write an Essay, 253K–253L

UNIT 2 Unit Assessment

INFORMAL

Informal Assessment

- Comprehension, 144B, 166, 167, 171F, 171H; 174B, 198, 199, 203F, 203H; 206B, 220, 221, 225F, 225H; 228B, 238, 239, 243F, 243H; 246B, 249, 253F
- Vocabulary, 171J, 203J, 225J, 243J, 253J

Performance Assessment

- Scoring Rubrics, 171L, 203L, 225L, 243L, 253L
- Research and Inquiry, 141, 255
- Writing Process, 171K, 203K, 225K, 243K, 253K
- Listening, Speaking, Viewing Activities, 142E, 142/143, 144C, 144–169, 171D, 171K–L; 172E, 172/173, 174C, 174–201, 203D, 203K–L; 204E, 204/205, 206C, 206–223, 225D, 225K–L; 226E, 226/227, 228C, 228–241, 243D, 243K–L; 244E, 244/245, 246C, 246–251, 253D, 253K–L
- Portfolio, 171L, 203L, 225L, 243L, 253L
- Writing, 171K–L, 203K–L, 225K–L, 243K–L, 253K–L, 255A–F
- Cross-Curricular Activities, 142E, 144C, 146, 148, 154, 156; 174C, 182, 186, 190, 192; 206C, 208, 210, 218; 228C, 232, 234, 236

Leveled Practice

Practice, Reteach, Extend

- **Comprehension**
  - Cause and Effect, 38, 42, 52, 56
  - Draw Conclusions, 43, 50, 64
  - Compare and Contrast, 45, 49, 57, 66
  - Important and Unimportant Information, 59, 63, 70
- **Vocabulary Strategies**
  - Context Clues, 44, 58, 72
  - Antonyms and Synonyms, 51, 65, 71
- **Study Skills**
  - Reference Sources, 41, 48, 55, 62, 69

FORMAL

Selection Assessments

- **Skills and Vocabulary Words**
  - *City Green*, 11–12
  - *The Sun, the Wind and the Rain*, 13–14
  - *Dream Wolf*, 15–16
  - *Spiders at Work*, 17–18
  - *Web Wonders*, 19–20

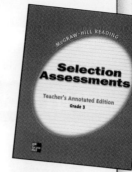

Unit 2 Test

- **Comprehension**
  - Cause and Effect
  - Draw Conclusions
  - Compare and Contrast
  - Important Information
- **Vocabulary Strategies**
  - Context Clues
  - Antonyms and Synonyms
- **Study Skills**
  - Reference Sources

Grammar and Spelling Assessment

- **Grammar**
  - Nouns, 37, 43, 49, 55, 61, 63–64
- **Spelling**
  - Syllable Patterns, 38
  - Words with Consonant Clusters, 44
  - Words with Consonant Clusters, 50
  - Plurals, 56
  - Words from Science, 62
  - Unit 2 Assessment, 63–64

Diagnostic/Placement Evaluation

- Individual Reading Inventory, 31–32
- Running Record, 33–34
- Grade K Diagnostic/Placement
- Grade 1 Diagnostic/Placement
- Grade 2 Diagnostic/Placement
- Grade 3 Diagnostic/Placement

Test Preparation

- TAAS Preparation and Practice Booklet, 30–39
- See also Test Power in Teacher's Edition, 171, 203, 225, 243, 253

Assessment Checklist

Student .... **Grade** ....

Teacher ....

	City Green	The Sun, the Wind and the Rain	Dream Wolf	Spiders at Work	Web Wonders	Assessment Summary
LISTENING/SPEAKING						
Participates in oral language experiences						
Listens and speaks to gain knowledge of culture						
Speaks appropriately to audiences for different purposes						
Communicates clearly						
READING						
Uses a variety of word identification strategies: • Syllable Patterns						
• Initial Consonant Clusters						
• Context Clues						
• Antonyms and Synonyms						
Reads with fluency and understanding						
Reads widely for different purposes in varied sources						
Develops an extensive vocabulary						
Uses a variety of strategies to comprehend selections: • Cause and Effect						
• Draw Conclusions						
• Compare and Contrast						
• Important and Unimportant Information						
Responds to various texts						
Analyzes the characteristics of various types of texts						
Conducts research using various sources: • Reference Sources						
Reads to increase knowledge						
WRITING						
Writes for a variety of audiences and purposes						
Composes original texts using the conventions of written language such as capitalization and penmanship						
Spells proficiently						
Composes texts applying knowledge of grammar and usage						
Uses writing processes						
Evaluates own writing and writing of others						

+ Observed   – Not Observed

Introducing the Theme

Nature Links

Nature can give us new ideas.

PRESENT THE THEME Read the theme statement to students. Encourage them to think of how nature inspires people to create things or see things in fresh ways. For example, attempts at making airplanes may have been inspired by watching birds fly. Help students understand that humans are part of the web of life. Ask what is meant by a web of life. How are people linked to their environment?

READ THE POEM Ask students to describe fog. What does it look like? Have students imagine fog rolling in as you read aloud "Fog" by Carl Sandburg. Ask how Sandburg's description differs from a scientific description. What words might scientists use to describe fog? In what ways is fog like a cat? (It is quiet; it stays awhile, then leaves.)

LISTENING LIBRARY AUDIOCASSETTES

GROUP **MAKE CONNECTIONS** Have students preview the unit by reading the selection titles and looking at the illustrations. Then have them work in small groups to brainstorm a list of ways that the stories, poems, and the *Time for Kids* magazine article relate to the theme Nature Links.

Groups can then compare their lists as they share them with the class.

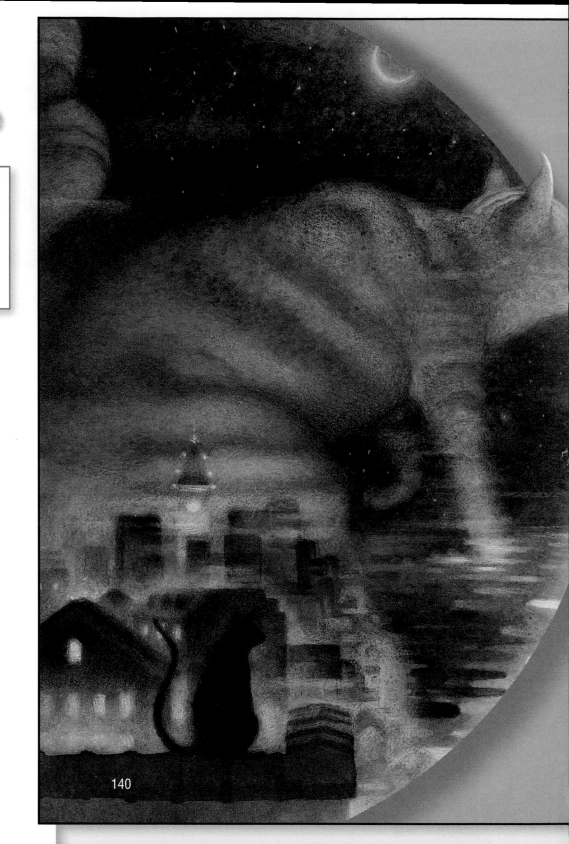

THEME SUMMARY

Each of the selections relates to the unit theme Nature Links as well as the global theme Connections. These thematic links will help students to make connections across texts.

City Green Marcy and her neighbors transform a vacant lot.

The Sun, the Wind and the Rain A girl learns about erosion.

Dream Wolf Two lost children dream of a wolf that saves them.

Spiders at Work Spiders weave intricate webs through a fascinating process.

Web Wonders Spider silk is the strongest thread scientists have found.

UNIT 2

Fog

The fog comes
on little cat feet.

It sits looking
over harbor and city
on silent haunches
and then moves on.

by Carl Sandburg

141

LEARNING ABOUT POETRY

Literary Devices Read the poem and have students listen for words that describe how a cat behaves. Point out that the poet gives the fog lifelike characteristics, such as having feet, sitting on haunches, and moving away. Be sure students understand the meanings of the words *haunches* and *harbor*.

Poetry Activity Suggest that students use movement to help them understand and interpret the poem. Have them pantomime walking on "little cat feet," looking over a scene while sitting "on silent haunches," and finally walking away.

Research and Inquiry

Theme Project: Community as Ecosystem Have students brainstorm ways to preserve plants native to the local area. They can research what others are doing. Have teams analyze their local environment and select an area they'd want to beautify or revitalize.

List What They Know Have students list what they know about the local ecosystem.

Ask Questions and Identify Resources Ask students to brainstorm questions they would need to answer to generate a proposal to present to a town or city council. Have them list possible resources.

QUESTIONS	POSSIBLE RESOURCES
• What things can damage plants? • How can we create a wildlife habitat? • What are the native wildflowers? • What products or pesticides are safe?	• Invite a naturalist to talk. • Visit a local garden center. • Contact the Humane Society.

interNET CONNECTION Have students visit ***www.mhschool.com/reading.***

Create a Presentation When their research is complete, students will present their plan for beautifying and revitalizing their community. Encourage students to submit their proposals to local councils. Students might make posters to publicize their ideas, initiate a letter-writing campaign, or start an Adopt-a-Park project. See Wrap Up the Theme, page 255.

City Green

Selection Summary: **Marcy and her neighbors convince a skeptical old man that things can be turned around for good by turning a vacant lot into a beautiful community garden.**

Listening Library Audiocassette

INSTRUCTIONAL
Pages 144–171

About the Author/Illustrator: Before Dyanne DiSalvo-Ryan begins a book, she says she can see the whole thing. Sometimes she takes a lot of photographs, sometimes she does historical research, and sometimes she draws from her own ideas. Ms. DiSalvo-Ryan says that *City Green* was inspired by a garden lot she often passed. She says, "From fire escapes to gum spots I see life in the buildings and movement on the sidewalks."

Resources for
Meeting Individual Needs

LEVELED BOOKS

EASY
Pages 171A, 171D

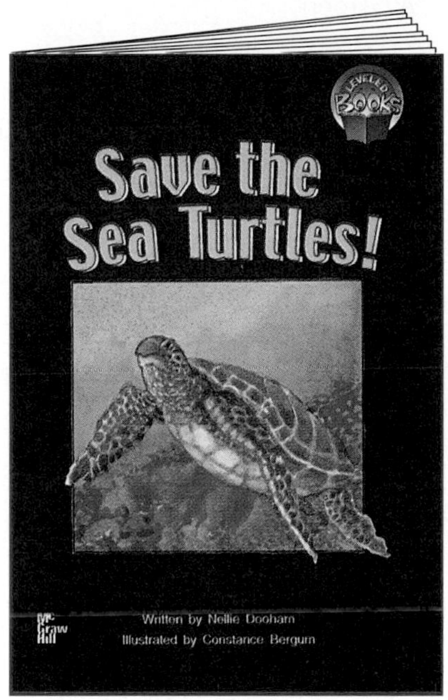

INDEPENDENT
Pages 171B, 171D

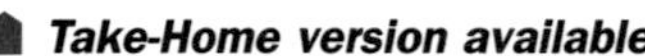
Take-Home version available

CHALLENGE
Pages 171C, 171D

LEVELED PRACTICE

Reteach, 38-44
blackline masters with reteaching opportunities for each assessed skill

Practice, 38-44
workbook with Take-Home Stories and practice opportunities for each assessed skill and story comprehension

Extend, 38-44
blackline masters that offer challenge activities for each assessed skill

ADDITIONAL RESOURCES

- **Language Support Book,** pp. 41-48
- **Take-Home Story, Practice** p. 39a
- **Alternate Teaching Strategies,** pp. T60-T66
- **Selected Quizzes Prepared by** 

Phonics CD-ROM provides extra phonics support.

interNET CONNECTION Research & Inquiry ideas. Visit ***www.mhschool.com/reading.***

Suggested Lesson Planner

Available on CD-ROM

READING AND LANGUAGE ARTS	 DAY 1 Focus on Reading and Skills	 DAY 2 Read the Literature
Comprehension Vocabulary Phonics/Decoding Study Skills Listening, Speaking, Viewing, Representing	 **Read Aloud and Motivate,** 142E "A Garden" **Develop Visual Literacy,** 142/143 ☑ **Introduce Cause and Effect,** 144A–144B **Teaching Chart 31** **Reteach, Practice, Extend,** 38	**Build Background,** 144C Develop Oral Language **Vocabulary,** 144D *area* *halfway* *schedule* *excitement* *heap* *stems* **Teaching Chart 32** **Word Building Manipulative Cards** **Reteach, Practice, Extend,** 39  **Read the Selection,** 144–167 Guided Instruction ☑ Cause and Effect **Minilessons,** 147, 149, 151, 153, 159, 161, 165 **Cultural Perspectives,** 150
 Curriculum Connections	 **Fine Arts,** 142/143	 **Social Studies,** 146
Writing	 **Writing Prompt:** Write an essay about someone you know. Give the person's first name, the name of the city in which he or she lives, and tell what he or she likes to do.	 **Writing Prompt:** Think about something the people in your community could do together. Write a paragraph about it.  **Journal Writing,** 167 Quick-Write
Grammar	**Introduce the Concept: Common and Proper Nouns,** 171M Daily Language Activity 1. Sometimes ali saves cans. Ali 2. My Cat purrs loudly. cat 3. The Boy went out. boy **Grammar Practice Book,** 33	**Teach the Concept: Common and Proper Nouns,** 171M Daily Language Activity 1. Aunt mae worked on monday. Mae, Monday 2. We met on groundhog day. Groundhog Day 3. We went to new york city. New York City **Grammar Practice Book,** 34
Spelling	**Pretest: Syllable Patterns,** 171O **Spelling Practice Book,** 33–34	**Explore the Pattern: Syllable Patterns,** 171O **Spelling Practice Book,** 35

Meeting Individual Needs

☑ = Skill Assessed in Unit Test

DAY 3 Read the Literature

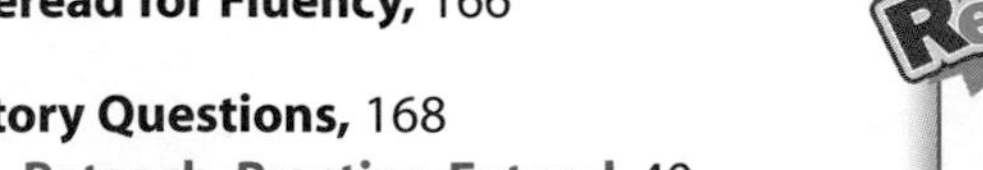

Reread for Fluency, 166

Story Questions, 168
Reteach, Practice, Extend, 40
Story Activities, 169

Study Skill, 170
☑ Reference Sources
Teaching Chart 33
Reteach, Practice, Extend, 41

Test Power, 171

Read the Leveled Books,
Guided Reading
Syllable Patterns
☑ Cause and Effect
☑ Instructional Vocabulary
Phonics **CD-ROM**

Social Studies, 146 Science, 148

Writing Prompt: Have you ever been to a park or a garden or another place you found beautiful? Write a paragraph describing the place.

Writing Process: Explanatory Writing, 171K
Prewrite, Draft

Review and Practice: Common and Proper Nouns, 171N
Daily Language Activity
1. I celebrate halloween. Halloween
2. Will luis move his Car? Luis, car
3. Please come to lina's Party. Lina's, party
Grammar Practice Book, 35

Practice and Extend: Syllable Patterns, 171P
Spelling Practice Book, 36

DAY 4 Build Skills

Read the Leveled Books and Self-Selected Books

☑ **Review Cause and Effect,** 171E–171F
Teaching Chart 34
Reteach, Practice, Extend, 42
Language Support, 46

☑ **Introduce Draw Conclusions,** 171G–171H
Teaching Chart 35
Reteach, Practice, Extend, 43
Language Support, 47

Drama, 154

Writing Prompt: Write a news story about upcoming community events. Tell where to go and who to contact. Use abbreviations.
Writing Process: Explanatory Writing, 171K
Revise
Meeting Individual Needs for Writing, 171L

Review and Practice: Common and Proper Nouns, 171N
Daily Language Activity
1. They will arrive on friday, Nov 4. Friday, Nov.
2. Ask mrs. li to meet us in New york. Mrs. Li, York
3. I watered mary's rosebush. Mary's
Grammar Practice Book, 36

Proofread and Write: Syllable Patterns, 171P
Spelling Practice Book, 37

DAY 5 Build Skills

Read Self-Selected Books

☑ **Introduce Context Clues,** 171I–171J
Teaching Chart 36
Reteach, Practice, Extend, 44
Language Support, 48

Listening, Speaking, Viewing, Representing, 171L
Make a Video
Make Mini-Gardens

Minilessons, 147, 149, 153, 159, 161, 165

Phonics Review,
Syllable Patterns, 151
Phonics/Phonemic Awareness Practice Book, 43–46

CD-ROM

Math, 156

Writing Prompt: Do you think one person can do something to change his or her neighborhood? Write about it.

Writing Process: Explanatory Writing, 171K
Edit/Proofread, Publish

Assess and Reteach: Common and Proper Nouns, 171N
Daily Language Activity
1. Ani called mr. hammer. Mr. Hammer
2. The Date is tues., Oct 9. date, Tues., Oct.
3. Is feb short for february? Feb., February
Grammar Practice Book, 37–38

Assess and Reteach: Syllable Patterns, 171P
Spelling Practice Book, 38

Language Arts

Read Aloud and Motivate

A Garden

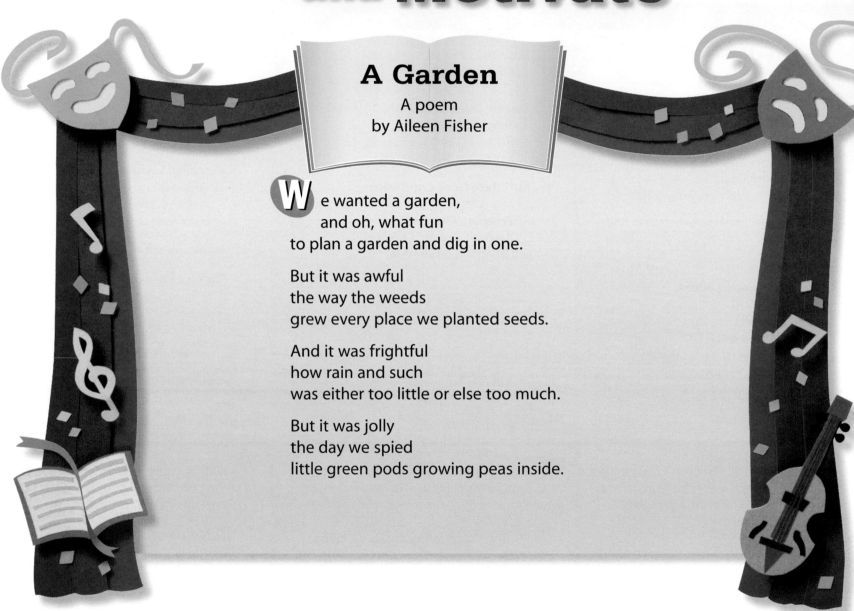

A poem
by Aileen Fisher

We wanted a garden,
and oh, what fun
to plan a garden and dig in one.

But it was awful
the way the weeds
grew every place we planted seeds.

And it was frightful
how rain and such
was either too little or else too much.

But it was jolly
the day we spied
little green pods growing peas inside.

Oral Comprehension

LISTENING AND SPEAKING Motivate students to think about sequence as you read this poem to them. Ask them to note the sequence of events as you read. When you have finished, ask, "What was the first thing that happened in this poem?" Then ask, "Can you remember whether the weeds grew first or the rain came?" Reread the poem to students and ask them to join in as you clap out the rhythm of the poem.

Activity Encourage students to create a storyboard showing the different events in this poem. Invite students to label each picture in the storyboard.

▶ **Visual**

Develop Visual Literacy

Fine Arts

Anthology pages 142-143

Stories in Art

Murals are usually painted in a public place for everyone to enjoy. Often members of a community work together to paint a mural.

Look at this mural. What can you tell about it? What might have happened to make the people hug the city? How do you think the artist who painted the mural feels about his community?

Look again at the painting. What is the most unusual thing about it? Why?

Together Protect the Community
by John Pitman Weber, 1976
Located on Diversity Street, Chicago

142 143

Objective: Identify Cause and Effect

VIEWING In this handsome mural, people are holding a whole community in their arms. Ask whether children have seen murals in their own neighborhoods. If so, what do they imagine the actual size of this work to be? Have students discuss some of the reasons that people paint murals. Ask students how they think the artist who painted the mural feels about the community.

Read the page with students, encouraging individual interpretations of the painting.

Ask students to identify what might have happened to make the people hug the city. For example:

- Everybody started to play wonderful music.
- Everybody is proud of the community.

REPRESENTING Students can create a mural to celebrate their school community. Encourage them to work collaboratively on a single large roll or sheets of butcher paper. You might hang the mural in the hall outside your classroom door.

Students will recognize and infer cause-and-effect relationships.

TEACHING TIP

INSTRUCTIONAL Have students role-play to develop an understanding of cause and effect. For example, volunteers may tell a joke, riddle, or story. Have students record the effects of each volunteer's actions. Have them record their causes and effects in a simple flow chart.

Introduce Cause and Effect

PREPARE

Discuss Cause-and-Effect Experiences Tell students to pretend they will have a big science test on Monday. Ask: What do you predict will happen if you study hard? What might happen if you do not study?

TEACH

Define Cause and Effect Write the words *CAUSE* and *EFFECT* on the chalkboard. Guide students to understand that an effect is what happens and a cause is why it happens.

The 12th Street Summer Project

Three years ago, the 12th Street boys and girls had a terrible summer. They never had anything to do. By the next year, Marcy had an idea. She knew just how they could keep busy all summer. Marcy told all of her friends she was having a meeting. All of the kids on the block came.

At the meeting she said, "This summer we will keep busy. If we all pitch in we can sell lemonade all summer long." When the summer ended they put all the money together. They had earned over $100. Now they could buy their own 12th Street basketball hoop and net. Because of the hoop, they would always have a great summer.

Teaching Chart 31

Read the Story and Model the Skill Display **Teaching Chart 31**. Have students pay attention to clue words that signal cause-and-effect relationships as the story is read.

MODEL I know that some words act as clues to causes and effects. For example, the word *because* is a clue to a cause. The words that follow *because* tell why something happened. Having a great summer is the effect of having the hoop.

Identify Cause and Effect Have students underline causes with one line and effects with two lines, and circle any clue words.

PRACTICE

Create a Cause-and-Effect Chart (GROUP)

Using a Cause-and-Effect chart, have students record the missing causes and effects of the story. Have volunteers complete the chart.
▶**Logical/Visual**

CAUSE	EFFECT
The boys and girls on 12th Street had nothing to do all summer.	They had a terrible summer.
Marcy told all of her friends she was having a meeting.	They all came to the meeting.
They sold lemonade all summer.	The 12th Street boys and girls kept busy all summer.
They earned over $100.	They bought a hoop and net.
They could play basketball.	They always had a great summer.

ASSESS/CLOSE

Infer Cause and Effect

Have students predict what the effect might be if someone broke the hoop. (Possible response: They might sell lemonade for another summer.)

Meeting Individual Needs for Comprehension

EASY	ON-LEVEL	CHALLENGE

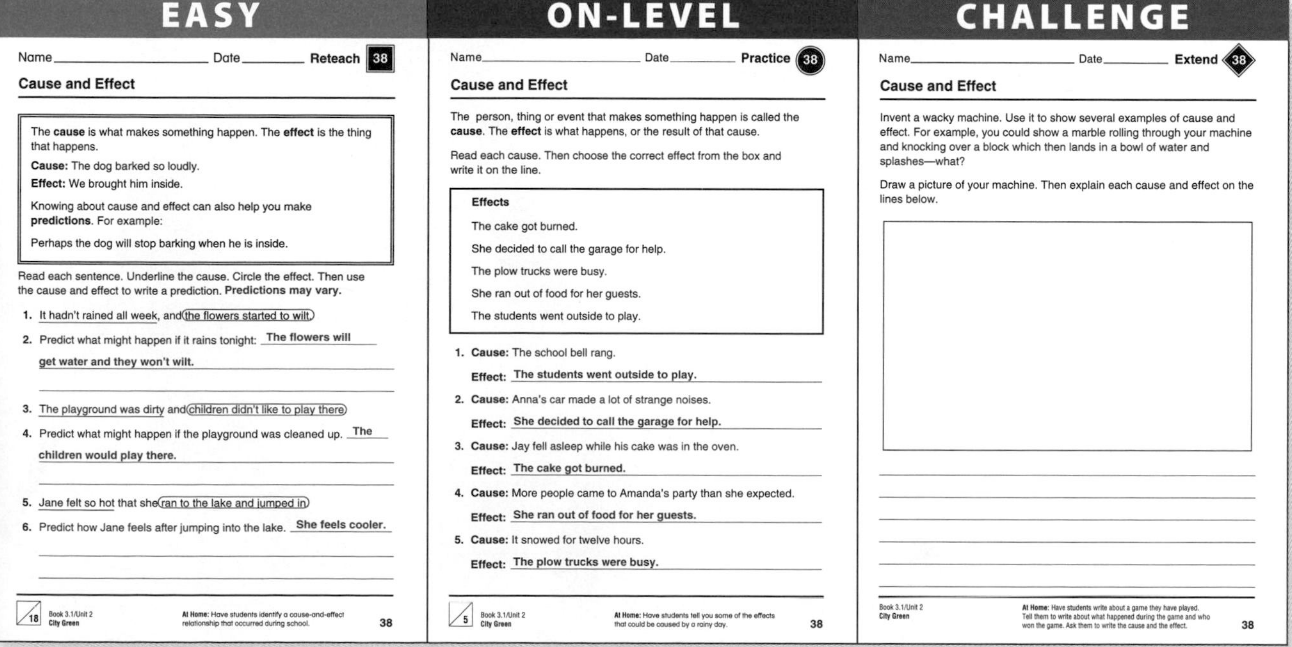

Name__________ Date______ Reteach 38

Cause and Effect

The **cause** is what makes something happen. The **effect** is the thing that happens.
Cause: The dog barked so loudly.
Effect: We brought him inside.
Knowing about cause and effect can also help you make **predictions**. For example:
Perhaps the dog will stop barking when he is inside.

Read each sentence. Underline the cause. Circle the effect. Then use the cause and effect to write a prediction. **Predictions may vary.**

1. It hadn't rained all week, and the flowers started to wilt.
2. Predict what might happen if it rains tonight: The flowers will get water and they won't wilt.
3. The playground was dirty and children didn't like to play there.
4. Predict what might happen if the playground was cleaned up. The children would play there.
5. Jane felt so hot that she ran to the lake and jumped in.
6. Predict how Jane feels after jumping into the lake. She feels cooler.

18 Book 3.1/Unit 2 City Green — At Home: Have students identify a cause-and-effect relationship that occurred during school. 38

Name__________ Date______ Practice 38

Cause and Effect

The person, thing or event that makes something happen is called the **cause**. The **effect** is what happens, or the result of that cause.

Read each cause. Then choose the correct effect from the box and write it on the line.

Effects
The cake got burned.
She decided to call the garage for help.
The plow trucks were busy.
She ran out of food for her guests.
The students went outside to play.

1. **Cause:** The school bell rang.
Effect: The students went outside to play.
2. **Cause:** Anna's car made a lot of strange noises.
Effect: She decided to call the garage for help.
3. **Cause:** Jay fell asleep while his cake was in the oven.
Effect: The cake got burned.
4. **Cause:** More people came to Amanda's party than she expected.
Effect: She ran out of food for her guests.
5. **Cause:** It snowed for twelve hours.
Effect: The plow trucks were busy.

5 Book 3.1/Unit 2 City Green — At Home: Have students tell you some of the effects that could be caused by a rainy day. 38

Name__________ Date______ Extend 38

Cause and Effect

Invent a wacky machine. Use it to show several examples of cause and effect. For example, you could show a marble rolling through your machine and knocking over a block which then lands in a bowl of water and splashes—what?

Draw a picture of your machine. Then explain each cause and effect on the lines below.

Book 3.1/Unit 2 City Green — At Home: Have students write about a game they have played. Tell them to write about what happened during the game and who won the game. Ask them to write the cause and the effect. 38

Reteach, 38 | Practice, 38 | Extend, 38

SELECTION Connection

Students will apply cause and effect when they read *City Green* and the Leveled Books.

ALTERNATE TEACHING STRATEGY

CAUSE AND EFFECT

For a different approach to teaching this skill, see page T60.

Build Background

Social Studies

Anthology and Leveled Books

Evaluate Prior Knowledge

CONCEPT: COMMUNITY PROJECTS In these stories communities work together. Have students share experiences they have had or heard about in which a community worked together on a specific project.

THINK ABOUT YOUR COMMUNITY Have a volunteer define *community*. Help students to consider all the types of people that live and work in their community. Have students create a word web of their community members. ▶ **Logical/Visual**

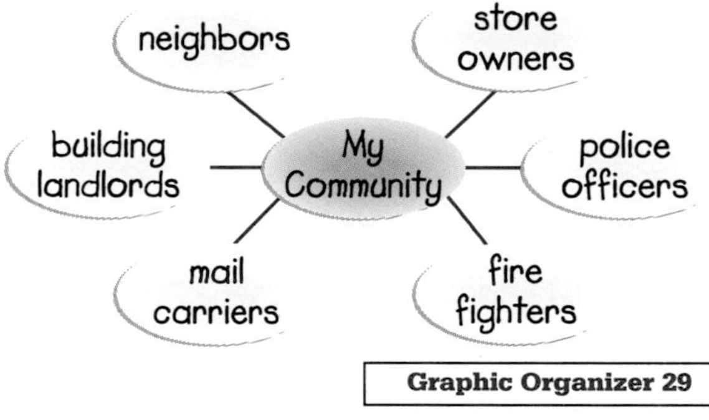

Graphic Organizer 29

WRITE A LETTER WRITING Have students write a letter to their neighbors inviting them to join the Community Garden. Tell students to let their neighbors know where and when the garden work will begin, and what they can do to help make the garden a success.

Develop Oral Language

NAME THE VEGETABLES ESL Have students orally identify a variety of different vegetables, using real vegetables or photographs.

Then have students brainstorm to describe each vegetable's color, taste, size, and texture. Record the descriptions on the chalkboard.

Explain to students that gardeners often label the seeds that they plant. Have students draw and label the vegetables they discussed. Attach the drawings to craft sticks and display them on the bulletin board.

TEACHING TIP

MANAGEMENT After you begin the chart listing community jobs, explain the Write a Letter activity. Have students continue working on these activities.

While students are working, present the Develop Oral Language activity to students who need help with oral language facility.

LANGUAGE SUPPORT

ESL See the Language Support Book, pages 41–44, for teaching suggestions for Build Background and Vocabulary.

Vocabulary

Key Words

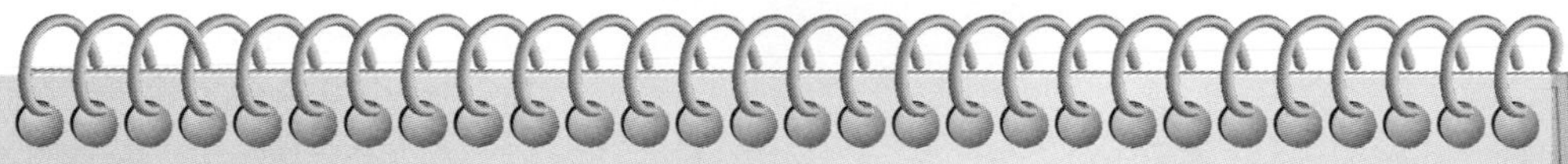

Marcy Gets Ready

1. Marcy is filled with excitement as she happily plans Mama's birthday party. **2.** She makes up a schedule that shows what she will do each day. **3.** The first task on her schedule is to clean up the whole living-room area. **4.** Marcy folds a large heap, or pile, of laundry. **5.** Next she trims the long stems from the fresh roses she bought. **6.** "Gee," she thinks, "Mama will be home soon and I'm only halfway finished preparing for the party!"

Teaching Chart 32

Vocabulary in Context

IDENTIFY VOCABULARY WORDS
Display **Teaching Chart 32** and read the passage with students. Have volunteers circle each vocabulary word and underline other words that are clues to its meaning.

DISCUSS MEANINGS Ask questions like these to help clarify word meanings:

- Would excitement cause you to be quiet or loud?
- What would you include in your schedule for Saturday?
- Which is your favorite area in your house?
- Would you carry a heap of books in one hand?
- Do the stems of flowers have petals?
- If you do something halfway, have you finished it?

Practice

DEMONSTRATE WORD MEANING Have a volunteer select one Vocabulary Card and describe the word to the class. Whoever guesses the word chooses the next word card. ▶ **Linguistic/Kinesthetic**

Word Building Manipulative Cards

DRAW PICTURES AND WRITE SENTENCES WRITING Have students draw a picture for each word and write definitions on separate sheets. Have partners exchange papers and match definitions to pictures. Have students refer to the Glossary as needed. ▶ **Linguistic/Interpersonal**

Definitions

excitement (p. 159) the condition of being stirred up or aroused

schedule (p. 148) a list of times, events, or things to do

area (p. 166) a particular space, region, or section

heap (p. 148) a collection of things piled together

stems (p. 162) the main parts of a plant that support the leaves and flowers

halfway (p. 148) to or at half the distance, partial

SPELLING/VOCABULARY CONNECTIONS

See the Spelling Challenge Words, pages 171O–171P.

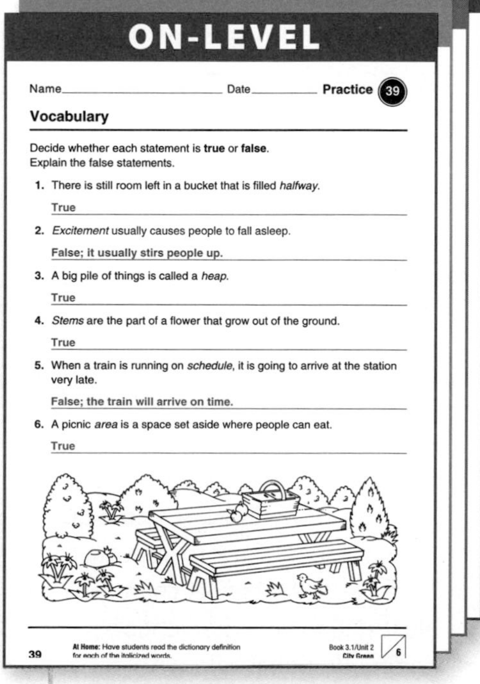

ON-LEVEL

Name______________ Date________ Practice 39

Vocabulary

Decide whether each statement is **true** or **false**. Explain the false statements.

1. There is still room left in a bucket that is filled *halfway*.
   True
2. *Excitement* usually causes people to fall asleep.
   False; it usually stirs people up.
3. A big pile of things is called a *heap*.
   True
4. *Stems* are the part of a flower that grow out of the ground.
   True
5. When a train is running on *schedule*, it is going to arrive at the station very late.
   False; the train will arrive on time.
6. A picnic *area* is a space set aside where people can eat.
   True

39 At Home: Have students read the dictionary definition for each of the italicized words. Book 3.1/Unit 2 City Green 5

Take-Home Story 39a
Reteach 39
Practice 39 • **Extend 39**

Guided Instruction

Preview and Predict

Have students preview the story by reading the title and looking at the pictures. During their **picture walk**, encourage them to find clues that tell what might be causing characters to look sad or happy.

- Based on picture clues, where do you think this story takes place?
- What clues do you see that this story is realistic fiction? (The characters and surroundings look real.) ***Genre***
- What do you think this story will be about?
- Why do you think the characters look happy in some of the pictures?

Have students record their predictions about the story.

PREDICTIONS	WHAT HAPPENED
The story takes place in the city.	
The flowers cause people to be happy.	

Set Purposes

What do students want to find out by reading this story? For example:

- What is a "city green"?

Meet DyAnne DiSalvo-Ryan

As a child, DyAnne DiSalvo-Ryan drew all the time. She recalls, "I always loved a sharp pencil and a new piece of paper." People would ask if she wanted to be an artist someday. She'd say, "I'm an artist already."

DiSalvo-Ryan hopes her drawings will feel familiar to children. She wants them "to be able to see themselves or their neighbors" in her art.

DiSalvo-Ryan's stories often grow out of her own experiences. *Uncle Willie and the Soup Kitchen* is based on her volunteer work at a soup kitchen. The garden lot she always passed on the way there inspired *City Green.*

144

Meeting Individual Needs • Grouping Suggestions for Strategic Reading

EASY

Shared Reading Read the story together with students or have them use the **Listening Library Audiocassette.** Have students record important events in a Cause-and-Effect chart. Guided Instruction and Intervention prompts offer additional help with decoding and comprehension.

ON-LEVEL

Guided Reading Preview the story words on page 145. You may want to have the students read the story first on their own. Then as you read the story together or use the **Listening Library Audiocassette,** have students use the Cause-and-Effect chart to record important events and why they happened.

CHALLENGE

Reading Independently Have students identify important changes that occur and what causes them. Have them complete a Cause-and-Effect chart as shown on page 145. After reading they can use the chart to check their predictions.

by DyAnne DiSalvo-Ryan

Guided Instruction

Cause and Effect

Strategic Reading Paying attention to cause and effect will help you understand why certain events happen in the story. Before we begin reading, let's set up a Cause-and-Effect chart so we can keep notes about important events and why they happen.

CAUSE	EFFECT

1 **CAUSE AND EFFECT** Look at the girl in the picture. What do you think is the cause of her happiness? (The girl is surrounded by beautiful flowers. Flowers usually make people feel good. The girl is happy because she is surrounded by flowers.)

Story Words

These words may be unfamiliar to students. Have them write each definition and pronunciation, using the Glossary on page 388.

- rubble, p. 148
- lease, p. 153
- petition, p. 153

LANGUAGE SUPPORT

A blackline master of the Cause-and-Effect chart is available in the **Language Support Book**. Point out that many of the events in *City Green* happen for a particular reason. Tell students that by noting cause and effect they will better appreciate this story.

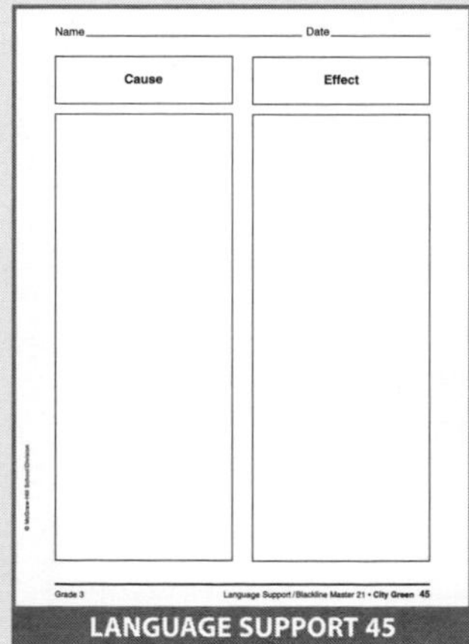

Name_______________ Date_______

Cause	Effect

Grade 3 Language Support/Blackline Master 21 • City Green 45

LANGUAGE SUPPORT 45

Guided Instruction

2 CAUSE AND EFFECT Here we learn that a building has been torn down. What caused this event? (The building was unsafe.)

MODEL As I read about events in a story, I observe how one event will cause another to happen. I know that keeping track of the causes and effects of events will help me better understand the story. I'm going to look for what happens because the building has been torn down. It could be important to the story plot.

There used to be a building right here on this lot. It was three floors up and down, an empty building nailed up shut for as long as I could remember. My friend Miss Rosa told me Old Man Hammer used to live there—some other neighbors too. But when I asked him about that, he only hollered, "Scram."

Old Man Hammer, hard as nails.

2 3 Last year two people from the city came by, dressed in suits and holding papers. They said, "This building is unsafe. It will have to be torn down."

146

Activity

Cross Curricular: Social Studies

MAP SKILLS Display local maps. Discuss children's neighborhoods. Ask:

- Do we live in a city or town?
- What cities are we near?

RESEARCH AND INQUIRY Have students copy an outline map of their state and label their town and important landmarks. ▶ **Mathematical/Spatial**

interNET CONNECTION Students can learn more about their state by visiting ***www.mhschool.com/reading.***

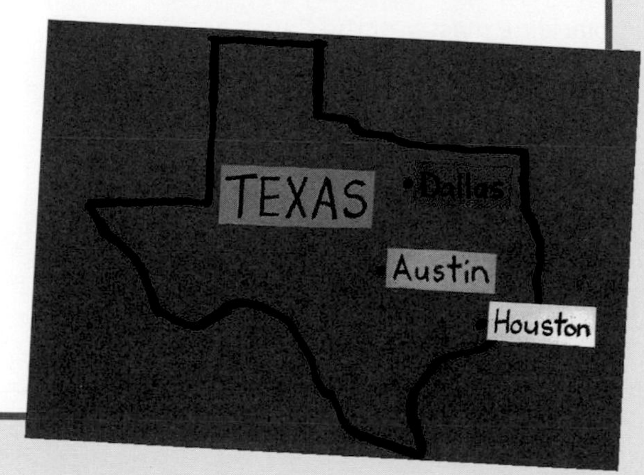

Guided Instruction

3 Often an author lets readers know what characters are like by both their actions and words. What can you tell so far about the person telling the story? How can you tell? (She is interested in her neighborhood. She asks about the empty building.) What can you tell about Old Man Hammer? (He is grouchy and likes to keep to himself. He tells the girl to "scram" when she asks him questions.) ***Character***

Minilesson

REVIEW/MAINTAIN

Prefixes

Have students reread the second to last sentence. Explain that adding the prefix *un-* to a word changes its meaning. Ask a volunteer to:

- write *unsafe* on the chalkboard.
- draw a line between the syllables.
- use the base word *safe* in a sentence and use it with the prefix *un-* in a sentence.
- tell how *un-* changes a word's meaning.

Activity Have partners add the prefix *un-* to the following base words: *used, tie, wrap, lucky, popular*. Have students write sentences using the base words and the words with the prefix *un-* added.

Guided Instruction

4 **CAUSE AND EFFECT** Look at the people in the picture. What is causing them to feel sad? Let's write the cause and effect in our chart.

CAUSE	EFFECT
The building was torn down.	The neighbors are all sad.

5 The last paragraph describes how Miss Rosa and the narrator plant seeds every spring. What steps to complete this task are mentioned here? (steps: clean the cans, buy the seeds, scoop the dirt, and fill the cans halfway) ***Steps in a Process***

By winter a crane with a wrecking ball was parked outside. Mama gathered everyone to watch from our front window. In three slow blows that building was knocked into a heap of pieces. Then workers took the rubble away in a truck and filled the hole with dirt.

Now this block looks like a big smile with one tooth missing. Old Man Hammer sits on his stoop and shakes his head. "Look at that piece of junk land on a city block," Old Man Hammer says. "Once that building could've been saved. But nobody even tried."

And every day when I pass this lot it makes me sad to see it. Every single day.

5 Then spring comes, and right on schedule Miss Rosa starts
6 cleaning her coffee cans. Miss Rosa and I keep coffee cans outside our windowsills. Every year we buy two packets of seeds at the hardware store—sometimes marigolds, sometimes zinnias, and one time we tried tomatoes. We go to the park, scoop some dirt, and
7 fill up the cans halfway.

148

Activity

Cross Curricular: Science

WEATHER This story takes place in spring. Ask students what they know about the seasons. List their ideas on the chalkboard.

RESEARCH AND INQUIRY Have students work in groups. Assign one season to each group. Have each group make a poster showing scenes that relate to their assigned season. ▶ **Spatial/Logical**

Winter In Our Town
Winter means you can build a snowman.

Guided Instruction

6 **CAUSE AND EFFECT** Why do you think Miss Rosa and the narrator use coffee cans to plant seeds? Why don't they plant them somewhere else? (They live in the city, and there are probably no gardens to plant seeds.)

7 Can you predict what might happen next? Explain why you think so. (The characters will plant a garden. They have planted seeds in coffee cans, and they can use the empty lot for a garden.) ***Make Predictions***

LANGUAGE SUPPORT

ESL Help students learn words related to cities. Ask them to name as many items as they can from the pictures and text they have read so far. Make a web for the words. Encourage students to add other words to the web.

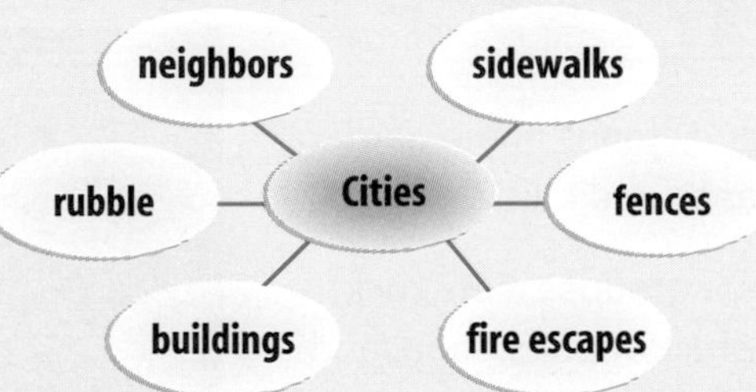

Minilesson

REVIEW/MAINTAIN

Character

Remind students that a character's actions and words help a reader to understand what that character is like. This helps the reader to better understand the story.

- Have students reread the second paragraph on page 148. Ask: What does Old Man Hammer do? What does he say?

Activity Have students make a web with Old Man Hammer as the center. Have them add as many words as they can to describe him, based on his actions and words.

Guided Instruction

8 **CAUSE AND EFFECT** Miss Rosa and the narrator realize the lot is one big pile of dirt. What effect does this have on them? Let's add the answer to our chart.

CAUSE	EFFECT
The building was torn down.	The neighbors are all sad.
The lot is filled with dirt.	Miss Rosa and the narrator decide to dig a garden.

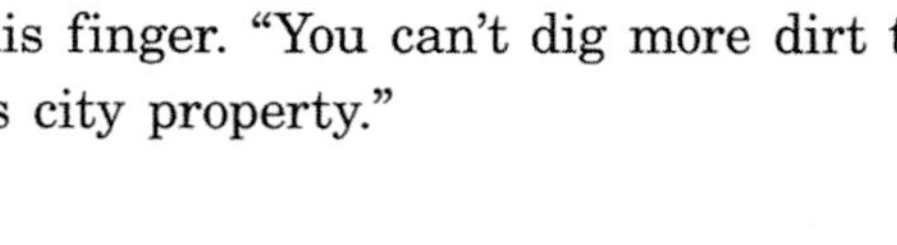

This time Old Man Hammer stops us on the way to the park. "This good for nothin' lot has plenty of dirt right here," he says.

Then all at once I look at Miss Rosa. And she is smiling back at me. "A *lot* of dirt," Miss Rosa says.

"Like one big coffee can," I say.

That's when we decide to do something about this lot.

8 Quick as a wink I'm digging away, already thinking of gardens and flowers. But Old Man Hammer shakes his finger. "You can't dig more dirt than that. This lot
9 is city property."

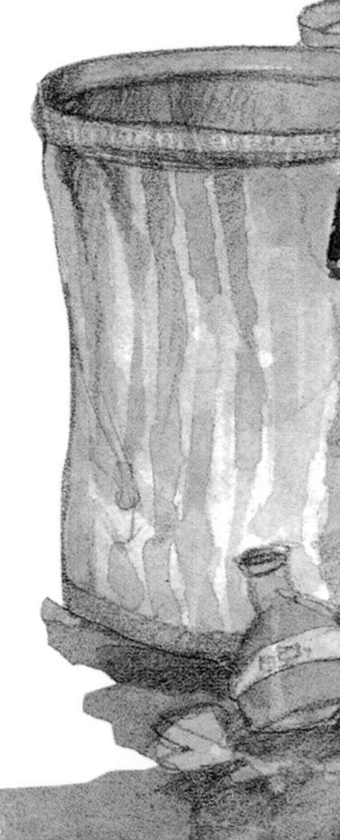

150

CULTURAL PERSPECTIVES

JAPANESE GARDENS In Japan there are special gardens known as rock gardens. Here is how to create them:

- Spread sand along the ground.
- Make wavy lines through the sand to represent water.
- Arrange rocks and stones in the garden to resemble islands and hills.

Activity Have groups create rock gardens. Provide shallow pans, sand, and rocks. Students can use combs to make waves and then arrange the rocks.
▶ **Kinesthetic/Spatial**

Guided Instruction

9 **CAUSE AND EFFECT** The characters want to dig more dirt, but Old Man Hammer tells them they can't. What cause, or reason, does he give them? (He tells them the lot is city property.)

PHONICS KIT
HANDS-ON ACTIVITIES AND PRACTICE

Minilesson

REVIEW/MAINTAIN

Syllable Patterns

Have students look at the words *Hammer* and *coffee* on page 150.

- Ask students what these words have in common. (They both contain double consonants.)
- Ask how the words would be divided into syllables. (between the first two consonants) Which syllable is accented? (first)
- Point out that in a two-syllable word with a double consonant, the first syllable usually has a short-vowel sound.

Activity Have students brainstorm and list other double-consonant words such as *happy* and *sorry*.

LANGUAGE SUPPORT

ESL Ask students to tell what has happened in the story so far. (A building has been torn down. The people on the block are unhappy. Miss Rosa and the little girl have started to dig dirt for their coffee can gardens.) Then ask: What idea do Miss Rosa and Marcy have? (They can plant a garden in the lot.) What does Mr. Hammer think about their idea? (He says they can't do it because the lot belongs to the city, not to them.)

Guided Instruction

10 **CAUSE AND EFFECT** Miss Rosa's and Marcy's actions have a big effect on the neighborhood. In your chart, list the cause (what they do) and the effect.

CAUSE	EFFECT
The lot is filled with dirt.	Miss Rosa and the narrator decide to dig a garden.
The lot is city property.	The neighbors decide to rent the lot from the city.

11 Old Man Hammer had an opinion about what would happen with the petition. What was his opinion? What facts proved him wrong? (He believed nothing would happen with the petition. The city accepted the petition and the neighbors rented the lot.) ***Fact and Opinion***

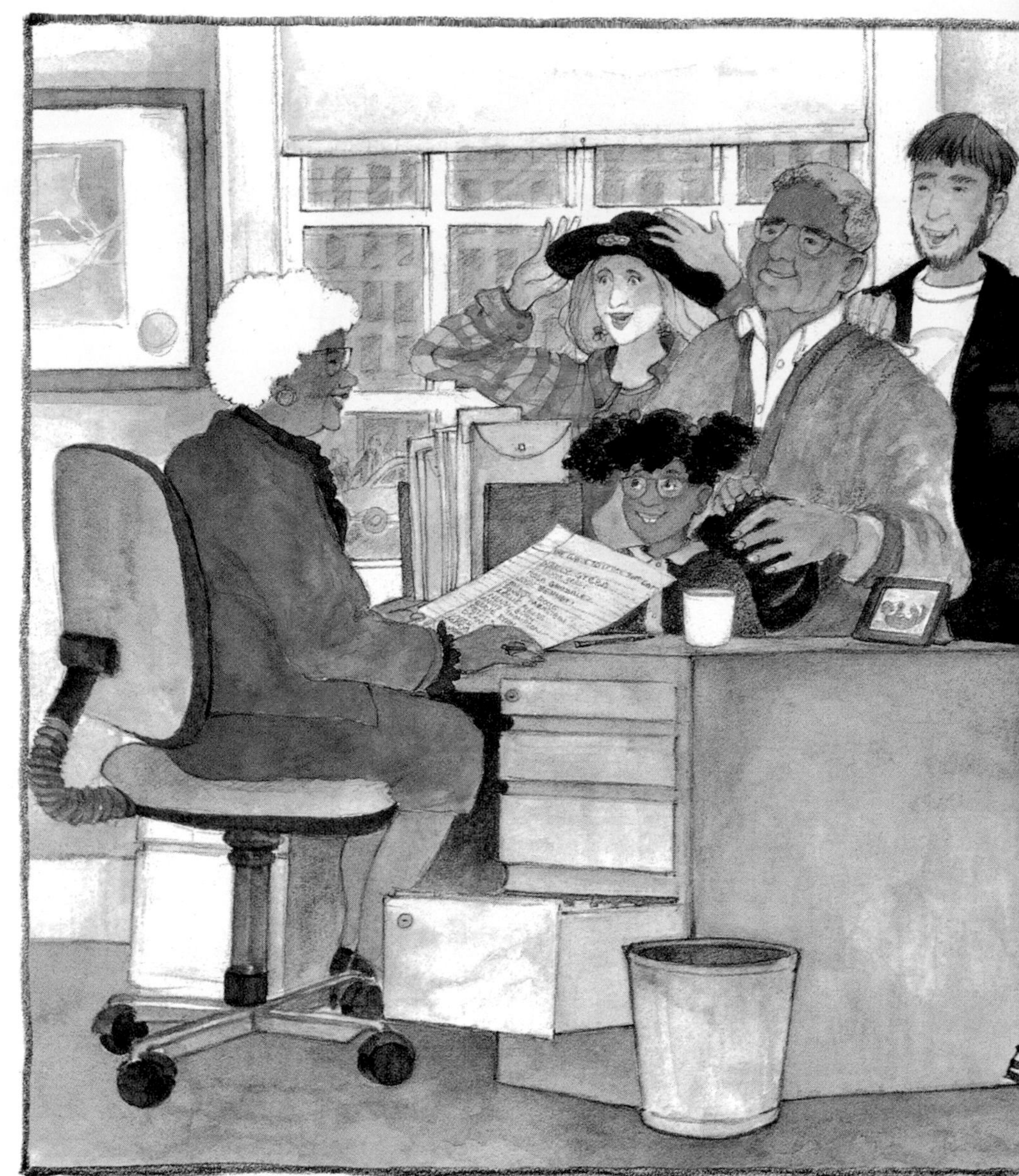

152

Visual Literacy

VIEWING AND REPRESENTING

The author doesn't tell us how the people feel about going to city hall. Look at the illustration and describe how the people feel. How can you tell? (They are excited and happy. You can tell by their smiles and hand gestures.)

Now look back at the illustrations on pages 148 and 149. What do the people feel like at this point of the story? How are their faces and hand gestures different? (They are upset and sad. They have sad and worried faces. One person has her hands covering her eyes.)

Miss Rosa and I go to see Mr. Bennett. He used to work for the city. "I seem to remember a program," he says, "that lets people rent empty lots."

That's how Miss Rosa and I form a group of people from our block. We pass around a petition that says: WE WANT TO LEASE THIS LOT. In less than a week we have plenty of names. 

"Sign with us?" I ask Old Man Hammer.

"I'm not signin' nothin'," he says. "And nothin' is what's gonna happen." 

But something did.

The next week, a bunch of us take a bus to city hall. We walk up the steps to the proper office and hand the woman our list. She checks her files and types some notes and makes some copies. "That will be one dollar, please."

We rent the lot from the city that day. It was just as simple as that.

Saturday morning I'm up with the sun and looking at this lot. My mama looks out too. "Marcy," she says, and hugs me close. "Today I'm helping you and Rosa." 

153

Guided Instruction

12 Think about how Old Man Hammer has reacted to all of the events so far. Based on his words and actions, what kind of a person do you think he is? Do you like his character? Why or why not? Support your answers with events from the story. (Possible response: He shakes his head and says that the building could have been saved. This shows he feels disappointed and sad. He stops them from digging, won't sign the petition, and is grouchy. This shows he has stopped trying to change things. I don't like his character because he is so negative.) *Character*

Minilesson

REVIEW/MAINTAIN

Main Idea

Review that the main idea of a selection answers the question: *What is it about?*

- Have students discuss the main idea on this page. (The neighbors work together to get permission to rent the lot.)

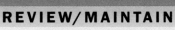

Activity Have partners write the main idea and then list details from the page that support it. What title might they give this page?

Guided Instruction

13 **CAUSE AND EFFECT** Everyone except Old Man Hammer is working together to clean up the lot. What effect does the work have? (The lot is beginning to look good.)

TEACHING TIP

INSTRUCTIONAL Point out to students that the characters aren't just throwing things away, but recycling items, too. Help them find the word *recycle* in the illustration. Talk about recycling programs in your community. Have students share how they help recycle.

13

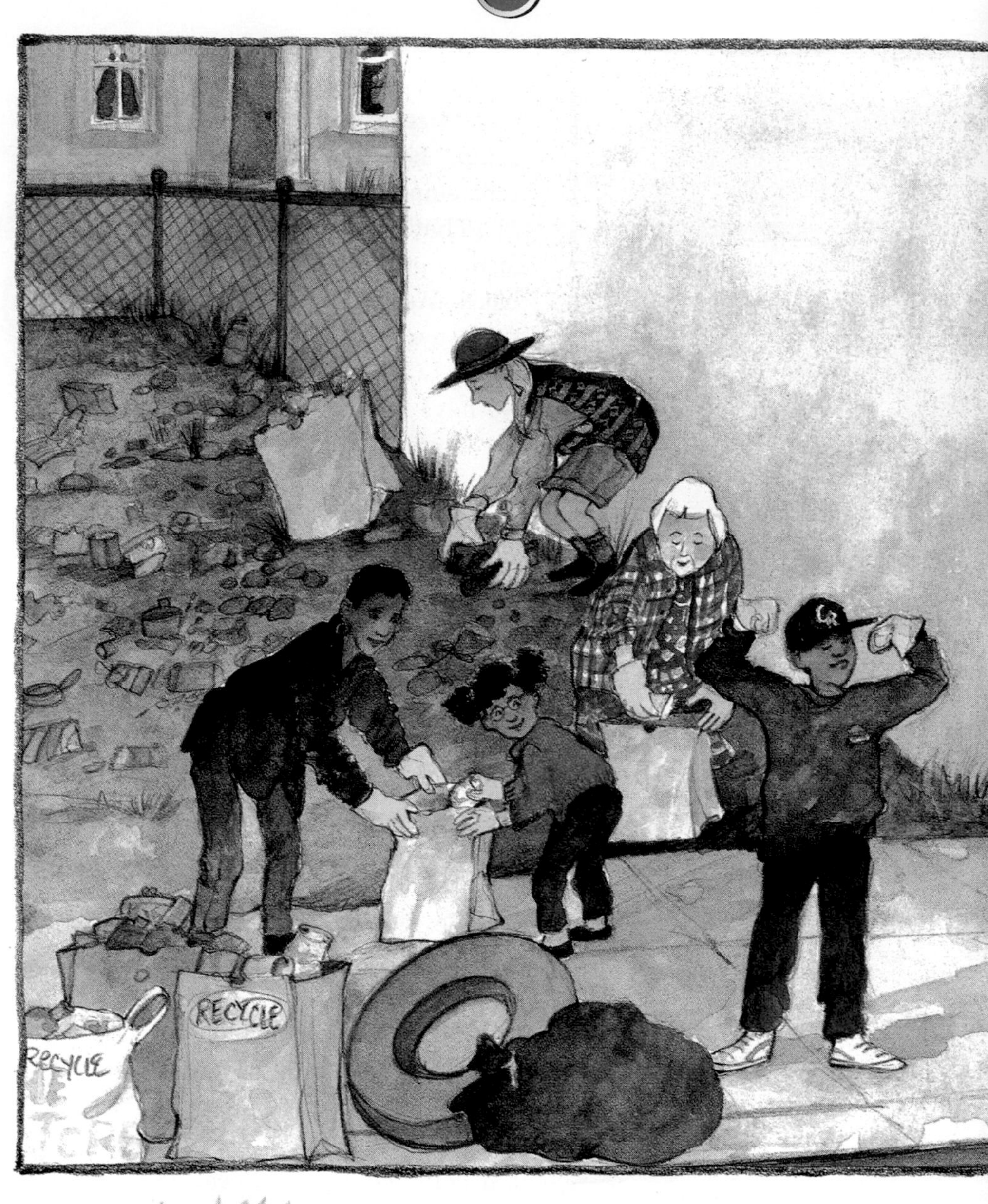

154

Activity

Cross Curricular: Drama

FABLES Explain that the phrase "sour grapes" comes from Aesop's tale about the fox and the grapes. Because the fox could not reach the grapes he wanted, he pretended that they were sour and not worth having. Discuss why Mama uses this term to refer to Old Man Hammer.

Have partners create and perform a short skit demonstrating "sour grapes". Have students role-play frustrated animals that can't perform certain tasks, such as a chicken trying to fly or a fish trying to walk.

▶ **Kinesthetic/Interpersonal**

After shopping, Mama empties her grocery bags and folds them flat to carry under her arm. "Come on, Mrs. B.," Mama tells her friend. "We're going to clear this lot."

Then what do you know but my brother comes along. My brother is tall and strong. At first, he scratches his neck and shakes his head just like Old Man Hammer. But Mama smiles and says, "None of that here!" So all day long he piles junk in those bags and carries them to the curb.

Now, this time of day is early. Neighbors pass by and see what we're doing. Most say, "We want to help too." They have a little time to spare. Then this one calls that one and that one calls another.

"Come on and help," I call to Old Man Hammer.

"I'm not helpin' nobody," he hollers. "You're all wastin' your time."

Sour grapes my mama'd say, and sour grapes is right.

Just before supper, when we are good and hungry, my mama looks around this lot. "Marcy," she says, "you're making something happen here."

155

Guided Instruction

14 **DRAW CONCLUSIONS** What conclusion can you draw about how Mama feels about Old Man Hammer's behavior? Support your conclusion with evidence from this page. (Mama disapproves of Old Man Hammer's behavior. Marcy says that her mother would use "sour grapes" to refer to his attitude.)

15 What has happened in the story so far? Who would like to give a summary? Be sure to mention only the main events. (Answers will vary. Possible answer: Marcy and her neighbors rent an empty city lot to make a garden. Everyone helps clean up the lot except Old Man Hammer. He is cranky and thinks the garden is a waste of time.) *Summarize*

LANGUAGE SUPPORT

ESL Ask students to explain in their own words what is happening on this Saturday morning. Ask questions such as: What are the people doing? (picking up trash, cleaning out the lot) How many people are helping? (five people) Point to each person in the picture and ask: Who is this? (Marcy, Mama, Marcy's brother, Miss Rosa, a woman, Mr. Hammer) Point to Mr. Hammer and ask: What does Mr. Hammer say when Marcy asks him to help? (He says he won't help. He thinks that the idea for a garden won't work.)

Guided Instruction

16 **CAUSE AND EFFECT** Marcy's brother asks why Old Man Hammer is so cranky these days. What does Marcy think is the cause of his crankiness? (She thinks he might miss the old building.)

SELF-MONITORING

STRATEGY

REREADING Rereading part of the story can remind readers about information they may have skipped or forgotten.

MODEL I'm not sure what causes Old Man Hammer to be so cranky. When I reread this page I see that he might miss his building. I don't remember why Marcy says "*his* building." I'll go back to the beginning. When I reread the first paragraph on page 146, I see that he used to live in this building. Now I know why he is so cranky.

156

Activity

Cross Curricular: Math

GARDEN PLOT Have students pretend they will select a plot for their community garden. Draw four rectangles on the chalkboard with the following measurements:

1. 40′ x 20′
2. 60′ x 30′
3. 25′ x 10′
4. 70′ x 40′

Have students find the total area of all four lots by completing the chart. Which lot has the largest area? Which has the smallest area? Which lot would you select and why? ▶ **Mathematical/Spatial**

Lot	Length	Width	Area in Square Feet
1.	40	20	800
2.	60	30	1800
3.	25	10	250
4.	70	40	2800

Next day the city drops off tools like rakes and brooms, and a Dumpster for trash. Now there's even more neighbors to help. Miss Rosa, my brother, and I say "Good morning" to Old Man Hammer, but Old Man Hammer just waves like he's swatting a fly.

"Why is Old Man Hammer so mean and cranky these days?" my brother asks.

"Maybe he's really sad," I tell him. "Maybe he misses his building." 16

"That rotten old building?" My brother shrugs. "He should be happy the city tore down that mess." 17

"Give him time," Miss Rosa says. "Good things take time."

Mr. Bennett brings wood—old slats he's saved—and nails in a cup. "I knew all along I saved them for something," he says. "This wood's good wood."

Then Mr. Rocco from two houses down comes, carrying two cans of paint. "I'll never use these," he says. "The color's too bright. But here, this lot could use some brightening up."

157

Guided Instruction

17 **CAUSE AND EFFECT** Let's write down the causes and effects we've identified so far. How do they help us understand the story? (They show each important event and why it happened.)

CAUSE	EFFECT
The lot is city property.	The neighbors decide to rent the lot from the city.
Everyone but Old Man Hammer works on the lot.	The lot is cleaned up.

P/I **CONTEXT CLUES** Read the word *Dumpster* in the first sentence on page 157. Can you guess what the word *Dumpster* means after reading the sentence? Try to define the word. (a large container for trash)

P/I PREVENTION/INTERVENTION

CONTEXT CLUES Have students reread the first sentence on this page. Discuss how the words in the sentence help explain the meaning of *Dumpster*. Point out that since a dumpster is "for trash" it is probably a large container that holds trash.

Have students review the picture on page 154. Point out that this is a large lot filled with a lot of garbage. Have students consider how large the dumpster would have to be to hold all the trash. Tell students that some dumpsters are as big as a truck.

Guided Instruction

18 **CAUSE AND EFFECT** Marcy sees Old Man Hammer walking to the back of the garden at night. What caused him to go there when no one else was around? (He didn't want the others to see him; he didn't want anyone to know that he was interested in the garden.)

19 Marcy tells her mama that she thinks Old Man Hammer has planted some seeds. Do you think she is right? Why or why not? (Answers may vary.) ***Make Predictions***

P/I **DECODING/CONTEXT CLUES** Near the end of the first paragraph on page 159, look for the word spelled *s-h-o-v-e-l*. (*shovel*) Read the sentence, then try to sound out the word. Do any of the other words in the sentence help?

158

PREVENTION/INTERVENTION

DECODING/CONTEXT CLUES
Write the word *shovel* on the chalkboard. Have students separate the word into syllables. Ask: Should we write *shov • el* or *sho • vel*?

Work together to sound out each version. (The first would have a short *o*; the second a long *o*.) Point out that students can figure out the word by using context clues.

Ask: According to the sentence, what is Sonny doing? (turning over dirt) What word do you know that names something that begins with the sound /sh/ and ends with /əl/ and is used to turn over dirt? (*shovel*)

Well, anyone can tell with all the excitement that something is going on. And everyone has an idea about what to plant—strawberries, carrots, lettuce, and more. Tulips and daisies, petunias, and more! Sonny turns the dirt over with a snow shovel. Even Leslie's baby tries to dig with a spoon.

For lunch, Miss Rosa brings milk and jelly and bread and spreads a beach towel where the junk is cleared. By the end of the day a fence is built and painted as bright as the sun.

Later, Mama kisses my cheek and closes my bedroom door. By the streetlights I see Old Man Hammer come down his steps to 18
open the gate and walk to the back of this lot. He bends down quick, sprinkling something from his pocket and covering it over with dirt.

In the morning I tell my brother. "Oh, Marcy," he says. "You're dreaming. You're wishing too hard."

But I know what I saw, and I
tell my mama, "Old Man 
Hammer's planted some seeds."

20

159

Guided Instruction

20 Reread the third paragraph on this page. What conclusions can you draw about Old Man Hammer through his actions? (Answers may vary: Old Man Hammer really wants to participate in the garden. He might be too embarrassed to let anyone know that he hopes the garden will succeed. He is afraid of another disappointment.) ***Draw Conclusions***

Minilesson

REVIEW/MAINTAIN

Setting

Remind students that the setting of a story tells where and when the story takes place. Knowing the time and place of events helps a reader follow the action.

- Ask students to describe the setting and how it changes in this part of the story.

Activity Have students make a chart to show story events for each time of the day:

MORNING	NOON	END OF THE DAY	NIGHT
Everyone is digging.	Miss Rosa brings lunch.	The fence is finished.	Old Man Hammer plants seeds.

Guided Instruction

21 **CAUSE AND EFFECT** Marcy now knows for sure that Old Man Hammer planted seeds. What does she think caused him to plant them there? What clues lead her to this conclusion?

MODEL I think Marcy believes Old Man Hammer planted his seeds in the back because that's where his room used to be. She thinks this because Mrs. Wells planted her seeds where her grandmother's bedroom used to be. Marcy probably remembers that Old Man Hammer also lived in the building that was torn down.

22 Look at the picture on this page. Then read the last paragraph. How do you think the author wants the reader to feel about Old Man Hammer? Did the author do a good job? Why or why not? (Possible response: The author wants the reader to feel sorry for Old Man Hammer. Yes, she did a good job because the picture shows him all alone and sad.) ***Author's Craft***

21 Right after breakfast, I walk to the back of this lot. And there it is—a tiny raised bed of soil. It is neat and tidy, just like the rows we've planted. Now I know for sure that Old Man Hammer planted something. So I pat the soil for good luck and make a little fence to keep the seeds safe.

Every day I go for a look inside our garden lot. Other neighbors stop in too. One day Mrs. Wells comes by. "This is right where my grandmother's bedroom used to be," she says. "That's why I planted my flowers there."

22 I feel sad when I hear that. With all the digging and planting and weeding and watering, I'd forgotten about the building that had been on this lot. Old Man Hammer had lived there too. I go to the back, where he planted his seeds. I wonder if this was the place where his room used to be.

160

23

Guided Instruction

23 **CAUSE AND EFFECT** What do you predict the effect of Old Man Hammer planting his seeds might be? (Answers may vary.)

Minilesson

REVIEW/MAINTAIN

Make Predictions

Remind students that making predictions can help readers focus on the plot and understand characters. Have students read page 161 and:

- predict what will happen to Old Man Hammer's seeds.
- predict if the garden will be a success.

Activity Have students revise these predictions as they read the story.

Guided Instruction

24 **CAUSE AND EFFECT** Old Man Hammer has changed from the beginning of the story to now. How has he changed? What event made him change? (I think Old Man Hammer no longer feels so negative because his flowers began to grow.)

I look down. Beside my feet, some tiny stems are sprouting. Old Man Hammer's seeds have grown! I run to his stoop. "Come with me!" I beg, tugging at his hand. "You'll want to see."

I walk him past the hollyhocks, the daisies, the peppers, the rows of lettuce. I show him the strawberries
24 that I planted. When Old Man Hammer sees his little garden bed, his sour grapes turn sweet. "Marcy, child."
25 He shakes his head. "This lot was good for nothin'. Now it's nothin' but good," he says.
26

162

Fluency

READ DIALOGUE

Have groups of three take turns acting out a brief skit showing the events on this page.

- Have one student be the narrator and read the prose part of the text.
- Have two other students read the dialogue for Marcy and Old Man Hammer and act out the words the narrator reads.
- Encourage students to use both facial and verbal expression as they play their parts.

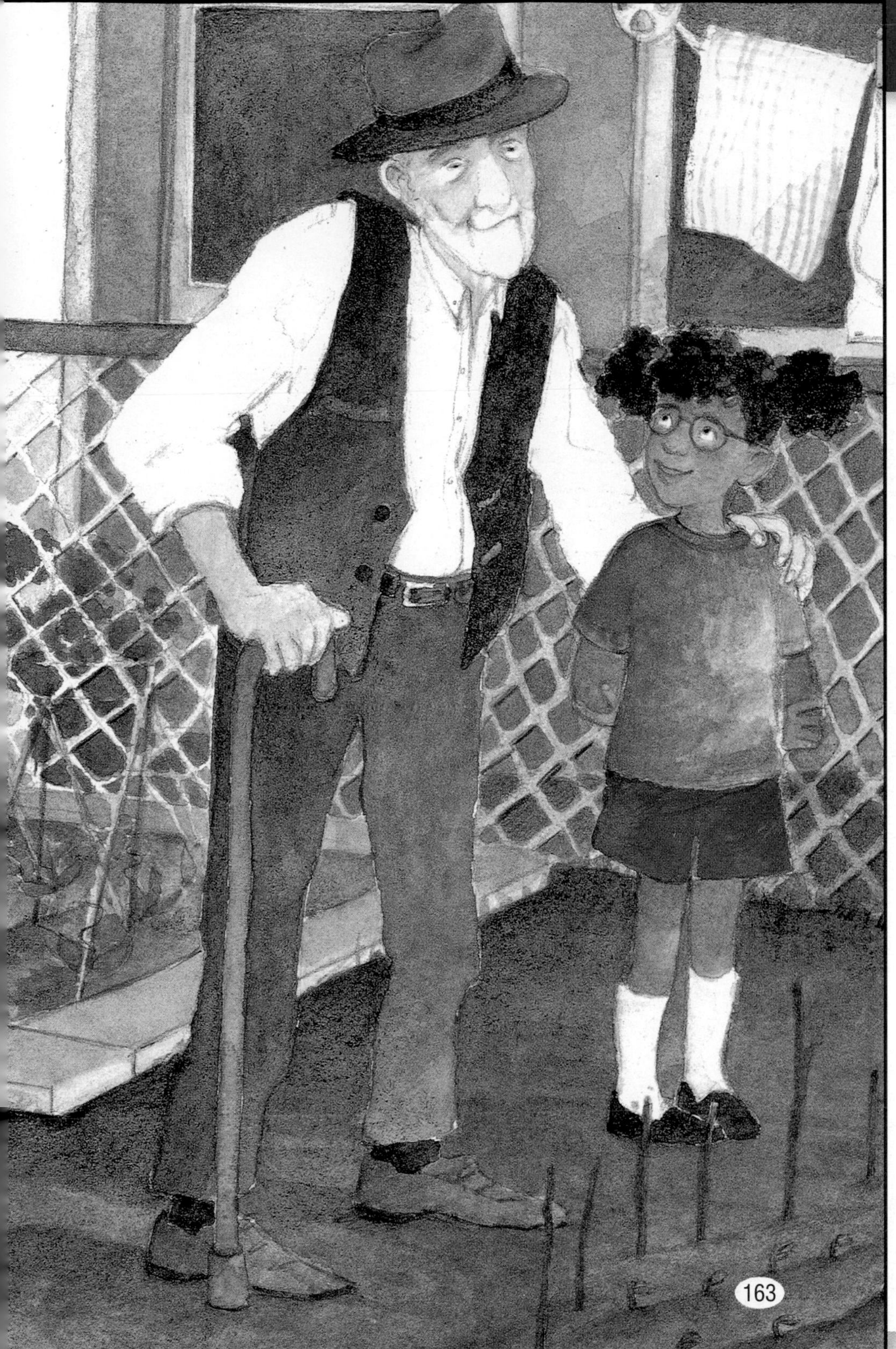

Guided Instruction

25 What is the main idea of the last paragraph on page 162? What details are given to support it? (Old Man Hammer is no longer angry about the garden. He tells Marcy, "It's nothin' but good.") ***Main Idea***

26 What is your opinion of Old Man Hammer now? Do you like him? Why or why not? What is your opinion of Marcy? Would you want her as a friend? Why or why not? (Answers may vary, but students should support opinions with evidence from the story.) ***Make Judgments and Decisions***

Guided Instruction

27 What was the main problem that Marcy faced in making the community garden? (Old Man Hammer was very negative and discouraging about the garden.) What did Marcy do to help solve her problem? (Marcy continued her work in the garden even though Old Mr. Hammer said "You're all wastin' your time." She kept trying to encourage him until finally he saw that the garden was a success.) ***Problem and Solution***

TEACHING TIP

MANAGEMENT Every Monday, give students a basic spelling pre-test. Let them replace every word they already know how to spell with an unfamiliar word from a special bonus list you have posted. This usually results in a different spelling list for each student.

Soon summertime comes, and this lot really grows. It fills with vegetables, herbs, and flowers. And way in the back, taller than anything else, is a beautiful patch of yellow sunflowers. Old Man Hammer comes every day. He sits in the sun, eats his lunch, and sometimes comes back with supper.

Nobody knows how the sunflowers came—not Leslie, my brother, or Miss Rosa. Not Mr. Bennett, or Sonny, or anyone else. But Old Man Hammer just sits there smiling at me. We know whose flowers they are. 27

29

165

Guided Instruction

28 What do you think of Old Man Hammer now? How has his character changed since the beginning of the story? (Old Man Hammer is very different at the end of the story. He is friends with Marcy and visits the garden at least once every day. He admits that the lot is "nothin' but good." He seems to be much happier and more friendly now that he knows that the garden is a success.) *Analyze Character*

29 **DRAW CONCLUSIONS** What conclusions can you draw about the neighbors who worked in the garden? What might they like or dislike? (Possible answer: The neighbors who worked in the garden were very hard-working people. They enjoyed being outdoors and liked gardening. They also enjoyed working in their community and liked their neighbors.)

Minilesson

REVIEW/MAINTAIN

Fact and Opinion

Write the definitions for fact and opinion on the chalkboard. Ask students whether the following statements are fact or opinion:

- Old Man Hammer is a bad person.
- Marcy's garden is the prettiest garden in the city.
- The neighbors are renting the lot to build a garden.

Activity Have students keep a Fact/Opinion chart as they read the story.

Guided Instruction

30 CAUSE AND EFFECT Let's think back about the story and complete our Cause-and-Effect chart.

CAUSE	EFFECT
The building was torn down.	The neighbors are all sad.
The lot is filled with dirt.	Miss Rosa and the narrator decide to dig a garden.
The lot is city property.	The neighbors decide to rent the lot from the city.
Everyone but Old Man Hammer works on the lot.	The lot is cleaned up.
The garden is a success.	Everyone, including Old Man Hammer, enjoys the garden.

RETELL THE STORY Using their Cause-and-Effect charts as a reference, have volunteers retell the main events of the story. Then have partners summarize the story in one or two sentences. Have them focus on the main characters' problems and how they are resolved.

STUDENT SELF-ASSESSMENT

- How did examining cause and effect help me understand the story?
- How did the Cause-and-Effect chart help me?
- When might I use this strategy again?
- In what other reading could the chart help me?

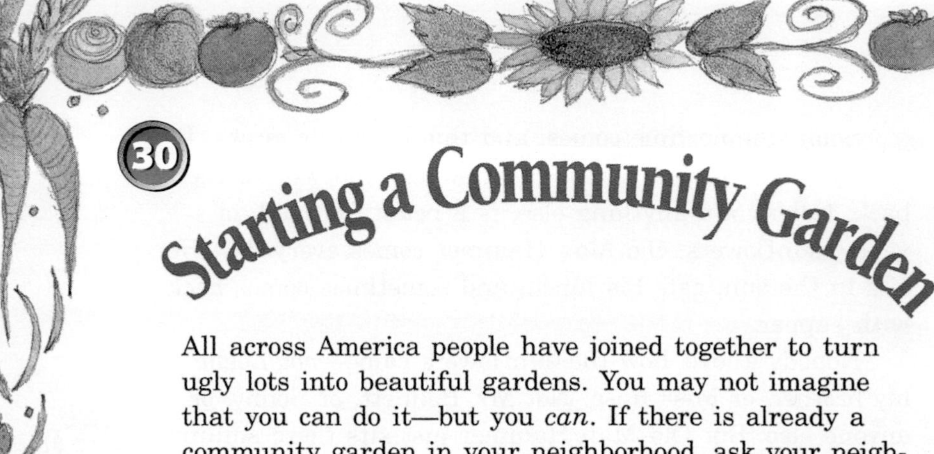

30

Starting a Community Garden

All across America people have joined together to turn ugly lots into beautiful gardens. You may not imagine that you can do it—but you *can*. If there is already a community garden in your neighborhood, ask your neighbors how they got started. But if you are the first on your block to "make something happen," this is what you can do:

1. Find an interested grown-up who wants to help you: a parent or guardian, a teacher, a librarian, or a neighbor.
2. Find out the address of the lot. This is very important. You may have to talk to neighbors or look at the address of the buildings next door. Example: The lot I am interested in is on Main Street. It is between 75 Main Street and 81 Main Street.
3. While you are finding out the address of the lot, get in touch with the local gardening program in your area (see end of this note). Say that you are interested in starting a garden. Since every city is different, your local program will be able to steer you in the right direction.
4. Find out who the owner is. The Department of Records at your local city hall can help. Look in the telephone book for the address of city hall in your area.

166

REREADING FOR *Fluency*

Have students role-play the end of the story with a partner. Encourage students to narrate or read characters' lines with feeling.

READING RATE You may want to evaluate an individual student's reading rate. Have the student read aloud from *City Green* for one minute. Ask the student to attach a self-stick note after the last word read. Then count the number of words he or she has read.

In order to assess small groups or the entire class together, have students count the words they read and record their own scores.

A Running Record form provided in **Diagnostic/Placement Evaluation** will help you evaluate reading rate(s).

5. If the lot is owned by the city, the people at city hall can help you get permission to use the lot. Usually there is a small fee. If the lot is owned by an individual person or group, you will need to get permission from that person or group to use the lot.

6. Once you get permission to use the lot, it's yours to name!

There are hundreds of gardening programs that are ready to help community gardeners with information, soil, seeds, fencing, and more.

To find out the community gardening program that is nearest you, write to:

American Community Gardening Association
325 Walnut Street
Philadelphia, PA 19106

Community gardens bring people together. Join the work and join the fun!

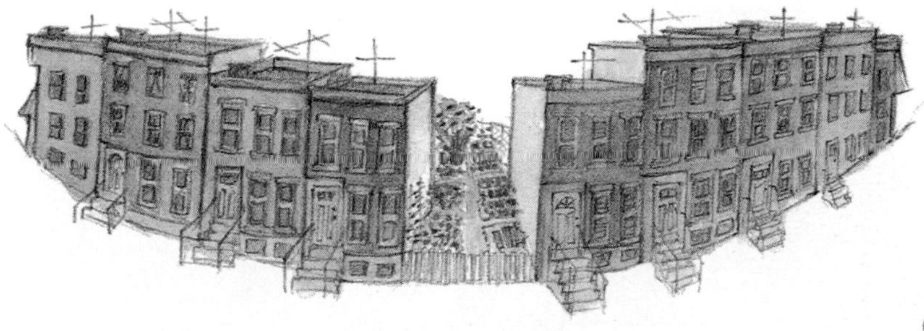

167

LITERARY RESPONSE

QUICK-WRITE Invite students to share their opinions about the characters in this story. Have them choose two of the following characters and tell what they liked about them. Have them support their opinions with events from the story.

JOURNAL

- Miss Rosa
- Marcy
- Old Man Hammer
- Marcy's mother

ORAL RESPONSE Have students share their journal writings and discuss whether or not they liked the story ending and why.

Guided Instruction

Return to Predictions and Purposes

Review with students their story predictions and reasons for reading the story. Were their predictions correct? Did they find out what they wanted to know?

PREDICTIONS	WHAT HAPPENED
The story takes place in the city.	The story mainly takes place in an empty lot on a block in a city.
The flowers cause people to be happy.	The neighbors change an empty lot into a garden. This makes everyone happy, even Old Man Hammer.

INFORMAL ASSESSMENT

ANALYZE CAUSE AND EFFECT

HOW TO ASSESS

Students should realize that an important effect was the change in Old Man Hammer's attitude. The success of the garden, especially his own sunflowers, caused him to realize that sometimes things do work out.

- Can the students identify cause-and-effect relationships in the story?
- Ask students to point out an important effect in the story.
- Have them describe the cause of this effect.

FOLLOW UP

If students have trouble identifying an important effect and its cause, have them describe Old Man Hammer and how he changed from the beginning of the story to the end. Ask them then to explain what made him change.

Story Questions

Have students discuss their answers.

Answers:

1. The lot looked like a big hole covered with dirt and garbage. *Literal/Setting*
2. Old Man Hammer was upset because he used to live in that building. *Inferential/ Cause and Effect*
3. Answers will vary. Possible answer: Yes, because it was such a success. *Inferential/ Make Predictions*
4. This story is mainly about a community working together to improve their neighborhood. *Critical/Summarize*
5. Both characters would probably get along. They are both very nostalgic for the past. *Critical/Reading Across Texts*

Write a Plan For a full writing process lesson related to this suggestion, see pages 171K–171L.

Story Questions & Activities

1. What did the lot look like at the beginning of the story?
2. Why was Old Man Hammer so upset about the building that was torn down?
3. Do you think the people on the block will plant the garden again next year? Why or why not?
4. What is this story mainly about?
5. If Old Man Hammer met the grandfather from "Grandfather's Journey," how would they get along? What might they talk about?

Write a Plan

Write a plan for a neighborhood garden. Explain how neighbors should choose a place, prepare it, and decide what to plant there. Check that your plan seems logical and well-organized.

Meeting Individual Needs

EASY

Name________________ Date________ **Reteach 39**

Vocabulary

area excitement halfway heap schedule stems

Choose a word from the box to finish each sentence. Write it on the line.

1. She looked at a ___schedule___ to see what she should do first.
2. The flower ___stems___ are growing strong and straight.
3. We will plant a garden in the ___area___ inside the fence.
4. Going to the zoo, the happy children were filled with ___excitement___.
5. We stopped to rest ___halfway___ up the hill.
6. We found a ___heap___ of rocks.

/6

Story Comprehension **Reteach 40**

Think about the story "City Green." Then underline the correct answer to each question.

1. What happens to the building at the beginning of the story?
   a. People move into the building. b. The building is knocked down.
2. What do Marcy and Rosa want to do in the empty lot?
   a. plant a garden b. make an area for animals
3. Who do Rosa and Marcy rent the empty lot from?
   a. the city b. Old Man Hammer
4. What secret do Rosa and Old Man Hammer share?
   a. He planted flowers. b. He paid for the empty lot.

39-40 **At Home:** Have students tell what they would plant if they had their own garden. Then have them draw a picture of their garden. Book 3.1/Unit 2 **City Green** /4

McGraw-Hill School Division

Reteach, 40

ON-LEVEL

Name________________ Date________ **Practice 40**

Story Comprehension

Think about "City Green." Then complete the chart below.
Answers may vary.

1. **Setting of the Story:** a city neighborhood
2. **Main Characters:** Marcy, Old Man Hammer, Miss Rosa, Marcy's mother and brother

Beginning of the Story

3. An old building was torn down, leaving behind an empty city lot.
4. The empty lot became filled with trash and litter.
5. Old Man Hammer said nothing good will ever come of the empty lot.

Middle of the Story

6. Marcy and Miss Rosa passed around a petition to lease the lot from the city.
7. Everyone in the neighborhood helped to clean up the lot and plant a garden.
8. One night, Marcy saw Old Man Hammer planting seeds in the garden.

End of the Story

9. Marcy begged Old Man Hammer to come see his seedlings in the garden.
10. When summer came, Marcy and Old Man Hammer enjoyed sitting in the garden near the sunflowers.

40 **At Home:** Have students identify and discuss problems on their street or in their own community. Book 3.1/Unit 2 **City Green** /10

McGraw-Hill School Division

Practice, 40

CHALLENGE

Name________________ Date________ **Extend 39**

Vocabulary

area excitement halfway heap schedule stems

Use words from the box to write a story about planting a garden. Exchange stories with a partner. Read the story. Then provide an illustration for your partner's story.

Extend 40

Story Comprehension

Select a part of the story "City Green" to write as a play. Describe the plot of your play below.

Decide on the characters you will need and who will play them. Write a script telling what the characters will say. Rehearse the play. Then act it out for your class.

39–40 **At Home:** Have students tell what they learned from "City Green." Book 3.1/Unit 2 **City Green**

McGraw-Hill School Division

Extend, 40

Design a Garden

Think about the kind of garden you would like to have. What shape would your garden be? Would you plant flowers, vegetables, or both? Draw and label a design for the garden.

Make a Speech

Brainstorm some ways that you, like Marcy, could make your environment better. Think of a project that would improve your school, home, or community. Prepare a speech about your project. Explain why other people should help, too.

Find Out More

Start a garden right in your classroom! First find out what plants grow well indoors. Choose one plant. Then find out what you can do to help the plant grow. Does it need sun or shade? How often should you water it?

169

Story Activities

Design a Garden

Materials: large sheets of white paper, felt-tipped markers or crayons, rulers

PARTNERS First have partners choose the vegetables or flowers for their garden. Then have partners sketch a diagram of their garden to determine the number of rows they will need.

Make a Speech

ONE Once students choose the topic for their speech, have them list the ways the project will help to improve their neighborhoods.

Find Out More

RESEARCH AND INQUIRY Students can

PARTNERS interview local florists or nursery owners for growing tips, and to find out which plants grow well in your area. Have students first brainstorm a list of questions to ask.

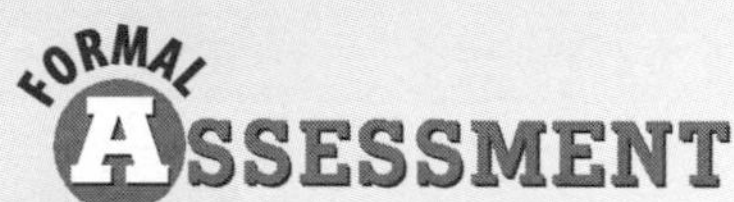

For more information about gardening have students visit ***www.mhschool.com/reading.***

FORMAL ASSESSMENT

After page 169, see the Selection Assessment.

Study Skills

Reference Sources

TESTED OBJECTIVES

Students will find information in a telephone directory.

PREPARE Look over the sample section of a telephone directory with students. Display **Teaching Chart 33**.

TEACH Bring in a telephone directory to show students. Review the parts of a telephone directory including the guide words, location of emergency numbers, yellow pages, and white pages.

PRACTICE Have students answer the questions **1–5**, then review the answers. **1.** 113 River Street; 555-7871 **2.** Roberto **3.** Phyllis's Pet Shop **4.** Park Hwy **5.** Possible response: You can use it to find addresses and phone numbers of people and stores you need.

ASSESS/CLOSE Have students write the phone number and address of a place where they can buy pies and cakes.

STUDY SKILLS

Use a Telephone Directory

In "City Green," neighbors work together to create something beautiful. People working together on a project often need to call each other. A telephone directory gives the names, addresses, and phone numbers of people and businesses in an area.

TELEPHONE DIRECTORY

128 PHOTO—POLLARD

Photo Phinishers 12 Beltway 555-4235	Pittman Gale 64 River St 555-6987
Phung Yan Chu 16 Center Ave 555-0971	Pittman Roger MD 1245 Santa Ana Blvd 555-9898
PHYLLIS'S PET SHOP 1166 Park Hwy **555-8920**	Pitts Loleta 133 Allen Way 555-6348
Pickard Nell 18 Dysart Ave 555-5681	Pizel John 501 Whitney Ave 555-6324
Pickard Roberto 9 Day St 555-6514	**PLAINVILLE BOAT SHOP** 1621 Park Hwy **555-9852**
Pickett Ana 809 Buena Vista 555-8942	Plante Kevan 113 River St 555-7421
Picovsky Susan 62 Wood St 555-6574	Plante Sylvia 113 River St 555-7871
Pidgeon C G 920 Main St 555-9821	Pletcher Arlen 75 Wood St 555-6314
Pie & Cake Co 622 Park Hwy 555-6355	Plumisto LeRoy 441 River St 555-6387
Piedra Bill 51 Horace St 555-3531	Plummer David 35 Main St 555-6871
Piedras Mike 23 Stuart Ave 555-6584	

Use the telephone directory to answer these questions.

1. What are Sylvia Plante's address and telephone number?
2. What is Mr. Pickard's first name?
3. Where would you go if you wanted to buy a canary?
4. On what street is the Plainville Boat Shop?
5. Why is a telephone directory useful?

Meeting Individual Needs

EASY

Name________ Date______ **Reteach 41**

Use a Telephone Directory

A **telephone directory** is a collection of names listed in alphabetical order. Both business and residential listings are included. Addresses and phone numbers are listed after the names.

Use this page from a telephone directory to answer the questions that follow.

658 LEWIS — LITTLE

LEWIS
Daniel 2 Woodchuck St 545-6785
Harold 34 Juniper Ave 677-9898
LEYDON
Thea 55 Krandle Blvd 432-4567
LI
Fung 637 23rd St 990-3212
Ping Wa 22 Sea View 877-3465
LIBERMAN SEE ALSO LIEBERMAN
LIBERMAN
Mario 321 Broadway 451-3234
LIDLE
Leonard 345 Tiger Rd 677-3458
Phyllis 441 Pond Trail 993-7575

1. What is Thea Leydon's phone number? 432-4567
2. What is Harold Lewis's address? 34 Juniper Ave.
3. Write the two ways the name Liberman is spelled in this directory. Liberman, Lieberman
4. How many different people have the last name Li? two: Fung and Ping Wa
5. What is the phone number of the person named Lidle who lives on Pond Trail? 993-7575

5 Book 3.1/Unit 2 City Green — **At Home:** Have students write two more questions using the telephone directory. Ask them to answer the questions. 41

Reteach, 41

ON-LEVEL

Name________ Date______ **Practice 41**

Use a Telephone Directory

102 **Garage Doors—Gas**

Garage Doors
Clegg Brothers
45 Simpson St 555-3423
T.J.'s Garage Supplies
523 Maple Ln 555-6520
Garbage Removal
See Rubbish and Garbage Removal
Garden Centers—plants, supplies
Chestnut Hill Farms
456 Harrison Blvd 555-0456
Harry's Garden World
Route 5 + Gray Way 555-4589
Montclair Mall 555-1111
Garden Furniture
Chestnut Hill Farms
456 Harrison Blvd 555-0456
Moon River Junction
626 Good Hope Rd 555-8734

Pretend you're building a garden. Use the section of the Yellow Pages shown here to help you.

1. Which two stores sell plants? Chestnut Hill Farms, Harry's Garden World
2. Which store sells both both plants and garden furniture? Chestnut Hill Farms
3. What's the phone number of Moon River Junction? 555-8734
4. Pretend you need to remove garbage from your garden. Where would you look in these Yellow Pages? Rubbish and Garbage Removal
5. Which two stores sell garage doors? Clegg Brothers and T.J.'s Garage Supplies

5 Book 3.1/Unit 2 City Green — **At Home:** Ask students to explain why they would not find listings of stores that sell fans on this page. 41

Practice, 41

CHALLENGE

Name________ Date______ **Extend 41**

Use a Telephone Directory

Bennet & Co. 10 3rd Street	555.8835	Hammar O. M. 11 3rd Street	555-1323
Bennett Sam 101 Broad Street	555-3497	Hammer's Supplies 29 3rd Street	555-6574
Bennett's Cakes 32 3rd Street	555-1483	Hammor's Pet Shop 2 3rd Street	555-9032

Suppose you live on 3rd Street. You want to get a group of 3rd Street business owners together to sponsor clean-up of the local park. You know the last names of the business owners. You don't have their telephone numbers. Here are the names of the business people you want to call. List the correct telephone numbers for these people. Then, tell how you found the correct number.

1. Mr. Hammer 555-6574
   How did you decide his telephone number?
   He is the Hammer spelled with an -er on 3rd Street.
2. Mr. Bennett 555-1483
   How did you decide his telephone number?
   He is the Bennett spelled with two t's on 3rd Street.

Describe what you will do to clean up the park.

Book 3.1/Unit 2 City Green — **At Home:** Have students use the local telephone directory to look up three businesses. Have them list the businesses' names in alphabetical order followed by their numbers. 41

Extend, 41

TEST POWER

Test Tip

Pay attention to the details in the story.

DIRECTIONS:
Read the story. Then read each question about the story.

SAMPLE

The Important Meeting

Jack's mother paused at the front door. "Do you have your key to the house, Jack?" she asked. "My meeting might run late this afternoon. I might not be home when school gets out."

Jack smiled and nodded. "Don't worry, Mom," he said. "I have it. You go ahead—don't be late!"

Jack's mother had opened her own gas station five years ago. He knew that the meeting today was important to her. She was meeting with the banker to open a new gas station.

"Don't forget your briefcase, Mom," Jack reminded her.

"Thanks, Jack," his mother called. "See you tonight! Wish me luck!"

1 Why might Jack's mother come home late?

- ○ She had a flat tire.
- ○ She did not have a key.
- ● She had a meeting.
- ○ She had to work.

2 How did Jack feel about his mother's business?

- ○ Worried
- ○ Angry
- ● Hopeful
- ○ Confused

Why are your answers correct?

171

ITBS/TEST PREPARATION

TERRANOVA/TEST PREPARATION

SAT 9/TEST PREPARATION

Test Power

THE PRINCETON REVIEW

Read the Page

Have students read the story. Instruct students to pay careful attention to the events in the story as they read.

Discuss the Questions

QUESTION 1: This question refers to a cause-and-effect relationship. The story begins with Jack's mother saying she "might not be home" when he returns from school. Remind the students to ask why as they read through the story.

QUESTION 2: This question requires students to understand Jack's feelings. Discuss what information in the story is a clue to how Jack feels. One clue: Jack "smiled" after his mom said she would be late. Also, Jack "knew the meeting was important to her." Ask students: How might Jack feel? Use process of elimination.

Leveled Books

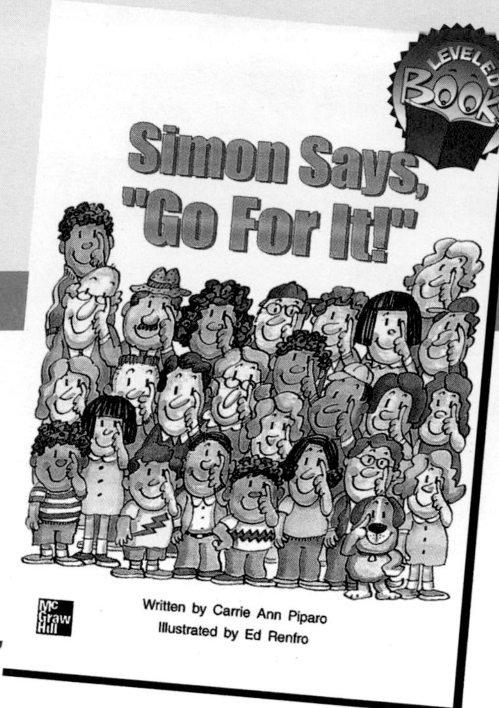

LEVELED BOOKS
Simon Says, "Go For It!"
Written by Carrie Ann Piparo
Illustrated by Ed Renfro
Mc Graw Hill

EASY

Simon Says, "Go For It!"

Syllable Patterns

☑ **Cause and Effect**

☑ **Instructional Vocabulary:** ***area, excitement, halfway, heap, schedule, stems***

Answers to Story Questions

1. The biggest game of Simon Says.
2. They asked their friends to ask other people, which created a growing amount of people who could participate in the record attempt. They also distributed fliers and received free publicity from the radio and newspaper.
3. No. People started volunteering to provide things such as juice or free fliers without being asked.
4. The story is about two girls who rely on the cooperation of many other people to achieve a goal that is much too big for them to accomplish on their own.
5. Answers will vary.

Story Questions and Writing Activity

1. What was the record Leah and Amy wanted to set?
2. How did the two girls get a record-setting crowd to attend the game?
3. Do you think getting free juice was on their "To Do List?" Why or why not?
4. What is the story mostly about?
5. If the Simon Says game was to be played in Marcy's neighborhood, how do you think she would spread the word about it?

Make a Pictograph

Think of some activities you can do with a friend, such as jumping jacks. Ask your friend to make tally marks in groups of five to keep track of how many jumping jacks you can do in two minutes. Then switch roles. Make a pictograph that shows how many jumping jacks each of you performed.

from *Simon Says, "Go For It!"*

Guided Reading

PREVIEW AND PREDICT Conduct a **picture walk** through page 10. Have students predict what the story will be about.

SET PURPOSES Students should discuss what they want to find out by reading the story. List their purposes on the chalkboard.

READ THE BOOK Use the following prompts while students read or after they have read the story independently.

Pages 2–3 What gave Leah the idea to set a record? (reading the *Guinness Book of World Records*) What are the girls' first ideas for setting a record? (a pogo stick, not cleaning their rooms) Why do they decide against these ideas? (too hard, parents would disapprove) ***Cause and Effect***

Pages 4–5 So far, who is excited about playing Simon Says? (Charles) Why? (They'll be famous.) ***Cause and Effect***

Page 9: Find the word *letter* on this page. Say the word slowly, clapping out each syllable. How many syllables does *letter* have? Where would you divide the word to show the two syllables? ***Phonics and Decoding***

Pages 13–16: What were some of the things the kids did to advertise the game? (passed out fliers, visited classrooms, and so on) What was the result of all the publicity? (They set a record.) ***Cause and Effect***

RETURN TO PREDICTIONS AND PURPOSES Review students' predictions and purposes for reading. Which predictions were correct?

LITERARY RESPONSE Discuss these questions:

- Each person in the story had a job to do. What were some of those jobs?
- Which of those jobs would you be good at doing?

Also see the story questions and activity in *Simon Says, "Go For It!"*

See the Phonics **CD-ROM** for practice with syllable patterns.

Leveled Books

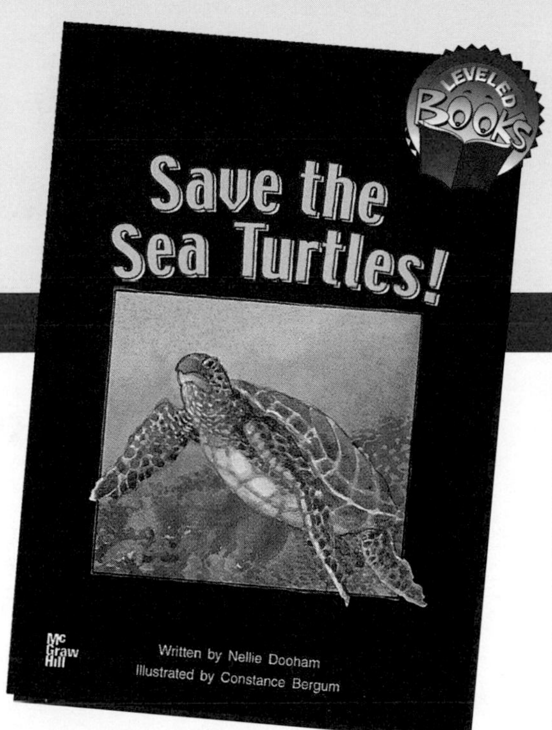

LEVELED
BOOKS
Save the Sea Turtles!
Written by Nellie Dooham
Illustrated by Constance Bergum
Mc Graw Hill

INDEPENDENT

Save the Sea Turtles!

- ☑ **Cause and Effect**
- ☑ **Instructional Vocabulary:** ***area, heap, excitement, halfway, schedule, stems***

Guided Reading

PREVIEW AND PREDICT Discuss each illustration up to page 13. Ask: What do you think Tomás finds? What do you think will happen in the story?

SET PURPOSES Students should decide what they want to find out as they read the story. Have them write down three questions they would like to have answered.

READ THE BOOK Use the following support prompts while students read or after they have read independently.

Page 3: What is Tomás looking for? (treasure) What does he find instead? (eggs) ***Cause and Effect***

Page 5: Why does Tomás think that mother sea turtles don't care about their eggs? (They leave the eggs and go back to the sea.) ***Cause and Effect***

Pages 10–11: Is Tomás correct when he says: "There must be more sea turtles in the ocean than there are stars in the sky"? What might happen to the sea turtle eggs? ***Cause and Effect***

Page 12: Which word tells you what Tomás is feeling when Ana suggests he cover the turtle eggs with sand? (excitement) ***Vocabulary***

Page 15: Why does Tomás mark the spot of the nest? (so that it can be found again) ***Cause and Effect***

Page 16: Why did the people build fences and number nests? (because they love the turtles and want to help them) ***Cause and Effect***

RETURN TO PREDICTIONS AND PURPOSES Review students' predictions and reasons for reading. Which predictions were correct? Which were not? Were their questions answered?

LITERARY RESPONSE Discuss these questions:

- Why was it hard for Tomás to wait for the eggs to hatch?
- Why weren't the hatchlings from other nests as wonderful as those from nest 3?
- What do you think happened to the turtle hatchlings?

Also see the story questions and activity in *Save the Sea Turtles!*

Answers to Story Questions

1. Tomás found a nest of sea turtle eggs.
2. The sea turtle had to swim to the beach where it was born, crawl up on the beach, choose a spot and dig a hole for the nest. A sea turtle's body is made for swimming in the ocean.
3. The eastern coast of Florida. Loggerheads only build nests there or on an island in the Middle East.
4. This story is about a boy who finds turtle eggs and, after learning about loggerheads from his cousin, helps hatchlings get to the sea.
5. Both stories are about community projects. In *City Green* the people grow their own flowers and vegetables. In this story, the people don't get anything but the satisfaction of knowing that they helped out.

Story Questions and Writing Activity

1. What did Tomás find in the sand?
2. What did the mother sea turtle have to do before she could lay her eggs? Why was this difficult to do?
3. Where does this story take place? How do you know?
4. What is the story mostly about?
5. How is this story like *City Green*? How is it different?

My Journey to the Sea

Each hatchling must break out of its own shell and climb out of the sandy nest. Then all the hatchlings head together towards the brightest horizon. Find out about the dangers facing these young sea turtles. Then write a paragraph from one hatchling's point of view that tells about the journey from the nest to the sea.

from *Save the Sea Turtles!*

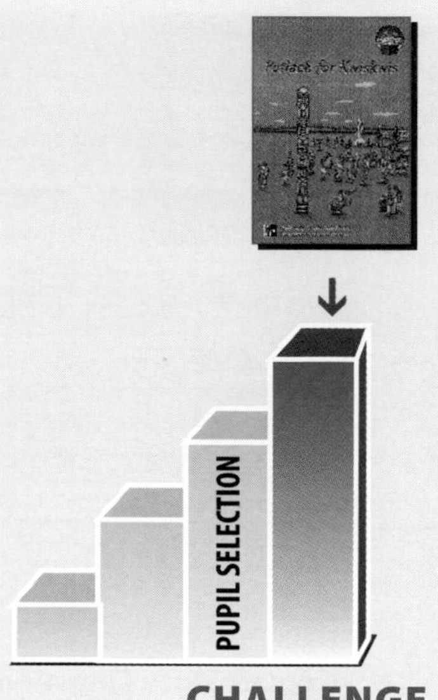

Leveled Books

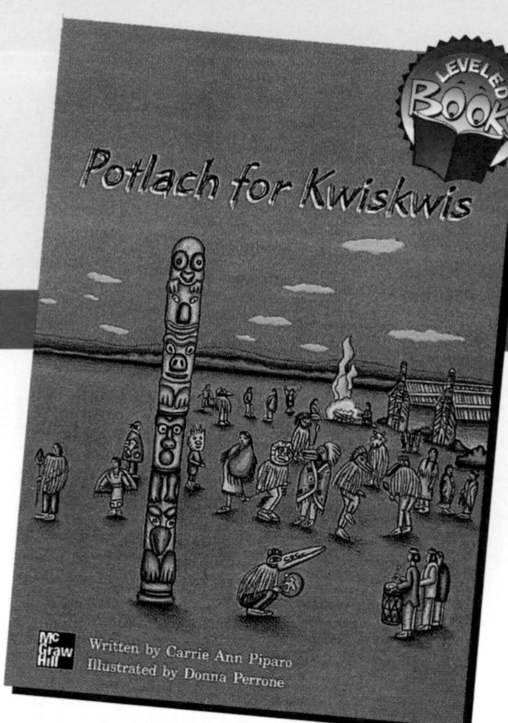

LEVELED BOOKS
Potlach for Kwiskwis
Written by Carrie Ann Piparo
Illustrated by Donna Perrone

CHALLENGE

Potlatch for Kwiskwis

- ☑ **Cause and Effect**
- ☑ **Instructional Vocabulary:** ***area, excitement, halfway, heap, schedule, stems***

Answers to Story Questions

1. A potlatch is a celebration of gift-giving and feasting.
2. She had wanted a name that was beautiful and graceful.
3. Running Wolf. He was the guest who accepted the blanket.
4. It is about the preparation for a potlatch and how Kwiskwis was given her grown-up name.
5. Answers will vary.

Story Questions and Writing Activity

1. What is a potlatch?
2. Why didn't Kwiskwis like her new name at first?
3. Who will hold the next potlatch? How was it decided?
4. What is this story mostly about?
5. In what ways were the neighbors in *City Green* and the guests at the potlatch similar? How were they different?

Potlatch Gifts

Draw an outline of a longhouse. On the inside, show the gifts that might be given at a potlatch. What is this potlatch celebrating? Write a paragraph that explains your drawing.

from *Potlatch for Kwiskwis*

Guided Reading

PREVIEW AND PREDICT Have students look through the illustrations up to page 15. Ask: What might the story be about? What might a potlatch be? What happens at a potlatch? What do you think will happen at this one?

SET PURPOSES Students should decide what they want to find out as they read the story. Have them write down three questions they would like to have answered.

READ THE BOOK Ask students to read the story independently. Then return to the story, using the following prompts to guide discussion.

Page 2: Read the second sentence on this page. What do you think the author means by using the word *buzzed* with the word excitement? (Everyone is busy and talking.) *Vocabulary*

Page 5: Why is Kwiskwis concerned? (She will have to give away her necklace.) Why might she have to do so? (Sometimes the host gives away everything.) *Cause and Effect*

Page 6: What are some festivities that occur at a potlatch? (food, dancing, exchange of gifts) *Setting*

Page 13: How does Kwiskwis feel at first about her new name? (disappointed) Why? (She had hoped she would be named after a fawn or a swan.) *Cause and Effect*

Page 14: Why was Kwiskwis given the name Fox-That-Laughs? (She's clever, quick, and happy.) How does she feel once she understands the reasons for her new name? *Cause and Effect*

RETURN TO PREDICTIONS AND PURPOSES Review students' predictions and reasons for reading. Ask: Did you figure out what a *potlatch* is?

LITERARY RESPONSE Discuss these questions:

- Why might the hosts of a potlatch give away everything they own?
- Why does Kwiskwis give Weesa her shell necklace?
- Based on their names and their characters in the story, what are Kwiskwis's parents like?

Also see the story questions and activity in *Potlatch for Kwiskwis.*

Connecting Texts

CLASS DISCUSSION Start a Community Project word web on the chalkboard. Call on volunteers from each reading level to tell what the community project was in each story. Add their suggestions to the word web. Discuss with students how each project was successful, based on how the people in the community worked together. You can add these ideas to the word web as well. Then ask:

- What do you think was the most interesting way in which people cooperated?
- What ideas do these stories give you for community projects that you could start?

Community Projects

- City Green: community garden
- Simon Says, "Go for It!": setting a world record
- Save the Sea Turtles: saving sea turtles
- Potlatch for Kwiskwis: potlatch celebration

Viewing/Representing

GROUP PRESENTATIONS Have each group choose one of these presentations for the story they read.

PANTOMIME Have students act out two or three scenes from the story in pantomime, showing how the characters felt about working and celebrating together.

SONG Ask students to write a song about the story, setting the words to a familiar tune such as "Row, Row, Row Your Boat." Provide copies so that the class can join in.

AUDIENCE RESPONSE Have the audience tell what they liked most about each performance. Suggest that audience members ask questions about what the performers liked most about each story.

Research and Inquiry

Have students ask themselves: What are some celebrations and festivals that I know about? What does my family or community do to make these celebrations happen? Invite students to do the following:

- Choose a celebration or festival that is celebrated in their family or local community.
- Interview a parent or other adult about how people work together to make the festival happen. Are there costumes? Is there food? Who raises money to pay for the festival?
- Present their findings to the class.

inter*NET CONNECTION** Students can find out more about local festivities by visiting ***www.mhschool.com/reading.

TESTED OBJECTIVES

Students will recognize and infer cause-and-effect relationships.

TEACHING TIP

INSTRUCTIONAL Point out to students that cause-and-effect relationships can often be found in their own lives. For example, if a student studies hard and does well on a test, the effect is doing well, and the cause is studying hard. Invite students to think of other cause-and-effect relationships.

Review Cause and Effect

PREPARE

Discuss Cause and Effect

Review: To identify cause and effect in a story, ask the questions: What happened? Why did it happen? Ask students how they predicted the effect the garden would have on the characters in the selection they just read.

TEACH

Read "Miss Rosa's Garden" and Model the Skill

Miss Rosa's Garden

Miss Rosa loved her vegetable garden. One year she planted rows of beans, carrots, tomatoes, and lettuce. She took very good care of her garden. Miss Rosa fed her plants plant food, watered them, and carefully weeded the rows. "With a little luck from the weather, " said Miss Rosa, "I'll have plenty of vegetables this year!"

Finally, all of Miss Rosa's work paid off. The weather was perfect all spring and summer. Her garden was a great success. Her garden grew so many vegetables that she was able to share them with her neighbors. Due to her success, she was known as the best gardener on the block.

Teaching Chart 34

Discuss events in the passage that have cause-and-effect relationships.

MODEL The third sentence tells me that Miss Rosa took good care of her garden. That could be the beginning of a cause-and-effect relationship. I think she would expect to have good results **because** of her efforts. The words *due to* in the last sentence are clues that point to the cause that follows. I'll look for the effects, or results, of her good care as I read.

PRACTICE

Make Inferences about Cause and Effect

Have students underline the causes and circle the effects in "Miss Rosa's Garden." Point out that they should find a cause for each effect in the following questions. ▶ **Logical/Interpersonal**

- What caused the garden to be a success?
- Why was she able to give her neighbors her vegetables?
- Why was she considered the block's best gardener?

ASSESS/CLOSE

Identify Cause and Effect

Have students create a cause-and-effect flowchart. Have them use the following information in their charts, using initials *C* for Cause and *E* for Effect: shared vegetables, garden grew, weather perfect, loved garden, best gardener, took care of garden.

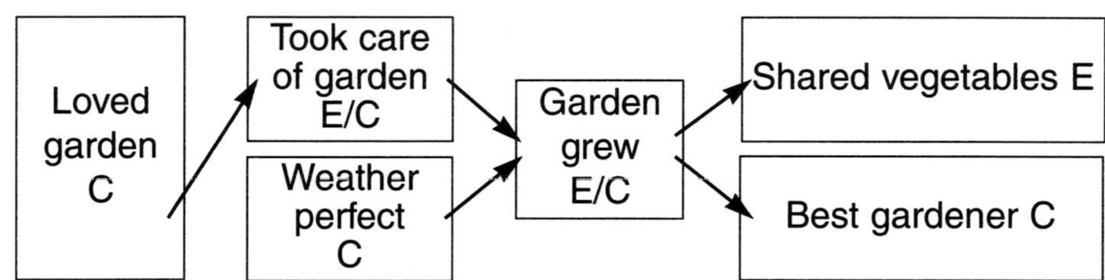

ALTERNATE TEACHING STRATEGY

CAUSE AND EFFECT

For a different approach to teaching this skill, see page T60.

SELF-SELECTED Reading

Students may choose from the following titles.

ANTHOLOGY

- *City Green*

LEVELED BOOKS

- *Simon Says, "Go For It!"*
- *Save the Sea Turtles*
- *Potlatch for Kwiskwis*

Bibliography, pages T76–T77

Meeting Individual Needs for Comprehension

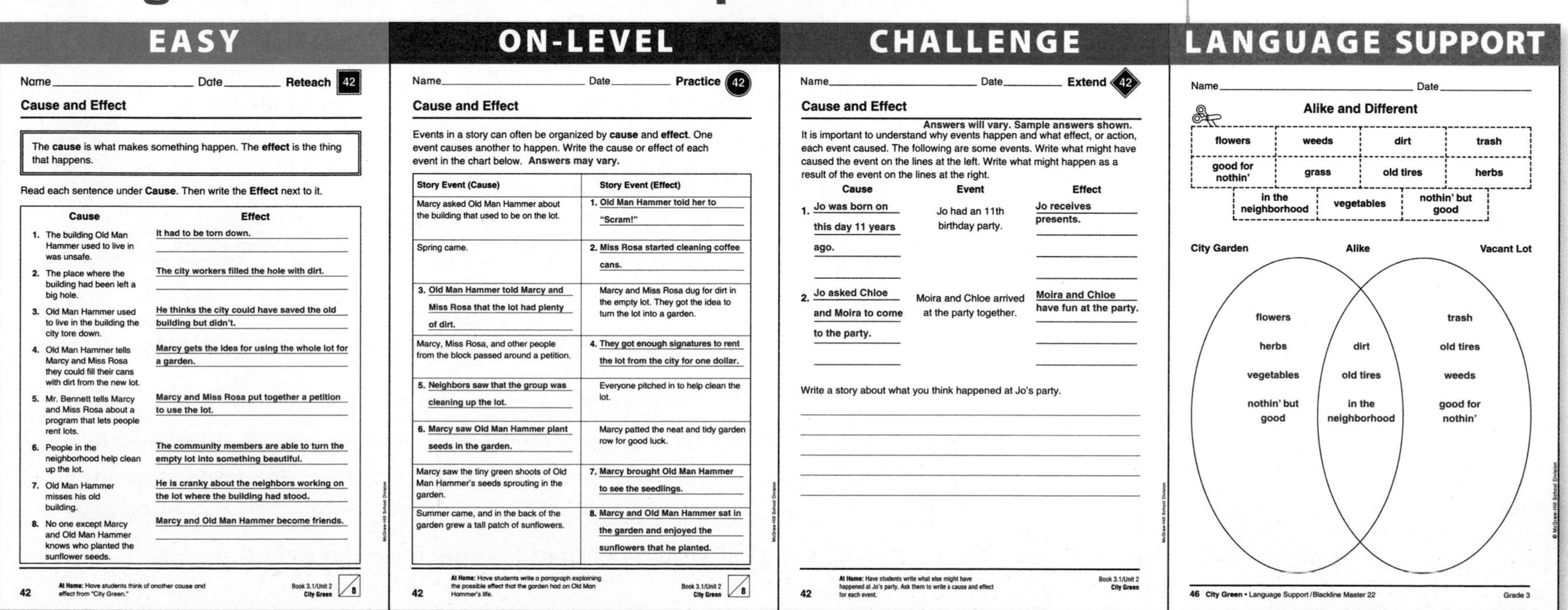

EASY

Name________ Date______ **Reteach 42**

Cause and Effect

The **cause** is what makes something happen. The **effect** is the thing that happens.

Read each sentence under **Cause**. Then write the **Effect** next to it.

Cause	Effect
1. The building Old Man Hammer used to live in was unsafe.	It had to be torn down.
2. The place where the building had been left a big hole.	The city workers filled the hole with dirt.
3. Old Man Hammer used to live in the building the city tore down.	He thinks the city could have saved the old building but didn't.
4. Old Man Hammer tells Marcy and Miss Rosa they could fill their cans with dirt from the new lot.	Marcy gets the idea for using the whole lot for a garden.
5. Mr. Bennett tells Marcy and Miss Rosa about a program that lets people rent lots.	Marcy and Miss Rosa put together a petition to use the lot.
6. People in the neighborhood help clean up the lot.	The community members are able to turn the empty lot into something beautiful.
7. Old Man Hammer misses his old building.	He is cranky about the neighbors working on the lot where the building had stood.
8. No one except Marcy and Old Man Hammer knows who planted the sunflower seeds.	Marcy and Old Man Hammer become friends.

42 **At Home:** Have students think of another cause and effect from "City Green." Book 3.1/Unit 2 **City Green** 8

McGraw-Hill School Division

Reteach, 42

ON-LEVEL

Name________ Date______ **Practice 42**

Cause and Effect

Events in a story can often be organized by **cause** and **effect**. One event causes another to happen. Write the cause or effect of each event in the chart below. **Answers may vary.**

Story Event (Cause)	Story Event (Effect)
Marcy asked Old Man Hammer about the building that used to be on the lot.	1. Old Man Hammer told her to "Scram!"
Spring came.	2. Miss Rosa started cleaning coffee cans.
3. Old Man Hammer told Marcy and Miss Rosa that the lot had plenty of dirt.	Marcy and Miss Rosa dug for dirt in the empty lot. They got the idea to turn the lot into a garden.
Marcy, Miss Rosa, and other people from the block passed around a petition.	4. They got enough signatures to rent the lot from the city for one dollar.
5. Neighbors saw that the group was cleaning up the lot.	Everyone pitched in to help clean the lot.
6. Marcy saw Old Man Hammer plant seeds in the garden.	Marcy patted the neat and tidy garden row for good luck.
Marcy saw the tiny green shoots of Old Man Hammer's seeds sprouting in the garden.	7. Marcy brought Old Man Hammer to see the seedlings.
Summer came, and in the back of the garden grew a tall patch of sunflowers.	8. Marcy and Old Man Hammer sat in the garden and enjoyed the sunflowers that he planted.

42 **At Home:** Have students write a paragraph explaining the possible effect that the garden had on Old Man Hammer's life. Book 3.1/Unit 2 **City Green** 8

McGraw-Hill School Division

Practice, 42

CHALLENGE

Name________ Date______ **Extend 42**

Cause and Effect

Answers will vary. Sample answers shown.

It is important to understand why events happen and what effect, or action, each event caused. The following are some events. Write what might have caused the event on the lines at the left. Write what might happen as a result of the event on the lines at the right.

Cause	Event	Effect
1. Jo was born on this day 11 years ago.	Jo had an 11th birthday party.	Jo receives presents.
2. Jo asked Chloe and Moira to come to the party.	Moira and Chloe arrived at the party together.	Moira and Chloe have fun at the party.

Write a story about what you think happened at Jo's party.

42 **At Home:** Have students write what else might have happened at Jo's party. Ask them to write a cause and effect for each event. Book 3.1/Unit 2 **City Green**

McGraw-Hill School Division

Extend, 42

LANGUAGE SUPPORT

Name________ Date______

Alike and Different

flowers	weeds	dirt	trash
good for nothin'	grass	old tires	herbs
in the neighborhood	vegetables	nothin' but good	

City Garden	Alike	Vacant Lot
flowers		trash
herbs	dirt	old tires
vegetables	old tires	weeds
nothin' but good	in the neighborhood	good for nothin'

46 **City Green** • Language Support/Blackline Master 22 Grade 3

Language Support, 46

TESTED **OBJECTIVES**

Students will draw conclusions based on two or more pieces of information.

TEACHING TIP

INSTRUCTIONAL Have students draw conclusions about situations familiar to them. Ask: What conclusion can you make about whether or not you should study for tests? What information supports your conclusion?

Introduce Draw Conclusions

PREPARE

Discuss Drawing Conclusions

Explain: Often an author gives readers clues about characters without directly stating what they are like or how they feel. By using two or more ideas or pieces of information, readers can draw conclusions that will make the characters and the story easier to understand.

TEACH

Read "Marcy's Visit" and Model the Skill

Read "Marcy's Visit" with students. Focus students' attention on Marcy's expectations about what will happen based on her experiences.

Marcy's Visit

Marcy and Mama took the train to see Marcy's grandma. Marcy was very excited. Her grandma lived in the country, far from the busy, noisy city. The train left the city and headed into the green hills. She knew the stop was coming soon because she recognized an old red barn and a large pond.

Finally they reached Grandma's house. Marcy raced into the house, down the hall, and straight into the kitchen. She knew Grandma would be there cooking for them, as usual. Marcy gave Grandma a big hug.

Teaching Chart 35

Help students think about Marcy's experiences and expectations.

MODEL As I read the story, I look for information that can help me find reasons for why things happen. I see that Marcy was excited about visiting her grandmother. She knew where the train would stop and exactly where her grandmother would be. Therefore, I can conclude that she has visited her grandmother many times in the past.

PRACTICE

Create a Draw Conclusions Chart

Work together with students to create and complete a chart showing conclusions they can draw based on story clues.

▶ **Logical/Interpersonal**

STORY CLUE	CONCLUSION
Marcy knew her train stop.	Marcy had taken the train ride before.
Marcy knew Grandma would be in the kitchen "as usual."	Marcy was familiar with visiting her grandmother's house.

ASSESS/CLOSE

Use a Chart to Draw Conclusions

Have students create a chart listing events from their own lives and conclusions they have drawn from them.

ALTERNATE TEACHING STRATEGY

DRAW CONCLUSIONS

For a different approach to teaching this skill, see page T62.

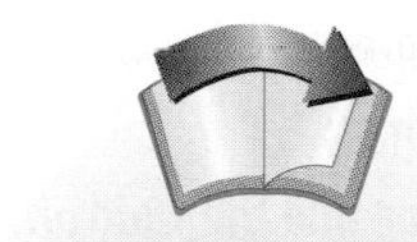

LOOKING AHEAD

Students will apply this skill as they read the next selection, *The Sun, the Wind and the Rain.*

Meeting Individual Needs for Comprehension

EASY

Name________ Date______ **Reteach 43**

Draw Conclusions

A **conclusion** is an answer based on information. You can **draw conclusions** based on information in a story or information you know from your own life.

Read the story. Then use information in the story and from your own life to draw conclusions. **Answers will vary.**

Keri was very excited as she got ready for Earth Day. This year she was in charge of games for little children.

She drew trees and flowers on brown lunch bags for a game she made up called "Little Trash Hunt." Keri bought enough balloons for all the children. Then she packed flower seeds and craft sticks so that everyone could plant a little garden. They could mark the places they planted with sticks. Then they would blow up their balloons and tie the balloon strings to the sticks.

"For the time being, it will be a balloon garden," Keri laughed.

1. About how old is Keri? **older than the little children**
2. Has Keri ever celebrated Earth Day before? Explain. **Yes. It says "This year," so she was probably involved last year too.**
3. In the story, how long is it until Earth Day? **It is probably very soon since Keri is getting ready for it.**
4. Why does Keri say, "For the time being, it will be a balloon garden"? **It will take a while for the flowers to grow.**

4 Book 3.1/Unit 2 **City Green** | **At Home:** Have students draw some conclusions based on the statement, "I am getting up early tomorrow." | 43

Reteach, 43

ON-LEVEL

Name________ Date______ **Practice 43**

Draw Conclusions

To draw a **conclusion** about a character or an event in a story, you use facts from the story. You also use your own knowledge and experience. Drawing conclusions as you read can help you better understand a story.

Answer each question below. Base your conclusion on your own experience and on information from "City Green." **Answers may vary.**

1. What kind of person is Marcy? **She is friendly, thoughtful, concerned, and involved with her neighborhood.**
2. What details from the selection helped you to draw that conclusion? **She knew everyone and kept trying to be friends with Old Man Hammer.**
3. What kind of relationship did Old Man Hammer and his neighbors have? **Not very friendly.**
4. What details from the selection helped you to draw your conclusion? **Old Man Hammer hollered "scram" to Marcy when she asked him a question. He yelled to the neighbors that they were all wasting their time working to build the community garden.**
5. Why did Old Man Hammer secretly plant seeds? **The old building meant a lot to him. Deep down inside, he was really a nice man.**
6. What details from the selection helped you draw that conclusion? **He used to live there; he sat with Rosa in the finished garden.**

6 Book 3.1/Unit 2 **City Green** | **At Home:** Have students draw a conclusion about the effect the community garden had on the neighborhood. | 43

Practice, 43

CHALLENGE

Name________ Date______ **Extend 43**

Draw Conclusions

You should draw a conclusion based on information you know from your own experience or from information you research. Read each problem below. Then find out more about the problem. Ask a teacher or family member, look in library books, or use a computer to search for more information. Then write your conclusion. Give reasons for your conclusion.

1. Many buildings are getting very old. Should they be torn down? Should they be fixed up? Why do you think as you do? **Answers will vary, but should give valid reasons for the conclusion drawn.**
2. Many areas are covered with litter and garbage. Should we help clean those areas up? Is that someone else's problem? Why do you think as you do? **Answers will vary, but should give valid reasons for the conclusion drawn.**

Book 3.1/Unit 2 **City Green** | **At Home:** Have students discuss what they think should be done to solve one of the problems. | 43

Extend, 43

LANGUAGE SUPPORT

Name________ Date______

Climb the Stairs

Your conclusion:

Why?

How?

Where?

When?

What?

Who?

Grade 3 | Language Support/Blackline Master 23 • **City Green** 47

Language Support, 47

TESTED **OBJECTIVES**

Students will learn to use general context clues and syntax (word order) to figure out the meaning of unfamiliar words.

MATERIALS

- **Teaching Chart 36**

TEACHING TIP

INSTRUCTIONAL Context clues are presented in different ways, such as:

- a comma and the word *or:* They coerced, or forced, him to go to the party.
- a dash: They were dumbfounded—speechless.
- examples: Many animals are feline, such as lions and tigers.

Introduce Context Clues

PREPARE

Discuss Meaning of Context Clues

Explain: Using general context clues, such as nearby words, can help a reader figure out the meaning of unfamiliar words. Sometimes the position of the unfamiliar word in the sentence and its part of speech can help a reader figure out its meaning.

TEACH

Read the Passage and Model the Skill

Have students read the passage on **Teaching Chart 36.**

Darryl and Max

Marcy's older brother, Darryl, and his best friend, Max, sat on the front stoop. As they sat outside on the steps of their building, they talked about some of the careers, or jobs, they wanted when they grew up.

"This garden has given me an idea. I think I'll be a landscaper someday. That way I can design parks and gardens in other cities," said Darryl.

"I want to be a journalist so I can write interesting stories for newspapers or television," said Max. They talked about their ideas until it was time for supper.

Teaching Chart 36

Circle and discuss the word *stoop* to demonstrate use of context clues and word order as strategies for figuring out meaning.

MODEL I'm not sure what the word *stoop* means. It comes after the verb *sat*, so I know it must have something to do with where someone sits. If I read the words in the next sentence, I see they are sitting outside on the steps of their building. So *stoop* must mean the steps outside a building.

Underline the meaning of *stoop*. Then circle the word *careers* and ask a volunteer to underline the words that tell them what the word means. Point out the word *or* and the commas as signals that identify a definition is given.

PRACTICE

Identify Context Clues

Have volunteers underline the context clues they can use to help them figure out the meanings of *landscaper* and *journalist*. Then have them explain what they think each word means.

▶ **Linguistic/Interpersonal**

ASSESS/CLOSE

Create Context Clues and Use Word Order

Have students make up meanings for the following nonsense words. Then have them use the words in sentences that contain context clues to their meanings. Encourage students to use syntax clues.

squizzle **maving** **plink**

You may wish to model an example:

squizzle: to squirt

Jamie squizzled the water gun at me and I got all wet.

Have students illustrate their sentences.

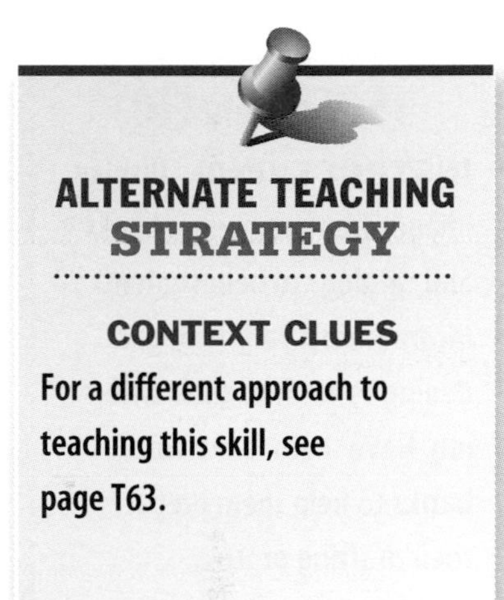

ALTERNATE TEACHING STRATEGY

CONTEXT CLUES

For a different approach to teaching this skill, see page T63.

Meeting Individual Needs for Vocabulary

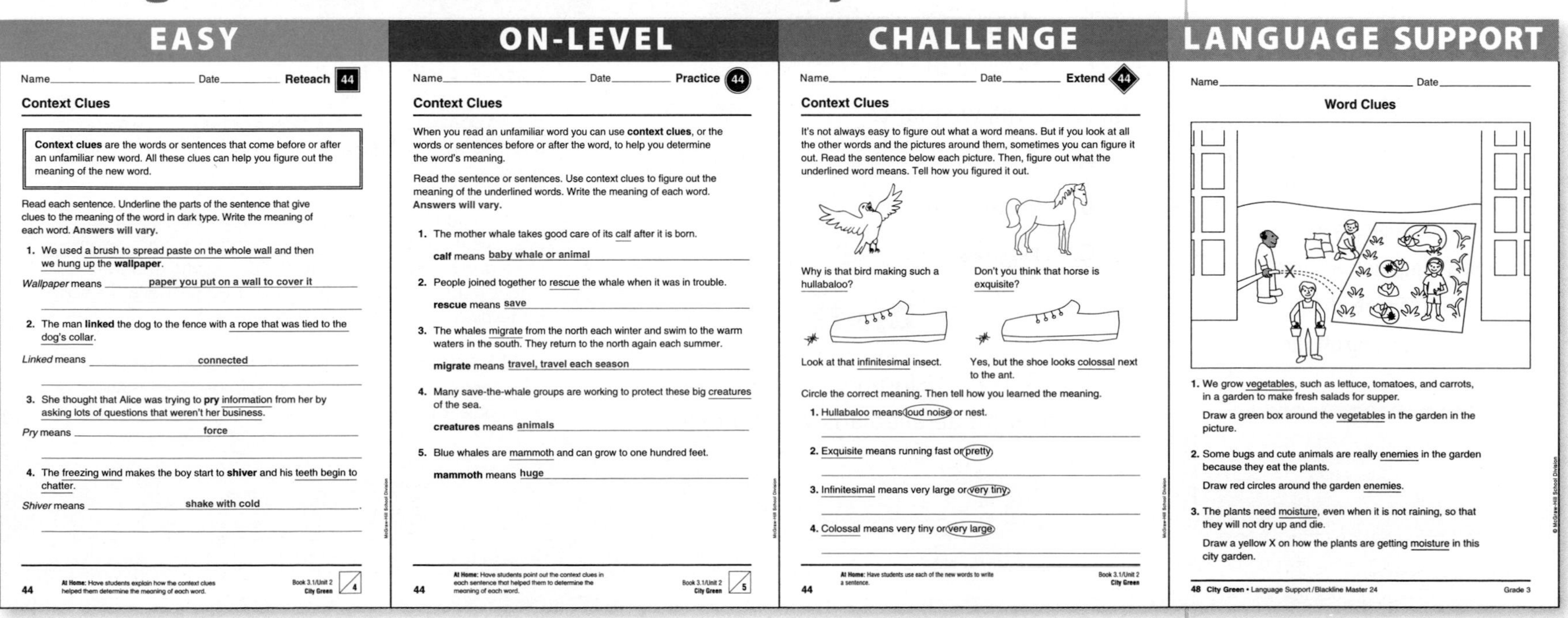

EASY

Name________ Date________ **Reteach 44**

Context Clues

Context clues are the words or sentences that come before or after an unfamiliar new word. All these clues can help you figure out the meaning of the new word.

Read each sentence. Underline the parts of the sentence that give clues to the meaning of the word in dark type. Write the meaning of each word. Answers will vary.

1. We used a brush to spread paste on the whole wall and then we hung up the **wallpaper**.

Wallpaper means paper you put on a wall to cover it

2. The man **linked** the dog to the fence with a rope that was tied to the dog's collar.

Linked means connected

3. She thought that Alice was trying to **pry** information from her by asking lots of questions that weren't her business.

Pry means force

4. The freezing wind makes the boy start to **shiver** and his teeth begin to chatter.

Shiver means shake with cold.

44 **At Home:** Have students explain how the context clues helped them determine the meaning of each word. Book 3.1/Unit 2 **City Green** 4

McGraw-Hill School Division

ON-LEVEL

Name________ Date________ **Practice 44**

Context Clues

When you read an unfamiliar word you can use **context clues**, or the words or sentences before or after the word, to help you determine the word's meaning.

Read the sentence or sentences. Use context clues to figure out the meaning of the underlined words. Write the meaning of each word. **Answers will vary.**

1. The mother whale takes good care of its calf after it is born.

calf means baby whale or animal

2. People joined together to rescue the whale when it was in trouble.

rescue means save

3. The whales migrate from the north each winter and swim to the warm waters in the south. They return to the north again each summer.

migrate means travel, travel each season

4. Many save-the-whale groups are working to protect these big creatures of the sea.

creatures means animals

5. Blue whales are mammoth and can grow to one hundred feet.

mammoth means huge

44 **At Home:** Have students point out the context clues in each sentence that helped them to determine the meaning of each word. Book 3.1/Unit 2 **City Green** 5

McGraw-Hill School Division

CHALLENGE

Name________ Date________ **Extend 44**

Context Clues

It's not always easy to figure out what a word means. But if you look at all the other words and the pictures around them, sometimes you can figure it out. Read the sentence below each picture. Then, figure out what the underlined word means. Tell how you figured it out.

Why is that bird making such a hullabaloo?

Don't you think that horse is exquisite?

Look at that infinitesimal insect.

Yes, but the shoe looks colossal next to the ant.

Circle the correct meaning. Then tell how you learned the meaning.

1. Hullabaloo means (loud noise) or nest.
2. Exquisite means running fast or (pretty).
3. Infinitesimal means very large or (very tiny).
4. Colossal means very tiny or (very large).

44 **At Home:** Have students use each of the new words to write a sentence. Book 3.1/Unit 2 **City Green**

McGraw-Hill School Division

LANGUAGE SUPPORT

Name________ Date________

Word Clues

1. We grow vegetables, such as lettuce, tomatoes, and carrots, in a garden to make fresh salads for supper.

   Draw a green box around the vegetables in the garden in the picture.

2. Some bugs and cute animals are really enemies in the garden because they eat the plants.

   Draw red circles around the garden enemies.

3. The plants need moisture, even when it is not raining, so that they will not dry up and die.

   Draw a yellow X on how the plants are getting moisture in this city garden.

48 **City Green** • Language Support/Blackline Master 24 Grade 3

© McGraw-Hill School Division

Reteach, 44 **Practice, 44** **Extend, 44** **Language Support, 48**

GRAMMAR/SPELLING CONNECTIONS

See the 5-Day Grammar and Usage Plan on common and proper nouns, pages 171M–171N.

See the 5-Day Spelling Plan on pages 171O–171P.

TEACHING TIP

INSTRUCTIONAL Display images from gardening books and catalogs to help students incorporate a variety of gardening terms into their writing. Have them make **word banks** to help them prepare their drafting process.

TECHNOLOGY TIP

Encourage students to save their writing periodically as they write on a computer. Remind them always to save their work before shutting off the computer.

Explanatory Writing

Prewrite

WRITE A PLAN Present the following assignment: Write a plan for a neighborhood garden. Discuss with students different ways that neighbors might choose a place, prepare it, and decide what to plant there.

FOCUSING QUESTIONS Have students list questions they will answer in their plan. They will need to answer *what, where,* and *how* questions.

Strategy: Make an Outline Have students follow the outline sequence below.

Topic: Planning a Garden

I. Where will we choose to plant our garden?
- A. in an empty lot
- B. on a rooftop
- C. in a plot of land at the park

II. How will we prepare our garden?
- A. buy or borrow tools
- B. clean up the grounds
- C. fertilize the soil

III. What will we plant?
- A. flowers
- B. vegetables
- C. bushes

Draft

FREE WRITE Using the outline, students can free write detailed answers for every entry.

Revise

SELF-QUESTIONING Ask students to assess their drafts.

- Are my ideas well-organized and in logical order?
- Am I missing any important details or steps?
- Do my sentences support the main idea?

Edit/Proofread

CHECK FOR ERRORS Have students reread their plans and correct any errors in spelling, grammar, and punctuation.

Publish

EXCHANGE PLANS After finishing their plans, students can then exchange plans and discuss what they liked best about one another's writing.

Planning a Neighborhood Garden

The first thing you must do when planning a neighborhood garden is to decide where you will plant it. Think about the places you will plant it. Think about the places you can use in your neighborhood, such as an empty lot, a rooftop, or an empty plot of land at a local park.

Once you have a place for your garden, you must prepare it for planting. First, get together with neighbors and buy or borrow tools for digging and for cleaning up. Remove any garbage, then prepare the soil by turning it over and watering it.

The final step is deciding what to plant. Find out what grows best in your area. Will you plant flowers or vegetables? Decide which, then get the seeds and plant.

Presentation Ideas

MAKE A VIDEO Have students pretend they are at a city council meeting presenting their plan. Videotape or tape-record students making their presentation and show the tape. ▶ **Speaking/Listening**

MAKE MINI-GARDENS Have students follow their plans and make mini-gardens in aluminum pans. Students can display their gardens and their plans in the classroom or in the library. ▶ **Viewing/Representing**

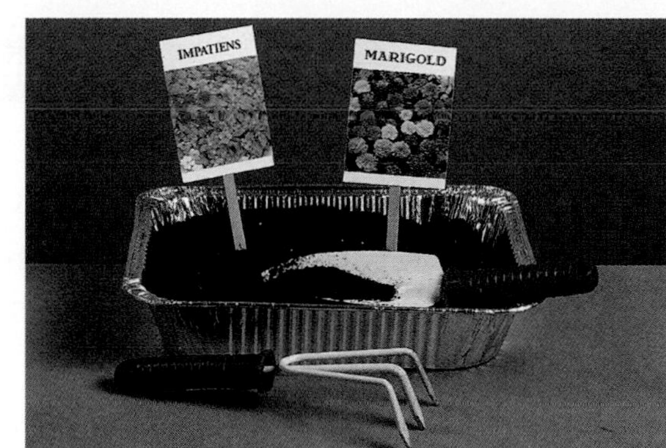

Consider children's creative efforts, possibly adding a plus (+) for originality, wit, and imagination.

Scoring Rubric

Excellent	Good	Fair	Unsatisfactory
4: The writer • clearly explains each step of the plan in order. • provides details in each paragraph that support the topic covered in the paragraph. • completely answers each question in the outline.	**3:** The writer • explains each step briefly in order. • provides at least one detail in each paragraph supporting the topic. • answers each question in the outline.	**2:** The writer • partially explains each step, but ideas may not be in logical order. • includes some details that support the topic, but may also include irrelevant details. • answers at least two of the questions in the outline.	**1:** The writer • has not explained each step and ideas are out of order. • gives details that are unrelated to the topic of each paragraph. • does not answer the questions presented in the outline.

0: The writer leaves the page blank or fails to respond to the writing task. The writer does not address the topic or simply paraphrases the prompt. The response is illegible or incoherent.

COMMUNICATION TIPS

SPEAKING You may wish to have students rehearse their speeches before recording them.

REPRESENTING Before they plant the seeds, students can draw a diagram of what their garden will look like.

LANGUAGE SUPPORT

ESL Have ESL students label as many parts of their garden plans as they can in English and the rest in their first language. English-fluent students can help them translate those words.

PORTFOLIO Invite students to include their plans or another writing project in their portfolios.

Meeting Individual Needs for Writing

EASY

Give Directions Have students choose a place on school property where they would plant a garden. Have them write directions on how to get to that place from the school entrance. Students can then draw a map to go with their directions.

ON-LEVEL

How-To Pamphlet Have students write a *How to Care for Your Garden* pamphlet. Have them include information on the tools needed, the necessity of weeding and watering, and how sunlight can affect a garden. Have students create illustrations to go with their pamphlet.

CHALLENGE

Interview Students can pretend they are interviewing Marcy from *City Green*. Have them write out both parts of the interview in which they ask Marcy about how she was able to create such a successful garden.

5 Day Grammar and Usage Plan

LANGUAGE SUPPORT

ESL In a group, have students say their names and then hold up an object and say, "This is a pencil (book, ruler, and so on)." Identify common and proper nouns.

DAILY LANGUAGE ACTIVITIES

Write the Daily Language Activity on the chalkboard each day or use **Transparency 6**. Have students correct the sentences orally.

Day 1
1. Sometimes ali saves cans. Ali
2. My Cat purrs loudly. cat
3. The Boy went out. boy

Day 2
1. Aunt mae worked on monday. Mae, Monday
2. We met on groundhog day. Groundhog Day
3. We went to new york city. New York City

Day 3
1. I celebrate halloween. Halloween
2. Will luis move his Car? Luis, car
3. Please come to lina's Party. Lina's, party

Day 4
1. They will arrive on friday, Nov 4. Friday, Nov.
2. Ask mrs. li to meet us in New york. Mrs. Li, York
3. I watered mary's rosebush. Mary's

Day 5
1. Ani called mr. hammer. Mr. Hammer
2. The Date is tues., Oct 9. date, Tues., Oct.
3. Is feb short for february? Feb., February

Daily Language Transparency 6

DAY 1 Introduce the Concept

Oral Warm-Up Read aloud: *Sally has a dog named Ginger*. Ask students which words name someone or something: A *noun* names a person, place, or thing.

Introduce Nouns Explain that *dog* is a *common noun*, but *Ginger* is a *proper noun* because it names a particular dog. Present:

Common and Proper Nouns

- A **common noun** names any person, place, or thing.
- A **proper noun** names a special person, place, or thing, and begins with a capital letter.

Present the Daily Language Activity. Have students correct orally. Then have students make three sentences using common and proper nouns.

WRITING Assign the daily Writing Prompt on page 142C.

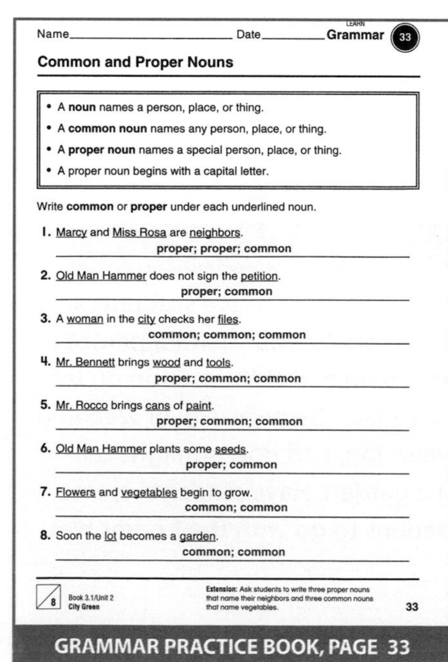
Name________ Date________ LEARN Grammar 33

Common and Proper Nouns

- A **noun** names a person, place, or thing.
- A **common noun** names any person, place, or thing.
- A **proper noun** names a special person, place, or thing.
- A proper noun begins with a capital letter.

Write **common** or **proper** under each underlined noun.

1. Marcy and Miss Rosa are neighbors.
   proper; proper; common
2. Old Man Hammer does not sign the petition.
   proper; common
3. A woman in the city checks her files.
   common; common; common
4. Mr. Bennett brings wood and tools.
   proper; common; common
5. Mr. Rocco brings cans of paint.
   proper; common; common
6. Old Man Hammer plants some seeds.
   proper; common
7. Flowers and vegetables begin to grow.
   common; common
8. Soon the lot becomes a garden.
   common; common

8 Book 3.1/Unit 2 City Green

Extension: Ask students to write three proper nouns that name their neighbors and three common nouns that name vegetables.

33

GRAMMAR PRACTICE BOOK, PAGE 33

DAY 2 Teach the Concept

Review Nouns Have students explain the difference between proper and common nouns. Ask them which kind of noun is capitalized.

Introduce Days, Months, and Holidays Point out that the word *day* is used for any day of the week, while *Monday* names a particular day. Present:

Days, Months, and Holidays

- The name of a day, month, or holiday begins with a capital letter.

Present the Daily Language Activity. Then have students write two sentences—one giving the present date and one describing a holiday. Have volunteers write their sentences on the chalkboard. Ask the rest of the class to check their capitalization.

Have students write three sentences using a day, month, and holiday.

WRITING Assign the daily Writing Prompt on page 142C.

Name________ Date________ LEARN AND PRACTICE Grammar 34

Proper Nouns: Days, Months, Holidays

- The name of a day, month, or holiday begins with a capital letter.

Complete the sentences by writing the name of the day, month, or holiday correctly.

1. Marcy gets up early on **Saturday**. saturday
2. On **Sunday**, the city drops off tools. sunday
3. A good time to plant seeds is **April**. april
4. Many flowers bloom in **May**. may
5. The garden is filled with plants by **July**. july
6. Pumpkins grow in **October**. october
7. People like pumpkins for **Halloween**. halloween
8. I like pumpkin pie for **Thanksgiving**. thanksgiving

34 **Extension:** Invite students to make up riddles about days, months, and holidays. Have students take turns writing the answers on the board.

Book 3.1/Unit 2 City Green 8

GRAMMAR PRACTICE BOOK, PAGE 34

Common and Proper Nouns

Review and Practice

Learn from the Literature Review common and proper nouns. Read the third sentence on page 146 of *City Green:*

> **My friend Miss Rosa told me Old Man Hammer used to live there—some other neighbors too.**

Ask students to identify the proper and common nouns in the sentence. Point out that the word *Miss* in Miss Rosa is a *title*. A title such as *Miss, Mr.*, or *Ms.* is part of a name, and should be capitalized.

Identify Types of Nouns Present the Daily Language Activity. Then ask students to read the last paragraph on page 153 of *City Green* and to list common and proper nouns.

WRITING Assign the daily Writing Prompt on page 142D.

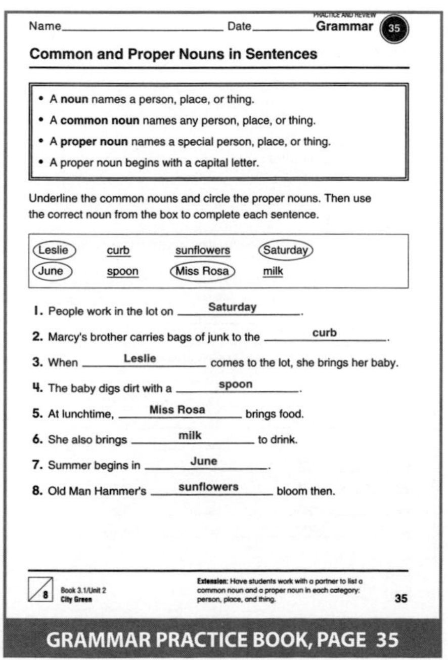

Name__________ Date__________ PRACTICE AND REVIEW Grammar 35

Common and Proper Nouns in Sentences

- A **noun** names a person, place, or thing.
- A **common noun** names any person, place, or thing.
- A **proper noun** names a special person, place, or thing.
- A proper noun begins with a capital letter.

Underline the common nouns and circle the proper nouns. Then use the correct noun from the box to complete each sentence.

Leslie	curb	sunflowers	Saturday
June	spoon	Miss Rosa	milk

1. People work in the lot on Saturday.
2. Marcy's brother carries bags of junk to the curb.
3. When Leslie comes to the lot, she brings her baby.
4. The baby digs dirt with a spoon.
5. At lunchtime, Miss Rosa brings food.
6. She also brings milk to drink.
7. Summer begins in June.
8. Old Man Hammer's sunflowers bloom then.

8 Book 3.1/Unit 2 City Green

Extension: Have students work with a partner to list a common noun and a proper noun in each category: person, place, and thing.

35

GRAMMAR PRACTICE BOOK, PAGE 35

Review and Practice

Review Nouns Ask students to find the nouns from the Daily Language Activity for Days 1 through 3 and to use them in new sentences. Introduce the Daily Language Activity for Day 4.

Mechanics and Usage Tell students that some proper nouns and titles have short forms. Display the following and list examples:

Abbreviations

- An abbreviation is the shortened form of a word. It begins with a capital letter and ends with a period.
- Abbreviate most titles of people before names. Examples: *Mrs., Mr., Ms., Dr.*
- You can abbreviate days of the week and months of the year.

WRITING Assign the daily Writing Prompt on page 142D.

Name__________ Date__________ MECHANICS Grammar 36

Abbreviation of Proper Nouns

- An abbreviation is a shortened form of a word.
- An abbreviation begins with a capital letter and ends with a period.
- Abbreviate titles of people before names.
  Mrs. Ms. Mr. Dr.
- You can abbreviate days of the week.
- You can also abbreviate most months.

Proofread the sentences. Write each abbreviation correctly.

1. Mama's friend mrs B helps clean the lot. Mrs.
2. From two houses down, mr Rocco comes. Mr.
3. One day, mrs Wells talks about her grandmother. Mrs.
4. mr Bennett doesn't know about the sunflowers. Mr.
5. On mon, Old Man Hammer sits in the garden. Mon.
6. He also comes on tues and every other day. Tues.
7. In aug, Marcy sees him sitting in the sun. Aug.
8. In jan, he probably won't come. Jan.

36

Extension: Have partners look through newspapers and magazines for abbreviations and underline them.

Book 3.1/Unit 2 City Green 8

GRAMMAR PRACTICE BOOK, PAGE 36

Assess and Reteach

Assess Use the Daily Language Activity and page 37 of the Grammar Practice Book for assessment.

Reteach Tell students to write down all the rules they have learned about proper and common nouns.

Ask students to turn to the illustration on page 154. Have them list the holiday objects and people in the picture on the chalkboard. Guide them to include the holiday and holiday decorations they see. Ask them to identify each as a proper or common noun according to the rules they have learned. Have them make up names with the titles *Mr., Miss,* or *Mrs.* for the people not identified in the story.

Use page 38 of the **Grammar Practice Book** for additional reteaching.

WRITING Assign the daily Writing Prompt on page 142D.

Name__________ Date__________ TEST Grammar 37

Common and Proper Nouns

A. If the underlined noun is a common noun, write **common**. If the underlined noun is a proper noun, write **proper**.

1. The building was unsafe. common
2. Old Man Hammer used to live in it. proper
3. A crane parked on the street. common
4. Workers knocked down the building. common
5. Miss Rosa took dirt from the lot. proper

B. Find the abbreviation of a proper noun in each sentence. Write it on the line.

6. One of the neighbors was Mr. Rocco. Mr.
7. Mrs. Wells was another neighbor. Mrs.
8. Apr. is a good month for gardens. Apr.
9. Dec. is not a good month for gardens. Dec.
10. Mr. Bennett is a neighbor also. Mr.

10 Book 3.1/Unit 2 City Green

37

GRAMMAR PRACTICE BOOK, PAGE 37

GRAMMAR PRACTICE BOOK, PAGE 38

5 Day Spelling Plan

LANGUAGE SUPPORT

To help students hear the number of syllables in each word, read the Spelling Words aloud one at a time. Have students repeat and clap each time they hear a vowel sound.

DICTATION SENTENCES

Spelling Words

1. Open the book and read the first page.
2. The battle was soon over.
3. She likes school even more this year.
4. Blow out the candle.
5. The lake is frozen.
6. I like to eat carrots.
7. Be silent so I can hear the birds.
8. Most animals are not lazy.
9. The sandwich has lettuce in it.
10. The chair is made of maple wood.
11. The fellow with the black shoes is my father.
12. He has read fifty books.
13. The corn has a sweet flavor.
14. She left the bottle of water by her desk.
15. The hat is floppy because it is too large.

Challenge Words

16. Do not walk through that area.
17. The children are filled with excitement.
18. I am halfway through the book.
19. She jumped over a heap of dirt.
20. Keep to the schedule for school.

DAY 1 Pretest

Assess Prior Knowledge Use the Dictation Sentences at the left and **Spelling Practice Book** page 33 for the pretest. Allow students to correct their own papers. If students have trouble, have partners give each other a mid-week test on Day 3. Students who require a modified list may be tested on the first eight words.

Spelling Words		Challenge Words
1. **open**	9. **lettuce**	16. area
2. battle	10. maple	17. excitement
3. even	11. fellow	18. halfway
4. candle	12. fifty	19. heap
5. frozen	13. flavor	20. schedule
6. **carrots**	14. bottle	
7. silent	15. floppy	
8. lazy		

*Note: Words in **dark type** are from the story.*

Word Study On page 34 of the **Spelling Practice Book** are word study steps and an at-home activity.

Name__________ Date______ PRETEST SPELLING 33

Syllable Patterns

Pretest Directions
Fold back the paper along the dotted line. Use the blanks to write each word as it is read aloud. When you finish the test, unfold the paper. Use the list at the right to correct any spelling mistakes. Practice the words you missed for the Posttest.

To Parents
Here are the results of your child's weekly spelling Pretest. You can help your child study for the Posttest by following these simple steps for each word on the word list:
1. Read the word to your child.
2. Have your child write the word, saying each letter as it is written.
3. Say each letter of the word as your child checks the spelling.
4. If a mistake has been made, have your child read each letter of the correctly spelled word aloud, and then repeat steps 1-3.

Parent/Child Activity:
Play a rhyming game with your child by taking turns saying as many rhyming words as you both can think of for each spelling word.

1. _____ 1. open
2. _____ 2. battle
3. _____ 3. even
4. _____ 4. candle
5. _____ 5. frozen
6. _____ 6. carrots
7. _____ 7. silent
8. _____ 8. bottle
9. _____ 9. lazy
10. _____ 10. lettuce
11. _____ 11. maple
12. _____ 12. fellow
13. _____ 13. fifty
14. _____ 14. flavor
15. _____ 15. floppy

Challenge Words
_____ area
_____ excitement
_____ halfway
_____ heap
_____ schedule

15 Book 3.1/Unit 2 City Green 33

SPELLING PRACTICE BOOK, PAGE 33

WORD STUDY STEPS AND ACTIVITY, PAGE 34

DAY 2 Explore the Pattern

Sort and Spell Words Write and say the words *open* and *battle*. Ask students whether the first syllable of each word has a long- or short-vowel sound. (*open*, long *o*; *battle*, short *a*) Have students sort the Spelling Words as below.

Vowel sound in the first syllable

Long		Short	
open	lazy	battle	lettuce
even	maple	candle	fellow
frozen	flavor	carrots	fifty
silent		bottle	floppy

Syllable Patterns. Have students divide the Spelling Words into syllables. If the first syllable has a long-vowel sound, the word is usually divided after the vowel. (This is an *open syllable*. Examples: *e-ven*, *ma-ple*.) If the first syllable has a short-vowel sound, the word is usually divided after the next consonant, often between two consonants. (This is a *closed syllable*. Examples: *can-dle, bat-tle*.)

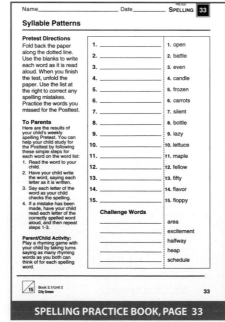

Name__________ Date______ EXPLORE THE PATTERN SPELLING 35

Syllable Patterns

open	candle	silent	lettuce	fifty
battle	frozen	bottle	maple	flavor
even	carrots	lazy	fellow	floppy

Syllable Practice
Write the spelling words that contain a long-vowel sound in the first syllable.

1. open 2. even 3. frozen
4. silent 5. lazy 6. maple
7. flavor

Write the spelling words that contain a short-vowel sound in the first syllable.

8. battle 9. candle 10. carrots
11. bottle 12. lettuce 13. fellow
14. fifty 15. floppy

Pattern Power!
Write the spelling words with each of these patterns.

fl
16. flavor
17. floppy

le
21. maple
22. battle
23. candle
24. bottle

en
18. frozen
19. open
20. even

y
25. lazy
26. fifty
27. floppy

27 Book 3.1/Unit 2 City Green 35

SPELLING PRACTICE BOOK, PAGE 35

Syllable Patterns

DAY 3 Practice and Extend

Word Meanings: Prefixes Explain to students that the prefixes are letters added to the beginning of words that change the words' meaning. Tell students that *re*-means *again* and *un*- means *not*. Ask students what *untrue* means. (not true) Have students form new words by adding *re*- to the words *open, do, write,* and *read*, and *un*- to *even, frozen, kind*, and *cover*. Then have them write a context sentence for each new word.

Glossary Remind students that multisyllable words in the Glossary have bullets (•) to show how they are divided into syllables. Have partners:

- write each Challenge Word.
- look up each Challenge Word in the Glossary to find its syllabication.
- write the syllabication and the number of syllables next to each Challenge Word.

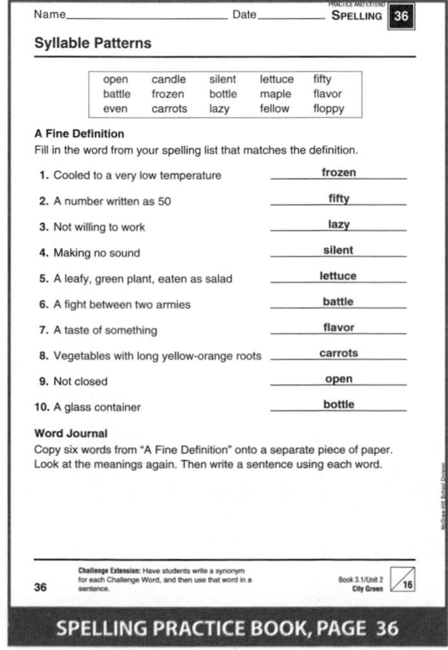

Name________________ Date________ PRACTICE AND EXTEND SPELLING 36

Syllable Patterns

open	candle	silent	lettuce	fifty
battle	frozen	bottle	maple	flavor
even	carrots	lazy	fellow	floppy

A Fine Definition

Fill in the word from your spelling list that matches the definition.

1. Cooled to a very low temperature ____frozen____
2. A number written as 50 ____fifty____
3. Not willing to work ____lazy____
4. Making no sound ____silent____
5. A leafy, green plant, eaten as salad ____lettuce____
6. A fight between two armies ____battle____
7. A taste of something ____flavor____
8. Vegetables with long yellow-orange roots ____carrots____
9. Not closed ____open____
10. A glass container ____bottle____

Word Journal

Copy six words from "A Fine Definition" onto a separate piece of paper. Look at the meanings again. Then write a sentence using each word.

36 **Challenge Extension:** Have students write a synonym for each Challenge Word, and then use that word in a sentence. Book 3.1/Unit 2 City Green 16

SPELLING PRACTICE BOOK, PAGE 36

DAY 4 Proofread and Write

Proofread Sentences. Write these sentences on the chalkboard, including the misspelled words. Ask students to proofread, circling incorrect spellings and writing the correct spellings. There are two spelling errors in each sentence.

Rabbits like carots and letuce for breakfast. (carrots, lettuce)

Sillent snow fell on the frozin ground. (silent, frozen)

Have students create additional sentences with errors for partners to correct.

WRITING Have students use as many spelling words as possible in the daily Writing Prompt on page 142D. Remind students to proofread their writing for errors in spelling, grammar, and punctuation.

Name________________ Date________ PROOFREAD AND WRITE SPELLING 37

Syllable Patterns

Proofreading Activity

There are seven spelling mistakes in this paragraph. Circle the misspelled words. Write the words correctly on the lines below.

It was a laysy sunny day. The gate by the garden was opun. Jean Marie saw a rabbit with flopee ears hop away. The girl knew there was trouble, because she and the rabbit were having an ongoing battel all summer long. She quickly checked her plants. Jean Marie found three were missing. All the leaves of the lettus plants were chewed. Then she spotted a bottul on the ground. Some mapil syrup had spilled from it. "There's nothing this rabbit won't eat!" she thought to herself.

1. ____lazy____ 2. ____open____ 3. ____floppy____
4. ____battle____ 5. ____lettuce____ 6. ____bottle____
7. ____maple____

Writing Activity

Write a description of a vegetable garden. Use at least three list words in your description.

10 Book 3.1/Unit 2 City Green 37

SPELLING PRACTICE BOOK, PAGE 37

DAY 5 Assess and Reteach

Assess Students' Knowledge Use page 38 of the **Spelling Practice Book** or the Dictation Sentences on page 171O for the posttest.

Personal Word List Have students keep lists of words that name or describe foods in their journals. Have them start with spelling words from this week to begin their lists. For example; words that name foods: *lettuce, carrots;* words that describe foods: *frozen, maple.* Encourage them to add to their lists as they come across other food-related words.

JOURNAL

Students should refer to their word lists during later writing activities.

Name________________ Date________ POSTTEST SPELLING 38

Syllable Patterns

Look at the words in each set. One word in each set is spelled correctly. Use a pencil to color in the circle in front of that word. Before you begin, look at the sample sets of words. Sample A has been done for you. Do Sample B by yourself. When you are sure you know what to do, you may go on with the rest of the page.

Sample A
Ⓐ aipron
Ⓑ aprone
● apron
Ⓓ appron

Sample B
● settle
Ⓕ setle
Ⓖ cettle
Ⓗ settal

1. ● carrots Ⓑ karots Ⓒ karrots Ⓓ carits
2. Ⓔ mapul ● maple Ⓖ mayple Ⓗ mapel
3. Ⓐ flayver ● flavor Ⓒ flavore Ⓓ flaiver
4. Ⓔ evin Ⓕ evon Ⓖ evun ● even
5. Ⓐ felow Ⓑ felloe ● fellow Ⓓ felluh
6. ● open Ⓕ owpen Ⓖ opun Ⓗ oppen
7. Ⓐ battul Ⓑ batle ● battle Ⓓ batel
8. ● silent Ⓕ sylent Ⓖ silen Ⓗ silunt
9. Ⓐ lettuse Ⓑ letuce ● lettuce Ⓓ lettace
10. Ⓔ flopy Ⓕ flopee ● floppy Ⓗ floppey
11. Ⓐ layzee ● lazy Ⓒ lazey Ⓓ lasy
12. Ⓔ candel Ⓕ kandle Ⓖ candul ● candle
13. Ⓐ botle Ⓑ botlle Ⓒ bottal ● bottle
14. Ⓔ fiffty Ⓕ phifty ● fifty Ⓗ fiftee
15. ● frozen Ⓑ frowzen Ⓒ frosen Ⓓ frozin

38 Book 3.1/Unit 2 City Green 15

SPELLING PRACTICE BOOK, PAGE 38

The Sun, the Wind and the Rain

Selection Summary Students will read about two mountains, one created by Earth, and one created by a girl. As the mountains erode, students will learn the different ways nature causes change.

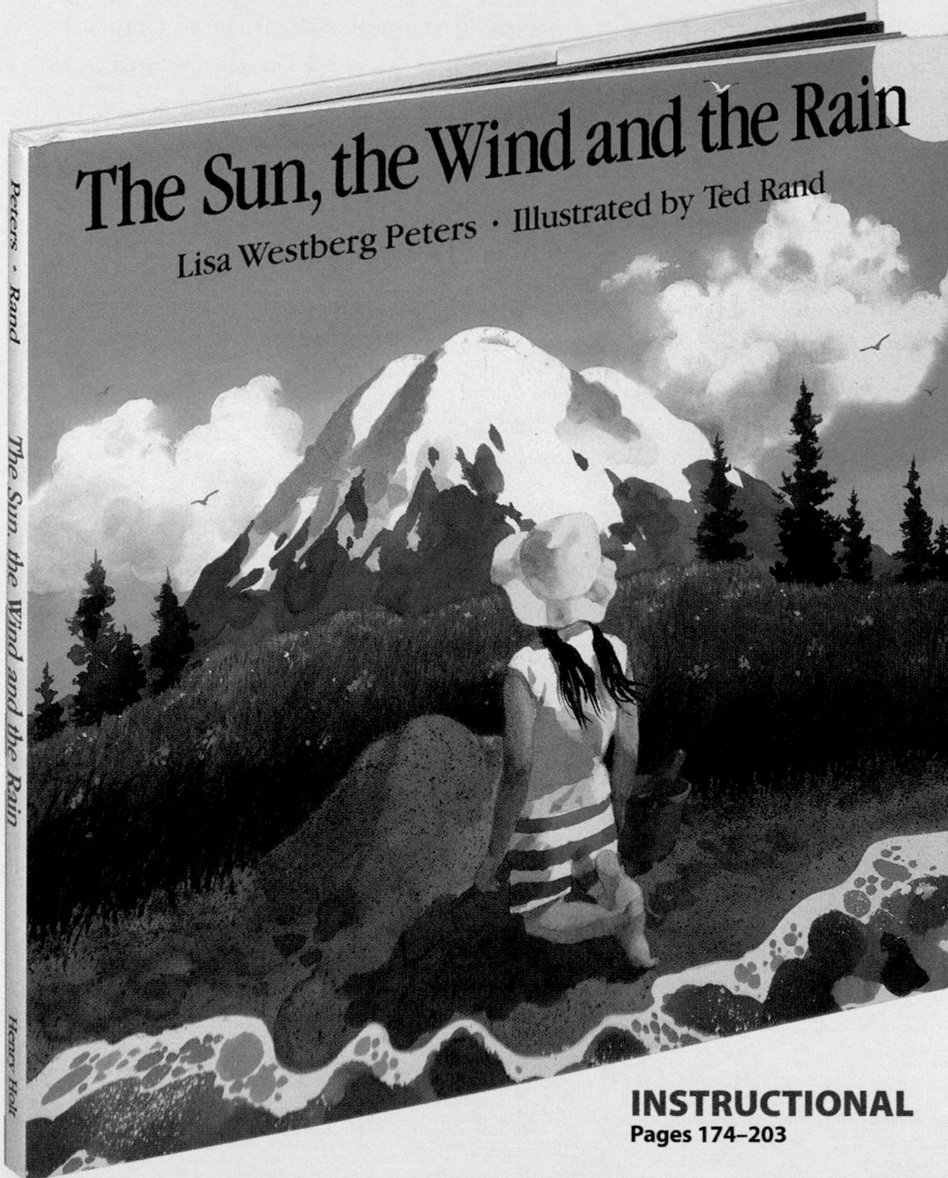

Listening Library Audiocassette

INSTRUCTIONAL
Pages 174–203

About the Author Lisa Westberg Peters wanted to write a book for children that would explain geology and how mountains change over time. "I was lucky enough to take some good geology courses and several unforgettable trips into the mountains," she says.

About the Illustrator Ted Rand painted a picture of Mt. Rainier in the state of Washington on the cover of *The Sun, the Wind and the Rain*. "I'd like to encourage young readers to draw and enjoy the fun of it," says Mr. Rand.

Resources for
Meeting Individual Needs

LEVELED BOOKS

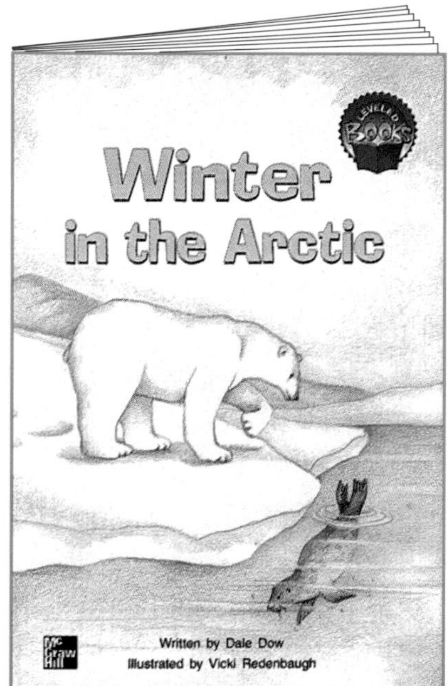

EASY
Pages 203A, 203D

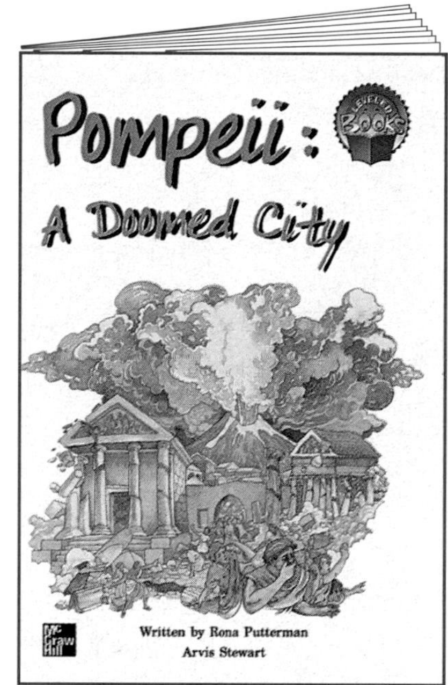

INDEPENDENT
Pages 203B, 203D

Take-Home version available

CHALLENGE
Pages 203C, 203D

LEVELED PRACTICE

Reteach, 45–51
blackline masters with reteaching opportunities for each assessed skill

Practice, 45–51
workbook with Take-Home stories and practice opportunities for each assessed skill and story comprehension

Extend, 45–51
blackline masters that offer challenge activities for each assessed skill

ADDITIONAL RESOURCES

- **Language Support Book** 49–56
- **Take-Home Story, Practice** p. 46a
- **Alternate Teaching Strategies** T60–T66
- **Selected Quizzes Prepared by** Accelerated Reader

Suggested Lesson Planner

Available on CD-ROM

READING AND LANGUAGE ARTS	DAY 1 Focus on Reading and Skills	 DAY 2 Read the Literature
• Comprehension • Vocabulary • Phonics/Decoding • Study Skills • Listening, Speaking, Viewing, Representing	 **Read Aloud and Motivate,** 172E "The Hurricane" **Develop Visual Literacy,** 172/173 ☑ **Introduce Compare and Contrast,** 174A–174B **Teaching Chart 37** **Reteach, Practice, Extend,** 45	**Build Background,** 174C Develop Oral Language **Vocabulary,** 174D *canyons* *grains* *peaks* *flowed* *handful* *traded* **Teaching Chart 38** **Word Building Manipulative Cards** **Reteach, Practice, Extend,** 46  **Read the Selection,** 174–199 Guided Instruction ☑ Compare and Contrast ☑ Draw Conclusions **Minilessons,** 183, 185, 187, 189, 193, 197 **Cultural Perspectives,** 178
 • Curriculum Connections	 **Fine Arts,** 172/173	 **Science,** 174C
• Writing	 **Writing Prompt:** You are going to make a lake on a beach. What materials will you need? How will you use them? Write a paragraph to explain.	 **Writing Prompt:** You are making a movie. Y need rain coming down a window. What v you do? Write a short explanation.  **Journal Writing,** 199 Quick-Write
• Grammar	**Introduce the Concept: Singular and Plural Nouns,** 203M Daily Language Activity 1. The earth has many mountain. (mountains) 2. Four rock fell down this hill. (rocks) 3. Several animal live here. (animals) **Grammar Practice Book,** 39	**Teach the Concept: Singular and Plural Nouns,** 203M Daily Language Activity 1. Many stream flow through these mountain. (streams, mountains) 2. Most city are built near river. (cities, rivers) 3. Fox live on these mountain. (foxes, mountains) **Grammar Practice Book,** 40
• Spelling	**Introduce: Words with Consonant Clusters,** 203O **Spelling Practice Book,** 39–40	**Explore the Pattern: Words with Consonant Clusters,** 203O **Spelling Practice Book,** 41

Meeting Individual Needs

☑ = **Skill Assessed in Unit Test**

DAY 3 Read the Literature

Reread for Fluency, 198

Story Questions, 200
Reteach, Practice, Extend, 47
Story Activities, 201

Study Skill, 202
☑ Reference Sources
Teaching Chart 39
Reteach, Practice, Extend, 48

Test Power, 203
TAAS Preparation and Practice Book, 32–33

Read the Leveled Books,
Guided Reading
Consonant Clusters
☑ Compare and Contrast
☑ Instructional Vocabulary
 **CD-ROM**

 **Music,** 186 **Social Studies,** 182

 **Writing Prompt:** What would you do if you spent a day at the beach? Write a paragraph describing different things you might see and do.

Writing Process: Explanatory Writing, 203K
Prewrite, Draft

Review and Practice: Singular and Plural Nouns, 203N
Daily Language Activity
1. They hiked on three path. (paths)
2. We filled many box with sand. (boxes)
3. Many country don't have enough rain. (countries)

Grammar Practice Book, 41

Practice and Extend: Words with Consonant Clusters, 203P
Spelling Practice Book, 42

DAY 4 Build Skills

Read the Leveled Books and Self-Selected Books

☑ **Review Compare and Contrast** 203E–203F
Teaching Chart 40
Reteach, Practice, Extend, 49
Language Support, 54

☑ **Review Draw Conclusions,** 203G–203H
Teaching Chart 41
Reteach, Practice, Extend, 50
Language Support, 55

 **Science,** 190

 **Writing Prompt:** List at least four things you might need for a trip to the mountains. Then tell why you need each one.

Writing Process: Explanatory Writing, 203K
Revise

Meeting Individual Needs for Writing, 203L

Review and Practice: Singular and Plural Nouns, 203N
Daily Language Activity
1. Do you like to make sand castle? (castles)
2. The animals eat berries from those bush. (bushes)
3. The boy told two story. (stories)

Grammar Practice Book, 42

Proofread and Write: Words with Consonant Clusters, 203P
Spelling Practice Book, 43

DAY 5 Build Skills

Read Self-Selected Books

☑ **Introduce Antonyms and Synonyms,** 203I–203J
Teaching Chart 42
Reteach, Practice, Extend, 51
Language Support, 56

Listening, Speaking, Viewing, Representing, 203L
Discuss Drawings
On-Location Broadcast

Minilessons, 183, 185, 187, 189, 197

Phonics Review,
Consonant Clusters, 189
Phonics/Phonemic Awareness Practice Book, 13–18
 **CD-ROM**

 **Math,** 192

 **Writing Prompt:** Describe what happens when it rains. Where does the water come from? Where does it go?

Writing Process: Explanatory Writing, 203K
Edit/Proofread, Publish

Assess and Reteach: Singular and Plural Nouns, 203N
Daily Language Activity
1. Elizabeth made two pile of sand. (piles)
2. The girl's two hobby involved pebbles and sand. (hobbies)
3. Who picked those bunch of flowers? (bunches)

Grammar Practice Book, 43–44

Assess and Reteach: Words with Consonant Clusters, 203P
Spelling Practice Book, 44

Language Arts

Read Aloud and Motivate

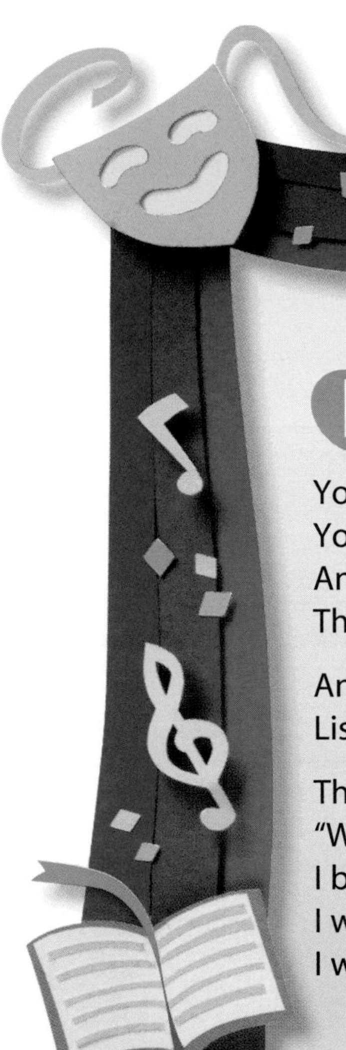

The Hurricane

a poem by Ashley Bryan

I cried to the wind,
"Don't blow so hard!
You've knocked down my sister
You're shaking
And tossing and tilting
The tree!"

And would the wind listen,
Listen to me?

The wind howled,
"Whooree!
I blow as I wish
I wish
I wish
I crush and
I splash and
I rush and
I swish."

I cried to the wind,
"Don't blow so wild!
You're chasing the clouds
You're whirling
And swishing and swirling
The sea!"

And would the wind listen,
Listen to me?

Continued on pages T2–T5

Oral Comprehension

LISTENING AND SPEAKING Encourage students to listen to the rhythm and rhyme as you read aloud this poem about the wind. When you are finished, ask students if they thought the rhythm of the poem sounded like the wind. Have students discuss what details they like about the poem. Ask them why they think the poet used words like *wish, swish,* and *splash*.

Activity Have students create paintings based on the images in the poem. Ask students to think about these images and decide which ones they wish to include in their painting. Remind them that the painting does not need to be realistic. Suggest they think of a title for their painting.

▶ **Visual/Intrapersonal**

Develop Visual Literacy

Works of Art

Anthology pages 172–173

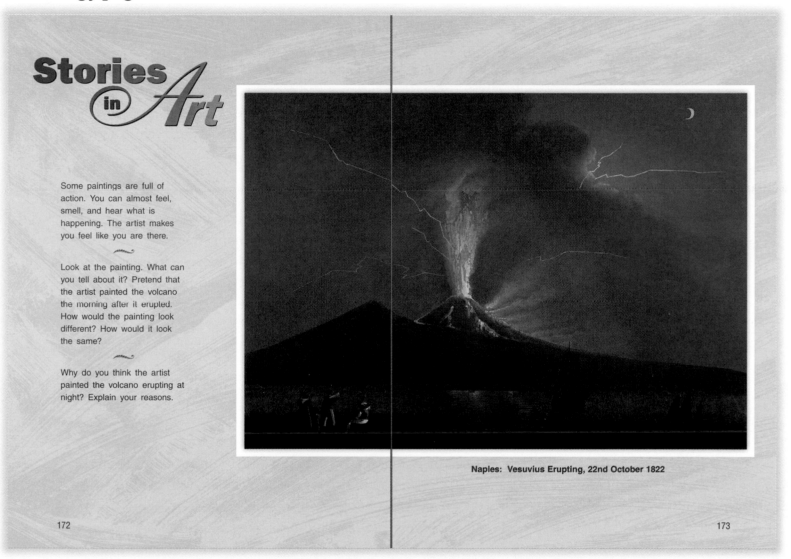

Stories in Art

Some paintings are full of action. You can almost feel, smell, and hear what is happening. The artist makes you feel like you are there.

Look at the painting. What can you tell about it? Pretend that the artist painted the volcano the morning after it erupted. How would the painting look different? How would it look the same?

Why do you think the artist painted the volcano erupting at night? Explain your reasons.

Naples: Vesuvius Erupting, 22nd October 1822

172 173

Objective: Introduce Compare and Contrast

VIEWING This vivid painting of a volcano erupting captures the magnitude and power of the event. Discuss with students what they see in the foreground, the middle ground, and the background. Invite them to close their eyes and describe the details that appear in the sky. Afterward, ask, "What areas of the painting are light or bright? What areas are dark?" Have students note that the darkness is not only realistic but also adds to the mood of the painting.

Read the page with students, encouraging individual interpretations of the painting.

Ask students to describe how the scene might look the morning after the volcano erupted. For example:

- The volcano would probably look different. Fire wouldn't be shooting into the sky.
- It would be light out. There might be ash or lava on the ground.

REPRESENTING Have students think of an earthquake, tornado, cyclone, or volcanic eruption. Invite students to draw their own picture of the event.

TESTED OBJECTIVES

Students will compare and contrast things that happen in a story.

LANGUAGE SUPPORT

ESL Show a picture of the city and a picture of the countryside. As you discuss how these pictures are alike and different, have students help you fill in a chart on the chalkboard that shows their responses.

Introduce Compare and Contrast

PREPARE

Compare Objects in Nature

Have students choose two objects in nature, such as a stone and a blade of grass, to compare and contrast. Tell them to touch and look at each object carefully. Ask: How are these objects different? How are they alike? What would happen to each of these objects in a strong wind?

TEACH

Define Compare and Contrast

Tell students: When you compare or contrast, or think how things are the same or different, you learn more about them. Thinking about how objects, people, and events in a story are the same or different can help you to understand what is happening in the story.

Jake Digs Two Tunnels

One Saturday morning, Jake wanted to dig a tunnel for his trucks. The weather was warm, and so was the dirt. It was hard, dry, and dusty, too. As he worked, a strong wind came and blew some of the dirt right back into the tunnel. Then rain began pouring down. Jake sighed and went back into the house. He would never be able to use that tunnel.

When the rain let up, Jake took his shovel, and went outside again. The first tunnel was gone, but the rain had made the earth softer, wetter, and easier to dig—much better for tunnel building. Jake started working again. The weather had gotten cooler, and the dirt felt cold in his hands. Jake kept digging, and soon he was happily racing trucks through his tunnel.

Teaching Chart 37

Read the Story and Model the Skill

Display **Teaching Chart 37**. As they read the story, have students pay attention to clues about similarities and differences.

MODEL The title of the story tells me that I will read about a boy who digs two tunnels. As I read, I will look for ways in which the tunnels are alike and different.

Compare and Contrast

Have students underline clues that describe how the second tunnel is different from the first.

SELECTION Connection

Students will understand how to compare and contrast story elements when they read *The Sun, the Wind and the Rain* and the Leveled Books.

PRACTICE

Create a Venn Diagram

Work with students to create a Venn diagram that contrasts the two tunnels. In the center circle, students should show how the two tunnels are alike. ▶**Visual/Logical**

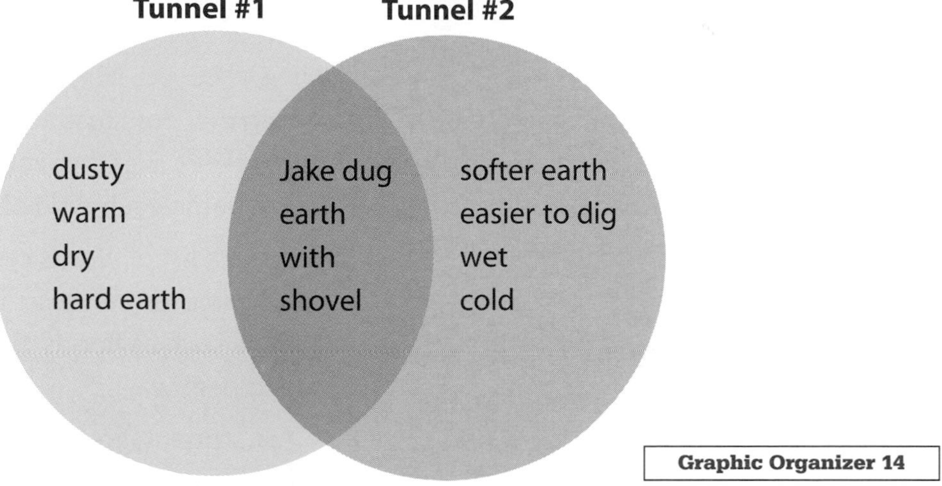

Graphic Organizer 14

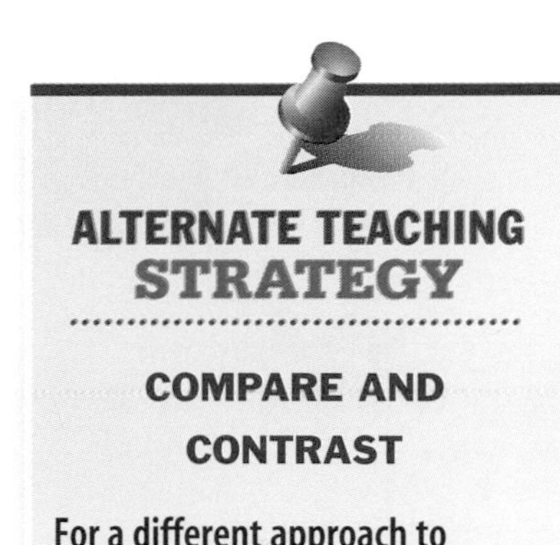

ALTERNATE TEACHING STRATEGY

COMPARE AND CONTRAST

For a different approach to teaching this skill, see page T64.

ASSESS/CLOSE

Compare and Contrast

If there had been no rain storm, how would that have changed what happened in the story? Would the title of the story stay the same? How might it change? (The wind and rain would not have filled up the first tunnel, and Jake would have been able to race trucks through it. He would not have had to start over and dig a second tunnel. The title of the story would be different. It might be: "Jake Digs a Tunnel.")

Meeting Individual Needs for Comprehension

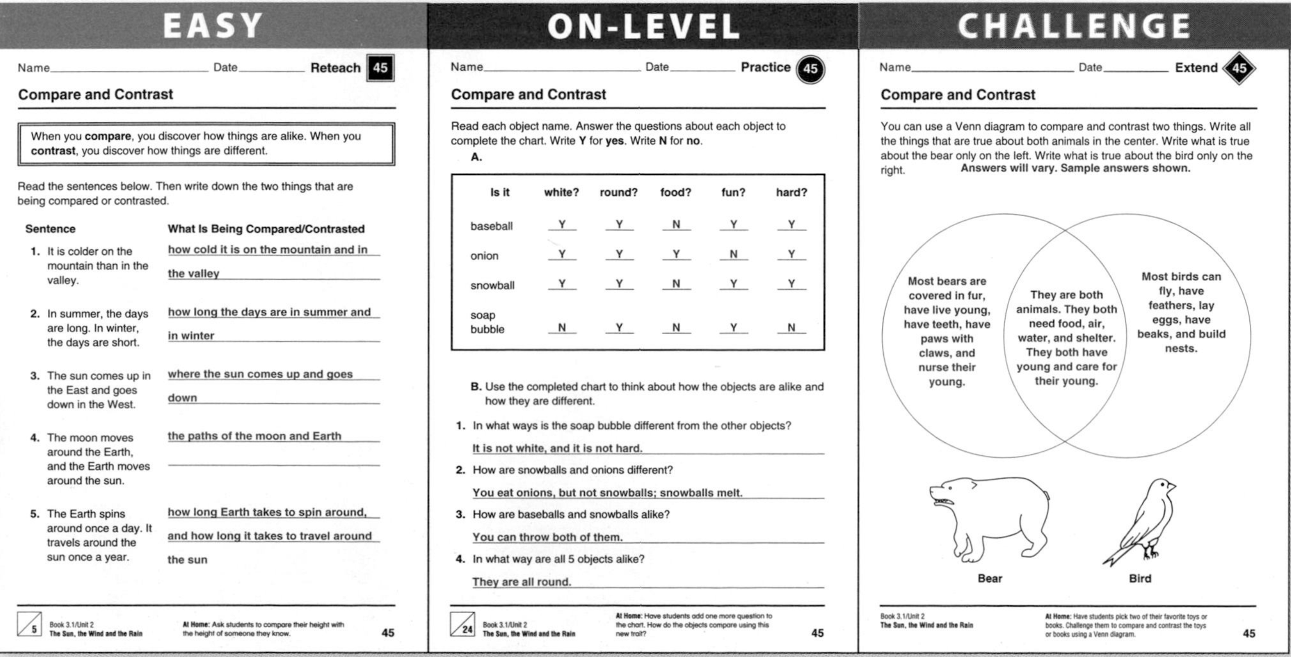

EASY

Name________ Date______ Reteach 45

Compare and Contrast

When you **compare**, you discover how things are alike. When you **contrast**, you discover how things are different.

Read the sentences below. Then write down the two things that are being compared or contrasted.

Sentence	What Is Being Compared/Contrasted
1. It is colder on the mountain than in the valley.	how cold it is on the mountain and in the valley
2. In summer, the days are long. In winter, the days are short.	how long the days are in summer and in winter
3. The sun comes up in the East and goes down in the West.	where the sun comes up and goes down
4. The moon moves around the Earth, and the Earth moves around the sun.	the paths of the moon and Earth
5. The Earth spins around once a day. It travels around the sun once a year.	how long Earth takes to spin around, and how long it takes to travel around the sun

5 Book 3.1/Unit 2 **The Sun, the Wind and the Rain**

At Home: Ask students to compare their height with the height of someone they know. 45

Reteach, 45

ON-LEVEL

Name________ Date______ Practice 45

Compare and Contrast

Read each object name. Answer the questions about each object to complete the chart. Write **Y** for **yes**. Write **N** for **no**.

A.

Is it	white?	round?	food?	fun?	hard?
baseball	Y	Y	N	Y	Y
onion	Y	Y	Y	N	Y
snowball	Y	Y	N	Y	Y
soap bubble	N	Y	N	Y	N

B. Use the completed chart to think about how the objects are alike and how they are different.

1. In what ways is the soap bubble different from the other objects?
   It is not white, and it is not hard.
2. How are snowballs and onions different?
   You eat onions, but not snowballs; snowballs melt.
3. How are baseballs and snowballs alike?
   You can throw both of them.
4. In what way are all 5 objects alike?
   They are all round.

24 Book 3.1/Unit 2 **The Sun, the Wind and the Rain**

At Home: Have students add one more question to the chart. How do the objects compare using this new trait? 45

Practice, 45

CHALLENGE

Name________ Date______ Extend 45

Compare and Contrast

You can use a Venn diagram to compare and contrast two things. Write all the things that are true about both animals in the center. Write what is true about the bear only on the left. Write what is true about the bird only on the right. **Answers will vary. Sample answers shown.**

Book 3.1/Unit 2 **The Sun, the Wind and the Rain**

At Home: Have students pick two of their favorite toys or books. Challenge them to compare and contrast the toys or books using a Venn diagram. 45

Extend, 45

Build Background

Anthology and Leveled Books

Science

Evaluate Prior Knowledge

CONCEPT: CHANGES IN NATURE This selection and the Leveled Books explore how nature changes and affects the things around it. Invite students to share what they already know about changes in the weather as an example of changes in nature.

CREATE A CHART Invite students to think about what happens to a pile of sand on the beach when the sun shines on it, when the wind blows, and when it rains.

Sun	Wind	Rain
dries out sand	blows sand around	makes pile wet
	makes pile smaller	hard rain could wash it away

Graphic Organizer 30

DESCRIBE YOURSELF Invite students to

GROUP WRITING

write short paragraphs describing how their appearances and moods might change during different weather conditions. Invite them to illustrate their paragraphs.

Develop Oral Language

DISCUSS WEATHER Provide photographs ESL or illustrations of different weather conditions. Help students name each type of weather.

- Write a list of words or phrases on the chalkboard that describe weather conditions such as floods, blizzards, tornados, and heat waves.
- Ask students to read the words aloud.
- Invite students to pantomime how it would feel to be outside in each type of weather.
- Discuss how weather can affect the environment.

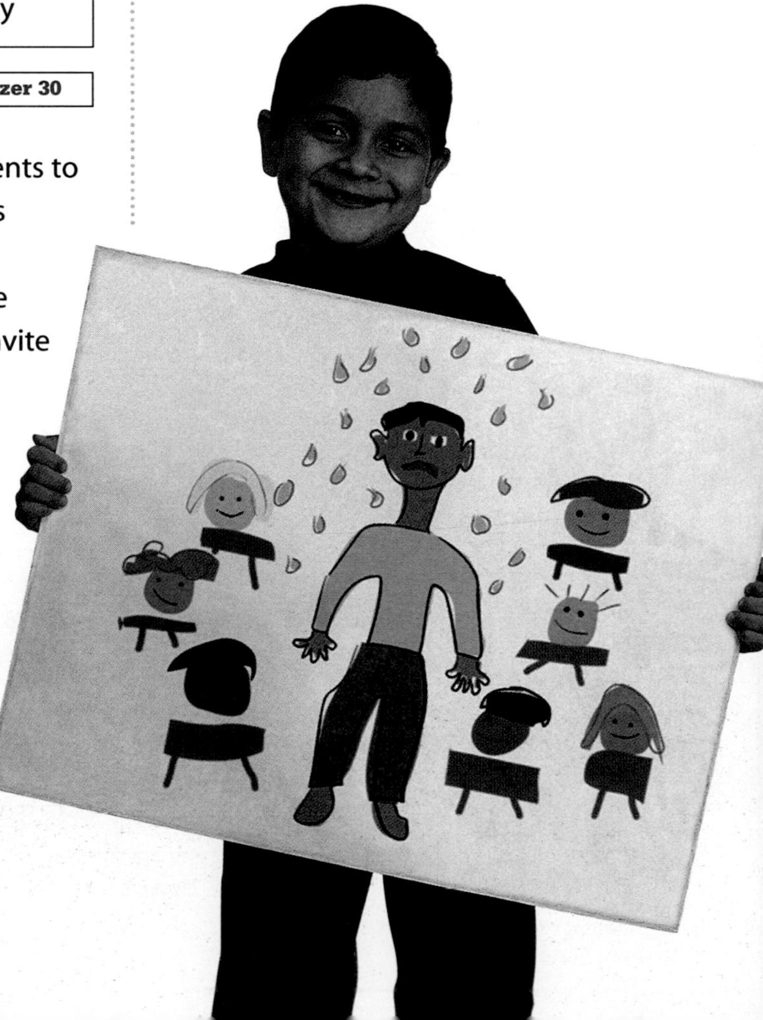

TEACHING TIP

MANAGEMENT While students are working on their paragraphs for the Describe Yourself activity, present the Develop Oral Language activity to students who need help with oral language.

LANGUAGE SUPPORT

See Language Support Book, pages 49–52, for teaching suggestions for Build Background and Vocabulary.

Vocabulary

Key Words

From Snow to Slush

1. The high peaks of the mountains were covered in snow. **2.** As the sun rose and changed the temperature during the day, snow was traded for slush. **3.** Elizabeth knelt down and picked up a handful of the slush. **4.** It melted even more and flowed right out of her hand! **5.** She mixed the slush with tiny grains of dirt from the mountain and made a little ball. **6.** Then she threw the ball far down into the deep canyons below.

Teaching Chart 38

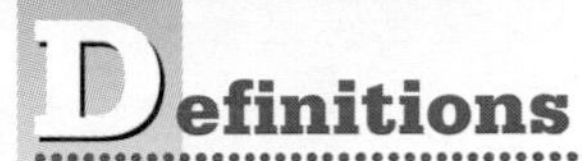

Definitions

peaks (p. 182) pointed ends or top parts of something, especially mountains

traded (p. 190) gave away something to get something else

handful (p. 193) the amount of something that fits in your hand

flowed (p. 188) moved like a liquid, like a stream of water

grains (p. 183) tiny bits

canyons (p. 182) long, narrow valleys between high hills or mountains

SPELLING/VOCABULARY CONNECTIONS

See Spelling Challenge Words, pages 203O–203P.

Vocabulary in Context

IDENTIFY VOCABULARY WORDS Display **Teaching Chart 38** and read the passage with students. Have volunteers circle each vocabulary word and underline other words that are clues to its meaning.

DISCUSS MEANINGS Ask questions like these to help clarify word meanings:

- What is a peak shaped like?
- Have you ever traded something for something else? What did you trade?
- Would you rather have a handful or a bucketful of your favorite treat? Why?
- If water is moving in a stream, is it stopping or flowing?
- Is it possible to count the grains of sand on a beach? Why or why not?
- Where would you most likely see canyons, in a flat area or a hilly area? Why?

Practice

DRAW CLUES Students can work in pairs. One student chooses a vocabulary card and draws a clue about its meaning. The partner guesses the vocabulary word, and then students switch roles. ▶ **Spatial/Linguistic**

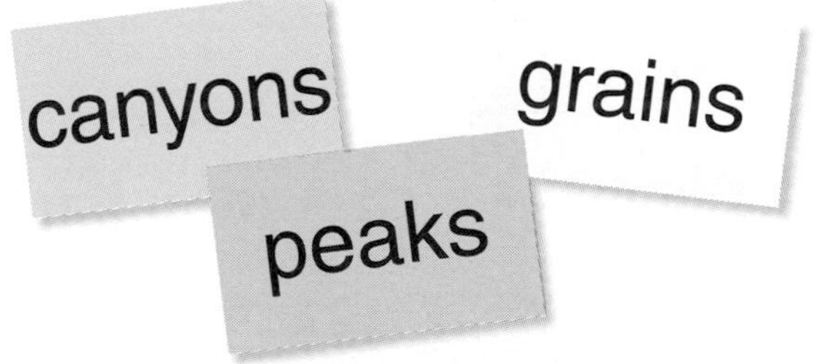

Word Building Manipulative Cards

SOLVE PUZZLES Have partners hide the vocabulary words in word search puzzles. They can exchange papers and circle the hidden vocabulary words. Have students refer to the Glossary as needed. ▶ **Interpersonal/Linguistic**

WRITING

ON-LEVEL

A Mountain of Fun

Molly mixed paper, paste, and water. She wanted to use the material to make something. "I will make two mountains with tall *peaks*," she said. When the mountains were finished, Cliff placed sand in the *canyons* between the mountains. It took a large *handful* of sand to completely cover the canyon floor. "The *grains* will stick to the sticky surface and look like the dirt of a canyon," Cliff told Molly.

Next, Molly painted the mountain gray and Cliff painted the canyon brown. Then they *traded* places and added on another layer of paint.

Molly and Cliff stepped back to look at their finished model. There was just one thing missing. Molly knew what it was. Slowly she painted a strip of blue through the canyon. The water looked like it *flowed*.

1. What is another word for the top of a mountain?
   the peak
2. Where did Cliff place sand?
   in the canyons
3. How much sand did Cliff use?
   a handful
4. What did the blue that Molly painted onto the model look like?
   flowing water
5. What did Molly do to help make the model?
   She made the mountains and painted on the water.

5 Book 3.1/Unit 2 **The Sun, the Wind and the Rain**

At Home: Encourage students to name any famous mountains or canyons they know about. Where are they? Have they ever been to them?

46A

Take-Home Story 46a
Reteach 46
Practice 46 • Extend 46

Guided Instruction

Preview and Predict

Have students read the title and look for pictures that show how the sun, wind, and rain change things.

- Which objects can be compared and contrasted on pages 182 and 183?
- How can comparing things help you understand the story?
- What is this story probably about?
- Will the story be a realistic one or a fantasy? How can you tell? (The pictures look real.) *Genre*

Have students record their predictions.

PREDICTIONS	WHAT HAPPENED
The two mountains will be compared and contrasted.	
The sun, wind, and rain will play important roles.	

Set Purposes

What do students want to find out by reading the story? For example:

- Why are the sun, wind, and rain important?
- What part does the girl play in the story?

The Sun, the Wind

The Sun, the Wind and the Rain
Lisa Westberg Peters · Illustrated by Ted Rand

by Lisa Westberg Peters
Illustrated by Ted Rand

174

Meeting Individual Needs • Grouping Suggestions for Strategic Reading

EASY	ON-LEVEL	CHALLENGE
Read Together Read the story with students or have them use the **Listening Library Audiocassette**. Have students use the Compare/Contrast chart to record important information as they read the story. Guided Instruction and Intervention prompts offer additional help with decoding, vocabulary, and comprehension.	**Guided Reading** Preview the story words on page 175. Read the story with students using the Guided Instruction. You may want to have students read the story or play the **Listening Library Audiocassette** first on their own. Help them make a Compare/Contrast chart.	**Read Independently** Remind students that comparing and contrasting can help them understand what the author is trying to explain. Have students set up a Compare/Contrast chart as on page 175. They can use their charts to help summarize the author's ideas.

and the Rain

This is the story of two mountains. The earth made one. Elizabeth in her yellow sun hat made the other.

175

Guided Instruction

Compare and Contrast

Draw Conclusions

Strategic Reading Comparing and contrasting can help you understand what happens in a story.

Before we begin reading, let's create Compare/Contrast charts to help us discover how the two mountains are alike and different.

REAL MOUNTAIN	SAND MOUNTAIN

1 **COMPARE AND CONTRAST** On the cover, Elizabeth is looking at a mountain. In the picture, Elizabeth is digging sand on a beach to make her mountain. Compare the sizes of the two mountains. (Elizabeth's mountain is very tiny compared to the other mountain.)

Story Words

The words below may be unfamiliar. Have students check their meanings and pronunciations in the Glossary on page 388.

- eons, p. 178
- crumble, p. 184
- jagged, p. 190

LANGUAGE SUPPORT

A blackline master of the Compare/Contrast chart is available in the **Language Support Book**.

Guided Instruction

2 **COMPARE AND CONTRAST** This picture shows the inside of a mountain. What would the inside of Elizabeth's mountain look like? How would it look different from the one in the picture? Why did the illustrator draw a picture like this?

MODEL I know that Elizabeth is making her mountain out of wet sand. The inside of Elizabeth's mountain would look very much like the outside. Her mountain was never fiery, hot and soft, or rock hard. Drawing a picture of something that is explained in the story can help readers to understand it better.

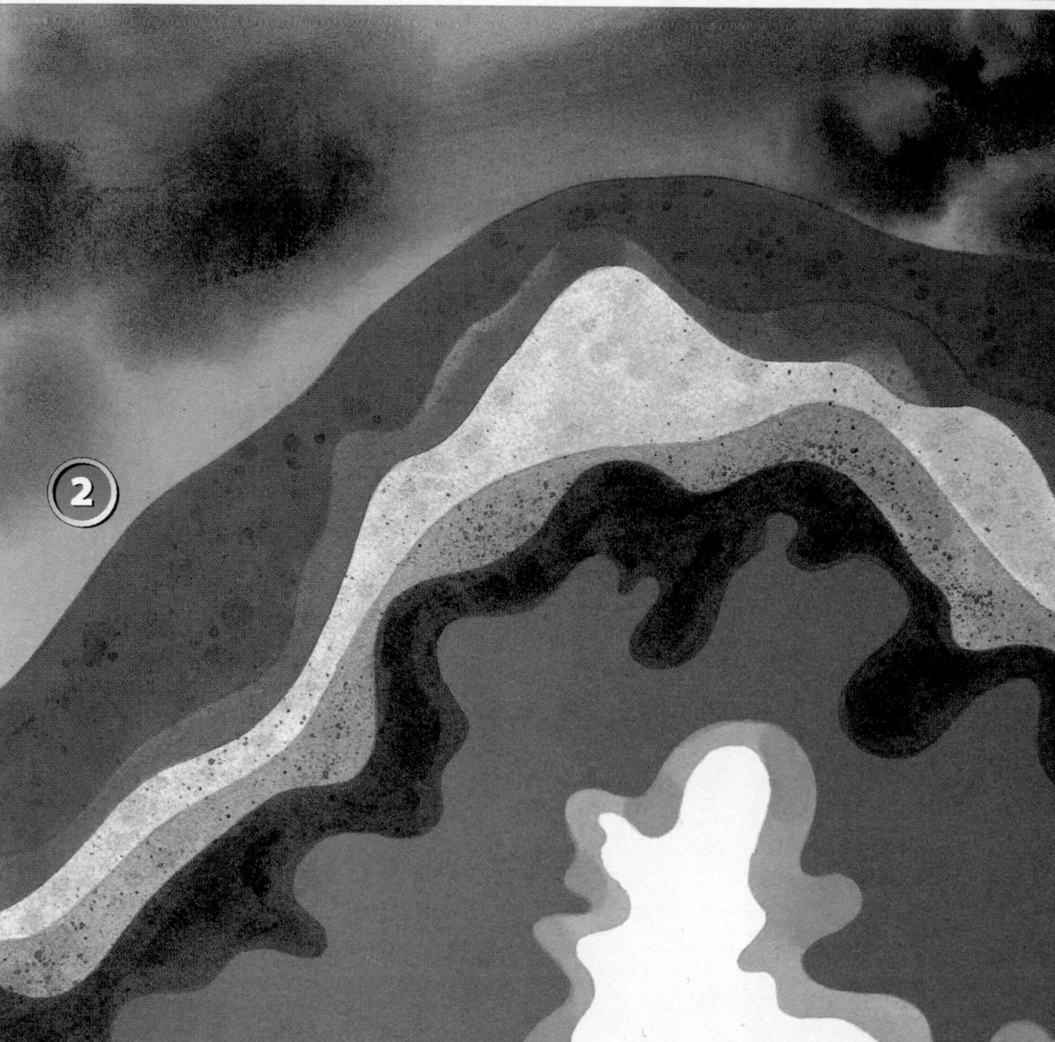

The earth made its mountain millions of years ago. It began as a pool underground, first fiery hot and soft, then cold and rock-hard.

176

Visual Literacy

VIEWING AND REPRESENTING

Discuss the style of the illustration on pages 176–177. Ask: Is it realistic or more like a cartoon? (It is like a cartoon because it is not something that can really be shown realistically.)

Have students compare this illustration with the illustration on page 180. Ask them to look at how the mountain has been drawn. Does it look like a real mountain? Why did the illustrator choose to draw this mountain in a more realistic style? (It looks real because there is snow and grass and trees on and near it just as in real life. He may have chosen this style because this is how Elizabeth really sees the mountain.)

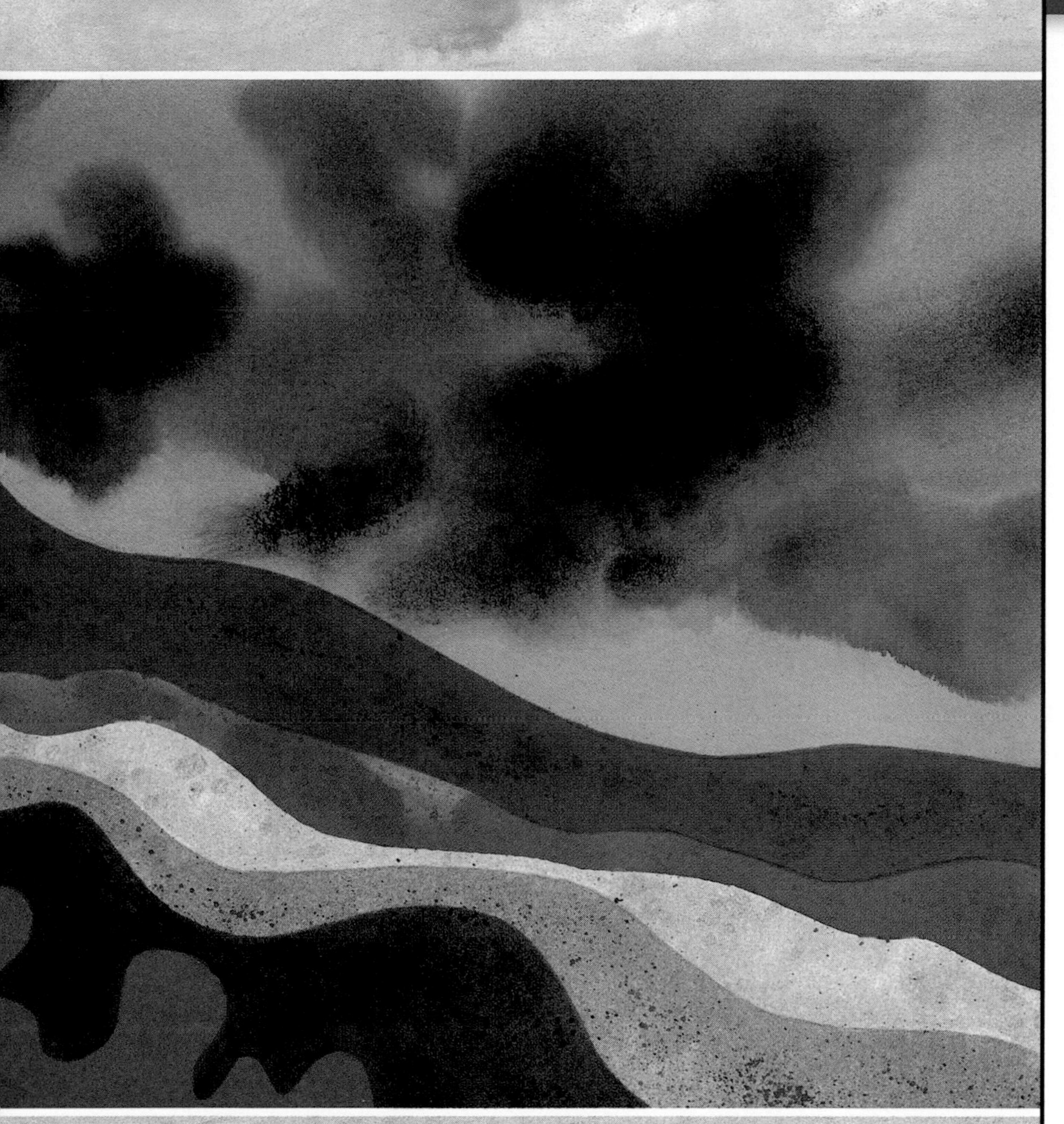

Elizabeth made hers on the beach today with bucketsful of wet sand. 

177

Guided Instruction

3 COMPARE AND CONTRAST The author says that the story is about a real mountain made millions of years ago and about a sand mountain made today by a girl named Elizabeth. We can see here how the author is comparing and contrasting the two mountains. Let's write what we learned about the mountains so far on our charts.

REAL MOUNTAIN	SAND MOUNTAIN
It is made of hot, soft materials. It took millions of years to form.	It is made of sand and water. It took one day to make.

Guided Instruction

4 **COMPARE AND CONTRAST** How does the illustration on this page compare with the illustration on page 177? How has the mountain changed? (Cracks have formed at the top. The shape of the mountain is different.) How are these two illustrations helpful in understanding the story?

MODEL I think the illustrations help me understand how mountains are created. I can see how a new mountain gets bigger over time. The pictures will also help me see the similarities and differences between the real mountain and Elizabeth's sand mountain.

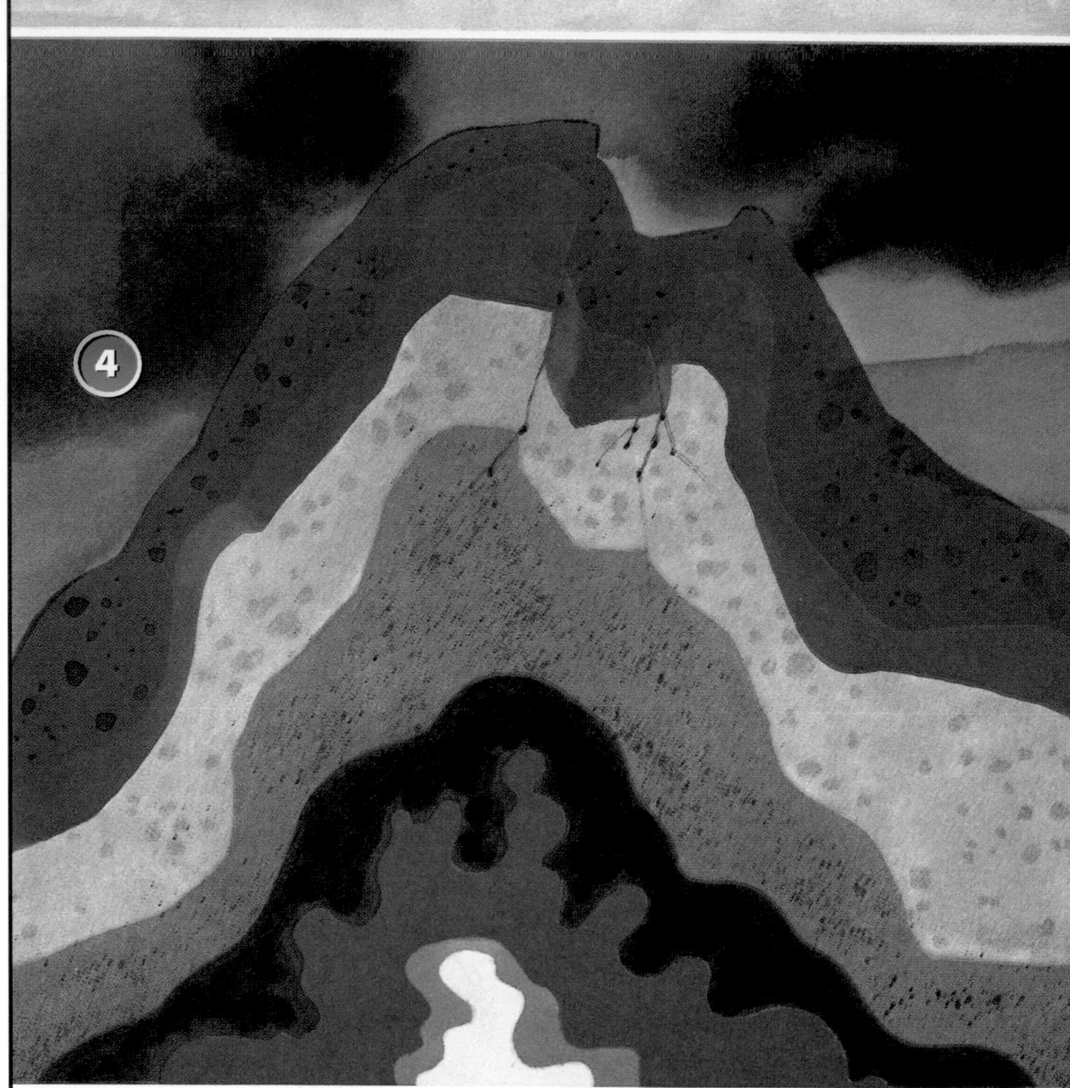

Eons passed. The earth cracked and shifted until the rock of its mountain slowly rose.

178

CULTURAL PERSPECTIVES

SUN HATS People have different ways of protecting themselves from the sun's powerful rays. In Mexico people wear wide-brimmed hats made of straw called *sombreros*. What other kinds of sun hats have you seen?

RESEARCH AND INQUIRY Have students research sun hats from other countries and make sample paper hats.

▶ **Spatial/Interpersonal**

Elizabeth quickly piled her sand high. She patted it smooth all the way around.

179

Guided Instruction

5 **DRAW CONCLUSIONS** You have already seen how the illustrator uses different styles for different reasons. Why do you think he has drawn Elizabeth in a box? (He wanted to show two different scenes at once. He wanted to show how much bigger and more powerful-looking the real mountain was. Drawing the two scenes this way helps to contrast their differences.)

p/i **CONTEXT CLUES** Read the first sentence on page 178. What do you think the word *Eons* means? Do you think it took eons for Elizabeth to make her mountain?

p/i PREVENTION/INTERVENTION

CONTEXT CLUES Ask students to reread the text on pages 178–179. Ask them to point to words in the text that give clues about the meaning of *Eons*, such as *passed* and *slowly*. Also point out the phrase "millions of years ago" on page 176 as another clue to its meaning. Have students cover the word *Eons* and give suggestions for other words or phrases that could be used in its place.

Guided Instruction

6 **COMPARE AND CONTRAST** Elizabeth has finished building her mountain. Let's use the words and pictures to compare and contrast the two mountains. How are they alike? How are they different?

REAL MOUNTAIN	SAND MOUNTAIN
It is made of hot, soft materials. It took millions of years to form.	It is made of sand and water. It took one day to make.
The earth cracked and shifted, causing the mountain to rise.	Elizabeth piled the sand high and her mountain got bigger.

The earth mountain sparkled against the sky. Furry animals walked in its lush green valleys.

180

Fluency

READ WITH EMPHASIS

PARTNERS Have partners take turns reading the text you have covered so far. Point out descriptive words they may want to emphasize, such as *sparkled* and *proud*.

Remind students to:

- think about how Elizabeth is feeling while they read about her.
- pause briefly at commas.
- pause at the ends of sentences.

Elizabeth's mountain stood almost as tall as she, with twigs for trees and pebbles for animals. Elizabeth was proud of her fine sand mountain. 6 7

181

Guided Instruction

7 **COMPARE AND CONTRAST/DRAW CONCLUSIONS** Elizabeth is dressed in shorts and a T-shirt. Do you think she is dressed correctly? What type of weather is happening at the beach? Look at the snow-capped mountain. What kind of clothing do you think Elizabeth would wear up there? Do you think she would be comfortable in shorts and a T-shirt? (She is dressed appropriately for the beach, but she would need to wear warmer clothes on the mountain.)

TEACHING TIP

MANAGEMENT To help out the substitute teacher, leave the phonetic pronunciation of your students' names on the seating chart. Include nick-names children prefer. This will help with classroom management and, at a time when classrooms are culturally diverse, can help students and teacher get acquainted more quickly.

Guided Instruction

8 **COMPARE AND CONTRAST** How did the sun and the wind affect both the earth mountain and Elizabeth's mountain? Did the same things happen to both of them, or did different things happen? How do the illustrations help you to understand what happened to the mountains? (The same things happened to both mountains, but it took longer for the earth mountain to show the effects. The illustration shows Elizabeth's mountain losing sand because of the wind.)

9 **DRAW CONCLUSIONS** Look at the illustration on page 183. Do you think Elizabeth is feeling proud and happy now? Why or why not? (Elizabeth is probably feeling uncomfortable because she has sand in her eyes.)

The sun beat down, day after day, year after year, on the earth mountain's sharp peaks. The wind howled through its canyons.

182

Activity

Cross Curricular: Social Studies

MOUNTAIN FACTS Provide reference books and explain that the highest mountains in the world are in the Himalayan range in Asia.

Have students:

- find out more about these mountains, such as how they were formed, how old they are, and whether or not they contain volcanoes.
- make informational posters about what they have learned.

▶ **Intrapersonal/Spatial**

Mt. Everest, 29,028 feet or 8,848 meters high, is the highest mountain in the Himalayas and the world.

8

9

Elizabeth's mountain baked in the afternoon heat. The breeze loosened a few grains of sand and blew them into Elizabeth's eyes and hair. 10

183

Guided Instruction

10 **DRAW CONCLUSIONS** Elizabeth has not spoken during this story. What clues in the story help you to know things about Elizabeth? Is speaking the only way you learn about a character?

TEACHING TIP

MANAGEMENT As you work with students on the Language Support activity, invite partners to discuss Elizabeth's character. Have them draw pictures of Elizabeth doing other activities they think she might like. Ask them to write a descriptive paragraph about the type of character they imagine Elizabeth to be.

LANGUAGE SUPPORT

ESL Help students understand how the word *baked* is used on page 183. Ask them to name things that are usually baked, such as pies, fish, or bread. Encourage them to describe or act out how it might feel to be "baked." Ask what is needed to bake something. (heat)

Provide students with kitchen clay so they can mold small mountains. Using a light source, model what has happened to the earth mountain in the story. Guide them to see that their mountains are getting dry and hard under the hot light. Have students name words that describe these changes and list them on the chalkboard.

Minilesson

REVIEW/MAINTAIN

Cause and Effect

Have students look at the illustration on page 183. Ask: Why is Elizabeth covering her eyes? (The breeze loosened a few grains of sand and blew them into her eyes and hair. She is protecting her eyes from more sand being blown into them.) Explain that this is an example of cause and effect—how one event causes another.

Activity Ask students to brainstorm what could cause a sand mountain on the beach to crumble. Map students' ideas on the chalkboard.

Guided Instruction

11 **COMPARE AND CONTRAST** How does the rain change the real mountain? Does it change the sand mountain in the same way? Let's fill in our chart that compares the real mountain with Elizabeth's sand mountain.

REAL MOUNTAIN	SAND MOUNTAIN
It is made of hot, soft materials. It took millions of years to form.	It is made of sand and water. It took one day to make.
The earth cracked and shifted, causing the mountain to rise.	Elizabeth piled the sand high and her mountain got bigger.
The sun, the wind, and the rain broke it apart after many years.	The sun, the wind, and the rain broke it apart in a short time.

SELF-MONITORING

STRATEGY

ASK FOR HELP Think of all the people and resources that could help you find out the meaning of an unfamiliar word.

MODEL I really do not understand what the word *seeped* means. Who could I ask or where could I look to find out the meaning of the word? I could ask a parent, a teacher, a librarian, or a friend, or I could look in the dictionary.

Countless rainstorms pounded the earth mountain. The water seeped into its rocks, making them crumble, then tumble into small streams.

184

An afternoon shower blew in suddenly and Elizabeth watched as the water began to destroy the mountain she had worked so hard to build. Her tears fell as freely as the rain.

185

Guided Instruction

(12) COMPARE AND CONTRAST Compare how Elizabeth felt in different kinds of weather. How did she feel when it was sunny? How did she feel when it was windy? How did she feel when it started to rain? Contrast Elizabeth's feelings with how she would feel if these things happened while she was flying a kite on the beach.

Minilesson

REVIEW/MAINTAIN

Suffixes

Explain that suffixes can be added to words to change their meaning. Use the words *countless* on page 184 and *suddenly* on page 185 to discuss suffixes.

- Explain that *count* (tell how many) + *-less* (cannot be) = *countless* (cannot be counted)
- Explain that *sudden* (unexpected) + *-ly* (in a way) = *suddenly* (in an unexpected way)

Activity Invite partners to find words in the story that end with *-less* and *-ly* as well as the suffix *-ful*. Encourage students to discuss the meaning of each word.

Guided Instruction

13 **COMPARE AND CONTRAST** Compare what the rain is doing now to the two mountains. What is similar? What is different?

Invite students to make sound effects to show the difference between the streams rushing down the two mountains. *Role-Play*

The small streams rushed together to become a raging river. The river gouged a deep valley. It ground the earth mountain's rough rocks into smooth pebbles.

186

Activity

Cross Curricular: Music

WEATHER DANCES Explain that many artists, musicians, writers, and dancers have been inspired by nature.

- Invite small groups of students to create a dance or movement that depicts the effects of the sun, wind, and rain on the Earth.
- Encourage students to choose different kinds of music to accompany their performances.

▶ **Musical/Kinesthetic**

Elizabeth could see the rain carving little valleys into her mountain. Tiny rivers carried the sand down the beach. 13

14

187

Guided Instruction

14 What do you think will happen to Elizabeth's mountain? (It will probably get smaller.) *Make Predictions*

DECODING/CONTEXT CLUES Look at the second sentence on page 186. What's the third word in the second sentence? *(gouged)* Let's sound it out. Can you find any clues to the meaning of the word?

PREVENTION/INTERVENTION

DECODING/CONTEXT CLUES
Write the word *gouged* on the chalkboard. Elicit that the letters *ou* make the sound /ou/. Blend the sounds in the word together to read *gouged*.

g ou g ed gouged

Then point out the ending *-ed* in *gouged*. Discuss how an *-ed* ending usually signals a verb. Help students use context clues to understand the word's meaning. For example: I know that a valley is a low place between hills or mountains. That makes me think that as the river flowed down the mountain, it must have cut or carved out the land around it. *Gouged* must mean cut or carved.

Minilesson

REVIEW/MAINTAIN

Make Inferences

Remind students that they can find clues to understanding a character both in the story and in what they already know about people.

- Have students study the illustration of Elizabeth on page 187. She was crying when it first began to rain, but now she is only looking at her mountain.
- Discuss Elizabeth's character. Is Elizabeth the type of person who would feel sorry for herself all the time? Why not?

Activity Have students imagine and describe other situations in which something unfortunate happens to Elizabeth's mountain. What might she do next in each situation?

Guided Instruction

15 **COMPARE AND CONTRAST** How are the pictures on page 188 and page 189 alike? How are they different? What happened to the earth mountain? What happened to Elizabeth's mountain? Let's fill in our chart.

REAL MOUNTAIN	SAND MOUNTAIN
It is made of hot, soft materials. It took millions of years to form.	It is made of sand and water. It took one day to make.
The earth cracked and shifted, causing the mountain to rise.	Elizabeth piled the sand high and her mountain got bigger.
The sun, the wind, and the rain broke it apart after many years.	The sun, the wind, and the rain broke it apart in a short time.
The river ground pebbles into sand and dumped it onto a plain. The mountain remains.	Smaller streams of water carried the sand off the mountain. The mountain shrunk down.

As the river flowed away from the earth mountain, it ground pebbles into sand and dumped the sand on a broad plain. Then it emptied into the sea.

188

15

Elizabeth saw the sand from her mountain spread silently into small fans. She wiped away her tears. 

189

Guided Instruction

16 What do you think Elizabeth is thinking now? What does the story tell you? (She wiped away her tears.) Do you think that Elizabeth is going to go home? Do you think she will fix her mountain or make another? What do you predict Elizabeth will do next? *Make Predictions*

PHONICS KIT
HANDS-ON ACTIVITIES AND PRACTICE

Minilesson

REVIEW/MAINTAIN

Consonant Clusters

Have students pronounce the words *ground, broad* and *plain* on page 188.

- Ask students what sounds they hear at the beginning of these words. (/gr/, /br/, and /pl/)
- Ask how the sounds /gr/, /br/, and /pl/ are spelled in these words. *(gr, br, pl)*

Activity Have students brainstorm and list other words that begin with *gr, br,* and *pl.* (for instance: *great, bring, please*)

Phonics CD-ROM Have students use the interactive phonics activities on the CD-ROM for more reinforcement.

LANGUAGE SUPPORT

ESL Ask students to explain in their own words how the river on the earth mountain "ground pebbles into sand." You may wish to give students actual pebbles to hold in their hands and have them grind the pebbles together. Explain that if they did that long enough, the pebbles would break into smaller and smaller pieces until they became sand.

Guided Instruction

17 **COMPARE AND CONTRAST** How are the mountains alike now? How are they different?

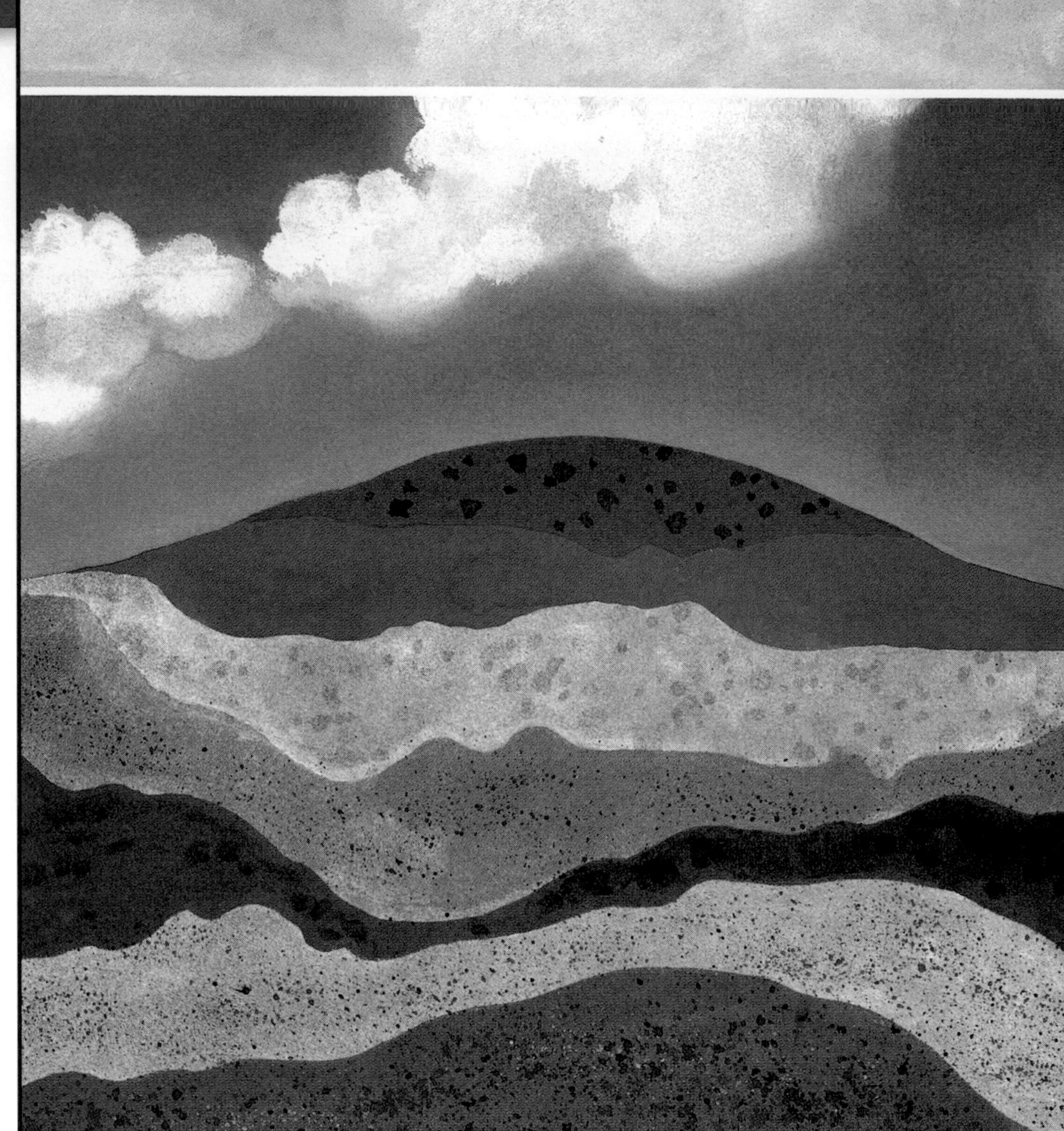

In just a blink of earth time, the earth mountain traded rocks for sand, jagged peaks for flat layers.
190

Activity

Cross Curricular: Science

MAGICAL VOLCANOES Explain to students that they can make their own volcano. Make sure every student wears safety goggles during this experiment.

- First, have students make a mountain out of sand or clay with a small crater in the top and tracks down the sides.
- Next, pour a liberal amount of baking soda into the crater. Then mix a cup of vinegar with red food coloring.
- Last, pour the vinegar onto the baking soda and watch the volcano erupt!

▶ **Spatial/Logical**

After a few minutes, the shower was over. Elizabeth's mountain was just a bump on the beach.

19
20

191

Guided Instruction

18 What does the picture on page 191 show you about how Elizabeth is feeling? Let your face show how you would feel if a rainstorm flattened a sand mountain you'd worked hard to make. *Character/Pantomime*

19 **COMPARE AND CONTRAST** The first sentence on page 190 says, "In just a blink of earth time, . . ." How long does it take you to blink your eyes? Is it a short or a long amount of time? Earth has been around for billions of years. How long do you think a blink of earth time would be? How is an earth-time blink different from the time it takes a person to blink?

20 **DRAW CONCLUSIONS** You have seen how one mountain is formed in the story. Do you think other mountains are formed in the same way? Why or why not?

Guided Instruction

21 **COMPARE AND CONTRAST** Elizabeth is making a new mountain. Do you think a new earth mountain is beginning? Why or why not?

21 The thick and heavy layers of sand sank down, down, down into the earth until they were squeezed into layers of sandstone.

192

Activity

Cross Curricular: Math

MAKING GRAPHS Ask students to talk about the mountains that they have seen or climbed. Ask them how high they think these mountains are and graph their responses. Discuss the graph.

RESEARCH AND INQUIRY Have partners graph the heights of four well-known mountains in the world.
▶**Mathematical/Spatial**

*inter***NET** CONNECTION Students can learn more about mountains by visiting ***www.mhschool.com/reading***.

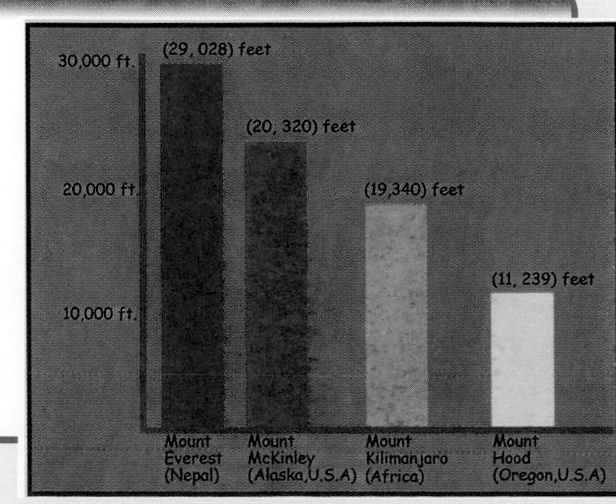

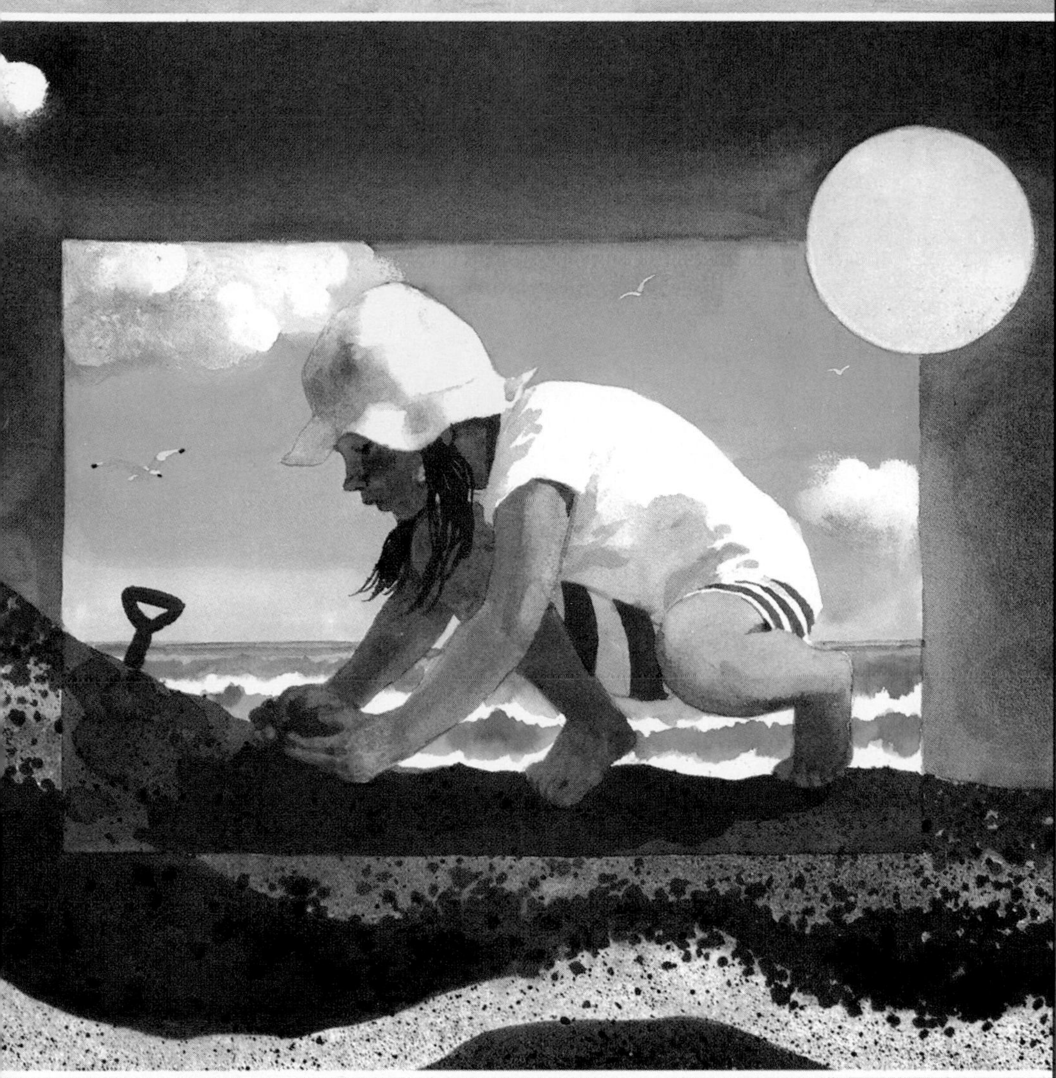

Elizabeth scooped up a handful of sand from one of the small fans on the beach. She smiled. It was wet and hard—just right. This time she hurried, for the sun was dropping in the sky. 

193

Guided Instruction

22 **COMPARE AND CONTRAST** How is Elizabeth feeling now compared with how she felt after the rainstorm had flattened her mountain? What was bad about the rainstorm? What was good about the rainstorm? (The storm destroyed her mountain, but now the sand was wet and hard—just right.)

Minilesson

REVIEW/MAINTAIN

Sequence of Events

Review that events in a story are told in an order, or sequence.

- Have students look back at pages 177–193 to find the order of steps Elizabeth took to create her mountain.

Activity Have students create a list, using sequence clue words such as *next* and *then*, to show the sequence of Elizabeth's actions.

Guided Instruction

23 **COMPARE AND CONTRAST** How did each new mountain come about? Let's record our comparisons on our chart.

REAL MOUNTAIN	SAND MOUNTAIN
It is made of hot, soft materials. It took millions of years to form.	It is made of sand and water. It took one day to make.
The earth cracked and shifted, causing the mountain to rise.	Elizabeth piled the sand high and her mountain got bigger.
The sun, the wind, and the rain broke it apart after many years.	The sun, the wind, and the rain broke it apart in a short time.
The river ground pebbles into sand and dumped it onto a plain. The mountain remains.	Smaller streams of water carried the sand off the mountain. The mountain shrunk down.
The earth cracked and shifted again. A new mountain is formed.	Using handfuls of sand, Elizabeth makes a new mountain.

23 The earth cracked and shifted again. Bending and breaking, the sandstone layers slowly rose to become a new mountain.

194

Elizabeth finished her new sand mountain. She brushed sand off her hands, picked up her bucket, and walked back up the beach. 24

195

Guided Instruction

24 **DRAW CONCLUSIONS/COMPARE AND CONTRAST** How do you think Elizabeth feels now that her new mountain is finished? Do you think she feels the same as she did after she made her first mountain? What might be different about how Elizabeth feels now?

P/I **COMPOUND WORDS** What kind of a word is *sandstone?* (compound word) What two smaller words make up this word? *(sand, stone)* What is sandstone? (a stone or rock made of sand)

P/I PREVENTION/INTERVENTION

COMPOUND WORDS Write *sandstone* on the chalkboard. Ask a volunteer to draw a line dividing it into two smaller words. Ask students the meanings of *sand* and *stone.* Guide them to see how understanding the meanings of small words in a compound word can help them to define the whole word.

Ask students to think of other compound words they know and list them on the chalkboard. Repeat this process of dividing and defining compound words with students.

Guided Instruction

25 **COMPARE AND CONTRAST** Elizabeth walks on the new earth mountain. What do you think would happen if she walked on her new sand mountain? What does this tell you about the differences between Elizabeth's mountain and the earth mountain?

REAL MOUNTAIN	SAND MOUNTAIN
It is made of hot, soft materials. It took millions of years to form.	It is made of sand and water. It took one day to make.
The earth cracked and shifted, causing the mountain to rise.	Elizabeth piled the sand high and her mountain got bigger.
The sun, the wind, and the rain broke it apart after many years.	The sun, the wind, and the rain broke it apart in a short time.
The river ground pebbles into sand and dumped it onto a plain. The mountain remains.	Smaller streams of water carried the sand off the mountain. The mountain shrunk down.
The earth cracked and shifted again. A new mountain is formed.	Using handfuls of sand, Elizabeth makes a new mountain.
It is large but has tiny grains of sand in it.	It is small and has tiny grains of sand in it.

26 **DRAW CONCLUSIONS** How are grains of sand made? Does knowing what wind, sun, and rain do to mountains give you any idea?

25 Elizabeth is walking on the new earth mountain. She steps carefully up the steep path from the beach.

When she stops to rest, she sees a smooth mound of sand far below. It looks very small.

196

As she turns to leave, Elizabeth reaches out to touch the sandstone wall. Tiny grains of sand fall on her shoulders.

26

197

Guided Instruction

27 **COMPARE AND CONTRAST** Compare the illustration of Elizabeth and the earth mountain on pages 196–197 with the illustration of Elizabeth and her sand mountain on page 195. What is different? What is the same?

28 **DRAW CONCLUSIONS** Why do you think Elizabeth wanted to touch the earth mountain? (She wanted to see what it was made of.) Do you think she was surprised that sand fell off the mountain's wall? Why or why not?

Minilesson

REVIEW/MAINTAIN

Summarize

Remind students that summarizing is telling the main events of a story.

- Ask students to summarize what has happened to Elizabeth's mountain so far. Have them include how she felt about these events. They can refer to their Compare/Contrast charts.

Activity Have students work in pairs to role-play Elizabeth and her sand mountain. Encourage them to act out the main points of their summaries.

Guided Instruction

29 **COMPARE AND CONTRAST** In this picture, Elizabeth looks very small compared to the earth mountain. Compare the way this picture looks with the other pictures in the story. What makes this picture different? (Elizabeth, the earth mountain, and the sand mountain are all in one picture.) Is there another picture in the book that looks similar to this one? (Yes, the cover of the book has Elizabeth, the earth mountain, and the sand mountain all in the same picture.)

RETELL THE STORY Ask volunteers to describe the major events of the story. Students may refer to their charts. Then have partners write one or two sentences that summarize the story. Have them focus on the main character's problem and how it is solved. *Summarize*

STUDENT SELF-ASSESSMENT

- How did using the strategy of comparison and contrast help me to understand the story?
- How did the Comparison/Contrast charts help me?

TRANSFERRING THE STRATEGY

- When might I try using this strategy again?
- In what other reading could the chart help me?

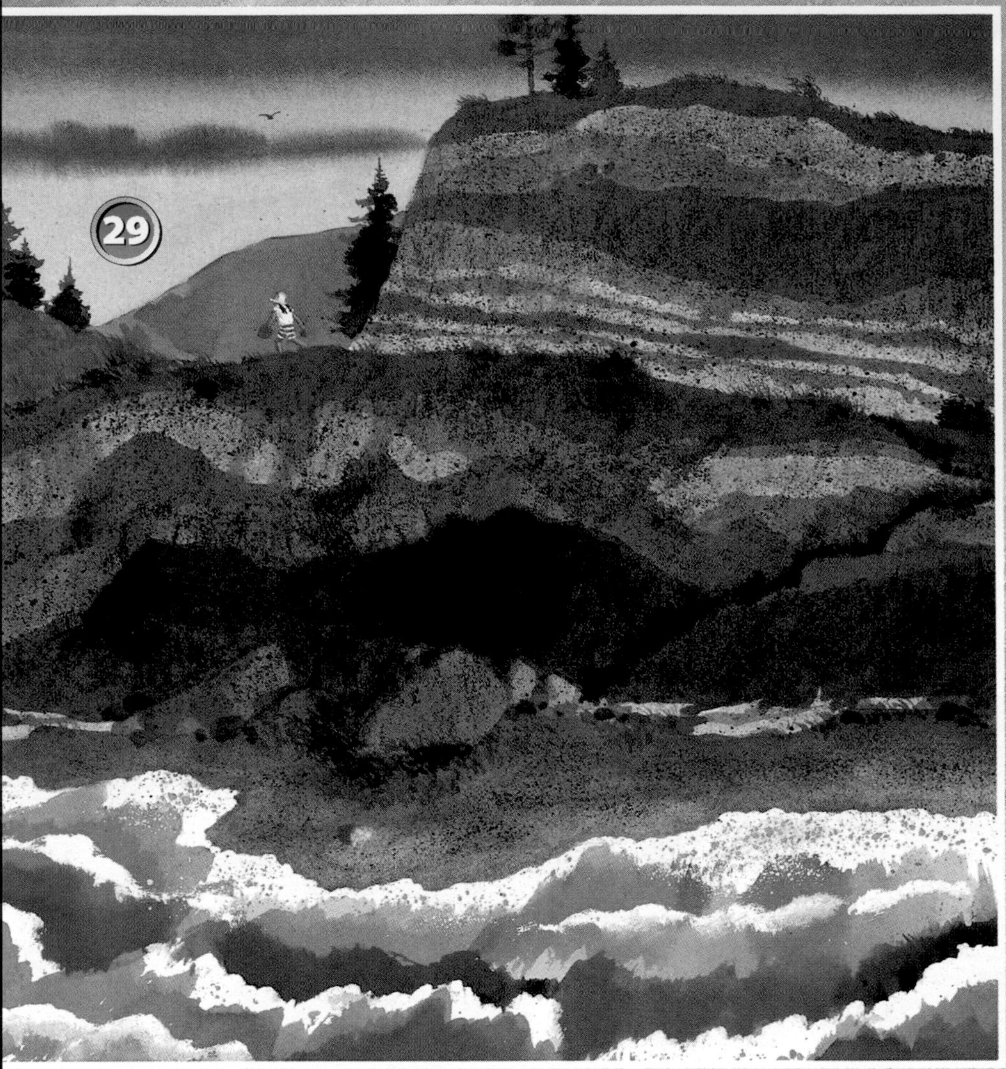

She brushes them off and watches them fall to the ground, where they will stay for just a while . . . in the sun, the wind and the rain.

198

REREADING FOR *Fluency*

PARTNERS Have partners take turns reading each page of the story. Encourage students to give positive feedback to their partners.

READING RATE You may want to evaluate an individual student's reading rate. Have the student read aloud from *The Sun, the Wind and the Rain.* Ask the student to place a self-stick note after the last word read. Then count the number of words he or she has read.

Alternatively, you could assess small groups or the whole class together by having students count words and record their own scores.

A Running Record form provided in **Diagnostic/Placement Evaluation** will help you evaluate reading rate(s).

Meet Lisa Westberg Peters

Lisa Westberg Peters wanted to write a book for children that would explain geology and how mountains change over time.

"I was lucky enough to take some good geology courses and several unforgettable trips into the mountains," she said. Then she visited a mountain along the coast in Washington State and wrote the story that became *The Sun, the Wind and the Rain.*

Meet Ted Rand

Ted Rand says the mountain painted on the cover of *The Sun, the Wind and the Rain* is Mt. Rainier in the Cascade Range in Washington State. He says that the beach and shoreline are very much like those on Puget Sound and along the Pacific Coast.

"I'd like to encourage young readers to draw and enjoy the fun of it. Drawing is a second language to me, and I hope it becomes that to you," Mr. Rand says.

LITERARY RESPONSE

QUICK-WRITE Invite students to record their thoughts about the story. These questions might help them get started:

JOURNAL

- How would you describe Elizabeth's experience at the beach?
- How does Elizabeth's experience making her mountain compare to an experience you have had making something?

ORAL RESPONSE Have students share their journal writings and discuss what part of the story they enjoyed most.

Guided Instruction

Return to Predictions and Purposes

Review with students their story predictions and reasons for reading the story. Were their predictions correct? Did they find out what they wanted to know?

PREDICTIONS	WHAT HAPPENED
The two mountains will be compared and contrasted.	The two mountains were made differently. They were both broken down by the sun, wind, and rain.
The sun, wind, and rain will play important roles.	The sun, wind, and rain had different ways of breaking down both mountains. The sun, wind, and rain caused similar things to happen to each mountain.

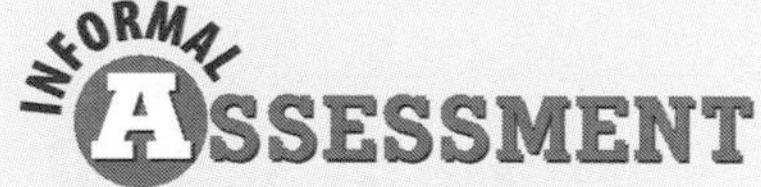

COMPARE AND CONTRAST

HOW TO ASSESS
Students should realize that the text and illustrations helped them to compare and contrast the sand mountain with the real mountain.

- Have students describe specific things they realized about the two mountains as they compared and contrasted different parts.

FOLLOW UP If students have trouble understanding the importance of the illustrations in this story, have them try to compare and contrast the text as they cover up the illustrations. They can also try the same procedure while covering up the text. Guide them to see how much information is missing in both cases.

Story Questions

Have students discuss or write answers to the questions on page 200.

Answers:

1. She makes a new one. *Literal/Sequence*
2. Elizabeth used piles of sand; the earth mountain was formed from a fiery pool. *Inferential/Compare and Contrast*
3. The sun, wind, and rain help form and change mountains. *Inferential/Draw Conclusions*
4. Changes in nature affect the earth in different ways. *Critical/Summarize*
5. Marcy and Elizabeth both find solutions to problems. *Critical/Reading Across Texts*

Write an Essay For a full writing process lesson on Explanatory Writing, see pages 203K–203L.

Story Questions & Activities

1. What does Elizabeth do after the rain washes away her mountain?
2. How was the way Elizabeth made her mountain different from the way Earth made its mountain?
3. Why is "The Sun, the Wind and the Rain" a good title for this selection?
4. What is the main idea of this selection?
5. How are Elizabeth and Marcy from "City Green" alike or different?

Write an Essay

Write an essay that tells how a rainstorm or snowstorm changes a place. Choose a place you know well, such as your backyard or a playing field. Use lively, descriptive words.

Meeting Individual Needs

EASY

Name__________ Date______ Reteach 46

Vocabulary

Draw a line from each clue to the correct word.

1. moved smoothly — flowed
2. tiny pieces of sand — grains
3. deep valleys — canyons
4. how much you can hold in each hand — handful
5. the tops of mountains — peaks
6. one thing exchanged for another — traded

(Words: canyons, grains, flowed, traded, handful, peaks) /6

Story Comprehension Reteach 47

Think about "The Sun, the Wind and the Rain." Circle the answer to complete each sentence.

1. The main idea of story is to show us ______
   a. the history of sand castles. **(b. how mountains are made.)**
2. The story compares ______
   (a. the sand mountain with the earth mountain.) b. the sun with the earth mountain.
3. Over time, the rushing rivers make ______
   (a. valleys.) b. mountain peaks.
4. Over many years, the sun, the wind, and the rain ______ the mountain.
   a. cannot change **(b. change the shape of)**

46–47 At Home: Have students use each of the vocabulary words in a sentence. Book 3.1/Unit 2 The Sun, the Wind and the Rain /4

Reteach, 47

ON-LEVEL

Name__________ Date______ Practice 47

Story Comprehension

Answer the following questions about "The Sun, the Wind and the Rain."

1. Where does this story take place? The story takes place by the ocean and on the beach.
2. What two mountains are looked at in the story? The mountains are the earth mountain and Elizabeth's sand mountain.
3. What kind of information does the story tell about the real mountain? The story tells about the way that the mountain is built and the way it breaks apart.
4. What happens when rivers rush down the earth mountain? The rivers cut valleys into the mountain and grind the rocks into pebbles.
5. What makes Elizabeth cry? Elizabeth cries when rain begins to destroy her sand mountain.
6. Why don't either of the mountains stay the same? The sun, the wind, and the rain break them apart.

47 At Home: Have students draw a picture of one of the scenes described in "The Sun, the Wind, and the Rain." Book 3.1/Unit 2 The Sun, the Wind and the Rain /6

Practice, 47

CHALLENGE

Name__________ Date______ Extend 46

Vocabulary

canyons	flowed	grains	handful	peaks	traded

Write a paragraph about nature. Use as many vocabulary words from the box as you can. Then erase the vocabulary words or cover them with tape. Exchange paragraphs with a partner and fill in the blanks.

Extend 47

Story Comprehension

A book reviewer writes about books. The reviewer summarizes the book, then states an opinion about it. Write a review of "The Sun, the Wind and the Rain." Summarize the story. Then tell what you thought of it. Was it good or bad? Would you recommend it to a friend? Would you make any changes to the story?

46–47 At Home: Ask students to describe Elizabeth's mountain and include what it looks like, how she built it, and where it is. Book 3.1/Unit 2 The Sun, the Wind and the Rain

Extend, 47

Check for Weathering

The sun, wind, rain, and ice can cause things to become dried, worn, cracked, or faded. This process is called **weathering**. With an adult, go outside and look for signs of weathering. Look at buildings. Look at streets. Look at sidewalks. List different examples of weathering that you find.

Paint with Sand

On a poster, draw the layers of a mountain. Choose a different color of sand for each layer. Then cover one layer on the poster with glue. Sprinkle colored sand over the glue. Shake off any extra sand. Then do the same for each of the other layers.

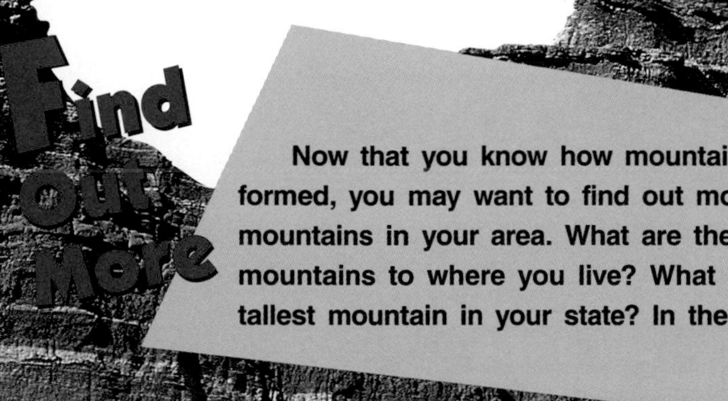

Find Out More

Now that you know how mountains are formed, you may want to find out more about mountains in your area. What are the closest mountains to where you live? What is the tallest mountain in your state? In the country?

201

Story Activities

Check for Weathering

Materials: paper, felt-tipped markers

GROUP Discuss the meaning of weathering. If possible, take students outside to inspect the effects of weathering on the school building and surroundings. Have them touch surfaces and describe the textures. Ask them if they think weathering makes surfaces look old or new. Have them illustrate their weathered surfaces.

Paint with Sand

Materials: poster, colored sand, glue, pencil

ONE Invite students to make their posters similar to the diagram of a mountain's layers in the story. Have them consider what each layer is before they sprinkle on sand. They may wish to leave room around the edges of the mountain to label each layer.

Find Out More

Materials: local and state maps, paper, felt-tipped markers

RESEARCH AND INQUIRY Discuss GROUP what students know about the mountains nearby. Then have them go to the library to find and list three new facts about these mountains. Have students compare their findings.

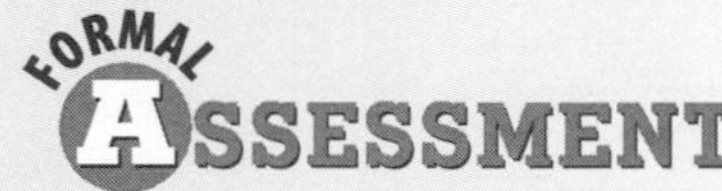

For more more information on the topic go to ***www.mhschool.com/reading***.

FORMAL ASSESSMENT

After page 201, see the Selection Assessment.

Study Skills

REFERENCE SOURCES

OBJECTIVES

Students will learn to use a dictionary to find out spelling, meaning, or pronunciation of words.

PREPARE Display **Teaching Chart 39.**

TEACH Explain that a dictionary can help students find out about unfamiliar words.

PRACTICE Have students answer questions 1–5. Review the answers with them.
1. The science that deals with the structure and physical changes of the Earth or other planets that are made mostly of rocks. **2.** noun **3.** Look at the letters and the marks in parentheses after *gerbil,* then find the meanings of these marks in the pronunciation key.
4. gerbil. You can look at the second guide word. **5.** portrait

ASSESS/CLOSE Have students make a list of troublesome words.

STUDY SKILLS

Use a Dictionary

When you are reading a science selection such as "The Sun, the Wind and the Rain," it helps to keep a dictionary handy. You can use the dictionary to look up the spelling, meaning, or pronunciation of words.

geology/gerbil

geology The science that deals with the structure and physical changes of the earth or other planets that are mostly made of rocks.
ge•ol•o•gy (jē ol′ ə jē) *noun, plural* **geologies.**

geometry The branch of mathematics that deals with the measurement and relation of points, lines, angles, plane figures, and solids.
ge•om•e•try (jē om′ i trē) *noun, plural* **geometries.**

Georgia A state in the southeastern United States. Its capital is Atlanta.
Geor•gia (jôr′ jə) *noun.*

geranium A plant with bright red, pink, white, or lavender flowers. The leaves of some geraniums have a scent.
ge•ra•ni•um (jə rā′ nē əm) *noun, plural* **geraniums.**

gerbil A small rodent that is native to deserts in Africa and Asia. It lives in a burrow and is sometimes kept as a pet.
ger•bil (jûr′ bil) *noun, plural* **gerbils**

Use the dictionary page to answer these questions.

1. What does the word *geology* mean?
2. Is *geranium* an adjective or noun?
3. If you want to know how to say the word *gerbil*, what should you do?
4. What is the last word on the page? How do you know?
5. Entries for the words *portrait* and *pose* appear on a later page. Which entry would come first?

Meeting Individual Needs

EASY

Name________ Date______ **Reteach 48**

Use a Dictionary

A **dictionary** tells you what a word means. It also shows you how to say it, spell it, and divide it.

CRAYON—CUTE

crayon (krā′on) 1. a colored wax stick for drawing **noun**
2. to draw or write with a crayon **verb**
cream (krēm) 1. the part of milk with the most fat **noun**
2. the best part of something **noun**
crocodile (krok′ə dīl′) an animal with short legs, a long tail, and thick scaly skin **noun**
cry (krī) 1. to have tears come out of the eyes
2. to call loudly, shout **verb**
cup (kup) 1. a small bowl with a handle **noun**
cupboard (kub′ərd) a cabinet with shelves **noun**
cupcake (kup′cāk′) a small cake **noun**
cute (kūt) charming, delightful, pretty **adjective**

Study the dictionary page. Use it to answer the questions.

1. What is the first definition of *cry*? **to have tears come out of the eyes**
2. Is *crocodile* a noun or a verb? **noun**
3. How do you pronounce *cream*? **krēm**
4. Write the word that is an adjective. **cute**
5. Which of the three words with *cup* in them means something to eat? **cupcake**

5 Book 3.1/Unit 2 **The Sun, the Wind and the Rain** **At Home:** Have students list all the nouns in the dictionary page above in alphabetical order. Then have them find the one word that is a verb. 48

Reteach, 48

ON-LEVEL

Name________ Date______ **Practice 48**

Use a Dictionary

Place each of the dictionary parts below in its proper place.

sizzle
adjective
sidewalk
to make music with your voice
SIDE
(sīz)

1. **SIDE** —SIZZLE
2. **sidewalk** 1. a path by the side of a street (sīd′wôk) *noun*
3. **silly** 1. lacking common sense, foolish (sil′ē) ***adjective***
4. **sing** 1. **to make music with your voice** (sing) *verb*
5. **size** 1. the amount of space an object takes up **(sīz)** *noun*
6. **sizzle** 1. to make a hissing sound (siz′əl) *verb*

6 Book 3.1/Unit 2 **The Sun, the Wind and the Rain** **At Home:** Ask students to look up the word silt and to put it in its proper place in the above dictionary page, writing in the definition, pronunciation, and part of speech. 48

Practice, 48

CHALLENGE

Name________ Date______ **Extend 48**

Use a Dictionary

Answers may vary. Sample answers are shown.
Here are some words to define. Write a list of the steps you will take to find the word in the dictionary. Then define each word and use it in a sentence.

Step 1. **Find the first letter of the word.**
Step 2. **Look for guide words.**
Step 3. **Find the word.**

1. pebble **a small rounded stone**
   Sentences will vary.
2. loosen **to make or become loose**
   Sentences will vary.
3. breeze **a gentle wind**
   Sentences will vary.
4. tumble **to roll and turn; to fall**
   Sentences will vary.
5. jagged **having a sharply uneven edge or surface**
   Sentences will vary.
6. sandstone **rock made of sand held together by a natural cement**
   Sentences will vary.

Book 3.1/Unit 2 **The Sun, the Wind and the Rain** **At Home:** Have students show you how to look up a word in the dictionary. 48

Extend, 48

TEST POWER

Test Tip
As you read the story, think about what the characters are doing.

DIRECTIONS:
Read the story. Then read each question about the story.

SAMPLE

Reggie's Flat Tire

Officer Brown saw that Reggie had a big frown, so he asked him what was wrong.

"My bike has a flat tire," Reggie said. "It won't hold air anymore."

Officer Brown smiled and went to his police car. He had a tire-patch kit in the car for emergencies. He got the kit out and looked at Reggie's tire.

"It looks like you rode over a tack," he said. "See this hole? It's tiny, but that is where your tire is losing air."

"Can it be fixed?" Reggie asked. He was nervous because he did not have enough money for a new tire.

"Oh, yes," Officer Brown said. "Would you please hand me that roll of patch tape? I will fix your tire."

1 How did Reggie feel about getting a new tire?

- ○ Happy
- ● Worried
- ○ Excited
- ○ Lonely

2 Who was going to fix the bicycle tire?

- ○ Reggie
- ● Officer Brown
- ○ Reggie's mother
- ○ The repairman

203

ITBS/TEST PREPARATION

TERRANOVA/TEST PREPARATION

SAT 9/TEST PREPARATION

Test Power

THE PRINCETON REVIEW

Read the Page

Have students read the story. Instruct students to pay attention to what the characters say to one another.

Discuss the Questions

QUESTION 1: This question requires students to understand Reggie's feelings about getting a new tire. Discuss what facts in the story are clues to Reggie's feelings. Reggie asks if the tire can "be fixed," and the story states that "he did not have enough money for a new tire." Ask students: What does that tell you about how Reggie feels?

QUESTION 2: This question requires students to recall facts from the story. Instruct students to refer back to the story. Ask: Who talked to Reggie about his tire? (Officer Brown) Then have students read through the answer choices.

Leveled Books

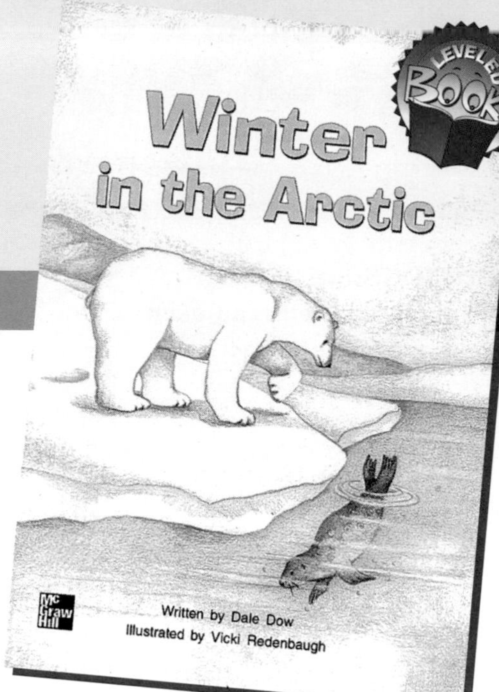

EASY

Winter in the Arctic

Consonant Clusters

☑ **Compare and Contrast**

☑ **Instructional Vocabulary:** ***canyons, flowed, grain, handful, peaks, traded***

Guided Reading

PREVIEW AND PREDICT Conduct a **picture walk**. Ask students what the story might be about. Have students record their predictions.

SET PURPOSES Students should decide what they want to find out from the story. Have students write down five questions.

READ THE BOOK Use the following questions as students read or after they have read the story independently.

Page 2: Find the word *peaks* in the second paragraph. What word in the same sentence can help you figure out the meaning of *peaks?* (mountain) What do you think a peak is? ***Vocabulary***

Pages 6–7: Find the word *ground* on page 6. What two letters make up the consonant cluster? (*gr*) Turn to page 7. Can you find two words that begin with the consonant cluster *gr*? (*grows, grains*) ***Phonics and Decoding***

Page 7: How does the ptarmigan change from winter to summer? (Its feathers change from white in the winter to brown in the summer.) How might this change in color help the bird? (It can camouflage in the snow in winter and in the sand in summer.) ***Compare and Contrast/Draw Conclusions***

Page 10: How are Arctic foxes and Snowy owls alike? (They both hunt lemmings and change color in different seasons.) ***Compare and Contrast***

RETURN TO PREDICTIONS AND PURPOSES Review students' predictions and reasons for reading. Were all their questions answered?

LITERARY RESPONSE Discuss these questions:

- How are winter and spring in the Arctic different? How are they the same?
- What are some ways animals cope with the Arctic winter?

Also, see the story questions and activity in *Winter in the Arctic*.

See the Phonics **CD-ROM** for practice using consonant clusters.

Answers to Story Questions

1. The Arctic tundra is in the far, far north.
2. It is too cold for them during the winter.
3. Possible answers include: They wear thick, heavy clothing; they build fires or heat their homes; they stay inside where it is warm.
4. Arctic animals have found ways to deal with the cold, winter weather.
5. Answers will vary.

Story Questions and Writing Activity

1. Where is the Arctic tundra?
2. Why do you think some animals leave the Arctic during the winter?
3. What might people who live near the Arctic do to make it through the long, cold winter?
4. What is the main idea of the book?
5. Compare what you have learned about the Arctic in this book with the setting in *The Sun, the Wind, and the Rain.* How are the two settings different? How are they alike?

I Can Change!

Choose an animal that changes in order to survive the Arctic winter. Draw a picture of how the animal looks during the summer. Then draw a picture of how the animal looks in the winter. Draw how the tundra looks in each season. Label your drawings.

from *Winter in the Arctic*

Leveled Books

INDEPENDENT

Pompeii: A Doomed City

☑ **Compare and Contrast**
☑ **Instructional Vocabulary:** ***canyons, flowed, grains, handful, peaks, traded***

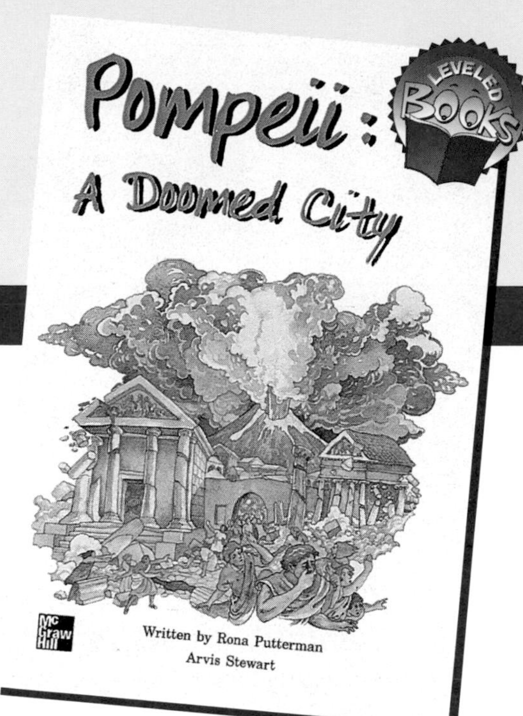

Guided Reading

PREVIEW AND PREDICT Have students read the title and chapter titles. Then conduct a **picture walk**. Ask: Where and when does the story take place? What might the story be about?

SET PURPOSES Students should jot down a purpose for reading. For example, they may want to find out what happened to the people of ancient Pompeii.

READ THE BOOK Have students read the story independently. When they finish, return to the text to apply strategies.

Pages 2–3: Contrast Pompeii before and after the earthquake in A.D. 62. (Pompeii had had many homes, shops, and other buildings. They were destroyed by the earthquake.) *Compare and Contrast*

Pages 8–9: Find the word *flowed* in the first paragraph. What flowed? (streams of lava and mud) Do you think these streams stopped or moved steadily if they flowed? *Vocabulary*

Pages 14–15: Compare what people can see in Pompeii today to what people saw in Pompeii 1,500 years ago. (They can see some homes and gardens. They can see news and ads written on the walls.) *Compare and Contrast*

Page 16: Will Mount Vesuvius erupt again? Explain. (Probably. It has erupted more than 30 times since its major eruption in A.D. 79) *Make Predictions*

RETURN TO PREDICTIONS AND PURPOSES Review students' predictions and reasons for reading. Which predictions were correct? Which were not?

LITERARY RESPONSE Discuss these questions:

- How is Pompeii "frozen in time"?
- What would you like to find in the ruins of Pompeii?

Also see the story questions and activity in *Pompeii: A Doomed City.*

INDEPENDENT

Answers to Story Questions

1. Pompeii is located in southern Italy.
2. Scientists might learn even more about life in an ancient Roman town. They might discover more art and other important finds.
3. People living near the mountain might be killed. Towns near Vesuvius might be destroyed.
4. Pompeii was a lively, important city until Vesuvius erupted in A.D. 79. Vesuvius changed life in Pompeii forever.
5. Both mountains are very old. Both change over time. Both can break apart into smaller pieces.

Story Questions and Writing Activity

1. Where is the city of Pompeii located?
2. What might scientists learn by digging out the rest of Pompeii?
3. What might happen if Vesuvius erupted again?
4. What is the main idea of the book?
5. In what ways are Vesuvius and the earth mountain in *The Sun, the Wind and the Rain* alike?

Illustrating the Past

Draw a before and after picture of Pompeii. On one side of the page, show Pompeii as it might have looked on the morning of August 24, A.D. 79. On the other side of the page, show Pompeii as it looks now. Below each picture write a short paragraph that explains why people might want to visit Pompeii as it was then and as it is now.

from *Pompeii: A Doomed City*

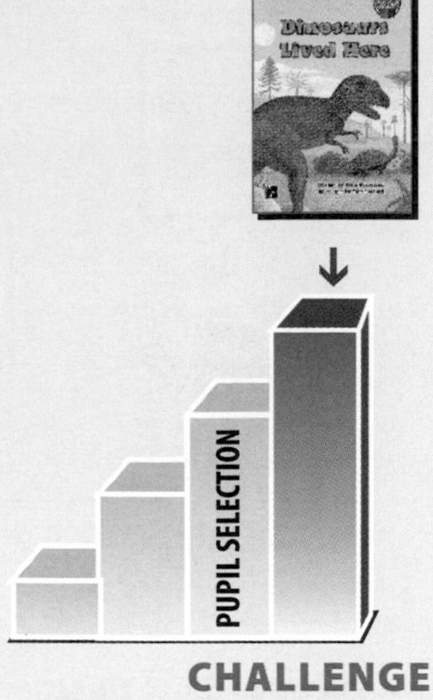

Leveled Books

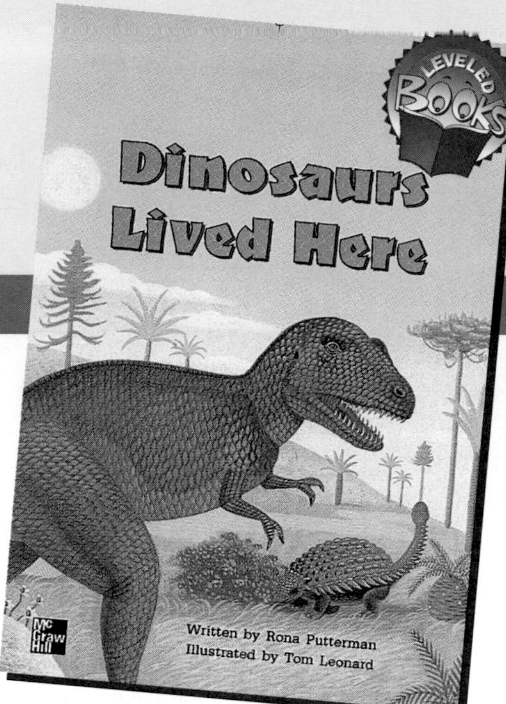

LEVELED BOOKS
Dinosaurs Lived Here
Written by Rona Putterman
Illustrated by Tom Leonard

CHALLENGE

Dinosaurs Lived Here

- ☑ **Compare and Contrast**
- ☑ **Instructional Vocabulary:** ***canyons, flowed, grains, handful, peaks, traded***

Answers to Story Questions

1. The first dinosaurs lived more than 220 million years ago. The last dinosaurs died out 65 million years ago.
2. The long neck of the Massospondylus probably allowed it to eat leaves at the tops of trees.
3. Because it was so big.
4. Conditions in the U.S. Midwest make it easier to collect fossils; the Antarctic is very cold and icy.
5. Earth and the creatures that lived here were very different millions of years ago.

Story Questions and Writing Activity

1. How long ago did the dinosaurs live?
2. Why do you think Massospondylus had such a long neck?
3. Why do you think scientists have found more fossils in the western United States than they have in Antarctica?
4. What is the main idea of the book?
5. What do you think Elizabeth's reaction might have been if she had found a dinosaur fossil on the beach?

Everything Changes!

Ask an older family member or neighbor how your hometown has changed over the years. What has remained the same? Write a paragraph describing what has stayed the same and what has changed. Tell what brought about the changes.

from *Dinosaurs Lived Here*

Guided Reading

PREVIEW AND PREDICT Conduct a **picture walk**, then ask students: Where and when did dinosaurs live? What might the story be about?

SET PURPOSES Students should decide what they want to find out from the story. Have students write down five questions.

READ THE BOOK Use the following questions to guide students' reading or after they have read the story independently.

Pages 2–3: How did Earth look different during the time when dinosaurs lived than it looks today? (Possible answer: Some scientists think that it was one big continent. Today this continent is broken into several pieces.) ***Compare and Contrast***

Pages 4–5: Compare and contrast the *Lesothosaurus* with the *Massospondylus*. (The *Lesothosaurus* was 3 feet long and the *Massospondylus* was 20 feet long. Both were plant eaters.) ***Compare and Contrast***

Page 11: Find the word *canyons* in the first paragraph. What are the words around it? (*pits, valleys*) How do the words help you determine the meaning of *canyons*? ***Vocabulary***

Pages 12–13: How might sand help preserve dinosaur fossils? (The fossils were protected because they were covered by sand.) ***Draw Conclusions***

Pages 14–15: How is Antarctica different today than it was in the time of the dinosaurs? (Now it's cold and icy instead of warm and mild.) ***Compare and Contrast***

RETURN TO PREDICTIONS AND PURPOSES Review students' predictions and purposes. Which predictions were correct? Were their questions answered?

LITERARY RESPONSE Discuss these questions:

- How were the Triassic and Jurassic periods different?
- What interests you most about dinosaurs?

Also see the story questions and activity in *Dinosaurs Lived Here*.

Connecting Texts

STORY CHARTS Write the story titles on a chart. Lead a discussion with students about the changes in nature that take place in each story:

- How do nature's changes affect people?
- How do nature's changes affect animals?
- How has nature changed over time?

Call on volunteers from each reading level and write their suggestions on the chart.

The Sun, the Wind and the Rain	Winter in the Arctic	Pompeii: A Doomed City	Dinosaurs Lived Here
There are two mountains, one created millions of years ago and one created in the sand by a young girl. The mountains wear down but get built up again.	Animals of the Arctic have special ways to deal with changes in weather. Spring brings new life to the Arctic.	Pompeii was once a great city in what is now Italy. Mount Vesuvius erupted, burying Pompeii and its people in ash and lava. Archeologists study the ruins of Pompeii in search of clues to life in the past.	Dinosaurs roamed and ruled Earth millions of years ago when Earth had one giant continent. Dinosaurs and Earth evolved. Scientists are not sure why dinosaurs died out.

Viewing/Representing

GROUP PRESENTATIONS Divide the class into groups, one for each of the four books read in the lesson. (For *The Sun, the Wind and the Rain*, combine students of different reading levels.) Have each group compare and contrast how nature affected what happened in their story. Have groups write and illustrate what happened before and after a natural occurrence.

AUDIENCE RESPONSE Have the audience tell what facts they found interesting in each group's presentation. Allow time for questions.

Research and Inquiry

MORE ABOUT CHANGES IN NATURE Invite students to do the following:

- Make a list of events in nature that happen quickly and a list of events that have happened slowly over time.
- Look up *archeology* and *paleontology* in the encyclopedia.
- Look around your room or classroom. What might an archeologist be able to learn about you? Write a report on your "discoveries."

*inter***NET** **CONNECTION** Have students log on to ***www.mhschool.com/reading*** for links to Web pages about archeology.

TESTED OBJECTIVES

Students will compare and contrast elements in a story.

LANGUAGE SUPPORT

ESL Have English-language learners and students with limited language skills work with partners to draw pictures of the two different houses in the story on Teaching Chart 40.

Review Compare and Contrast

PREPARE

Discuss Comparison of Story Elements

Review: Thinking about how objects, people, and events in a story are the same or different can help you to understand what is happening in the story. When you think about how things are alike or different, you learn more about them.

TEACH

Read "Two Houses" and Model the Skill

Ask students to pay close attention to what is alike and what is different about the two houses as you read **Teaching Chart 40**.

Two Houses

Elizabeth took a walk to the beach. On the way she saw a big house made of stone. Its roof was made of red clay tiles. Elizabeth made a house of stone, too. She collected little pebbles near the beach. She used hard mud for the roof. Soon, it started to rain. The big stone house became wet and slippery. Elizabeth's stone house turned wet and slippery, too. It rained harder and harder. The roof of the house that Elizabeth made fell in. The roof of the stone house stayed strong and kept the family inside dry. Elizabeth ran home to get warm.

Teaching Chart 40

Discuss clues in the passage that help readers use comparison and contrast to understand a story better.

MODEL I can tell by the word *too* in the story that something is the same as something else. I am not surprised that the roof of the big stone house did not fall in because it is made of stronger materials than the roof of the house that Elizabeth made.

PRACTICE

Compare and Contrast

Have partners discuss what is the same and what is different about the two houses. One partner can underline clues in "Two Houses" that are the same, while the other partner circles clues that are different. Have them write a list of similarities and a list of differences.

▶ **Linguistic/Interpersonal**

SAME	DIFFERENT
Made of stone	different roofs
	different size
	different outcome in rain

ASSESS/CLOSE

Compare and Contrast Characters

Have students compare and contrast the good and bad characters in a familiar tale, such as "The Three Little Pigs" or "Jack and the Beanstalk." Have each group create Compare and Contrast charts for the different characters and their situations at different points in the story.

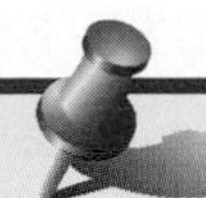

ALTERNATE TEACHING STRATEGY

COMPARE AND CONTRAST

For a different approach to teaching the skill, see page T64.

SELF-SELECTED Reading

Students may choose from the following titles.

ANTHOLOGY

- *The Sun, The Wind and The Rain*

LEVELED BOOKS

- *Winter in the Arctic*
- *Pompeii: A Doomed City*
- *Dinosaurs Lived Here*

Bibliography, pages T76–T77

Meeting Individual Needs for Comprehension

EASY

Name__________ Date______ **Reteach 49**

Compare and Contrast

When you **compare** and **contrast**, you point out how things are alike and how they are different. Authors often use comparison and contrast to describe things.

Think about the story "The Sun, the Wind and the Rain." Show how Elizabeth's mountain and the earth mountain are alike and different. Then answer the questions that follow.

	Earth's Mountain	Elizabeth's Mountain
What are they made of?	1. rock	2. wet sand
How long did they take to make?	3. many years	4. one day
How did they grow?	5. It rose higher as it cracked and shifted.	6. Elizabeth piled the sand higher.
What did the sun, wind, and rain do to each one over time?	7. broke it apart	8. broke it apart

9. In what ways are the two mountains alike? They were both broken apart by the sun, the wind, and the rain.
10. Name two ways in which the mountains are different. Answers will vary but should reflect answers 1–6.

49 **At Home:** Show students two objects such as a fork and a spoon, and have students describe how they are alike and how they are different. Book 3.1/Unit 2 **The Sun, the Wind and the Rain** 10

Reteach, 49

ON-LEVEL

Name__________ Date______ **Practice 49**

Compare and Contrast

Think about "The Sun, the Wind and the Rain." In what ways are the earth mountain and Elizabeth's mountain alike? How are they different? Complete the chart to compare the two mountains.

	earth mountain	Elizabeth's mountain
Formed when?	long ago	built today
Made of what?	rock and sandstone	wet sand
How big?	reaching up into the sky	as tall as a child
Rain does what?	destroys it and carries it to sea	destroys it and carries it to sea

Why do you think the author wrote about the two kinds of mountains? Circle your answer.

- to show how big they are
- to show mountain canyons
- (to show how mountains change over time)

49 **At Home:** Have students share experiences they have had at the beach or the mountains. Encourage them to focus on the sights and sounds. Book 3.1/Unit 2 **The Sun, the Wind and the Rain** 5

Practice, 49

CHALLENGE

Name__________ Date______ **Extend 49**

Compare and Contrast

Answers will vary. Sample answers are given.

Think about how animals and plants are alike and different. Fill out the chart to compare a pine tree and an owl.

Alike

1. They are both living organisms.
2. Both need water, air, and food.
3. Both live in the same habitat.

Different

4. Pine tree makes its own food. Owl finds and eats food.
5. Pine tree cannot move except to grow toward sunlight. Owl can fly anywhere.
6. Owls lay eggs to reproduce. Pine trees reproduce seeds protected in cones.

7. What might you title this table? "The Owl and the Pine Tree"; "Compare the Owl and the Pine Tree"

49 **At Home:** Have students write a paragraph about the owl and the pine tree using the information they listed in the compare and contrast chart. Book 3.1/Unit 2 **The Sun, the Wind and the Rain**

Extend, 49

LANGUAGE SUPPORT

Name__________ Date______

Two Mountains

made of sand	made slowly	plants	small size
sandstone	made today	millions of years ago	water destroys
very big	sun bakes	made quickly	can make again

Elizabeth's Mountain: made of sand, small size, made today, made quickly, can make again

Alike: plants, water destroys, sun bakes

Earth's Mountain: made slowly, sandstone, millions of years ago, very big

54 **The Sun, the Wind, and the Rain** • Language Support/Blackline Master 26 Grade 3

Language Support, 54

Students will draw conclusions based on a passage.

TEACHING TIP

INSTRUCTIONAL After you have discussed the skill, ask students to turn to the person next to them and explain or discuss the skill, telling what it means and giving an example.

Review Draw Conclusions

PREPARE

Discuss Drawing Conclusions Explain: As you read, you get more information about characters, settings, and events. You can use this information to answer questions or draw conclusions about what is happening in the story.

TEACH

Read "Elizabeth's Day" and Model the Skill Read the passage "Elizabeth's Day" with students. Focus students' attention on clues about Elizabeth's mood during her experiences.

Elizabeth's Day

With the sun high above her, Elizabeth smiled at the beach. She looked up at her favorite mountain. She would make a mountain, too. Elizabeth worked very hard shoveling sand into her bucket. She piled the sand high on the beach. When she was finished, she added twigs for trees. Elizabeth was proud of her work.

The sun dried out her sand mountain. The wind blew some of the sand into her eyes. Then rain washed away her mountain. Elizabeth cried. Later, she made a new mountain, even bigger than the first, and went home.

Teaching Chart 41

Invite a volunteer to underline a sentence about Elizabeth's mood at the start of her day. Help students to understand how they could draw the conclusion that she was happy.

MODEL I know that Elizabeth was really looking forward to making a sand mountain. She worked hard on it, and tried to make it look the same as her favorite mountain. When the wind and rain ruined her mountain, she was really sad. I think that when she made a new mountain, she was happy again.

PRACTICE

Create a Draw Conclusions Chart

Help groups create a Draw Conclusions chart. ▶ **Visual/Interpersonal**

FACT	CONCLUSION
Elizabeth smiled at the beach.	Elizabeth was happy to be there.
Elizabeth made a sand mountain.	Elizabeth liked playing with sand.

ASSESS/CLOSE

Make a Draw Conclusions Web

Have students create a Draw Conclusions web. Ask them to describe Elizabeth in the outer circles and write their conclusion about her in the center.

Graphic Organizer 29

ALTERNATE TEACHING STRATEGY

DRAW CONCLUSIONS

For a different approach to teaching this skill, see page T62.

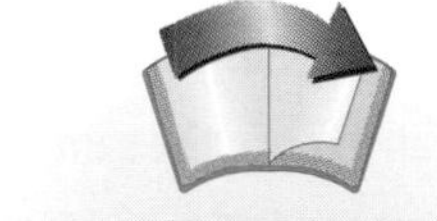

LOOKING AHEAD

Students will apply this skill as they read the next selection, *Dream Wolf*.

Meeting Individual Needs for Comprehension

EASY

Name________ Date________ **Reteach 50**

Draw Conclusions

When you **draw conclusions**, you make a decision based on the facts. You can draw conclusions about story characters based on what they say and do.

Read the story. Then circle the correct conclusion.

All summer, Andy had been hard at work fixing up an old boat. At last it was ready. Andy went to find Mr. Ray to see if he could have a sailing lesson that afternoon.

Mr. Ray looked up at the sky. "Not today, it's too windy."

"Don't we need wind?" asked Andy.

"Not this much. I think a big storm is blowing up."

As Andy watched the clouds rolling over the ocean, he realized he hadn't noticed the changing weather. Tall waves crashed onto shore. The wind started to blow hard and Andy dug his chin into the collar of his jacket.

"Why don't you help me put the covers on these boats," said Mr. Ray. "Then we'll go inside and have something hot to drink and watch the storm. It should be a pretty good show."

1. Where do Andy and Mr. Ray live?
   (by the sea) in the mountains
2. What information helped you draw your conclusion?
   There was a storm. (Andy had a boat and wanted to learn to sail.)
3. Does Andy know Mr. Ray very well?
   (yes) no
4. What information helped you draw your conclusion?
   They lived nearby. (Andy asked him to teach him to sail.)

Book 3.1/Unit 2 **The Sun, the Wind and the Rain** — **At Home:** Discuss with students what conclusion they might draw if the weather forecast was for rain. 50

Reteach, 50

ON-LEVEL

Name________ Date________ **Practice 50**

Draw Conclusions

A conclusion is what you decide after you have read a story. You can also use your own experience to help you **draw conclusions**.

Draw your conclusions about the story by answering each question. **Answers may vary.**

Annie took a lot of pictures. There was one rock that looked like a bridge and another that looked like a wise old owl.

Annie wondered out loud if people had ever lived in this wonderful place.

"I'll show you something and you can decide for yourself," her father said.

It was already getting dark when they parked the car next to an enormous rock. Annie was astonished to see drawings of the horses and people.

"Native Americans made these pictures hundreds of years ago. Aren't they beautiful?" Annie's father said.

"Can we come back tomorrow when it's light enough for me to take a picture?"

1. Do you think Annie enjoyed her trip? yes
2. What information from the story helped you to draw your conclusion? She took pictures of the rocks; she liked the pictures on the rock; she said it was a wonderful place.
3. Where might Annie and her father be? Definitely in America, because "Native Americans" made the pictures on the wall, maybe in the West.
4. Had people ever lived in the place Annie visited? Explain. Yes, people made pictures on the wall hundreds of years ago.

Book 3.1/Unit 2 **The Sun, the Wind and the Rain** — **At Home:** Have students draw conclusions about whether or not Annie's father had ever visited this place before. 50

Practice, 50

CHALLENGE

Name________ Date________ **Extend 50**

Draw Conclusions

Telephone Tale

Sometimes when people pass information from person to person, the information can change. See what will happen with a story you start.

Get together with a group of your classmates. You are the story starter. Make up a story about an animal. It may be a story about a pet monkey that gets loose and into trouble. Write your story on paper so that you can compare it to the story the group ends up with.

Have your group sit together. Tell your story quietly to the person next to you. When you are done, ask him or her to pass the story on to the next person. Ask the last person who hears the story to write it down on a piece of paper.

As a group, compare the two stories. Under the columns below, list how the stories were the same. List how the stories were different.

Answers will vary.

Similarities	Differences

What conclusions can you draw from this "telephone tale"?

Book 3.1/Unit 2 **The Sun, the Wind and the Rain** — **At Home:** Have students continue the telephone tale they started in their group. 50

Extend, 50

LANGUAGE SUPPORT

Name________ Date________

Draw What Happened

Your conclusion:

Why?

How?

Where?

When?

What?

Who?

Grade 3 — Language Support/Blackline Master 27 • **The Sun, the Wind, and the Rain** 55

Language Support, 55

TESTED OBJECTIVES

Students will identify and use antonyms and synonyms.

MATERIALS

- Teaching Chart 42

TEACHING TIP

INSTRUCTIONAL Explain to students that synonyms are words that have the same or almost the same meaning. For example, the synonyms *big* and *large* mean exactly the same thing. *Leap* and *jump,* however, have slightly different meanings. (A leap is a big jump.)

Introduce Antonyms and Synonyms

PREPARE

Define Antonym and Synonym

Explain: *Synonyms* are words that have the same or almost the same meaning. *Antonyms* are words that have opposite meanings.

TEACH

Read the Passage and Model the Skill

Have students read the passage on **Teaching Chart 42.** Encourage them to look for antonyms and synonyms.

Two Mountains

Deep underground, a soft, fiery, hot pool formed. Slowly, the pool turned cold and rock-hard. It became a large earth mountain. Years later, on a nearby beach, Elizabeth scooped up buckets of wet sand. She quickly made a small sand mountain. She patted it smooth.

The sun made her little mountain dry. The wind blew grains of sand high into the air. A rainstorm came and beat down on the earth mountain's rocks. Elizabeth's mountain was washed away in the shower. The rough rocks of the earth mountain were not.

Teaching Chart 42

Help students identify a pair of synonyms and antonyms.

MODEL I know that the word *hot* in the first sentence and the word *cold* in the second sentence mean opposite things. They must be antonyms. The words *fiery* and *hot* in the first sentence both describe the same word (*pool*) and seem to mean nearly the same thing. They must be synonyms.

Have students tell how *fiery* and *hot* mean almost the same thing, but not exactly the same thing.

PRACTICE

Identify Antonyms and Synonyms

Have volunteers underline a pair of synonyms in "Two Mountains." Then have them circle a pair of antonyms. Invite the class to find and list other pairs of synonyms and antonyms in the passage.

PARTNERS

Have partners write and illustrate a pair of words that are antonyms and a pair of words that are synonyms. ▶ **Visual/Spatial**

ASSESS/CLOSE

Explore More Antonyms and Synonyms

Have students work in groups to think of other pairs of antonyms and pairs of synonyms. Then encourage groups to collaborate on sorting, classifying, and identifying related words. Invite each group to draw a set of pictures or cartoons that show synonyms.

ALTERNATE TEACHING STRATEGY

ANTONYMS AND SYNONYMS

For a different approach to teaching this skill, see page T65.

Meeting Individual Needs for Vocabulary

EASY

Name______ Date______ Reteach 51

Antonyms and Synonyms

An **antonym** is a word that has the opposite, or nearly opposite, meaning as another word.
A **synonym** is a word that has the same, or nearly the same, meaning as another word.

Write ***S*** if the word pairs are synonyms. Write ***A*** if the word pairs are antonyms.

1. big / giant S
2. small / tiny S
3. pleasant / mean A
4. shower / rainstorm S
5. breaking / cracking S
6. soft / rock-hard A
7. fiery / hot S
8. hilly / flat A
9. rough / smooth A
10. slowly / quickly A
11. near / far A
12. happy / cheerful S

51 **At Home:** Have students name a synonym and an antonym for *tired.* Book 3.1/Unit 2 **The Sun, the Wind and the Rain** 12

Reteach, 51

ON-LEVEL

Name______ Date______ Practice 51

Antonyms and Synonyms

Antonyms are words that have the opposite, or nearly opposite, meaning.

Synonyms are words that have the same, or nearly the same, meaning.

Antonyms	Synonyms
hot, cold	large, big

Choose a word from the list on the right that is a synonym or antonym for the word on the left. Write the word on the first line. On the second line, write **S** if the word pairs are synonyms. Write **A** if the word pairs are antonyms.

1. shout	yell	S	different
2. like	dislike	A	won
3. help	aid	S	distrust
4. less	more	A	dislike
5. noisy	quiet	A	yell
6. unusual	different	S	quiet
7. believe	distrust	A	down
8. lost	won	A	aid
9. angry	mad	S	more
10. up	down	A	mad

51 **At Home:** Have students name a synonym and an antonym for **chilly.** Book 3.1/Unit 2 **The Sun, the Wind and the Rain** 20

Practice, 51

CHALLENGE

Name______ Date______ Extend 51

Antonyms and Synonyms

Antonyms are words that have opposite meanings. Synonyms are words that have the same or similar meanings. Read the words in the first box. Write an antonym for each word.

rough hard dry light small

Antonyms Answers may vary. Sample answers are given.

1. smooth rough
2. soft hard
3. wet dry
4. heavy light
5. big small

Look at the words in the second box. Write a synonym for each word.

wind rush hairy sharp-edged help

Synonyms Answers may vary. Sample answers are given.

6. breeze wind
7. hurry rush
8. furry hairy
9. jagged sharp-edged
10. aid help

Look at the picture. Use some of the words in the boxes to write about it.

51 **At Home:** Ask students to select two sets of antonyms and synonyms. Have them write sentences using one set of antonyms or one set of synonyms in each sentence. Book 3.1/Unit 2 **The Sun, the Wind and the Rain**

Extend, 51

LANGUAGE SUPPORT

Name______ Date______

Match It

Cracking	Gouge	Smooth
Fiery	Cold	Jagged
Rainstorm	Quickly	Bump

Opposite of hot cold	Opposite of slowly quickly	Opposite of rough smooth
Same as hot fiery	Same as carve gouge	Same as breaking cracking
Same as shower rainstorm	Opposite of flat jagged	Opposite of mountain bump

56 The Sun, the Wind, and the Rain • Language Support/Blackline Master 28 Grade 3

Language Support, 56

GRAMMAR/SPELLING CONNECTIONS

See the 5-Day Grammar and Usage Plan on pages 203M–203N.

See the 5-Day Spelling Plan on words with consonant clusters on pages 203O–203P.

TECHNOLOGY TIP

Write the title of your essay in bold type. Use a bigger size of type for the title. This will make it stand out from the rest of the essay.

Explanatory Writing

Prewrite

WRITE AN ESSAY Present this writing assignment: Write an essay that tells how a rainstorm or snowstorm changes a place. Choose an outdoor place that you know well, such as your backyard or a playing field. Use lively, descriptive words.

VISUALIZING AND DRAWING After students choose a place, invite them to close their eyes and picture it in the sun, a rainstorm, or snowstorm. Have students make drawings of their place in each weather condition.

Strategy: Make a Venn Diagram Ask students to fill in a Venn diagram to describe their place in two different weather conditions. Suggest that they:

- label the outer circles of the Venn diagram with each type of weather.
- write distinguishing details of each weather condition in outer circles.
- write characteristics that stay the same in different weather conditions in the central part of the diagram.

Draft

USE THE VENN DIAGRAM As students write their essays, they should refer to their Venn diagrams to help them organize information. Suggest that they write about their place in one weather condition first, and then how it changes in the second weather condition. Lastly, they can use information from the central part of the diagram to tell how their place stays the same in both weather conditions.

Revise

TAKING TIME OUT Have students work in pairs. They can make revision suggestions based on personal experience.

Edit/Proofread

CHECK FOR ERRORS Students should reread their essays to correct spelling, grammar, punctuation, and incomplete sentences.

Publish

MATCH ESSAYS WITH DRAWINGS Display students' sketches and drawings from the Prewriting activity. As students read their essays aloud, classmates can match the drawing(s) with what has been read. Have students explain how they made their choice.

MY BACKYARD

My backyard changes all the time. It is always there, but the sun, the wind, and the rain make it look different.

When the sun shines on my backyard, all of the flowers look bright. All the birds sing when it is sunny. When my mother cuts the grass, it smells good.

Once, on a windy day, a big branch broke off our maple tree. I was sad to see that branch break. I used to swing on it.

My backyard looks different now, but it is always there. The birds always sing.

Presentation Ideas

DISCUSS DRAWINGS Have students discuss their drawings from the Prewriting activity. Elicit comments on how visualizing and drawing helped them to write their essays.

▶ **Viewing/Representing**

ON-LOCATION BROADCAST Have students imagine they are broadcasting a weather report from their chosen place. How would they change their style of reading?

▶ **Speaking/Listening**

Consider students' creative efforts, possibly adding a plus (+) for originality, wit, and imagination.

Scoring Rubric

Excellent	Good	Fair	Unsatisfactory
4: The writer • clearly presents the main idea at the beginning of the essay. • incorporates facts and details in a logical way. • includes descriptive and colorful details to enhance the given facts.	**3:** The writer • presents a main idea and develops it with facts and examples. • attempts to enhance facts with descriptive details. • communicates clearly and logically.	**2:** The writer • attempts to present a topic. • may present vague details and facts. • may have trouble with sequence.	**1:** The writer • may not present a topic. • may present vague or irrelevant facts or details. • has not understood the assignment.

0: The writer leaves the page blank or fails to respond to the writing task. The student does not address the topic or simply paraphrases the prompt. The response is illegible.

Meeting Individual Needs for Writing

EASY

Postcard Have students draw a postcard showing where they live. On the back of their postcard, invite them to write a few sentences about it and how the weather is affecting it. Help them to address, stamp, and mail the cards.

ON-LEVEL

Journal Entry Ask students to pretend that they are Elizabeth and write a journal entry about making a sand mountain on the beach. Have students recall the different emotions Elizabeth felt as the weather changed her sand mountain.

CHALLENGE

Paragraph Ask students to write a short passage about what would have happened to Elizabeth's sand mountain during a natural disaster, such as a hurricane, earthquake, or tidal wave. Discuss with students the effects of these weather conditions on the earth mountain as well.

COMMUNICATION TIPS

REPRESENTING Have students walk through the audience with their drawings so others can see the details clearly.

LISTENING As students listen to the essays, have them think about the scenes being described. Ask them to tell how listening to an essay compares with reading it.

LANGUAGE SUPPORT

ESL Different countries may experience unusual weather. Ask students who have lived abroad or visited other countries to describe weather conditions they experienced there.

PORTFOLIO Invite students to include their essays or another writing project in their portfolios.

5 Day Grammar and Usage Plan

LANGUAGE SUPPORT

ESL **Write *brush, beach,* and *fox* on the board. Circle the final *sh, ch,* or *x*. Add *es* to form the plural. Have students write other words with the same last letters and then add *es*.**

DAILY LANGUAGE ACTIVITIES

Write the Daily Language Activities on the chalkboard each day or use **Transparency 7**. Have students correct sentences orally.

Day 1

1. The earth has many mountain. mountains
2. Four rock fell down this hill. rocks
3. Several animal live here. animals

Day 2

1. Many stream flow through these mountain. streams; mountains
2. Most city are built near river. cities; rivers
3. Fox live on these mountain. foxes; mountains

Day 3

1. They hiked on three path. paths
2. We filled many box with the sand. boxes
3. Many country don't have enough rain. countries

Day 4

1. Do you like to make sand castle? castles
2. The animals eat berries from those bush. bushes
3. The boy told two story. stories

Day 5

1. Elizabeth made two pile of sand. piles
2. The girl's two hobby involved pebbles and sand. hobbies
3. Who picked those bunch of flowers? bunches

Daily Language Transparency 7

DAY 1 Introduce the Concept

Oral Warm-Up Read this sentence aloud: I have two cats, but you have only one cat. Ask students why the first *cat* in the sentence ends in *-s*.

Introduce Plural Nouns Point out that the words *singular* and *plural* are similar to the words *single* and *plus*. Present and discuss:

Singular and Plural Nouns

- A **singular noun** names one person, place, or thing.
- A **plural noun** names more than one person, place, or thing.
- Add *-s* to form the plural of most singular nouns.

Present the Daily Language Activity and have students correct it orally. Then have them write two sentences using singular nouns and two sentences using plural nouns.

Assign the daily Writing Prompt on page 172C.

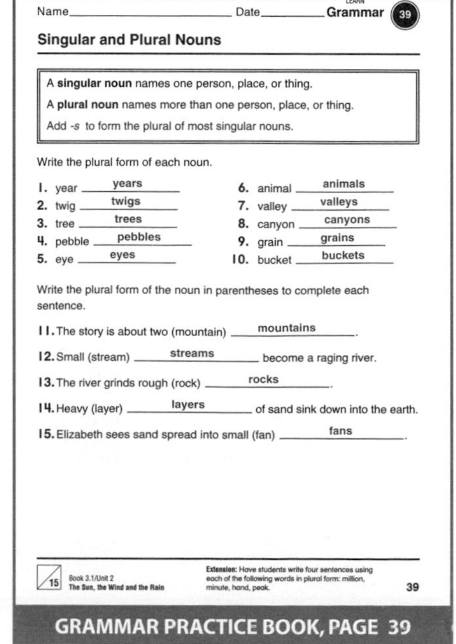
Name_______________ Date_______ LEARN Grammar 39

Singular and Plural Nouns

A **singular noun** names one person, place, or thing.
A **plural noun** names more than one person, place, or thing.
Add *-s* to form the plural of most singular nouns.

Write the plural form of each noun.

1. year years
2. twig twigs
3. tree trees
4. pebble pebbles
5. eye eyes
6. animal animals
7. valley valleys
8. canyon canyons
9. grain grains
10. bucket buckets

Write the plural form of the noun in parentheses to complete each sentence.

11. The story is about two (mountain) mountains.
12. Small (stream) streams become a raging river.
13. The river grinds rough (rock) rocks.
14. Heavy (layer) layers of sand sink down into the earth.
15. Elizabeth sees sand spread into small (fan) fans.

15 Book 3.1/Unit 2 **The Sun, the Wind and the Rain**

Extension: Have students write four sentences using each of the following words in plural form: million, minute, hand, peak. 39

GRAMMAR PRACTICE BOOK, PAGE 39

DAY 2 Teach the Concept

Review Singular and Plural Nouns Have students give the plural form of *mountain, hat,* and *year*.

Introduce the *-es* Ending Ask students to say the plural form of *beach*. Explain that adding an *e* to the *-s* helps us to pronounce the plural of *beach*. Present:

Adding *-es*

- Add *-es* to form the plural of singular nouns that end in *s, sh, ch,* or *x*.
- To form the plural of nouns ending in a consonant and *y*, change *y* to *i* and add *-es*.

Present the Daily Language Activity and have students correct it orally. Then have them write the plural forms of *grass, brush, peach, fox,* and *city*.

Assign the daily Writing Prompt on page 172C.

Name_______________ Date_______ LEARN AND PRACTICE Grammar 40

Forming Plural Nouns

- Add *-es* to form the plural of singular nouns that end in *s, sh, ch,* or *x*.
- To form the plural of nouns ending in a consonant and *y*, change the *y* to *i* and add *-es*.

Change each word to a plural noun.

1. story stories
2. beach beaches
3. pass passes
4. crack cracks
5. wish wishes
6. day days
7. sky skies
8. path paths
9. box boxes
10. bunch bunches

Write the plural form of each noun in parentheses.

11. My family takes (journey) journeys to the mountains.
12. I look for birds in the (branch) branches of trees.
13. I also look for birds in (bush) bushes.
14. I see birds eating (berry) berries.
15. Sometimes at night we see (fox) foxes.

40 **Extension:** Have students take turns writing singular nouns that end in s, x, ch, sh, and y. Have other students write the plurals of these words.

Book 3.1/Unit 2 **The Sun, the Wind and the Rain** 15

GRAMMAR PRACTICE BOOK, PAGE 40

Singular and Plural Nouns

DAY 3 Review and Practice

Learn from the Literature Review plural nouns. Read page 187 of *The Sun, the Wind and the Rain.*

> **Elizabeth could see the rain carving little valleys into her mountain. Tiny rivers carried the sand down the beach.**

Ask students to identify all singular and plural nouns. Then ask them to make the singular nouns plural. Remind them that since *beach* ends in *ch*, they must add *-es*.

Form Plural Nouns Present the Daily Language Activity and have students correct the sentences orally. Write on the chalkboard the words *class, coach, leash, box,* and *kitty*. Ask each student to choose one of these words and write a sentence using its plural form.

Assign the daily Writing Prompt on page 172D.

Name__________ Date______ PRACTICE AND REVIEW Grammar 41

Using Plural Nouns in Sentences

- Add *-s* to form the plural of most singular nouns.
- Add *-es* to form the plural of singular nouns that end in *s, sh, ch,* or *x.*
- To form the plural of nouns ending in a consonant and *y*, change the *y* to *i* and add *-es.*

Complete each sentence with the correct singular or plural noun in parentheses.

1. Two (family, families) families went to the beach.
2. The parking lot was full of (car, cars) cars.
3. Many (bus, buses) buses stopped at the beach.
4. The children swam in the (ocean, oceans) ocean.
5. One child made a sand (mountain, mountains) mountain.
6. Some children picked up (shell, shells) shells.
7. They put them in a small (box, boxes) box.
8. Someone found a big white (feather, feathers) feather.
9. Everyone ate (sandwich, sandwiches) sandwiches.
10. Then they ate juicy (peach, peaches) peaches.

10 Book 3.1/Unit 2 The Sun, the Wind and the Rain

Extension: Invite students to draw a picture that shows the families at the beach. Then have students use singular and plural nouns to label people, places, and things in their pictures. 41

GRAMMAR PRACTICE BOOK, PAGE 41

DAY 4 Review and Practice

Review Singular and Plural Nouns Ask students to explain how most plurals are formed. (by adding *-s*) Have them explain how the plurals *watches* and *babies* are formed. (Add *-es*; change *y* to *i* and add *-es*.) Then present the Daily Language Activity.

Mechanics and Usage Before students begin the daily Writing Prompt on page 172D, explain how to use commas in a series. Give an example such as: *Nancy, Tom, and Kim walked on the beach.* Present:

> **Commas**
>
> Use commas to separate three or more words in a series.

Point out that some people do not use the comma before *and,* as in the title of the story. Ask students how they would change the title to match the above rule.

Assign the daily Writing Prompt on page 172D.

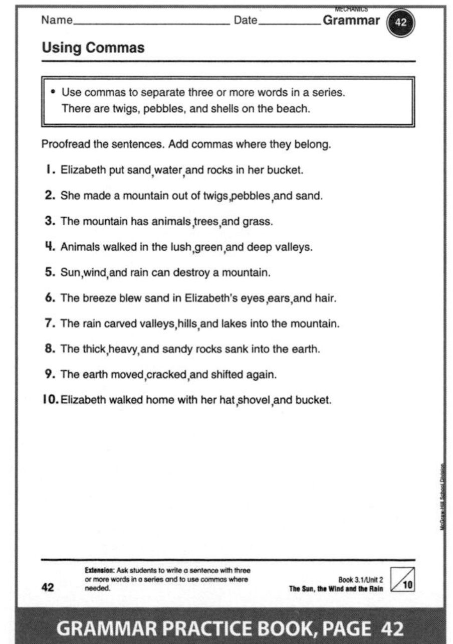

Name__________ Date______ MECHANICS Grammar 42

Using Commas

- Use commas to separate three or more words in a series. There are twigs, pebbles, and shells on the beach.

Proofread the sentences. Add commas where they belong.

1. Elizabeth put sand, water, and rocks in her bucket.
2. She made a mountain out of twigs, pebbles, and sand.
3. The mountain has animals, trees, and grass.
4. Animals walked in the lush, green, and deep valleys.
5. Sun, wind, and rain can destroy a mountain.
6. The breeze blew sand in Elizabeth's eyes, ears, and hair.
7. The rain carved valleys, hills, and lakes into the mountain.
8. The thick, heavy, and sandy rocks sank into the earth.
9. The earth moved, cracked, and shifted again.
10. Elizabeth walked home with her hat, shovel, and bucket.

42 **Extension:** Ask students to write a sentence with three or more words in a series and to use commas where needed.

Book 3.1/Unit 2 The Sun, the Wind and the Rain 10

GRAMMAR PRACTICE BOOK, PAGE 42

DAY 5 Assess and Reteach

Assess Use the Daily Language Activity and page 43 of the **Grammar Practice Book** for assessment.

Reteach Have students review orally the rules for forming the plurals of nouns ending in *s, sh, ch, x,* and a consonant plus *y*.

Ask students to write the singular form of the nouns in the Daily Language Activities on one side of an index card and their plural forms on the other side. Pin the cards, singular side up, on the bulletin board. Play a game in which two teams compete to give the most correct plural forms for the nouns written on the cards.

Use page 44 of the **Grammar Practice Book** for additional reteaching.

Assign the daily Writing Prompt on page 172D.

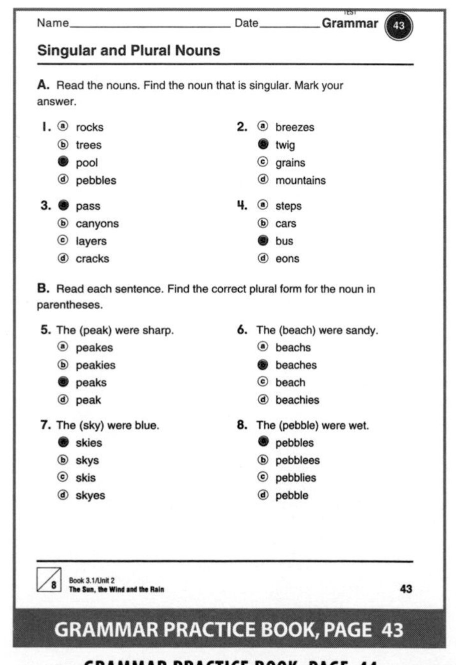

Name__________ Date______ TEST Grammar 43

Singular and Plural Nouns

A. Read the nouns. Find the noun that is singular. Mark your answer.

1. ⓐ rocks ⓑ trees ● pool ⓓ pebbles
2. ⓐ breezes ● twig ⓒ grains ⓓ mountains
3. ● pass ⓑ canyons ⓒ layers ⓓ cracks
4. ⓐ steps ⓑ cars ● bus ⓓ eons

B. Read each sentence. Find the correct plural form for the noun in parentheses.

5. The (peak) were sharp. ⓐ peakes ⓑ peakies ● peaks ⓓ peak
6. The (beach) were sandy. ⓐ beachs ● beaches ⓒ beach ⓓ beachies
7. The (sky) were blue. ● skies ⓑ skys ⓒ skis ⓓ skyes
8. The (pebble) were wet. ● pebbles ⓑ pebblees ⓒ pebblies ⓓ pebble

8 Book 3.1/Unit 2 The Sun, the Wind and the Rain 43

GRAMMAR PRACTICE BOOK, PAGE 43

GRAMMAR PRACTICE BOOK, PAGE 44

5 Day Spelling Plan

LANGUAGE SUPPORT

List the following letters in two columns on chart paper: *b, c, f, g, p* in column 1; *r, l* in column 2. Help students hear and identify the sounds of blends by saying a spelling word and having them pick one letter from column 1 and one from column 2 to spell the initial sound they hear.

DICTATION SENTENCES

Spelling Words

1. Do not block the window.
2. Push the brake now.
3. The cat acts crazy if you scare her.
4. There was a red flash in the sky.
5. The baby can grab her toe.
6. Her plate is clean.
7. The loud noise made him blink.
8. The creek is too broad to jump over.
9. The leaves crumble because they are dry.
10. The animals were caught in a flood.
11. A bird is a grand pet to have.
12. Many famous people have been blind.
13. A winter day can be brisk.
14. The flame blew through the window.
15. We caught plenty of fish in the river.

Challenge Words

16. We walked through the deep canyons.
17. The rain flowed off of the roof.
18. What grains grow in the fields?
19. I have a handful of bread for the birds.
20. That roof on the old house has many peaks.

DAY 1 Pretest

Assess Prior Knowledge Use the Dictation Sentences at the left and **Spelling Practice Book** page 39 for the pretest. Allow students to correct their own papers. If students have trouble, have partners give each other a midweek test on Day 3. Students who require a modified list may be tested on the first eight words.

Spelling Words		Challenge Words
1. block	9. **crumble**	16. canyons
2. brake	10. flood	17. flowed
3. crazy	11. grand	18. grains
4. flash	12. blind	19. handful
5. grab	13. brisk	20. **peaks**
6. plate	14. flame	
7. **blink**	15. plenty	
8. **broad**		

*Note: Words in **dark type** are from the story.*

Word Study On page 40 of the **Spelling Practice Book** are word study steps and an at-home activity.

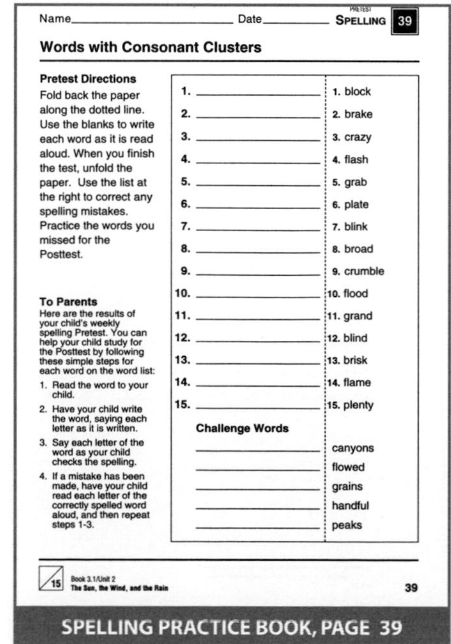

Name________ Date________ PRETEST SPELLING 39

Words with Consonant Clusters

Pretest Directions
Fold back the paper along the dotted line. Use the blanks to write each word as it is read aloud. When you finish the test, unfold the paper. Use the list at the right to correct any spelling mistakes. Practice the words you missed for the Posttest.

1. ______	1. block
2. ______	2. brake
3. ______	3. crazy
4. ______	4. flash
5. ______	5. grab
6. ______	6. plate
7. ______	7. blink
8. ______	8. broad
9. ______	9. crumble
10. ______	10. flood
11. ______	11. grand
12. ______	12. blind
13. ______	13. brisk
14. ______	14. flame
15. ______	15. plenty
Challenge Words	
______	canyons
______	flowed
______	grains
______	handful
______	peaks

To Parents
Here are the results of your child's weekly spelling Pretest. You can help your child study for the Posttest by following these simple steps for each word on the word list:

1. Read the word to your child.
2. Have your child write the word, saying each letter as it is written.
3. Say each letter of the word as your child checks the spelling.
4. If a mistake has been made, have your child read each letter of the correctly spelled word aloud, and then repeat steps 1-3.

15 Book 3.1/Unit 2 The Sun, the Wind, and the Rain 39

SPELLING PRACTICE BOOK, PAGE 39

WORD STUDY STEPS AND ACTIVITY, PAGE 40

DAY 2 Explore the Pattern

Sort and Spell Words Say the words *blue* and *brown*. Ask students what two sounds they hear in the beginning of each word. These words contain initial consonant blends *bl* and *br*. Tell students this week's spelling words begin with two consonants blended together. Have them sort the words by spelling pattern.

Words beginning with:

bl	br	cr
block	brake	crazy
blink	broad	crumble
blind	brisk	
fl	**gr**	**pl**
flash	grab	plate
flood	grand	plenty
flame		

Word Wall Have students try to make silly sentences using only words that begin with consonant blends shown on the word wall. Have them display their sentences on the word wall.

Name________ Date________ EXPLORE THE PATTERN SPELLING 41

Words with Consonant Clusters

block	flash	blink	flood	brisk
brake	grab	broad	grand	flame
crazy	plate	crumble	blind	plenty

Pattern Power!
Write the spelling words that have these spelling patterns.

bl	br	cr
1. block	4. brake	7. crazy
2. blink	5. broad	8. crumble
3. blind	6. brisk	
fl	**gr**	**pl**
9. flash	12. grab	14. plate
10. flood	13. grand	15. plenty
11. flame		

Words Within Words
Write the spelling word that contains the small word.

16. risk	brisk	17. and	grand
18. lock	block	19. ate	plate
20. ash	flash	21. ink	blink
22. rake	brake	23. lent	plenty
24. am	flame	25. road	broad

25 Book 3.1/Unit 2 The Sun, the Wind, and the Rain 41

SPELLING PRACTICE BOOK, PAGE 41

Words with Consonant Clusters

DAY 3 Practice and Extend

Word Meaning: Synonyms Explain to students that a *synonym* is a word that has the same or about the same meaning as another word. Have partners work together to match synonyms with spelling words. Have partners share and compare their answers.

Display synonyms such as *stop* (brake), *great* (grand); *broad* (wide); for students to match.

Glossary Explain to students that most words in the Glossary are listed under their base word. The entry for the base word may include other verb forms or the plural of the word. Have partners:

- write each Challenge Word.
- look up each Challenge Word in the Glossary
- if the Challenge Word is listed under a base word, write the base word and whether the Challenge Word is a plural or a verb form.

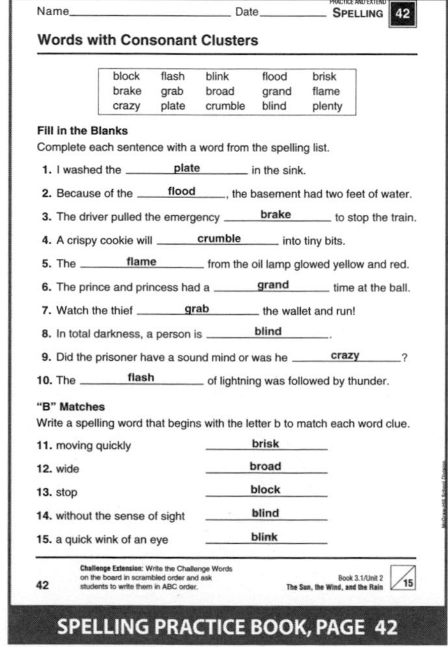

Name_______________ Date_______ PRACTICE AND EXTEND SPELLING 42

Words with Consonant Clusters

block	flash	blink	flood	brisk
brake	grab	broad	grand	flame
crazy	plate	crumble	blind	plenty

Fill in the Blanks

Complete each sentence with a word from the spelling list.

1. I washed the ___plate___ in the sink.
2. Because of the ___flood___, the basement had two feet of water.
3. The driver pulled the emergency ___brake___ to stop the train.
4. A crispy cookie will ___crumble___ into tiny bits.
5. The ___flame___ from the oil lamp glowed yellow and red.
6. The prince and princess had a ___grand___ time at the ball.
7. Watch the thief ___grab___ the wallet and run!
8. In total darkness, a person is ___blind___.
9. Did the prisoner have a sound mind or was he ___crazy___?
10. The ___flash___ of lightning was followed by thunder.

"B" Matches

Write a spelling word that begins with the letter b to match each word clue.

11. moving quickly ___brisk___
12. wide ___broad___
13. stop ___block___
14. without the sense of sight ___blind___
15. a quick wink of an eye ___blink___

42 **Challenge Extension:** Write the Challenge Words on the board in scrambled order and ask students to write them in ABC order. Book 3.1/Unit 2 **The Sun, the Wind, and the Rain** 15

SPELLING PRACTICE BOOK, PAGE 42

DAY 4 Proofread and Write

Proofread Sentences Write these sentences on the chalkboard, including the misspelled words. Ask students to proofread, circling incorrect spellings and writing the correct spellings. There are two spelling errors in each sentence.

The (falash) of light made me (bllink). (flash, blink)

(Grabb) the (braek) and pull it. (grab, brake)

Have students create additional sentences with errors for partners to correct.

WRITING Have students use as many Spelling Words as possible in the daily Writing Prompt on page 172D. Remind students to proofread their writing for errors in spelling, grammar, and punctuation.

Name_______________ Date_______ PROOFREAD AND WRITE SPELLING 43

Words with Consonant Clusters

Proofreading Activity

There are six spelling mistakes in these directions. Circle the misspelled words. Write the words correctly on the lines below.

If you plan to travel by foot:

1. Go one (blauk) west.
2. Walk at a (brissk) pace.
3. Then skip across the (brawd) avenue.
4. Never mind, (grabb) a taxi instead!

If you plan to travel by car:

5. Slam on the emergency (brak) when you reach the driveway.
6. Then (flasch) your headlights three times.

1. ___block___ 2. ___brisk___ 3. ___broad___
4. ___grab___ 5. ___brake___ 6. ___flash___

Writing Activity

Write a set of directions telling how to get to a certain place. You could explain, for example, how to get to your school or to your nearest library. Number each step. Use at least four spelling words.

10 Book 3.1/Unit 2 **The Sun, the Wind, and the Rain** 43

SPELLING PRACTICE BOOK, PAGE 43

DAY 5 Assess and Reteach

Assess Students' Knowledge Use page 44 of the **Spelling Practice Book** or the Dictation Sentences on page 203O for the posttest.

Personal Word List Have students identify their own "drive me crazy" spelling demons in this week's words. They can list the words they have trouble with in groups according to their blends, then in the future, add any words they have difficulty with to the appropriate categories.

JOURNAL

Students should practice spelling these words and refer to them during later writing activities.

Name_______________ Date_______ POSTTEST SPELLING 44

Words with Consonant Clusters

Look at the words in each set. One word in each set is spelled correctly. Use a pencil to color in the circle in front of that word. Before you begin, look at the sample sets of words. Sample A has been done for you. Do Sample B by yourself. When you are sure you know what to do, you may go on with the rest of the page.

Sample A: (A) truk ● truck (C) truak (D) druck

Sample B: (E) blaime (F) blamme ● blame (H) blaym

1. ● flash (B) flashh (C) flasch (D) flach
2. ● crumble (F) crumbel (G) krumble (H) crummble
3. (A) flud (B) fludd (C) flod ● flood
4. (E) brissk ● brisk (G) brysk (H) brisck
5. ● broad (B) brawd (C) browd (D) broud
6. ● plate (F) playte (G) plaite (H) plaet
7. (A) blynk (B) blenk ● blink (D) blienk
8. (E) crazee ● crazy (G) crazie (H) krazy
9. ● blind (B) bliand (C) blinde (D) blynd
10. (E) flayme (F) flaim ● flame (H) flaym
11. (A) grabbe ● grab (C) grabb (D) grabe
12. (E) plentie (F) plennty ● plenty (H) plenity
13. (A) granned (B) gran (C) grande ● grand
14. (E) brayk ● brake (G) braik (H) braick
15. (A) blauk ● block (C) blawk (D) blok

44 Book 3.1/Unit 2 **The Sun, the Wind and the Rain** 15

SPELLING PRACTICE BOOK, PAGE 44

Lesson Overview

Dream Wolf

Selection Summary: **In this North American folk tale, two children are lost in the hills surrounding their village, until a wolf comes to them in their dreams to help them find their way home.**

Listening Library Audiocassette

INSTRUCTIONAL
Pages 206–225

About the Author/Illustrator: Though born in England, Paul Goble is a leading interpreter of Native American folklore for children. His retellings of Native American myths and legends such as *Dream Wolf* have won many awards. His books introduce young readers to the Sioux, Blackfoot, and Cheyenne cultures and help to preserve rich Native American traditions of storytelling.

Resources for

Meeting Individual Needs

LEVELED BOOKS

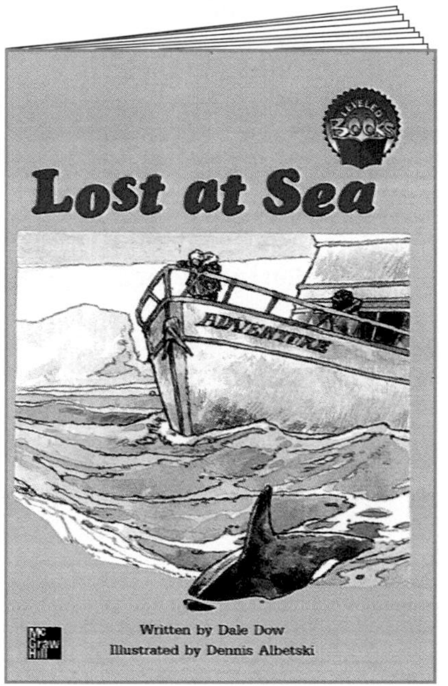

EASY
Pages 225A, 225D

INDEPENDENT
Pages 225B, 225D

Take-Home version available

CHALLENGE
Pages 225C, 225D

LEVELED PRACTICE

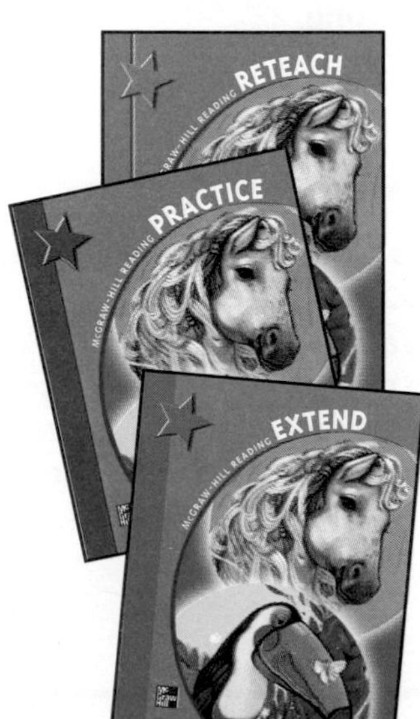

Reteach, 52–58
blackline masters with reteaching opportunities for each assessed skill

Practice, 52–58
workbook with Take-Home Stories and practice opportunities for each assessed skill and story comprehension

Extend, 52–58
blackline masters that offer challenge activities for each assessed skill

ADDITIONAL RESOURCES

- **Language Support Book** 57–64
- **Take-Home Story, Practice** p. 53a
- **Alternate Teaching Strategies** T60–T66
- **Selected Quizzes Prepared by** Accelerated Reader

Suggested Lesson Planner

Available on CD-ROM

READING AND LANGUAGE ARTS	DAY 1 Focus on Reading and Skills	DAY 2 Read the Literature
• Comprehension • Vocabulary • Phonics/Decoding • Study Skills • Listening, Speaking, Viewing, Representing	 **Read Aloud and Motivate,** 204E "Seeing the Animals" **Develop Visual Literacy,** 204/205 ✓ **Review Cause and Effect,** 206A–206B **Teaching Chart 43** **Reteach, Practice, Extend,** 52	**Build Background,** 206C Develop Oral Language **Vocabulary,** 206D *buffalo* *echoes* *ripe* *darkness* *herds* *shelter* **Teaching Chart 44** **Word Building Manipulative Cards** **Reteach, Practice, Extend,** 53  **Read the Selection,** 206–221 Guided Instruction ✓ Cause and Effect ✓ Draw Conclusions **Minilessons,** 209, 213, 215, 217, 219 **Cultural Perspectives,** 216
• Curriculum Connections	 **Fine Arts,** 204/205	 **Social Studies,** 206C
• Writing	 **Writing Prompt:** Imagine you got lost in a big city. What would you do? Who might you turn to for help? Explain in a paragraph.	 **Writing Prompt:** Write a paragraph about animals with whom country people share their space, such as horses, pigs, cows, deer, and sheep.  **Journal Writing,** 221 Quick-Write
• Grammar	**Introduce the Concept: Irregular Plural Nouns,** 225M Daily Language Activity 1. The mans jumped on the horse. (men) 2. The childs were lost. (children) 3. Her tooths are sharp. (teeth) **Grammar Practice Book,** 45	**Teach the Concept: Irregular Plural Nouns,** 225M Daily Language Activity 1. Two mooses ate berries. (moose) 2. I have a flock of sheeps. (sheep) 3. The park has many deers. (deer) **Grammar Practice Book,** 46
• Spelling	**Introduce: Words with Consonant Clusters,** 225O **Spelling Practice Book,** 45–46	**Explore the Pattern: Words with Consonant Clusters,** 225O **Spelling Practice Book,** 47

Meeting Individual Needs

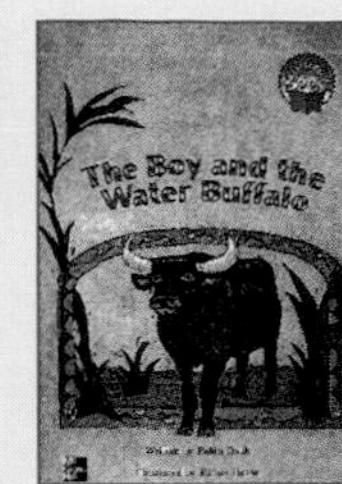

 = **Skill Assessed in Unit Test**

DAY 3 Read the Literature

Reread for Fluency, 220

Story Questions, 222
Reteach, Practice, Extend, 54
Story Activities, 223

Study Skills, 224
☑ Reference Sources
Reteach, Practice, Extend, 55

Test Power, 225

Read the Leveled Books,
Guided Reading
Consonant Clusters
☑ Cause and Effect
☑ Instructional Vocabulary

 **CD-ROM**

 **Math,** 208

 **Writing Prompt:** Write a short description of an animal. Tell about the different parts of its body.

Writing Process: Explanatory Writing, 225K
Prewrite, Draft

Review and Practice: Irregular Plural Nouns, 225N
Daily Language Activity
1. The mooses ate grass. (moose)
2. The sheeps stay in the field. (sheep)
3. Three mouses saved them. (mice)
Grammar Practice Book, 47

Practice and Extend: Words with Consonant Clusters, 225P
Spelling Practice Book, 48

DAY 4 Build Skills

 **Read the Leveled Books and Self-Selected Books**

☑ **Review Cause and Effect,** 225E–225F
Teaching Chart 46
Reteach, Practice, Extend, 56
Language Support, 62

☑ **Review Compare and Contrast,** 225G–225H
Teaching Chart 47
Reteach, Practice, Extend, 57
Language Support, 63

 **Science,** 210

 **Writing Prompt:** If you had the chance to talk to Tiblo what would you ask him? Write a short list of questions as well as the answers he might give.

Writing Process: Explanatory Writing, 225K Revise
Meeting Individual Needs for Writing, 225L

Review and Practice: Irregular Plural Nouns, 225N
Daily Language Activity
1. The wolf has white tooths. (teeth)
2. All the womans were glad. (women)
3. The bear has big foots. (feet)
Grammar Practice Book, 48

Proofread and Write: Words with Consonant Clusters, 225P
Spelling Practice Book, 49

DAY 5 Build Skills

 **Read Self-Selected Books**

☑ **Review Context Clues,** 225I–225J
Teaching Chart 48
Reteach, Practice, Extend, 58
Language Support, 64

Listening, Speaking, Viewing, Representing, 225L
Create a Book Cover
Conduct an Interview

Minilessons, 213, 215, 217, 219

Phonics Review,
Consonant Clusters, 209
Phonics/Phonemic Awareness Practice Book, 13–18

 **CD-ROM**

 **Social Studies,** 218

 **Writing Prompt:** Write a short follow-up story in which the wolf leads other groups of people home.

Writing Process: Explanatory Writing, 225K
Edit/Proofread, Publish

Assess and Reteach: Irregular Plural Nouns, 225N
Daily Language Activity
1. Tiblo spoke about the mans. (men)
2. The childs ran along the path. (children)
3. The deers meet by the pond. (deer)
Grammar Practice Book, 49–50

Assess and Reteach: Words with Consonant Clusters, 225P
Spelling Practice Book, 50

Language Arts

Read Aloud and Motivate

Seeing the Animals

a poem by Joseph Bruchac

Their eyes are
not our eyes,
yet we can see
ourselves in them.

We do not walk
the ways they walk,
yet we follow
their footprints in sand.

Sometimes they come
to us, when we
hold their silence
they understand.

When they live with us
we must give them respect,
though most stay apart
like the bird which is hidden
yet touches us with its song.

Sometimes we think
that we humans can live
without them,
but we are wrong.

Oral Comprehension

LISTENING AND SPEAKING Ask students to draw conclusions about the way the author feels about animals as you read the poem. When you have finished, ask, "What do you think the author was saying about people and animals in this poem?" Then ask, "Which words in the poem helped you draw your conclusion?"

Activity Encourage students to create animal masks. Have them draw an animal's face on a piece of cardboard. Then help them attach yarn or string to the cardboard so they can wear the masks. Encourage students to wear their masks and imitate the movements of the animal depicted.

▶ **Visual/Kinesthetic**

Develop Visual Literacy

Works of Art

Anthology pages 204-205

Stories in Art

Some paintings tell part of a story. You can see what is happening, but you might wonder what caused it.

Look at this painting. What is happening? What do you think happened to make the dog carry a suitcase? What might happen next?

Look at the painting again. How does it make you feel? Why?

A. BIRNBAUM

Family Going Shopping
by Aaron Birnbaum, 1993

204 205

Objective: Identify Cause and Effect

VIEWING Ask students to suggest another title for this painting, such as *Family Vacation*. Ask: "What is unusual about the scene?" (The characters appear to float; the dog has a suitcase.) Read the page with students, encouraging individual interpretations of the painting.

Ask students to discuss cause and effect in relation to the picture. For example:

- Having the people float lends an air of fantasy to the piece. Also, floating suggests happiness.
- The smiling faces and the childlike style suggest joy, perhaps because of a trip or a wonderful afternoon out.

REPRESENTING Have students draw or paint family scenes that convey certain moods, such as excitement, happiness, or confusion.

TESTED **OBJECTIVES**

Students will identify cause-and-effect relationships.

LANGUAGE SUPPORT

ESL Have students look at the picture on the cover of the book on page 206. Ask them to act out two verbs, or action words, shown in the picture (*flying* and *walking*). Have volunteers write these words on the chalkboard.

Review Cause and Effect

PREPARE

Discuss Importance of Cause and Effect Ask students why it is helpful to know why something happens—the cause—in order to understand what happens—the effect. Encourage them to discuss ways they can use such knowledge to solve problems.

TEACH

Define Cause and Effect Explain to students that events are often related to each other. For example, one night Jason forgets to set his alarm clock. The next morning he oversleeps. Forgetting to set the alarm clock is the "cause." Oversleeping is the "effect."

Why Brian Broke His Ankle

Brian fell and broke his ankle. He asked his mother, "Mom, why did I break my ankle?" She said, "Because I told you that tree was dangerous, and you climbed it anyway!" But Brian had climbed trees and fallen before, and hadn't broken anything. So he asked the doctor, "Why did I break my ankle?" The doctor said, "Because you fell with all your weight on the weakest part of your ankle." The doctor's answer made Brian feel better. Maybe someday he would be a doctor, so he could help people understand why things happen.

Teaching Chart 43

Read the Story and Model the Skill Display **Teaching Chart 43.** As the story is read, have students pay attention to the possible causes of the accident.

MODEL The title of the story tells me *what* happened—Brian broke his ankle. That is the effect. It makes me wonder *why* the accident happened, or the causes.

The word *because* often is the sign of a cause.

PRACTICE

Create a Cause-and-Effect Chart

Ask students to underline the possible causes of Brian's accident. Ask them if Brian's mother and the doctor might both have been right. Using a Cause-and-Effect chart, have students record the possible causes of Brian's accident. Ask them which event they think had the closest connection to the effect. ▶ **Interpersonal/Logical**

CAUSE	EFFECT
Brian climbed a tree.	Brian broke his ankle.
Brian fell on his ankle.	Brian broke his ankle.

ASSESS/CLOSE

Make Inferences about Cause and Effect

Ask students to think of three possible *effects* of Brian having a broken ankle. Provide this sentence frame, and have them complete it three ways: *Because he broke his ankle, Brian* ... (possible answers: *could not play sports; had to wear a cast; had a hard time getting around.*)

SELECTION Connection

Students will apply cause and effect when they read *Dream Wolf* and the Leveled Books.

ALTERNATE TEACHING STRATEGY

CAUSE AND EFFECT

For a different approach to teaching this skill, see page T60.

Meeting Individual Needs for Comprehension

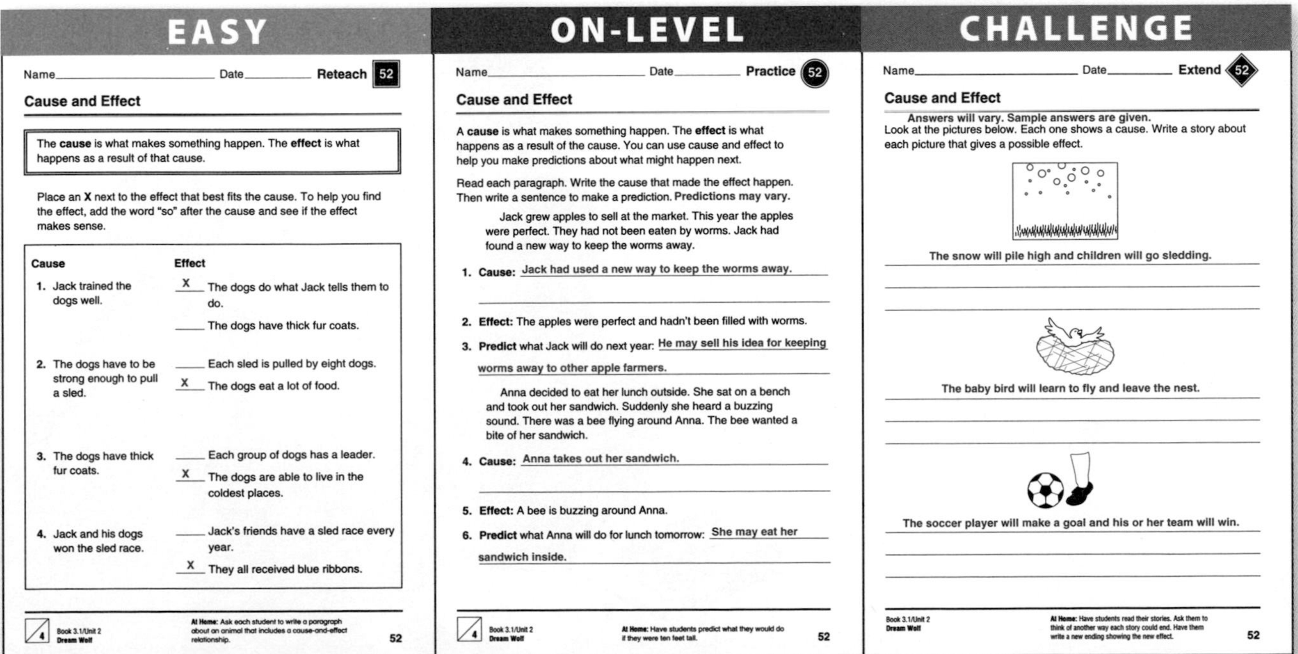

EASY

Name__________ Date______ Reteach 52

Cause and Effect

The **cause** is what makes something happen. The **effect** is what happens as a result of that cause.

Place an **X** next to the effect that best fits the cause. To help you find the effect, add the word "so" after the cause and see if the effect makes sense.

Cause	Effect
1. Jack trained the dogs well.	X The dogs do what Jack tells them to do. ___ The dogs have thick fur coats.
2. The dogs have to be strong enough to pull a sled.	___ Each sled is pulled by eight dogs. X The dogs eat a lot of food.
3. The dogs have thick fur coats.	___ Each group of dogs has a leader. X The dogs are able to live in the coldest places.
4. Jack and his dogs won the sled race.	___ Jack's friends have a sled race every year. X They all received blue ribbons.

Book 3.1/Unit 2 Dream Wolf — At Home: Ask each student to write a paragraph about an animal that includes a cause-and-effect relationship. 52

ON-LEVEL

Name__________ Date______ Practice 52

Cause and Effect

A **cause** is what makes something happen. The **effect** is what happens as a result of the cause. You can use cause and effect to help you make predictions about what might happen next.

Read each paragraph. Write the cause that made the effect happen. Then write a sentence to make a prediction. **Predictions may vary.**

Jack grew apples to sell at the market. This year the apples were perfect. They had not been eaten by worms. Jack had found a new way to keep the worms away.

1. **Cause:** Jack had used a new way to keep the worms away.
2. **Effect:** The apples were perfect and hadn't been filled with worms.
3. **Predict** what Jack will do next year: He may sell his idea for keeping worms away to other apple farmers.

Anna decided to eat her lunch outside. She sat on a bench and took out her sandwich. Suddenly she heard a buzzing sound. There was a bee flying around Anna. The bee wanted a bite of her sandwich.

4. **Cause:** Anna takes out her sandwich.
5. **Effect:** A bee is buzzing around Anna.
6. **Predict** what Anna will do for lunch tomorrow: She may eat her sandwich inside.

Book 3.1/Unit 2 Dream Wolf — At Home: Have students predict what they would do if they were ten feet tall. 52

CHALLENGE

Name__________ Date______ Extend 52

Cause and Effect

Answers will vary. Sample answers are given.

Look at the pictures below. Each one shows a cause. Write a story about each picture that gives a possible effect.

The snow will pile high and children will go sledding.

The baby bird will learn to fly and leave the nest.

The soccer player will make a goal and his or her team will win.

Book 3.1/Unit 2 Dream Wolf — At Home: Have students read their stories. Ask them to think of another way each story could end. Have them write a new ending showing the new effect. 52

Reteach, 52 — Practice, 52 — Extend, 52

Build Background

Social Studies

Anthology and Leveled Books

Evaluate Prior Knowledge

CONCEPT: ANIMALS HELPING PEOPLE These stories deal with the different ways in which animals interact with and/or help people. Encourage students to brainstorm some kinds of animals that help people today. (seeing-eye dogs, watchdogs, herding dogs, pets that cheer up the residents of nursing homes)

NEW USES FOR ANIMALS Have students think of animals that they like and list the things these animals can do. Then have them create new ways these activities might be used to help humans. Ask them to make a chart with three columns: the first stating the kind of animal, the second listing its activity, and the third showing a new use for this activity. ▶**Logical/Visual**

ANIMAL	ACTIVITY	NEW USE
dolphin	dives deep	Equipped with a TV camera, it can send back pictures of the ocean depths.
dog	fetches balls	It can be trained to retrieve tennis balls that fall into bushes.

Graphic Organizer 30

THE IDEAL PET Have students work in pairs to write a list of traits their ideal pet might have.

PARTNERS WRITING

Develop Oral Language

PETS IN DIFFERENT CULTURES

ESL Tell students that people in almost every culture have pets. Explain that one very popular pet is the dog. Tell students that there are different breeds of dogs all over the world. Present a picture book of dogs and tell students which country they came from. (The Pekinese is from China, Chihuahua is from Mexico, and so on.)

- Ask volunteers to name a breed of dog found in their family's native country.
- Write a list of words students use to describe pets, such as *friendly, smart, protective, gentle, playful,* and so on.
- Have students use these descriptive words or phrases in sentences.

TEACHING TIP

MANAGEMENT Before you present the Ideal Pet activity, explain to students that they should choose traits that the animal will have. While partners are working together on the activity, present the Develop Oral Language activity to students who need help with oral language facility.

LANGUAGE SUPPORT

See Language Support Book, pages 57–60, for teaching suggestions for Build Background and Vocabulary.

Vocabulary

Key Words

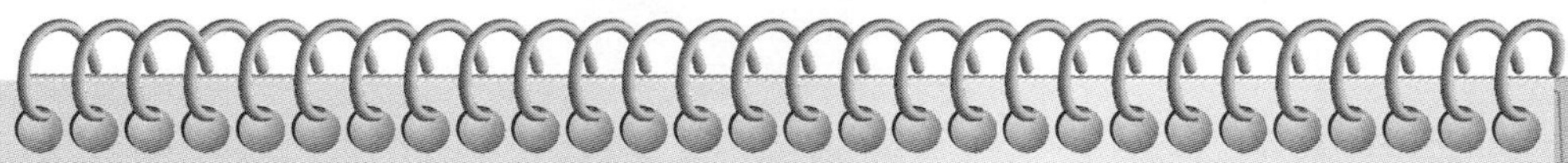

Tiblo's Wish

1. Tiblo longed to become a man so he could hunt the great, shaggy animals called buffalo. **2.** In the darkness of night, the grown men would sit around a fire. **3.** They would tell stories about the buffalo that traveled together in great herds over the hills and plains. **4.** Tiblo liked to help his mother pick berries, because she let him eat the ripe ones that were fully grown and sweet. **5.** He also liked to watch her prepare the buffalo skins so they could be made into tents to shelter the people from rain and wind. **6.** Just the same, he would sigh longingly whenever he heard the echoes of the hunters' shouts coming back from the hills.

Teaching Chart 44

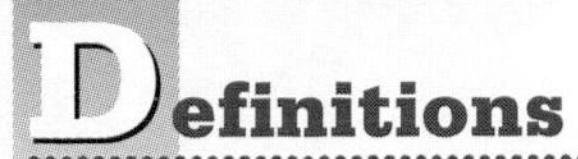

buffalo (p. 207) a large, shaggy, wild ox

darkness (p. 211) a time of no, or very little, light

herds (p. 207) groups of animals living together

ripe (p. 207) fully grown and developed

shelter (p. 211) to protect

echoes (p. 209) sounds that are repeated

SPELLING/VOCABULARY CONNECTIONS

See the Spelling Challenge Words, pages 225O–225P.

Vocabulary in Context

IDENTIFY VOCABULARY WORDS Display **Teaching Chart 44** and read the passage with students. Have volunteers circle each vocabulary word and underline other words that are clues to their meanings.

DISCUSS MEANINGS Ask questions like these to help clarify word meanings:

- What do buffalo look like?
- What base word do you recognize in the word *darkness*?
- When animals travel in herds, are they alone or together?
- What do peaches look and taste like when they are ripe?
- If a tent keeps out rain, does it shelter you?
- While in a tunnel, have you ever shouted to hear the echo of your voice?

Practice

DEMONSTRATE WORD MEANING Have students draw pictures for each Vocabulary Card. Then scramble the cards and pictures in separate piles and ask students to take turns matching the picture with the card. ▶ **Visual/Linguistic**

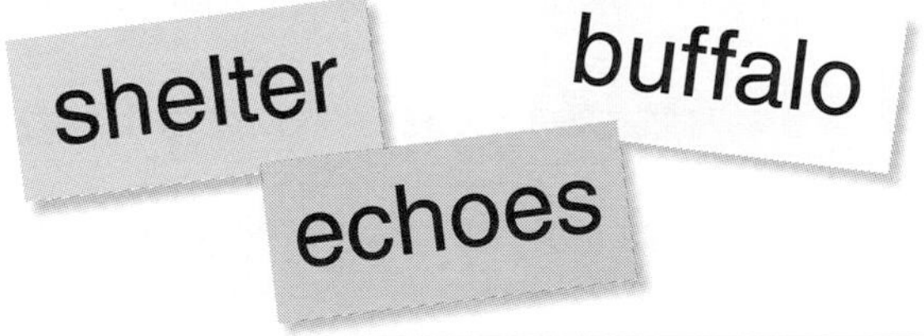

Word Building Manipulative Cards

BUILD A STORY Have partners write a short story together. Tell them to take turns making up sentences with vocabulary words until they have no more words left. ▶ **Linguistic/Oral**

WRITING PARTNERS

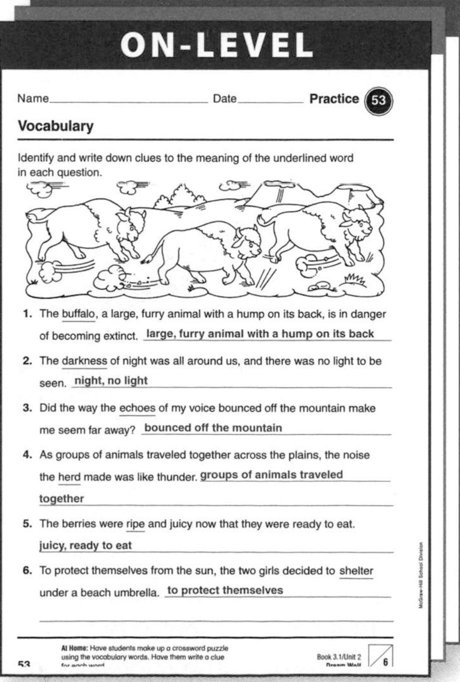

ON-LEVEL

Name________________ Date__________ Practice 53

Vocabulary

Identify and write down clues to the meaning of the underlined word in each question.

1. The buffalo, a large, furry animal with a hump on its back, is in danger of becoming extinct. large, furry animal with a hump on its back
2. The darkness of night was all around us, and there was no light to be seen. night, no light
3. Did the way the echoes of my voice bounced off the mountain make me seem far away? bounced off the mountain
4. As groups of animals traveled together across the plains, the noise the herd made was like thunder. groups of animals traveled together
5. The berries were ripe and juicy now that they were ready to eat. juicy, ready to eat
6. To protect themselves from the sun, the two girls decided to shelter under a beach umbrella. to protect themselves

At Home: Have students make up a crossword puzzle using the vocabulary words. Have them write a clue

53 Book 3.1/Unit 2 6

McGraw-Hill School Division

Take-Home Story 53a
Reteach 53
Practice 53 • **Extend 53**

Guided Instruction

Preview and Predict

Have students read the title and preview the story, looking for clues that will help them draw conclusions.

- Where do you think the story takes place?
- Why do you think that this story might be a folk tale? (The story begins, "In the old days . . ." In the pictures, the wolf seems to be acting like a human.) ***Genre***
- Which pictures offer the best clues about the story's meaning?

Have students record their predictions about the story and its possible outcome.

PREDICTIONS	WHAT HAPPENED
Two children get lost.	
They meet a wolf.	

Set Purposes

What do students want to find out by reading the story? For example:

- Why did the children get lost?
- What was the result of their meeting the wolf?

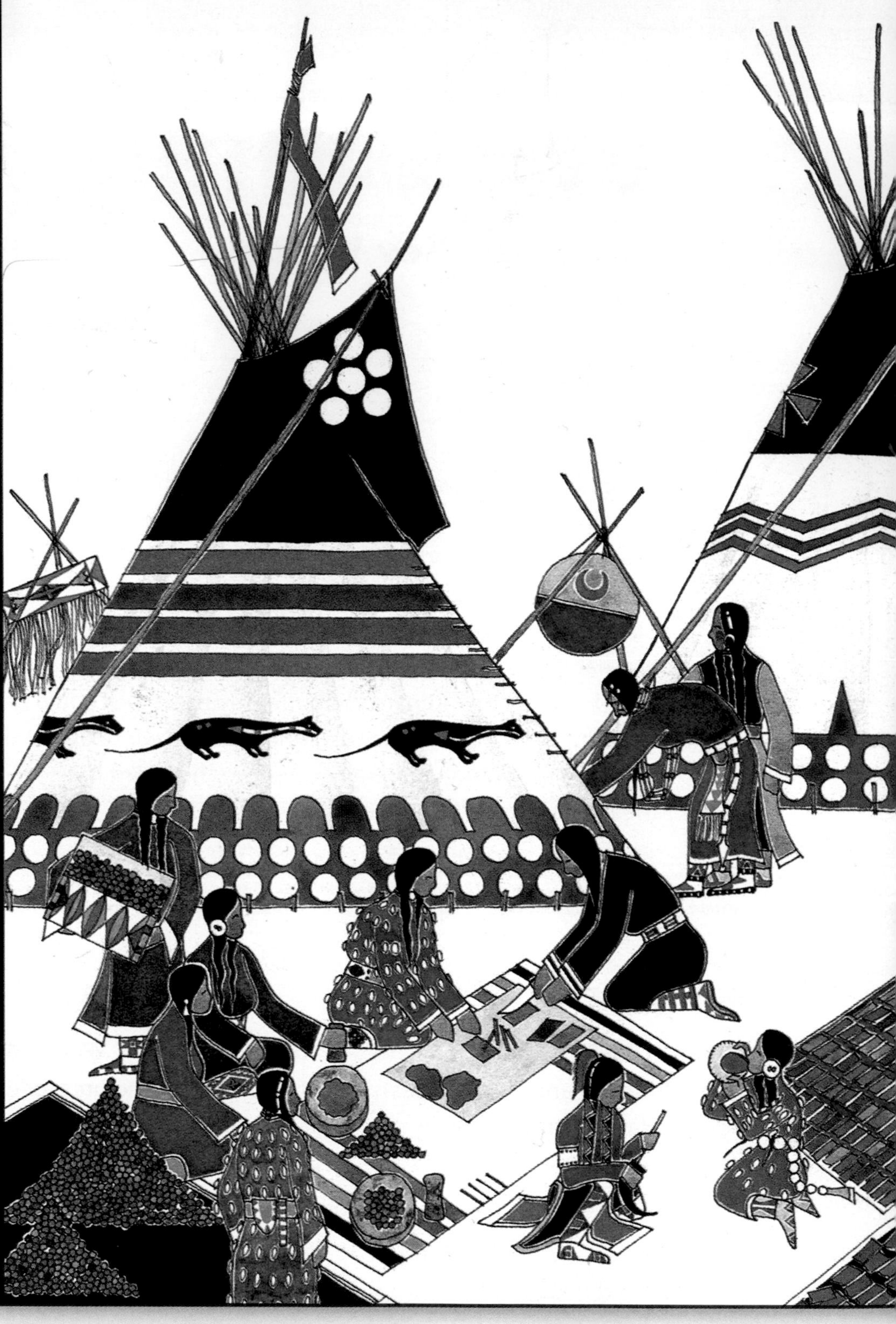

Meeting Individual Needs • Grouping Suggestions for Strategic Reading

EASY

Read Together Read the story or have students use the **Listening Library Audiocassette**. Have them use the Cause-and-Effect chart to record the story's events. As they read, have them adjust their predictions, if necessary. Guided Instruction and Intervention prompts offer help with decoding, vocabulary, and comprehension.

ON-LEVEL

Guided Reading Preview the story words listed on page 207. Then choose from the Guided Instruction questions as you read the story with students or after they have played the **Listening Library Audiocassette**. Have them use the Cause-and-Effect chart to record meaningful information during reading.

CHALLENGE

Read Independently Have students set up a Cause-and-Effect chart. Tell them that noticing cause and effect will help them to make inferences about the characters. After reading, students can write the reasons why Tiblo was not afraid of the wolf.

Dream Wolf

by Paul Goble

In the old days the people travelled over the plains. They followed the great herds of buffalo.

Every year when the berries were ripe, they would leave the plains and go up into the hills. They made camp in a valley where the berry bushes grow. Everyone picked great quantities. They mashed the berries into little cakes which they dried in the sun. These they stored in painted bags for the winter. 1

Tiblo (tee-blow) was too young to play with the older boys. He and his little sister, Tanksi (tawnk-she), had to go berry-picking with their mother and the other women and children.

207

Guided Instruction

 **Cause and Effect**

 **Draw Conclusions**

Strategic Reading Paying attention to cause and effect and drawing conclusions will help you understand why things happen in the story.

Before we begin reading, let's prepare a Cause-and-Effect chart so we can record important information about the story.

CAUSE	EFFECT

1 **CAUSE AND EFFECT** What causes the people to leave the Plains and go up into the hills? (The people need to find food, so they go to the hills to pick berries.)

Story Words

Have students check the meanings and pronunciations of these words in the Glossary beginning on page 388:

- Tiblo, p. 207
- Tanksi, p. 207
- den, p. 213
- haunches, p. 215
- kinship, p. 219

LANGUAGE SUPPORT

This chart is available as a blackline master in the **Language Support Book**.

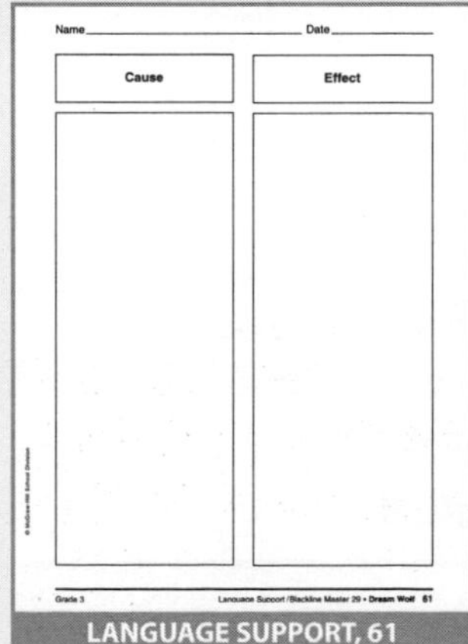
Name________ Date________

Cause	Effect

LANGUAGE SUPPORT, 61

Guided Instruction

2 **DRAW CONCLUSIONS** How might going to a different place affect the characters in the story? (The children might get lost.)

3 **CAUSE AND EFFECT** Most stories answer the questions, "What happened?" and, "Why?" Sometimes the causes are left for the reader to figure out. For example, why do you suppose the children are left alone in an area where wild animals live?

MODEL Looking at the pictures usually helps me understand what is happening and why. From the picture on these two pages, I can tell the children are used to being in the wilderness and aren't afraid of wild animals. That's why their family allows them to explore this area on their own.

Activity

Cross Curricular: Math

GROUP NUMBERS TO 10 Explain to students that Native Americans used certain small objects for money. Give students beads, beans, and shells. You might use dry pasta shells. Have students:

- assign a value to each object (2 beans = 1 bead; 5 beads = 1 shell).
- distribute "money" evenly among pairs of students.
- make a list of things they would like to buy. Partners can take turns buying and selling. Have them record the amounts of money they make and spend.

▶ **Mathematical/Logical**

I bought 2 erasers
for 1 bead.
I sold 1 notebook
for 1 shell.

Tiblo was soon tired of picking, and too full to eat any more. When nobody was looking he slipped away with Tanksi to climb the hills.

They climbed up and up among the rocks and cedar trees where bighorn sheep and bears live. Soon they could hardly hear the berry-pickers laughing and calling to each other far below. Tiblo wanted to reach the top. They climbed on.

They never noticed the sun starting to go down behind the hills.

It was getting dark when Tiblo knew they had to go back home. In the twilight every hill and valley looked the same.  He did not know which way to go. He called out. . . . Only the echoes answered him. 

209

Guided Instruction

4 Why do you think Tiblo wants to climb to the top? (The boy seems to be pointing at something in the distance. This suggests that the children are enjoying the sights in the new area.) Do you think the children are in danger? Why or why not? (Since there are no adults watching them, they may be in danger of getting lost. The wild animals are probably not a danger to the children, because the animals aren't paying attention to them.) Identify the animals in the picture. *Make Inferences*

P/I **DECODING/CONTEXT CLUES** Look at the second paragraph. Find the word in the first sentence that's spelled *c-e-d-a-r*. (*cedar*) Let's sound it out. Can you find any clues to the word's meaning?

PHONICS KIT
HANDS-ON ACTIVITIES AND PRACTICE

Minilesson

REVIEW/MAINTAIN

Consonant Clusters

Have students pronounce the words *slipped* on page 209, and *speaking* on page 211.

- Ask students what sounds they hear at the beginning of these words. (/sl/ and /sp/)
- Tell students that two consonants blended together at the beginning of a word are called *initial consonant clusters*.

Activity Have students brainstorm and list other words that begin with *sl* and *sp*.

Phonics CD-ROM Have students use the interactive phonics activities on the CD-ROM for more reinforcement.

P/I PREVENTION/INTERVENTION

DECODING/CONTEXT CLUES Write *cedar* on the chalkboard. Remind students that the letter *c* can make a hard sound as in *car* and it can also make a soft sound as in *cent*. Point out that when the letter *c* is followed by the vowels *e* or *i*, it makes the sound /s/.

Then have students pronounce the word first with a long *e* sound and then with a short *e* sound. Ask them which one they think is correct. Help students use context clues to also find the word's meaning. (*Cedar* is describing the trees, so *cedar* is a kind of tree.)

Guided Instruction

5 Do you think Tiblo and Tanksi will get home safely? Explain why you think they will or won't. (The wolf lay down beside them and kept them warm. The children will probably be all right.) ***Make Predictions***

Activity

Cross Curricular: Science

THE WOLVES RETURN There have been attempts to return wolves to areas where they once lived. Some farmers fear the wolves will kill their animals.

RESEARCH AND INQUIRY Think of methods that might be used to control wolves. Then research what methods are actually used. Make a Predictions/What Happened chart. ▶ **Logical/Spatial**

Predictions	What Happened
Farmers make stronger fences.	Radio collars used on wolves keep track of them.

They wandered on. Tiblo was lost. Darkness closed around them. It grew colder. They were tired and hungry, and Tanksi began to cry.

Speaking of happy things, Tiblo found a small cave among the rocks. They crawled inside to shelter for the night.

The children were tired, and in a little while they fell asleep. Tiblo had a dream.

He dreamed that a wolf with shining eyes entered the cave. In his dream he felt the wolf's hot breath and its rough tongue licking his face. The wolf lay down beside him. His shaggy fur was like a blanket which kept Tiblo and Tanksi warm. 

The sun was already shining into the mouth of the cave when Tiblo opened his eyes again.

Tiblo woke up his sister. They crawled out of the cave into the warm sunshine. He took Tanksi by the hand, and they set off walking down the hill.  

211

Guided Instruction

6 DRAW CONCLUSIONS/CAUSE AND EFFECT You can draw conclusions, or make an informed decision about something, by looking at cause-and-effect relationships. First let's fill in our chart. What causes and effects can we list for the story so far?

CAUSE	EFFECT
The people leave the Plains to pick berries in the hills.	Tiblo and Tanksi don't know their way around the new place.
Tiblo and Tanksi wander away.	They get lost.
When it gets dark, the children feel cold and tired.	Tiblo looks for shelter and finds a cave.

7 DRAW CONCLUSIONS Now let's use what we've learned to draw a conclusion. Read the last paragraph on page 211. Tiblo and Tanksi have just slept and it is now daytime. How may these two facts have affected the children? (They were no longer tired and felt a little better.)

LANGUAGE SUPPORT

ESL Point to the picture of the wolf on page 210 and ask students to describe the wolf. Ask: What does the wolf look like? (It has shining eyes.) Where does it come from? (The story says it enters the cave.) What does the wolf do to Tiblo? (It licks Tiblo with its tongue. It lies down next to Tiblo.) Does the wolf help or hurt Tiblo? (It helps Tiblo. It keeps him warm all night.) Where is the wolf when the children wake up in the morning? (It isn't in the cave.)

Guided Instruction

8 We have learned that Tiblo and Tanksi are lost and have spent the night in a cave. What do you think will happen next? (The children meet a new wolf. This wolf looks more real than the one in the picture on page 210. Since the wolf in the cave was friendly, this one may be friendly, too. Maybe he will help the children.) ***Make Predictions***

TEACHING TIP

INSTRUCTIONAL As students read, explain that stories can help us to understand our own feelings. Ask students if they have ever overcome their fear of something. How did they do that? Point out that Tiblo dreams of something that at first frightened him. As the dream goes on, he learns that the dream wolf is friendly. Then he is not afraid to ask the real wolf for help.

Visual Literacy

VIEWING AND REPRESENTING

Discuss the illustrations on pages 210 and 212. What time of day was the artist trying to depict in the picture on page 210? Why do you think the illustrator has made that wolf look different from the wolf in the picture on page 212? (It is probably night, because the wolf's face appears to be shining out of the dark. His eyes are very bright. The illustrator may have made the two wolves look different because one was a dream wolf and one was real.)

When the children came to a stream, they stopped to drink. Suddenly Tiblo saw that a wolf was sitting on some rocks close by, watching them. At once he remembered his dream. 8

"O Wolf," Tiblo said, "we are lost. Mother will be crying. Help us to find our way home again." 

The wolf panted and smiled. "My children, do not worry. I will help you. Last night you slept in my den. Follow me now, and I will take you home."

213

Guided Instruction

9 **CAUSE AND EFFECT** Look at the picture on page 212. Why do you think Tiblo is waving to the wolf? (Maybe he thinks this wolf will be as friendly as the one in his dream.) Let's add to our chart.

CAUSE	EFFECT
The people leave the Plains to pick berries in the hills.	Tiblo and Tanksi don't know their way around the new place.
Tiblo and Tanksi wander away.	They get lost.
When it gets dark, the children feel cold and tired.	Tiblo looks for shelter and finds a cave.
Tiblo dreams about a friendly wolf.	He asks a wolf to lead them home.

Minilesson

REVIEW/MAINTAIN

Make Inferences

Have students look back at pages 209 and 211 to find clues about how Tiblo and Tanksi are feeling. (Tiblo was tired of picking berries and too full to eat; both were tired, cold, and hungry; Tanksi began to cry.) Point out the "feeling" word clues. (*tired, cold, hungry, cry*)

Activity Have students print words that describe emotions on index cards. You may want students to brainstorm a list together. (*happy, sad, tired, bored, angry, excited*) Ask students to act out the feelings written on the cards. Have other students try to infer the feeling being shown. Students then show the word on the card.

Guided Instruction

10 **DRAW CONCLUSIONS** Look at the picture on this page. What conclusion do you draw when you see the wolf walking peacefully with Tiblo and Tanksi? (He doesn't mean to hurt them. He is guiding them back to the camp.)

Fluency

READ WITH EXPRESSION

PARTNERS Have partners take turns reading aloud page 215. Point out that this page describes the children's happiness at being home and their gratitude toward the wolf, and ask them to express these feelings as they read.

Remind students to:

- think about how Tiblo and Tanksi are feeling and to read with expression.
- pause briefly at a comma.
- pause at the ends of sentences.
- vary the speed of reading depending on the tone of the passage.

The wolf trotted off. He looked back to see that the children were following. From time to time he trotted ahead out of sight, but he always returned.

At last the wolf led them to a hilltop. The children were filled with joy to see their home in the valley below. The wolf sat back on his haunches and smiled. And then he trotted off back toward the hills. The children begged him to come and live with them. 

Guided Instruction

11 DRAW CONCLUSIONS The children beg the wolf to come and live with them. Do you think he will move into their village? Give a reason for your answer. (He will not agree because he is at home in the wild.)

P/i WORD STRUCTURE Look at the second paragraph. What is the last word in the first sentence? *(hilltop)* Can you find any clues to the word's meaning?

P/i PREVENTION/INTERVENTION

WORD STRUCTURE Tell students that some words are made up of two smaller words. They can sometimes figure out the meaning of these words by breaking them into smaller parts. Ask students what words they can find in *hilltop*. (*hill* and *top*) Then have them give the definition of the word. (the highest part of a hill)

Ask students to define other compound words. Use familiar words, such as *newspaper* and *homemade*, that will help students understand the technique of defining compound words by breaking them into parts.

Minilesson

REVIEW/MAINTAIN

Sequence of Events

Review with students that events in a story are told in a certain order, or sequence. Why is the sequence of events important in a story? Ask:

- What would have happened if Tiblo and Tanksi had met the real wolf *before* the dream wolf?
- How would the story change if the children had been afraid of the real wolf?

Activity Have students create a picture storyboard of the events that happen in the story.

Guided Instruction

(12) The children and the wolf have become friends. Look at the men on horseback. Where do you think they're going? (to bring the children home) Do you think these people will also befriend the wolf? (Yes, once they understand that the wolf has saved the children.) ***Make Predictions***

SELF-MONITORING

STRATEGY

ASKING QUESTIONS Tell students that it is important that they learn to check their understanding of what they read. Tell them that one way to do this is to ask themselves questions as they read.

MODEL Why did Tiblo dream about a wolf? Sometimes I dream about things that worry me. Maybe Tiblo was worried that he and his sister would be harmed by an animal while they were lost. His dream may have helped to make him feel safe.

"No," the wolf called back, "I like to wander from place to place with my friends. Listen for me in the evenings! You will hear me calling, and you will know that I never forget you."

People in the camp saw the children coming down the hill. The men jumped on to their horses, and galloped out to bring them home. Everyone was happy that the children were safe.

(12)

CULTURAL PERSPECTIVES

PLAINS TRADITIONS Explain that once there were more than 35 nations of Native Americans living on the Plains. Among these were the Arapaho, Sioux, Pawnee, and Cheyenne.

RESEARCH AND INQUIRY Have students find some common traditions of the Plains Indians. Have them display their findings on the bulletin board.

▶ **Spatial/Interpersonal**

interNET* CONNECTION** Students can learn more about Native Americans by visiting ***www.mhschool.com/reading.

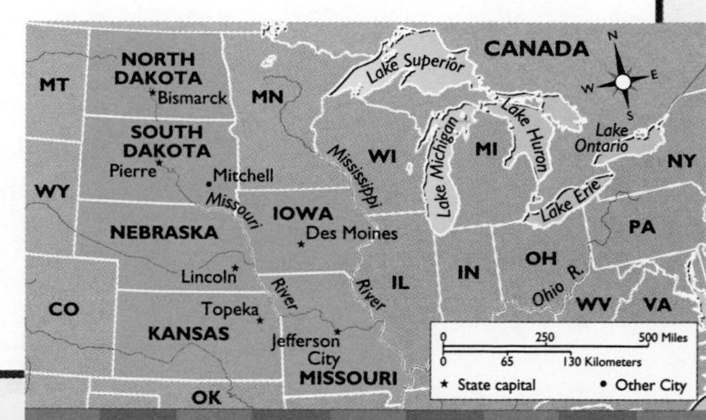

Guided Instruction

13 DRAW CONCLUSIONS The children have been away from home overnight. What do you think their parents will say to them when they see them again? What will the children say to their parents? Role-play the conversation you think Tiblo and Tanksi might have with their parents.
Character/Role-Play

Minilesson

REVIEW/MAINTAIN

Suffixes

Compile a list of familiar words to which the suffix *-ful* can be added. You may want to include these words from the story: *joy*, *forget*, and *thank*.

- Have students add the suffix *-ful* to each word and tell how the new ending changes its meaning.

Activity Ask students to suggest other endings, such as *-ness* and *-less*. Have them form pairs. One partner can suggest an ending and the other can supply words to which that ending can be added. The first partner can then explain how the new ending changes the meaning of the base word.

Guided Instruction

(14) **DRAW CONCLUSIONS** Look at the picture on pages 218–219. What do the people seem to be doing? (They seem to be giving a party for the wolf and bringing him presents.) What conclusion can you draw from this observation? (The people are grateful to the wolf.)

Activity

Cross Curricular: Social Studies

PLAINS HORSES Explorers from Spain brought the horse to America. Some horses made their way to the Great Plains to become an important part of Native American life.

RESEARCH AND INQUIRY Have students find pictures that show how the Plains people decorated their horses. Then ask students to write brief reports and illustrate them. ▶ **Linguistic**

Tiblo told how the wolf had brought them home. Everyone walked into the hills to thank the wolf. They spread a blanket for him to sit on. They gave him necklaces and other beautiful gifts.

There has been close kinship with the Wolf People for as long as anyone can remember. That is what they say. 

Guided Instruction

15 **MAKE INFERENCES** Do you think that people who live in the Plains area today feel the same kinship with the wolf that the characters in this story did? Explain. (Most people today are afraid of wolves. Farmers worry that wolves will kill their farm animals.)

TEACHING TIP

MANAGEMENT As students read aloud, make observations about fluency and decoding skills. Classify problems by type, such as:

- reading rate
- fluency, accuracy, and expression
- decoding, using letter-sound correspondences
- recognizing common vowel spelling patterns

Minilesson

REVIEW/MAINTAIN

Summarize

Explain to students that summarizing a story means stating the main events in proper sequence. Compare a story detail, which should not be included in a summary, with a main event, which should be included.

Ask children to review the Cause-and-Effect chart to help them summarize the selection.

Activity Tell students that an outline is one kind of summary. Help students make an outline of the story.

Guided Instruction

16 **CAUSE AND EFFECT** Use the Cause-and-Effect chart. How did the main events affect the characters and cause other events?

CAUSE	EFFECT
The people leave the Plains to pick berries in the hills.	Tiblo and Tanksi don't know their way around the new place.
Tiblo and Tanksi wander away.	They get lost.
When it gets dark, the children feel cold and tired.	Tiblo looks for shelter and finds a cave.
Tiblo dreams about a friendly wolf.	He asks a wolf to lead them home.
The wolf brings the children home.	The village people become friends with the wolf.

RETELL THE STORY Ask volunteers to tell the major events of the story. Students may refer to their charts. Then have partners write one or two sentences that summarize the story. Have them focus on the main characters' problem and how it is solved. *Summarize*

STUDENT SELF-ASSESSMENT

- How did analyzing cause-and-effect relationships help me understand the story?
- How did making the Cause-and-Effect chart help me?

TRANSFERRING THE STRATEGY

- When might I try using this strategy again?
- In what other reading could the chart help?

The wolves are no longer heard calling in the evenings at berry-picking time. Hunters have killed and driven them away with guns and traps and poisons. People say that the wolves will return when we, like Tiblo and Tanksi, have the wolves in our hearts and dreams again.

220

REREADING FOR *Fluency*

Have the class choral read a section of the story. Encourage students to use punctuation as clues for changes in pausing and inflection.

READING RATE You may want to evaluate a student's reading rate. Have the student read aloud from *Dream Wolf* for one minute. Ask the student to place a self-stick note after the last word read. Then count the number of words he or she has read.

Alternatively, you could assess small groups or the whole class together by having students count words and record their own scores.

A Running Record form provided in **Diagnostic/Placement Evaluation** will help you evaluate reading rate(s).

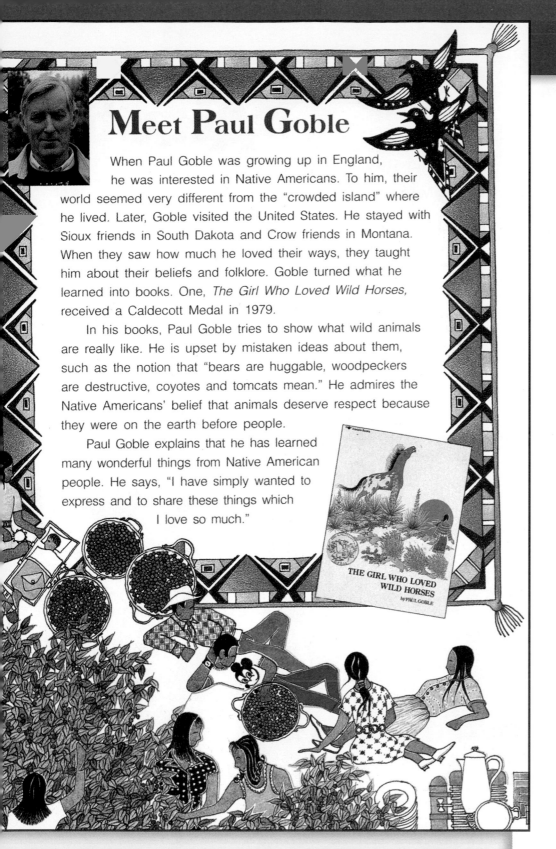

Meet Paul Goble

When Paul Goble was growing up in England, he was interested in Native Americans. To him, their world seemed very different from the "crowded island" where he lived. Later, Goble visited the United States. He stayed with Sioux friends in South Dakota and Crow friends in Montana. When they saw how much he loved their ways, they taught him about their beliefs and folklore. Goble turned what he learned into books. One, *The Girl Who Loved Wild Horses,* received a Caldecott Medal in 1979.

In his books, Paul Goble tries to show what wild animals are really like. He is upset by mistaken ideas about them, such as the notion that "bears are huggable, woodpeckers are destructive, coyotes and tomcats mean." He admires the Native Americans' belief that animals deserve respect because they were on the earth before people.

Paul Goble explains that he has learned many wonderful things from Native American people. He says, "I have simply wanted to express and to share these things which I love so much."

THE GIRL WHO LOVED WILD HORSES by PAUL GOBLE

LITERARY RESPONSE

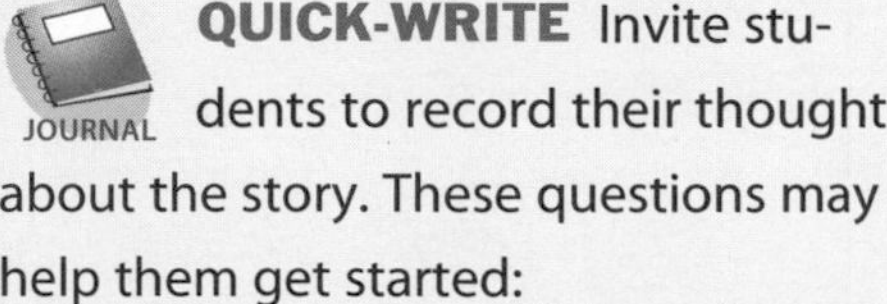

QUICK-WRITE Invite students to record their thoughts about the story. These questions may help them get started:

- Have you ever had an experience in which an animal has helped you? How does your experience compare with Tiblo's story?
- What did you like most about this story?

ORAL RESPONSE Invite students to share their feelings about the wolf and the villagers with the class. Encourage them to refer to the pictures as well as to the text.

Guided Instruction

Return to Predictions and Purposes

Have students review their Predictions chart.

How does the actual outcome of the story compare with their predictions?

PREDICTIONS	WHAT HAPPENED
Two children get lost.	They find shelter in a cave.
They meet a wolf.	The wolf guides them home.

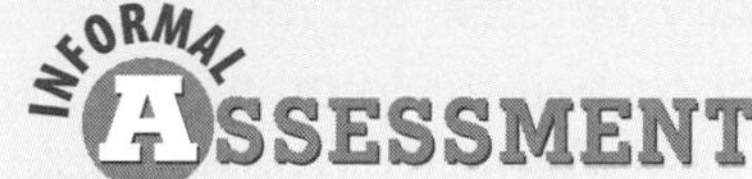

ANALYZE CAUSE AND EFFECT

HOW TO ASSESS

- Have students review the effects of each event in the story and compare them with the predictions they made.
- Ask students if the story changed what they thought about wolves.

Students should recognize that as a result of Tiblo's experience with the wolf, Tiblo and the other village people learned to respect all wolves.

FOLLOW UP If students have trouble analyzing cause and effect, ask them what the villagers might have felt about the wolf if he had harmed the children.

Story Questions

Have students discuss or write answers to the questions on page 222.

Answers:

1. They were wandering around a new area alone. *Literal/Cause and Effect*
2. The dream encouraged Tiblo to ask the real wolf for help. *Inferential/Conclusions*
3. It explains that people once felt close to wild animals. *Inferential/Cause and Effect*
4. This story is mainly about two children who make friends with a wolf and are saved by it. *Critical/Summarize*
5. Answers will vary. Possible answer: The wolf in this story is helpful. In other stories, wolves are often harmful. *Critical/Reading Across Texts*

Write Directions For a full writing process lesson on explanatory writing, see pages 225K–225L.

Story Questions & Activities

1. What were Tiblo and Tanksi doing when they got lost?
2. How did Tiblo's dream help the two children get home? Explain.
3. Legends often explain why things are the way they are. What might this legend explain?
4. What is this story mostly about?
5. How is the wolf in this story different from wolves in other stories that you know?

Write Directions
Pretend you are the wolf in the story. Write directions for Tiblo and Tanksi to get home. Should they turn right at a big rock? Left at a stream? Be sure to give the directions in a clear, simple order.

Meeting Individual Needs

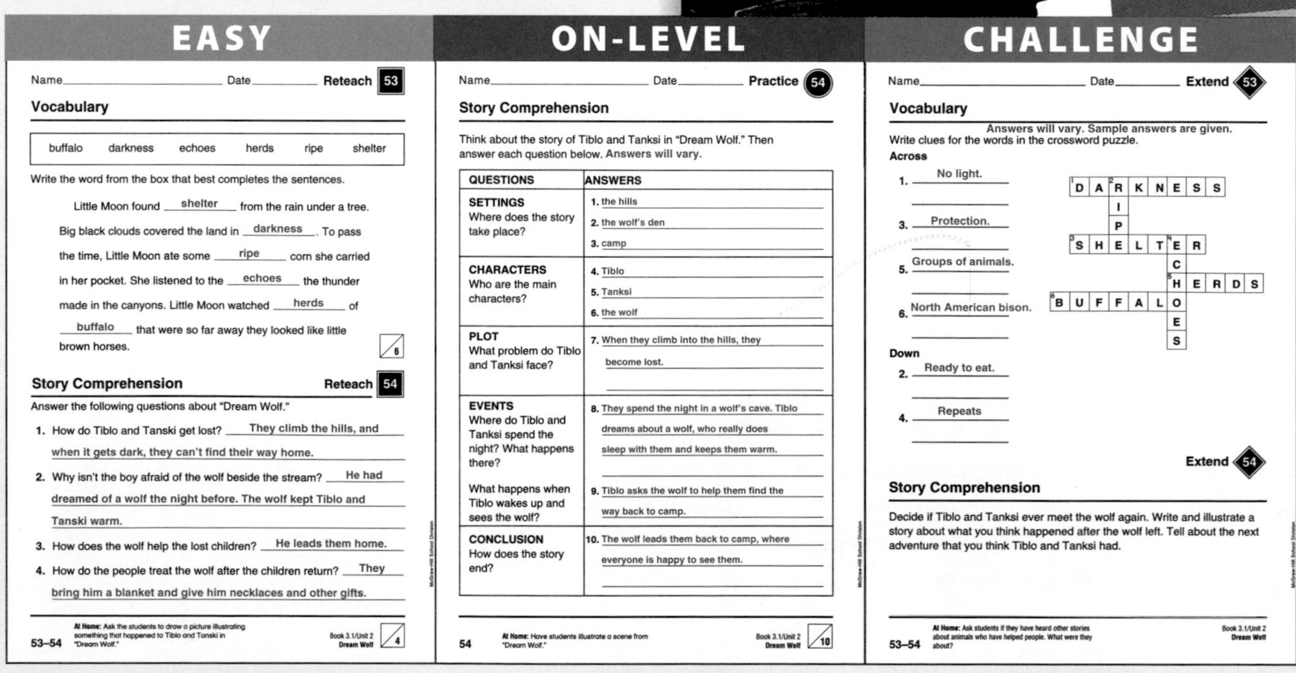

EASY

Name________ Date______ **Reteach 53**

Vocabulary

buffalo darkness echoes herds ripe shelter

Write the word from the box that best completes the sentences.

Little Moon found shelter from the rain under a tree. Big black clouds covered the land in darkness. To pass the time, Little Moon ate some ripe corn she carried in her pocket. She listened to the echoes the thunder made in the canyons. Little Moon watched herds of buffalo that were so far away they looked like little brown horses. /6

Story Comprehension **Reteach 54**

Answer the following questions about "Dream Wolf."

1. How do Tiblo and Tanski get lost? They climb the hills, and when it gets dark, they can't find their way home.
2. Why isn't the boy afraid of the wolf beside the stream? He had dreamed of a wolf the night before. The wolf kept Tiblo and Tanski warm.
3. How does the wolf help the lost children? He leads them home.
4. How do the people treat the wolf after the children return? They bring him a blanket and give him necklaces and other gifts.

53–54 **At Home:** Ask the students to draw a picture illustrating something that happened to Tiblo and Tanski in "Dream Wolf." Book 3.1/Unit 2 **Dream Wolf** /4

Reteach, 54

ON-LEVEL

Name________ Date______ **Practice 54**

Story Comprehension

Think about the story of Tiblo and Tanksi in "Dream Wolf." Then answer each question below. Answers will vary.

QUESTIONS	ANSWERS
SETTINGS Where does the story take place?	1. the hills 2. the wolf's den 3. camp
CHARACTERS Who are the main characters?	4. Tiblo 5. Tanksi 6. the wolf
PLOT What problem do Tiblo and Tanksi face?	7. When they climb into the hills, they become lost.
EVENTS Where do Tiblo and Tanksi spend the night? What happens there?	8. They spend the night in a wolf's cave. Tiblo dreams about a wolf, who really does sleep with them and keeps them warm.
What happens when Tiblo wakes up and sees the wolf?	9. Tiblo asks the wolf to help them find the way back to camp.
CONCLUSION How does the story end?	10. The wolf leads them back to camp, where everyone is happy to see them.

54 **At Home:** Have students illustrate a scene from "Dream Wolf." Book 3.1/Unit 2 **Dream Wolf** /10

Practice, 54

CHALLENGE

Name________ Date______ **Extend 53**

Vocabulary

Answers will vary. Sample answers are given.
Write clues for the words in the crossword puzzle.

Across
1. No light.
3. Protection.
5. Groups of animals.
6. North American bison.

Down
2. Ready to eat.
4. Repeats

1 DARKNESS
2 RIPE
3 SHELTER
4 ECHOES
5 HERDS
6 BUFFALO

Extend 54

Story Comprehension

Decide if Tiblo and Tanksi ever meet the wolf again. Write and illustrate a story about what you think happened after the wolf left. Tell about the next adventure that you think Tiblo and Tanksi had.

53–54 **At Home:** Ask students if they have heard other stories about animals who have helped people. What were they about? Book 3.1/Unit 2 **Dream Wolf**

Extend, 54

Draw Pictures

Pretend that a wolf goes to visit a skunk. What might be fun about the visit? What might some problems be? Draw a series of pictures showing what might happen. Write a caption for each picture.

Make a Map

Find out which part of the United States is called the Great Plains. Trace a map of the United States, label each state, and then shade in the area that makes up the Great Plains.

Find Out More

Did you know that some kinds of wild animals, such as wolves, live in groups but others do not? Research three different types of animals that live in groups. Also find out what the group is called. For example, a group of wolves is called a pack.

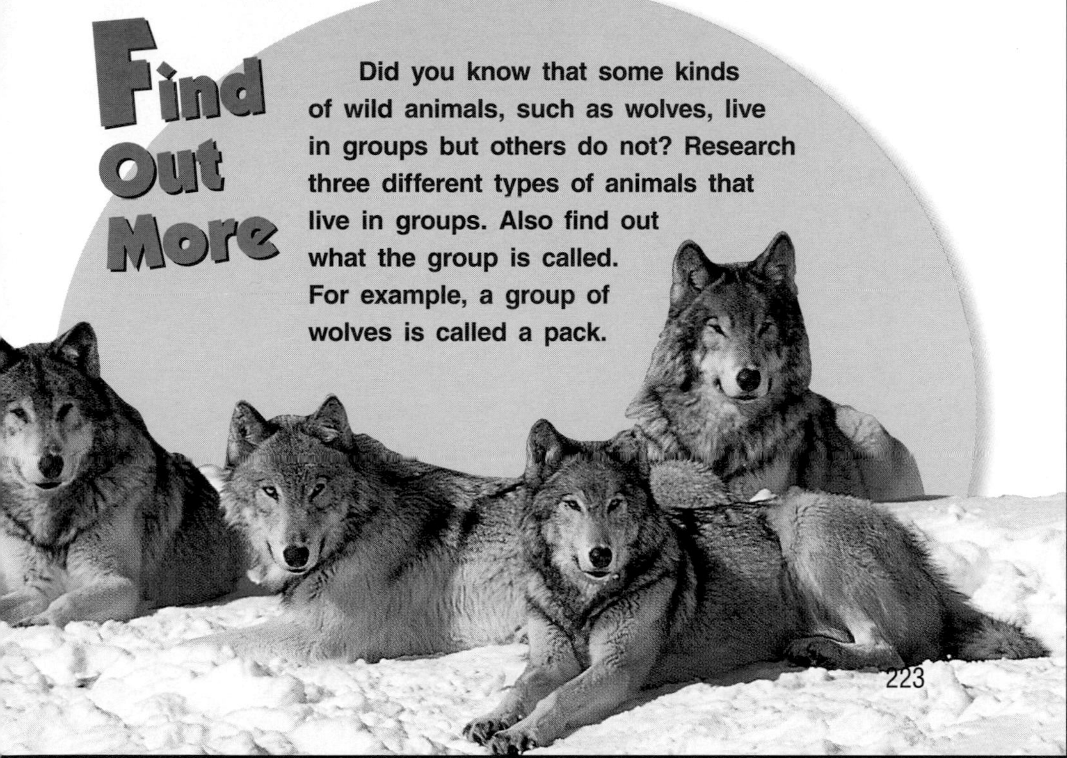

223

Story Activities

Draw Pictures

Materials: construction paper, felt-tipped markers, colored pencils, crayons

GROUP Ask groups to brainstorm a list of ways that a wolf and a skunk might have fun together. Have them think about the characteristics of both animals. Ask each student to illustrate and caption the events of the wolf's visit. Have the groups present their finished pictures as storyboards.

Make a Map

Materials: map of the United States with each state easily identifiable, tracing paper, pencils, colored pencils

PARTNERS Have students use an encyclopedia or atlas to identify the Great Plains. Ask them to use their colored pencils to shade in this area.

Find Out More

PARTNERS **RESEARCH/INQUIRY** Encourage students to use at least three different resources to identify their animal groups. Have students check out the science and reference section of their school library and the Internet. Then have them hold a panel discussion on their findings.

interNET CONNECTION See ***www.mhschool.com/reading*** for more information on the topic.

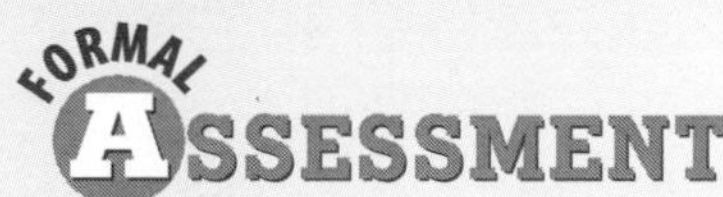

FORMAL ASSESSMENT

After page 223, see the Selection Assessment.

Study Skills

REFERENCE SOURCES

Students will:

- use the encyclopedia to find information.
- identify entry words and guide words.

PREPARE Display **Teaching Chart 45.** Have students look at encyclopedias to become familiar with them. Ask students how they differ from a dictionary.

TEACH Review how guide words help us to find the entries we want. Have students look up a few entries. Point out that some entries may just refer to others.

PRACTICE Have students answer questions 1–5. Review their answers. **1.** 26 Volumes **2.** Volume 19 **3.** Sioux Falls College, Sioux Indians **4.** North Dakota, South Dakota, Nebraska, Montana (also Wyoming) **5.** Schools, Colleges, and Universities

ASSESS/CLOSE Have students brainstorm a list of Native American nations. Then use encyclopedias to research where in the United States these groups were or are located.

Use an Encyclopedia

An encyclopedia is a set of books that contains information on many subjects. Each book within the set is called a volume. The volumes are arranged in alphabetical order. So are the entries inside each volume.

Sioux Falls College, *See under* SCHOOLS, COLLEGES, AND UNIVERSITIES.

Sioux Indians, the popular name of a large tribe of North American Indians who lived in North Dakota, South Dakota, Nebraska, Montana, and Wyoming. Calling themselves the Dakota, they were known as the Sioux, after a French name given them. They were divided into the Santee, Yankton, and Teton groups.

Like other Plains Indians, the Sioux hunted buffalo, which provided them with food, hides for clothing and teepees, and bone and horn for implements.

Use the set of encyclopedias and the sample entries to answer these questions.

1. How many volumes are in this set of encyclopedias?
2. In which volume will you find an entry called "Sioux Indians"?
3. What are the two entries shown in the sample?
4. What are four states where the Sioux lived?
5. For more information on Sioux Falls College, what is another entry that you should check in this set of encyclopedias?

Meeting Individual Needs

EASY

Name________ Date______ **Reteach 55**

Use an Encyclopedia

An **encyclopedia** gives you information on different subjects. Bigger encyclopedias are divided into separate books. The topics inside each book are listed in alphabetical order.

1	2	3	4	5	6	7	8	9	10	11	12	13	14	15	16	17	18	19	20	21	22	23	24
A	B	C	D	E	F	G	H	I	J	K	L	M	N	O	P	Q/R	S–Sn	So–Sz	T	U	V	W/X Y/Z	Index

Use the letters on the encyclopedias to help you answer these questions.

1. What is the number of the book where a word beginning with the letter **B** could be found? 2
2. Which book has topics that begin with the letters **Q** and **R**? 17 or Q/R
3. What book would tell you about Native Americans? 14 or N
4. Would South Dakota and Squirrels be in the **S–Sn** or the **So–Sz** book? the So–Sz book
5. Which book contains a listing of all the topics found in the other books? the index

5 Book 3.1/Unit 2 **Dream Wolf** **At Home:** Have students list five subjects and then write the number and letter of the book where each could be found. 55

Reteach, 55

ON-LEVEL

Name________ Date______ **Practice 55**

Use an Encyclopedia

Natural Bridge—Navigation

Natural Bridge is a bridge made from stone by nature. Wind or rain or rivers carved away the stone over many years. Usually softer stone is removed from under harder stone. A bridge of harder stone is all that remains.

Nauru is a small island country in the Pacific Ocean. It is the third smallest nation in the world. Monaco and Vatican City are smaller. It's greatest resource is phosphate, a substance used to make fertilizer.

Navajo, a Native American group who have lived in the southwestern United States since around 1000 A.D. They are the largest Native American group in the United States. Many members still live in houses called hogans, made of earth and logs. See also Indian, American

Naval Reserve. See Navy, United States

Fill in the blank spaces below based on the encyclopedia page.

Entry Words:

Natural bridge
Nauru
Navajo
Naval Reserve

Cross-References:

See also Indian, American
See Navy, United States

Guide Words:

Natural bridge
navigation

8 Book 3.1/Unit 2 **Dream Wolf** **At Home:** Ask students if they would look on this page for information about narwhal whales. Why or why not? 55

Practice, 55

CHALLENGE

Name________ Date______ **Extend 55**

Use an Encyclopedia

You and your family are on the way to pick berries to make pies and cakes. You want to make sure you get berries that will be sweet and tasty. You also want to make sure that any berries you pick can be used in food.

Here are some different kinds of berries you could pick. Describe how you would find out about each one in an encyclopedia. Then pick one of these berries to research in your school library's encyclopedia. Write what you find out on another piece of paper.

boysenberry
elderberry
strawberry
blackberry
raspberry

Let's Go Berry-Picking

Answers will vary, but should demonstrate understanding of how to look up a subject in an encyclopedia.

Book 3.1/Unit 2 **Dream Wolf** **At Home:** Have students research information about wolves. 55

Extend, 55

TEST POWER

Test Tip
Read each answer choice carefully. Then choose the best one.

DIRECTIONS:
Read the story. Then read each question about the story.

SAMPLE

The Polar Bear Club

In some parts of the country, groups of people celebrate the New Year in a special way. In towns near the ocean, people go for a swim in the freezing cold water on the first day in January! One of these groups of people is called the Polar Bear Club.

All kinds of people are members of the Polar Bear Club. They swim in the ocean even in the middle of the winter!

"There's nothing as fun as freezing water filled with warm hearts," says Joe Cabona. "I don't stay in for long," Joe says. "But I stay in long enough to celebrate the New Year. Then my friends and I all go over to someone's house and drink hot apple cider. It's a special occasion!"

1 In this story, the word occasion means—

- ○ water
- ○ heart
- ○ person
- ● event

2 Why do the Polar Bear Club members swim in the ocean in January?

- ● To celebrate the New Year
- ○ They like cold water
- ○ So they can catch a cold
- ○ To warm their hearts

225

Test Power

THE PRINCETON REVIEW

Read the Page

Instruct students to ask themselves *why?* or *how?* when they come across facts in the story. Line 2 says, "people celebrate . . . in a special way." *Why* do they celebrate? *How* do they celebrate?

Discuss the Questions

QUESTION 1: This question asks students to define a word in context. Explain to students that even if they don't know what a word means, they can look for clues in the surrounding sentences. The characters are celebrating a special occasion. Ask: What does that mean? Refer back to the story.

QUESTION 2: This question requires students to locate information in the story. Shorter stories are full of information. Instruct students to refer back to the story.

ITBS/TEST PREPARATION

TERRANOVA/TEST PREPARATION

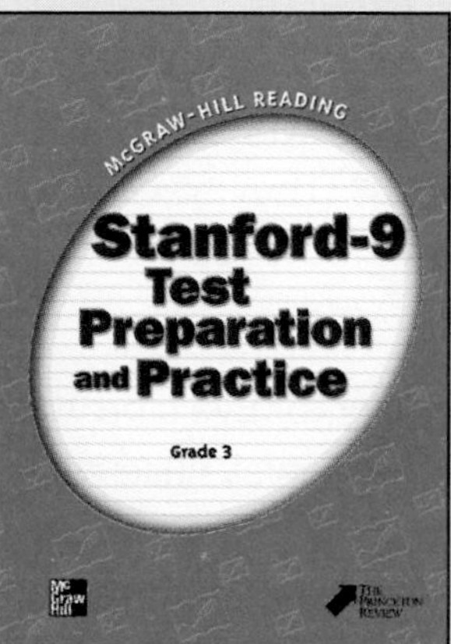

SAT 9/TEST PREPARATION

Answers to Story Questions

1. Danny is sick and needs a doctor.
2. If they didn't try it, Danny would probably get even sicker. If they did try it, they might hit the ice and damage the ship.
3. Dad and Eva probably took Danny to see a doctor.
4. The story is about a young girl who has a good idea. The idea is to follow an orca towards land.
5. Answers will vary.

Story Questions and Writing Activity

1. Why do Eva and Dad want to reach land quickly?
2. What did Dad and the captain have to consider when they made the decision to follow the orca?
3. What do you think happened once the ship reached land?
4. What is the story mostly about?
5. Do you think *Dream Wolf* would have been able to help Eva? Why or why not?

What Do You See?

Suppose that you are standing on the deck of the *Adventure*. Draw what you see. Write a title for your drawing. Label the items in your drawing.

from *Lost at Sea*

Leveled Books

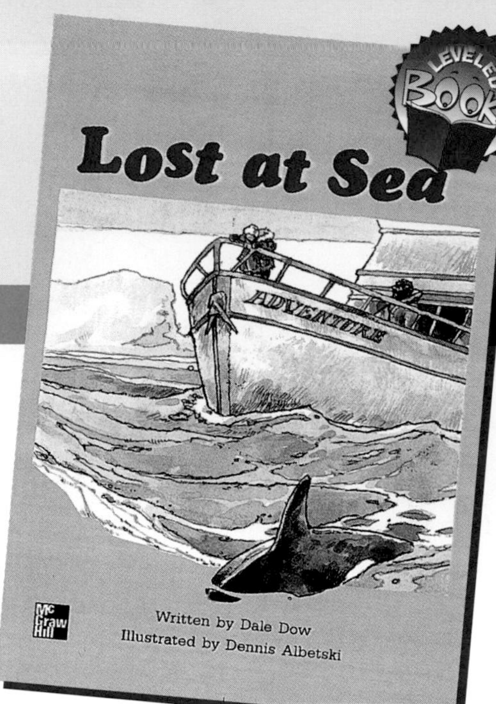

EASY

Lost at Sea

Consonant Clusters

☑ **Cause and Effect**

☑ **Instructional Vocabulary:** ***herds, ripe, shelter, darkness, buffalo, echoes***

Guided Reading

PREVIEW AND PREDICT Conduct a **picture walk** up to page 10. Have students discuss illustrations. Ask: What can you tell from the title? Do you think the characters are in danger?

SET PURPOSES Have students write down questions that they would like to have answered by the story. For example, one question might be: How will the characters get back to shore?

READ THE BOOK Have students read the story independently. After they have read the story, use the questions below to guide students' rereading of the story.

Page 2: Where does the story take place? (the ocean) ***Setting***

Page 4: What did Eva mean when she said the orcas traveled in *herds*? (They traveled in groups.) What did Eva's father call groups of whales? (pods) ***Vocabulary***

Page 6: Why is it necessary for Eva's brother to get back to shore right away? (He is seriously sick and needs a doctor.) ***Cause and Effect***

Page 14: Why did the captain decide to follow Eva's plan? (it was their only hope of reaching shore.) ***Make Inferences***

Page 16: Find the words *screamed*, *sprang*, and *splashed*. What other words begin with the same consonants as these three words? ***Phonics and Decoding***

RETURN TO PREDICTIONS AND PURPOSES Review students' predictions and reasons for reading. Which predictions were accurate? Which questions were answered?

LITERARY RESPONSE Discuss these questions:

- Do you think the captain would have followed the orcas to shore if Eva hadn't suggested it? Why or why not?
- Have you ever had an idea that helped solve a problem?

Also see the story questions and activity in *Lost at Sea*.

See the Phonics **CD-ROM** for practice using initial consonant clusters.

Leveled Books

INDEPENDENT

The Clever Jackal

- Cause and Effect
- Instructional Vocabulary: *echoes, buffalo, shelter, ripe, darkness, herds*

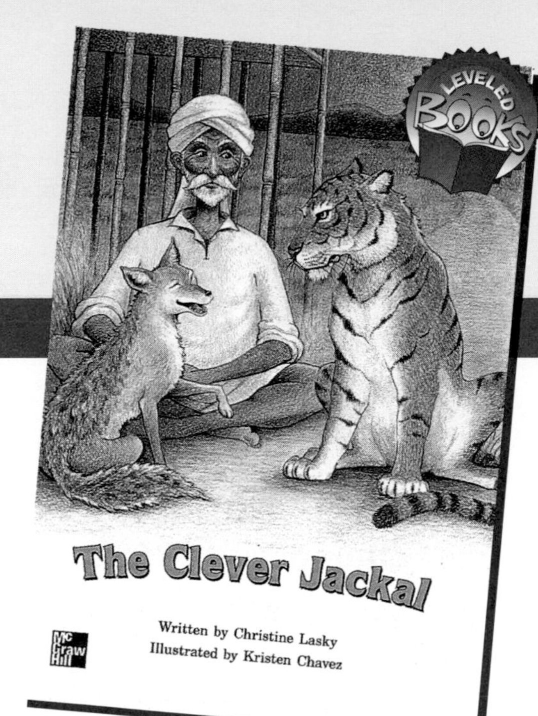

LEVELED Books
The Clever Jackal
Written by Christine Lasky
Illustrated by Kristen Chavez
Mc Graw Hill

Guided Reading

PREVIEW AND PREDICT Conduct a **picture walk** to page 9. Have students discuss the illustrations. Ask: Do you think the man should let the tiger out of its cage? What do you think is going to happen to the man?

SET PURPOSES Have students write down questions that they would like to have answered by the story. For example, one question might be: Does the jackal get the tiger back into its cage?

READ THE BOOK Have students read the story independently. After they have read the story, return to the text to apply strategies.

Page 5: What happens after the man frees the tiger? (The tiger decides to eat the man.) *Sequence of Events*

Page 7: How does the water buffalo feel about pulling a plow? (He is angry.) *Make Inferences*

Page 8–9: What kind of shelter might a tree give? (It might protect creatures from the hot sun and from strong winds.) *Vocabulary*

Page 12–16: Why did the tiger go back into the cage? (because the jackal tricked him) *Cause and Effect*

RETURN TO PREDICTIONS AND PURPOSES Review students' predictions and reasons for reading. Which predictions were accurate? How did students arrive at their predictions?

LITERARY RESPONSE Discuss these questions:

- What was the man's first thought about setting the tiger free?
- Do you think the man was wrong to feel sorry for the tiger? How else might he have been kind to the tiger without putting himself in danger?

Also see the questions and activity in *The Clever Jackal*.

Answers to Story Questions

1. The main characters are an elderly man, a tiger, and a jackal.
2. The water buffalo and the tree helped people, but people didn't treat them well.
3. The tiger would probably eat the man.
4. The story is about how the jackal outsmarts the tiger and saves the man's life.
5. Answers will vary.

Story Questions and Writing Activity

1. Who are the main characters of the story?
2. Why did the water buffalo and the tree refuse to help the elderly man?
3. What do you think would happen if the man freed the tiger again?
4. What is the story mostly about?
5. If Tiblo and Tansi from *Dream Wolf* visited the man in this story, what ideas about animals might they share? How might their views be different?

Thank You!

Draw a picture that shows how the man might reward the jackal. Write a short conversation the two might have together.

from *The Clever Jackal*

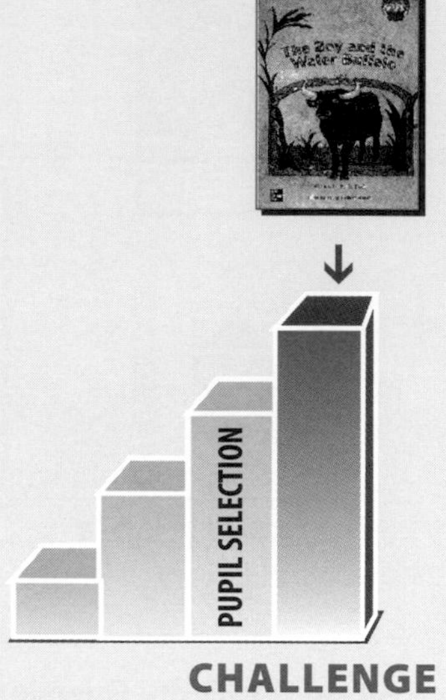

Leveled Books

CHALLENGE

The Boy and the Water Buffalo

- ☑ **Cause and Effect**
- ☑ **Instructional Vocabulary:** ***darkness, buffalo, echoes, shelter, ripe, herds***

Answers to Story Questions

1. It takes place in Indonesia.
2. A feast appeared.
3. The boy might have never found his way home.
4. The story is about a buffalo with magic horns that helps a boy who has become lost.
5. Answers will vary.

Story Questions and Writing Activity

1. Where does the story take place?
2. What happened when the boy rubbed the buffalo's horns?
3. What might have happened if the boy had not trusted the buffalo?
4. What is the story mostly about?
5. If the boy from this story met Tiblo from *Dream Wolf,* what might they talk about?

Make a Wish!

Imagine that you are the boy returning to your village. How would you convince your neighbors and family that the magic horns work? Write an explanation. Tell what you would wish for and why.

from *The Boy and the Water Buffalo*

Guided Reading

PREVIEW AND PREDICT Conduct a **picture walk** up to page 11. Ask: Will the buffalo help the boy find his way home? Have students record their predictions.

SET PURPOSES Students should decide what they want to learn before they read the story. Have students write down questions that they would like to have answered by the story. For example, they might ask, "Why do wonderful things, like the appearance of feasts, happen around the buffalo?"

READ THE BOOK Have students read the story independently. After they have read the story, return to the text to apply strategies.

Pages 2–3: Why does the boy go into the mountains? (to escape the heat) ***Cause and Effect***

Page 4–5: How was this water buffalo different from other water buffaloes? (It had golden horns and could talk.) ***Compare and Contrast***

Page 10: Are ripe berries usually sweet and juicy or sour and dry? (sweet and juicy) ***Vocabulary***

Pages 12–13: What happened to the buffalo while the boy slept? (It disappeared.) ***Plot***

Page 14–16: How did the boy convince the villagers that his story was true? (He used the buffalo horns to make a feast appear.) ***Cause and Effect***

RETURN TO PREDICTIONS AND PURPOSES Review students' predictions and reasons for reading.

LITERARY RESPONSE Discuss these questions:

- What would you have done if you had been lost like the boy in the story?
- What lesson about growing up do you think this story teaches?

Also see the questions and activity in *The Boy and the Water Buffalo.*

Connecting Texts

CAUSE-AND-EFFECT CHARTS Write the story titles on a chart. Discuss with students the causes and effects of the events in the stories. Call on volunteers from each reading level and write their suggestions on the chart.

Dream Wolf	Lost at Sea	The Clever Jackal	The Boy and the Water Buffalo
• Because Tiblo had dreamed of a kind wolf, he trusted the wolf that saved him. • Because the villagers were grateful to the wolf they became friendly to all wolves.	• Seeing the orca caused Eva to think of her idea. • Because the orca could find a path through the ice, it showed the captain the way to shore.	• Because the tiger was a hungry predator, he wanted to eat the man. • Because the jackal was clever, he got the tiger back into his cage.	• Because the buffalo was different from other buffalo, the boy trusted it. • Because the boy used the horn to produce a feast, the villagers believed him.

Viewing/Representing

GROUP PRESENTATIONS Divide the class into groups, one for each of the four books read in the lesson. (For *Dream Wolf* combine students of different reading levels.) Have each group act out the story using puppets made from socks.

AUDIENCE RESPONSE Ask students to pay attention to each group's presentation. Allow time for questions after each presentation. Encourage students to ask the characters why they acted as they did.

Research and Inquiry

MORE ABOUT ANIMALS HELPING PEOPLE Have students discuss how some animals, such as guide dogs, help people. Invite students to do the following:

- Write to societies that train animals to help people and ask for information about the skills animals can learn.
- Ask people who have pets about the ways their pets may help them (act as company, provide protection, make them laugh).
- Invite an expert on working animals to come and talk to the class about their subject.

*inter***NET CONNECTION** Have students visit ***www.mhschool.com/reading*** for links to Web sites about animals helping people.

OBJECTIVES

Students will identify and set up cause-and-effect relationships.

TEACHING TIP

MANAGEMENT Turn magnetic photos into learning centers. Mount worksheets, workbook pages, and activity cards in the books. Students take albums to their desks and work with wipe-off crayons. Place answer keys at the back of each book for self-checking.

Review Cause and Effect

PREPARE

Discuss Cause and Effect Review how "one thing leads to another" in a story, and how some events cause effects—new events that affect the characters.

TEACH

Read "From the Stream" and Model the Skill Ask students to pay close attention to cause and effect as you read the **Teaching Chart 46** passage with them.

From the Stream

Since Tiblo had survived a night away from home with a wolf, he was sure he would be allowed to play with the older boys. But his mother said that he was still too young and made him stay with the women. Tiblo just had to prove himself. But what could he do?

He remembered the wolf stopping at a beautiful stream on their way home. In that stream were the biggest fish Tiblo had ever seen.

So, when no one was looking, Tiblo ran off toward the stream. If he was lucky, he would bring home the biggest fish in the stream.

Teaching Chart 46

Discuss clues that would help readers to make predictions about new events as they think about how the events affect each other.

MODEL Near the end of the first paragraph, it says that Tiblo wants to prove himself. This could be the beginning of a cause-and-effect relationship. I'll look out for the effect. I know that sometimes when people are trying to prove themselves they do something risky. I wonder if that will be the effect this time.

PRACTICE

Make Predictions About Cause and Effect

Ask students to underline clues in "From the Stream" that can help them to make predictions about the outcome. Have students focus on what effects they think Tiblo's actions will have. Help them set up a Cause-and-Effect chart such as this: ▶ **Spatial/Interpersonal**

CAUSE AND EFFECT
Because Tiblo wants to prove himself,
he sneaks off to the stream.
Because Tiblo sneaks off to the stream,
______________________________.

ASSESS/CLOSE

Brainstorm Endings and Provide Causal Events

Have students brainstorm a list of possible endings for the passage they have just read. Then ask them to decide what actions Tiblo must take to obtain each desired outcome. Have them complete their chart.

ALTERNATE TEACHING STRATEGY

CAUSE AND EFFECT

For a different approach to teaching this skill, see page T60.

SELF-SELECTED Reading

Students may choose from the following titles.

ANTHOLOGY

- *Dream Wolf*

LEVELED BOOKS

- *Lost at Sea*
- *The Clever Jackal*
- *The Boy and the Water Buffalo*

Bibliography, pages T76–T77

Meeting Individual Needs for Comprehension

EASY

Name______________ Date________ **Reteach 56**

Cause and Effect

In a story, events cause other events to happen. Events also affect how characters respond. The following example shows a **cause** and its **effect.**

Cause	Effect
People drive away the wolves.	People don't hear the wolf call in summer anymore.

Think about what happened in "Dream Wolf." Then read each cause before writing down the effect it had.

1. **Cause:** The berries in the valleys get ripe at the end of each summer. What effect does this have on the people living on the plains?
   Effect: The people leave the plains to camp near the berry bushes.
2. **Cause:** The boy and girl are tired of picking fruit with their mother. What do they do?
   Effect: They climb into the hills.
3. **Cause:** The sun went down while the children were up in the hills. How does the darkness affect the children?
   Effect: The darkness causes the children to get lost.
4. **Cause:** The boy has a good dream about a wolf. How does this dream affect how the boy feels when he sees a wolf?
   Effect: When the boy sees a wolf the next day, he is not afraid to ask for help.

56 **At Home:** Ask students to tell you what might cause the wolves to come back to the land described in "Dream Wolf." Book 3.1/Unit 2 **Dream Wolf** 4

Reteach, 56

ON-LEVEL

Name______________ Date________ **Practice 56**

Cause and Effect

In "Dream Wolf," things happen that cause other events to occur. Answer the following questions about **cause** and **effect**.

1. Why do the people move from the plains to the hills and valleys? The berry bushes are ripe in the valleys.
2. What did Tiblo do when he became tired of picking berries? He decided to sneak off into the hills with Tanksi.
3. What effect did the sun going down have on the two children? They got lost.
4. While the children slept, a wolf came into the cave and kept them warm. What effect did this have on Tiblo's dreams? It caused Tiblo to have a dream about a wolf.
5. The wolf led the children back to their camp. What did the children then ask the wolf? They asked the wolf to live with them.
6. What did the people in the camp do when they saw the children coming down the hill? They galloped out on horses to bring the children home.
7. What has caused wolves to disappear from the hills where they used to live? Hunters have killed the wolves and driven them away.
8. When do the people say the wolves will return? When we have the wolves in our hearts and dreams again.

56 **At Home:** Have students draw a picture of a wolf. Book 3.1/Unit 2 **Dream Wolf** 8

Practice, 56

CHALLENGE

Name______________ Date________ **Extend 56**

Cause and Effect

Many things happen in the fall as the temperature changes. No matter where you live, the change in temperatu/e and amount of sun cause things to happen. Describe some of the effects that fall causes where you live.

1. About what time does the sun set at the beginning of August where you live? Answers will vary. Sample answers are shown.
   About what time does the sun set at the beginning of October?
   ____
2. Describe some effects that the change in temperature and the amount of sunlight has on plants where you live.
   The leaves fall.
   The flowers stop blooming.
   Fruit ripens.
3. Describe some effects that fall has on animals where you live.
   Birds fly south.
   Animals hibernate.
   Squirrels hide nuts.
4. Write a paragraph that tells what happens in the fall to plants, animals, and you.
   ____

56 **At Home:** Have students describe what happens to the plants where they live between October and January. Book 3.1/Unit 2 **Dream Wolf**

Extend, 56

LANGUAGE SUPPORT

Name______________ Date________

Cause and Effect

	If this...	Then what...	Infer easy or hard.
1.	We are lost.	Draw an unhappy boy and girl.	This is hard for the characters.
2.	We sleep with a wolf.	Draw boy and girl petting wolf.	This is easy for the characters.
3.	We see adults.	Draw the children safe with adults.	This is easy for the characters.

62 **Dream Wolf** • Language Support/Blackline Master 30 Grade 3

Language Support, 62

OBJECTIVES

Students will compare and contrast a character's experiences with their own.

LANGUAGE SUPPORT

ESL Show students two pieces of cloth, both of the same material but different colors. Ask students how they are alike and how they are different.

Review Compare and Contrast

PREPARE

Discuss Cause and Effect Explain to students that *to compare* is to point out the similarities between things and *to contrast* is to point out the differences between things.

TEACH

Read "Tiblo Shares His Adventure" and Model the Skill Have students read "Tiblo Shares His Adventure." Ask students to think about how this story compares to their own lives.

Tiblo Shares His Adventure

Each night after their evening meal, the people of the village gathered around the campfire to share their experiences of the day. Tiblo was very excited when it was his turn to speak. He told all the villagers about sleeping in the wolf's den and how, at first, he thought it was all a dream. Then he told about how the wolf led Tanski and him home, teaching them special things about nature along the way.

The people of the village felt proud. They praised Tiblo for befriending the wolf. Everyone agreed that he had been brave. It was then decided that Tiblo could play with the older boys.

Teaching Chart 47

Ask students to underline details that are like their own lives, and circle those that are different. Have students explain their choices.

MODEL After dinner I like to sit in the living room and read. The people in Tiblo's village don't have books or TVs. They sit around the campfire instead. That's very different. One thing is the same, though. They love to talk about and share their experiences. So do I.

PRACTICE

Create a Venn Diagram

Have students create a Venn diagram. Help them get started.

▶ **Spatial/Logical**

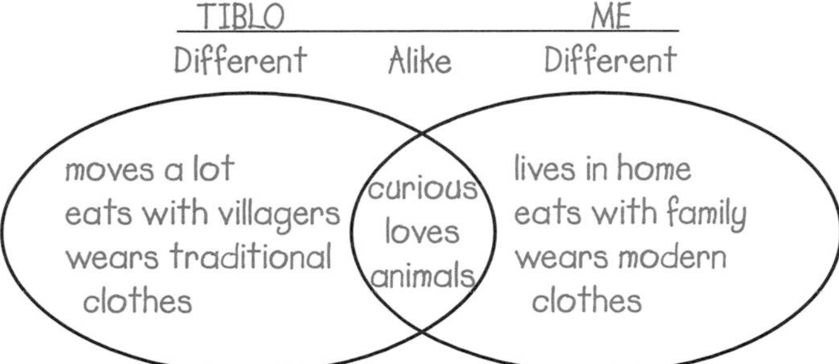

ASSESS/CLOSE

Compare/Contrast with Different Story

Have students create a Venn diagram of their favorite book or television show and their own lives. Have them summarize the similarities and differences.

ALTERNATE TEACHING STRATEGY

COMPARE AND CONTRAST

For a different approach to teaching this skill, see page T64.

LOOKING AHEAD

Students will apply this skill as they read the next selection, *Spiders at Work*.

Meeting Individual Needs for Comprehension

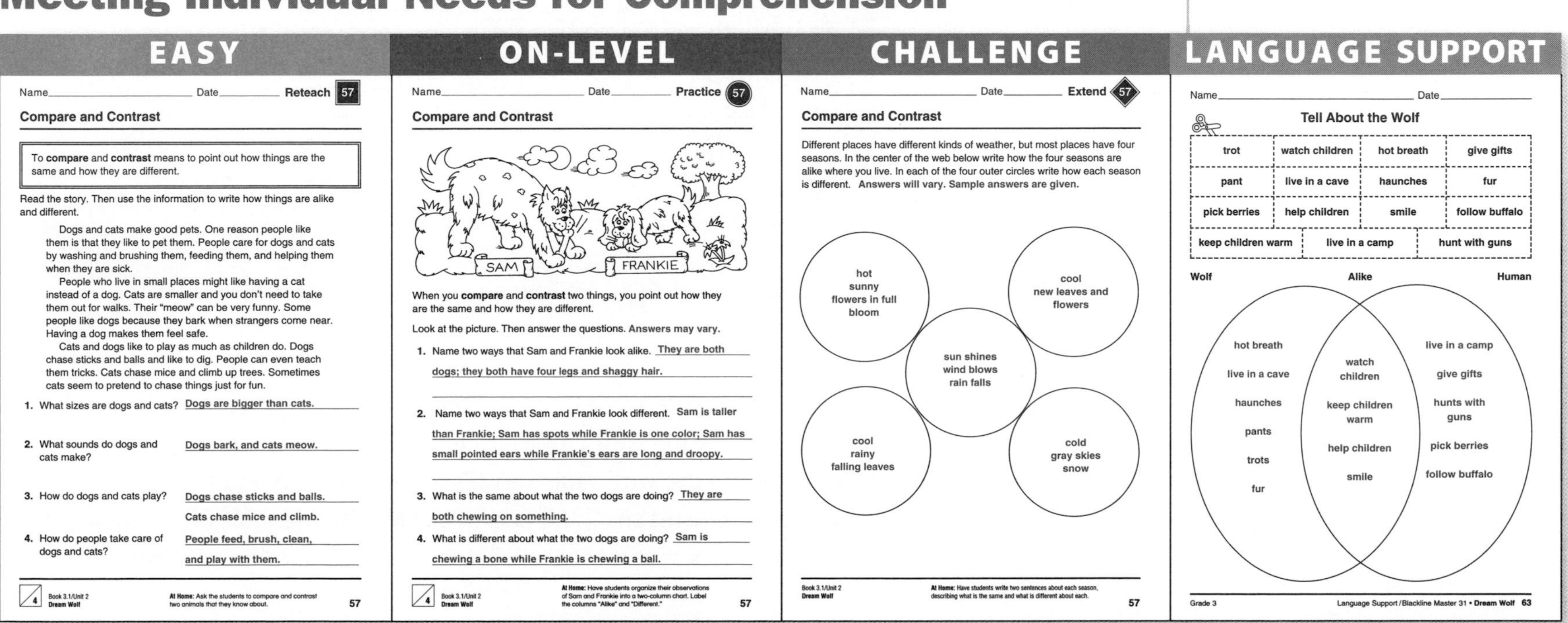

EASY

Name________ Date______ **Reteach 57**

Compare and Contrast

To **compare** and **contrast** means to point out how things are the same and how they are different.

Read the story. Then use the information to write how things are alike and different.

Dogs and cats make good pets. One reason people like them is that they like to pet them. People care for dogs and cats by washing and brushing them, feeding them, and helping them when they are sick.

People who live in small places might like having a cat instead of a dog. Cats are smaller and you don't need to take them out for walks. Their "meow" can be very funny. Some people like dogs because they bark when strangers come near. Having a dog makes them feel safe.

Cats and dogs like to play as much as children do. Dogs chase sticks and balls and like to dig. People can even teach them tricks. Cats chase mice and climb up trees. Sometimes cats seem to pretend to chase things just for fun.

1. What sizes are dogs and cats? **Dogs are bigger than cats.**
2. What sounds do dogs and cats make? **Dogs bark, and cats meow.**
3. How do dogs and cats play? **Dogs chase sticks and balls. Cats chase mice and climb.**
4. How do people take care of dogs and cats? **People feed, brush, clean, and play with them.**

4 Book 3.1/Unit 2 **Dream Wolf** — **At Home:** Ask the students to compare and contrast two animals that they know about. 57

ON-LEVEL

Name________ Date______ **Practice 57**

Compare and Contrast

SAM FRANKIE

When you **compare** and **contrast** two things, you point out how they are the same and how they are different.

Look at the picture. Then answer the questions. **Answers may vary.**

1. Name two ways that Sam and Frankie look alike. **They are both dogs; they both have four legs and shaggy hair.**
2. Name two ways that Sam and Frankie look different. **Sam is taller than Frankie; Sam has spots while Frankie is one color; Sam has small pointed ears while Frankie's ears are long and droopy.**
3. What is the same about what the two dogs are doing? **They are both chewing on something.**
4. What is different about what the two dogs are doing? **Sam is chewing a bone while Frankie is chewing a ball.**

4 Book 3.1/Unit 2 **Dream Wolf** — **At Home:** Have students organize their observations of Sam and Frankie into a two-column chart. Label the columns "Alike" and "Different." 57

CHALLENGE

Name________ Date______ **Extend 57**

Compare and Contrast

Different places have different kinds of weather, but most places have four seasons. In the center of the web below write how the four seasons are alike where you live. In each of the four outer circles write how each season is different. **Answers will vary. Sample answers are given.**

hot
sunny
flowers in full bloom

cool
new leaves and flowers

sun shines
wind blows
rain falls

cool
rainy
falling leaves

cold
gray skies
snow

Book 3.1/Unit 2 **Dream Wolf** — **At Home:** Have students write two sentences about each season, describing what is the same and what is different about each. 57

LANGUAGE SUPPORT

Name________ Date______

Tell About the Wolf

trot	watch children	hot breath	give gifts
pant	live in a cave	haunches	fur
pick berries	help children	smile	follow buffalo
keep children warm	live in a camp	hunt with guns	

Wolf — **Alike** — **Human**

Wolf: hot breath, live in a cave, haunches, pants, trots, fur

Alike: watch children, keep children warm, help children, smile

Human: live in a camp, give gifts, hunts with guns, pick berries, follow buffalo

Grade 3 — Language Support / Blackline Master 31 • **Dream Wolf** 63

Reteach, 57 **Practice, 57** **Extend, 57** **Language Support, 63**

Review Context Clues

TESTED OBJECTIVES

Students will use context clues including syntax (word order) to determine the meanings of unfamiliar words.

MATERIALS

- **Teaching Chart 48**
- **dictionary**

TEACHING TIP

INSTRUCTIONAL To help students understand the use of context clues, have them form pairs to play a game. Ask them to take turns with their partners giving clues and guessing the answer. ("I am a shaggy, wild animal that looks like a big dog." "You are a wolf.")

PREPARE

Discuss Meaning and Syntax

Explain to students that we can often determine the meaning of a word by looking at other words that are used before or after it and where it appears in a sentence. These words are called context clues. Context clues usually do not tell the exact meaning of an unfamilliar word; they just give readers a basic idea.

TEACH

Read the Passage and Model the Skill

Have students read the passage on **Teaching Chart 48.** Demonstrate the use of context clues and syntax as strategies for figuring out meaning.

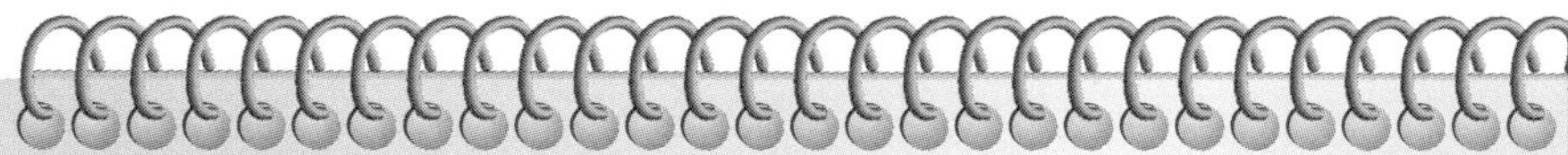

Tiblo's Friend

Tiblo sat on the rocks, waiting for the wolf to return to his den. The wolf had to come home soon. All of a sudden, Tiblo felt the wolf's shaggy fur brush his arm. The wolf sat on his haunches right in front of Tiblo. "Please come back to the village with me," Tiblo begged.

The wolf smiled. "If I didn't wander from place to place, how could I learn new things to teach you?"

Teaching Chart 48

MODEL I'm not sure what the word *shaggy* means. The two words next to it give me clues, though. From its position, I can tell *shaggy* is describing the wolf's fur. A wolf's fur is very long and thick. Maybe *shaggy* means "long and thick." Maybe the wolf's fur is so long and thick that it touches Tiblo's arm as the wolf walks by him.

PRACTICE

Identify Context Clues

Have students look for context clues to define the words *den*, *haunches*, *begged*, and *wander*. Have volunteers circle the words and then underline the context clues that help them to determine the meaning of the words. Then have groups use the clues and write what they think each word means. Afterward, encourage them to check their guesses using a dictionary.

▶ **Logical/Interpersonal**

Word	Possible Meaning
den	wolf's home
haunches	part of wolf's body used for sitting
begged	asked
wander	go from place to place

ASSESS/CLOSE

Practice Using Context Clues

Have students work in pairs, using the story words and vocabulary words below to write a paragraph. Encourage them to include context clues for each word's meaning.

shaggy den haunches begged darkness echoes buffalo herds

ALTERNATE TEACHING STRATEGY

CONTEXT CLUES

For a different approach to teaching this skill, see page T63.

Meeting Individual Needs for Vocabulary

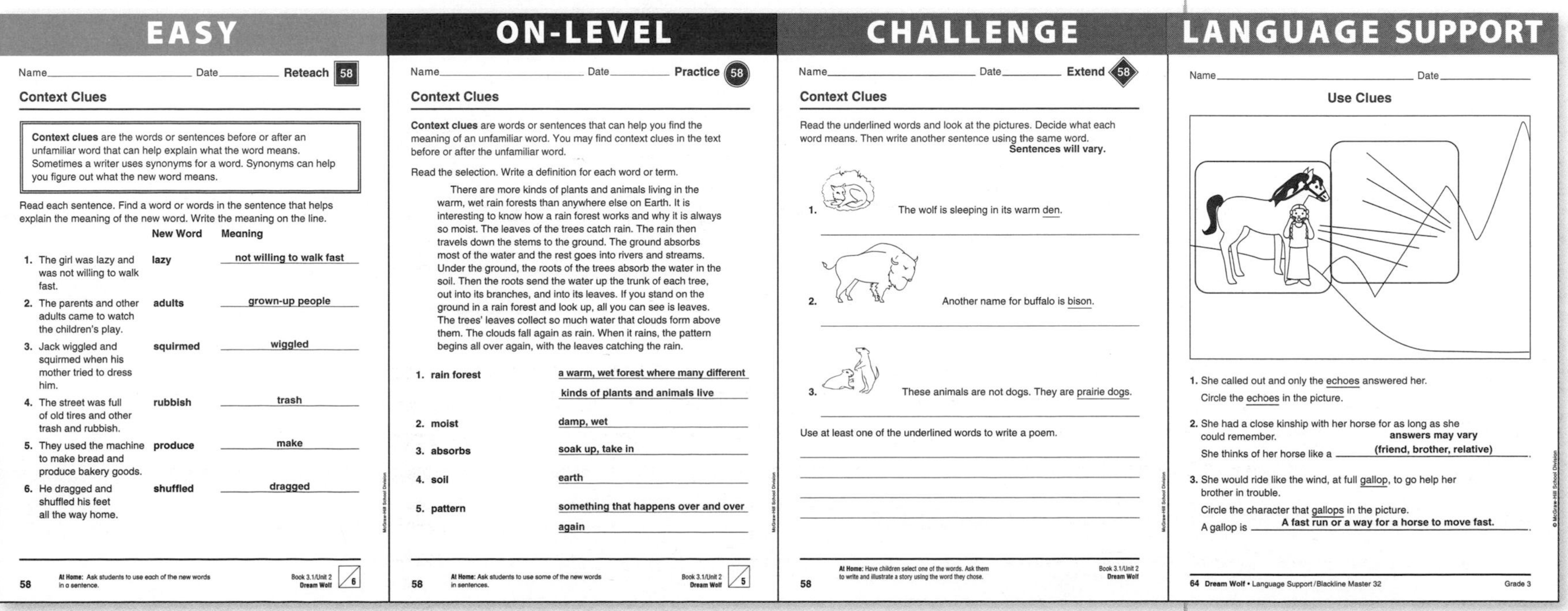

EASY

Name______ Date______ **Reteach 58**

Context Clues

Context clues are the words or sentences before or after an unfamiliar word that can help explain what the word means. Sometimes a writer uses synonyms for a word. Synonyms can help you figure out what the new word means.

Read each sentence. Find a word or words in the sentence that helps explain the meaning of the new word. Write the meaning on the line.

	New Word	Meaning
1. The girl was lazy and was not willing to walk fast.	**lazy**	**not willing to walk fast**
2. The parents and other adults came to watch the children's play.	**adults**	**grown-up people**
3. Jack wiggled and squirmed when his mother tried to dress him.	**squirmed**	**wiggled**
4. The street was full of old tires and other trash and rubbish.	**rubbish**	**trash**
5. They used the machine to make bread and produce bakery goods.	**produce**	**make**
6. He dragged and shuffled his feet all the way home.	**shuffled**	**dragged**

58 **At Home:** Ask students to use each of the new words in a sentence. Book 3.1/Unit 2 **Dream Wolf** 6

McGraw-Hill School Division

Reteach, 58

ON-LEVEL

Name______ Date______ **Practice 58**

Context Clues

Context clues are words or sentences that can help you find the meaning of an unfamiliar word. You may find context clues in the text before or after the unfamiliar word.

Read the selection. Write a definition for each word or term.

There are more kinds of plants and animals living in the warm, wet rain forests than anywhere else on Earth. It is interesting to know how a rain forest works and why it is always so moist. The leaves of the trees catch rain. The rain then travels down the stems to the ground. The ground absorbs most of the water and the rest goes into rivers and streams. Under the ground, the roots of the trees absorb the water in the soil. Then the roots send the water up the trunk of each tree, out into its branches, and into its leaves. If you stand on the ground in a rain forest and look up, all you can see is leaves. The trees' leaves collect so much water that clouds form above them. The clouds fall again as rain. When it rains, the pattern begins all over again, with the leaves catching the rain.

1. **rain forest** **a warm, wet forest where many different kinds of plants and animals live**
2. **moist** **damp, wet**
3. **absorbs** **soak up, take in**
4. **soil** **earth**
5. **pattern** **something that happens over and over again**

58 **At Home:** Ask students to use some of the new words in sentences. Book 3.1/Unit 2 **Dream Wolf** 5

McGraw-Hill School Division

Practice, 58

CHALLENGE

Name______ Date______ **Extend 58**

Context Clues

Read the underlined words and look at the pictures. Decide what each word means. Then write another sentence using the same word.
Sentences will vary.

1. The wolf is sleeping in its warm den.
2. Another name for buffalo is bison.
3. These animals are not dogs. They are prairie dogs.

Use at least one of the underlined words to write a poem.

58 **At Home:** Have children select one of the words. Ask them to write and illustrate a story using the word they chose. Book 3.1/Unit 2 **Dream Wolf**

McGraw-Hill School Division

Extend, 58

LANGUAGE SUPPORT

Name______ Date______

Use Clues

1. She called out and only the echoes answered her.
   Circle the echoes in the picture.
2. She had a close kinship with her horse for as long as she could remember. **answers may vary**
   She thinks of her horse like a **(friend, brother, relative)**.
3. She would ride like the wind, at full gallop, to go help her brother in trouble.
   Circle the character that gallops in the picture.
   A gallop is **A fast run or a way for a horse to move fast.**

64 **Dream Wolf** • Language Support/Blackline Master 32 Grade 3

Language Support, 64

GRAMMAR/SPELLING CONNECTIONS

See the 5-Day Grammar and Usage Plan on irregular plural nouns, pages 225M–225N.

See the 5-Day Spelling Plan on words with consonant clusters, pages 225O–225P.

TECHNOLOGY TIP

Help students to learn how to use the cut and paste functions on their computers. Tell them that they can use these functions to make faster changes in their writing.

Explanatory Writing

Prewrite

WRITE DIRECTIONS Present this writing assignment: Pretend that you are the wolf in the story. You want to help Tiblo and Tanksi return home. Write directions for them to get back to camp.

VISUALIZE IDEAS Have students visualize a landscape of woods and hills. Then ask them to make a list of typical landmarks found in such a scene (for example, big rocks, streams, bushes, and special kinds of trees).

Strategy: Make a Map Have students make a map of an imaginary place. They can mark the spot where Tiblo and Tanksi meet the wolf and the spot where the camp is located. Have them draw a route from the children to the camp, showing the major landmarks between these points and in which direction they turn at each landmark.

Draft

USE THE MAP Students should base their written directions on their prewriting map. Students' directions should be clear and include details to help guide the characters home. The map should help them to write the directions in a logical sequence. Remind students to number each step of their directions.

Revise

SELF-QUESTIONING Ask students to assess their drafts.

- Are my directions clear and in order?
- Do directions match map information?
- Have I included all necessary details?
- Have I used helpful time order words?

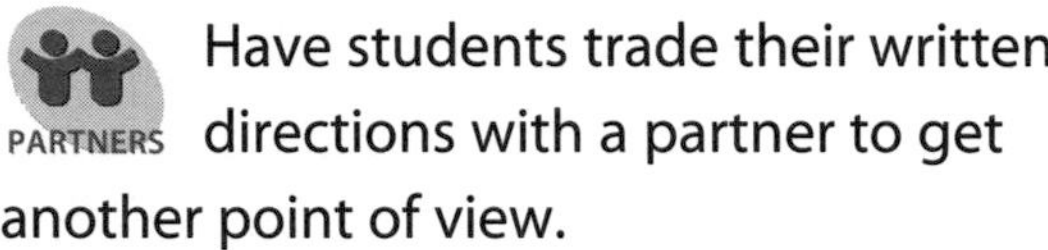

Have students trade their written directions with a partner to get another point of view.

Edit/Proofread

CHECK FOR ERRORS Students should reread their directions, checking spelling, grammar, word usage, and punctuation.

Publish

COMPILE A BOOK Have students compile a book of their maps and written directions.

The Way Back to Camp

The camp is located in the valley, on the right side of the hill. It will take 30 minutes to get there:

1. Follow the stream to the mossy rock.
2. When you get to the mossy rock, take the path that leads to the right around the bramble bushes.
3. Keep on this path until you get to the tallest cedar tree.
4. Leave the path and cross the meadow. The camp is on the other side.

Presentation Ideas

CREATE A BOOK COVER Have students draw a cover for their book.
▶Viewing/Representing

CONDUCT AN INTERVIEW Have partners take turns interviewing each other. The student being interviewed can pretend to be Tiblo or Tanksi. Tell them to use their written directions to give clear explanations of how they found their way back to camp.

▶Speaking/Listening

Consider student's creative efforts, possibly adding a plus (+) for originality, wit, and imagination.

Scoring Rubric

Excellent	Good	Fair	Unsatisfactory
4: The writer • presents the directions concisely and clearly. • presents the directions in proper sequence and with relevant detail. • uses time-order words and phrases effectively.	**3:** The writer • presents the directions in logical order. • includes some relevant details. • uses time-order words and phrases. • shows adequate awareness of the audience.	**2:** The writer • needs to be clearer about the sequence of steps. • uses a few time-order words and phrases. • includes only a few relevant details.	**1:** The writer • has poor use of details. • has used no time-order words. • has not presented distinct and logical steps. • has given vague or unclear directions.

0: The writer leaves the page blank or fails to respond to the writing task. The student does not address the topic or simply paraphrases the prompt. The response is illegible or incoherent.

Meeting Individual Needs for Writing

EASY

Invitation Have students write a letter to the wolf thanking him for his kindness and inviting him to a party celebrating the return of Tiblo and Tanksi. Students may include simple directions to the party as well as a brief description of what the party will include (food, games, and so on).

ON-LEVEL

Write a Diary Have students pretend to be Tiblo and Tanksi. Ask them to write an entry in their diary describing how they returned home after being lost. Encourage students to mention some of the emotions they had that day, including how they felt about the wolf.

CHALLENGE

News Article Have students write a short newspaper article about a meeting between Tiblo, Tanksi, and the wolf. Have them include information about who, what, where, when, and why. Encourage students to rewrite or revise their article if necessary.

COMMUNICATION TIPS

REPRESENTING Have students make sure their book covers relate in an interesting way to the maps and directions they have included.

LISTENING During the interviewing process, both students should practice good listening skills. Students being interviewed should listen to the entire question before answering it.

LANGUAGE SUPPORT

Have students create maps of the classroom. Hide items in various parts of the room. Ask students to use the maps to find the items. Then have them write a list of directions based on their maps.

PORTFOLIO Invite students to include their written directions or another writing project in their portfolios.

5 Day Grammar and Usage Plan

LANGUAGE SUPPORT

ESL On the board, list irregular singular and plural forms, such as *tooth/teeth*. Ask students to use each in a sentence. Then erase the plurals. Say a singular form, and have students give the plural.

DAILY LANGUAGE ACTIVITIES

Write the Daily Language Activities on the chalkboard each day or use **Transparency 8**. Have the students correct the sentences orally.

Day 1

1. The mans jumped on the horses. men
2. The childs were lost. children
3. Her tooths are sharp. teeth

Day 2

1. Two mooses ate berries. moose
2. I have a flock of sheeps. sheep
3. The park has many deers. deer

Day 3

1. The mooses ate grass. moose
2. The sheeps stay in the field. sheep
3. Three mouses saved them. mice

Day 4

1. The wolf has white tooths. teeth
2. All the womans were glad. women
3. The bear has big foots. feet

Day 5

1. Tiblo spoke about the mans. men
2. The childs ran along the path. children
3. The deers meet by the pond. deer

Daily Language Transparency 8

DAY 1 Introduce the Concept

Oral Warm-Up Read this sentence aloud: *The boys have many boxes.* Ask students to identify the plural nouns and tell how they are formed.

Introduce Irregular Plural Nouns Tell students that some nouns do not add *-s* or *-es*. Present:

> **Irregular Plural Nouns**
>
> Some nouns have special plural forms.

Write the following singular and plural nouns on the chalkboard: *man/men, woman/women, child/children, tooth/teeth, mouse/mice,* and *foot/feet.*

Present the Daily Language Activity and have students correct orally. Have students write a sentence for each irregular plural noun.

WRITING

Assign the daily Writing Prompt on page 204C.

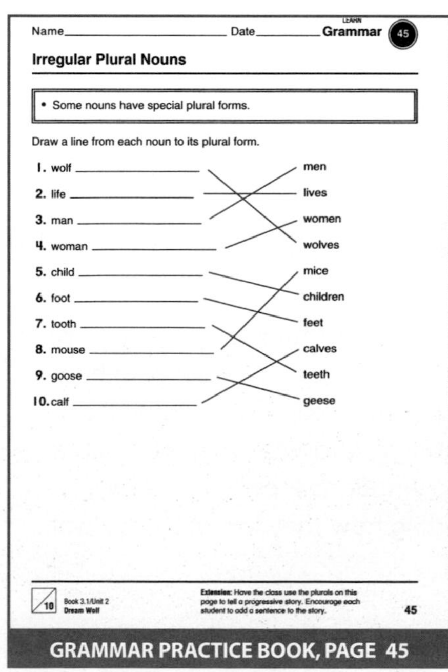

Name________________ Date________ LEARN Grammar 45

Irregular Plural Nouns

• Some nouns have special plural forms.

Draw a line from each noun to its plural form.

1. wolf — men
2. life — lives
3. man — women
4. woman — wolves
5. child — mice
6. foot — children
7. tooth — feet
8. mouse — calves
9. goose — teeth
10. calf — geese

10 Book 3.1/Unit 2 Dream Wolf

Extension: Have the class use the plurals on this page to tell a progressive story. Encourage each student to add a sentence to the story.

45

GRAMMAR PRACTICE BOOK, PAGE 45

DAY 2 Teach the Concept

Review Irregular Plural Nouns Review that the plural forms of some nouns do not end in *-s*. Ask students to form the plurals of *mouse* and *tooth*.

Introduce Nouns with Same Forms Tell students that some nouns do not change to show the plural. Present:

> **Irregular Plural Nouns**
>
> A few nouns have the same singular and plural forms.

Write the following singular and plural nouns on the chalkboard: *sheep/sheep, deer/deer, moose/moose.*

Present the Daily Language Activity. Then have students make charts showing the singular and plural forms for *man, woman, child, tooth, mouse, foot, sheep, deer, moose.*

WRITING

Assign the daily Writing Prompt on page 204C.

Name________________ Date________ LEARN AND PRACTICE Grammar 46

More Irregular Plural Nouns

• A few nouns are the same in both singular and plural forms.

Singular	Plural	Singular	Plural
sheep	sheep	fish	fish
deer	deer	trout	trout
buffalo	buffalo	salmon	salmon
moose	moose	scissors	scissors

Complete each sentence with the correct plural form of the noun in parentheses.

1. The children saw bighorn (sheep) ___sheep___ in the hills.
2. I have seen (deer) ___deer___ in a forest.
3. The Wolf People followed a herd of (buffalo) ___buffalo___.
4. I once saw two (moose) ___moose___.
5. Some forests have streams with (fish) ___fish___.
6. Rainbow (trout) ___trout___ live in streams.
7. I drew a picture of (salmon) ___salmon___ jumping in a stream.
8. When I find (scissors) ___scissors___, I will cut it out.

46

Extension: Have pairs of students pantomime the animals on this page. Invite classmates to guess the animals, using the correct plural forms.

Book 3.1/Unit 2 Dream Wolf 8

GRAMMAR PRACTICE BOOK, PAGE 46

Irregular Plural Nouns

DAY 3 Review and Practice

Learn from the Literature Review irregular plural nouns. Read aloud the third sentence on page 209 of *Dream Wolf:*

> **They climbed up and up among the rocks and cedar trees where bighorn sheep and bears live.**

Ask students to identify all the plural nouns in this sentence. Ask them which of these plurals is irregular.

Differentiate Between Singular Nouns and Plural Nouns Present the Daily Language Activity and have students correct the sentences orally.

Ask students to find the two plural nouns in the first paragraph on page 213 of *Dream Wolf*. Have them identify which plural noun is regular and which is irregular. *(rocks, children)*

WRITING Assign the daily Writing Prompt on page 204D.

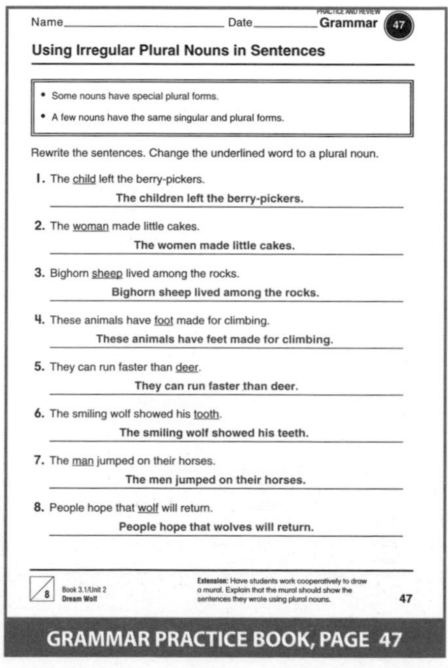

Name______ Date______ PRACTICE AND REVIEW Grammar 47

Using Irregular Plural Nouns in Sentences

- Some nouns have special plural forms.
- A few nouns have the same singular and plural forms.

Rewrite the sentences. Change the underlined word to a plural noun.

1. The child left the berry-pickers.
   The children left the berry-pickers.
2. The woman made little cakes.
   The women made little cakes.
3. Bighorn sheep lived among the rocks.
   Bighorn sheep lived among the rocks.
4. These animals have foot made for climbing.
   These animals have feet made for climbing.
5. They can run faster than deer.
   They can run faster than deer.
6. The smiling wolf showed his tooth.
   The smiling wolf showed his teeth.
7. The man jumped on their horses.
   The men jumped on their horses.
8. People hope that wolf will return.
   People hope that wolves will return.

8 Book 3.1/Unit 2 Dream Wolf

Extension: Have students work cooperatively to draw a mural. Explain that the mural should show the sentences they wrote using plural nouns. 47

GRAMMAR PRACTICE BOOK, PAGE 47

DAY 4 Review and Practice

Review Irregular Plural Nouns Write the singular nouns from the lesson on the chalkboard. Ask students to give the plural forms.

Mechanics and Usage Before students begin the daily Writing Prompt on page 204D, review sentence punctuation. Display and discuss:

Sentence Punctuation

- Every sentence begins with a capital letter.
- A statement ends with a period.
- A question ends with a question mark.
- A command ends with a period.
- An exclamation ends with an exclamation point.

WRITING Assign the daily Writing Prompt on page 204D.

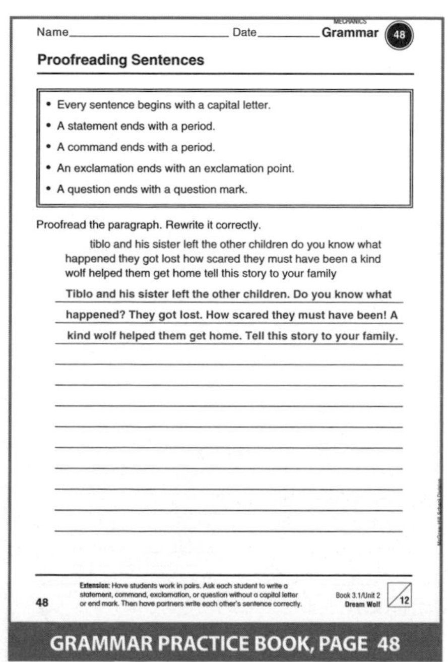

Name______ Date______ MECHANICS Grammar 48

Proofreading Sentences

- Every sentence begins with a capital letter.
- A statement ends with a period.
- A command ends with a period.
- An exclamation ends with an exclamation point.
- A question ends with a question mark.

Proofread the paragraph. Rewrite it correctly.

tiblo and his sister left the other children do you know what happened they got lost how scared they must have been a kind wolf helped them get home tell this story to your family

Tiblo and his sister left the other children. Do you know what happened? They got lost. How scared they must have been! A kind wolf helped them get home. Tell this story to your family.

48 Extension: Have students work in pairs. Ask each student to write a statement, command, exclamation, or question without a capital letter or end mark. Then have partners write each other's sentence correctly.

Book 3.1/Unit 2 Dream Wolf 12

GRAMMAR PRACTICE BOOK, PAGE 48

DAY 5 Assess and Reteach

Assess Use the Daily Language Activity and page 49 of the **Grammar Practice Book** for assessment.

Reteach Have students work in groups to draw pictures illustrating the singular and plural forms of the nouns in this lesson. Make sure students draw more than one thing for the picture representing the plural noun. Then ask students to write captions for their pictures.

Students can add their pictures to a classroom word wall, underlining the irregular plural noun in each caption.

Use page 50 of the **Grammar Practice Book** for additional reteaching.

WRITING Assign the daily Writing Prompt on page 204D.

Name______ Date______ TEST Grammar 49

Irregular Plural Nouns

A. Decide if the underlined noun is singular or plural. Write your answer on the line.

1. The children came to a stream. **plural**
2. Trout live in some streams. **plural**
3. A trout is a kind of salmon. **singular**
4. Deer are quiet animals. **plural**
5. A wolf has sharp teeth. **singular**

B. Write **yes** if the plural form of the underlined noun is correct. Write **no** if it is not correct.

6. Tiblo stayed with the womans. **No**
7. He and his sister saw sheep. **Yes**
8. They did not see any mooses. **No**
9. The Wolf People heard wolves call. **Yes**
10. The cattle ate the grass. **Yes**

10 Book 3.1/Unit 2 Dream Wolf 49

GRAMMAR PRACTICE BOOK, PAGE 49

GRAMMAR PRACTICE BOOK, PAGE 50

5 Day Spelling Plan

LANGUAGE SUPPORT

ESL On the board write *sp spend, sk skate, sl slept, str stream, scr scream, spr spring*. Say each blend and each sample word. Ask students to listen and repeat.

DICTATION SENTENCES

1. Do not spend too much money.
2. She stood on a hill near the stream.
3. That scream was scary.
4. I like spring weather.
5. His skate wheel came off.
6. We slept out in a tent.
7. This kind of spider can't hurt you.
8. My father is very strong.
9. It is my turn to scrub the pans.
10. Sprinkle water over the flame.
11. My skin is cold.
12. That sleeve is too short.
13. Tie a string around the bag.
14. There is a hole in the screen.
15. I would like a slice of bread.

Challenge Words

16. Buffalo walk through the fields.
17. We do not like the darkness of the night.
18. The echoes call back my name.
19. That piece of fruit is ripe.
20. Take shelter now from the rain.

DAY 1 Pretest

Assess Prior Knowledge Use the Dictation Sentences at the left and **Spelling Practice Book** page 45 for the pretest. Allow students to correct their own papers. If students have trouble, have partners give each other a midweek test on Day 3. Students who require a modified list may be tested on the first eight words.

Spelling Words		Challenge Words
1. spend	9. scrub	16. **buffalo**
2. **stream**	10. sprinkle	17. **darkness**
3. scream	11. skin	18. **echoes**
4. spring	12. sleeve	19. **ripe**
5. skate	13. string	20. **shelter**
6. **slept**	14. screen	
7. spider	15. slice	
8. strong		

*Note: Words in **dark type** are from the story.*

Word Study On page 46 of the **Spelling Practice Book** are word study steps and an at-home activity.

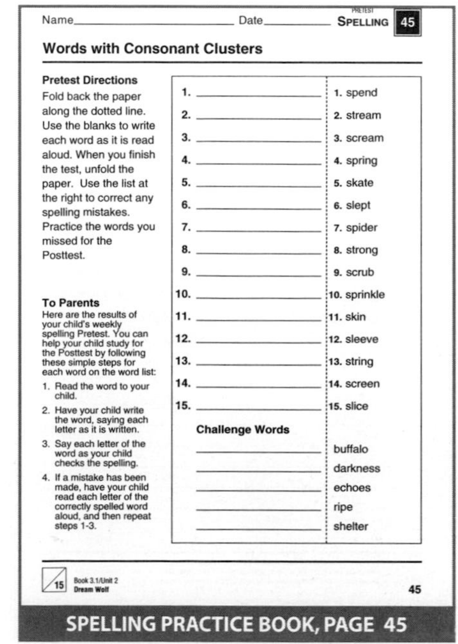

Name______________ Date________ PRETEST SPELLING 45

Words with Consonant Clusters

Pretest Directions
Fold back the paper along the dotted line. Use the blanks to write each word as it is read aloud. When you finish the test, unfold the paper. Use the list at the right to correct any spelling mistakes. Practice the words you missed for the Posttest.

To Parents
Here are the results of your child's weekly spelling Pretest. You can help your child study for the Posttest by following these simple steps for each word on the word list:
1. Read the word to your child.
2. Have your child write the word, saying each letter as it is written.
3. Say each letter of the word as your child checks the spelling.
4. If a mistake has been made, have your child read each letter of the correctly spelled word aloud, and then repeat steps 1-3.

1. ________ 1. spend
2. ________ 2. stream
3. ________ 3. scream
4. ________ 4. spring
5. ________ 5. skate
6. ________ 6. slept
7. ________ 7. spider
8. ________ 8. strong
9. ________ 9. scrub
10. ________ 10. sprinkle
11. ________ 11. skin
12. ________ 12. sleeve
13. ________ 13. string
14. ________ 14. screen
15. ________ 15. slice

Challenge Words
________ buffalo
________ darkness
________ echoes
________ ripe
________ shelter

15 Book 3.1/Unit 2 Dream Wolf 45

SPELLING PRACTICE BOOK, PAGE 45

WORD STUDY STEPS AND ACTIVITY, PAGE 46

DAY 2 Explore the Pattern

Sort and Spell Words Say the words *spice* and *stream*. Ask children what consonant sounds besides the /s/ sound they hear at the beginning of each word. Tell students this week's spelling words begin with the blends *sp, sk, sl, str, scr,* and *spr*.

Words beginning with:

sp	*sk*	*sl*
spend	skate	slept
spider	skin	sleeve
		slice

str	*scr*	*spr*
stream	scream	spring
strong	scrub	sprinkle
string	screen	

Word Wall Have students think of other words that begin with the blends *sp, sk, sl, str, scr,* and *spr* and add them to a classroom word wall, underlining the blend in each word.

Name______________ Date________ EXPLORE THE PATTERN SPELLING 47

Words with Consonant Clusters

spend spring spider sprinkle string
stream skate strong skin screen
scream slept scrub sleeve slice

Fill in the Blanks
Complete the sentences with words in the list that have the same spelling pattern.

sp
1. I never spend my whole allowance.
2. The spider crawled onto his foot.

sk
3. Don't skate on thin ice.
4. The sun and wind make my skin dry.

sl
5. It was so noisy I hardly slept.
6. The sleeve on my shirt was too short.
7. I'll have another slice of pie.

str
8. The stream made a bubbly sound.
9. He's strong enough to lift anything.
10. The balloon is only held by a string.

scr
11. The sudden sound made me scream.
12. We saw the movie on a very big screen.
13. If you scrub hard you can clean it.

spr
14. In the spring the snow melted.
15. A light sprinkle of rain made the flowers bloom.

Rhyme Time
Write the spelling words that rhyme with the words below.

cream stream scream
swing spring string
twice slice
state skate
stub scrub

22 Book 3.1/Unit 2 Dream Wolf 47

SPELLING PRACTICE BOOK, PAGE 47

Words with Consonant Clusters

DAY 3 Practice and Extend

Word Meaning: Antonyms Explain to students that an *antonym* is a word that has the opposite meaning or nearly the opposite meaning of another word. Have partners work together to match antonyms with Spelling Words. Have partners share and compare their answers.

Display antonyms such as *earn (spend); whisper (scream); fall (spring)*.

Glossary Have students:

- write an original definition for each Challenge Word.
- look up the definition for each word in the Glossary and check their work against it.
- discuss how their definitions compared with those in the Glossary.

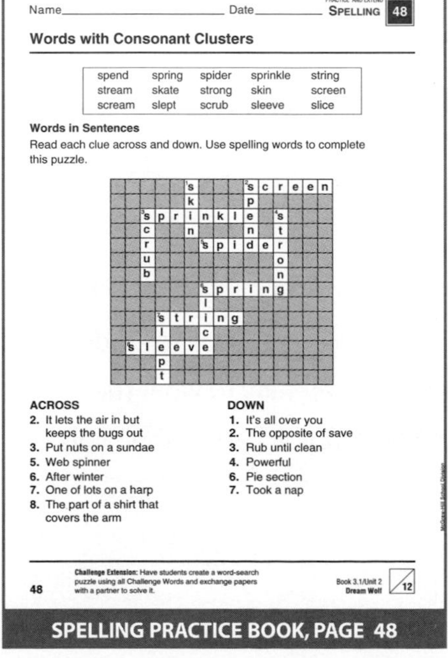

Name________________ Date__________ PRACTICE AND EXTEND SPELLING 48

Words with Consonant Clusters

spend	spring	spider	sprinkle	string
stream	skate	strong	skin	screen
scream	slept	scrub	sleeve	slice

Words in Sentences

Read each clue across and down. Use spelling words to complete this puzzle.

ACROSS
2. It lets the air in but keeps the bugs out
3. Put nuts on a sundae
5. Web spinner
6. After winter
7. One of lots on a harp
8. The part of a shirt that covers the arm

DOWN
1. It's all over you
2. The opposite of save
3. Rub until clean
4. Powerful
6. Pie section
7. Took a nap

48 **Challenge Extension:** Have students create a word-search puzzle using all Challenge Words and exchange papers with a partner to solve it. Book 3.1/Unit 2 **Dream Wolf** 12

SPELLING PRACTICE BOOK, PAGE 48

DAY 4 Proofread and Write

Proofread Sentences Write these sentences on the chalkboard, including the misspelled words. Ask students to proofread, circling incorrect spellings and writing the correct spellings. There are two spelling errors in each sentence.

When we walked by the straem we saw a spyder. (stream, spider)

The stringe on your sleave is white. (string, sleeve)

Have students create additional sentences with errors for partners to correct.

WRITING Have students use as many spelling words as possible in the daily Writing Prompt on page 204D. Remind students to proofread their writing for errors in spelling, grammar, and punctuation.

Name________________ Date__________ PROOFREAD AND WRITE SPELLING 49

Words with Consonant Clusters

Proofreading Activity

There are 6 spelling mistakes in this paragraph. Circle the misspelled words. Write the words correctly on the lines below.

Spring is a great time of year for Roger. He likes to spen time at the park. The trees have turned green with new leaves. Plants have started to bloom. Roger can scate along a special trail that takes him by the water. The streem looks inviting, but Roger knows it's too dangerous to play there. He'll just sprinckal some water on his face. The water feels cool on his scin and Roger wipes his face on his sleve. Maybe later Roger will fly his kite.

1. spend 2. skate 3. stream
4. sprinkle 5. skin 6. sleeve

Writing Activity

What season of the year do you like best? Write about it. Explain what you like most about your favorite season. Use four words from your spelling list. Circle any words you use that have consonant clusters.

10 Book 3.1/Unit 2 **Dream Wolf** 49

SPELLING PRACTICE BOOK, PAGE 49

DAY 5 Assess and Reteach

Assess Students' Knowledge Use page 50 of the **Spelling Practice Book** or the Dictation Sentences on page 225O for the posttest.

Personal Word List Have students add words from this week's list to their list of troublesome words in their journals.

JOURNAL

Students should continue to practice spelling these words and refer to them during later writing activities.

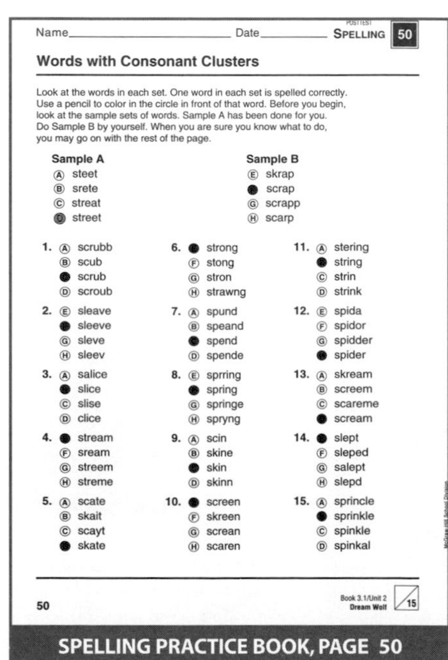

Name________________ Date__________ POSTTEST SPELLING 50

Words with Consonant Clusters

Look at the words in each set. One word in each set is spelled correctly. Use a pencil to color in the circle in front of that word. Before you begin, look at the sample sets of words. Sample A has been done for you. Do Sample B by yourself. When you are sure you know what to do, you may go on with the rest of the page.

Sample A: Ⓐ steet Ⓑ srete Ⓒ streat ● street

Sample B: Ⓔ skrap ● scrap Ⓖ scrapp Ⓗ scarp

1. Ⓐ scrubb Ⓑ scub ● scrub Ⓓ scroub
2. Ⓔ sleave ● sleeve Ⓖ sleve Ⓗ sleev
3. Ⓐ salice ● slice Ⓒ slise Ⓓ clice
4. ● stream Ⓕ sream Ⓖ streem Ⓗ streme
5. Ⓐ scate Ⓑ skait Ⓒ scayt ● skate
6. ● strong Ⓕ stong Ⓖ stron Ⓗ strawng
7. Ⓐ spund Ⓑ speand ● spend Ⓓ spende
8. Ⓔ sprring ● spring Ⓖ springe Ⓗ spryng
9. Ⓐ scin Ⓑ skine ● skin Ⓓ skinn
10. ● screen Ⓕ skreen Ⓖ screan Ⓗ scaren
11. Ⓐ stering ● string Ⓒ strin Ⓓ strink
12. Ⓔ spida Ⓕ spidor Ⓖ spidder ● spider
13. Ⓐ skream Ⓑ screem Ⓒ scareme ● scream
14. ● slept Ⓕ sleped Ⓖ salept Ⓗ slepd
15. Ⓐ sprincle ● sprinkle Ⓒ spinkle Ⓓ spinkal

50 Book 3.1/Unit 2 **Dream Wolf** 15

SPELLING PRACTICE BOOK, PAGE 50

Spiders at Work

Selection Summary Students will learn how spiders use their unique abilities to survive in the natural world. The dangerous black widow and tarantulas are among the spiders featured.

Listening Library Audiocassette

INSTRUCTIONAL
Pages 228–243

About the Author Diane Hoyt-Goldsmith has long been interested in the rich cultural diversity of the Americas and is well known for her books about cultural celebrations. Her message to students is, "If you want to write about other people, as I do, you must learn to listen carefully to what they say to you. Each and every person has a wonderful story to share. If you listen, you can be their voice."

Resources for

Meeting Individual Needs

LEVELED BOOKS

EASY
Pages 243A–243D

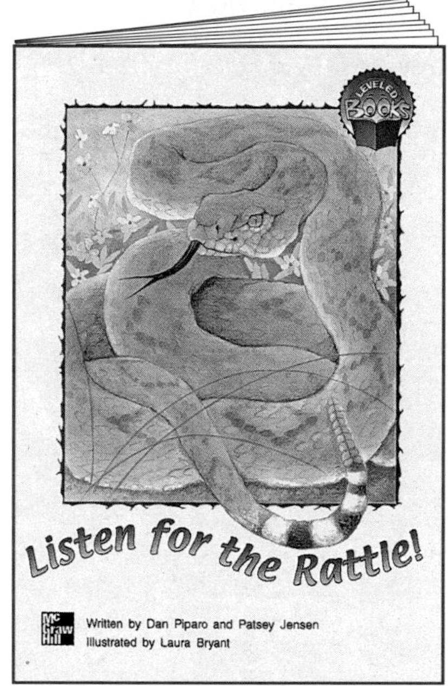

INDEPENDENT
Pages 243B, 243D

Take-Home version available

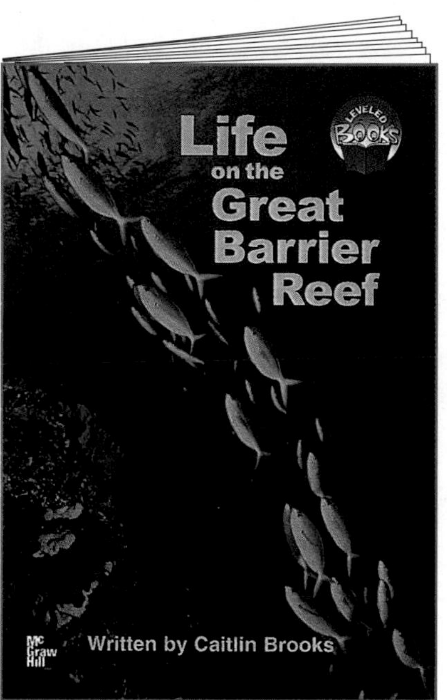

CHALLENGE
Pages 243C, 243D

LEVELED PRACTICE

Reteach, 59–65
blackline masters with reteaching opportunities for each assessed skill

Practice, 59–65
workbook with Take-Home Stories and practice opportunities for each assessed skill and story comprehension

Extend, 59–65
blackline masters that offer challenge activities for each assessed skill

ADDITIONAL RESOURCES

- **Language Support Book** 65–72
- **Take-Home Story, Practice** p. 60a
- **Alternate Teaching Strategies** T60–T66
- **Selected Quizzes Prepared by** Accelerated Reader

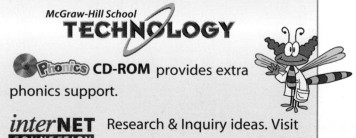

McGraw-Hill School
TECHNOLOGY

Phonics **CD-ROM** provides extra phonics support.

interNET CONNECTION Research & Inquiry ideas. Visit ***www.mhschool.com/reading.***

Suggested Lesson Planner

Available on CD-ROM

READING AND LANGUAGE ARTS	DAY 1 Focus on Reading and Skills	DAY 2 Read the Literature
• Comprehension • Vocabulary • Phonics/Decoding • Study Skills • Listening, Speaking, Viewing, Representing	 **Read Aloud and Motivate,** 226E "Spider on the Floor" **Develop Visual Literacy,** 226/227 ☑ **Introduce Important and Unimportant Information,** 228A–228B **Teaching Chart 49** **Reteach, Practice, Extend,** 59	**Build Background,** 228C Develop Oral Language **Vocabulary,** 228D ***capture*** ***ruin*** ***skills*** ***liquid*** ***serious*** ***struggles*** **Teaching Chart 50** **Word Building Manipulative Cards** **Reteach, Practice, Extend,** 60 Read **Read the Selection,** 228–239 Guided Instruction ☑ Important and Unimportant Information ☑ Compare and Contrast **Minilessons,** 231, 233, 235, 237 **Cultural Perspectives,** 236
• Curriculum Connections	 Fine Arts, 226/227	 Science, 228C
• Writing	 **Writing Prompt:** Write a description of an insect. Tell what it looks like and where it lives.	 **Writing Prompt:** What would you do if you saw a group of spiders? What would the spiders do? Write a description.  **Journal Writing,** 239 Quick-Write
• Grammar	**Introduce the Concept: Possessive Nouns,** 243M Daily Language Activity 1. The spiders web looks like lace. (spider's) 2. It is natures web maker. (nature's) 3. The black widows bite is strong. (widow's) **Grammar Practice Book,** 51	**Teach the Concept: Possessive Nouns,** 243 Daily Language Activity 1. Tarantulas bodies are hairy. (Tarantulas 2. Many mens hands have been bitten. (m 3. Spiders threats are serious. (Spiders') **Grammar Practice Book,** 52
• Spelling	**Introduce: Plurals,** 243O **Spelling Practice Book,** 51–52	**Explore the Pattern: Plurals,** 243O **Spelling Practice Book,** 53

Meeting Individual Needs

 = **Skill Assessed in Unit Test**

DAY 3 Read the Literature

Reread for Fluency, 238

Story Questions, 240
Reteach, Practice, Extend, 61
Story Activities, 241

Study Skill, 242
✓ Reference Sources
Teaching Chart 51
Reteach, Practice, Extend, 62
Test Power, 243

Read the Leveled Books,
Guided Reading
Consonant Clusters
✓ Important and Unimportant Information
✓ Instructional Vocabulary

 **CD-ROM**

 **Social Studies,** 230

Writing Prompt: Compare and contrast a spider with an insect. What is the same? What is different?

Writing Process: Explanatory Writing, 243K
Prewrite, Draft

Review and Practice: Possessive Nouns, 243N
Daily Language Activity
1. The fly is caught in the webs spokes. (web's)
2. Each spiders bite is deadly. (spider's)
3. This familys members are insects. (family's)

Grammar Practice Book, 53

Practice and Extend: Plurals, 243P
Spelling Practice Book, 54

DAY 4 Build Skills

 **Read the Leveled Books and Self-Selected Books**

✓ **Review Important and Unimportant Information,** 243E–243F
Teaching Chart 52
Reteach, Practice, Extend, 63
Language Support, 70

✓ **Review Draw Conclusions,** 243G–243H
Teaching Chart 53
Reteach, Practice, Extend, 64
Language Support, 71

 **Math,** 232

Writing Prompt: Imagine the most beautiful spider web in the world. Describe it.

Writing Process: Explanatory Writing, 243K
Revise

Meeting Individual Needs for Writing, 243L

Review and Practice: Possessive Nouns, 243N
Daily Language Activity
1. That webs threads are invisible. (web's)
2. The two legs purpose is special. (legs')
3. The girls mother told her a folk tale. (girl's)

Grammar Practice Book, 54

Proofread and Write: Plurals, 243P
Spelling Practice Book, 55

DAY 5 Build Skills

Read Self-Selected Books

✓ **Review Antonyms and Synonyms,** 243I–243J
Teaching Chart 54
Reteach, Practice, Extend, 65
Language Support, 72

Listening, Speaking, Viewing, Representing, 243L
Present Illustrations
Make a Speech

Minilessons, 231, 233, 235

Phonics Review,
Consonant Clusters, 237
Phonics/Phonemic Awareness Practice Book, 13–18

 **CD-ROM**

 **Science,** 234

Writing Prompt: Write a description of two boys as they might appear to a spider. Tell what it likes most and least about them.

Writing Process: Explanatory Writing, 243K
Edit/Proofread, Publish

Assess and Reteach: Possessive Nouns, 243N
Daily Language Activity
1. The Spider Womans skills were spinning and weaving. (Woman's)
2. She made blankets from the sheeps wool. (sheep's)
3. This rattlesnakes venom is deadly. (rattlesnake's)

Grammar Practice Book, 54–56

Assess and Reteach: Plurals, 243P
Spelling Practice Book, 56

Music

Read Aloud and Motivate

Spider on the Floor

a song by Bill Russell

There's a spider on the floor, on the floor.
There's a spider on the floor, on the floor.
Who could ask for any more than a spider on the floor?
There's a spider on the floor, on the floor.

Now the spider's on my leg, on my leg.
Oh, the spider's on my leg, on my leg.
Oh, he's really big! This old spider on my leg.
There's a spider on my leg, on my leg.

Now the spider's on my stomach, on my stomach.
Oh, the spider's on my stomach, on my stomach.
Oh, he's just a dumb old lummock, this old spider on my stomach.
There's a spider on my stomach, on my stomach.

Continued on pages T2-T5

Oral Comprehension

LISTENING AND SPEAKING Encourage students to listen carefully as you sing them this song about a wandering spider. Ask them to try and guess where the spider will move in each new verse. When you have finished singing, ask: "Did you guess where the spider was going to go next?" Then ask: "If you had a different place for the spider to go, what would it be? How would the verse go then?"

Activity Invite students to sing this song along with you. Encourage them to create hand gestures for each of the verses. They may also wish to make funny facial expressions as they sing.

▶ **Musical/Kinesthetic**

Develop Visual Literacy

Works of Art

Anthology pages 226-227

Stories in Art

Many animals have special features that help them get the food they need. A garden spider spins a web to catch its food. A harvester ant has strong jaws that help it chew seeds.

Look at the painting. What can you tell about this hummingbird? How will its bill help it to sip nectar from the flowers? What details do you notice about the flowers?

Look at the painting again. What do you think are the important details in the picture?

Ruby-Throat & Columbine
by Robert Bateman, 1983

226

227

Objective: Identify Important and Unimportant Information

VIEWING This painting captures a moment in nature in which a hummingbird approaches flowers. Encourage students to note how the hummingbird seems to be both still and in motion at the same time. Ask students to comment on the artist's use of color. Have they seen colors like these in gardens or parks?

Read the page with students, encouraging individual interpretations of the painting.

Ask students to describe some of the important details in the painting. For example:

- The bird's beak, long and narrow, is perfect for getting nectar from flowers.
- The flowers' blossoms point downwards.

REPRESENTING Have students write a short poem that will tell readers something interesting about a bird or a flower. Ask students to choose a particular type of bird or flower—for example, a rose or a robin.

Students will distinguish between important and unimportant information.

LANGUAGE SUPPORT

ESL Write the words *important* and *unimportant* on the chalkboard and have a volunteer define each word. To reinforce the meaning, have students use a two-column chart to organize important and unimportant information from a movie or TV show that everyone has seen.

Introduce Important and Unimportant Information

PREPARE

Relate a Plot Invite a volunteer to relate the plot of a movie. Ask students: Which takes longer, watching a movie or telling what it is about? Why? What information do you throw out when you want to tell about a movie quickly?

TEACH

Read the Story and Model the Skill Tell students: It is easier to hold on to what you learn if you can tell the difference between important and unimportant information. One way to do this is by thinking about the purpose or main idea of a story. Another way is to bear in mind what exactly you are trying to learn.

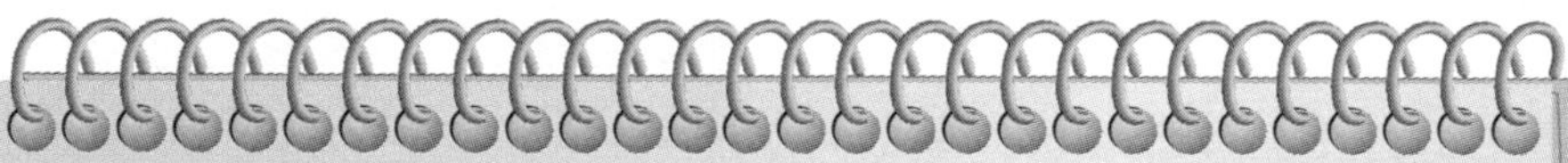

Pet Care

Jake has three pets. He has a canary named Bloggie, a dog named Jasper, and a goldfish named Spot. He got all three pets on his tenth birthday. Jake loves animals, even though they take a lot of care. Every morning he changes Bloggie's water and gives him a fresh piece of lettuce. Then he takes Jasper out for a long walk. Afterwards, he pours him a big bowl of dog food and fresh water. Then he takes the box of fish food and carefully taps out a little bit for Spot. Only then does Jake have time for his own breakfast.

Teaching Chart 49

Display **Teaching Chart 49**. As the story is being read, have students pay attention to what is the important information. After you model the skill, have students underline the important information.

MODEL The title of the story lets me know that I'm going to be learning about how to care for pets. As I read, I will look for information that is most important to that purpose.

PRACTICE

Create Inverted Triangle

Work with students to create an Inverted Triangle that shows information from the most important to the least important. ▶ **Visual/Logical**

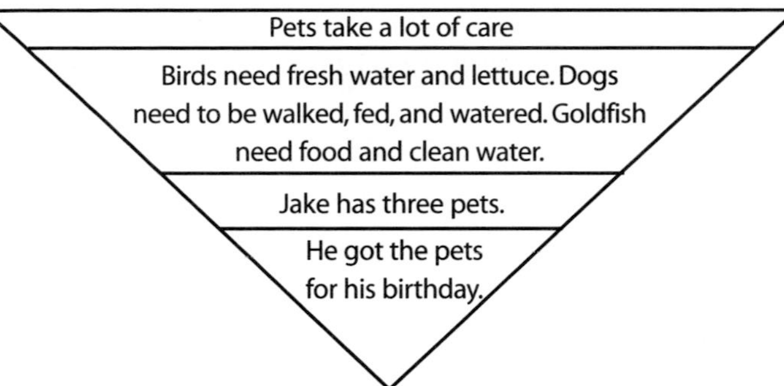

Pets take a lot of care
Birds need fresh water and lettuce. Dogs need to be walked, fed, and watered. Goldfish need food and clean water.
Jake has three pets.
He got the pets for his birthday.

ASSESS/CLOSE

Identify Important and Unimportant Information

If the title of the story were "All About Jake," how would that change what is important information in the story? Why? (The number of pets, how he got them, and when he has his breakfast would become important information because they tell specific things about Jake.)

SELECTION Connection

Students will distinguish between important and unimportant information when they read *Spiders at Work* and the Leveled Books.

ALTERNATE TEACHING STRATEGY

IMPORTANT AND UNIMPORTANT INFORMATION

For a different approach to teaching this skill, see page T66.

Meeting Individual Needs for Comprehension

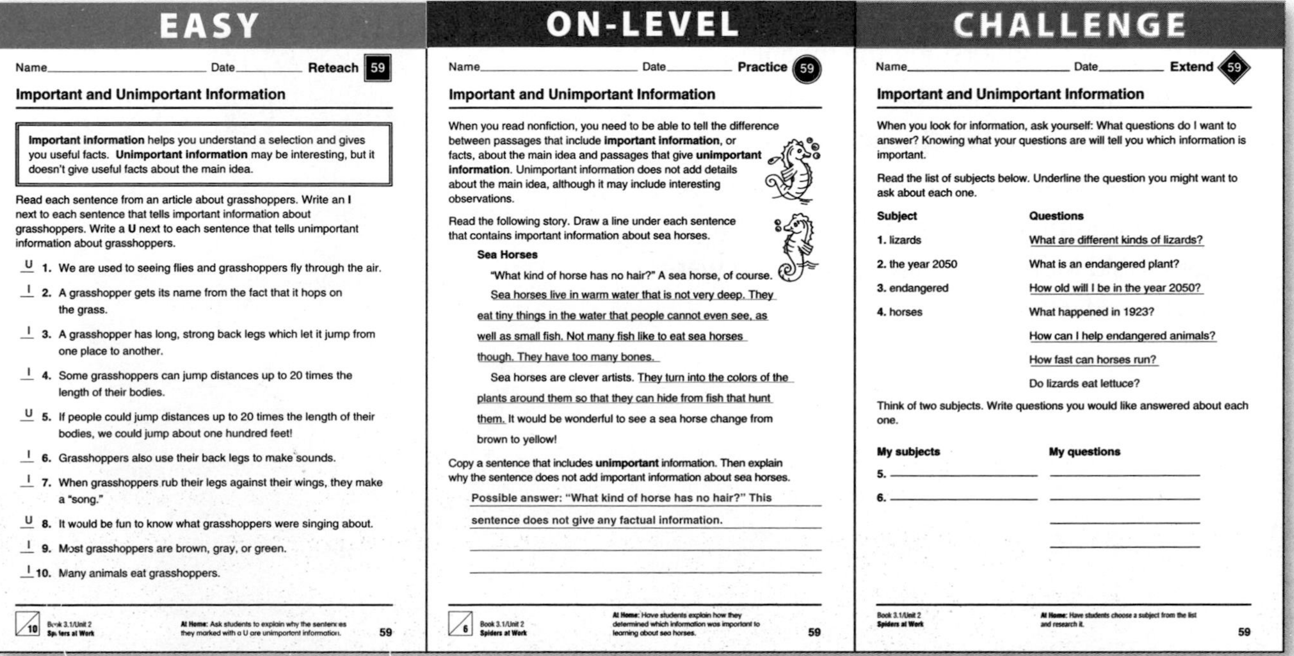

EASY

Name______________ Date________ **Reteach 59**

Important and Unimportant Information

Important information helps you understand a selection and gives you useful facts. **Unimportant information** may be interesting, but it doesn't give useful facts about the main idea.

Read each sentence from an article about grasshoppers. Write an **I** next to each sentence that tells important information about grasshoppers. Write a **U** next to each sentence that tells unimportant information about grasshoppers.

U 1. We are used to seeing flies and grasshoppers fly through the air.
I 2. A grasshopper gets its name from the fact that it hops on the grass.
I 3. A grasshopper has long, strong back legs which let it jump from one place to another.
I 4. Some grasshoppers can jump distances up to 20 times the length of their bodies.
U 5. If people could jump distances up to 20 times the length of their bodies, we could jump about one hundred feet!
I 6. Grasshoppers also use their back legs to make sounds.
I 7. When grasshoppers rub their legs against their wings, they make a "song."
U 8. It would be fun to know what grasshoppers were singing about.
I 9. Most grasshoppers are brown, gray, or green.
I 10. Many animals eat grasshoppers.

10 Book 3.1/Unit 2 Spiders at Work

At Home: Ask students to explain why the sentences they marked with a U are unimportant information. 59

Reteach, 59

ON-LEVEL

Name______________ Date________ **Practice 59**

Important and Unimportant Information

When you read nonfiction, you need to be able to tell the difference between passages that include **important information**, or facts, about the main idea and passages that give **unimportant information**. Unimportant information does not add details about the main idea, although it may include interesting observations.

Read the following story. Draw a line under each sentence that contains important information about sea horses.

Sea Horses

"What kind of horse has no hair?" A sea horse, of course. Sea horses live in warm water that is not very deep. They eat tiny things in the water that people cannot even see, as well as small fish. Not many fish like to eat sea horses though. They have too many bones.

Sea horses are clever artists. They turn into the colors of the plants around them so that they can hide from fish that hunt them. It would be wonderful to see a sea horse change from brown to yellow!

Copy a sentence that includes **unimportant** information. Then explain why the sentence does not add important information about sea horses.

Possible answer: "What kind of horse has no hair?" This sentence does not give any factual information.

6 Book 3.1/Unit 2 Spiders at Work

At Home: Have students explain how they determined which information was important to learning about sea horses. 59

Practice, 59

CHALLENGE

Name______________ Date________ **Extend 59**

Important and Unimportant Information

When you look for information, ask yourself: What questions do I want to answer? Knowing what your questions are will tell you which information is important.

Read the list of subjects below. Underline the question you might want to ask about each one.

Subject	Questions
1. lizards	What are different kinds of lizards?
2. the year 2050	What is an endangered plant?
3. endangered	How old will I be in the year 2050?
4. horses	What happened in 1923?
	How can I help endangered animals?
	How fast can horses run?
	Do lizards eat lettuce?

Think of two subjects. Write questions you would like answered about each one.

My subjects	My questions
5. ______	______
6. ______	______

Book 3.1/Unit 2 Spiders at Work

At Home: Have students choose a subject from the list and research it. 59

Extend, 59

Build Background

Anthology and Leveled Books

Science

Evaluate Prior Knowledge

CONCEPT: HOW ANIMALS PROTECT THEMSELVES These selections deal with information explaining the various ways different animals protect themselves. Encourage students to share what they already know about how different animals protect themselves.

CREATE CATEGORY WEBS Have students brainstorm ways animals protect themselves and then create a web showing each form of protection. ▶ **Logical/Visual**

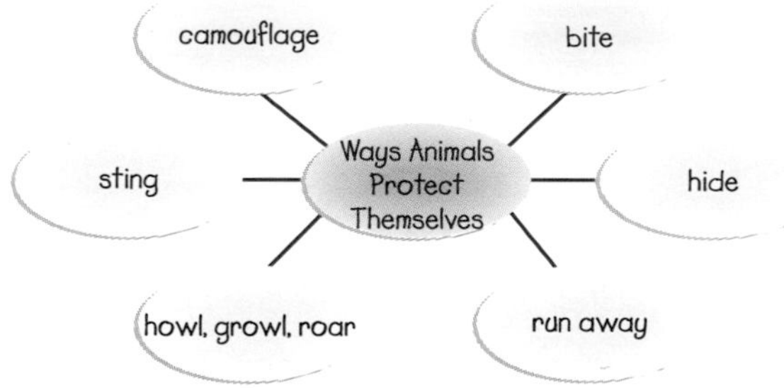

CAMOUFLAGE YOURSELVES After

making sure that students understand the meaning of *camouflage*, invite them to think about how they would camouflage themselves if they were going to hide. Then have them write a short paragraph telling what their camouflage would look like, where they would want to hide, and why.

Develop Oral Language

DISCUSS ANIMAL HABITATS Provide ESL books and magazines that contain pictures of animals in their natural habitats. Help students to

- name and describe the animals such as: furry rabbit, huge giraffe, fat hippo, and so on.
- describe the animal's environment using such terms as: *jungle*, *desert*, *mountains*, *forests*, and so on.
- point to elements in the pictures and use gestures in the discussion.
- write the animals' names and the various descriptive words and phrases on the chalkboard and read the words aloud.

TEACHING TIP

MANAGEMENT Display pictures and books of animals in camouflage or about animal protection for students to browse through. Encourage students to comment on the pictures.

LANGUAGE SUPPORT

ESL See Language Support Book, pages 65–68, for teaching suggestions for Build Background and Vocabulary.

Vocabulary

Key Words

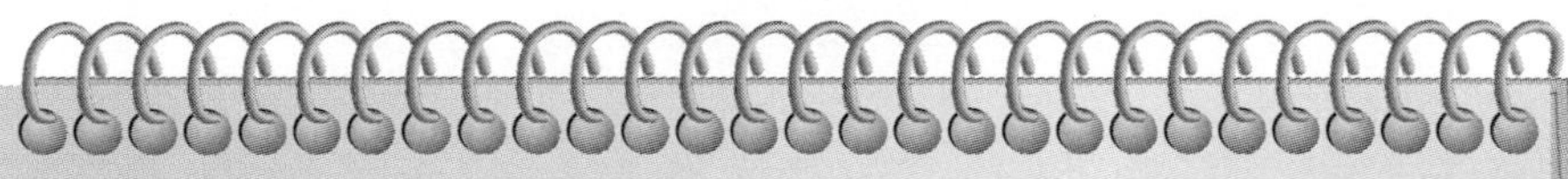

A Spider and Its Web

1. Spiders spin webs to capture their prey. **2.** The prey struggles and struggles but cannot free itself. **3.** If you don't look where you are going, you might step on a web and ruin it. **4.** To make a web, spiders spray a liquid silk that becomes hard and strong when it dries. **5.** Some spider bites can cause serious sickness and even death. **6.** Native Americans tell a story of Spider Woman who used her skills at spinning and weaving to help people.

Teaching Chart 50

Vocabulary in Context

IDENTIFY VOCABULARY WORDS Display **Teaching Chart 50** and read the passage with students. Have volunteers circle each vocabulary word and underline other words that are clues to its meaning.

DISCUSS MEANINGS Ask questions like these to help clarify word meanings:

- Would a cat capture a mouse or a cow?
- If you struggle to do something, is it easy or hard to do?
- How would you feel if someone was to ruin something you worked hard on?
- Would a straw or a fork be better for drinking a liquid?
- If someone is sick, is that serious or funny?
- Are painting and singing skills?

Practice

ACT OUT WORD MEANING Have a volunteer pick a vocabulary card from the top of a pile and act out the word's meaning. Whoever guesses the correct word picks the next word, acts it out, and so on.
▶ **Lingusitic/Kinesthetic**

Word Building Manipulative Cards

WRITE RIDDLES Have partners write riddles for which the answers are vocabulary words. Have them exchange papers and write the answers to the riddles. Have students refer to their Glossaries as needed.
▶ **Linguistic/Interpersonal**

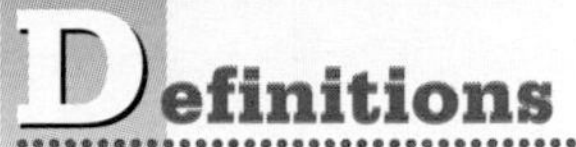

capture (p. 231) to catch or hold a person, animal or thing

struggles (p. 233) makes a great effort

ruin (p. 236) to destroy

liquid (p. 231) a form of matter, such as water or milk, that is not a gas or solid and can be poured

serious (p. 233) dangerous

skills (p. 238) powers or abilities to do things

SPELLING/VOCABULARY CONNECTIONS

See Spelling Challenge Words, page 2430.

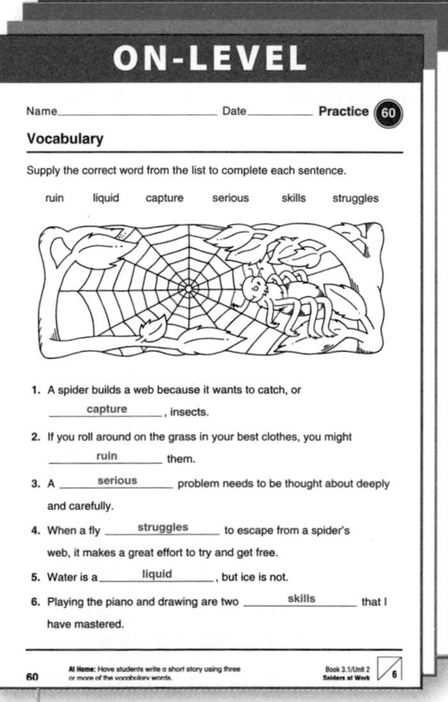

ON-LEVEL

Name______ Date______ Practice 60

Vocabulary

Supply the correct word from the list to complete each sentence.

ruin liquid capture serious skills struggles

1. A spider builds a web because it wants to catch, or ___capture___, insects.
2. If you roll around on the grass in your best clothes, you might ___ruin___ them.
3. A ___serious___ problem needs to be thought about deeply and carefully.
4. When a fly ___struggles___ to escape from a spider's web, it makes a great effort to try and get free.
5. Water is a ___liquid___, but ice is not.
6. Playing the piano and drawing are two ___skills___ that I have mastered.

60 **At Home:** Have students write a short story using three or more of the vocabulary words. Book 3.1/Unit 2 Spiders at Work 6

Take-Home Story 60a
Reteach 60
Practice 60 • **Extend 60**

Guided Instruction

Preview and Predict

Have students read the title and preview the photographs, looking for clues as to what will be important about the selection.

- Do you think the information in the columns will be important?
- What is this selection probably about?
- Will the selection be nonfiction or fiction? How can you tell? (Nonfiction; the titles and the photographs show that facts will be taught about spiders.) *Genre*

Have students record their predictions about the selection.

PREDICTIONS	WHAT HAPPENED
There are different kinds of spiders.	
The story will explain how and why spiders make webs.	

Set Purposes

What do students want to find out by reading the selection? For example:

- Are all spiders dangerous?
- What do tarantulas eat?

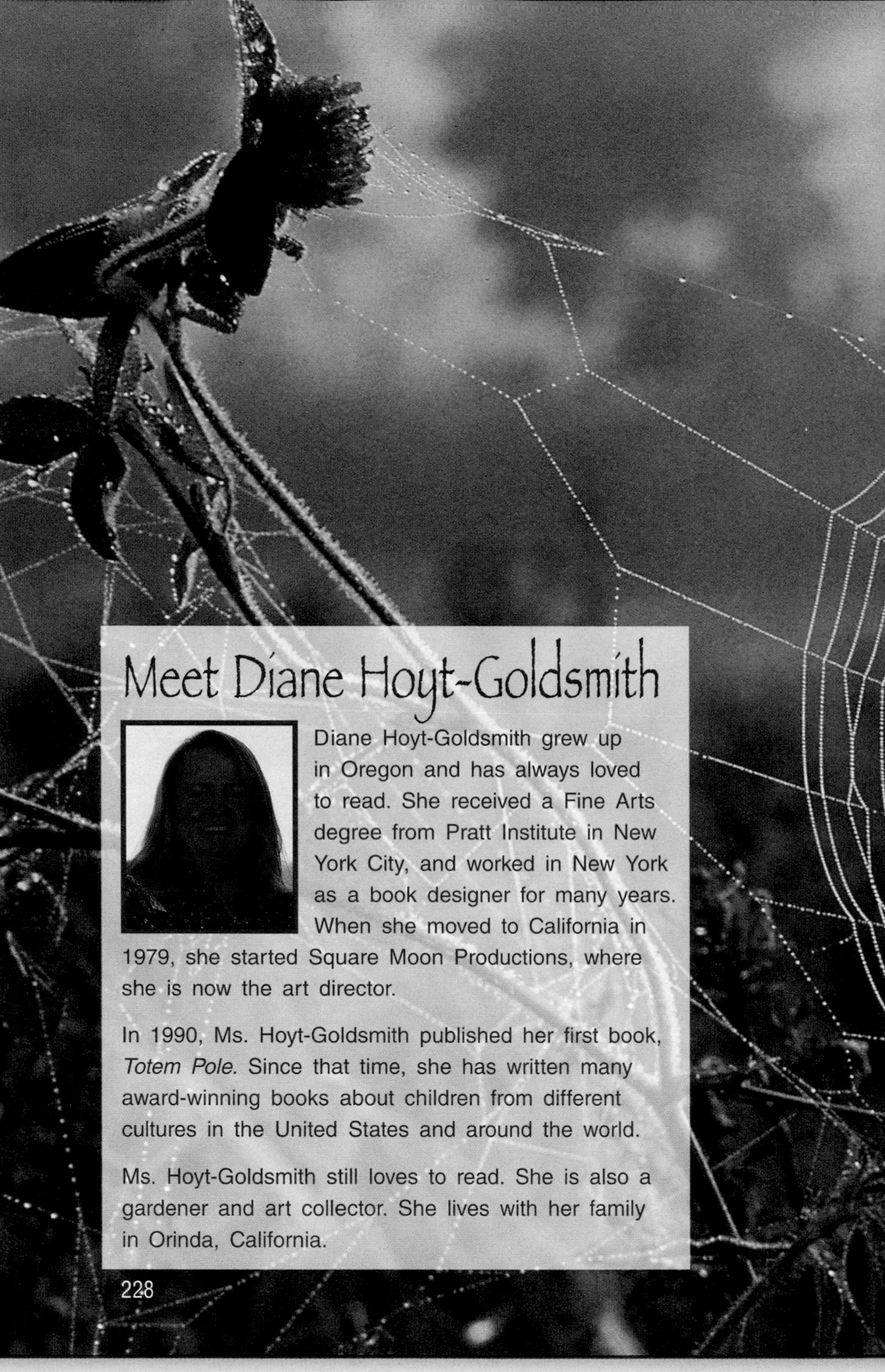

Meet Diane Hoyt-Goldsmith

Diane Hoyt-Goldsmith grew up in Oregon and has always loved to read. She received a Fine Arts degree from Pratt Institute in New York City, and worked in New York as a book designer for many years. When she moved to California in 1979, she started Square Moon Productions, where she is now the art director.

In 1990, Ms. Hoyt-Goldsmith published her first book, *Totem Pole.* Since that time, she has written many award-winning books about children from different cultures in the United States and around the world.

Ms. Hoyt-Goldsmith still loves to read. She is also a gardener and art collector. She lives with her family in Orinda, California.

228

Meeting Individual Needs • Grouping Suggestions for Strategic Reading

EASY

Read Together Read the selection with students or have them use the **Listening Library Audiocassette.** Have students use the Important and Unimportant Information web as they compare and contrast the spiders in the selection. Guided Instruction and Intervention prompts offer additional help with decoding, vocabulary, and comprehension.

ON-LEVEL

Guided Reading Preview the story words listed on page 229. Read the selection with the class using the Guided Instruction. You may want to have students read the story or play the **Listening Library Audiocassette** first on their own. Ask them to use the Important and Unimportant Information web to record information during reading.

CHALLENGE

Read Independently Remind students that comparing and contrasting story elements can help them understand what the author is trying to explain. Have students set up an Important and Unimportant Information web. After reading, they can use their charts to help summarize the author's ideas.

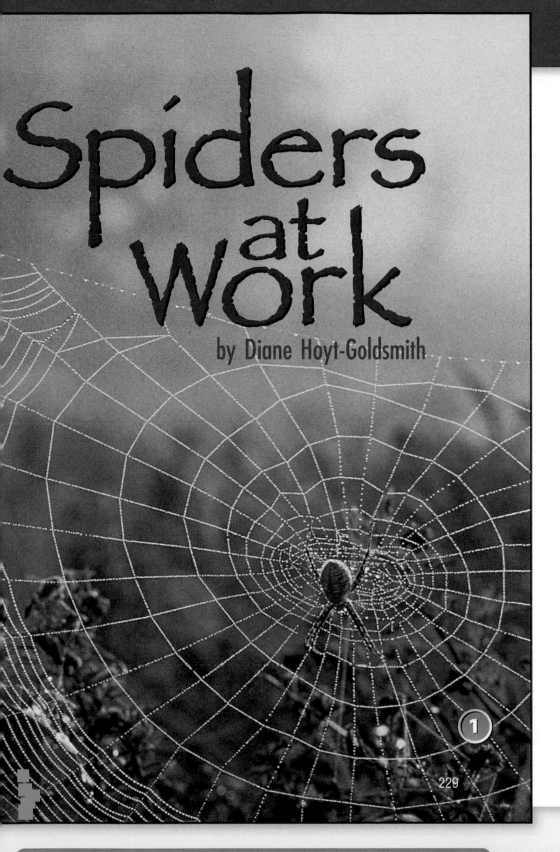

Spiders at Work

by Diane Hoyt-Goldsmith

1

229

Guided Instruction

☑ Important and Unimportant Information

☑ Compare and Contrast

Strategic Reading Identifying important and unimportant information while you read will help you remember important facts. Let's prepare a word web so we can write down story notes.

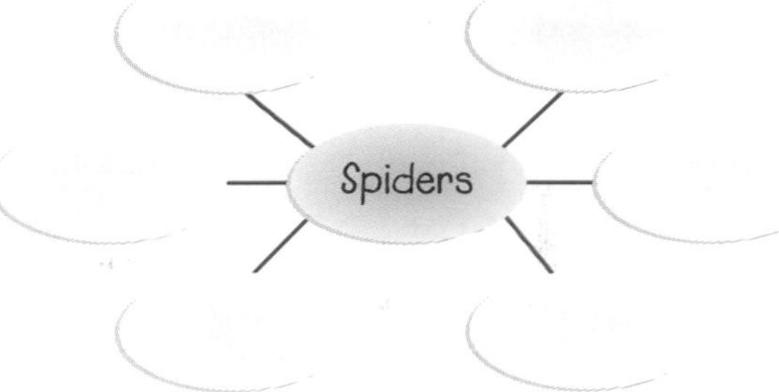

1 **IMPORTANT AND UNIMPORTANT INFORMATION** If you did not know the title of this story, what clues does the picture give you about what will be important to this story? (It will probably be about spiders.)

Story Words

The words below may be unfamiliar. Have students check their meanings and pronunciations in the Glossary.

- prey, p. 231
- tarantula, p. 232
- black widow, p. 232
- daddy-longlegs, p. 236
- arachnids, p. 237
- feelers, p. 237

LANGUAGE SUPPORT

A blackline master of the Important and Unimportant Information web is available in the **Language Support Book.**

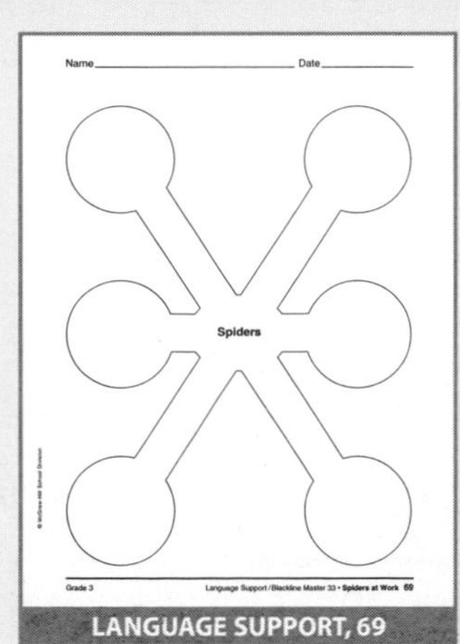

LANGUAGE SUPPORT, 69

Guided Instruction

2 IMPORTANT AND UNIMPORTANT INFORMATION What is the most important point about the garden spider? What is an unimportant detail that you learn about the spider and its web?

MODEL There is a lot of important information on this page. I think the most important things are that the garden spider can spin a web, and that it traps insects to eat. If I don't have this information, none of the other information on the page will make sense. It is not so important for me to know that the web looks like lace, although it is a detail that helps me understand the main idea better.

Nature's Web Maker

The tiny creature called a spider spins a web that is both beautiful and useful. Although it looks like lace, 2 the web is a deadly trap.

Hanging in the space between two plants, the threads that make up the web are almost invisible. A fly buzzes into the web and gets stuck. Then the spider runs out and wraps the insect up in sticky threads. Next the spider carries the fly away to eat it.

The garden spider is one of nature's best builders. Let's look at how it makes its web between two plants.

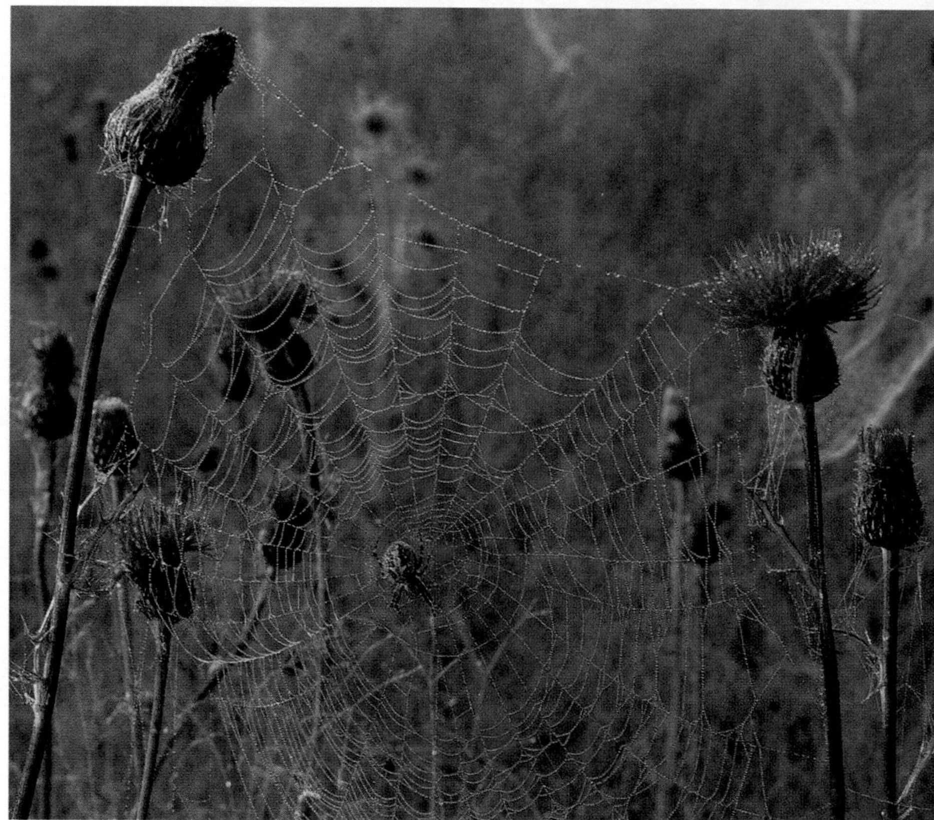

230

Activity

Cross Curricular: Social Studies

SPIDER MAPS Explain to students that spiders are found all over the world. Provide a large map of the world. As they read, they can draw the spiders they learn about on sticky notes, label them and paste them onto the map.

RESEARCH AND INQUIRY Have students research facts about other spiders. They can then add them to the map.
▶ **Spatial/Visual**

interNET CONNECTION Students can learn more facts about spiders by visiting ***www.mhschool.com/reading***.

First, the spider makes a bridge line by spinning out a long silk thread. The silk begins as a liquid that the spider sprays from its body. When the silk hits the air, it hardens into the strongest fiber found in nature.

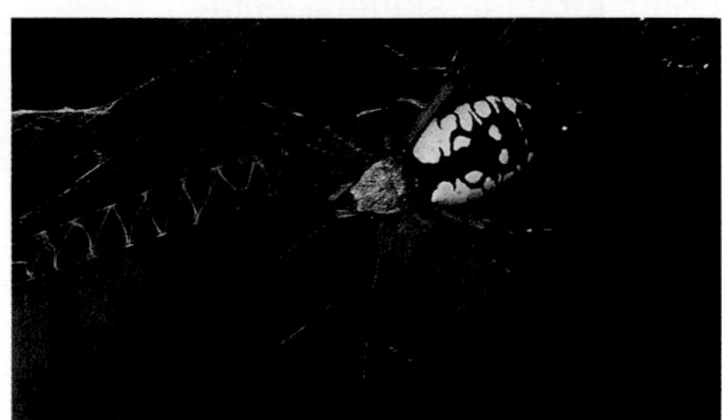

Air currents blow one end of this thread to another plant where it sticks. The spider travels along the bridge line it has made. It drops another line down to a plant below and travels down it. Then it comes back up with another silk thread to make a triangle.The spider keeps spinning. Back and forth, up and down, the spider goes. The web now looks something like the spokes of a wheel. Then the spider lays the trap—a long thread of sticky silk that spirals around the spokes until it reaches the center of the wheel. When the spider gets a victim, it can race down the spokes because they are dry, not sticky, and capture its prey. 3

FACTOIDS

Water spiders have their homes and raise their young under water, in air-tight, balloon-shaped webs.

Spiders can be fast. The fastest spider in the world can run 330 times its own body length in 10 seconds. A person can only run 50 times his or her body length in that time.

231

Guided Instruction

3 IMPORTANT AND UNIMPORTANT INFORMATION Are the facts important for understanding the selection so far? What are the sidebars? (extra information or fun facts about spiders) Let's write the important information that we have learned so far on our webs.

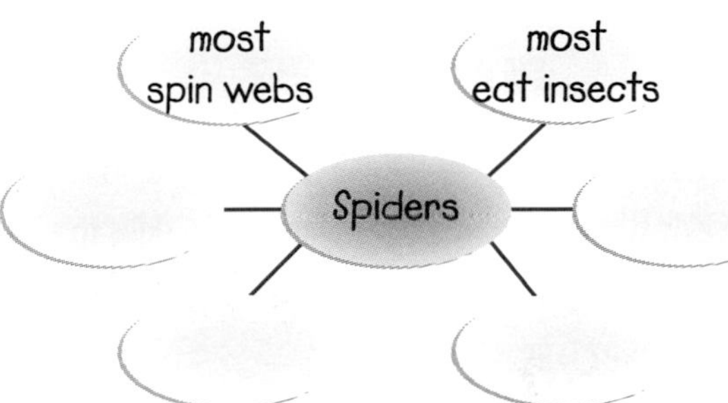

LANGUAGE SUPPORT

ESL Help students understand the concept of *spinning webs.* Write *spinning* on the chalkboard and have a volunteer demonstrate how something moves in a circular way when it spins. Now point out that the author is using the word *spinning* in a different way here. To *spin* means to *make thread or yarn.* Provide students with photographs of yarn or thread being spun from wool.

Minilesson

REVIEW/MAINTAIN

Context Clues

Review with students that words and phrases surrounding unfamiliar words can help in figuring out their meaning. Have students find the word *silk* in the first paragraph of page 231. Then ask:

- What clues can you find around the word *silk* that help you understand what the word means? (long thread; strongest fiber found in nature)

Activity Invite partners to help each other write down context clues for unfamiliar words as they read the selection. Students may record their clues in a chart.

Guided Instruction

4 Let's reread the first sentence in every paragraph on page 232. What do all of these sentences tell you? (They each tell the main idea of each paragraph.) Do the sentences following the first sentences give readers supporting details or main ideas? (supporting details) ***Main Idea***

TEACHING TIP

MANAGEMENT As students read aloud, make observations about fluency and decoding skills to determine where help may be needed. Classify problems by type, such as:

- reading rate
- fluency, accuracy, and expression
- decoding, using letter-sound correspondences
- recognizing common vowel spelling patterns

Spiders, Spiders, Everywhere

4 There are many different kinds of spiders. Some spiders make webs to catch their food in the air. Others hunt for insects on the ground.

Spiders can be found anywhere on Earth. They live in jungles near the sea. They live on the top of the highest mountains. Because spiders travel by clinging to wind-blown silk threads (a kind of travel called ballooning), they have also been found miles up in the sky and hundreds of miles out to sea.

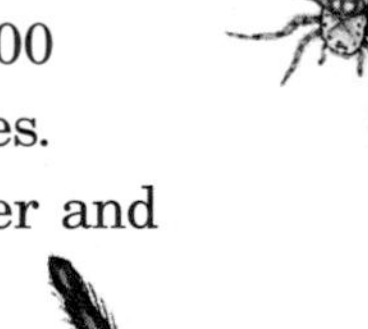

Spiders come in many sizes. Some are as small as the head of a pin. A few are much larger. The bird eating tarantulas of South America can be as long as ten inches with their legs spread.

There are more than 30,000 species of spiders living in the world—that we know about. Scientists believe the total number of kinds of spiders may be anywhere from 50,000 to 100,000. More than 2,000 different kinds of spiders live in the United States. Two of the best-known are the black widow spider and the tarantula.

232

Activity

Cross Curricular: Math

GRAPHS Review with students how graphs help illustrate certain facts. Present the following data and help students create either bar graphs or pictographs about spiders:

- A common spider lays 100 eggs; a tarantula lays 2,000 eggs; a jumping spider lays 75 eggs; a fisher spider lays 1,700 eggs.
- A dwarf spider is 2 mm long; the South American tarantula is 25 cm long; a cellar spider is 5 cm long; a bolas spider is 2 cm long.

▶ **Mathematical/Spatial**

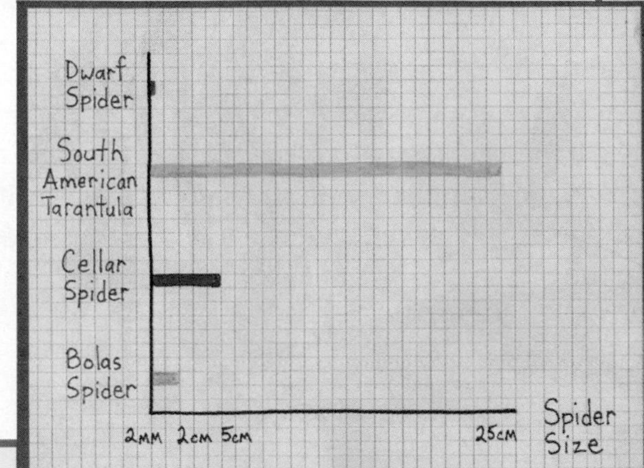

The Dangerous Black Widow

The female black widow has a poisonous bite that can cause humans serious illness and even death. But the black widow is even more dangerous to her mate. From time to time she kills and eats him. This behavior isn't unusual among spiders—many other kinds do the same thing.

Black widows have a small, shiny black body. On the bottom there is a red or yellow mark shaped like an hourglass. Black widows can be found everywhere in the United States except Alaska.

The poison in the black widow's bite is very strong. The spider uses it to kill the insects it eats. The black widow makes a web to catch an insect. When she has one in her trap, she throws a few sticky threads over it. As the insect struggles to get free, the black widow bites and kills it. Then she can eat it whenever she wants to.

233

Guided Instruction

5 IMPORTANT AND UNIMPORTANT INFORMATION If you found a black widow spider, what information on this page would be most important for you to know? (Black widow spiders have a poisonous bite that can cause humans serious illness and even death.)

P/I CONTEXT CLUES Read aloud the word *poisonous* in the first sentence on page 233. What do you think the word *poisonous* means?

PREVENTION/INTERVENTION

CONTEXT CLUES Ask students to point to words in the text that give clues about the meaning of the word *poisonous. (bite, serious illness, death)* Help them conclude that something that is poisonous can injure or kill. Then have them read the last paragraph on page 233, which contains the word *sticky*. Ask students to point to words in the text that give clues about the meaning of the word *sticky. (struggles to get free)* Then help them define *sticky*.

Minilesson

REVIEW/MAINTAIN

Make Generalizations

Remind students that they can combine information they already know with new information in a story to make generalizations.

- Have students think about how many people feel when they see a spider. Ask: *Are people afraid of spiders? Why?*
- Ask students to make generalizations about what people would do if they saw a black widow spider and a common garden spider. Discuss how knowledge about different spiders might affect people's reactions.

Activity Have students draw cartoon showing how most people react to spiders.

Guided Instruction

6 IMPORTANT AND UNIMPORTANT INFORMATION Sometimes the information in a story can be important to some readers and unimportant to others. If you were doing a report on the bird-eating tarantulas of South America, which information on pages 232–234 would be important to you? Which information would be unimportant?

MODEL If I know the reason I am reading something, it helps me to focus on information that is important to me. I want to find information about the South American bird-eating tarantula. On page 232, I find information about its size. On page 234, I learn that it lives in trees and eats small birds. The rest of the information is unimportant to me.

7 COMPARE AND CONTRAST How are tarantulas like black widows? (They are both spiders; they both eat insects; they can both be dangerous to humans.) How are tarantulas and black widows different? (Black widows have a much more poisonous bite than tarantulas; black widows spin webs and tarantulas wait for insects to come near them.

FACTOIDS

The poison in the bite of the black widow spider is more deadly than the venom of a rattlesnake.

6 The bird spider tarantula of South America lives in trees and eats small birds.

Tarantulas have lived on Earth since the time of the dinosaurs.

Most spiders live only for a year or so. Female tarantulas, however, can live to be 35 years old or more.

234

Black widow spiders do not bite people very often. If the spider is left alone, it won't hurt anyone. The best advice is to avoid any spider with a shiny, black body and a red or yellow mark on the bottom.

Tarantulas—Deadly Monsters?

Most tarantulas aren't very dangerous, but they look like they are! Unlike other spiders, the tarantula can be huge—anywhere from the size of a quarter to the size of an outstretched human hand. Its body is covered with hair.

Although tarantulas look like monsters, most kinds have a bite no more powerful than a bee sting. The tarantula likes to be left alone in a quiet, dark place. In fact, some people think that tarantulas make good pets.

The hairs on the tarantula's body help it to defend itself. When in danger, the tarantula drops some of its hairs. Each hair has a tiny barb at the end. This barb is as sharp as a fish hook and can hurt the skin and eyes of an enemy.

Activity

Cross Curricular: Science

SILK Tell students that spiders spin webs from silk threads. Explain that other creatures can spin silk, including lacewings and caterpillars.

RESEARCH AND INQUIRY Have students research facts about animals that produce silk. Have them focus on how and why the animals produce silk. Have students share their findings with the class.

▶ **Linguistic/Logical**

These hairs also pose the spider's greatest threat to humans, because they can cause an allergic reaction in some people.

Although tarantulas have eight eyes, they can't see very well. They hide and wait for an insect to come to them. The hairs on the tarantula's body and legs help it to sense when something is getting close. The 7
tarantula feeds on all kinds of beetles, grasshoppers, and caterpillars. 8

Guided Instruction

8 IMPORTANT AND UNIMPORTANT INFORMATION What important information have we learned on these last few pages? Are all spiders poisonous? (no) Are there may different kinds of spiders? (yes) Let's fill in our webs.

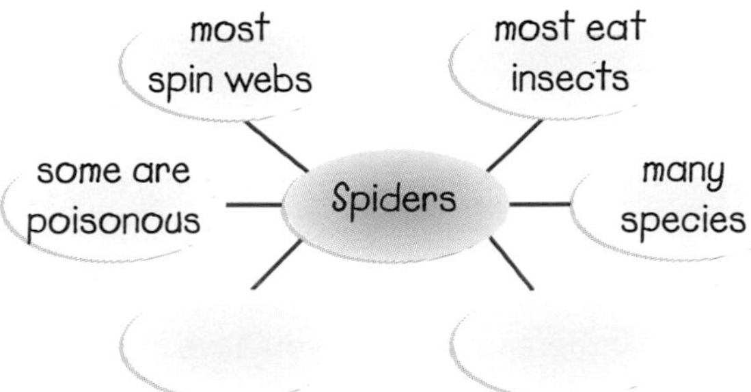

P/I PHONICS AND DECODING Read the word *huge* in the second paragraph on page 234. How is the long *u* sound spelled? (*u–e*)

P/I PREVENTION/INTERVENTION

PHONICS AND DECODING Write the word *huge* on the chalkboard. Ask students to read the word aloud. What vowel sound do they hear? (/ū/) What letters spell the sound? (*u–e*)

Have students brainstorm a list of words with the / sound spelled *u–e*. (Examples: *tube, rude, cute*) Then have students write sentences that include words from their list.

Minilesson

REVIEW/MAINTAIN

Main Idea

Review that a main idea is the most important point in a paragraph or story.

- Have students reread the text on pages 234–235. Then ask them to tell you the main idea of each paragraph.
- Ask: *Where do you usually find the main idea of a paragraph?* (in the first sentence)

Activity Students can take turns locating the main ideas for each paragraph that has been read so far. Record students' responses on the chalkboard and discuss whether all the information listed is important or unimportant.

Guided Instruction

9 IMPORTANT AND UNIMPORTANT INFORMATION If you were writing a report about daddy-longlegs, what information on page 236 might be important to you? (They are not spiders. They eat grasshoppers and locusts which can ruin a farmer's crops.)

SELF-MONITORING

STRATEGY

REREAD Rereading what you have already read can help you remember the important information in a story.

MODEL I can't remember all the facts I have read so far. There was a lot of information. Some of it was important and some of it was not so important. I think I'll quickly glance at the pages I have read. I probably won't need to go back and read every word because I have already read them.

The Daddy-longlegs

Certain creatures that we may think are spiders are not. Daddy-longlegs are a good example of this. They look like spiders because they are part of the same family. Like many spiders, daddy-longlegs are helpful to
9 humans. They eat insects that are harmful. For example, they like to eat grasshoppers and locusts—insects that can ruin a farmer's crops. They also like to eat flies and mosquitoes. These insects spread sickness to humans.

Can you guess how the daddy-longlegs got its name? It has very long legs. Two of its legs are even longer than all the others.

These two legs have a special purpose. The daddy-longlegs uses them to touch things as it passes. The fine hairs on these legs help it to hear. There are also dark spots on the legs that help it to smell and taste.

Each of the daddy-longlegs' eight legs ends with a tiny hook. It uses these to grab onto things as it walks over them.

236

CULTURAL PERSPECTIVES

SPIDER STORIES Explain that spiders belong to a group of animals called arachnids. They are named after Arachne, a girl in a Greek legend who was a skilled weaver. She bragged that she could weave better than Athena, the goddess of arts and crafts. They held a weaving contest and Arachne won. Athena was angry at losing the contest, so she turned Arachne into a spider.

Have partners research more legends and folk tales about spiders. Invite them to record their findings in cartoons, poems, or dramatizations.
▶ **Linguistic/Interpersonal**

Although they look alike, spiders and insects are different. Spiders belong to a family of their own. Spiders are called Arachnids (ah-RACK-nids). Scorpions, ticks, and daddy-longlegs are also arachnids.

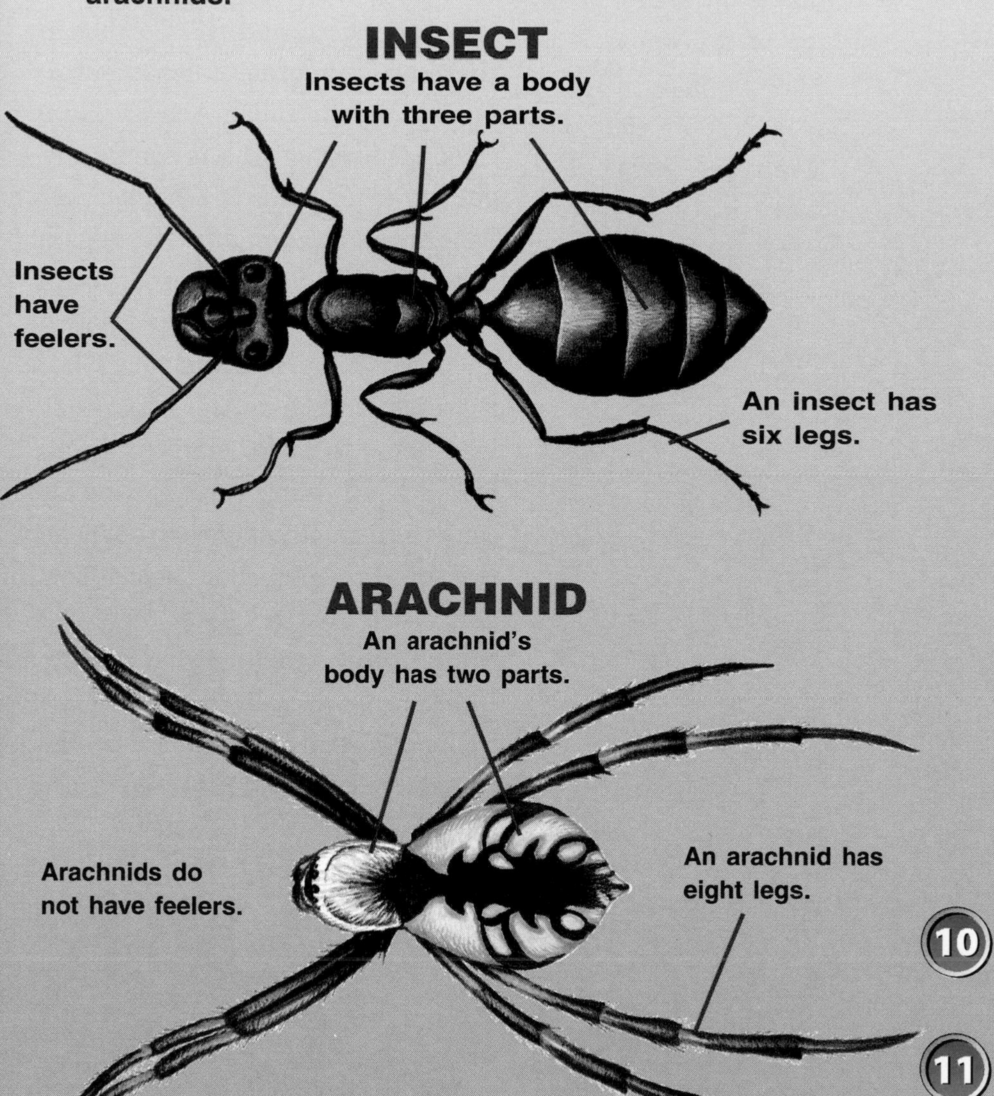
INSECT
Insects have a body with three parts.
Insects have feelers.
An insect has six legs.
ARACHNID
An arachnid's body has two parts.
Arachnids do not have feelers.
An arachnid has eight legs.
10
11

237

Guided Instruction

10 **COMPARE AND CONTRAST** How are insects and arachnids the same? (They look similar; both have bodies with many legs.) How are they different? (Insects have six legs and arachnids have eight; insects have a body with three parts and arachnids have a body with two parts; insects have feelers and arachnids do not.)

11 **IMPORTANT AND UNIMPORTANT INFORMATION** What important fact did we learn from reading page 237? (Spiders are not insects. They are arachnids.)

LANGUAGE SUPPORT

ESL Create a two-column chart on the chalkboard to review the differences between insects and arachnids. Write characteristics (feelers, number of body parts, number of legs) as row headings along the left side of the chart, and write the words *insect* and *arachnid* as column headings across the top. Ask students to take turns filling in information on the chart. Discuss the information in the completed chart.

PHONICS KIT
HANDS-ON ACTIVITIES AND PRACTICE

Minilesson

REVIEW/MAINTAIN

Consonant Clusters

Write the word *spiders* on the chalkboard. Review /sp/ by saying it aloud together. Have a volunteer underline the letters that make /sp/ in *spiders*. Continue with the word *special* for /sp/, *spread* for /spr/, and *skills* for /sk/.

Brainstorm a list of other words with the initial consonant clusters *sp, spr, sk,* such as *spot, spit, sprinkle, spring, skin,* and *skate.*

Activity Have students work in pairs to write poems about spiders using /sp/*sp*, /spr/*spr*, and /sk/*sk* words.

Guided Instruction

12 IMPORTANT AND UNIMPORTANT INFORMATION What is the most important information on page 238? (Spiders have been used in stories and folk tales all over the world.) Let's add this information to our webs.

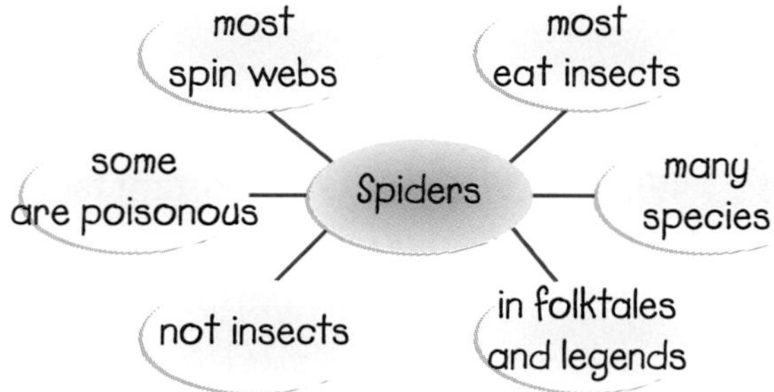

RETELL THE STORY Have volunteers retell the selection in their own words. They may use their Important and Unimportant Information webs for reference. Guide them to focus on the main ideas of each part of the selection. *Summarize*

STUDENT SELF-ASSESSMENT

- How did distinguishing between important and unimportant information help me to understand the story?
- How did the Important and Unimportant Information web help me?

TRANSFERRING THE STRATEGY

- When might I use this strategy again?
- In what other reading could the web help me?

FACTOIDS

Did you know a daddy-longlegs can swim? It's so light it can stand on the surface of the water to take a drink.

It takes about one hour for a spider to spin a web.

12 Spiders in Storie

In many parts of the world, spide have been featured in stories and folk tales. In Africa and the Caribbean, there are humorous tales about a famous spider called Anansi. He is a clever character who is constantly getting in and out of trouble. Native Americans have many folk tales abou the spider. In one of these, the Navah tell of Spider Woman. She knew all about spinning and weaving. She use these skills to help the first people learn how to make blankets that would keep them warm during the cold winters. She showed them how to take the wool from their sheep and spin it into thread. Then they dyed th thread bright colors, using dyes made from plants. Finally, on a wooden loor Spider Woman taught the Navaho ho to weave the thread into beautiful patterns. Like the web of the spider, these blankets are both beautiful and useful.

238

REREADING FOR *Fluency*

GROUP Students can form two groups. One group rereads the story while the other group reads the text in the sidebar columns. After reading, groups can exchange parts.

READING RATE You may want to evaluate a student's reading rate. In a quiet area of the classroom, have the student read aloud from *Spiders at Work* for one minute. Ask the student to place a self-stick note after the last word read. Then count the number of words he or she has read. Alternatively, you could assess small groups or the whole class together by having students count words and record their own scores.

A Running Record form provided in **Diagnostic/Placement Evaluation** will help you evaluate reading rate(s).

The Master Weaver

Round and round, up and down, a hungry spider rushes to weave its web. Later it will rest, waiting for an insect to come by. Nature's web maker knows how to create something beautiful. The web, however, is also useful. It is the key to this spider's survival.

239

Guided Instruction

Return to Predictions and Purposes

Review with students their story predictions and reasons for reading the story. Were their predictions correct? Did they find out what they wanted to know?

PREDICTIONS	WHAT HAPPENED
There are different kinds of spiders.	There are more than 30,000 species of spiders.
The story will explain how and why spiders make webs.	Some spiders weave webs out of long silk thread in order to capture their prey.

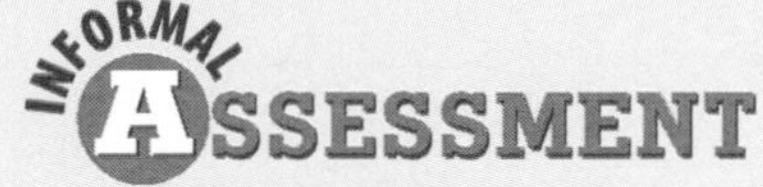

INFORMAL ASSESSMENT

IMPORTANT AND UNIMPORTANT INFORMATION

HOW TO ASSESS

Students should realize that distinguishing between important and unimportant information in a story can help them organize the facts.

- Ask students to explain the difference between important and unimportant information.
- Have students tell some information they found important in the article.

FOLLOW UP

If students have trouble understanding the difference between important and unimportant information, have them think about their own experiences. For example, ask about safety procedures during a fire drill. Ask: *What is the most important thing to remember during a fire drill?*

LITERARY RESPONSE

QUICK-WRITE Invite students to record their thoughts about the story. These questions may help them get started:

JOURNAL

- What spider would you most like to have as a pet?
- What would you do if you saw a black widow spider?
- What fact about spiders did you find most interesting?
- Were you afraid of spiders before reading the article? How do you feel about them now?

ORAL RESPONSE Have students share their journal writings and discuss what part of the article they found the most interesting.

Story Questions

Have students discuss or write answers to the questions on page 240.

Answers:

1. Silk thread from its body. *Literal/Logical*
2. No, because a black widow's bite can kill a person, and a tarantula's bite is no more powerful than a bee sting. *Literal/Compare and Contrast*
3. They can kill insects that spread disease. *Inferential/Make Inferences*
4. There are many spiders in the world, both helpful and harmful. *Critical/Summarize*
5. Answers will vary: A spider might help the children by weaving a map using its threads. *Critical/Reading Across Texts*

Write a Report For a full lesson related to explanatory writing, see the lesson on pages 243K–243L.

Story Questions & Activities

1. What does a spider use to make a web?
2. Is a tarantula more poisonous than a black widow? Explain.
3. In what ways are spiders helpful to people?
4. What is the main idea of this selection?
5. In "Dream Wolf", a wolf helped two children find their way home. How might a spider have helped the children in that story?

Write a Report

Select a type of spider that you would like to learn more about. Write a report on your spider. Include lots of fun facts and a diagram.

Meeting Individual Needs

EASY

Name__________ Date______ **Reteach 60**

Vocabulary

captures liquid ruin serious skills struggles

Write the word from the list that best completes each sentence.

Spiders are __serious__ about their work. They use all their __skills__ to build a trap to catch their food. First, they make a __liquid__ that turns into a hard thread. Then they use the thread to spin a web that __captures__ flies. No matter how much it __struggles__ a fly can't get out of the web. However, sometimes the stuck insect can tear and __ruin__ the carefully made web. 6

Story Comprehension **Reteach 61**

Write the letter of the word or phrase that correctly completes each sentence about "Spiders at Work."

1. This story was mainly written to __a__.
   a. teach about spiders b. to tell funny stories about spiders c. make people like spiders
2. The spider could not build a web without __b__.
   a. another spider's help b. thread c. plants
3. Black widows can hurt people with their __c__.
   a. barbed hairs b. pointed legs c. poison bites
4. Daddy-longlegs walk with the help of __a__.
   a. small hooks b. shoes c. a kind of glue

60–61 **At Home:** Ask students to tell you what they recall about daddy-longlegs, black widows, and tarantulas. Book 3.1/Unit 2 **Spiders at Work** 4

McGraw-Hill School Division

Reteach, 61

ON-LEVEL

Name__________ Date______ **Practice 61**

Story Comprehension

Use the story "Spiders at Work" to help you answer these questions.

1. How many legs does a spider have? __eight legs__
2. What is a bridge line? __A bridge line is the first line in a spider's web.__
3. How can you tell if a spider is a black widow? __Black widows have shiny black bodies with a red or yellow mark on the bottom.__
4. Why do people need to look out for black widow spiders? __Black widows have a poisonous bite.__
5. What kind of spiders do some people keep as pets? __tarantulas__
6. How did the daddy-longlegs get its name? __It has very long legs.__
7. Name some places that spiders can be found. __They can be found all over the world, including jungles, mountains, up in the sky, and even out at sea.__
8. According to a Navaho folk tale, what did Spider Woman teach the Navaho people to do? __She taught them how to spin wool into thread and weave it into blankets.__

61 **At Home:** Ask students to imagine what it would be like to be a spider. Have them write a short story about a day as a spider. Book 3.1/Unit 2 **Spiders at Work** 8

McGraw-Hill School Division

Practice, 61

CHALLENGE

Name__________ Date______ **Extend 60**

Vocabulary

capture liquid ruin serious skills struggles

Concentration Game

Write each vocabulary word on a different card. Write the definitions on other cards. Place the cards face down. Play a matching game with a partner. Turn over two cards at a time. If the word matches the definition, keep both cards and play again. If the cards don't match, turn them both over and let your partner have a turn.

Extend 61

Story Comprehension

What did you find out about spiders? Write and illustrate a booklet about spiders. Include the most interesting facts from "Spiders at Work." Then share the booklet with your class.

60–61 **At Home:** Have students use some of the words in the box to write some facts about spiders. Book 3.1/Unit 2 **Spiders at Work**

Extend, 61

Make a Web

Look up pictures of spider webs. Then create your own web. Using a pencil, lightly draw a web on a piece of construction paper. Glue colorful yarn to the lines. Make a spider out of construction paper and paste it to your web.

Interview a Spider

Choose your favorite kind of spider. Write a list of questions that you would like to ask it. With a partner, act out the roles of the spider and a reporter interviewing the spider. Then switch roles.

Find Out More

Black widows are poisonous spiders. What other kinds of spiders are poisonous? Find out more about poisonous spiders. Choose six of them and make a poster. Draw the six spiders, label them, and include facts about each.

241

Story Activities

Make a Web

Materials: pencil, construction paper, colorful yarn, glue, scissors

ONE Provide photographs of many different types of spiders and their webs. Encourage students to make sketches of these webs, as well as those in the photographs.

Interview a Spider

Materials: paper and pencil

PARTNERS Provide interviews from magazines for students to read. Have students present their spider interviews to the class. Encourage them to act spiderlike when playing the spider by using a different voice and appropriate gestures.

Find Out More

Materials: reference materials, poster board, felt-tipped markers

RESEARCH AND INQUIRY Students may GROUP wish to use the Internet to find out more about spiders.

interNET CONNECTION For more information on spiders, go to ***www.mhschool.com/reading***.

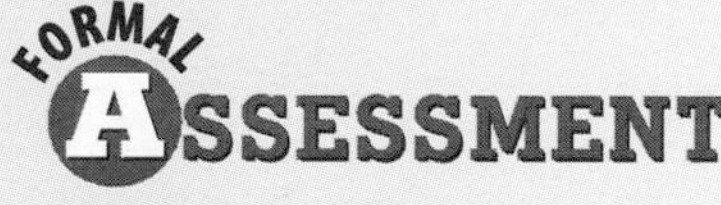

After page 241, see the Selection Assessment.

Study Skills

REFERENCE SOURCES

TESTED OBJECTIVES

Students will:

- use guide words in a dictionary.
- use the pronunciation key.

PREPARE Preview the dictionary insert and display **Teaching Chart 51.**

TEACH Remind students that dictionaries can provide definitions as well as other information about words. Have students list the types of information that can be found in a dictionary.

PRACTICE Have students answer questions 1–5. Review the answers with them. **Answers: 1.** *spider–spiral* **2.** spindle **3.** noun **4.** *i* in *it* **5.** noun

ASSESS/CLOSE Have partners create a list of words, exchange papers, and look up each other's words. For each word, have them list the definition and the part of speech.

STUDY SKILLS

Use a Dictionary

The words in a **dictionary** are arranged alphabetically. **Guide words** at the top tell you the first and last word on the page. **Word Histories** tell you the origin of some words.

spider — spiral **S**

spider A small animal with four pairs of legs, a body divided into two parts, and no wings. Most spiders spin webs to catch insects for food. **spi•der** (spī′ dər) *noun, plural* **spiders.**

Most spiders spin webs so they can catch insects for food.

spike 1. A, heavy nail used to hold rails to railroad ties. 2. Any sharp, pointed object or part that sticks out: *Baseball shoes have* ***spikes*** *on the soles.* **spike** (spīk) *noun, plural* **spikes.**

spin 1. To turn around quickly: *The car's wheels* ***spun*** *in the mud. The child* ***spun*** *the top.* 2. To make thin fibers into thread. 3. To make a web or cocoon by giving off a sticky substance that hardens into thread: *Spiders* ***spin*** *webs.* 4. To tell: *Our counselor at camp was good at* ***spinning*** *ghost stories.* 5. To feel dizzy: *The sun made my head* ***spin****. Verb.*
spin (spin) *verb,* **spun, spinning;** *noun, plural* **spins.**

spindle A stick or rod on or around which something is turned. Fibers of cotton are spun into thread from a spindle. **spin•dle** (spin′dəl) *noun, plural* **spindles.**

spine 1. The column of bones in the back; backbone. Look up backbone for more information. 2. A sharp, pointed growth on a plant or animal. *The quills of a porcupine are* ***spines.*** **spine** (spīn) *noun, plural* **spines.**

spiral A curve that keeps winding. A spiral may wind inward and outward or downward and upward. Some springs are spirals. *Noun.*
• To move in or take the shape of a spiral. *Verb.*
• Having the shape or form of a spiral: *a* **spiral** *staircase. Adjective.*
spi•ral (spī′rəl) *noun, plural* **spirals;** *verb,* **spiraled, spiraling;** *adjective.*

This building is built in the shape of a spiral

PRONUNCIATION KEY

at āpe fär câre end mē it īce pîerce hot ōld sông fôrk
oil out up ūse rüle pu̇ll tûrn chin sing shop thin this
hw in white; zh in treasure. The symbol ə stands for the unstressed vowel sound in about, taken, pencil, lemon, and circus.

Use the dictionary to answer these questions.

1. What are the **guide words** for this dictionary page?
2. What word comes before *spine*?
3. Is the word *spike* an adjective or a noun?
4. Does the *i* in *spindle* sound like the *i* in *ice* or the *i* in *it*? Use the pronunciation to help you decide.
5. Is the word *spindle* an adjective or a noun?

Meeting Individual Needs

EASY

Name________ Date________ **Reteach 62**

Use a Dictionary

Dictionaries can give you more than definitions. Hard-to-pronounce words can be sounded out with a pronunciation key. You can also learn how to spell the plural of a word. A dictionary also tells you which part of speech a word can be.

meet to come together with someone (mēt) **verb**
merry cheerful and jolly (mer′ē) **adjective**
mitten a warm covering for the hand (mit′ən) **noun**
mosquito a small insect with two wings (mə skē′ tō) **noun**
muscle a body tissue made of strong fibers (mus′əl) **noun**

Complete the blanks in the dictionary entries below.

WORD	DEFINITION	PRONUNCIATION	PART OF SPEECH
mitten	1. a warm covering for the hand	(mit′ ən)	*noun*
merry	1. cheerful and jolly	(mer′ē)	*adjective*
mosquito	1. a small insect with two wings	(mə skē′tō)	*noun*
meet	1. to come together with someone	(mēt)	*verb*
muscle	1. a body tissue made of strong fibers	(mus′əl)	*noun*

5 Book 3.1/Unit 2 **Spiders at Work** **At Home:** Have students write the nouns from the list above and use each in a sentence. 62

Reteach, 62

ON-LEVEL

Name________ Date________ **Practice 62**

Use a Dictionary

The word-history section of a dictionary entry tells how the word entered our language. *ME* stands for Middle English, an older form of English. *OE* stands for Old English, an even older form of English. *Fr* stands for French, and *OFr* stands for old French. Latin is also an old language.

leg the part of the body that is used for standing or walking *noun* (leg) ME *leggr.*

capture to grab or hold *verb* (kap′ chər) OFr< Latin *captura*

insect a small animal without a backbone *noun* (in sekt′) Latin *insectum*

spin to turn around and around *verb* (spin) ME *spinnen*

weave to spin a web or cocoon *verb* (wēv) OE *wefan*

Fill in the blanks in the chart below.

WORD	PRONUNCIATION	DEFINITION	PART OF SPEECH	ORIGIN
leg	(leg)	the part of the body that is used for standing or walking	noun	ME *leggr*
spin	(spin)	to turn around and around	verb	ME *spinnen*
weave	(wēv)	to spin a web or cocoon	verb	OE *wefan*
insect	(in′sekt)	a type of small animal without a backbone	noun	Latin *insectum*
capture	(kap′ cher)	to grab or hold	verb	OFr< Latin *captura*

6 Book 3.1/Unit 2 Spiders at Work **At Home:** Ask students to look in an dictionary and find another word that comes from Middle English, Old English, French, Old French, or Latin. 62

Practice, 62

CHALLENGE

Name________ Date________ **Extend 62**

Use a Dictionary

Answers will vary. Sample answers are shown.

A. Use a dictionary. Find out what each word means.

1. dangerous full of danger
2. allergy a condition in which a person is made sick by something that is harmless to most people
3. sting to prick painfully, usually with a sharp or poisonous stinger
4. tarantula a large hairy spider mistakenly believed to be dangerous

B. Use the words to write a story about Ned the tarantula.

Stories will vary.

Book 3.1/Unit 2 **Spiders at Work** **At Home:** Have students write as many sentences as they can using the word **sting** in different ways. 62

Extend, 62

TEST POWER

Test Tip
As you read, think about what is happening in the story.

DIRECTIONS:
Read the story. Then read each question about the story.

SAMPLE

Homework for Linda

Linda's father picked up her homework assignments from her teacher, Mr. Smith.

> **Math:**
> Complete the problems in Chapter 11. They are similar to the ones you did last week.
> **Spelling:**
> You spelled all of the words correctly last week! Your spelling work is complete this week.
> **Reading:**
> Finish reading *Mystery Island.* The book report will be due next week. Your book reports have been excellent. Keep up the good work!
> **Geography:**
> Highlight the capitals on the map of the United States.
> Get well soon!
> —Mr. Smith and your classmates

1 According to the letter, Linda does NOT have work in —

- ○ math
- ● spelling
- ○ geography
- ○ reading

2 From Mr. Smith's note, Linda probably thinks that her teacher is —

- ○ angry
- ○ bored
- ● caring
- ○ unkind

Why are your answers correct?

243

Test Power

THE PRINCETON REVIEW

Read the Page

Have students read *all* of the information on the page. Explain that shorter stories are full of important details.

Discuss the Questions

QUESTION 1: This question requires students to follow directions. Direct students back to the story. As a group, work through the answer choices. As you discuss what Linda needs to accomplish in math, have the students explain why this is not the correct answer choice.

QUESTION 2: This question requires students to determine what Linda probably thinks about her teacher. Based on the information in the story, what clues are given about Mr. Smith's personality? In the letter he said, "Keep up the good work"; in closing, "Get well soon." Use process of elimination to figure out the answer.

ITBS/TEST PREPARATION

TERRANOVA/TEST PREPARATION

SAT 9/TEST PREPARATION

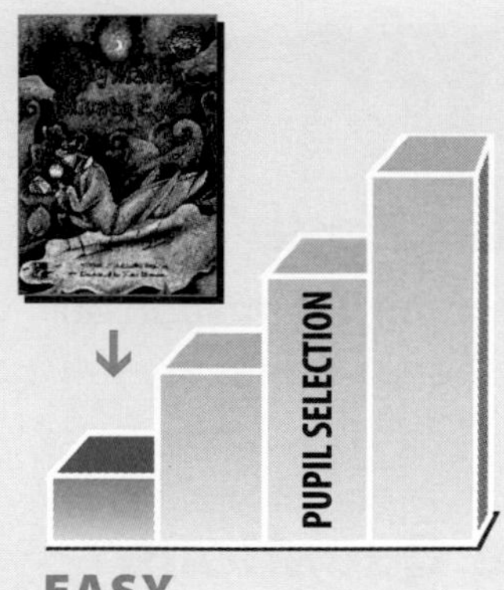

Leveled Books

EASY

Perry Mantis, Private Eye

Consonant Clusters

☑ **Important and Unimportant Information**

☑ **Instructional Vocabulary**
capture, liquid, ruin, serious, skills, struggles

Guided Reading

PREVIEW AND PREDICT Conduct a **picture walk** up to pages 6–7. Have students discuss illustrations and predict what the story is about. Chart their ideas.

SET PURPOSES Have students write down questions they would like the story to answer. For example: Why would a praying mantis make a good detective?

READ THE BOOK Use the following questions as students read or after they have read the story independently.

Pages 2–3: What word begins with the /str/ sound on these pages? *(strange)* ***Phonics and Decoding***

Pages 4–5: What does the word *skills* mean? (ability) ***Instructional Vocabulary***

Pages 6–7: Is it important for Honey Bee to tell Mantis about her earrings? Why or why not? (Yes, because it shows a crime was committed.) ***Important and Unimportant Information***

Pages 8–9: Why does Mantis want to avoid Buster the Bat? (Buster wants to catch Mantis.) ***Cause and Effect***

Pages 14–15: Who stole Honey Bee's earrings? How do you know? (Rusty the Roach. Petey asks him about the earrings.) ***Draw Conclusions***

Page 16: How did Perry Mantis trick Rusty? (He pretended to be Sting the Wasp.) ***Plot***

RETURN TO PREDICTIONS AND PURPOSES Review students' predictions and reasons for reading. Which predictions were accurate?

LITERARY RESPONSE Discuss these questions:

- Why do you think Mantis was the hero of this story?
- What mystery did Mantis solve?

Also see the story questions and activity in *Perry Mantis, Private Eye.*

See the Phonics **CD-ROM** for practice in consonant clusters.

Answers to Story Questions

1. Perry could blend into any surroundings.
2. No, the dream was not important in helping him solve the crime.
3. Sting the Wasp will probably be upset and angry. Rusty will find out he had been tricked.
4. The story tells how Perry Mantis, a praying mantis private eye, finds Ms. Honey Bee's earrings.
5. Possible answer: a month's worth of flies.

Story Questions and Writing Activity

1. Why did Ms. Honey Bee choose Perry Mantis to solve the case of the missing earrings?
2. Did Perry's dream about the cricket help him solve the crime?
3. What will happen when Rusty the Roach runs into Sting the Wasp?
4. What is the story mostly about?
5. Based on what you learned in *Spiders at Work,* what would Sam Spider probably have wanted from Sting in exchange for the earrings?

Who Would Be a Good Detective?

Draw a picture of another animal that might make a good detective. Use three or four sentences to tell why your animal would make a good private eye.

from *Perry Mantis, Private Eye*

Leveled Books

INDEPENDENT

Listen for the Rattle!

- ☑ **Important and Unimportant Information**
- ☑ **Instructional Vocabulary** ***capture, liquid, ruin, serious, skills, struggles***

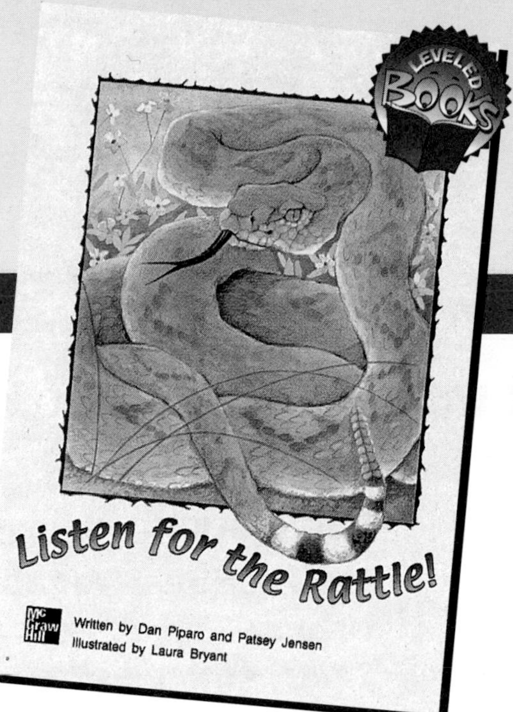

Leveled Books
Listen for the Rattle!
Written by Dan Piparo and Patsey Jensen
Illustrated by Laura Bryant

Guided Reading

PREVIEW AND PREDICT Conduct a **picture walk** to pages 6–7. As students discuss the illustrations, have them predict what the story is about. Chart their ideas.

SET PURPOSES Have students write questions about why they want to read the story. For example: Why do the girls know so much about snakes?

READ THE BOOK Use the following questions as students read or after they have read the story independently.

Pages 2–3: Does it matter that Anita's bike is bigger than María's? Why or why not? (no) ***Important and Unimportant Information***

Pages 6–7: Why does Anita tell the family two things about snakes that are not true? (She wanted to scare them.) ***Draw Conclusions***

Page 8: What does the word *struggles* mean? (make a great effort) ***Instructional Vocabulary***

Page 10: How do snakes help farmers? (They eat rodents and bugs that ruin crops.) ***Cause and Effect***

Pages 14–16: How are María and Anita different? How are they the same? (María likes to scare people. Anita does not. They both know a lot about snakes.) ***Compare and Contrast***

RETURN TO PREDICTIONS AND PURPOSES Review students' predictions. Ask which predictions were accurate and why. Have students review their purposes for reading. Did they find out what they wanted to know?

LITERARY RESPONSES Discuss these questions:

- Why do you think the girls shared their knowledge of snakes with the tourist family?
- What would you have done in their place?
- Did this story make you want to learn more about animal behavior?

Also see the Story Questions and activity in *Listen for the Rattle!*

INDEPENDENT

Answers to Story Questions

1. Anita and María are the main characters in the story.
2. It takes place at a store near the Grand Canyon in Arizona.
3. Snakes will not attack you if you leave them alone.
4. Anita and María give some tourists useful information about snakes.
5. Answers will vary.

Story Questions and Writing Activity

1. Who are the main characters in the story?
2. Where do you think the story takes place?
3. What is the most important fact Anita tells the tourists?
4. What is the story mostly about?
5. Compare what you learned here with *Spiders at Work.* How are spiders and snakes alike? How are they different?

Where are the Grand Canyon snakes?

Find a map of Arizona in an atlas or the encyclopedia. Draw the map. Mark where the Grand Canyon is on the map. Then draw a rattlesnake around the border of the map. Write three interesting facts about rattlesnakes on the bottom of the map.

from *Listen for the Rattle!*

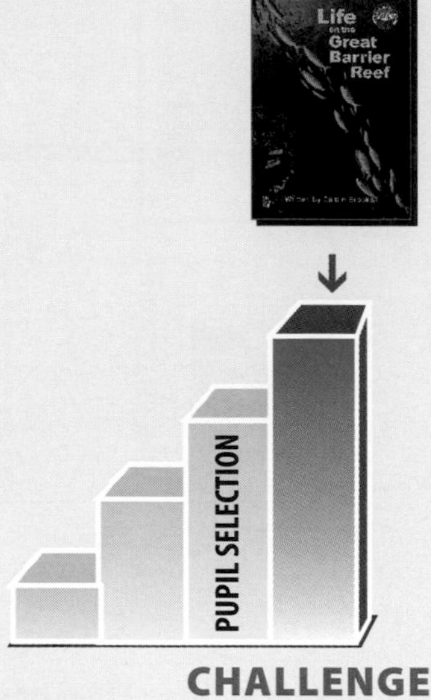

Leveled Books

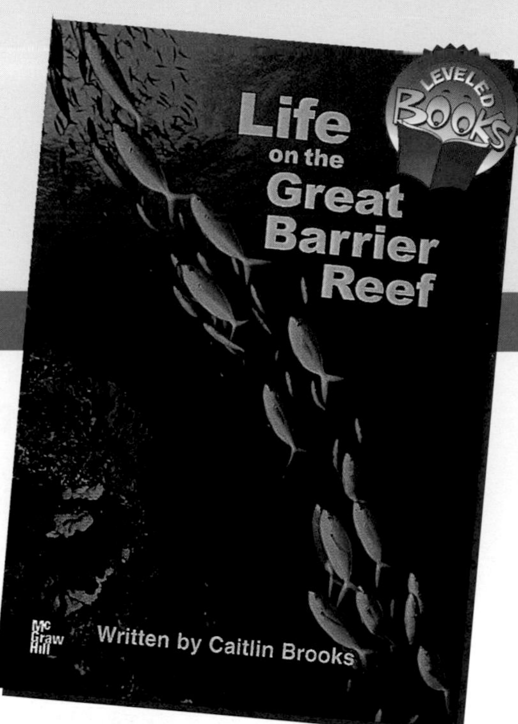

CHALLENGE

Life on the Great Barrier Reef

- ☑ **Important and Unimportant Information**
- ☑ **Instructional Vocabulary** ***capture, liquid, ruin, serious, skills, struggles***

Guided Reading

PREVIEW AND PREDICT Conduct a **picture walk** up to page 8. Have students discuss illustrations. Ask them to predict what the story will be about. Chart their ideas.

SET PURPOSES Have students write down questions they hope to find answers to by reading the story. For example: What kinds of dangerous animals live on a reef?

READ THE BOOK Use the following questions as students read or after they have read the story independently.

Pages 2–3: How is coral different from a plant? (It looks like a plant, but it is really a tiny animal.) ***Compare and Contrast***

Pages 4–5: How do you think some of the different kinds of coral get their names? (from their shapes) ***Draw Conclusions***

Page 8: What does the word *liquid* mean? How does the octopus use the dark liquid it shoots when it is afraid? (uses liquid as a screen to hide itself) ***Vocabulary***

Page 11: If you were a diver, would you need to know facts about tiger sharks? Why or why not? (Yes. Tiger sharks sometimes attack divers.) ***Important and Unimportant Information***

Pages 14–15: How are dolphins and sea cows alike? (They are both mammals.) ***Compare and Contrast***

RETURN TO PREDICTIONS AND PURPOSES Review students' predictions. Have students review their purposes in reading. Did they find out what they wanted to know?

LITERARY RESPONSE Discuss these questions:

- Why would you describe the reef as a huge undersea garden?
- Why is it important not to disturb the life undersea?

Also see the story questions and activity in *Life on the Great Barrier Reef.*

Answers to Story Questions

1. The Great Barrier Reef is the largest coral reef in the world.
2. A coral reef is made of the hard shells of dead coral.
3. Its shell is very hard. When a giant clam closes it, its enemies can't harm it.
4. The story is about the different kinds of animals found in the Great Barrier Reef.
5. Both are patient hunters; spiders move about on their webs, while coral spend all their lives in one place.

Story Questions and Writing Activity

1. What is the Great Barrier Reef?
2. Why is a coral reef hard?
3. How does the giant clam protect itself?
4. What is the story mostly about?
5. How are spiders similar to coral? In what ways are they different?

Choose Your Favorite

Draw a picture of your favorite fish from the coral reef. You may choose a fish from the story or choose one from a reference book. Label your picture. Then write a paragraph that tells about the fish and why you like it.

from *Life on the Great Barrier Reef*

Connecting Texts

SUMMARIZE Write the story titles on a chart. Discuss with students what happened in each story. Have them focus on the important events in each selection. Call on volunteers from each reading level and challenge them to summarize their story in three sentences.

Spiders at Work	Perry Mantis, Private Eye	Listen for the Rattle!	Life on the Great Barrier Reef
• Spiders weave webs to catch insects for food. • There are many different kinds of spiders. • Spiders are arachnids like ticks and daddy longlegs.	• Perry is a private eye who can make himself almost invisible. • Honey Bee hires him to get back her earrings from the June Bug Gang. • Perry tricks Rusty Roach into giving back the earrings.	• Anita and Maria are sisters who know a lot about snakes. • A family of tourists is afraid of snakes until the girls explain what to watch out for. • The girls help the family feel safer as they leave on a camping trip.	• Australia's Great Barrier Reef is made from dead coral. • Many interesting creatures—both harmless and dangerous—live on the reef. • Visitors to the reef must take care not to harm it.

Viewing/Representing

GROUP PRESENTATIONS Divide the class into groups, one for each of the four books read in the lesson. (For *Spiders at Work*, combine students of different reading levels.) Have each group create charts with columns labeled Animal and Home; then fill them in for each selection. Have each group present its chart to the class.

AUDIENCE RESPONSE Ask students to pay attention to each group's presentation. Allow time for questions after each presentation.

Research and Inquiry

MORE ABOUT ANIMALS Have students ask themselves: Why are some people so frightened of spiders, snakes, and sharks? Then invite them to do the following:

- Use school library resources to research information about these animals.
- Plan a visit to a natural history museum.

*inter***NET** CONNECTION Have students log on to ***www.mhschool.com/reading*** for information about spiders, snakes, and sharks.

OBJECTIVES

Students will distinguish between important and unimportant information.

TEACHING TIP

INSTRUCTIONAL To aid in comprehension, encourage students to visualize the information given.

Review Important and Unimportant Information

PREPARE

Discuss Important and Unimportant Information Remind students that knowing the main idea in the selection will help them to better distinguish between important and unimportant information.

TEACH

Read "Owning a Tarantula" and Model the Skill Ask students to distinguish between important and unimportant information as you read the **Teaching Chart 52** passage with them.

Owning a Tarantula

Some people buy tarantulas, and keep them as pets. If you decide to have a pet tarantula, you should know how to take care of it. First, it is important that you keep it in a safe cage. This can be an aquarium, a plastic shoe box, or a gallon glass jar. Make sure there are a few small holes at the top of the cage. Put soil and sand at the bottom of the cage.

Secondly, know what to feed it. Most tarantulas eat worms and crickets, but some larger tarantulas like to eat mice. Remember to give it water as well. And be careful holding it. Tarantulas can get badly hurt if you drop them.

Teaching Chart 52

Discuss how readers can distinguish between important and unimportant information in this passage.

MODEL The main idea of this passage is to tell how to take care of a tarantula. Knowing that other people have tarantulas as pets doesn't tell me how to take care of them. Therefore that is not important information for me.

PRACTICE

Distinguish Between Important and Unimportant Information

Have students underline the important information in "Owning a Tarantula." Ask: If the purpose of your reading this passage is to find out how to take care of a tarantula, then what information becomes the most important? (All the information after the word *First* in the first paragraph.)

ASSESS/CLOSE

Write about Places and Discuss Important Information

Brainstorm a list of places that various students have visited, such as the zoo, the ocean, another country, a museum, and so on. Ask students to each pick a place and write a short essay about it. Invite partners to read each other's papers and discuss what they think is important information and why.

ALTERNATE TEACHING STRATEGY

IMPORTANT AND UNIMPORTANT INFORMATION

For a different approach to teaching this skill, see page T66.

SELF-SELECTED Reading

Students may choose from the following titles.

ANTHOLOGY

- *Spiders at Work*

LEVELED BOOKS

- *Perry Mantis, Private Eye*
- *Listen for the Rattle!*
- *Life on the Great Barrier Reef*

Bibliography, pages T76–T77

Meeting Individual Needs for Comprehension

EASY

Name__________ Date______ **Reteach 63**

Important and Unimportant Information

When you read nonfiction, you need to be able to tell the difference between important information and unimportant information. **Important information** gives information about the main ideas. **Unimportant information** may be interesting, but not useful for understanding the main idea.

What information would be useful if you were going to write a report on spiders? Read each pair of sentences about spiders. Write an **X** next to the sentence in each pair that contains important information that you could use in your factual report.

1. X The fastest spider in the world can run 330 times the length of its own body in ten seconds.
   __ A person can only run 50 times his or her length in that time.
2. __ Tarantulas look like monsters.
   X Tarantulas have eight eyes, but they still don't see very well.
3. __ Most children know the song about the spider and the rain.
   X Most spiders live only for a year or so.
4. X The spider makes a bridge line by spinning out a long thread.
   __ All builders should study the garden spider.
5. __ Can you guess how the daddy-longlegs got its name?
   X Dark spots on the spider's legs help the spider to smell and taste.

63 **At Home:** Ask students how they decided which information would be useful in writing a report about spiders. Book 3.1/Unit 2 **Spiders at Work** 5

Reteach, 63

ON-LEVEL

Name__________ Date______ **Practice 63**

Important and Unimportant Information

People often read stories like "Spiders at Work" in order to answer questions that they have. Keeping such purposes in mind can help you sort out **important information** from **unimportant information**.

Decide whether or not each statement below is important to the given purpose. Write an **X** next to the information that is important.

Purpose: To find out which spiders can hurt people

___ 1. The web looks pretty, but it is a trap for flies and other bugs.
X 2. Black widow spiders do not bite people very often.
X 3. The tarantula's bite is about as strong as a bee sting.
___ 4. Spiders belong to a family of their own.

Purpose: To find out how a spider builds its web

X 5. The air helps the spider by blowing the bridge line from one plant to another.
___ 6. Daddy-longlegs eat flies and mosquitoes.
X 7. The spider keeps building by going back and forth, and up and down.
X 8. The spider spins a sticky thread in a circle.

Purpose: To find out where spiders live

___ 9. Some spiders are as small as the head of a pin.
X 10. Water spiders have their homes under water.
___ 11. Ants have six legs, and spiders have eight legs.
X 12. One spider in South America lives in trees and eats small birds.

63 **At Home:** Ask students to illustrate one of the sentences on the page. Book 3.1/Unit 2 **Spiders at Work** 12

Practice, 63

CHALLENGE

Name__________ Date______ **Extend 63**

Important and Unimportant Information

We draw. We write. We talk. Sometimes we sign. We do these activities to communicate. When you communicate directions or instructions, you need to make sure you communicate what is most important.

Write how to make a peanut butter and jelly sandwich. Make sure you write exactly what to do. Keep it simple.

Answers will vary, but should list exact steps in making the sandwich. For example: Get two pieces of bread. Get peanut butter and open the jar. Get jelly and open the jar. With a knife, carefully spread the peanut butter on one side of one piece of bread. Use the knife to spread the jelly on one side of the other piece of bread. Put the bread together with the jelly side and the peanut butter side facing each other.

Ask a friend or family member to follow your instructions and make a peanut butter and jelly sandwich.

Now tell someone how to make a peanut butter and jelly sandwich by speaking. You can use gestures. Compare the two sandwiches. Explain why one looks better than the other.

Write down any of the information in your directions that was unimportant.

Answers will vary.

Explain how you could do a better job of telling or writing how to make the sandwich.

Answers will vary.

63 **At Home:** Have students tell how to make another kind of sandwich they like to eat. Remind them to include only the important steps. Book 3.1/Unit 2 **Spiders at Work**

Extend, 63

LANGUAGE SUPPORT

Name__________ Date______

Spider Web

silk threads	catches food	sticky threads
different sizes	wheel shape	one hour to spin
everywhere	beautiful	for travel

silk threads
catches food
sticky threads
wheel shape
for travel

70 **Spiders at Work** • Language Support/Blackline Master 34 Grade 3

Language Support, 70

TESTED OBJECTIVES

Students will draw conclusions.

TEACHING TIP

INSTRUCTIONAL Remind students that readers must draw conclusions based on evidence that the author gives and what they know from their own experience.

Review Draw Conclusions

PREPARE

Discuss Draw Conclusions

Remind students that drawing a conclusion from a selection means to arrive at a decision or realization based on information that you have learned while reading. Explain that drawing conclusions helps you think about and make decisions about the information you've learned.

TEACH

Read "The House Spider" and Model the Skill

Ask students to think about whether or not they would want a house spider in their house as you read the **Teaching Chart 53** passage with them.

The House Spider

Some people don't like spiders. They think that all spiders are dangerous and hurt people. But that's not true. A lot of common spiders are quite shy and their fangs are too small or weak to harm humans.

One of these types of spiders might be found in your own home, and, as a matter of fact, is called a house or cobweb spider. This spider likes to spin its web in the dark corners of a room. It hangs upside down while waiting for its prey to come along. If you don't like the idea of a spider in your house, stop and think about the harmful insects it eats, like mosquitoes and flies.

Teaching Chart 53

Ask a volunteer to find and underline two facts about the house spider. Help students decide if this is enough information to draw a conclusion about whether or not it might be helpful to have a house spider in the house.

MODEL These two facts lead me to the conclusion that house spiders don't hurt humans. But still, I would want more information before I decide if it's good to have a house spider in the house. I'll find more facts in the passage before I draw my conclusion.

PRACTICE

Use a Fact List to Draw Conclusions Have students list facts that will help them draw a conclusion about whether or not they would want a house spider in their home. Afterwards, invite them to discuss these facts and share their conclusions.
▶ **Logical/Visual**

House Spider Facts
shy
fangs are too weak to harm humans
found in many homes
spins webs in dark corners
eats insects from your home

ASSESS/CLOSE

Play a Game of Twenty Questions Explain the game rules: A volunteer thinks of a person, place, or thing. The rest of the class is allowed to ask twenty questions in order to guess what the student is thinking of. The volunteer can only answer "yes" or "no." Point out that students are using the facts they are learning to draw conclusions about what the volunteer is thinking.

ALTERNATE TEACHING STRATEGY

DRAW CONCLUSIONS
For a different approach to teaching this skill, see page T62.

LOOKING AHEAD
Students will apply this skill as they read the next selection, *Web Wonders*.

Meeting Individual Needs for Comprehension

EASY

Name______ Date______ Reteach 64

Draw Conclusions

A conclusion is always based on information. To **draw conclusions** about a story or a character, use the information the author gives you as well as what you know from your own life.

Read the story. Then answer each question.

Alix wasn't very excited when she woke up on Saturday. Because she had promised to help her parents clean out the barn, she would miss going ice skating with her friends. Instead, she guessed, she would spend the day brushing spiders out of her hair.

Kicking the snow off her boots, Alix went inside the old barn. Her mother was cleaning the floor. Each time her father washed another window, more light streamed into the room. As she explored the corners with her dust cloth, Alix discovered a doll's crib and a child's rocking chair.

"Look at these beautiful old things," Alix said, "I wonder who they belonged to."

1. What is Alix going to do today? clean out a barn with her parents
2. What information from the story lets you know what she will do? She has to help her parents, she goes to the barn, her mother cleans, her father washes windows, Alix dusts with a dust cloth.
3. What time of year is it? winter
4. What clues tell you the time of year? Alix will not be able to go ice skating; she kicks the snow off her boots.
5. What did Alix want to do today? go ice skating

5 Book 3.1/Unit 2 **Spiders at Work** **At Home:** Ask students to draw conclusions about whether Alix is a person who keeps her word. 64

Reteach, 64

ON-LEVEL

Name______ Date______ Practice 64

Draw Conclusions

You can **draw conclusions** based on information from a story or from your own life. You can often draw conclusions from just a few clues.

Draw a conclusion from each passage below.

1. Sometimes, Jeff and Bill would fight over their toys. When this happened, their grandmother played games with them so they would forget why they were fighting.
   Conclusion: What can you tell about the boys' grandmother?
   She is patient and knows how to keep children from fighting.
2. The flowers had just started to peek out from beneath the ground. The park was full of people wearing jackets and hats that they didn't need.
   Conclusion: What time of year is it? How do you know? Spring; the flowers are coming up and the weather is warm.
3. Kim decided to try out for the baseball team. Her brother said she was better than he had been at her age.
   Conclusion: Is Kim's brother older or younger? older
4. "It is too bad that so many people are afraid of spiders. Most spiders don't bite! Many are even helpful. They eat bugs that might bite you," said Jack.
   Conclusion: How does Jack feel about spiders? He likes spiders.
5. May spilled her milk. Her teacher still had something kind to say about May. May's teacher was good when things went wrong.
   Conclusion: What is May's teacher like? She is kind.

5 Book 3.1/Unit 2 **Spiders at Work** **At Home:** Have students draw another conclusion about each of the passages. 64

Practice, 64

CHALLENGE

Name______ Date______ Extend 64

Draw Conclusions

A conclusion is what you decide to think about something based on what you see, what you already know, and on any other information you have. Look at each of the pictures below. Draw a conclusion about what is happening in each one. Answers will vary. Sample answers are shown.

1. The rabbit and the turtle are having a tea party.
2. The rabbit fell off his bike.
3. The rabbit and turtle are running a race.

Choose one picture. Write a story about it on another piece of paper.

Book 3.1/Unit 2 **Spiders at Work** **At Home:** Have students write another scenario for what might be happening in each picture. 64

Extend, 64

LANGUAGE SUPPORT

Name______ Date______

Should You Be Afraid?

	Black Widows	Trantulas
Who?		
What?		
When?		
Where?		
How?		
Why?		

Conclusion:

1. Yes, you should be afraid of Black Widows because
2. No, you should not be afraid of Black Widows because
3. Yes, you should be afraid of Tarantulas because
4. No, you should not be afraid of Tarantulas because

Grade 3 Language Support/Blackline Master 35 • **Spiders at Work** 71

Language Support, 71

Review Antonyms and Synonyms

OBJECTIVES

Students will identify antonyms and synonyms.

MATERIALS

- **Teaching Chart 54**

TEACHING TIP

INSTRUCTIONAL Remind students that looking at a word's prefix or suffix can help define the word.

- The prefix *ant-* as in *antonyms*, means *"against."*
- The prefix *syn-* as in *synonym*, means *"with."*

Show students how to use a thesaurus when looking for synonyms and antonyms.

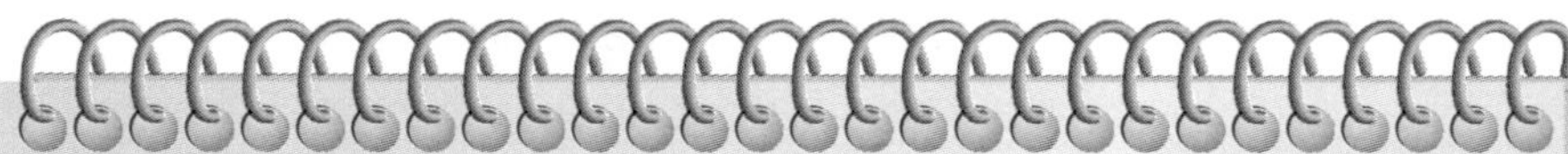

PREPARE

Review Antonyms and Synonyms

Explain: Synonyms are words that have similar meanings. Antonyms are words that are opposite in meaning. Knowing the synonyms and antonyms of words can improve your understanding when you read. It also gives you more words to choose from for your own writing.

TEACH

Read the Passage and Model the Skill

Have students read the passage on **Teaching Chart 54**. Encourage them to look for antonyms and synonyms.

Spider's Web

Have you ever seen a web shining with light from the early morning sun? Have you noticed how the dew clings to the strands of the web like tiny little diamonds?

A web is made from silk which starts off as a liquid but soon becomes solid. Spiders spend anywhere from twenty-five minutes to weave a little web to several hours for a large one.

A spider web is so beautiful and lovely to look at that, it is hard to imagine its main purpose is to be a deadly trap for insects.

Teaching Chart 54

Model identifying an antonym.

MODEL To help me better understand the passage's meaning, I will look for antonyms and synonyms. For example, I see a sentence containing two words that are antonyms, *liquid* and *solid*. This sentence helps me see how the silk in a spider web changes.

Have students discuss how knowing the synonym or antonym helps make the information clearer.

PRACTICE

Identify Synonyms and Antonyms

Have volunteers circle words in **Teaching Chart 54** that are synonyms and underline words that are antonyms. Then help the class brainstorm a list of adjectives and write them on the chalkboard. Challenge students to give synonyms and antonyms for the words and write these on the chalkboard as well. ▶ **Linguistic/Visual**

ASSESS/CLOSE

Write Using Antonyms and Synonyms

Assess students' understanding of synonyms and antonyms by having them write a paragraph using at least six of the listed words, including two synonyms and two antonyms.

ALTERNATE TEACHING STRATEGY

ANTONYMS AND SYNONYMS

For a different approach to teaching this skill, see page T65.

Meeting Individual Needs for Vocabulary

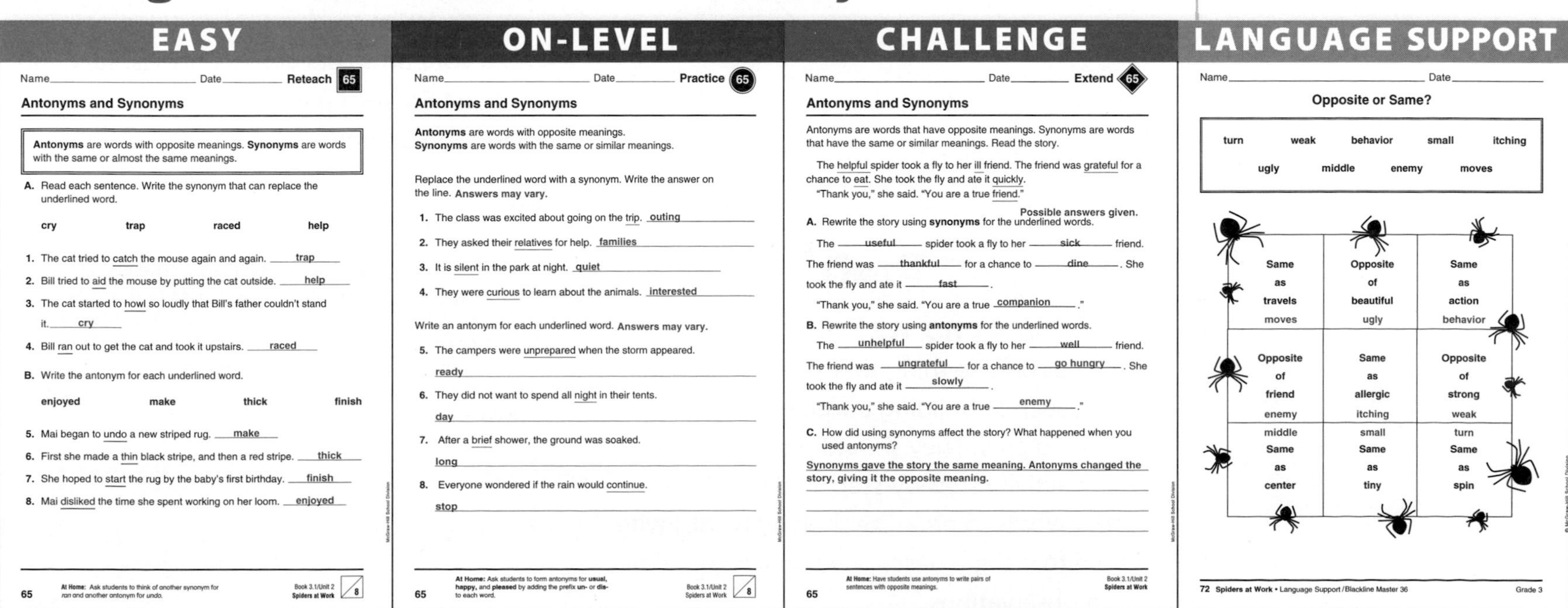

EASY

Name______________ Date________ **Reteach 65**

Antonyms and Synonyms

Antonyms are words with opposite meanings. **Synonyms** are words with the same or almost the same meanings.

A. Read each sentence. Write the synonym that can replace the underlined word.

cry **trap** **raced** **help**

1. The cat tried to catch the mouse again and again. trap
2. Bill tried to aid the mouse by putting the cat outside. help
3. The cat started to howl so loudly that Bill's father couldn't stand it. cry
4. Bill ran out to get the cat and took it upstairs. raced

B. Write the antonym for each underlined word.

enjoyed **make** **thick** **finish**

5. Mai began to undo a new striped rug. make
6. First she made a thin black stripe, and then a red stripe. thick
7. She hoped to start the rug by the baby's first birthday. finish
8. Mai disliked the time she spent working on her loom. enjoyed

65 **At Home:** Ask students to think of another synonym for *ran* and another antonym for *undo*. Book 3.1/Unit 2 **Spiders at Work** 8

ON-LEVEL

Name______________ Date________ **Practice 65**

Antonyms and Synonyms

Antonyms are words with opposite meanings.
Synonyms are words with the same or similar meanings.

Replace the underlined word with a synonym. Write the answer on the line. **Answers may vary.**

1. The class was excited about going on the trip. outing
2. They asked their relatives for help. families
3. It is silent in the park at night. quiet
4. They were curious to learn about the animals. interested

Write an antonym for each underlined word. **Answers may vary.**

5. The campers were unprepared when the storm appeared. ready
6. They did not want to spend all night in their tents. day
7. After a brief shower, the ground was soaked. long
8. Everyone wondered if the rain would continue. stop

65 **At Home:** Ask students to form antonyms for **usual, happy,** and **pleased** by adding the prefix **un-** or **dis-** to each word. Book 3.1/Unit 2 Spiders at Work 8

CHALLENGE

Name______________ Date________ **Extend 65**

Antonyms and Synonyms

Antonyms are words that have opposite meanings. Synonyms are words that have the same or similar meanings. Read the story.

The helpful spider took a fly to her ill friend. The friend was grateful for a chance to eat. She took the fly and ate it quickly.

"Thank you," she said. "You are a true friend."

Possible answers given.

A. Rewrite the story using **synonyms** for the underlined words.

The useful spider took a fly to her sick friend. The friend was thankful for a chance to dine. She took the fly and ate it fast.

"Thank you," she said. "You are a true companion."

B. Rewrite the story using **antonyms** for the underlined words.

The unhelpful spider took a fly to her well friend. The friend was ungrateful for a chance to go hungry. She took the fly and ate it slowly.

"Thank you," she said. "You are a true enemy."

C. How did using synonyms affect the story? What happened when you used antonyms?

Synonyms gave the story the same meaning. Antonyms changed the story, giving it the opposite meaning.

65 **At Home:** Have students use antonyms to write pairs of sentences with opposite meanings. Book 3.1/Unit 2 **Spiders at Work**

LANGUAGE SUPPORT

Name______________ Date________

Opposite or Same?

turn **weak** **behavior** **small** **itching**
ugly **middle** **enemy** **moves**

Same as travels moves	Opposite of beautiful ugly	Same as action behavior
Opposite of friend enemy	Same as allergic itching	Opposite of strong weak
middle Same as center	small Same as tiny	turn Same as spin

72 **Spiders at Work** • Language Support/Blackline Master 36 Grade 3

Reteach, 65 **Practice, 65** **Extend, 65** **Language Support, 72**

Explanatory Writing

GRAMMAR/SPELLING CONNECTIONS

See the 5-Day Grammar and Usage Plan on Apostrophes, pages 243M–243N.

See the 5-Day Spelling Plan on pages 243O–243P.

TECHNOLOGY TIP

Use the thesaurus to find synonyms for words. Instead of using the same word over and over, find a word that means almost the same thing in the thesaurus.

Prewrite

WRITE A REPORT Present this writing assignment: Select a type of spider that you would like to learn more about. Write a report explaining something that your chosen spider does. Include lots of fun facts and a diagram.

LIST QUESTIONS Ask students to think about all the things they need to know about what their spider does. Partners can work together to decide which questions are most important. As they research, students can make a separate list of fun facts to include in their report.

Strategy: Make a Word Web Have students draw word webs showing the different facts they find out about their spiders.
For example:

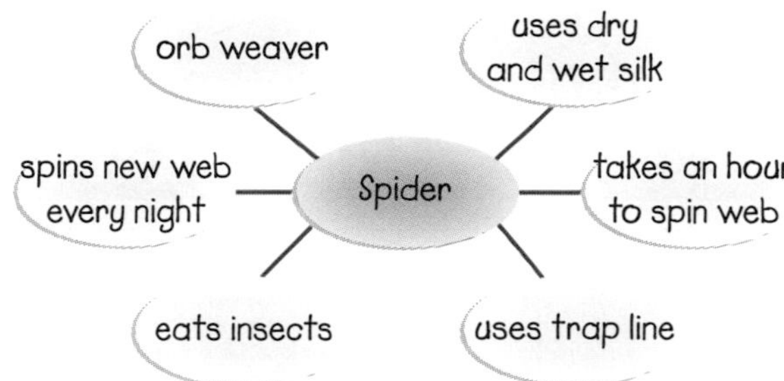

Draft

USE THE WORD WEB Remind students to focus on one thing that their topic spider does, such as building a web or nest, or catching prey. They should present the animal's activity step-by-step, and use time-order words to organize their material. Invite them to include descriptive details, and their own observations.

Revise

SELF-QUESTIONING Have students assess their drafts by asking themselves:

- Is each step in the spider's activity clear?
- Can a reader "see" what the spider is doing?
- Did I use important descriptions and vivid details?

Have partners exchange reports and give feedback on the information presented in each report.

Edit/Proofread

CHECK FOR ERRORS Students should reread their reports for spelling, grammar, and punctuation. Have them check to make sure their language is clear and appropriate.

Publish

SHARE SPIDERS Students can read their reports to the class. As they listen to the reports, invite students to jot down notes for a vote on spider characteristics, such as Scariest Spider, Funniest Spider, or Best Web-Spinner.

The Golden Spider Catches Dinner

Golden spiders are orb weavers. They weave round webs made out of both wet and dry silk. This kind of spider uses a trap line to catch its prey. The spider attaches a line to the center of the web. Then it hides in its nest and holds onto the line. When an insect lands in the web, the line moves and the spider comes out and gets it. Golden spiders weave a new web every night. It takes about an hour.

Presentation Ideas

PRESENT ILLUSTRATIONS Have students present detailed illustrations of their spiders, labeling each part.
▶ **Representing/Viewing**

MAKE A SPEECH Students can use their reports to make speeches about why their spider is the best spider. After all the speeches have been made, students can vote for a King and a Queen of all spiders.
▶ **Speaking/Listening**

Consider students' creative efforts, possibly adding a (+) for originality, wit, and imagination.

Scoring Rubric

Excellent	Good	Fair	Unsatisfactory
4: The writer • presents a well-researched, detailed explanation of a spider activity. • organizes each step of the activity in a time-order. • enhances facts with description and relevant observation.	**3:** The writer • correctly explains one spider activity. • presents a step-by-step process in proper sequence. • may explore some descriptive detail.	**2:** The writer • attempts to explain a spider activity. • may not follow a complete step-by - step order. • may provide few, or vague, supporting details.	**1:** The writer: • may not grasp the assignment. • may show extreme lack of organization. • may present disconnected facts, details, or observations.

0: The writer leaves the page blank or fails to respond to the writing tasks. The student does not address the topic or simply paraphrases the prompt. The response is illegible or incoherent.

COMMUNICATION TIPS

VIEWING Have students pay careful attention to details in their illustrations.

SPEAKING Remind students that persuasive speakers make eye contact with the audience, vary their tone, and speak clearly. Have them keep the goal of their speech in mind as they talk.

LANGUAGE SUPPORT

ESL Students from other countries may be familiar with spiders or other insects that are native to that land. Invite them to write and share information about these creatures with the class.

PORTFOLIO Invite students to include their reports or another writing project in their portfolios.

Meeting Individual Needs for Writing

EASY

Spider Poster Have students create a spider poster explaining the various types of webs spiders can weave. Encourage them to draw other elements of a spider's world, such as its food and its enemies. Remind students to clearly label their posters.

ON-LEVEL

Keep a Diary Have students write a diary entry from the point of view of an insect who managed to escape from a spider's web. Ask them to include how they felt while they were trapped, and how they managed to escape.

CHALLENGE

Life as a Spider Ask students to think about how their life would change if they had as many arms and legs as a spider. Invite them to write a report on their day as a human with eight arms and legs. What special things could they achieve? Would it change how they play a sport or an instrument?

5 Day Grammar and Usage Plan

LANGUAGE SUPPORT

ESL Have each student show something that belongs to him or her. Have the class respond by saying the possessive form. Example: *Ben's pencil.*

DAILY LANGUAGE ACTIVITIES

Write the Daily Language Activities on the chalkboard each day or use **Transparency 9**. Have students correct the sentences orally.

Day 1

1. The spiders web looks like lace. spider's
2. It is natures web maker. nature's
3. The black widows bite is strong. widow's.

Day 2

1. Tarantulas bodies are hairy. Tarantulas'
2. Many mens hands have been bitten. men's
3. Spiders threats are serious. Spiders'

Day 3

1. The fly is caught in the webs spokes. web's
2. Each spiders bite is deadly. spider's
3. This familys members are insects. family's

Day 4

1. That webs threads are invisible. web's
2. The two legs purpose is special. legs'
3. The girls mother told her a folk tale. girl's

Day 5

1. The Spider Womans skills were spinning and weaving. Woman's
2. She made blankets from the sheeps wool. sheep's
3. This rattlesnakes venom is deadly. rattlesnake's

Daily Language Transparency 9

DAY 1 Introduce the Concept

Oral Warm-Up Read aloud: *Sara's watch stopped ticking.* Have students identify to whom the watch belongs. Explain that the most common way to say "the watch that belongs to Sara" or "the watch that Sara owns" is to say "Sara's watch."

Introduce Possessive Nouns A noun that shows ownership is a possessive noun. Present the following:

Possessive Nouns

- A **possessive noun** is a noun that shows who or what owns or has something.
- Add an **apostrophe (')** and an *s* to a singular noun to make it possessive.

Present the Daily Language Activity and have students correct orally. Then have students write the possessive form for the following: *the bone that belongs to the dog, the cap that the girl owns, the brother of Pedro.*

WRITING

Assign the daily Writing Prompt on page 226C.

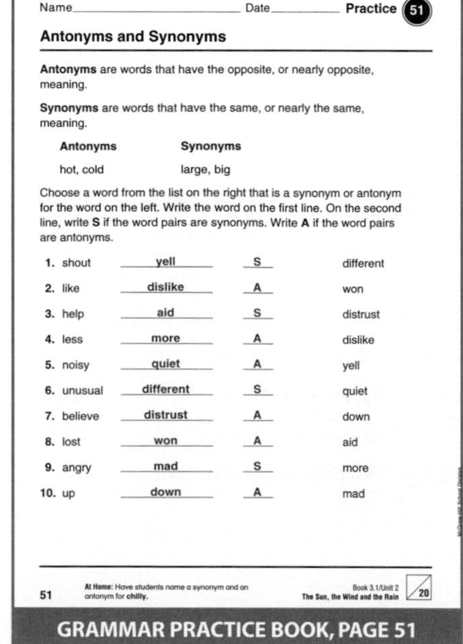

Name________ Date________ **Practice 51**

Antonyms and Synonyms

Antonyms are words that have the opposite, or nearly opposite, meaning.

Synonyms are words that have the same, or nearly the same, meaning.

Antonyms	Synonyms
hot, cold	large, big

Choose a word from the list on the right that is a synonym or antonym for the word on the left. Write the word on the first line. On the second line, write **S** if the word pairs are synonyms. Write **A** if the word pairs are antonyms.

1.	shout	yell	S	different
2.	like	dislike	A	won
3.	help	aid	S	distrust
4.	less	more	A	dislike
5.	noisy	quiet	A	yell
6.	unusual	different	S	quiet
7.	believe	distrust	A	down
8.	lost	won	A	aid
9.	angry	mad	S	more
10.	up	down	A	mad

51 **At Home:** Have students name a synonym and an antonym for **chilly.** Book 3.1/Unit 2 The Sun, the Wind and the Rain 20

GRAMMAR PRACTICE BOOK, PAGE 51

DAY 2 Teach the Concept

Review Singular Possessives Ask students to define a possessive noun and give an example of one.

Introduce Plural Possessives Plural nouns can also be possessive. Present and discuss:

Plural Possessive Nouns

- Add an apostrophe to make most plural nouns possessive.
- Add an apostrophe and *s* to form the plural possessive of plural nouns that do not end in *s*.

Present the Daily Language Activity. Then write the following on the chalkboard: *the room that belongs to the boys, the shoes owned by the children.* Have students write a sentence about each, using a possessive noun.

WRITING

Assign the daily Writing Prompt on page 226C.

Name________ Date________ **Practice 52**

Cause and Effect

A **cause** is what makes something happen. The **effect** is what happens as a result of the cause. You can use cause and effect to help you make predictions about what might happen next.

Read each paragraph. Write the cause that made the effect happen. Then write a sentence to make a prediction. **Predictions may vary.**

Jack grew apples to sell at the market. This year the apples were perfect. They had not been eaten by worms. Jack had found a new way to keep the worms away.

1. **Cause:** Jack had used a new way to keep the worms away.
2. **Effect:** The apples were perfect and hadn't been filled with worms.
3. **Predict** what Jack will do next year: He may sell his idea for keeping worms away to other apple farmers.

Anna decided to eat her lunch outside. She sat on a bench and took out her sandwich. Suddenly she heard a buzzing sound. There was a bee flying around Anna. The bee wanted a bite of her sandwich.

4. **Cause:** Anna takes out her sandwich.
5. **Effect:** A bee is buzzing around Anna.
6. **Predict** what Anna will do for lunch tomorrow: She may eat her sandwich inside.

4 Book 3.1/Unit 2 Dream Wolf **At Home:** Have students predict what they would do if they were ten feet tall. 52

GRAMMAR PRACTICE BOOK, PAGE 52

Possessive Nouns

DAY 3 Review and Practice

Learn from the Literature Review possessive nouns. Read the sentence on page 233 of *Spiders at Work*.

> **The poison in the black widow's bite is very strong.**

Ask students to identify the possessive noun and what belongs to it. (black widow's, bite)

Identify Possessive Nouns Present the Daily Language Activity and have students correct orally.

Have students look through the story to find more possessive nouns. They can make a two-column chart—one column identifying the noun and the other column identifying its possessive form. For example, *nature* is a noun; *nature's web maker* shows the noun in possessive form.

Assign the daily Writing Prompt on page 226D.

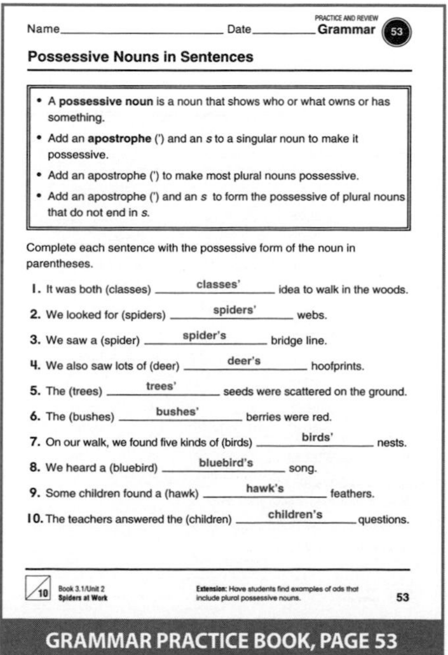

Name__________ Date__________ PRACTICE AND REVIEW Grammar 53

Possessive Nouns in Sentences

- A **possessive noun** is a noun that shows who or what owns or has something.
- Add an **apostrophe** (') and an *s* to a singular noun to make it possessive.
- Add an apostrophe (') to make most plural nouns possessive.
- Add an apostrophe (') and an *s* to form the possessive of plural nouns that do not end in *s*.

Complete each sentence with the possessive form of the noun in parentheses.

1. It was both (classes) **classes'** idea to walk in the woods.
2. We looked for (spiders) **spiders'** webs.
3. We saw a (spider) **spider's** bridge line.
4. We also saw lots of (deer) **deer's** hoofprints.
5. The (trees) **trees'** seeds were scattered on the ground.
6. The (bushes) **bushes'** berries were red.
7. On our walk, we found five kinds of (birds) **birds'** nests.
8. We heard a (bluebird) **bluebird's** song.
9. Some children found a (hawk) **hawk's** feathers.
10. The teachers answered the (children) **children's** questions.

10 Book 3.1/Unit 2 Spiders at Work

Extension: Have students find examples of ads that include plural possessive nouns.

53

GRAMMAR PRACTICE BOOK, PAGE 53

DAY 4 Review and Practice

Review Possessive Nouns Have students describe something about other students using the possessive form. For example: *Tim's eyes are brown.* Put some examples on the board. Then present the Daily Language Activity.

Mechanics and Usage Review the use of an apostrophe with possessive nouns.

Apostrophes in Possessives

- Add an apostrophe and an *s* to a singular noun to make it possessive.
- Add an apostrophe to make most plural nouns possessive.
- Add an apostrophe and *s* to form the possessive of plural nouns that do not end in *s*.

Assign the daily Writing Prompt on page 226D.

Name__________ Date__________ MECHANICS Grammar 54

Correcting Possessive Nouns

- Add an apostrophe (') and an *s* to a singular noun to make it possessive.
- Add an apostrophe (') to make most plural nouns possessive.
- Add an apostrophe (') and an *s* to form the possessive of plural nouns that do not end in *s*.

Rewrite each sentence. Use the correct possessive form of the underlined word.

1. Water <u>spiders</u> homes are underwater.
   Water spiders' homes are underwater.
2. A garden <u>spider</u> web is strong.
   A garden spider's web is strong.
3. Some spiders are as small as a <u>pin</u> head.
   Some spiders are as small as a pin's head.
4. Black widows can cause <u>humans</u> death.
   Black widows can cause humans' death.
5. A black <u>widow</u> bite is poisonous.
   A black widow's bite is poisonous.
6. <u>Rattlesnakes</u> venom is not as deadly.
   Rattlesnakes' venom is not as deadly.
7. In Africa, some <u>children</u> stories are about a spider.
   In Africa, some children's stories are about a spider.
8. The <u>story</u> main character is called Anansi.
   The story's main character is called Anansi.

54

Extension: Have students use the possessive nouns *spider's, spiders', bush's, bushes'* in sentences of their own and draw pictures to illustrate each sentence.

Book 3.1/Unit 2 Spiders at Work 8

GRAMMAR PRACTICE BOOK, PAGE 54

DAY 5 Assess and Reteach

Assess Use the Daily Language Activity and page 55 of the **Grammar Practice Book** for assessment.

Reteach Have students write each rule about possessive nouns on an index card. Dictate the following sentences and have students hold up the card that gives the rule for each noun. Then ask students to make up their own sentences.

Have students add their sentences to the classroom word wall and underline each possessive noun.

Assign the daily Writing Prompt on page 226D.

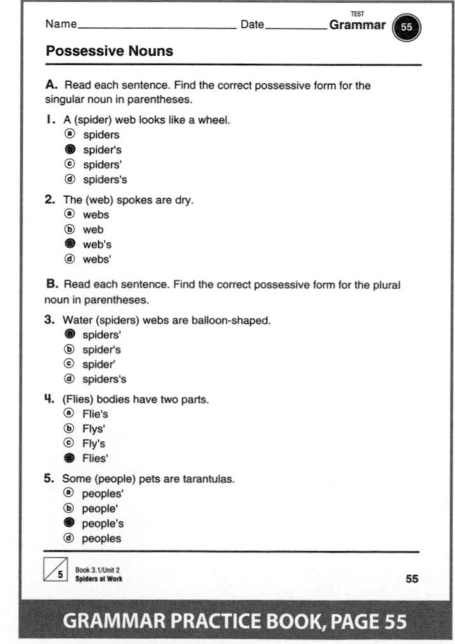

Name__________ Date__________ TEST Grammar 55

Possessive Nouns

A. Read each sentence. Find the correct possessive form for the singular noun in parentheses.

1. A (spider) web looks like a wheel.
   - ⓐ spiders
   - ● spider's
   - ⓒ spiders'
   - ⓓ spiders's
2. The (web) spokes are dry.
   - ⓐ webs
   - ⓑ web
   - ● web's
   - ⓓ webs'

B. Read each sentence. Find the correct possessive form for the plural noun in parentheses.

3. Water (spiders) webs are balloon-shaped.
   - ● spiders'
   - ⓑ spider's
   - ⓒ spider'
   - ⓓ spiders's
4. (Flies) bodies have two parts.
   - ⓐ Flie's
   - ⓑ Flys'
   - ⓒ Fly's
   - ● Flies'
5. Some (people) pets are tarantulas.
   - ⓐ peoples'
   - ⓑ people'
   - ● people's
   - ⓓ peoples

5 Book 3.1/Unit 2 Spiders at Work

55

GRAMMAR PRACTICE BOOK, PAGE 55

GRAMMAR PRACTICE BOOK, PAGE 56

5 Day Spelling Plan

LANGUAGE SUPPORT

ESL Review the difference between singular and plural nouns. Write on the chalkboard:

There is one ______.

There are many ______.

Point to different objects or people in the classroom, alternating between singular and plural nouns, and have students complete the sentences. Examples: *There is one teacher. There are many students.*

DICTATION SENTENCES

1. The blankets are made of wool.
2. That tree has large branches.
3. The flies are all around the horses.
4. The plane went over the mountains.
5. I went through three states.
6. Most libraries have many books.
7. She has three pairs of boots.
8. The farmers sell bunches of flowers.
9. Enemies do not like each other at all.
10. That dress has deep pockets.
11. Birds live in most jungles.
12. The fields are covered with daisies.
13. That book is three inches high.
14. He works for many companies.
15. He wrote down the addresses.

Challenge Words

16. A spider can capture flies.
17. The liquid in the dish is hot.
18. Rain will ruin her birthday party.
19. The player has many skills.
20. The farmer struggles to grow crops.

DAY 1 Pretest

Assess Prior Knowledge Use the Dictation Sentences at the left and **Spelling Practice Book** page 51 for the pretest. Allow students to correct their own papers. If students have trouble, have partners give each other a midweek test on Day 3. Students who require a modified list may be tested on the first eight words.

Spelling Words		Challenge Words
1. **blankets**	9. enemies	16. **capture**
2. branches	10. pockets	17. **liquid**
3. **flies**	11. **jungles**	18. **ruin**
4. **mountains**	12. daisies	19. **skills**
5. **states**	13. inches	20. **struggles**
6. libraries	14. companies	
7. pairs	15. addresses	
8. bunches		

*Note: Words in **dark type** are from the story.*

Word Study On page 52 of the **Spelling Practice Book** are word study steps and an at-home activity.

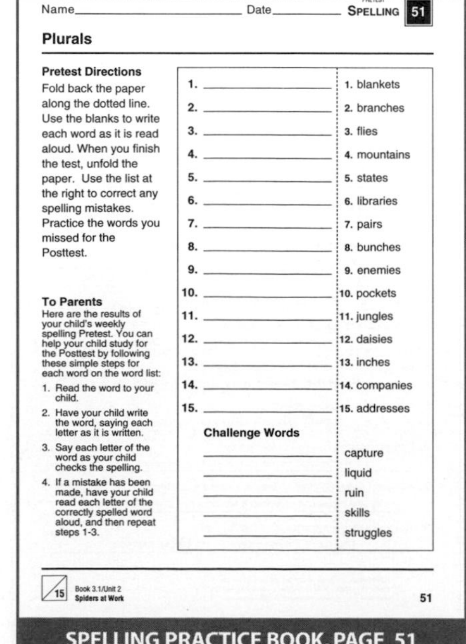

Name________________ Date__________ PRETEST SPELLING 51

Plurals

Pretest Directions
Fold back the paper along the dotted line. Use the blanks to write each word as it is read aloud. When you finish the test, unfold the paper. Use the list at the right to correct any spelling mistakes. Practice the words you missed for the Posttest.

To Parents
Here are the results of your child's weekly spelling Pretest. You can help your child study for the Posttest by following these simple steps for each word on the word list:
1. Read the word to your child.
2. Have your child write the word, saying each letter as it is written.
3. Say each letter of the word as your child checks the spelling.
4. If a mistake has been made, have your child read each letter of the correctly spelled word aloud, and then repeat steps 1-3.

1. ______ 1. blankets
2. ______ 2. branches
3. ______ 3. flies
4. ______ 4. mountains
5. ______ 5. states
6. ______ 6. libraries
7. ______ 7. pairs
8. ______ 8. bunches
9. ______ 9. enemies
10. ______ 10. pockets
11. ______ 11. jungles
12. ______ 12. daisies
13. ______ 13. inches
14. ______ 14. companies
15. ______ 15. addresses

Challenge Words
______ capture
______ liquid
______ ruin
______ skills
______ struggles

15 Book 3.1/Unit 2 Spiders at Work 51

SPELLING PRACTICE BOOK, PAGE 51

WORD STUDY STEPS AND ACTIVITY, PAGE 52

DAY 2 Explore the Pattern

Sort and Spell Words Write the words *blanket, bunch,* and *fly* on the chalkboard. Then write their plural forms. Review: To make most nouns plural, add *-s;* add *-es* if the word ends in *s, sh, ch,* or *x;* change *y* to *i* and add *-es* if the word ends in a consonant and *y.* All of the Spelling Words are plural nouns. Have students sort them according to the rule followed in forming them.

Add *s*	Add *es*	Change *y* to *i* and add *es*
blankets	branches	flies
mountains	bunches	libraries
pairs	inches	enemies
pockets	addresses	daisies
states		companies
jungles		

Word Wall Have students add to the list of plural nouns on the word wall.

Name________________ Date__________ EXPLORE THE PATTERN SPELLING 53

Plurals

blankets	mountains	pairs	pockets	inches
branches	states	bunches	jungles	companies
flies	libraries	enemies	daisies	addresses

This week's spelling list contains plural words. **Plurals** are words that name more than one thing.
Write the spelling words for each of these plural endings.

s
1. blankets
2. mountains
3. pairs
4. pockets
5. states
6. jungles

es
7. branches
8. bunches
9. inches
10. addresses

y to i + es
11. flies
12. libraries
13. enemies
14. daisies
15. companies

Find the Base Word
Write the base word of each plural noun.
16. blankets blanket 17. flies fly
18. branches branch

18 Book 3.1/Unit 2 Spiders at Work 53

SPELLING PRACTICE BOOK, PAGE 53

Plurals

Practice and Extend

Word Meaning: Base Words Explain to students that the base word of each Spelling Word is the singular form. Have students work in pairs to write the base words for Spelling Words. Review the spelling rules for forming plurals.

Glossary Have partners:

- write each Challenge Word.
- look up each Challenge Word and find the ones that have synonyms listed.
- write a synonym for each Challenge Word that has one listed.

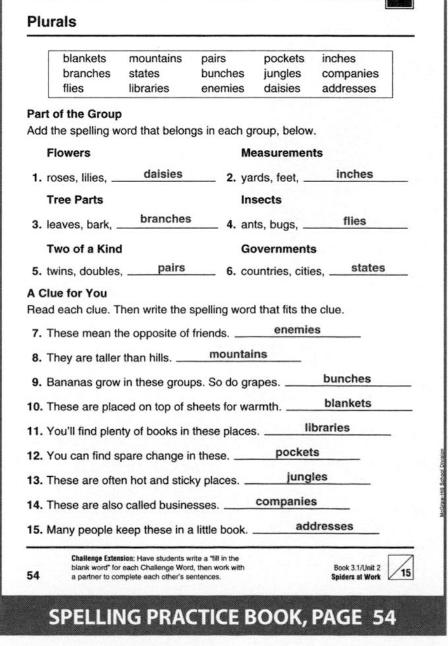

Name________ Date______ PRACTICE AND EXTEND SPELLING 54

Plurals

blankets	mountains	pairs	pockets	inches
branches	states	bunches	jungles	companies
flies	libraries	enemies	daisies	addresses

Part of the Group

Add the spelling word that belongs in each group, below.

Flowers
1. roses, lilies, daisies

Measurements
2. yards, feet, inches

Tree Parts
3. leaves, bark, branches

Insects
4. ants, bugs, flies

Two of a Kind
5. twins, doubles, pairs

Governments
6. countries, cities, states

A Clue for You

Read each clue. Then write the spelling word that fits the clue.

7. These mean the opposite of friends. enemies
8. They are taller than hills. mountains
9. Bananas grow in these groups. So do grapes. bunches
10. These are placed on top of sheets for warmth. blankets
11. You'll find plenty of books in these places. libraries
12. You can find spare change in these. pockets
13. These are often hot and sticky places. jungles
14. These are also called businesses. companies
15. Many people keep these in a little book. addresses

Challenge Extension: Have students write a "fill in the blank word" for each Challenge Word, then work with a partner to complete each other's sentences.

54 Book 3.1/Unit 2 Spiders at Work 15

SPELLING PRACTICE BOOK, PAGE 54

Proofread and Write

Proofread Sentences Write these sentences on the chalkboard, including the misspelled words. Ask students to proofread, circling incorrect spellings and writing the correct spellings. There are two spelling errors in each sentence.

He has three paires of pants with pocketes. (pairs, pockets)

Librarys have books about jungels. (libraries, jungles)

Have students create additional sentences with errors for partners to correct.

WRITING Have students use as many spelling words as possible in the daily Writing Prompt on page 226D. Remind students to proofread their writing for errors in spelling, grammar, and punctuation.

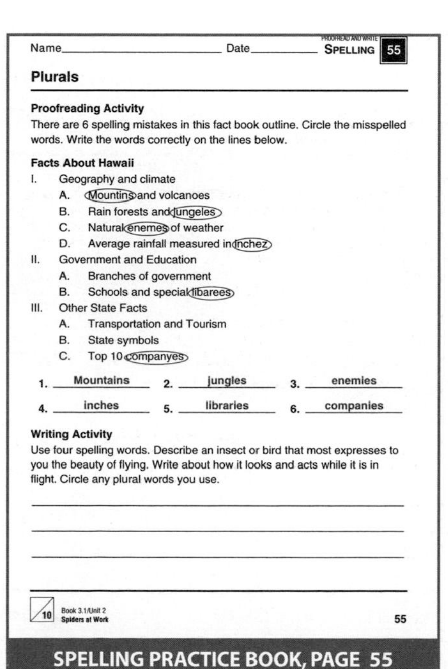

Name________ Date______ PROOFREAD AND WRITE SPELLING 55

Plurals

Proofreading Activity

There are 6 spelling mistakes in this fact book outline. Circle the misspelled words. Write the words correctly on the lines below.

Facts About Hawaii

I. Geography and climate
   A. Mountins and volcanoes
   B. Rain forests and jungeles
   C. Natural enemes of weather
   D. Average rainfall measured in inchez
II. Government and Education
   A. Branches of government
   B. Schools and special libarees
III. Other State Facts
   A. Transportation and Tourism
   B. State symbols
   C. Top 10 companyes

1. Mountains 2. jungles 3. enemies
4. inches 5. libraries 6. companies

Writing Activity

Use four spelling words. Describe an insect or bird that most expresses to you the beauty of flying. Write about how it looks and acts while it is in flight. Circle any plural words you use.

10 Book 3.1/Unit 2 Spiders at Work 55

SPELLING PRACTICE BOOK, PAGE 55

Assess and Reteach

Assess Students' Knowledge Use page 56 of the **Spelling Practice Book** or the Dictation Sentences on page 243O for the post test.

Personal Word List Have JOURNAL students list in their journals any words that they can use to describe a place or a setting. (For example: jungles, mountains, flies, daisies, branches) Have them add to the list as they come across other setting words in their reading.

Students can refer to their lists during later writing activities.

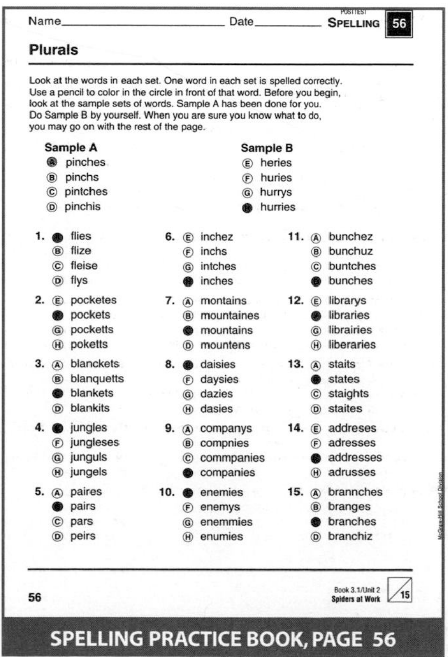

Name________ Date______ POSTTEST SPELLING 56

Plurals

Look at the words in each set. One word in each set is spelled correctly. Use a pencil to color in the circle in front of that word. Before you begin, look at the sample sets of words. Sample A has been done for you. Do Sample B by yourself. When you are sure you know what to do, you may go on with the rest of the page.

Sample A
● pinches
(B) pinchs
(C) pintches
(D) pinchis

Sample B
(E) heries
(F) huries
(G) hurrys
● hurries

1. ● flies (B) flize (C) fleise (D) flys
2. (E) pocketes ● pockets (G) pocketts (H) poketts
3. (A) blanckets (B) blanquetts ● blankets (D) blankits
4. ● jungles (F) jungleses (G) junguls (H) jungels
5. (A) paires ● pairs (C) pars (D) peirs
6. (E) inchez (F) inchs (G) intches ● inches
7. (A) montains (B) mountaines ● mountains (D) mountens
8. ● daisies (F) daysies (G) dazies (H) dasies
9. (A) companys (B) compnies (C) commpanies ● companies
10. ● enemies (F) enemys (G) enemmies (H) enumies
11. (A) bunchez (B) bunchuz (C) buntches ● bunches
12. (E) librarys ● libraries (G) librairies (H) liberaries
13. (A) staits ● states (C) staights (D) staites
14. (E) addreses (F) adresses ● addresses (H) adrusses
15. (A) brannches (B) branges ● branches (D) branchiz

56 Book 3.1/Unit 2 Spiders at Work 15

SPELLING PRACTICE BOOK, PAGE 56

Web Wonders

Selection Summary Students will read about the amazing silk that spiders produce, and about all the wonderful ways that scientists use it.

Listening Library Audiocassette

INSTRUCTIONAL
Pages 246–253

Resources for

Meeting Individual Needs

REVIEW

LEVELED BOOKS

EASY
Pages 253A, 253D

INDEPENDENT
Pages 253B, 253D

Take-Home version available

CHALLENGE
Pages 253C, 253D

LEVELED PRACTICE

Reteach, 66–72
blackline masters with reteaching opportunities for each assessed skill

Practice, 66–72
workbook with Take-Home Stories and practice opportunities for each assessed skill and story comprehension

Extend, 66–72
blackline masters that offer challenge activities for each assessed skill

ADDITIONAL RESOURCES

- **Language Support Book** 73–80
- **Take-Home Story, Practice** p. 67a
- **Alternate Teaching Strategies** T60–T66
- **Selected Quizzes Prepared by** 

Suggested Lesson Planner

Available on CD-ROM

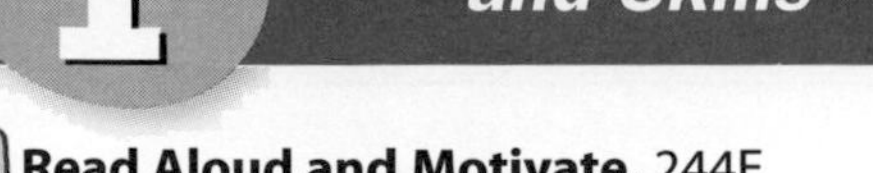

READING AND LANGUAGE ARTS	DAY 1 Focus on Reading and Skills	DAY 2 Read the Literature
• Comprehension • Vocabulary • Phonics/Decoding • Study Skills • Listening, Speaking, Viewing, Representing	Read **Read Aloud and Motivate,** 244E "Arachne the Spinner" **Develop Visual Literacy,** 244/245 ☑ **Review Compare and Contrast,** 246A–246B **Teaching Chart 55** **Reteach, Practice, Extend,** 66	**Build Background,** 246C Develop Oral Language **Vocabulary,** 246D ***crops*** ***earthquake*** ***hatch*** ***respect*** ***soldiers*** ***woven*** **Teaching Chart 56** **Word Building Manipulative Cards** **Reteach, Practice, Extend,** 67  **Read the Selection,** 246–249 Guided Instruction ☑ Compare and Contrast ☑ Draw Conclusions
 • Curriculum Connections	 **Fine Arts,** 244/245	 **Science,** 246C
• Writing	 **Writing Prompt:** Why do you think some people are afraid of spiders? What would you tell them?	 **Writing Prompt:** Compare how a spider makes a web and how a person sews on a missing button.  **Journal Writing,** 249 Quick Write
• Grammar	**Introduce the Concept: Sentence Combining with Nouns,** 253M Daily Language Activity 1. The spider has a web. The spider has a trap. The spider has a web and a trap. 2. I saw a spider. I saw a fly. I saw a spider and a fly. **Grammar Practice Book,** 57	**Teach the Concept: Sentence Combining with Nouns,** 253M Daily Language Activity 1. Spiders crawl. Lizards crawl. 2. Spiders lay eggs. Chickens lay eggs. 3. Farmers like spiders. Scientists like spiders. **Grammar Practice Book,** 58
• Spelling	**Pretest: Words from Science,** 253O **Spelling Practice Book,** 57–58	**Explore the Pattern: Words from Science,** 253O **Spelling Practice Book,** 59

Meeting Individual Needs

☑ = Skill Assessed in Unit Test

DAY 3 Read the Literature

Reread for Fluency, 248

Story Questions, 250
Reteach, Practice, Extend, 68
Story Activities, 251

Study Skill, 252
Reference Sources
Teaching Chart 57
Reteach, Practice, Extend, 69

Read the Leveled Books,
Guided Reading
Phonics Review
☑ Comprehension Review
 CD-ROM

 Art, 251

 **Writing Prompt:** Do you think car manufacturers would like to make bumpers that never get a dent? Why or why not?

Writing Process: Explanatory Writing, 253K
Prewrite, Draft

Review and Practice: Sentence Combining with Nouns, 253N
Daily Language Activity
1. The bug crawled. The ant crawled.
2. Spiders have eight legs. Spiders have eight eyes.
3. The ant got out. The fly got out.
Grammar Practice Book, 59

Practice and Extend: Words from Science, 253P
Spelling Practice Book, 60

DAY 4 Build and Review Skills

 **Read the Leveled Books and Self-Selected Books**

☑ **Review Important and Unimportant Information,** 253E–253F
Teaching Chart 58
Reteach, Practice, Extend, 70
Language Support, 78

☑ **Review Antonyms and Synonyms,** 253G–253H
Teaching Chart 59
Reteach, Practice, Extend, 71
Language Support, 79

 **Writing Prompt:** Write a letter to a friend telling him or her about some of the things spider silk can do.

Writing Process: Explanatory Writing, 253K Revise

Meeting Individual Needs for Writing, 253L

Review and Practice: Sentence Combining with Nouns, 253N
Daily Language Activity
1. Flies were caught. Birds were caught.
2. Len found a spider. Len found a firefly.
3. The bug died. The ant died.
Grammar Practice Book, 60

Proofread and Write: Words from Science, 253P
Spelling Practice Book, 61

DAY 5 Build and Review Skills

 **Read Self-Selected Books**

☑ **Review Context Clues,** 253I–253J
Teaching Chart 60
Reteach, Practice, Extend, 72
Language Support, 80

Listening, Speaking, Viewing, Representing, 253L
Picture That
Persuasive Speaking

 **Writing Prompt:** Silk makes things strong. Write about things you use that would be better if they were stronger.

Writing Process: Explanatory Writing, 253K
Edit/Proofread, Publish

Assess and Reteach: Sentence Combining with Nouns, 253N
Daily Language Activity
1. Spiders help crops. Spiders help flowers.
2. The babies are gone. The eggs are gone.
3. The spiders grew. The web grew.
Grammar Practice Book, 61–62

Assess and Reteach: Words from Science, 253P
Spelling Practice Book, 62

Language Arts

Read Aloud and Motivate

Arachne the Spinner

retold by
Geraldine McCaughrean

Once, when all cloths and clothes were woven by hand, there was a weaver called Arachne more skillful than all the rest. Her tapestries were so lovely that people paid a fortune to buy them. Tailors and weavers came from miles around just to watch Arachne at work on her loom. Her shuttle flew to and fro, and her fingers plucked the strands as if she were making music rather than cloth.

"The gods certainly gave you an amazing talent," said her friends.

"Gods? There's nothing the gods could teach me about weaving. I can weave better than any god or goddess."

Her friends turned rather pale. "Better not let the goddess Athene hear you say that."

"I don't care who hears it. I'm the best there is," said Arachne.

An old lady sitting behind her examined the yarns Arachne had spun that morning, feeling their delightful texture between finger and thumb.

Continued on pages T2–T5

Oral Comprehension

LISTENING AND SPEAKING Encourage students to think about character and setting as you read aloud this Greek myth. When you have finished, ask students, "How would you describe the character of Athene?" Then ask, "What do you think is the setting for this story? How do you know?" Discuss the ending of the story. Do students think Athene treated Arachne fairly?

Activity Help groups make their own tapestries. Create a simple loom by wrapping yarn loosely around a large book ten times. Demonstrate how to weave yarn through the strands encircling the book using a large paper clip as a shuttle. Encourage students to use different-colored yarns. Alternately, show pictures of tapestries and then have students draw the myth as if it were panels of a tapestry.

▶ **Kinesthetic/Visual**

Develop Visual Literacy

Anthology pages 244-245

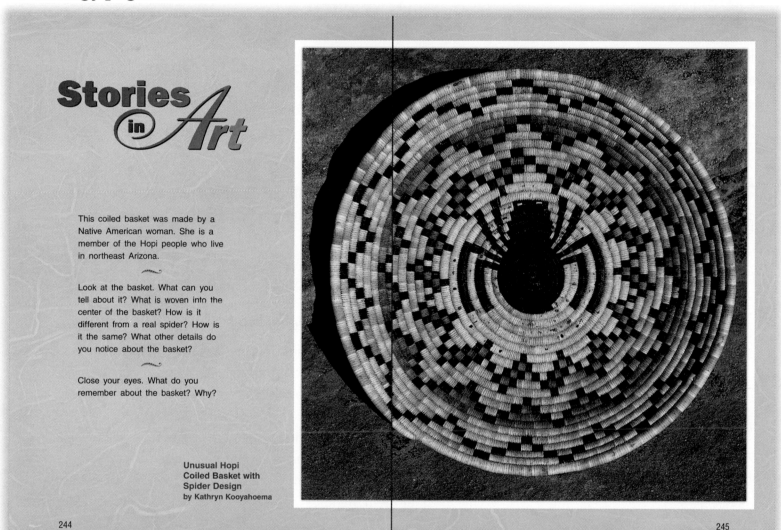

Stories in Art

This coiled basket was made by a Native American woman. She is a member of the Hopi people who live in northeast Arizona.

Look at the basket. What can you tell about it? What is woven into the center of the basket? How is it different from a real spider? How is it the same? What other details do you notice about the basket?

Close your eyes. What do you remember about the basket? Why?

Unusual Hopi Coiled Basket with Spider Design
by Kathryn Kooyahoema

244

245

Objective: Compare and Contrast

VIEWING This photograph shows a Hopi coiled basket with a spider design. The pattern of the basket is as intricate and symmetrical as the pattern of a spider's web. Ask students to close their eyes and visualize a spider's web and compare and contrast it with the photograph they have just seen. How are the two alike? How are they different?

Read the page with students, encouraging individual interpretations of the photograph.

Ask students to compare the handiwork of the basket with the handiwork of real spiders in nature. For example:

- Both can be viewed as works of art.
- The symmetrical pattern of the basket matches the symmetry of the spider's web. Have students note patterns that exist in nature.

REPRESENTING Have students reproduce floral or leaf patterns in drawings. Encourage them to use alternating colors to reinforce pattern motifs.

Review Compare and Contrast

TESTED OBJECTIVES

Students will compare and contrast as they read.

LANGUAGE SUPPORT

ESL Have students begin by comparing and contrasting animals such as dogs and cats. Then review vocabulary for comparing and contrasting a butterfly and a bee.

PREPARE

Use Compare and Contrast to Describe Ask volunteers to describe a bee to someone who has never seen any insect but a butterfly. Have them explain why it helps that person if you compare a bee to a butterfly.

TEACH

Define Compare and Contrast Remind students that comparing shows how things are alike and contrasting shows how they are different.

Grasshoppers and Praying Mantises

Scientists put grasshoppers and praying mantises into the group of insects called *orthoptera*. All orthoptera have the same kind of wings, go through the same stages of development, and chew their food.

But grasshoppers and praying mantises have important differences. Grasshoppers eat plants, and often destroy farmers' crops. Since praying mantises eat other insects, farmers consider them friends.

Teaching Chart 55

Read the Passage Aloud and Model the Skill Display **Teaching Chart 55**. Have students pay attention to similarities and differences as the passage is read.

MODEL The first paragraph tells me about some of the things that make grasshoppers and praying mantises alike. This helps me understand why scientists group them together. But the second paragraph explains what is different about them. This gives me a clearer picture of the two insects.

PRACTICE

Compare and Contrast Using a Venn Diagram Have students underline the similarities and circle the differences between the two insects described in the passage. Then have students create a Venn diagram to compare and contrast grasshoppers and praying mantises.

GRASSHOPPERS		PRAYING MANTISES
Different	**Alike**	**Different**
eat plants, destroy crops	both have same kind of wings; both develop in the same way; both chew their food	eat other insects; farmers consider them friends

ASSESS/CLOSE

Give Reasons for Comparing and Contrasting Ask students why scientists need to know how grasshoppers and praying mantises are alike. Then have them explain why farmers need to know how they are different.

Meeting Individual Needs for Comprehension

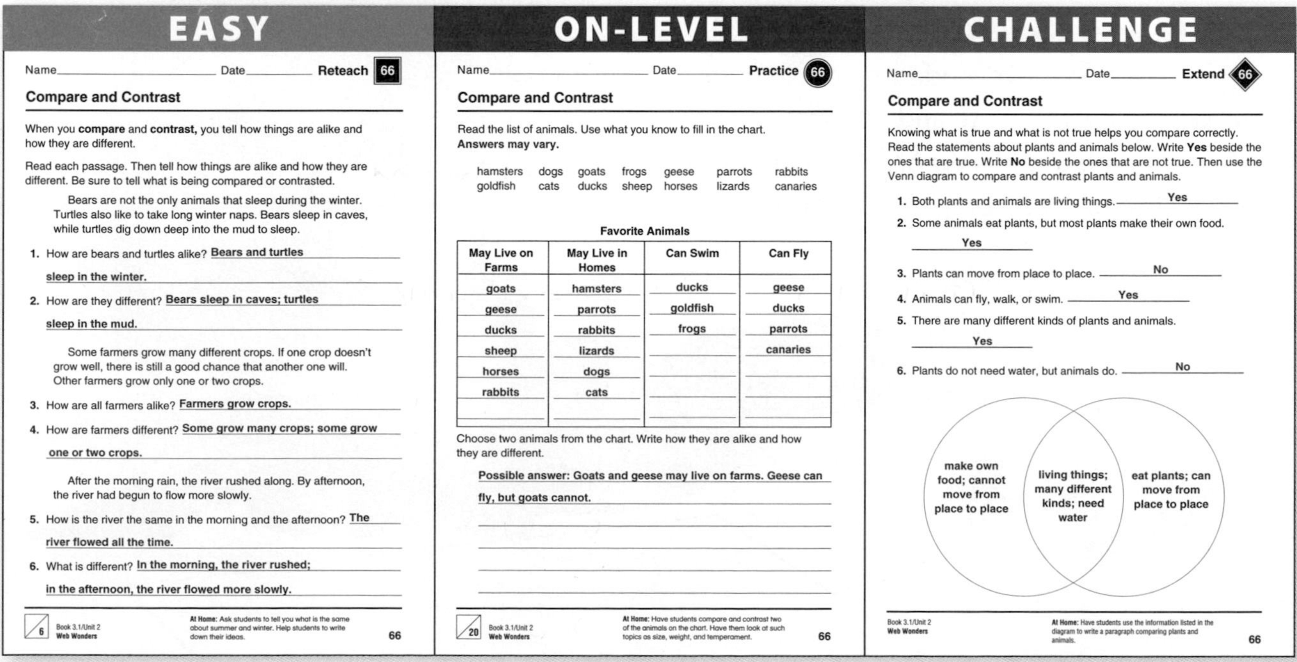

EASY

Name______________ Date__________ **Reteach 66**

Compare and Contrast

When you **compare** and **contrast,** you tell how things are alike and how they are different.

Read each passage. Then tell how things are alike and how they are different. Be sure to tell what is being compared or contrasted.

Bears are not the only animals that sleep during the winter. Turtles also like to take long winter naps. Bears sleep in caves, while turtles dig down deep into the mud to sleep.

1. How are bears and turtles alike? **Bears and turtles sleep in the winter.**
2. How are they different? **Bears sleep in caves; turtles sleep in the mud.**

Some farmers grow many different crops. If one crop doesn't grow well, there is still a good chance that another one will. Other farmers grow only one or two crops.

3. How are all farmers alike? **Farmers grow crops.**
4. How are farmers different? **Some grow many crops; some grow one or two crops.**

After the morning rain, the river rushed along. By afternoon, the river had begun to flow more slowly.

5. How is the river the same in the morning and the afternoon? **The river flowed all the time.**
6. What is different? **In the morning, the river rushed; in the afternoon, the river flowed more slowly.**

6 Book 3.1/Unit 2 **Web Wonders**

At Home: Ask students to tell you what is the same about summer and winter. Help students to write down their ideas. 66

Reteach, 66

ON-LEVEL

Name______________ Date__________ **Practice 66**

Compare and Contrast

Read the list of animals. Use what you know to fill in the chart. **Answers may vary.**

hamsters dogs goats frogs geese parrots rabbits
goldfish cats ducks sheep horses lizards canaries

Favorite Animals

May Live on Farms	May Live in Homes	Can Swim	Can Fly
goats	hamsters	ducks	geese
geese	parrots	goldfish	ducks
ducks	rabbits	frogs	parrots
sheep	lizards		canaries
horses	dogs		
rabbits	cats		

Choose two animals from the chart. Write how they are alike and how they are different.

Possible answer: Goats and geese may live on farms. Geese can fly, but goats cannot.

20 Book 3.1/Unit 2 **Web Wonders**

At Home: Have students compare and contrast two of the animals on the chart. Have them look at such topics as size, weight, and temperament. 66

Practice, 66

CHALLENGE

Name______________ Date__________ **Extend 66**

Compare and Contrast

Knowing what is true and what is not true helps you compare correctly. Read the statements about plants and animals below. Write **Yes** beside the ones that are true. Write **No** beside the ones that are not true. Then use the Venn diagram to compare and contrast plants and animals.

1. Both plants and animals are living things. **Yes**
2. Some animals eat plants, but most plants make their own food. **Yes**
3. Plants can move from place to place. **No**
4. Animals can fly, walk, or swim. **Yes**
5. There are many different kinds of plants and animals. **Yes**
6. Plants do not need water, but animals do. **No**

Book 3.1/Unit 2 **Web Wonders**

At Home: Have students use the information listed in the diagram to write a paragraph comparing plants and animals. 66

Extend, 66

SELECTION Connection

Students will compare and contrast when they read *Web Wonders* and the Leveled Books.

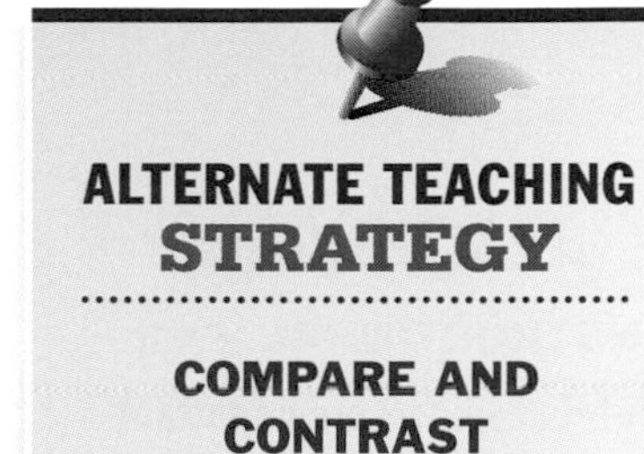

ALTERNATE TEACHING STRATEGY

COMPARE AND CONTRAST

For a different approach to teaching this skill, see page T64.

Build Background

Science

Evaluate Prior Knowledge

CONCEPT: WEBS This selection gives information about spider webs. Have students describe their experiences with spider webs, including where they found them and what they found interesting about them. Write key words from these descriptions on the chalkboard.

MAKE A WORD WEB Using the key words written on the board, have students create a word web about their experience of finding spider webs. ▶ **Logical/Visual**

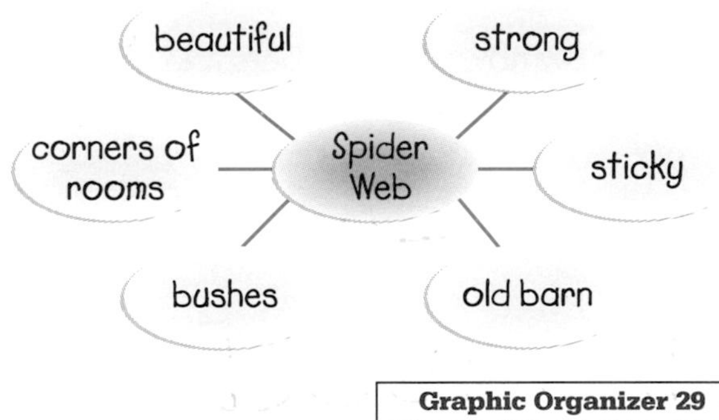

Graphic Organizer 29

WRITE AND ILLUSTRATE A STORY

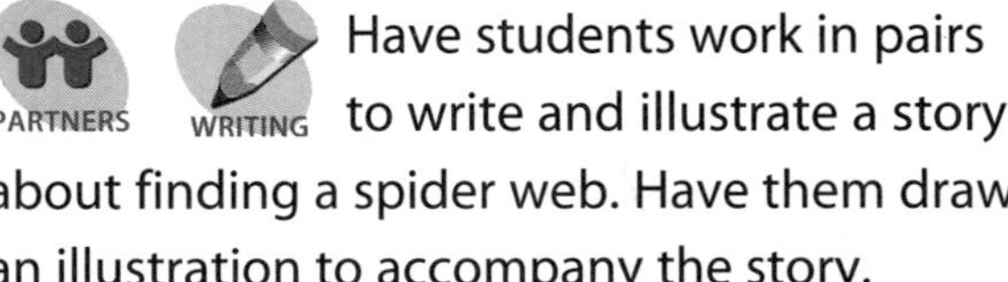

Have students work in pairs to write and illustrate a story about finding a spider web. Have them draw an illustration to accompany the story.

Develop Oral Language

APPRECIATING WEBS Bring in pictures of ESL spiders and spider webs and have students look back at *Spiders at Work*. Ask volunteers to describe the picture that they find most interesting.

Select key words used in the descriptions and write them on the chalkboard. Discuss the meaning of each word and have students use it in a sentence.

Then ask students to draw a picture of a spider web and label it, using one or more of the key words.

TEACHING TIP

INSTRUCTIONAL Point out that spiders are important characters in folk tales and legends. Tell students a traditional tale about a spider, such as one of the African stories about the spider Anansi.

LANGUAGE SUPPORT

ESL See Language Support Book, pages 73–76, for teaching suggestions for Build Background and Vocabulary.

Vocabulary

Key Words

Pablo's Discovery

1. An earthquake shook the ground and destroyed the dam that held the water back from Pablo's village. **2.** Water flooded the farmers' fields where their crops grew. **3.** The army sent soldiers to keep order and repair the damage. **4.** In a ruined barn, Pablo found a web woven by a spider. **5.** Baby spiders that had begun to hatch from the spider's eggs hung in the air on silky threads. **6.** Pablo had respect for spiders because they ate the insects that made the villagers sick.

Teaching Chart 56

Definitions

earthquake (p. 249) a shaking of the earth caused by underground movements

crops (p. 248) plants grown by farmers

soldiers (p. 247) people who serve in an army

woven (p. 247) formed by interlaced threads

hatch (p. 248) to come out of an egg

respect (p. 249) approval

Vocabulary in Context

IDENTIFY VOCABULARY WORDS Display **Teaching Chart 56** and read the passage with students. Have volunteers circle each vocabulary word and underline other words that are clues to its meaning.

DISCUSS MEANINGS Ask questions like these to help clarify word meanings:

- What happens to the ground during an earthquake?
- Why do farmers grow crops?
- What do soldiers do during battles? During disasters?
- Was your shirt woven from cotton or from silk thread?
- Name something that hatches from eggs.
- Do you respect or disapprove of honest people?

Practice

FINISHING SENTENCES Have partners take turns choosing Vocabulary Cards. The chooser makes up a sentence fragment that gives a clue to the selected word. The other student finishes the sentence using the word.
▶ **Kinesthetic/Linguistic**

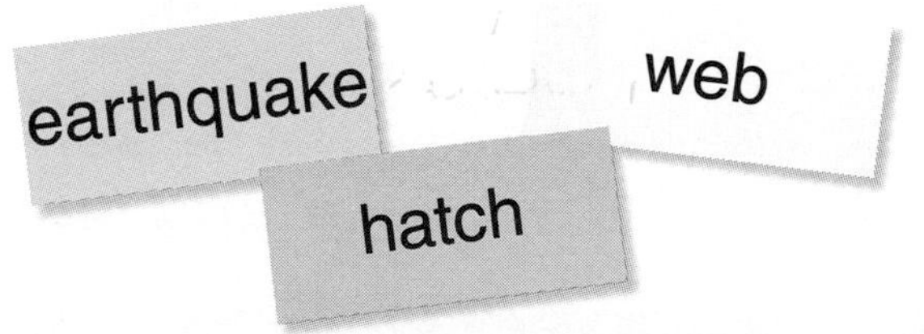

Word Building Manipulative Cards

MAKE SIMILES Have partners work together to use the vocabulary words in similes. For example, *When my brother stomps around, it feels like an earthquake is shaking the house.*
▶ **Linguistic/Oral**

SPELLING/VOCABULARY CONNECTIONS

See Spelling Challenge Words, pages 253O–253P.

ON-LEVEL

Name________ Date______ Practice 67

Vocabulary

Supply the correct words from the list to complete each sentence.
The same vocabulary word is used twice in each example.

crops earthquake hatch respect soldiers woven

1. __Crops__ are plants we grow for food. Wheat and corn are two kinds of __crops__ farmers grow in the United States.
2. When the ground started to shake, I knew we were having an __earthquake__. Luckily, no one was hurt during the __earthquake__, but some buildings were damaged.
3. The hen sits on her eggs to keep them warm until they __hatch__. Watch the eggs __hatch__ to see the little chicks!
4. I really admire and __respect__ Mrs. Jackson. As one of the best teachers at school, she has earned everyone's __respect__.
5. My cousins joined the army because they wanted to be __soldiers__. Besides fighting in wars, __soldiers__ also help to protect and rebuild cities and countries.
6. Some of the most beautiful blankets in the world are __woven__ by Native Americans. Yarn is carefully __woven__ together in different colored strips to make lovely patterns.

McGraw-Hill School Division

67 **At Home:** Have students use each vocabulary word in another sentence. Book 3.1/Unit 2 **Web Wonders** 12

Take-Home Story 67a
Reteach 67
Practice 67 • **Extend 67**

Guided Instruction

Preview and Predict

Lead students through a **picture walk**. Have them preview the article by skimming it, looking at the pictures, and reading the captions.

- Is this article fiction or nonfiction? What gives you a hint? (Nonfiction; it is illustrated by photographs.) ***Genre***
- What special ability of the spider does the author discuss?

Set Purposes

What do students want to find out by reading the selection? For example:

- What is special about spider silk?
- How can it be used by people?
- Why do spiders spin webs?

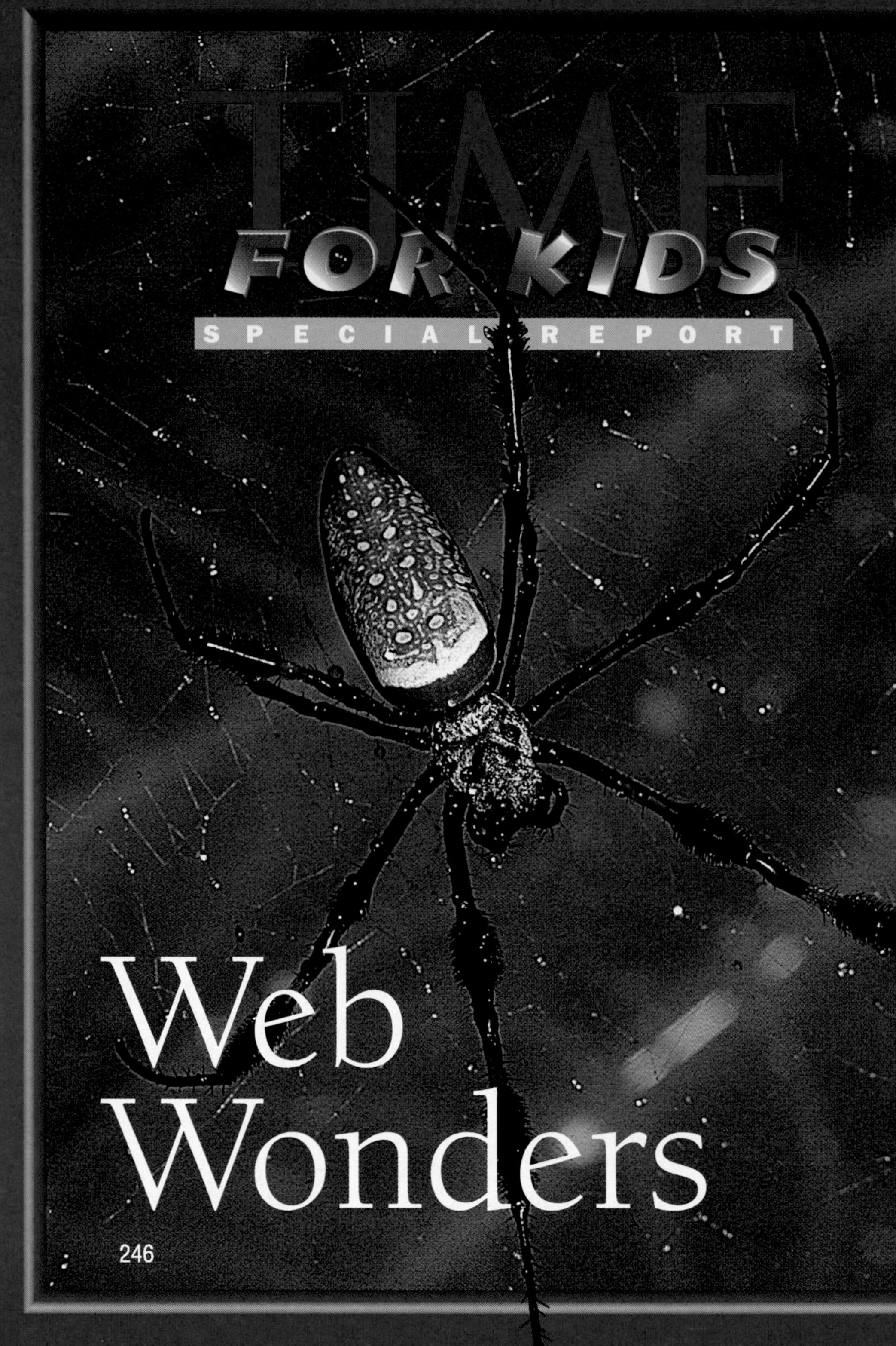

Meeting Individual Needs • Grouping Suggestions for Strategic Reading

EASY

Read Together Read the article with students or have them use the **Listening Library Audiocassette.** Have students use the Comparison/Contrast chart to record information about spiders. Guided Instruction prompts offer additional help with vocabulary and comprehension.

ON-LEVEL

Guided Reading Display the story words listed on page 247. Choose from the Guided Instruction questions as you read the article with students or after they have played the **Listening Library Audiocassette.** Have them use the Compare and Contrast chart to record meaningful information during reading.

CHALLENGE

Read Independently Remind students that using the skills of comparing and contrasting will help them understand the information given in the article. Have students set up a Compare and Contrast chart as on page 247. After reading, they can use their charts to summarize facts about spiders and their webs.

TIME FOR KIDS SPECIAL REPORT

A New Spin on Spider Silk

About 800 years ago, a ruler named Genghis Khan went to fight a war. An old story tells how enemy arrows bounced off his soldiers. What was their secret? Spider silk! It was woven into their clothes and their armor.

Today, scientists still have not come up with a thread stronger than the silk spiders use to spin their webs. (1)

Scientists think that a giant spider-silk web could stop a jet plane! And the strands of the web would only have to be as thick as a pencil.

Spiders cannot be raised on farms. (They eat one another.) So scientists are trying to make spider silk without the spiders! (2)

COVER: M.H. SHARP/PHOTO RESEARCHERS (SPIDER); CHARLES KREBS/TONY STONE IMAGES (WEB); LEFT: TIM FLACH/TONY STONE IMAGES

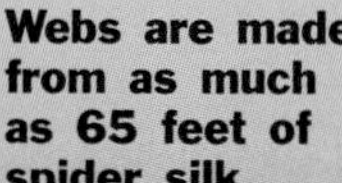

Webs are made from as much as 65 feet of spider silk.

247

Guided Instruction

Compare and Contrast

Draw Conclusions

As we read, let's make Venn diagrams to help us keep track of what we learn.

(1) **COMPARE AND CONTRAST** What fact did people hundreds of years ago know about spider silk that is still interesting to scientists today? (that it could be woven into material to make the material stronger) What are today's scientists doing that people didn't do in the past? (trying to make spider silk without spiders)

(2) **DRAW CONCLUSIONS** Why do you think people want to make spider silk? (They want to use it, as Genghis Khan did, to make ordinary materials stronger.)

Story Words

The words below may be unfamiliar. Have students check their meanings and pronunciations in the Glossary.

- Genghis Khan, p. 247
- dragonflies, p. 249

LANGUAGE SUPPORT

This Venn diagram is available as a blackline master in the **Language Support Book.**

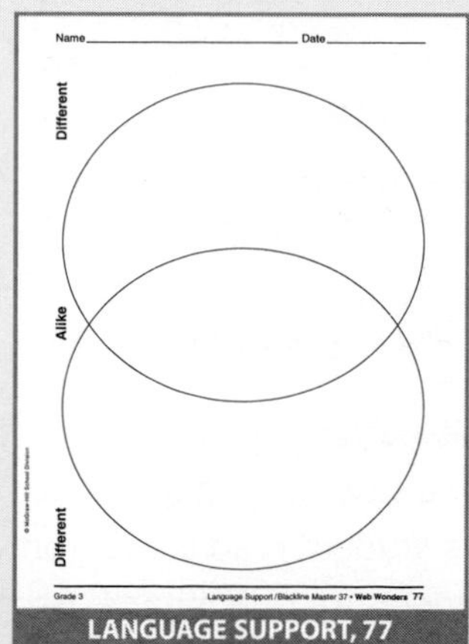

Name ____ Date ____

Different

Alike

Different

Grade 3 Language Support/Blackline Master 37 • Web Wonders 77

LANGUAGE SUPPORT, 77

Guided Instruction

3 **DRAW CONCLUSIONS** Why do farmers like to have spiders around? (Spiders eat insects that hurt their crops.)

4 **COMPARE AND CONTRAST** Let's use the Venn diagram to organize the information about real spider silk and human-made spider silk.

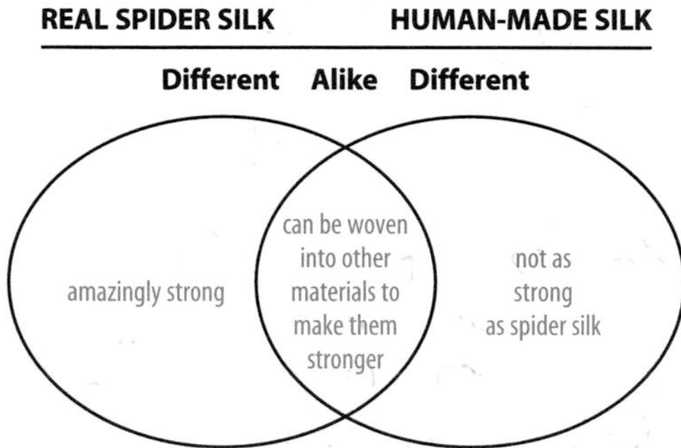

ORGANIZE INFORMATION Ask volunteers to summarize the important information in the article. They can use the Venn diagrams to help them organize the information they have learned by reading the article. *Summarize*

JOE MCDONALD/CORBIS

Baby spiders are called "spiderlings." Winds gently carry the spiderlings to new homes.

DID YOU KNOW? AMAZING SPIDER FACTS

- Baby spiders hatch from eggs. Then they spin a long silk line. They wait for a breeze to carry them to a new home. The wind has carried some baby spiders 200 miles away.
- Spiders spin sticky webs to catch insects. Then they eat them.
- The web of a golden silk spider is strong enough to trap a bird.
- Spiders have eight legs. Most have eight eyes.
- **3** Farmers like to have most spiders around. They eat insects that can hurt farm crops.

248

REREADING FOR *Fluency*

GROUP Organize the class into groups of five. Have each group member read one item in Did You Know? Encourage students to read clearly and expressively to engage the interest of their audience.

READING RATE You may want to evaluate a student's reading rate. Have the student read aloud from *Web Wonders* for one minute. Ask the student to place a stick-on note after the last word read. Then count the number of words he or she has read.

Alternatively, you could assess small groups or the whole class together by having students count words and record their own scores.

A Running Record form provided in **Diagnostic/Placement Evaluation** will help you evaluate reading rate(s).

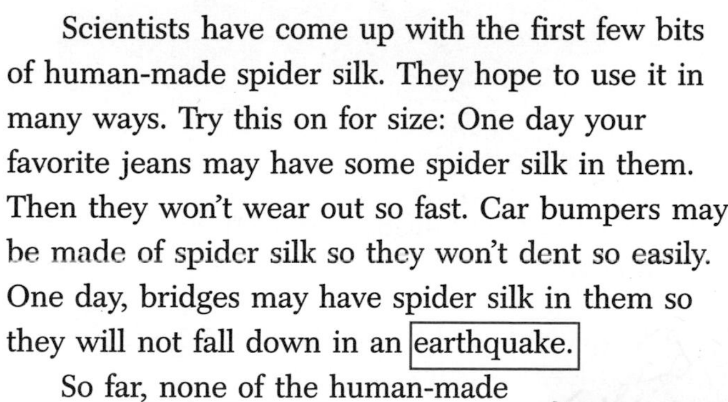

Scientists have come up with the first few bits of human-made spider silk. They hope to use it in many ways. Try this on for size: One day your favorite jeans may have some spider silk in them. Then they won't wear out so fast. Car bumpers may be made of spider silk so they won't dent so easily. One day, bridges may have spider silk in them so they will not fall down in an earthquake.

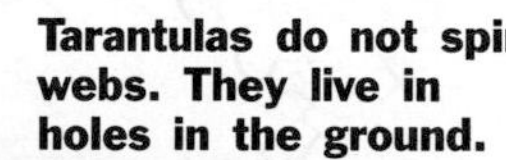

So far, none of the human-made silk is as strong as real spider silk. But scientists will continue to work on the problem.

The silk spiders make is a truly amazing fiber. That's one reason scientists have so much respect for spiders.

4

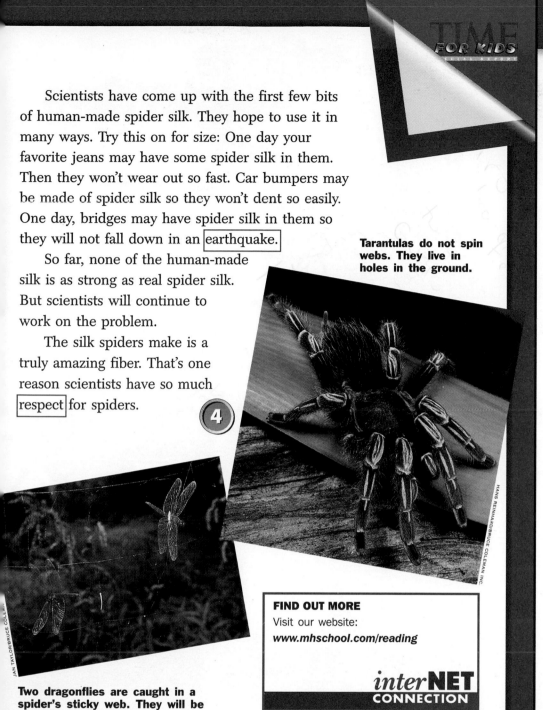

Tarantulas do not spin webs. They live in holes in the ground.

HANS REINHARD/BRUCE COLEMAN INC.

JAN TAYLOR/BRUCE COLEMAN

Two dragonflies are caught in a spider's sticky web. They will be a meal for the spider.

FIND OUT MORE
Visit our website:
www.mhschool.com/reading

*inter*NET CONNECTION

Based on an article in *TIME FOR KIDS.*

249

Guided Instruction

Return to Predictions and Purposes

Review with students their story predictions. Were their predictions correct? Did they find out what they wanted to know?

INFORMAL ASSESSMENT

COMPARE AND CONTRAST

HOW TO ASSESS Ask students to name one similarity and one difference between spider silk and ordinary thread.

Students should realize that both spider silk and ordinary thread are thin, and both can be used in making clothes. They should also see that the spider silk is tough, while thread is easy to tear.

FOLLOW UP If students have trouble comparing and contrasting spider silk with thread, have them review their Venn diagrams.

LITERARY RESPONSE

QUICK-WRITE Invite students to record their thoughts about the selection.

JOURNAL

- Are there any articles of clothing that you wish would last longer?

ORAL RESPONSE Have students share their journal writings and discuss the part of the article they enjoyed most.

RESEARCH AND INQUIRY Have students look up another human-made fiber, such as nylon or polyester. They can use a Venn diagram to compare and contrast that fiber with silk.

*inter*NET CONNECTION For more information on this topic, have students go to ***www.mhschool.com/reading***.

Story Questions

Have students discuss or write answers to the questions on page 250.

Answers:

1. Because they eat one another. *(Literal/Cause and Effect)*
2. Possible answer: It might never wear out. *(Inferential/Make Inferences)*
3. Possible answer: I am afraid of spiders. They probably like them for killing insects. *(Critical/Compare and Contrast)*
4. Scientists are trying to make a silk as strong as spider silk to strengthen cloth, metal, and other materials. *(Critical/Summarize)*
5. The kind that eats insects; many insects kill plants. *(Critical/Reading Across Texts)*

Write an Essay For a full lesson related to this suggestion, see the lesson on explanatory writing on pages 253K–253L.

Story Questions & Activities

1. Why can't spiders be raised on farms?
2. In what ways might a shirt of human-made spider silk be different from a cotton shirt?
3. How do you feel about spiders? How do you think farmers feel about them? Do you feel the same or different? Explain.
4. What is the main idea of this selection?
5. Which kinds of spiders do you think would be helpful to the community garden in "City Green"? Why?

Write an Essay

Choose one kind of spider. Write about what a day in the life of the spider would be like. Tell your story from a spider's point of view. Be sure to include where your spider lives, what it likes to eat, and what makes it unique.

Meeting Individual Needs

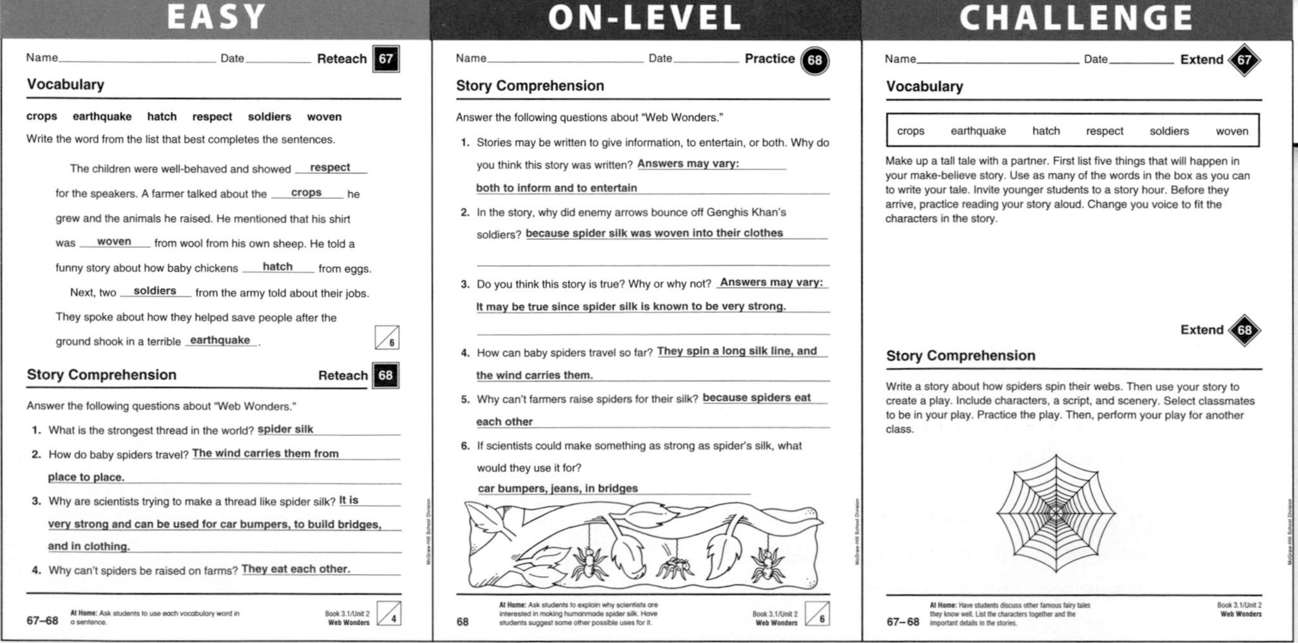

EASY

Name________ Date________ Reteach 67

Vocabulary

crops earthquake hatch respect soldiers woven

Write the word from the list that best completes the sentences.

The children were well-behaved and showed **respect** for the speakers. A farmer talked about the **crops** he grew and the animals he raised. He mentioned that his shirt was **woven** from wool from his own sheep. He told a funny story about how baby chickens **hatch** from eggs.

Next, two **soldiers** from the army told about their jobs. They spoke about how they helped save people after the ground shook in a terrible **earthquake**.

6

Story Comprehension Reteach 68

Answer the following questions about "Web Wonders."

1. What is the strongest thread in the world? **spider silk**
2. How do baby spiders travel? **The wind carries them from place to place.**
3. Why are scientists trying to make a thread like spider silk? **It is very strong and can be used for car bumpers, to build bridges, and in clothing.**
4. Why can't spiders be raised on farms? **They eat each other.**

67–68 **At Home:** Ask students to use each vocabulary word in a sentence. Book 3.1/Unit 2 **Web Wonders** 4

McGraw-Hill School Division

Reteach, 68

ON-LEVEL

Name________ Date________ Practice 68

Story Comprehension

Answer the following questions about "Web Wonders."

1. Stories may be written to give information, to entertain, or both. Why do you think this story was written? **Answers may vary: both to inform and to entertain**
2. In the story, why did enemy arrows bounce off Genghis Khan's soldiers? **because spider silk was woven into their clothes**
3. Do you think this story is true? Why or why not? **Answers may vary: It may be true since spider silk is known to be very strong.**
4. How can baby spiders travel so far? **They spin a long silk line, and the wind carries them.**
5. Why can't farmers raise spiders for their silk? **because spiders eat each other**
6. If scientists could make something as strong as spider's silk, what would they use it for? **car bumpers, jeans, in bridges**

68 **At Home:** Ask students to explain why scientists are interested in making humanmade spider silk. Have students suggest some other possible uses for it. Book 3.1/Unit 2 **Web Wonders** 6

McGraw-Hill School Division

Practice, 68

CHALLENGE

Name________ Date________ Extend 67

Vocabulary

crops earthquake hatch respect soldiers woven

Make up a tall tale with a partner. First list five things that will happen in your make-believe story. Use as many of the words in the box as you can to write your tale. Invite younger students to a story hour. Before they arrive, practice reading your story aloud. Change you voice to fit the characters in the story.

Extend 68

Story Comprehension

Write a story about how spiders spin their webs. Then use your story to create a play. Include characters, a script, and scenery. Select classmates to be in your play. Practice the play. Then, perform your play for another class.

67–68 **At Home:** Have students discuss other famous fairy tales they know well. List the characters together and the important details in the stories. Book 3.1/Unit 2 **Web Wonders**

McGraw-Hill School Division

Extend, 68

Create a Spider Diagram

Look up different types of spiders. Choose one and draw a diagram of it. Carefully label each part of the spider. Include some facts about your spider and write them under your diagram.

Draw a Spider Comic Strip

Create a comic strip about a baby spider being carried by the wind to a new home. Draw the panels and the characters in pencil. Add speech balloons. Then color in the strip with markers.

Find Out More

Spider babies are called spiderlings. Find out more about what different kinds of baby animals are called. Make a list of animals and the baby name for each animal. Compare your list with your classmates' lists.

251

Story Activities

Create a Spider Diagram

Materials: encyclopedia and other natural history resources, drawing materials

ONE Tell students that their diagram and facts must show how their spider differs from other spiders.

Draw a Spider Comic Strip

Materials: paper, colored pencils or felt-tipped markers

Encourage students to brainstorm ideas about story line, dialogue, and thought balloons. Ask them to consider what other characters they might include in addition to the baby spider.

Find Out More

RESEARCH AND INQUIRY Have partners use reference books and the Internet to create their lists. After partners have made and compared their lists, create a combined class list.

interNET CONNECTION For more information on spiders, have students go to ***www.mhschool.com/reading***.

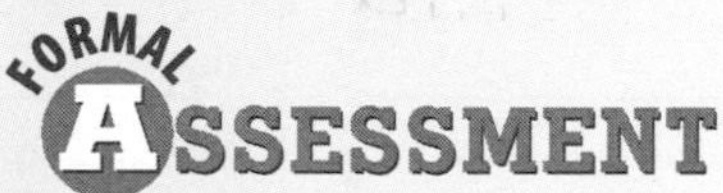

After page 251, see Selection and Unit Assessments.

Study Skills

REFERENCE SOURCES

TESTED **OBJECTIVES** Students will:

- find information in a dictionary.
- find information in an encyclopedia.
- choose the appropriate reference source.

PREPARE Look over the sample dictionary and encyclopedia selections with the students. Display **Teaching Chart 57.**

TEACH Show students a dictionary and an encyclopedia. Explain that a dictionary is usually one volume and an encyclopedia is many volumes. Review alphabetical order.

PRACTICE Have students answer questions **1–5.** Review the answers with them. **1.** encyclopedia **2.** Noun; it is identified as a noun in the dictionary. **3.** dictionary **4.** encyclopedia **5.** Encyclopedia; key words may vary, but should include *spider* and *web*.

ASSESS/CLOSE Have students write or tell two differences between insects and arachnids.

STUDY SKILLS

Use a Resource

A dictionary is an alphabetical listing of words that tells the meaning, pronunciation, and other information for each word. An encyclopedia is an alphabetical listing of subjects that gives detailed information about each subject.

spider A small animal with four pairs of legs, a body divided into two parts, and no wings. Most spiders spin webs to catch insects for food. **spi•der** (spī′ dər) *noun, plural* **spiders**.

DICTIONARY

Spider (spī′ dər), any of a large group of small invertebrates, or animals without backbones, that usually spin silken webs. Spiders, along with mites, ticks, and scorpions, belong to a group of animals known as arachnids. Although they are often confused with insects, arachnids differ from insects in that they lack antennae and have four pairs of legs instead of three. Another major difference is that the insect's body is divided into a head, a thorax, and an abdomen, while the spider's body consists of only two sections.

ENCYCLOPEDIA

Use the dictionary and encyclopedia entries to answer these questions.

1. Which resource would you use to find out the difference between spiders and insects?
2. Is *spider* a verb or a noun? How do you know?
3. Which resource would you use if you wanted a short description of what a spider is?
4. Which resource would you use if you wanted to look up detailed information about a spider?
5. Suppose you wanted to find out more about spider webs. Which resource would you use and what key words might you look under?

Meeting Individual Needs

EASY

Name________ Date______ Reteach 69

Use a Resource

Dictionaries list information about words. **Encyclopedias** list information about different topics.

Read the questions below. Then decide which reference source you would use to answer them. Write **dictionary** or **encyclopedia** in the space at the right. (Some of the questions could be answered by either reference source.)

1. Where could I find out how to pronounce *silk*? **dictionary**
2. Where could I find out about the history of silk-making? **encyclopedia**
3. Where could I find out how a silkworm spins a cocoon? **encyclopedia**
4. Where could I find out what part of speech *silk* is? **dictionary**
5. Where could I learn about changes in silk production? **encyclopedia**
6. Where could I learn the origin of the word *insect*? **dictionary or encyclopedia**
7. Where could I learn how many kinds of spiders there are? **encyclopedia**
8. Where could I find the definition of the word *tarantula*? **dictionary**

8 Book 3.1/Unit 2 **Web Wonders** **At Home:** Have students choose a word and decide where they would look to find out about it. Ask them to explain their answer. 69

Reteach, 69

ON-LEVEL

Name________ Date______ Practice 69

Use a Resource

Study the sample dictionary entry. Then take a careful look at the encyclopedia entry that is below it.

nylon a strong fabric manufactured from chemicals. Nylon is used to make thread, clothes, stockings, tires for automobiles, tents for camping, and many other things. **ny-lon** (nī′lon) *noun.*

nylon is the family name for a group of materials made from chemicals. Coal, water, and chemicals are blended to make a wide variety of products. Nylon can be both strong and flexible. In 1937, it was first used to replace silk in stockings. Wallace Carothers developed special ways to make nylon for the Dupont Company. The first nylon he produced melted at low temperatures. If you made a dress out of this early nylon, a hot iron would melt it. By adding other chemicals, the nylon we know today was created. Qiana is a type of nylon that is commonly used in modern clothes. It has many of the qualities of silk.

Now read the selections below. Decide if they might have come from a dictionary entry or an encyclopedia entry. Write *dictionary* or *encyclopedia* to answer the questions below.

1. Which resource tells the history of *nylon*? **encyclopedia**
2. Which resource defines *nylon* as a strong fabric manufactured from chemicals? **dictionary**
3. Which resource tells you how to pronounce *nylon*? **dictionary**
4. Which resource tells you about a type of *nylon* called Qiana? **encyclopedia**
5. Which resource tells you that *nylon* is a noun? **dictionary**

5 Book 3.1/Unit 2 **Web Wonders** **At Home:** Ask students where they might look to find predictions about how nylon will be used in the future. 69

Practice, 69

CHALLENGE

Name________ Date______ Extend 69

Use a Resource

There are many different places you can find information. When you need a definition of a word you can look in a dictionary. When you need to know where a country is, you can look on a map. When you want to learn about a topic, you can use an encyclopedia or search the Internet on a computer.

Read the questions below. Write the resource or resources that could give you the information you need to answer the question. It may be a dictionary, a map, an encyclopedia, or the Internet.

1. What does *hatch* mean? **dictionary**
2. Is a tarantula an arachnid that spins a web? **encyclopedia, Internet**
3. Where is South America? **map, encyclopedia, Internet**
4. How do spiders spin strong webs? **encyclopedia, Internet**
5. How far can the wind carry baby spiders? **encyclopedia, Internet**

Choose two questions to answer. Use a resource. Write the answers below.

Answers will vary.

Book 3.1/Unit 2 **Web Wonders** **At Home:** Have students use a resource to find out more about a topic of their own choice. 69

Extend, 69

TEST POWER

Test Tip

If the questions seem too hard, go back and read the story again.

DIRECTIONS:

Read the story. Then read each question about the story.

SAMPLE

The Amusement Park

Juanita likes animals and wants to learn about them. This flyer tells about the amusement park she is visiting.

> **WORLD OF SCIENCE WELCOMES YOU!**
>
> **The Secret World of Submarines**— Take a ride on a real submarine in Science Lake! See underwater creatures and plants.
>
> **Timberland Wolves**—Visit our new exciting Timberland Wolf <u>exhibit</u>. See live wolves in their natural habitat.
>
> **The Planetarium**—Come see how the night sky looks from the North Pole or the Equator. See how the planets move in space.

1 Why would Juanita like the Timberland Wolves attraction best?

- ○ She thinks contests are fun.
- ● She enjoys looking at stars.
- ● She likes animals.
- ○ She wants a new pet.

2 In the flyer, an <u>exhibit</u> is—

- ● a display
- ○ an animal
- ○ a telescope
- ○ a submarine

Why are your answers correct?

ITBS/TEST PREPARATION

TERRANOVA/TEST PREPARATION

McGRAW-HILL READING
Stanford-9
Test
Preparation
and Practice
Grade 3

SAT 9/TEST PREPARATION

Test Power

THE PRINCETON REVIEW

Read the Page

Have students read *all* of the information in the flyer, the questions, and the answer choices.

Discuss the Questions

QUESTION 1: This question refers specifically to the information before the flyer. Direct students back to that part of the story.

QUESTION 2: This question asks students to define a word in context. Have students look for clues in the surrounding sentences. The sentence following refers to the exhibit as a display. Upon examination of the answer choices, we find that display is a choice. Use process of elimination.

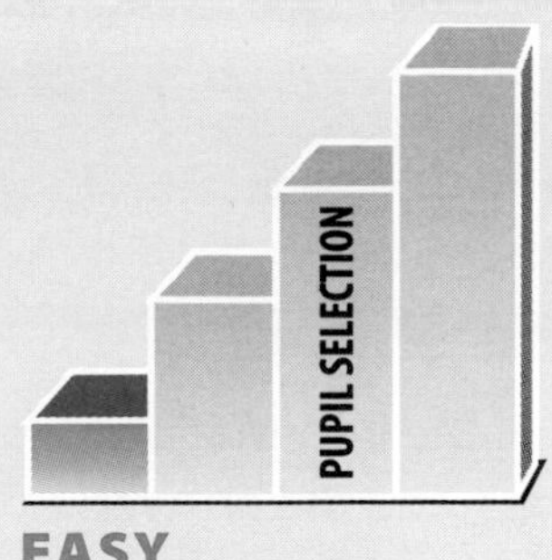

EASY

Self-Selected Reading
Leveled Books

EASY

UNIT SKILLS REVIEW

Phonics

☑ **Comprehension**

Help students self-select an Easy Book to read and apply phonics and comprehension skills.

Guided Reading

PREVIEW AND PREDICT Discuss the illustrations in the beginning of the book. As you take the **picture walk**, have students predict what the story will be about.

SET PURPOSES Have students write why they want to read the book. Have them share their purposes.

READ THE BOOK Use items like the following to guide students' reading, or after they have read the story independently. Model phonics and decoding strategies for students who need help.

- Look back through the book and search for words with closed syllables (short-vowel as in *winter*) and open syllables (long-vowel as in *program*). *Phonics and Decoding*
- Look through the book and search for words that use initial consonant clusters *br, gr, pl, str, sl, sp, spr,* and *sk*. *Phonics and Decoding*
- Identify a main event in the story. What are the cause and the effect of the main event in the story? *Cause and Effect*
- Look at the first four pages. Identify one important and one unimportant piece of information in those four pages. *Important and Unimportant Information*
- Compare and contrast two characters in the story. *Compare and Contrast*

RETURN TO PREDICTIONS AND PURPOSES Discuss students' predictions. Ask which were correct and why. Have students review their purposes for reading. Did they find out what they wanted to know?

LITERARY RESPONSE Have students discuss questions like the following:

- What part of the story was most interesting? Why?
- What other books or stories have you read with a similar setting?
- If you could change the ending of the story, how would you change it?

See the Phonics **CD-ROM** for practice with closed syllables and consonant clusters.

Phonics

- Syllable Patterns
- Consonant Clusters

☑ Comprehension

- Cause and Effect
- Compare and Contrast
- Important and Unimportant Information

Answers will vary. Have students cite examples from the story to support their answers.

EASY

Story Questions for Selected Reading

1. Did the story teach you anything new?
2. Did you find the story interesting? Why or why not?
3. What was your favorite illustration? Why?
4. If you could be a character in the story, who would you be? Why?
5. If you could change something about the story, what would it be?

Draw a Picture

Draw a picture of one scene from the book.

Self-Selected Reading
Leveled Books

INDEPENDENT

UNIT SKILLS REVIEW

Comprehension

Help students self-select an Independent Book to read and apply comprehension skills.

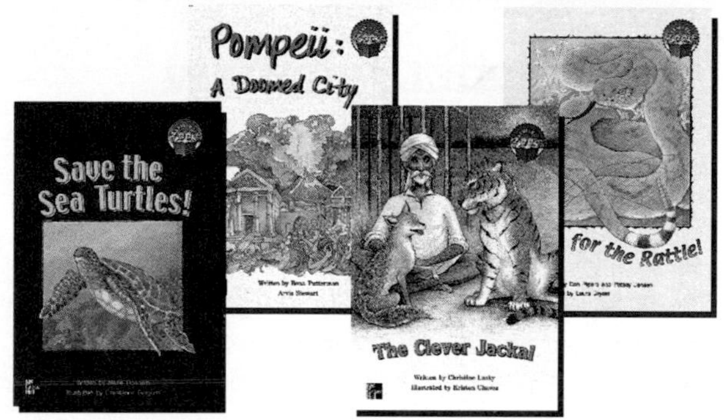

Guided Reading

PREVIEW AND PREDICT Discuss the illustrations in the beginning of the book. As you take the **picture walk**, have students predict what the story will be about. List their ideas. If the book has chapter headings, ask students to use the headings to predict what will happen.

SET PURPOSES Have students write why they want to read the book. Have them share their purposes.

READ THE BOOK Use items like the following to guide students' reading, or after they have read the book independently.

- Choose a main event in the story. What caused that main event to happen? *Cause and Effect*
- Tell one important and one unimportant piece of information in the story. How can you tell the difference? *Important and Unimportant Information*
- Compare and contrast the setting in the story with the town or city where you live. *Compare and Contrast*
- What conclusion can you draw about a character or event in the story? *Draw Conclusions*
- What is the main idea of the story? *Main Idea*

RETURN TO PREDICTIONS AND PURPOSES Have students review their predictions. Students can talk about whether their purposes were met, and if they have any questions the story left unanswered. For books with chapter headings, were the headings useful? How?

LITERARY RESPONSE The following questions will help focus students' responses:

- What new ideas or facts did you learn by reading the story?
- What other books or stories have you read about similar situations?
- If you were the writer of the story, what would you have done differently? Why?

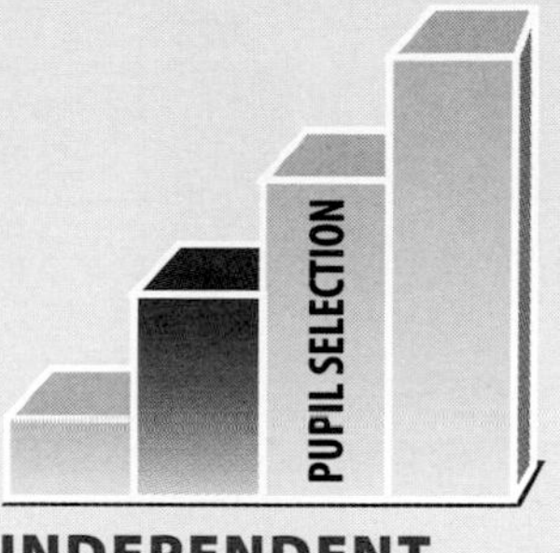

INDEPENDENT

Comprehension

- Cause and Effect
- Compare and Contrast
- Important and Unimportant Information

Answers will vary. Have students cite examples from the story to support their answers.

INDEPENDENT

Story Questions for Selected Reading

1. What was the setting of the story?
2. Did you find the subject of the story interesting? Why or why not?
3. How could you find out more about the story subject? Where would you look?
4. Which do you enjoy reading more: fiction or nonfiction? Explain your answer.
5. Which illustrations did you like best?

Make a Poster
Create a poster that tells why people might enjoy reading the book.

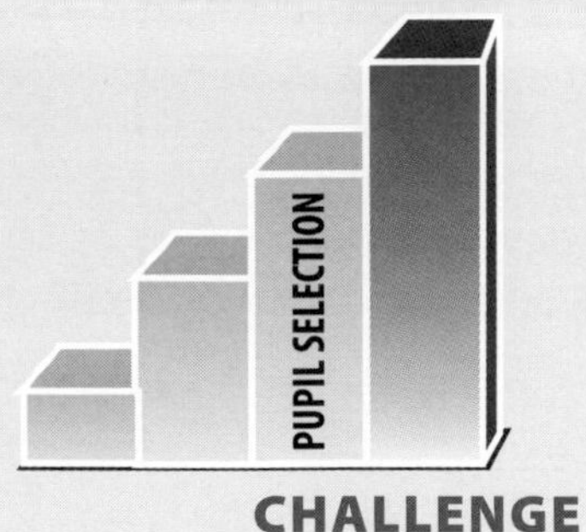

CHALLENGE

Comprehension

- Cause and Effect
- Compare and Contrast
- Important and Unimportant Information

Answers will vary. Have students cite examples from the story to support their answers.

CHALLENGE

Story Questions for Selected Reading

1. What was the main idea of the story?
2. Was the subject of the story a good choice? Why or why not?
3. Was there anything that surprised you about the story? What was it?
4. If you could change anything in the story, what would it be?
5. What did you learn from the story?

Write a Review

Write a review of the book telling what you liked and did not like about it.

Self-Selected Reading
Leveled Books

CHALLENGE

UNIT SKILLS REVIEW

Comprehension

Help students self-select a Challenge Book to read and apply comprehension skills.

Guided Reading

PREVIEW AND PREDICT Discuss the illustrations in the beginning of the book. As you take the **picture walk,** have students predict what the story will be about. List their ideas. If the book has chapter headings, ask students to use the headings to predict what will happen.

SET PURPOSES Have students write why they want to read the book. Have them share their purposes.

READ THE BOOK Use questions like the following to guide students' reading, or after they have read the book independently.

- What are the cause and the effect of a main event in the story? *Cause and Effect*
- Choose one important piece of information and explain why it is important. *Important and Unimportant Information*
- Compare and contrast the setting of the story with that of another story you have read. How are they alike? *Compare and Contrast*
- What was the author's purpose in writing the story? *Author's Purpose*
- What is a fact in the story? How can you tell? *Fact and Nonfact*

RETURN TO PREDICTIONS AND PURPOSES Discuss students' predictions. Ask which were close to the book's contents and why. For books with chapter headings, were the headings useful? How? Have students review their purposes for reading. Did they find out what they wanted to know?

LITERARY RESPONSE Have students discuss questions like the following:

- How would a different setting or time period affect the story?
- What interested you most about the story?
- Would you suggest turning this story into a movie? Why or why not?

Connecting Texts

VENN DIAGRAMS Have students compare two books. First, draw two Venn diagrams on the chalkboard. Write the following two story titles at the top of the first diagram: *Simon Says "Go for it!"* and *Save the Sea Turtles*. Write the following two titles at the top of the second diagram: *Pompeii: A Doomed City* and *Potlatch for Kwiskwis*. Have students use the Venn diagrams to compare and contrast these two sets of stories. What information about nature is presented in the stories? How are the stories alike? How are they different? Are the stories realistic or fantastic? Are the characters human or animal? Do they take place in the present or the past? Are the settings the same or different? Have students share their ideas with the class.

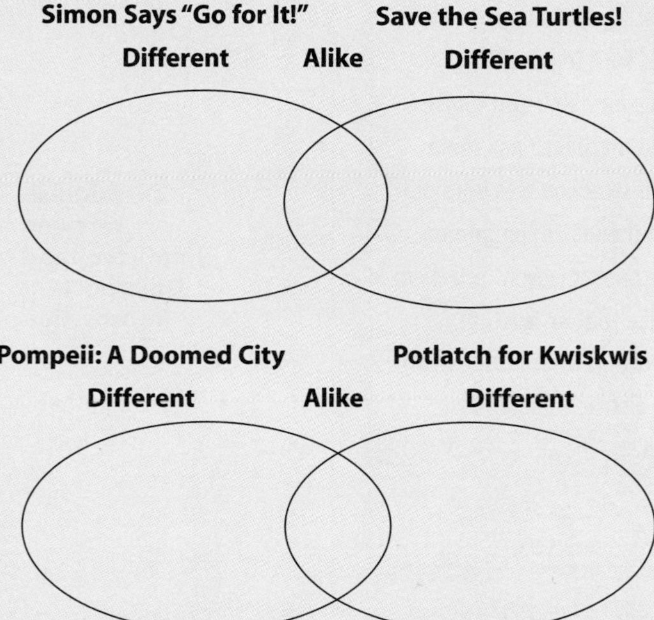

Viewing/Representing

GROUP PRESENTATIONS Have students divide into groups in which they have read some of the same titles. Have each group choose one title, then create plans for a Web site that advertises the book. Remind students that Web sites can make use of pictures as well as music and text. Have groups share their completed Web site plans with the class.

AUDIENCE RESPONSE Ask students to describe what they liked most about the Web site plans. Would they be interested in the books if they saw these Web sites on the Internet?

Research and Inquiry

CHOOSE A TOPIC Have students choose a topic to investigate in detail. They should do the following:

- Make a list of the things they want to know about a topic.
- Talk to teachers and librarians about the best way to research their topics.
- Take notes about their topics as they gather information.
- Keep their information in a notebook.

Have students log on to ***www.mhschool.com/reading*** for links to Web pages.

Students can write and draw what they learned in their journals.

TESTED OBJECTIVES

Students will distinguish between important and unimportant information.

TEACHING TIP

INSTRUCTIONAL Give students a series of instructions, such as: "Open your arithmetic book"; "Turn to page 24"; "Comb your hair"; and "Solve the first problem." Ask them which instruction was unimportant to the idea of beginning the arithmetic lesson. Tell them that, like that instruction, unimportant information in an article distracts or confuses readers.

Review Important and Unimportant Information

PREPARE

Recognizing Unimportant Information Ask students: If they were writing an essay about eagles, would the name of their pet parakeet be important or unimportant information? Have them explain their answers.

TEACH

Distinguish Between Important and Unimportant Information Tell students that the importance of information is strongly connected to the main idea of an article. Unimportant information has little or no connection to the main idea.

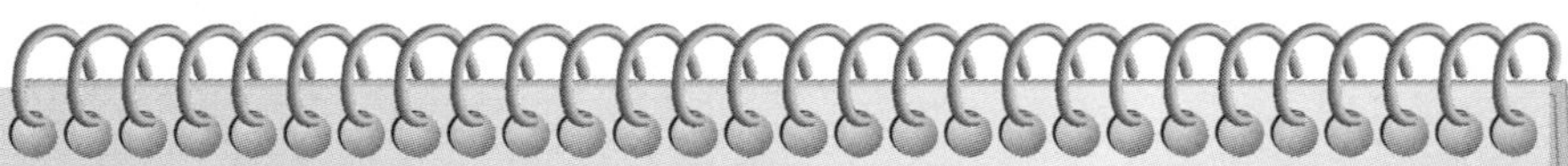

A Plant Like Steel

Natural materials can be as strong as human-made materials. For example, the stems of an Asian plant called *bamboo* are nearly as strong as steel. [Giant pandas eat bamboo.]

In the United States, engineers make steel frames for buildings. In Asia, however, engineers sometimes use bamboo. Bamboo frames bend so buildings made with bamboo are less likely to fall down during strong winds. [Typhoons are storms with strong winds.]

Teaching Chart 58

Read "A Plant Like Steel" and Model the Skill Help students to identify the facts that are connected and the facts that are not connected to the main idea of the passage.

MODEL I see that the main idea of this passage is that natural materials can be as strong as human-made materials. The idea that bamboo is a strong natural material is connected to the main idea. It is important information. That pandas eat bamboo has nothing to do with the strength of natural materials. It is unimportant information.

PRACTICE

Identify Important and Unimportant Information

Have students circle the main idea, underline important information, and bracket unimportant information. Discuss with students how you can recognize unimportant information in a piece of writing. Note that while important information tends to answer readers' questions, unimportant information may be interesting but does not relate to the main topic. ▶ **Linguistic/Logical**

ASSESS/CLOSE

Retell Fables Including Important and Unimportant Information

Organize the class into groups. Ask each group to choose a fable, such as "The Dog in the Manger" or "The Fox and the Grapes." Have the groups identify the main idea of the fable. Then have them work together to rewrite the story, including both important and unimportant information.

ALTERNATE TEACHING STRATEGY

DISTINGUISHING IMPORTANT AND UNIMPORTANT INFORMATION

For a different approach to teaching this skill, see page T66.

SELF-SELECTED Reading

Students may choose from the following titles.

ANTHOLOGY

- *Web Wonders*

LEVELED BOOKS

All titles for the unit.

Bibliography, pages T76–T77

Meeting Individual Needs for Comprehension

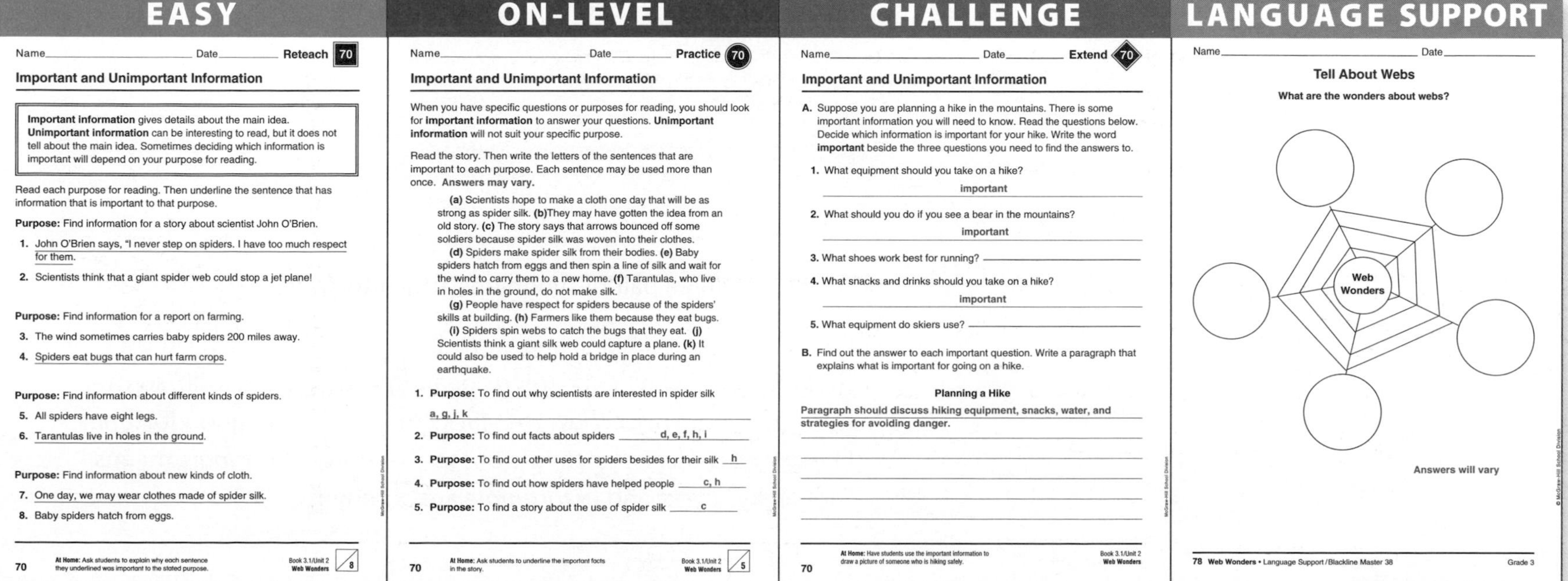

EASY

Name_____ Date_____ **Reteach 70**

Important and Unimportant Information

Important information gives details about the main idea. **Unimportant information** can be interesting to read, but it does not tell about the main idea. Sometimes deciding which information is important will depend on your purpose for reading.

Read each purpose for reading. Then underline the sentence that has information that is important to that purpose.

Purpose: Find information for a story about scientist John O'Brien.

1. John O'Brien says, "I never step on spiders. I have too much respect for them.
2. Scientists think that a giant spider web could stop a jet plane!

Purpose: Find information for a report on farming.

3. The wind sometimes carries baby spiders 200 miles away.
4. Spiders eat bugs that can hurt farm crops.

Purpose: Find information about different kinds of spiders.

5. All spiders have eight legs.
6. Tarantulas live in holes in the ground.

Purpose: Find information about new kinds of cloth.

7. One day, we may wear clothes made of spider silk.
8. Baby spiders hatch from eggs.

70 **At Home:** Ask students to explain why each sentence they underlined was important to the stated purpose. Book 3.1/Unit 2 **Web Wonders** 8

McGraw-Hill School Division

Reteach, 70

ON-LEVEL

Name_____ Date_____ **Practice 70**

Important and Unimportant Information

When you have specific questions or purposes for reading, you should look for **important information** to answer your questions. **Unimportant information** will not suit your specific purpose.

Read the story. Then write the letters of the sentences that are important to each purpose. Each sentence may be used more than once. **Answers may vary.**

(a) Scientists hope to make a cloth one day that will be as strong as spider silk. **(b)**They may have gotten the idea from an old story. **(c)** The story says that arrows bounced off some soldiers because spider silk was woven into their clothes.

(d) Spiders make spider silk from their bodies. **(e)** Baby spiders hatch from eggs and then spin a line of silk and wait for the wind to carry them to a new home. **(f)** Tarantulas, who live in holes in the ground, do not make silk.

(g) People have respect for spiders because of the spiders' skills at building. **(h)** Farmers like them because they eat bugs.

(i) Spiders spin webs to catch the bugs that they eat. **(j)** Scientists think a giant silk web could capture a plane. **(k)** It could also be used to help hold a bridge in place during an earthquake.

1. **Purpose:** To find out why scientists are interested in spider silk a, g, j, k
2. **Purpose:** To find out facts about spiders d, e, f, h, i
3. **Purpose:** To find out other uses for spiders besides for their silk h
4. **Purpose:** To find out how spiders have helped people c, h
5. **Purpose:** To find a story about the use of spider silk c

70 **At Home:** Ask students to underline the important facts in the story. Book 3.1/Unit 2 **Web Wonders** 5

McGraw-Hill School Division

Practice, 70

CHALLENGE

Name_____ Date_____ **Extend 70**

Important and Unimportant Information

A. Suppose you are planning a hike in the mountains. There is some important information you will need to know. Read the questions below. Decide which information is important for your hike. Write the word **important** beside the three questions you need to find the answers to.

1. What equipment should you take on a hike? important
2. What should you do if you see a bear in the mountains? important
3. What shoes work best for running? _____
4. What snacks and drinks should you take on a hike? important
5. What equipment do skiers use? _____

B. Find out the answer to each important question. Write a paragraph that explains what is important for going on a hike.

Planning a Hike

Paragraph should discuss hiking equipment, snacks, water, and strategies for avoiding danger.

70 **At Home:** Have students use the important information to draw a picture of someone who is hiking safely. Book 3.1/Unit 2 **Web Wonders**

McGraw-Hill School Division

Extend, 70

LANGUAGE SUPPORT

Name_____ Date_____

Tell About Webs

What are the wonders about webs?

Web Wonders

Answers will vary

78 **Web Wonders** • Language Support/Blackline Master 38 Grade 3

© McGraw-Hill School Division

Language Support, 78

OBJECTIVES

Students will identify antonyms and synonyms.

MATERIALS

- **Teaching Chart 59**
- **fairy tale *Cinderella***

TEACHING TIP

INSTRUCTIONAL Have students think of a favorite activity. Ask them for words that describe how the activity makes them feel, such as *excited, happy,* or *interested*. Then have them describe their feelings in other words that mean the same thing—*thrilled, cheerful,* or *curious*. Tell them that these words are *synonyms*. Next ask them to think of opposite words—*calm, sad,* or *bored*. Explain that these words are *antonyms*.

Review Antonyms and Synonyms

PREPARE

Define Antonyms and Synonyms Review with students that *antonyms* are words that mean the opposite of a particular word. *Synonyms* are words that mean the same, or almost the same. Ask a volunteer to give both an antonym and a synonym for *fast*. *(quick, slow)*

TEACH

Read "How Spiders Hunt" and Model the Skill Ask students to listen for synonyms and antonyms as you read the passage on **Teaching Chart 59** with them.

How Spiders Hunt

The cunning and crafty spider has a different and unusual way of hunting—it lies in wait for its victims, or ambushes them. The lucky spider knows that she has trapped an unfortunate insect when she feels the threads of her web move with the victim's struggles. The spider pounces on the insect and either bites it to death or injects poison into it. Although some poisonous spiders can be dangerous to humans, most are completely harmless to them.

Teaching Chart 59

Model identifying a pair of synonyms and antonyms.

MODEL The words *cunning* and *crafty* both describe *spider*. I know that they have similar meanings dealing with "having skill," so they must be synonyms. I know that *lucky* means "having good fortune." I know the prefix *un-* means "not," so the word *unfortunate* means "not lucky." *Lucky* and *unfortunate* are antonyms.

PRACTICE

Create a Synonyms and Antonyms Chart

Ask students to circle the synonyms and underline the antonyms on **Teaching Chart 59**. Have students make a chart of synonyms and antonyms using word pairs from "How Spiders Hunt." Challenge students to name either a synonym or antonym for each word pair.

▶ **Visual/Logical**

SYNONYMS	ANTONYMS
cunning, crafty	lucky, unfortunate
different, unusual	dangerous, harmless

ASSESS/CLOSE

Distinguish Between Synonyms and Antonyms in a Story

Have students use a Synonyms/Antonyms chart to distinguish between synonyms and antonyms that could be used to describe different characters in the fairy tale "Cinderella." Help them get started by giving them the following word pairs: *cruel, wicked; ugly, beautiful.* They should add at least two pairs of synonyms and two pairs of antonyms to the chart.

ALTERNATE TEACHING STRATEGY

ANTONYMS AND SYNONYMS

For a different approach to teaching this skill, see page T65.

Meeting Individual Needs for Vocabulary

EASY

Name________ Date______ **Reteach 71**

Antonyms and Synonyms

A **synonym** is a word that has the same, or almost the same, meaning as another word. The words *happy* and *cheerful* are synonyms. An **antonym** is a word that has the opposite meaning of another word. The words *happy* and *sad* are antonyms.

Write the letter of the word that has almost the same meaning as the first word.

1. lift __b__ **a.** get up **b.** raise **c.** add
2. trail __c__ **a.** peaks **b.** globe **c.** path

Write the letter of the word that has the opposite meaning of the first word.

3. up __b__ **a.** pick **b.** down **c.** spend
4. dark __a__ **a.** light **b.** early **c.** night

Choose a word from the list below that could complete each sentence. Choose a synonym for sentences with **S**. Choose an antonym for sentences with **A**.

stopped big slowly below

5. The mountain peaks were tall and white. **(S)** big
6. The man ran quickly up the hill. **(A)** slowly
7. The cups are above the sink. **(A)** below
8. The road ended and soon we were lost. **(S)** stopped

8 Book 3.1/Unit 2 **Web Wonders**

At Home: Have students think of some synonyms and antonyms for the following words: *sad, bright,* and *quick.*

71

Reteach, 71

ON-LEVEL

Name________ Date______ **Practice 71**

Antonyms and Synonyms

A **synonym** is a word that has the same, or almost the same, meaning as another word. An **antonym** is a word that has the opposite, or almost opposite, meaning of another word.

Synonyms: *beautiful, pretty* **Antonyms**: *quiet, noisy*

Choose the word from the box that is a synonym for the underlined word in each sentence. Write the word.

turned covered gripe heap wave

1. May watched the trees sway in the wind. wave
2. All the garden tools were in a pile in the corner. heap
3. Suddenly the rain changed into hail. turned
4. Clouds hid the mountain's peaks. covered
5. It didn't do any good to complain about the cold. gripe

In each group of four words, circle the two words that are either synonyms or antonyms. Write **synonym** if the words are synonyms and **antonym** if the words are antonyms.

6. (rough) (smooth) take hide antonym
7. sing (walk) (stride) branch synonym
8. (look) chase eat (stare) synonym
9. (pull) rush (push) sift antonym
10. gray (clean) (dirty) proud antonym

10 Book 3.1/Unit 2 **Web Wonders**

At Home: Have students tell if the following word pairs are synonyms or antonyms: **throw/catch; small/little; soft/hard; rest/nap.**

71

Practice, 71

CHALLENGE

Name________ Date______ **Extend 71**

Antonyms and Synonyms

A. Synonyms are words that have similar meanings. Read about some inventions that never made it. Then find a synonym in the box that you can use for the underlined words in the paragraphs.

destroyed live hoped earth sail person

Inventions That Never Got Off the Ground

In 1869, Leopold Trouvvelot tried to get caterpillars and silkworms to reproduce. He wished __hoped__ to produce caterpillars that could reside __live__ in American trees and spin silk. His experiment didn't work, but his caterpillars got loose and killed __destroyed__ a lot of trees.

In 1961, a "Rocket Belt" was invented. A human __person__ wearing it could fly __sail__ 80 feet off the ground __earth__ at 6 miles an hour. The problem was that there was only enough fuel for 21 minutes.

B. Antonyms are words with opposite meanings. Choose four words from the paragraphs above. Write an antonym for each word.

1. loose: caged
2. fly: walk
3. ground: air
4. problem: solution

Answers will vary. Possible answers are shown.

Book 3.1/Unit 2 **Web Wonders**

At Home: Challenge students to find as many other synonyms for the words in the box as they can.

71

Extend, 71

LANGUAGE SUPPORT

Name________ Date______

Word Wonders

tiny friend not kind weak admire
surprising usual bad guy huge tough

Word	Antonyms (opposite)	Synonyms (same)
enemy	friend	bad guy
strong	weak	tough
giant	tiny	huge
amazing	usual	surprising
respect	not kind	admire

Grade 3 Language Support / Blackline Master 39 • **Web Wonders** 79

Language Support, 79

Review Context Clues

OBJECTIVES

Students will use syntax and other context clues to understand the meaning of unfamiliar words.

MATERIALS

- **Teaching Chart 60**
- **dictionary**

TEACHING TIP

MANAGEMENT Before reviewing a concept, ask students to discuss with the person next to them what they remember about the concept. For example, ask students to explain to their neighbor how using word order and context clues can help them understand unfamiliar words. Tell the neighbor to ask questions or to add to the explanation.

PREPARE

Discuss Context, Unfamiliar Words, and Syntax Explain that context means the parts of a sentence or paragraph that surround a word or a particular group of words. Ask students how context and word order can give clues to unfamiliar words.

TEACH

Read "The Amazing Thread" and Model the Skill Have students read the passage on **Teaching Chart 60**. Suggest they listen for unfamiliar words, then look for clues to what the words mean.

The Amazing Thread

Professor Wunderbar clapped his hands and danced a little jig. He felt elated at what he had accomplished. "I've done it! I've made a thread as strong as silk! Max, my boy, this thread will make us famous!" he sang out. He continued to croon to himself as he looked up toward the ceiling of the lab. There, suspended by a golden thread through his harness, was the professor's pet elephant, Max.

Teaching Chart 60

Model how to use syntactic and other context clues to determine what *jig* might mean.

MODEL I'm not sure what *jig* means. Let me look at the word order of the sentence it's in. I can tell that *jig* is a noun, or naming word, because it follows the verb *danced*, the article *a*, and the adjective *little*. Since the professor is dancing, a *jig* must be a kind of dance.

PRACTICE

Use Context Clues to Understand Unfamiliar Words

Circle these words on the chart: *elated, accomplished, croon,* and *suspended*. Have volunteers underline context clues as to their meaning. Have groups discuss what each word might mean and then check their guesses in a dictionary. ▶ **Linguistic**

ASSESS/CLOSE

Write Context Sentences

Have students look up the words shown below in a dictionary. Then ask them to work with a partner to write one sentence using three of the words and giving context clues to their meanings.

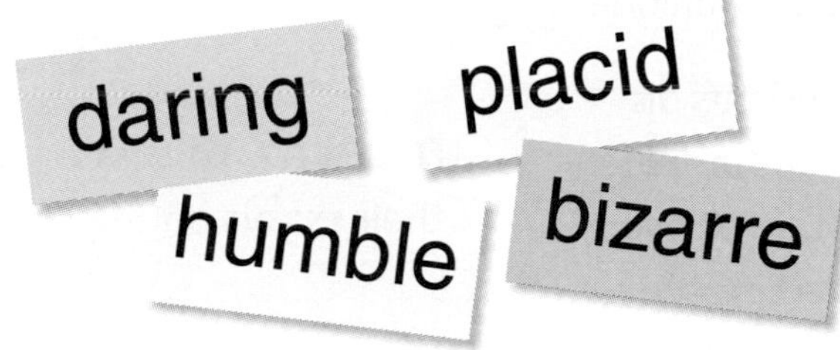

ALTERNATE TEACHING STRATEGY

CONTEXT CLUES

For a different approach to teaching this skill, see page T63.

Meeting Individual Needs for Vocabulary

EASY

Name________ Date________ **Reteach 72**

Context Clues

Context clues can help you decide if a new word is a noun or verb and help you understand its meaning. Sometimes the context may give a definition of a word or give examples.

Read each sentence. Write the meaning of the underlined word.

1. On holidays such as Thanksgiving, people like to get together with their friends and families.
   special days such as Thanksgiving
2. They make foods such as milk, butter, and cheese in their dairy.
   a place where people make milk, butter, and cheese
3. We saw a freight train, a train that carries goods and supplies rather than people.
   goods and supplies
4. The plane was soaring in the sky like a flying bird.
   moving through the air
5. He neglected his dog. For example, he sometimes forgot to feed him.
   not to give attention or care to something

72 **At Home:** Have students find a new word in a book they are reading and then try to use context clues to figure out the meaning of the word. Book 3.1/Unit 2 **Web Wonders** 5

Reteach, 72

ON-LEVEL

Name________ Date________ **Practice 72**

Context Clues

The words and sentences around a word can help you discover its meaning. **Context clues** can be synonyms, antonyms, or examples. Some sentences even provide an exact definition for a word.

Write a definition for each boldfaced word. Answers may vary.

1. It was an **error.** Luckily, we could fix the incorrect word.
   incorrect
2. They will **admit** everyone to the play. They will let in children first.
   let in
3. Many planets move in wide circles. For example, the earth **revolves** around the sun.
   move in wide circles
4. Erin wants to **adopt** a dog and take care of it at her home.
   take care of it
5. The afternoon seemed **endless.** The children thought it would go on forever.
   on forever
6. The soldier played the **bugle,** a small instrument like a trumpet, every morning and evening.
   a small instrument like a trumpet

72 **At Home:** Ask students to think of some context clues that could be used for the word **shelter.** Book 3.1/Unit 2 **Web Wonders** 6

Practice, 72

CHALLENGE

Name________ Date________ **Extend 72**

Context Clues

A. The underlined words in the sentences below are scrambled. Look at the picture and read the sentences to figure out what the words should be. Write the correct word next to the scrambled word.

This spider is spinning a silk ewb __web__. The silk web is trsgno __strong__ enough to capture a grasshopper. The strong web might even capture a ribd __bird__!

B. Draw your own picture. Write sentences about it. Include three scrambled words. Give your picture and sentences to a partner. Ask your partner to unscramble the words.

Scrambled words and sentences will vary.

72 **At Home:** Invite students to read a passage in a story. Encourage them to use context clues to figure out the meaning of any unfamiliar words. Book 3.1/Unit 2 **Web Wonders**

Extend, 72

LANGUAGE SUPPORT

Name________ Date________

Search for Clues

1. Arrows bounced off of the soldiers because spider silk was woven into the armor they were wearing over their clothes.
   Color the armor in the picture.
2. One day your favorite jeans may have some spider silk in them.
   Color the favorite jeans in the picture.
3. Car bumpers may be made of spider silk so they won't dent so easily when hit.
   Color the bumper in the picture.

80 **Web Wonders** • Language Support/Blackline Master 40 Grade 3

Language Support, 80

GRAMMAR/SPELLING CONNECTIONS

See the 5-Day Grammar and Usage Plan on Sentence Combining with Nouns, pages 253M–253N.

See the 5-Day Spelling Plan on Words from Science, pages 253O–253P.

TECHNOLOGY TIP

Help students use a search engine to find information about spiders.

Explanatory Writing

Prewrite

WRITE AN ESSAY Present this writing assignment: Choose one kind of spider. Write a step-by-step explanation of a day in the life of a spider. Tell your story from the spider's point of view. Be sure to include where it lives, what it likes to eat, and what makes it unique.

EXPLORE THE TOPIC Have students discuss the things that they learned about spiders in *Spiders at Work*, in the article *Web Wonders*, in the encyclopedia entry they read in Study Skills, and from their personal experience.

Strategy: List Facts Have students make a class list of all the facts they have learned about spiders. Then have them each choose one kind of spider. Guide them to chart their spider's activities in a step-by-step, chronological sequence.

Draft

Ask students to imagine themselves as the spider they chose to write about. Guide them to use their facts to construct an imaginative narrative of a step-by-step activity. Invite them to use vivid details to enhance the explanation.

Revise

FOCUS ON ELABORATION Have students ask themselves the following questions:

- Did I give each step in my spider's activity?
- Are the steps in chronological order?
- Did I describe what my spider looks like, does and sees?

PARTNERS

Have students trade essays with a peer and ask for suggestions.

Edit/Proofread

CHECK FOR ERRORS Students should reread their reports to check spelling, grammar, punctuation, and to ensure that they have included a clear beginning, middle, and end.

Publish

DISPLAY ESSAYS Students can display their essays on the classroom library table.

Lucy, the Brown Recluse Spider

by Mohammed Jones

I am a brown recluse spider. My name is Lucy. Even though the word "brown" is part of my name, I have a beautiful yellow-orange body. On my back, you can see a dark shape like a violin. I am almost half an inch long. I live in Kansas. I have relatives in Texas and in California.

I spend my day indoors. First I sit in my web and wait for small insects to get trapped there. Then I bite and poison them. I can poison people, too. But they do not die.

After I bite an insect, I attach them to my web so they cannot move.

Presentation Ideas

PICTURE THAT Have students research photos or drawings to make a model of their topic spider. ▶ **Viewing/Representing**

PERSUASIVE SPEAKING Have students give a one-minute speech telling about the good things that spiders do for the world.
▶ **Speaking/Listening**

Consider students' creative efforts, possibly adding a plus (+) for originality, wit, and imagination.

Scoring Rubric

Excellent	Good	Fair	Unsatisfactory
4: The writer • presents a well-researched, step-by-step explanation of a spider's activity, in proper sequence. • uses vivid description to enhance facts. • may make sophisticated observations.	**3:** The writer • clearly explains a step-by-step spider activity. • may enhance facts with detail or observations. • organizes material in chronological order.	**2:** The writer • attempts to explain a spider's activity. • may not present a step-by-step process. • may not elaborate with sufficient, or correct, detail.	**1:** The writer • may not present a step-by-step, factual report on spiders. • may list vague or irrelevant facts and details. • shows severe trouble with organization or language usage.

0: The writer leaves the page blank or fails to respond to the writing task. The student does not address the topic or simply paraphrases the prompt. The response is illegible or incoherent.

Meeting Individual Needs for Writing

EASY

Web Sight Have students draw a spider-web design with a spider in the middle. Have them label the drawing with a fact about the spider they researched.

ON-LEVEL

Spinning a Story Have students write a story from the point of view of an insect that escaped from a spider's web.

CHALLENGE

Letter to the Editor Have students pretend to be a spider who writes a letter to the editor of a scientific journal. The spider might complain of scientists trying to take away its job by developing artificial spider silk.

COMMUNICATION TIPS

REPRESENTING Students can use pipe cleaners, paint, paper, and glue to make model spiders. They can use wire or thread to suspend spiders in the air.

LISTENING Students can use gestures while making their persuasive speeches. Tell them to practice in front of a mirror.

LANGUAGE SUPPORT

ESL Before writing their final essays, ask ESL students to work with English-fluent partners to put together a list of vocabulary words covering the specific details and factual observations to include in their reports.

PORTFOLIO Remind students to place their essays in their portfolios after the essays have been displayed on the library table.

5 Day Grammar and Usage Plan

LANGUAGE SUPPORT

In a group, have each student tell two things he or she sees in the classroom. Example: *I see a chair and a table.*

DAILY LANGUAGE ACTIVITIES

Write the Daily Language Activities on the chalkboard each day or use **Transparency 10**. Have students combine sentences orally. Answers given for Day 1; remaining answers follow same pattern.

Day 1

1. The spider has a web. The spider has a trap. The spider has a web and a trap.
2. I saw a spider. I saw a fly. I saw a spider and a fly.
3. It ate a fly. It ate a beetle. It ate a fly and a beetle.

Day 2

1. Spiders crawl. Lizards crawl.
2. Spiders lay eggs. Chickens lay eggs.
3. Farmers like spiders. Scientists like spiders.

Day 3

1. The bug crawled. The ant crawled.
2. Spiders have eight legs. Spiders have eight eyes.
3. The ant got out. The fly got out.

Day 4

1. Flies were caught. Birds were caught.
2. Len found a spider. Len found a firefly.
3. The bug died. The ant died.

Day 5

1. Spiders help crops. Spiders help flowers.
2. The babies are gone. The eggs are gone.
3. The spiders grew. The web grew.

Daily Language Transparency 10

DAY 1 Introduce the Concept

Oral Warm-Up Ask students to listen to the following sentences carefully: *Ed has a dog. Ed has a bird.* Elicit ways to change the sentences into one sentence.

Introduce Sentence Combining Explain to students that they can make their writing more interesting by combining sentences. Use the sentences above as a model. Underline *Ed has* in each sentence. Explain that *and* is used to join the sentences, and words that repeat are left out.

Sentence Combining

Two sentences can be combined by joining two nouns with *and.*

Present the Daily Language Activity. Then have students write their own combined sentences, as above. Ask them to start by writing two simple sentences about spiders.

WRITING Assign the daily Writing Prompt on page 244C.

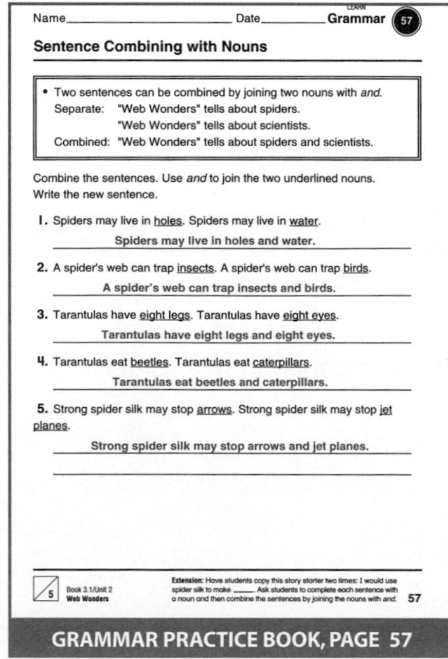

Name________ Date________ LEARN Grammar 57

Sentence Combining with Nouns

- Two sentences can be combined by joining two nouns with *and.*
  Separate: "Web Wonders" tells about spiders.
  "Web Wonders" tells about scientists.
  Combined: "Web Wonders" tells about spiders and scientists.

Combine the sentences. Use *and* to join the two underlined nouns. Write the new sentence.

1. Spiders may live in holes. Spiders may live in water.
   Spiders may live in holes and water.
2. A spider's web can trap insects. A spider's web can trap birds.
   A spider's web can trap insects and birds.
3. Tarantulas have eight legs. Tarantulas have eight eyes.
   Tarantulas have eight legs and eight eyes.
4. Tarantulas eat beetles. Tarantulas eat caterpillars.
   Tarantulas eat beetles and caterpillars.
5. Strong spider silk may stop arrows. Strong spider silk may stop jet planes.
   Strong spider silk may stop arrows and jet planes.

5 Book 3.1/Unit 2 **Web Wonders**

Extension: Have students copy this story starter two times: I would use spider silk to make ____. Ask students to complete each sentence with a noun and then combine the sentences by joining the nouns with *and.* 57

GRAMMAR PRACTICE BOOK, PAGE 57

DAY 2 Teach the Concept

Review Sentence Combining Ask students to explain how sentences can be combined using the word *and.*

Introduce Sentence Combining with Subjects Remind students that the subject of a sentence tells what or whom the sentence is about. Present:

Sentence Combining

- Some nouns are subjects of sentences.
- Sometimes two subjects can be joined with *and.*

Example: *The spider is tiny. Its eggs are tiny. The spider and its eggs are tiny.*

Then have students work in pairs to write about a spider and a fly. They can take turns writing a sentence, writing a second sentence with the same predicate, and then combining sentences by joining subjects.

WRITING Assign the daily Writing Prompt on page 244C.

Name________ Date________ LEARN AND PRACTICE Grammar 58

Combining Subjects

- Some nouns are the subjects of sentences. Sometimes two subjects can be joined with *and.*
  Separate: Adult spiders travel on threads in the wind.
  Spiderlings travel on threads in the wind.
  Combined: Adult spiders and spiderlings travel on threads in the wind.

Combine the subjects of the sentences. Write the new sentence.

1. Flies are meals for spiders. Dragonflies are meals for spiders.
   Flies and dragonflies are meals for spiders.
2. Tarantulas eat grasshoppers. Daddy-longlegs eat grasshoppers.
   Tarantulas and daddy-longlegs eat grasshoppers.
3. Bird spider tarantulas eat birds. Golden silk spiders eat birds.
   Bird spider tarantulas and golden silk spiders eat birds.
4. Farmers like spiders. Scientists like spiders.
   Farmers and scientists like spiders.
5. Spiders are making spider silk. Scientists are making spider silk.
   Spiders and scientists are making spider silk.

58 **Extension:** Arrange students in pairs. Have partners take turns generating and extending sentences. One partner thinks of a sentence with one noun in the subject. The other student extends the sentence by adding *and* and another noun. Book 3.1/Unit 2 **Web Wonders** 5

GRAMMAR PRACTICE BOOK, PAGE 58

Sentence Combining with Nouns

DAY 3 Review and Practice

Learn from the Literature Review combining sentences with nouns. Read the following sentence from page 247 of *Web Wonders*:

> **It was woven into their clothes and their armor.**

Ask students to identify the two nouns in the sentence, as well as the word that is used to join the nouns. (*clothes, armor, and*)

Combine Sentences Present the Daily Language Activity and have students combine sentences using *and*.

Have students write simple sentences containing facts about spiders. Then have students write other sentences which could be combined. Example: *Spiders lay eggs. Chickens lay eggs.* Then have students work together to combine sentences.

WRITING Assign the daily Writing Prompt on page 244D.

Name______ Date______ PRACTICE AND REVIEW Grammar 59

Combining Subjects and Objects

- Two sentences can be combined by joining two nouns with *and*.
  Separate: "Web Wonders" tells about spiders.
  "Web Wonders" tells about scientists.
  Combined: "Web Wonders" tells about spiders and scientists.
- Some nouns are the objects of sentences. Sometimes two objects can be joined with *and*.

Join each pair of sentences. Use *and* to join the nouns. Write the new sentence.

1. Elena read about spiders. Elena read about butterflies.
   Elena read about spiders and butterflies.
2. She learned about spider silk. She learned about human-made silk.
   She learned about spider and human-made silk.
3. Pang looked for spider webs. Elena looked for spider webs.
   Pang and Elena looked for spider webs.
4. Garden spiders spin webs. Golden silk spiders spin webs.
   Garden and golden silk spiders spin webs.
5. Pang drew pictures of webs. Pang drew pictures of spiders.
   Pang drew pictures of webs and spiders.
6. He drew a tarantula. He drew a black widow spider.
   He drew a tarantula and a black widow spider.
7. Tarantulas live in holes. Wolf spiders live in holes.
   Tarantulas and wolf spiders live in holes.
8. Spiders are living things. Plants are living things.
   Spiders and plants are living things.

8 Book 3.1/Unit 2 Web Wonders — Extension: Have students write a pair of sentences with similar ideas and then join the sentences by combining the nouns. 59

GRAMMAR PRACTICE BOOK, PAGE 59

DAY 4 Review and Practice

Review Sentence Combining Write the following on the chalkboard: *Carla has a _____ and a _____.* Have students supply nouns to complete the sentence. Then write: _____ *and* _____ *enjoy bowling.* Repeat the activity. Have students identify which nouns are subjects. Then present the Daily Language Activity.

Mechanics and Usage Before students begin the daily Writing Prompt on page 244D, review letter greetings and closings. Display and discuss:

Letter Punctuation

- Begin the greeting and closing in a letter with a capital letter.
- Use a comma after the greeting and the closing in a letter.

WRITING Assign the daily Writing Prompt on page 244D.

Name______ Date______ MECHANICS Grammar 60

Using Commas and Capital Letters in a Letter

- Begin the greeting and closing in a letter with a capital letter.
- Use a comma after the greeting in a letter.
- Use a comma after the closing in a letter.

Proofread this letter. Correct the capitalization and punctuation mistakes. Combine the underlined sentences. Rewrite the letter correctly on the lines.

dear uncle jack

we learned a lot about spiders today do you know how amazing spider webs are spider webs can trap birds. spider webs can trap flies

your niece
jan

(Greeting)
Dear Uncle Jack,

We learned a lot about spiders today.
Do you know how amazing spider webs are?
Spider webs can trap birds and flies.

(Closing)
Your niece,

(Your name)
Jan

60 Extension: Have students proofread their letters and use proofreading marks to show corrections. Then have students rewrite their letters correctly. Book 3.1/Unit 2 Web Wonders 14

GRAMMAR PRACTICE BOOK, PAGE 60

DAY 5 Assess and Reteach

Assess Use the Daily Language Activity and page 61 of the **Grammar Practice Book** for assessment.

Reteach Have students work in small groups. Distribute cards with a simple sentence written on each. Include pairs of sentences with the same predicate. For example: *Boys like to eat cake. Girls like to eat cake. We went to the store. We went to the park.* Ask students to read their sentences aloud in the group, and then work together to decide which pairs of sentences could be combined. Students holding these cards should work together to combine the sentences.

Have partners write their new sentences and add them to a classroom word wall.

Use page 62 of the **Grammar Practice Book** for additional reteaching.

WRITING Assign the daily Writing Prompt on page 244D.

Name______ Date______ TEST Grammar 61

Sentence Combining with Nouns

A. Write **yes** if the sentences can be combined by joining two nouns. Write **no** if they cannot be combined.

1. Webs catch flies. Webs catch bees. Yes
2. Spiders spin circles. Spiders spin triangles. Yes
3. Spiderlings are baby spiders. Spiderlings spin a silk line. No
4. Spider silk may be in jeans. Spider silk may be in coats. Yes

B. Each pair of sentences can be combined. Write the two nouns that can be joined with the word *and*. Use capital letters correctly.

5. Flies have six legs. Ants have six legs.
   Flies and ants
6. Ants do not spin webs. Tarantulas do not spin webs.
   Ants and tarantulas
7. Ants have feelers. Beetles have feelers.
   Ants and beetles
8. Tarantulas have no feelers. Daddy-longlegs have no feelers.
   Tarantulas and daddy-longlegs

8 Book 3.1/Unit 2 Web Wonders 61

GRAMMAR PRACTICE BOOK, PAGE 61

GRAMMAR PRACTICE BOOK, PAGE 62

5 Day Spelling Plan

LANGUAGE SUPPORT

Students may have trouble with some unusual spellings in this list, including short *e* spelled *ea* in *thread,* long *e* spelled *ey* in *prey*, /s/ spelled *sc* in *science,* and the silent *e* in *breathe*. Write these words on the chalkboard, highlight the difficult parts, and have students brainstorm ways to remember them.

DICTATION SENTENCES

1. The spider made a web.
2. The oil is sticky.
3. You need bait to catch fish.
4. Each cell of your body is tiny.
5. The new dress is made from silk.
6. She taught me how to weave.
7. What fiber is used in that hat?
8. It was made from thin strands of wool.
9. I saw a beetle on the ground.
10. The thread on the sleeve is red.
11. I want to know more about science.
12. A fang is a kind of tooth.
13. All animals have to breathe.
14. I do not like the taste of carrots.
15. A large bird will eat small prey.

Challenge Words

16. An earthquake can push a building down.
17. When will the egg hatch?
18. I respect my parents.
19. The soldiers carry flags.
20. The clothes were woven by hand.

DAY 1 Pretest

Assess Prior Knowledge Use the Dictation Sentences at the left and **Spelling Practice Book** page 57 for the pretest. Allow students to correct their own papers. If students have trouble, have partners give each other a midweek test on Day 3. Students who require a modified list may be tested on the first eight words.

Spelling Words		Challenge Words
1. **web**	9. beetle	16. **earthquake**
2. **sticky**	10. **thread**	17. **hatch**
3. bait	11. science	18. **respect**
4. cell	12. fang	19. **soldiers**
5. **silk**	13. breathe	20. **woven**
6. **weave**	14. taste	
7. **fiber**	15. prey	
8. **strands**		

*Note: Words in **dark type** are from the story.*

Word Study On page 58 of the **Spelling Practice Book** are word study steps and an at-home activity.

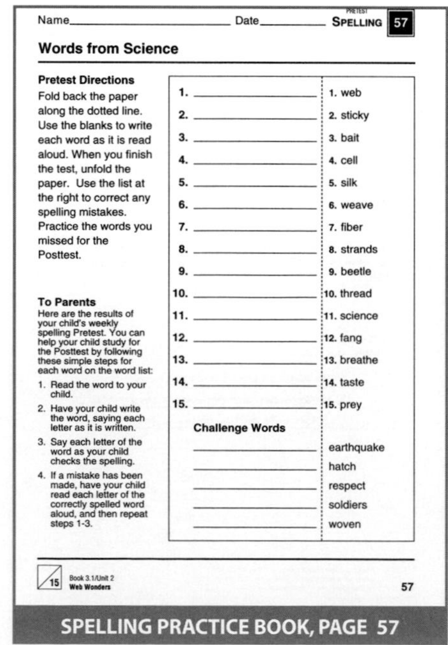

Name________ Date________ PRETEST SPELLING 57

Words from Science

Pretest Directions
Fold back the paper along the dotted line. Use the blanks to write each word as it is read aloud. When you finish the test, unfold the paper. Use the list at the right to correct any spelling mistakes. Practice the words you missed for the Posttest.

To Parents
Here are the results of your child's weekly spelling Pretest. You can help your child study for the Posttest by following these simple steps for each word on the word list:

1. Read the word to your child.
2. Have your child write the word, saying each letter as it is written.
3. Say each letter of the word as your child checks the spelling.
4. If a mistake has been made, have your child read each letter of the correctly spelled word aloud, and then repeat steps 1-3.

1. ______ 1. web
2. ______ 2. sticky
3. ______ 3. bait
4. ______ 4. cell
5. ______ 5. silk
6. ______ 6. weave
7. ______ 7. fiber
8. ______ 8. strands
9. ______ 9. beetle
10. ______ 10. thread
11. ______ 11. science
12. ______ 12. fang
13. ______ 13. breathe
14. ______ 14. taste
15. ______ 15. prey

Challenge Words

earthquake
hatch
respect
soldiers
woven

15 Book 3.1/Unit 2 **Web Wonders** 57

SPELLING PRACTICE BOOK, PAGE 57

WORD STUDY STEPS AND ACTIVITY, PAGE 58

DAY 2 Explore the Pattern

Sort and Spell Words Say the words *fang* and *weave*. Ask students what vowel sound they hear in each word. (short *a*; long *e*) Have students say each Spelling Word and sort them according to the categories below. For words with more than one syllable, they should sort by the vowel sound in the first syllable.

Words with:

short *a*	short *e*	short *i*
strands	web	sticky
fang	cell	silk
	thread	
long *a*	**long *e***	**long *i***
bait	weave	fiber
taste	beetle	science
prey	breathe	

Word Wall Have students find more science-related words with the vowel sounds listed above and add them to a classroom word wall.

Name________ Date________ EXPLORE THE PATTERN SPELLING 59

Words from Science

web	cell	fiber	thread	breathe
sticky	silk	strands	science	taste
bait	weave	beetle	fang	prey

Pattern Power

Write the spelling words with the short **e** sound.
1. web 2. cell 3. thread

Write the spelling words with the long **e** sound.
4. beetle 5. weave 6. breathe

Write the spelling words with the long **i** sound.
7. science 8. fiber

Write the spelling words with the short **i** sound.
9. silk 10. sticky

Write the spelling words with the long **a** sound.
11. bait 12. taste 13. prey

Write the spelling words with the short **a** sound.
14. strands 15. fang

15 Book 3.1/Unit 2 **Web Wonders** 59

SPELLING PRACTICE BOOK, PAGE 59

Words from Science

DAY 3 Practice and Extend

Word Meaning: Science Help students develop definitions for each of the Spelling Words, or have them work in groups, referring to science books and dictionaries. Then have groups write context sentences for the words.

Glossary Explain to students that sometimes one word can be used as more than one part of speech. Have students:

- write each Challenge Word.
- look up each Challenge Word in the Glossary.
- write the part of speech by each Challenge Word and circle the word that can be used as a noun or a verb. *(respect)*

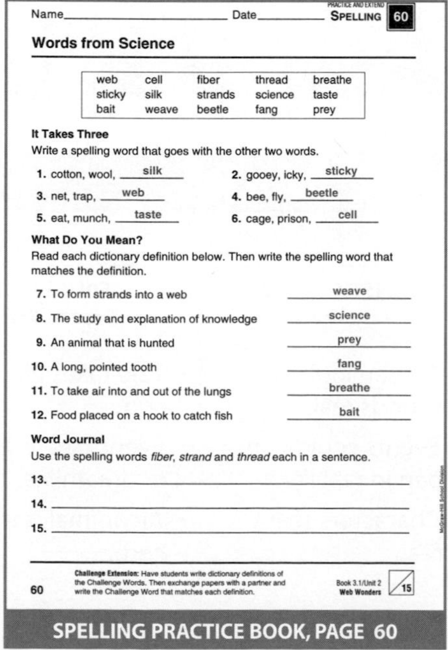

Name________ Date______ PRACTICE AND EXTEND SPELLING 60

Words from Science

web	cell	fiber	thread	breathe
sticky	silk	strands	science	taste
bait	weave	beetle	fang	prey

It Takes Three

Write a spelling word that goes with the other two words.

1. cotton, wool, silk
2. gooey, icky, sticky
3. net, trap, web
4. bee, fly, beetle
5. eat, munch, taste
6. cage, prison, cell

What Do You Mean?

Read each dictionary definition below. Then write the spelling word that matches the definition.

7. To form strands into a web — weave
8. The study and explanation of knowledge — science
9. An animal that is hunted — prey
10. A long, pointed tooth — fang
11. To take air into and out of the lungs — breathe
12. Food placed on a hook to catch fish — bait

Word Journal

Use the spelling words *fiber, strand* and *thread* each in a sentence.

13. ________
14. ________
15. ________

60 **Challenge Extension:** Have students write dictionary definitions of the Challenge Words. Then exchange papers with a partner and write the Challenge Word that matches each definition. Book 3.1/Unit 2 **Web Wonders** 15

McGraw-Hill School Division

SPELLING PRACTICE BOOK, PAGE 60

DAY 4 Proofread and Write

Proofread Sentences Write these sentences on the chalkboard, including the misspelled words. Ask students to proofread, circling incorrect spellings and writing the correct spellings. There are two spelling errors in each sentence.

Fish like the taest of bate. (taste, bait)

The beatle was the prai of the spider. (beetle, prey)

There were strandes of fibur on the floor (strands, fiber)

Have students create additional sentences with errors for partners to correct.

WRITING Have students use as many spelling words as possible in the daily Writing Prompt on page 244D. Remind students to proofread their writing for errors in spelling, grammar, and punctuation.

Name________ Date______ PROOFREAD AND WRITE SPELLING 61

Words from Science

Proofreading Activity

There are 6 spelling mistakes in this poem. Circle the misspelled words. Write the words correctly on the lines below.

Web Nonsense

This spider's name is Nicky.
Its web is gooey and stickey.
Its strandes are smooth as silck
Or very rich buttermilk.
You may well not believe
How gently Nicky can weeve
Each fine thread into a net.
That's when the trap is set!
For every fibur is a way
To trap some poor insect preay.

1. sticky 2. strands 3. silk
4. weave 5. fiber 6. prey

Writing Activity

Write four words that rhyme with the spelling words. Then write a nonsense poem using pairs of rhyming words. Use the poem above as a model.

Words That Rhyme	Your Nonsense Poem
7.	
8.	
9.	
10.	

10 Book 3.1/Unit 2 **Web Wonders** 61

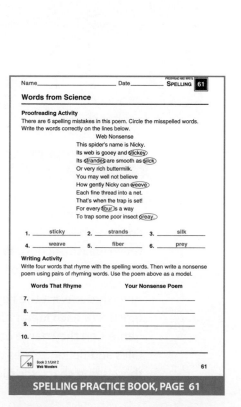

SPELLING PRACTICE BOOK, PAGE 61

DAY 5 Assess and Reteach

Assess Students' Knowledge Use page 62 of the **Spelling Practice Book** or the Dictation Sentences on page 253O for the posttest.

Personal Word List Have

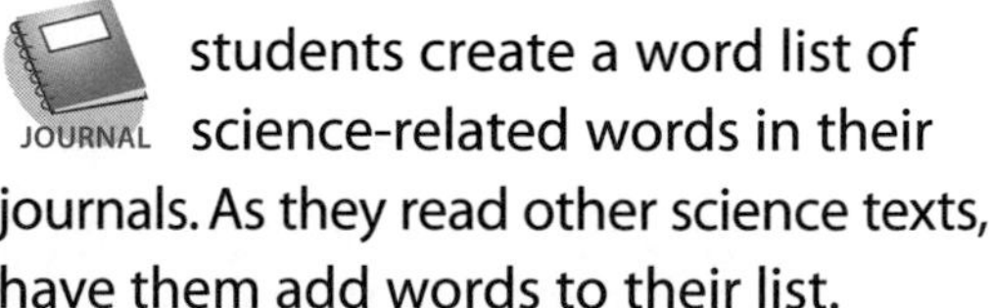

JOURNAL students create a word list of science-related words in their journals. As they read other science texts, have them add words to their list.

Students should continue to practice spelling these words and refer to them during later writing activities.

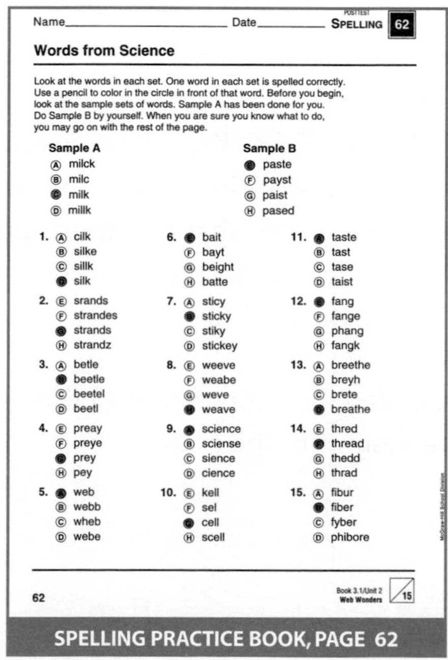

Name________ Date______ POSTTEST SPELLING 62

Words from Science

Look at the words in each set. One word in each set is spelled correctly. Use a pencil to color in the circle in front of that word. Before you begin, look at the sample sets of words. Sample A has been done for you. Do Sample B by yourself. When you are sure you know what to do, you may go on with the rest of the page.

Sample A	Sample B
Ⓐ milck	● paste
Ⓑ milc	Ⓕ payst
● milk	Ⓖ paist
Ⓓ millk	Ⓗ pased

1. Ⓐ cilk	6. ● bait	11. ● taste
Ⓑ silke	Ⓕ bayt	Ⓑ tast
Ⓒ sillk	Ⓖ beight	Ⓒ tase
● silk	Ⓗ batte	Ⓓ taist
2. Ⓔ srands	7. Ⓐ sticy	12. ● fang
Ⓕ strandes	● sticky	Ⓕ fange
● strands	Ⓒ stiky	Ⓖ phang
Ⓗ strandz	Ⓓ stickey	Ⓗ fangk
3. Ⓐ betle	8. Ⓔ weeve	13. Ⓐ breethe
● beetle	Ⓕ weabe	Ⓑ breyh
Ⓒ beetel	Ⓖ weve	Ⓒ brete
Ⓓ beetl	● weave	● breathe
4. Ⓔ preay	9. ● science	14. Ⓔ thred
Ⓕ preye	Ⓑ sciense	● thread
● prey	Ⓒ sience	Ⓖ thedd
Ⓗ pey	Ⓓ cience	Ⓗ thrad
5. ● web	10. Ⓔ kell	15. Ⓐ fibur
Ⓑ webb	Ⓕ sel	● fiber
Ⓒ wheb	● cell	Ⓒ fyber
Ⓓ webe	Ⓗ scell	Ⓓ phibore

62 Book 3.1/Unit 2 **Web Wonders** 15

McGraw-Hill School Division

SPELLING PRACTICE BOOK, PAGE 62

Wrap Up the Theme

Nature Links

Nature can give us new ideas.

REVIEW THE THEME Remind students that all of the selections in this unit relate to the theme Nature Links. In reading about nature, do students prefer fiction or nonfiction? Ask them to explain their choices. Has their reading made students more aware of the natural environment? What do they notice now about nature that they might not have noticed before?

READ THE POEM Read aloud the poem "Who Am I?" by Felice Holman. Besides the poet herself, what are the things mentioned in the first stanza? (trees, sky, sea) What is mentioned in stanza 2? (grass, sand, rocks) What conclusion does the speaker draw? (All things are interrelated.) Ask students to discuss how the shape of the poem supports what the poet says.

LISTENING LIBRARY AUDIOCASSETTE

GROUP **MAKE CONNECTIONS** Have students work in small groups to brainstorm a list of ways that the stories, poems, and the *Time for Kids* magazine article relate to the theme Nature Links.

Groups can then compare their lists as they share them with the class.

Who Am I?

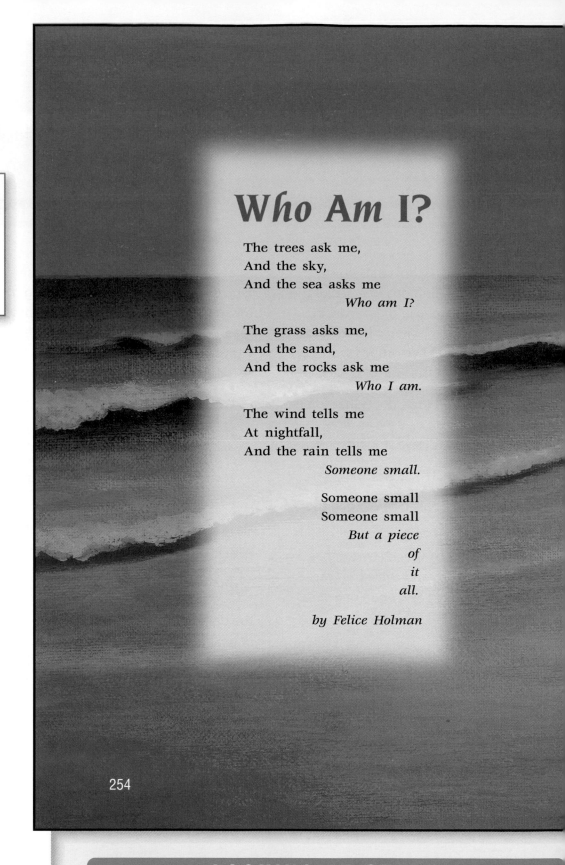

The trees ask me,
And the sky,
And the sea asks me
Who am I?

The grass asks me,
And the sand,
And the rocks ask me
Who I am.

The wind tells me
At nightfall,
And the rain tells me
Someone small.

Someone small
Someone small
But a piece
of
it
all.

by Felice Holman

254

LOOKING AT GENRE

Have students review *City Green* and *Dream Wolf*. What makes *City Green* realistic fiction? What makes *Dream Wolf* a folk tale?

Help students list the key characteristics of each literary form or genre. Can they name other folk tales and fiction stories that have these same characteristics?

REALISTIC FICTION *City Green*	FOLK TALE *Dream Wolf*
• Setting looks and sounds real. • Events could happen in real life. • Characters seem real.	• Tale takes place long ago. • Events seem magical or dreamlike. • An animal is the hero.

255

Research and Inquiry

Complete the Theme Project GROUP Have students work in teams to complete their group project. Remind students that the information they have gathered about habitats, native wildlife, and plants demonstrates the delicate balance of nature. Encourage them to share tasks of letter writing, poster making, and so on in ways that allow each member to contribute.

Make a Classroom Presentation Have teams take turns presenting their proposals and sharing what they have learned. Be sure to include time for questions from the audience.

Draw Conclusions Have students draw conclusions about what they have learned from researching their projects. Were human resources helpful? Were visits to local sites helpful? How does hands-on research differ from library research? Has the research inspired students to get involved with groups that work to keep the planet healthy? Do they think they could find information on such groups on the Internet?

Ask More Questions What additional questions do students have? What else would students like to do? Students who have applied their research to an actual task, such as creating a litter-free zone or a natural habitat, may be encouraged to continue this kind of community work.

LEARNING ABOUT POETRY

Literary Devices: Free Verse, Rhetorical Question Tell students that the poem, as an example of free verse, does not have a regular meter. Also explain that, while it includes rhymes, the poem does not have a regular rhyme scheme or pattern. Read the poem aloud a second time. Explain that the repetition of the rhetorical question "Who Am I?" suggests a person's attempts at figuring out where he or she belongs in the universe. Help students realize that the speaker's conclusion is one of being small, yet significant.

Poetry Activity Have students write a poem that answers the question: Who Am I? Students might want to use this poem as a model to follow when they write or choose another one.

UNIT 2

Writing Process

Explanatory Writing

CONNECT TO LITERATURE In *City Green*, the author explains how a community turned a vacant lot into a beautiful neighborhood garden. Have students name the steps that Miss Rosa and Marcy took to create the community garden. Make a chart and ask students to put the steps in the order that they happened.

GROUP

Here's a special gift you can make for a friend. First, collect magazine pictures of his or her favorite things. Cut out each picture in a different shape. Then, glue the pictures to a wooden or cardboard box. Next, you can paint stripes, dots or shapes around the lid, or decorate the box with colorful beads. Finally, ask a grown-up to varnish the box to make it waterproof. Your friend will love this present!

Prewrite

PURPOSE AND AUDIENCE Explain to students that they will write reports whose purpose is to inform and explain how to do a simple project for a friend or family member. Encourage students to think about purpose and audience as they write their reports.

STRATEGY: MAKE A LIST Invite students to think of a favorite project category. Ask them to choose a simple project from their category and have them list the materials and the steps they will need to complete the project.

Use **Writing Process Transparency 2A** as a model.

FEATURES OF EXPLANATORY WRITING

- **Informs how to complete a specific task.**
- **Presents step-by-step instructions.**
- **Uses time-order words to help set a logical sequence.**

TEACHING TIP

ORGANIZATION **Help students write their list of steps in a logical sequence of actions. Ask them to think carefully as they write, and consider the order of each step in the process.**

PREWRITE TRANSPARENCY

How to Make Breakfast for Mom

What you need	How to do it
1. cereal, banana, milk	1. fill bowl with cereal
2. butter knife	2. slice banana over the top
3. bowl, spoon, napkin	3. mix juice and water in pitcher
4. can of juice, water	4. pour juice into glass
5. pitcher and glass	5. pour milk over cereal
6. a flower	6. set table, and call Mom
	7. don't forget to give her the flower

McGraw-Hill School Division

Book 3.1/Unit 2: Explanatory Writing / Prewriting 2A

Draft

STRATEGY: EXPANDING ON IDEAS Ask students to start with a topic sentence that tells why their project is a fun thing to do. Then have them explain how to do their project in detail. Invite them to write freely, as if they were telling their idea to a friend. Remind them to check their lists for the project steps and materials.

Use **Writing Process Transparency 2B** to model a first draft.

LANGUAGE CONTROL Have students write time-order words next to each step on their project charts, such as *first, next,* and *finally.* Ask them to come up with additional words that can help to build a logical sequence. They can use a thesaurus to expand their lists. Have them save their time-order lists in their writing portfolios.

LANGUAGE SUPPORT

ESL Some students may find it helpful to write about something familiar that they have done several times before. Have them create a word bank of adjectives to help them describe each step in detail.

***DRAFT* TRANSPARENCY**

How to Make Breakfast for Mom

To surprise your mom, make your mom breakfast on a saturday morning. Go to the kitchen and get started. Put all your ingreadients on the counter—cereal, milk, a banana, and a can of juice. Pour cereal in your mom's favorite bowl. Next use a knife to slice a banana over the top. Mix up the juice with some water in a nice pitcher, and pour some in glass. Set the table and pour milk over the cereal. Do this last, so the cereal doesn't get soggy! Finally, call your mom to breakfast. And make sure to give her a flower

McGraw-Hill School Division

Book 3.1/Unit 2: Explanatory Writing / Drafting 2B

Revise

Have students look over their first drafts for sequence and clarity. Ask them to check that their steps are in a logical order. Invite them to think of descriptive details they can add to enliven their explanations.

Use **Writing Process Transparency 2C** for classroom discussion on the revision process. Ask students to comment on how revisions have improved the writing example they saw earlier.

STRATEGY: ELABORATION Students can compare their first drafts with their prewriting lists to be sure that they have included all the necessary steps and materials. Have them use the following questions to assess their writing:

- Have I made my project seem like it would be fun to do?
- Can a reader follow my step-by-step instructions?
- Do I need to include specific details to make the steps clearer?

TEACHING TIP

TEACHER CONFERENCE Help students individually to expand their drafts. Offer concrete ideas for how they might incorporate more detail into each step. Encourage them to use lots of action words to make their writing come alive. Ask them:

- Do you have a strong topic sentence?
- Do you think your explanation has enough step-by-step detail? Do you need to add any examples to help explain how to do a specific step?
- Picture yourself doing the project. Have you written the steps in the correct order?

REVISE TRANSPARENCY

How to Make Breakfast for Mom

To surprise your mom, make ~~your mom~~ [her a special] breakfast on a saturday morning. [When everyone's asleep.] Go to the kitchen and get started. [First,] Put all your ingreadients on the counter—cereal, milk, a banana, and a can of juice. [Then,] Pour cereal in your mom's favorite bowl. Next use a [butter] knife to slice a banana over the top. Mix up the juice with some water in a nice pitcher, and pour some in glass. Set the table and pour milk over the cereal. [Be sure to] Do this last, so the cereal doesn't get soggy! Finally, call your mom to breakfast. And [last but not least] make sure to give her a flower [when she sits down at the table!]

McGraw-Hill School Division

Book 3.1/Unit 2: Explanatory Writing / Revising 2C

Explanatory Writing

Edit/Proofread

After students finish revising their texts, have them proofread for final corrections and additions.

GRAMMAR/SPELLING CONNECTIONS

See the 5-Day Grammar and Usage Plans on nouns, pages 171M–171N, 203M–203N, 225M–225N, 243M–243N, and 253M–253N.

See the 5-Day Spelling Plans, pages 171O–171P, 203O–203P, 225O–225P, 243O–243P, and 253O–253P.

GRAMMAR, MECHANICS, USAGE

- Use a comma after time-order words.
- Use a comma between the day and year in a date.
- Begin proper nouns with a capital letter.

Publish

DISPLAY THE PROJECT REPORTS Have students illustrate and display their explanatory pieces.

Use **Writing Process Transparency 2D** as a proofreading model and **Writing Process Transparency 2E** to discuss presentation ideas for their writing.

***PROOFREAD* TRANSPARENCY**

How to Make Breakfast for Mom

To surprise your mom, make ~~your mom~~ [her a special] breakfast on ~~s~~ saturday morning. [When everyone's asleep,] Go to the kitchen and get started. [First,] Put all your ingreadients on the counter—cereal, milk, a banana, and a can of juice. [Then,] Pour cereal in your mom's favorite bowl. Next use a [butter] knife to slice a banana over the top. Mix up the juice with some water in a nice pitcher, and pour some in [a] glass. Set the table and pour milk over the cereal. [Be sure to] Do this last, so the cereal doesn't get soggy! Finally, call your mom to breakfast. And [last but not least,] make sure to give her a flower [when she sits down at the table!]

McGraw-Hill School Division

Book 3.1/Unit 2: Explanatory Writing / Proofreading 2D

***PUBLISH* TRANSPARENCY**

How to Make Breakfast for Mom

To surprise your mom, make her a special breakfast on Saturday morning. When everyone's asleep, go to the kitchen and get started. First, put all your ingredients on the counter—cereal, milk, a banana, and a can of juice. Then, pour cereal in your mom's favorite bowl. Next, use a butter knife to slice a banana over the top. Mix up the juice with some water in a nice pitcher, and pour some in a glass. Set the table and pour milk over the cereal. Be sure to do this last, so the cereal doesn't get soggy! Finally, call your mom to breakfast. And last but not least, make sure to give her a flower when she sits down at the table!

McGraw-Hill School Division

Book 3.1/Unit 2: Explanatory Writing / Publishing 2E

Presentation Ideas

SHARE THE ESSAYS Invite students to read aloud their essays to the class. Some students may want to try and make some of the projects that they learn about from their classmates. ▶ **Viewing/Speaking**

MAKE A CLASS HOW-TO BOOK Copy students' essays and create a book called *Fun Projects for Everyone.* Invite students to create a front and back cover for the book. ▶ **Viewing /Representing**

Assessment

SCORING RUBRIC When using the rubric, please consider students' creative efforts, possibly adding a plus (+) for originality, wit, and imagination.

SELF-ASSESSMENT Use the features of explanatory writing on page 255B in question form. Students can use the questions to self-assess their informative narratives.

COMMUNICATION TIPS

REPRESENTING Have students design posters to advertise the book. Students could sell the books to students to raise money for a charity, or for school-library books.

SPEAKING Have students read their essays aloud. Encourage them to experiment with movement to enhance their reading style.

Scoring Rubric: 6-Trait Writing

4 Excellent	3 Good	2 Fair	1 Unsatisfactory
Ideas & Content • presents a focused, interesting how-to process, with an extensive set of details.	Ideas & Content • presents a clear, interesting how-to process, with a set of details that shows knowledge of the topic.	Ideas & Content • has some control of a how-to explanation, but may not offer clear or thorough details.	Ideas & Content • does not explain a how-to process; writing may go off in several directions, without a sense of purpose.
Organization • clear time sequence moves the reader logically and smoothly through the process; steps and details are carefully placed.	Organization • logical sequence helps the reader to follow the process; details make sense and help to clarify the steps.	Organization • tries to structure a how-to process, but may have trouble ordering steps; reader may be confused by poorly-developed details.	Organization • has an extreme lack of organization; ideas are disconnected; no clear beginning or ending; few explicit connections made between ideas.
Voice • exceptionally strong personal style speaks directly to the reader, and enlivens content.	Voice • personal style reaches out to the reader, and shows who is behind the words.	Voice • communicates ideas in a predictable way; gives some hint of who is behind the words; may not show involvement with an audience.	Voice • is not involved in the topic; lacks a purpose and interaction with a reader.
Word Choice • thoughtful, imaginative use of accurate, specific language creates a vivid picture of the how-to process.	Word Choice • uses a variety of words that clarify the process; may experiment with new words or use everyday words in a fresh way.	Word Choice • attempts to use few new words; may not use specific or colorful words that create a picture of the how-to process.	Word Choice • does not use words that convey a picture of a process; some words may detract from the meaning of the text.
Sentence Fluency • varied, effective sentences flow with a natural rhythm; fragments, if used, work well and add interest.	Sentence Fluency • careful sentences are easy to read and understand; sentence lengths and patterns vary and fit together.	Sentence Fluency • may have trouble with more complex sentences; sentences are understandable, but may be choppy, rambling, or awkward.	Sentence Fluency • constructs incomplete, rambling, or confusing sentences; does not understand how words and sentences fit together.
Conventions • is skilled in most writing conventions; proper use of the rules of English enhances clarity and personal style; editing largely unnecessary.	Conventions • uses a variety of conventions correctly; some editing may be needed; errors are few and don't make the paper hard to understand.	Conventions • makes frequent noticeable mistakes which may interfere with a smooth reading of the text.	Conventions • makes repeated errors in spelling, word choice, punctuation and usage; sentence structures may be confused.

0: This piece is either blank, or fails to respond to the writing task. The topic is not addressed, or the student simply paraphrases the prompt. The response may be illegible or incoherent.

VOCABULARY

GROUP Assign one selection to each of five teams. Instruct each team to write sentences using at least two vocabulary words. Then have the teams read their sentences aloud. The first team to define each spelling word gets a point. The team with the most points wins.

Unit Review

City Green

area	halfway	schedule
excitement	heap	stems

The Sun, the Wind and the Rain

canyons	grains	peaks
flowed	handful	traded

Dream Wolf

buffalo	echoes	ripe
darkness	herds	shelter

Spiders at Work

capture	ruin	skills
liquid	serious	struggles

Web Wonders

crops	hatch	soldiers
earthquake	respect	woven

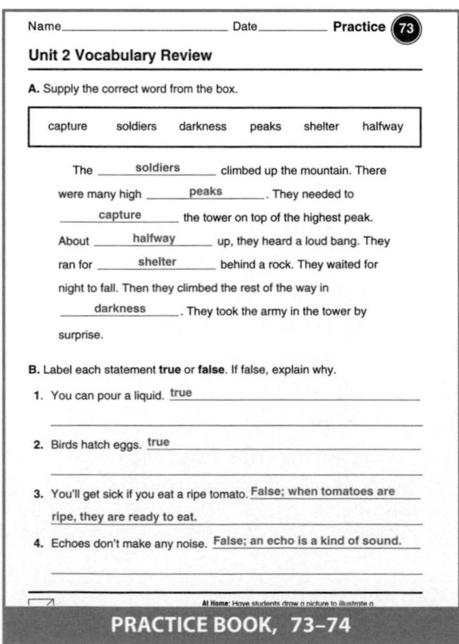

Name________ Date______ **Practice 73**

Unit 2 Vocabulary Review

A. Supply the correct word from the box.

capture	soldiers	darkness	peaks	shelter	halfway

The _soldiers_ climbed up the mountain. There were many high _peaks_. They needed to _capture_ the tower on top of the highest peak. About _halfway_ up, they heard a loud bang. They ran for _shelter_ behind a rock. They waited for night to fall. Then they climbed the rest of the way in _darkness_. They took the army in the tower by surprise.

B. Label each statement **true** or **false**. If false, explain why.

1. You can pour a liquid. true
2. Birds hatch eggs. true
3. You'll get sick if you eat a ripe tomato. False; when tomatoes are ripe, they are ready to eat.
4. Echoes don't make any noise. False; an echo is a kind of sound.

At Home: Have students draw a picture to illustrate a

PRACTICE BOOK, 73–74

GRAMMAR

PARTNERS Have each partner write a letter to a friend about visiting a special place. Then have them exchange letters. Next, have each partner identify all the nouns and proper nouns in the letter.

Unit Review

City Green
Common and Proper Nouns

The Sun, the Wind and the Rain
Singular and Plural Nouns

Dream Wolf
Irregular Plural Nouns

Spiders at Work
Possessive Nouns

Web Wonders
Sentence Combining with Nouns

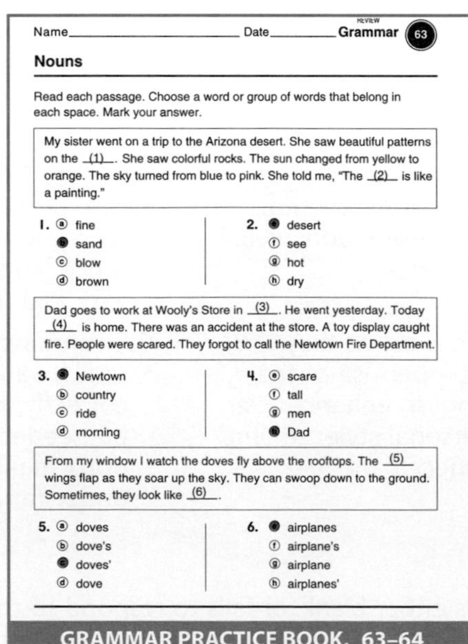

Name________ Date______ REVIEW **Grammar 63**

Nouns

Read each passage. Choose a word or group of words that belong in each space. Mark your answer.

My sister went on a trip to the Arizona desert. She saw beautiful patterns on the _(1)_. She saw colorful rocks. The sun changed from yellow to orange. The sky turned from blue to pink. She told me, "The _(2)_ is like a painting."

1. ⓐ fine ● sand ⓒ blow ⓓ brown
2. ● desert ⓕ see ⓖ hot ⓗ dry

Dad goes to work at Wooly's Store in _(3)_. He went yesterday. Today _(4)_ is home. There was an accident at the store. A toy display caught fire. People were scared. They forgot to call the Newtown Fire Department.

3. ● Newtown ⓑ country ⓒ ride ⓓ morning
4. ⓔ scare ⓕ tall ⓖ men ● Dad

From my window I watch the doves fly above the rooftops. The _(5)_ wings flap as they soar up the sky. They can swoop down to the ground. Sometimes, they look like _(6)_.

5. ⓐ doves ⓑ dove's ● doves' ⓓ dove
6. ● airplanes ⓕ airplane's ⓖ airplane ⓗ airplanes'

GRAMMAR PRACTICE BOOK, 63–64

SPELLING

Select a unit review word and write its definition on the chalkboard. Underneath the definition write a line for each letter. Call on volunteers to fill in the missing letters that spell the correct word.

Unit Review

Syllable Patterns
open
candle
frozen
lettuce
fellow

Plurals
branches
flies
mountains
libraries
inches

Consonant Clusters
brake
plate
blink
crumble
flood

Science Words
silk
fiber
beetle
fang
taste

Consonant Clusters
spend
spring
skate
strong
slice

Name__________ Date________ UNIT TEST SPELLING 63

Book 3.1/Unit 2 Review Test

Read each sentence. If an underlined word is spelled wrong, fill in the circle that goes with that word. If no word is spelled wrong, fill in the circle below NONE. Read Sample A, and do Sample B.

					NONE
A. Please close the door again.	A.	Ⓐ	Ⓑ	Ⓒ	●
B. The breeze kept me awacke.	B.	Ⓔ	Ⓕ	●	Ⓗ
1. Use the brayke to skate on the open road.	1.	●	Ⓑ	Ⓒ	Ⓓ
2. He had to blink when he blew out the candel.	2.	Ⓔ	Ⓕ	●	Ⓗ
3. I ate this slice of littuce.	3.	Ⓐ	Ⓑ	●	Ⓓ
4. Did you know that silke is not made by a beetle?	4.	Ⓔ	●	Ⓖ	Ⓗ
5. The fellowe likes to spend time in libraries.	5.	●	Ⓑ	Ⓒ	Ⓓ
6. The playte is full of frozen lettuce.	6.	●	Ⓕ	Ⓖ	Ⓗ
7. In spring, there was a flood in the mountians.	7.	Ⓐ	Ⓑ	●	Ⓓ
8. The flies are inshes away on the branches.	8.	Ⓔ	●	Ⓖ	Ⓗ
9. You cannot taste the fibber in lettuce.	9.	Ⓐ	●	Ⓒ	Ⓓ
10. The snake did not taste with his fang.	10.	Ⓔ	Ⓕ	Ⓖ	●

SPELLING PRACTICE BOOK, 63–64

SKILLS & STRATEGIES

Comprehension
- ☑ Cause and Effect
- ☑ Draw Conclusions
- ☑ Compare and Contrast
- ☑ Important and Unimportant Information

Vocabulary Strategy
- ☑ Context Clues
- ☑ Antonyms and Synonyms

Study Skills
- ☑ Reference Sources

Writing
- ☑ Explanatory Writing

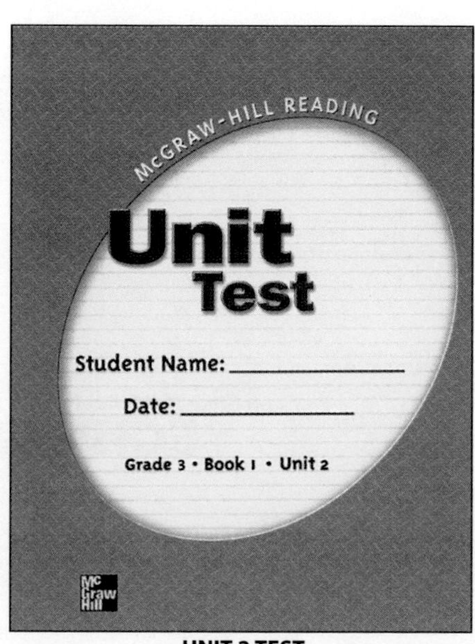

UNIT 2 TEST

Assessment Follow-Up

Use the results of the informal and formal assessment opportunities in the unit to help you make decisions about future instruction.

SKILLS AND STRATEGIES	Reteaching Blackline Masters	Alternate Teaching Strategies
Comprehension		
Cause and Effect	38, 42, 52, 56	T60
Draw Conclusions	43, 50, 64	T62
Compare and Contrast	45, 49, 57, 66	T64
Important and Unimportant Information	59, 63, 70	T66
Vocabulary Strategy		
Context Clues	44, 58, 72	T63
Antonyms and Synonyms	51, 65	T65
Study Skills		
Reference Sources	41, 48, 55, 62, 69	T61

	Alternate Writing Project–Easy	Unit Writing Process Lesson
Writing		
Explanatory Writing	171L, 203L, 225L, 243L, 253L	255A–255F

CD-ROM provides extra phonics support.

Research & Inquiry ideas. Visit ***www.mhschool.com/reading.***

Name______________________ Date__________

Fixing Fragments by Adding Subjects

- A **sentence fragment** is a group of words that does not express a complete thought.
- Some sentence fragments can be fixed by adding a subject.

Fix each fragment in the first column by adding a subject from the second column. Write the subject.

1. ______________ has white lines on it.
2. ______________ disappear from the wall.
3. ______________ waits for a letter.
4. ______________ makes the message clear.
5. ______________ hang on the wall.
6. ______________ fishes with his new rod.
7. ______________ picks flowers.
8. ______________ are black and white.
9. ______________ points the way to the zoo.
10. ______________ float in the air.

Gray dots
A clue
The prince
The wall
A sign
The king
Two pictures
Many kites
Flower centers
The princess

Extension: Invite students to take turns finding subjects from the story Opt: An Illusionary Tale. Then have them make a sentence about each subject.

Name________________________ Date__________

Writing Subjects to Complete Sentences

- Every sentence has a subject.
- The subject of a sentence tells what or whom the sentence is about.

Add a subject to each group of words. Write the sentence.

1. ____________________ is a land of surprises.

____

2. ____________________ has red and blue tape on it.

____

3. ____________________ may be taller than the queen.

____

4. ____________________ has a shade on it.

____

5. ____________________ catches a fish.

____

6. ____________________ looks in the mirror.

____

7. ____________________ stops by the sign.

____

8. ____________________ marches up the stairs of the tower.

____

Extension: Have one group of students write subjects about the Prince's party. Have another group write predicates. Invite students to match subjects and predicates to make sentences about the Prince's party.

Glossary

Introduce students to the Glossary by reading through the introduction and looking over the pages with them. Encourage the class to talk about what they see.

Words in a glossary, like words in a dictionary, are listed in **alphabetical order.** Point out the **guide words** at the top of each page that tell the first and last words appearing on that page.

Point out examples of **entries** and **main entries.** Read through a simple entry with the class, identifying each part. Have students note the order in which information is given: entry words(s), definition(s), example sentence, syllable division, pronunciation respelling, part of speech, plural/verb/adjective forms.

Note that if more than one definition is given for a word, the definitions are numbered. Note also the format used for a word that is more than one part of speech.

Review the parts of speech by identifying each in a sentence:

inter.	*adj.*	*n.*	*conj.*	*adj.*	*n.*
Wow!	**A**	**dictionary**	**and**	**a**	**glossary**
v.	*adv.*	*pron.*	*prep.*	*n.*	
tell	**almost**	**everything**	**about**	**words!**	

Explain the use of the **pronunciation key** (either the **short key,** at the bottom of every other page, or the **long key,** at the beginning of the glossary). Demonstrate the difference between **primary** stress and **secondary** stress by pronouncing a word with both.

Point out an example of the small triangle signaling a homophone. **Homophones** are words with different spellings and meanings but with the same pronunciation. Explain that a pair of words with the superscripts **1** and **2** are **homographs**—words that have the same spelling, but different origins and meanings, and in some cases, different pronunciations.

The **Word History** feature tells what language a word comes from and what changes have occurred in its spelling and/or meaning. Many everyday words have interesting and surprising stories behind them. Note that word histories can help us remember the meanings of difficult words.

Allow time for students to further explore the Glossary and make their own discoveries.

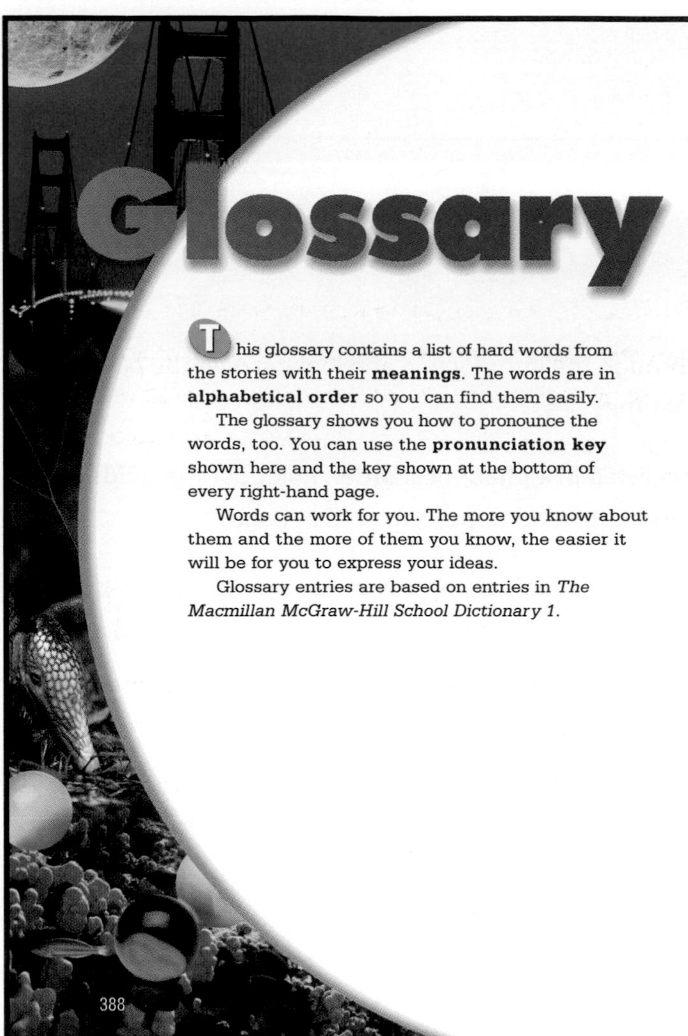

Glossary

This glossary contains a list of hard words from the stories with their **meanings**. The words are in **alphabetical order** so you can find them easily.

The glossary shows you how to pronounce the words, too. You can use the **pronunciation key** shown here and the key shown at the bottom of every right-hand page.

Words can work for you. The more you know about them and the more of them you know, the easier it will be for you to express your ideas.

Glossary entries are based on entries in *The Macmillan McGraw-Hill School Dictionary 1.*

388

Guide Words

adobe/banner

First word on the page — Last word on the page

Sample Entry

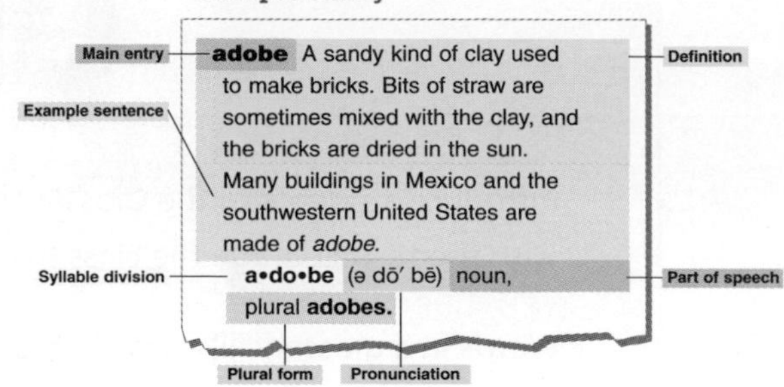

Main entry
Example sentence
Syllable division
Definition
Part of speech
Plural form
Pronunciation
adobe A sandy kind of clay used to make bricks. Bits of straw are sometimes mixed with the clay, and the bricks are dried in the sun. Many buildings in Mexico and the southwestern United States are made of adobe.
a•do•be (ə dō′ bē) noun, plural adobes.

a	at, bad	d	dear, soda, bad
ā	ape, pain, day, break	f	five, defend, leaf, off, cough, elephant.
ä	father, car, heart	g	game, ago, fog, egg
âr	care, pair, bear, their, where	h	hat, ahead
e	end, pet, said, heaven, friend	hw	white, whether, which
ē	equal, me, feet, team, piece, key	j	joke, enjoy, gem, page, edge
i	it, big, English, hymn	k	kite, bakery, seek, tack, cat
ī	ice, fine, lie, my	l	lid, sailor, feel, ball, allow
îr	ear, deer, here, pierce	m	man, family, dream
o	odd, hot, watch	n	not, final, pan, knife
ō	old, oat, toe, low	ng	long, singer, pink
ô	coffee, all, taught, law, fought	p	pail, repair, soap, happy
ôr	order, fork, horse, story, pour	r	ride, parent, wear, more, marry
oi	oil, toy	s	sit, aside, pets, cent, pass
ou	out, now	sh	shoe, washer, fish, mission, nation
u	up, mud, love, double	t	tag, pretend, fat, button, dressed
ū	use, mule, cue, feud, few	th	thin, panther, both,
ü	rule, true, food	th	this, mother, smooth
u̇	put, wood, should	v	very, favor, wave
ûr	burn, hurry, term, bird, word, courage	w	wet, weather, reward
ə	about, taken, pencil, lemon, circus	y	yes, onion
b	bat, above, job	z	zoo, lazy, jazz, rose, dogs, houses
ch	chin, such, match	zh	vision, treasure, seizure

389

Aa

adobe A sandy kind of clay used to make bricks. Bits of straw are sometimes mixed with the clay, and the bricks are dried in the sun. Many buildings in Mexico and the southwestern United States are made of *adobe.*
a•do•be (ə dō′ bē) *noun, plural* **adobes.**

Word History
The word **adobe** comes from the Spanish word of the same spelling, meaning "sun-dried brick." But the Spanish got this word from an even earlier Arabic word, *at-tob,* meaning "the brick."

anxious 1. Wanting very much; eager. I was *anxious* to make friends at my new school.
2. Nervous, worried or fearful about what may happen. My cousin was *anxious* about driving on the slippery roads.
anx•ious (angk′ shəs *or* ang′ shəs) *adjective.*

appendix A short, hollow pouch that is attached to the large intestine.
ap•pen•dix (ə pen′ diks) *noun, plural* **appendixes.**

applaud To show approval or enjoyment of something by clapping the hands. The children *applauded* the clown's funny tricks.
ap•plaud (ə plôd′) *verb,* **applauded, applauding.**

arachnid Any of a large group of small animals without a backbone. The body of an arachnid is divided into two parts. Arachnids have four pairs of legs and no antennae or wings. Spiders, scorpions, mites, and ticks are *arachnids.*
ar•ach•nid (ə rak′ nid) *noun, plural* **arachnids.**

area A particular space, region, or section. We moved from the city to a rural *area.*
ar•e•a (âr′ ē ə) *noun, plural* **areas.**

astonish To surprise very much; amaze. The news that I had won the contest *astonished* me.
▲**Synonym:** astound
as•ton•ish (ə ston′ ish) *verb,* **astonished, astonishing.**

Language Note
A **synonym** is a word that can be used for another word. A synonym for *astonish* is *surprise.*

390

attic The space just below the roof of a house. We use our *attic* to store trunks of old clothes.
at•tic (at′ ik) noun, plural **attics.**

autograph To write one's name in one's own handwriting. Will you *autograph* a copy of your book for me? *Verb.* —A person's signature written in that person's own handwriting. *Noun.*
au•to•graph (ô′ tə graf′) *verb,* **autographed, autographing;** *noun, plural* **autographs.**

Word History
The word **autograph** comes from the Greek words *autos,* meaning "self," and *graphein,* meaning "to write."

Bb

banner A flag or other piece of cloth that has a design and sometimes writing on it. The fans at the baseball game held up a *banner.*
ban•ner (ban′ ər) *noun, plural* **banners.**

beauty A quality that makes a person or a thing pleasing to look at, hear, or think about. The garden is a place of *beauty.*
beau•ty (bū′ tē) *noun, plural* **beauties.**

bewilder To confuse or puzzle; mix up. The student was *bewildered* by the math problem.
be•wil•der (bi wil′ dər) *verb,* **bewildered, bewildering.**

black widow A black spider. The female black widow is poisonous and has a red mark on her body. The female black widow is larger than the male.
black wi•dow (blak wid′ ō) *noun, plural* **black widows.**

blossom The flower of a plant or tree, especially one that produces fruit. We gathered *blossoms* from the apple trees. *Noun.*—To have flowers or blossoms; bloom. The peach trees *blossom* in the spring. *Verb.*
blos•som (blos′ əm) *noun, plural* **blossoms;** *verb,* **blossomed, blossoming.**

at; āpe; fär; câre; end; mē; it; īce; pîerce; hot; ōld; sông; fôrk; oil; out; up; ūse; rüle; pu̇ll; tûrn; chin; sing; shop; thin; this; **hw** in white; **zh** in treasure. The symbol ə stands for the unstressed vowel sound in about, taken, pencil, lemon, and circus.

391

bronco busting The act of taming and training wild horses. The cowboys spent part of each day *bronco busting.*
bron•co bust•ing (brong′ kō bust′ ing) *noun.*

buffalo **1.** A large North American animal that has a big shaggy head with short horns and a hump on its back; bison. **2.** Any of various oxen of Europe, Asia, and Africa.
buf•fa•lo (buf′ ə lō′) *noun, plural* **buffaloes** *or* **buffalos** *or* **buffalo.**

canyon A deep valley with very high, steep sides. A *canyon* often has a stream running through it.
can•yon (kan′ yən) *noun, plural* **canyons.**

capture To catch and hold a person, animal, or thing. The explorers *captured* the tiger in a large net. ▲**Synonyms:** take, seize
cap•ture (kap′ chər) *verb* **captured, capturing.**

ceiling The inside overhead surface of a room. The tall guest reached up and almost touched the *ceiling.*
ceil•ing (sē′ ling) *noun, plural* **ceilings.**

celebrate To observe or honor a special day or event with ceremonies and other activities. We *celebrated* Grandma's birthday with a big party.
cel•e•brate (sel′ ə brāt′) *verb,* **celebrated, celebrating.**

cent A coin of the United States and Canada. One hundred *cents* is equal to one dollar. ▲Other words that sound like this are **scent** and **sent.**
▲**Synonym:** penny
cent (sent) *noun, plural,* **cents.**

Language Note
A **homonym** is a word that sounds like another word but has a different meaning. A homonym for *cent* is *sent.*

combine To cause to mix together; blend. We *combined* eggs, flour, and milk to make the batter for the pancakes.
▲**Synonyms:** blend, mix
com•bine (kəm bīn′) *verb,* **combined, combining.**

concert A performance, usually a musical performance by a number of musicians. We went to a *concert* in the park.
▲**Synonyms:** show, recital, symphony
con•cert (kon′ sərt) *noun, plural* **concerts.**

conductor **1.** A person who leads a group of musicians. Our music teacher is also the *conductor* of the school orchestra. **2.** A person on a train or bus who collects fares and assists passengers. The *conductor* walked down the aisle and called out the name of the next stop.
con•duc•tor (kən duk′ tər) *noun, plural* **conductors.**

consonant A letter of the alphabet that is not a vowel. *Consonants* include the letters *b, d, f, g, m, p, t,* and others.
con•so•nant (kon′ sə nənt) *noun, plural* **consonants.**

continue **1.** To go on or do after stopping. We will *continue* the meeting after lunch. **2.** To keep on happening, being, or doing; go on without stopping. The rain had *continued* for two days.
con•tin•ue (kən tin′ ū) *verb,* **continued, continuing.**

cork The light, thick outer bark of a kind of oak tree. *Cork* is used for such things as bottle stoppers, insulation, and floats for rafts.
cork (kôrk) *noun, plural* **corks.**

correct Not having any mistakes; accurate. This is the *correct* answer to the arithmetic problem. *Adjective.* —To mark the mistakes in; change to make right. The teacher *corrected* our spelling tests. *Verb.*
cor•rect (kə rekt′) *adjective; verb,* **corrected, correcting.**

costume Clothes worn in order to look like someone or something else. I wore a cowboy *costume* to the Halloween party.
cos•tume (kos′ tüm *or* kos′ tūm) *noun, plural* **costumes.**

at; āpe; fär; câre; end; mē; it; īce; pîerce; hot; ōld; sông; fôrk; oil; out; up; ūse; rüle; pull; tûrn; chin; sing; shop; thin; <u>th</u>is; hw in white; zh in treasure. The symbol ə stands for the unstressed vowel sound in about, taken, pencil, lemon, and circus.

Glossary

creep To move slowly along the ground or over a surface. The wind *creeps* in through the window.
creep (krēp) *verb,* **crept, creeping.**

crooked Not straight; bent or curving. The path through the woods was very *crooked.*
▲**Synonyms:** bent, winding
crook•ed (krŭk′ id) *adjective.*

crop Plants that are grown to be used as a food or to be sold for profit. Wheat and corn are two *crops* grown in the Midwest.
crop (krop) *noun, plural* **crops.**

crumble **1.** To break into small pieces. The muffin *crumbled* when I tried to butter it. **2.** To fall apart or be destroyed. The old house is slowly *cumbling.*
crum•ble (krum′ bəl) *verb,* **crumbled, crumbling.**

daddy-longlegs A kind of bug that looks like a spider. A daddy-longlegs has a small, round body and eight very long, thin legs.
dad•dy long•legs (dad′ē lông′ legz′) *noun, plural* **daddy-longlegs.**

darkness A partial or total absence of light; the result of a light going out. The sun dipped behind the hilltops and *darkness* fell.
dark•ness (därk′ nis) *noun.*

dawn The first light that appears in the morning. We left our house before *dawn.*
▲**Synonym:** daybreak
dawn (dôn) *noun, plural* **dawns.**

deaf Not able to hear, or not able to hear well. The *deaf* children were using sign language to speak to one another
deaf (def) *adjective,* **deafer, deafest.**

decimal **1.** A period put before a decimal fraction. The periods in .5, .30, and .052 are *decimals.* **2.** A fraction with a denominator of 10, or a multiple of 10 such as 100 or 1,000. The *decimal* .5 is another way of writing $\frac{5}{10}$.
dec•i•mal (des′ ə məl) *noun, plural* **decimals.**

den A place where wild animals rest or sleep. The bear uses a cave as a *den* during its long winter sleep.
den (den) *noun, plural* **dens.**

disaster An event that causes much suffering or loss. The flood was a *disaster.*
▲**Synonyms:** tragedy, trouble
dis•as•ter (di zas′ tər) *noun, plural* **disasters.**

Word History
The word **disaster** comes from the Latin *dis,* meaning "away," and *astrum,* meaning "star."

dragonfly An insect that has a long, thin body and two pairs of wings. *Dragonflies* eat mosquitoes and live near fresh water.
drag•on•fly (drag′ ən flī′) *noun, plural* **dragonflies.**

eager Wanting very much to do something. A person who is *eager* is full of interest and enthusiasm.
▲**Synonym:** excited
ea•ger (ē′ gər) *adjective.*

earthquake A shaking or trembling of the ground. Earthquakes are caused by rock, lava, or hot gases moving deep inside the earth. Some *earthquakes* are so powerful that they cause the ground to split.
earth•quake (ûrth′ kwāk′) *noun, plural* **earthquakes.**

echo The repeating of a sound. Echoes are caused when sound waves bounce off a surface. We shouted "hello" and soon heard the *echo* of our voices.
ech•o (ek′ ō) *noun, plural* **echoes.**

embarrass To make someone feel shy, uncomfortable, or ashamed. My foolish mistake *embarrassed* me.
em•bar•rass (em bar′ əs) *verb,* **embarrassed, embarrassing.**

enormous Much greater than the usual size or amount; very large. The flood caused an *enormous* amount of damage.
▲**Synonyms:** large, gigantic
e•nor•mous (i nôr′ məs) *adjective.*

at; āpe; fär; câre; end; mē; it; īce; pîerce; hot; ōld; sông; fôrk; oil; out; up; ūse; rüle; pull; tûrn; chin; sing; shop; thin; <u>th</u>is; hw in white; zh in treasure. The symbol ə stands for the unstressed vowel sound in about, taken, pencil, lemon, and circus.

eon A very long period of time. That deposit of coal was formed *eons* ago.
e•on (ē′ ən *or* ē′ on) *noun, plural* **eons.**

Espino, Fernando
(es pē′ nō, fûr nän′ dō)

examine 1. To look at closely and carefully; check. We *examined* the baseball bat to be sure it wasn't cracked. **2.** To question in a careful way or test, usually to discover what a person knows. The lawyer *examined* the witness during the trial.
▲**Synonyms:** inspect, study
ex•am•ine (eg zam′ in) *verb,* **examined, examining.**

excitement The condition of being excited. We could hardly sleep because of our *excitement* about starting the trip tomorrow.
ex•cite•ment (ek sīt′ mənt) *noun.*

fade 1. To lose freshness; wither. The flowers *faded* after three days. **2.** To lose or cause to lose color or brightness. Blue jeans may *fade* when they are washed.
fade (fād) *verb,* **faded, fading.**

fan A person who is very interested in or enthusiastic about something. The *fans* ran up to the movie star.
▲**Synonym:** admirer
fan (fan) *noun, plural* **fans.**

feelers A part of an animal's body that is used for touching things. Many insects have *feelers* on their heads.
feel•er (fē′ lər) *noun, plural* **feelers.**

flex To bend. If your arm is tired, *flex* it to keep it loose.
flex (fleks) *verb,* **flexed, flexing.**

flow To move along steadily in a stream. Water *flows* through these pipes.
flow (flō) *verb,* **flowed, flowing.**

furniture Tables, chairs, beds, and other movable articles used in a home or office. Our living room is full of *furniture.*
fur•ni•ture (fûr′ ni chər) *noun.*

Gg

gaze To look at something a long time. We all *gazed* at the beautiful sunset. *Verb.*—A long steady look. Our *gaze* rested on the bear and its two playful cubs. *Noun.*
gaze (gāz) *verb,* **gazed, gazing;** *noun, plural* **gazes.**

Genghis Khan
(geng′ gis kän′)

gift 1. Something given; a present. This basketball was a *gift* from my parents. **2.** Talent; ability. That student has a *gift* for dancing.
gift (gift) *noun, plural* **gifts.**

grain 1. A tiny, hard piece of something. *Grains* of sand fell from the beach towel. **2.** The seed of wheat, corn, rice, oats, and other cereal plants. Breakfast cereal is made from *grains.*
grain (grān) *noun, plural* **grains.**

groan To make a deep, sad sound. I *groaned* when the doctors touched my injured ankle.
▲**Synonym:** moan ▲ Another word that sounds like this is **grown.**
groan (grōn) *verb,* **groaned, groaning.**

guard A person who is assigned to watch over things. The museum *guard* collected our tickets at the door. *Noun.*—To keep safe from harm or danger; protect. The dog *guarded* the house. *Verb.*
guard (gärd) *noun, plural* **guards;** *verb,* **guarded, guarding.**

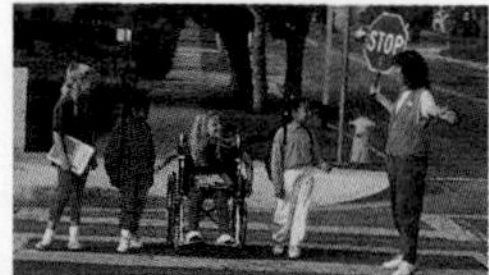

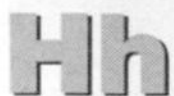

halfway To or at half the distance; midway. We climbed *halfway* up the mountain.
half•way (haf′ wā) *adverb.*

handful 1. The amount the hand can hold at one time. Each child took a *handful* of peanuts. **2.** A small number. Only a *handful* of people showed up.
hand•ful (hand′ fu̇l′) *noun, plural* **handfuls.**

at; āpe; fär; câre; end; mē; it; īce; pîerce; hot; ōld; sông; fôrk; oil; out; up; ūse; rüle; pu̇ll; tûrn; chin; sing; shop; thin; th͟is; hw in white; zh in treasure. The symbol ə stands for the unstressed vowel sound in about, taken, pencil, lemon, and circus.

hatch To come from an egg. We are waiting for these chicks to *hatch.*
hatch (hach) *verb,* **hatched, hatching.**

haunch A part of the body of a person or animal including the hip and upper thigh. The lion sat on its *haunches.*
haunch (hônch) *noun, plural* **haunches.**

heap A collection of things piled together. We left a *heap* of peanut shells on the kitchen table.
▲**Synonyms:** pile, load, mound
heap (hēp) *noun, plural* **heaps.**

herd A group of animals that live or travel together. A *herd* of cattle grazed in the pasture.
▲Another word that sounds like this is **heard.**
herd (hûrd) *noun, plural* **herds;** *verb,* **herded, herding.**

Ii

ill Not healthy or well; sick. Many children in our class were *ill.*
ill (il) *adjective.*

imaginary Existing only in the mind; unreal. Most people believe that elves are *imaginary.*
▲**Synonyms:** unreal, fictional
i•mag•i•nary (i maj′ə ner′ē) *adjective.*

include To have as part of the whole; contain. You don't have to buy batteries for that toy because they are already *included* in the box.
in•clude (in klüd′) *verb,* **included, including.**

instrument 1. A device for producing musical sounds. Our music teacher plays the guitar, flute, and several other *instruments.* **2.** A device used for doing a certain kind of work; tool. The dental hygienist used a sharp *instrument* to scrape my teeth.
in•stru•ment (in′strə mənt) *noun, plural* **instruments.**

invent 1. To make or think of for the first time; create. Do you know who *invented* the phonograph? **2.** To make up. I'm ashamed to say I *invented* an excuse for being late.
in•vent (in vent′) *verb,* **invented, inventing.**

Word History

The word **invent** comes from a Latin word meaning "to come upon" or "find." The word *invent* was originally used to describe the finding of an answer, the solution to a problem, or the means to do something.

Jj

jagged Having sharp points that stick out. Some eagles build nests on *jagged* cliffs.
jag•ged (jag′ id) *adjective.*

jingle To make or cause to make a tinkling or ringing sound. When the bell moved, it *jingled.*
jingle (jing′gəl) *verb,* **jingled, jingling.**

journey A long trip. The Pilgrims crossed the Atlantic on their *journey* to the New World.
jour•ney (jûr′ nē) *noun, plural* **journeys.**

kinship A relationship or close connection. There has always been a *kinship* between the two villages.
kin•ship (kin′ ship′) *noun, plural* **kinships.**

lasso A long rope with a loop. A *lasso* is used to catch animals. *Noun.*
—To catch with a lasso. The cowhands will *lasso* the steer. *Verb.*
las•so (la′sō *or* lasü′) *noun, plural* **lassos** *or* **lassoes;** *verb,* **lassoed, lassoing.**

lease To rent. The family *leased* a cabin for the summer. *Verb.*
—A written agreement for renting a house, apartment, or land. My parents signed a new *lease. Noun.*
lease (lēs) *verb,* **leased, leasing;** *noun, plural* **leases.**

at; āpe; fär; câre; end; mē; it; īce; pîerce; hot; ōld; sông; fôrk; oil; out; up; ūse; rüle; pu̇ll; tûrn; chin; sing; shop; thin; th͟is; hw in white; zh in treasure. The symbol ə stands for the unstressed vowel sound in about, taken, pencil, lemon, and circus.

legend A story passed down through the years that many people believe, but that is not entirely true. There are many *legends* about the knights of the Middle Ages.
leg•end (lej′ənd) *noun, plural* **legends.**

length The distance from one end to the other end. The *length* of a football field is 100 yards.
▲**Synonym:** measure
length (lengkth *or* length) *noun, plural* **lengths.**

liquid A form of matter that is not a solid or a gas. A liquid can flow easily. It can take on the shape of any container into which it is poured. Milk is a *liquid.*
liq•uid (lik′wid) *noun, plural* **liquids.**

Little League A baseball league for children under thirteen years of age. We play for the West Side *Little League* on Saturday.
Lit•tle League (lit′ əl lēg) *noun.*

locate 1. To put or settle in a particular place. The baker *located* the bakery in the shopping mall. **2.** To find the place or position of. He could not *locate* his glasses.
lo•cate (lō′kāt) *verb,* **located, locating.**

longhorn A breed of cattle with very long horns. *Longhorns* were once common in the southwestern United States.
long•horn (lông′ hôrn) *noun, plural* **longhorns.**

Mm

marvel To feel wonder and astonishment. We *marveled* at the acrobat's skill.
mar•vel (mär′vəl) *verb,* **marveled, marveling.**

McGwire, Mark
(mə gwir′, märk)

mischievous Playful but naughty. That *mischievous* child hid my slippers again.
mis•chie•vous (mis′chə vəs) *adjective.*

miserable 1. Very unhappy; wretched. We all felt *miserable* about losing our dog. **2.** Causing discomfort or unhappiness. I had a *miserable* cold.
▲**Synonyms:** sad, horrible, unpleasant
mis•er•a•ble (miz′ ər ə bəl) *adjective.*

mob To crowd around in excitement or anger. Shoppers *mobbed* the store during the big sale. *Verb.* —A large number of people; crowd. A *mob* is sometimes made up of people who are so angry or upset about something that they break the law and cause damage. *Noun.*
mob (mob) *verb,* **mobbed, mobbing;** *noun, plural* **mobs.**

mock Not real; imitation. In history class we had a *mock* battle with cardboard shields. *Adjective.*—To make fun of in a mean way. Instead of helping, they laughed and *mocked* me when I fell off my bike. *Verb.*
mock (mok) *adjective; verb,* **mocked, mocking.**

musician A person who is skilled in playing a musical instrument, composing music, or singing. My brother studied piano for years and became a talented *musician.*
mu•si•cian (mū zish′ ən) *noun, plural* **musicians.**

mustang A wild horse that lives on the American plains; bronco. We watched the *mustangs* go down to the river for a cool drink of water.
mus•tang (mus′tang) *noun, plural* **mustangs.**

Nn

New World North and South America; the Western Hemisphere.
New World (nü wûrld)

Nilsson, Kerstin
(Nil′sən, Kûr′stin)

northern lights Shining bands of light that can be seen in the night sky in the Northern Hemisphere. In the winter, you can see the *northern lights* in Alaska.
north•ern lights (nôr′thərn lits) *noun.*

at; āpe; fär; câre; end; mē; it; īce; pîerce; hot; ōld; sông; fôrk; oil; out; up; ūse; rüle; pu̇ll; tûrn; chin; sing; shop; thin; this; hw in white; zh in treasure. The symbol ə stands for the unstressed vowel sound in about, taken, pencil, lemon, and circus.

Oo

orchestra 1. A group of musicians playing together on various instruments. **2.** The area just in front of a stage in which the orchestra plays.
▲**Synonyms:** symphony, band
or•ches•tra (ôr′ kə strə) *noun, plural* **orchestras.**

Word History
The word **orchestra** comes from a Greek word meaning "dance area." In the theater of ancient Greece, one section of the stage was called the *orchestra.* It was there that a chorus of performers danced and sang during a performance.

Pp

palace A very large, grand building where a king, queen, or other ruler usually lives. In London, we got to visit Buckingham *Palace.*
pal•ace (pal′ is) *noun, plural* **palaces.**

Panama A country in Central America.
Pan•a•ma (pan′ ə mä′) *noun.*

pattern The way in which colors, shapes, or lines are arranged or repeated in some order. The wallpaper was printed with a pretty flower *pattern.*
▲**Synonym:** design
pat•tern (pat′ ərn) *noun, plural* **patterns.**

peak 1. A high mountain, or the pointed top of a high mountain. We could see the snowy *peaks* in the distance. **2.** A sharp or pointed end or top. If you stand on the *peak* of our roof, you can see the ocean.
▲**Synonyms:** mountain top, crest, summit
peak (pēk) *noun, plural* **peaks.**

pedestrian A person who travels on foot; walker. Sidewalks are for *pedestrians.*
ped•es•tri•an (pə des′trē ən) *noun, plural* **pedestrians.**

Word History
The word **pedestrian** comes to us from the Latin root *pedis,* meaning "on foot."

percussionist One who is skilled in playing percussion instruments, such as the drum, cymbal, xylophone, and piano. The *percussionist* in the orchestra played the bass drum and cymbals.
per•cus•sion•ist (pər kush′ ən ist) *noun, plural* **percussionists.**

petition A formal request that is made to a person in authority. All the people on our street signed a *petition* asking the city to put a stop sign on the corner. *Noun.*—To make a formal request to. The students in our school *petitioned* the principal to keep the library open on weekends. *Verb.*
pe•ti•tion (pə tish′ ən) *noun, plural* **petitions;** *verb,* **petitioned, petitioning.**

pitcher A baseball player who throws the ball to the batter. The *pitcher* stands near the middle of the diamond facing home place.
pitch•er (pich′ ər) *noun, plural* **pitchers.**

pitcher

prairie Flat or rolling land covered with grass. A *prairie* has few trees.
▲**Synonym:** plains
prai•rie (prâr′ ē) *noun, plural* **prairies.**

prey An animal that is hunted by another animal for food. Rabbits and birds are the *prey* of foxes.
prey (prā) *noun, plural* **prey.**

prong One of the pointed ends of an antler or of a fork or other tool. My grandmother's forks have only three *prongs.*
▲**Synonym:** point
prong (prông *or* prong) *noun, plural* **prongs.**

at; āpe; fär; câre; end; mē; it; īce; pîerce; hot; ōld; sông; fôrk; oil; out; up; ūse; rüle; pu̇ll; tûrn; chin; sing; shop; thin; this; hw in white; zh in treasure. The symbol ə stands for the unstressed vowel sound in about, taken, pencil, lemon, and circus.

pure 1. Nothing but. We won that game with *pure* luck. **2.** Not mixed with anything else. This bracelet is made of *pure* silver.
▲**Synonyms:** true, actual
pure (pyůr) *adjective,* **purer, purest.**

respect High regard or consideration. We show *respect* for our teacher. *Noun.*—To have or show honor or consideration for. I *respect* your opinion. *Verb.*
▲**Synonyms:** admiration, esteem
re•spect (ri spekt′) *noun; verb,* **respected, respecting.**

ripe Fully grown and ready to be eaten. The tomatoes in the garden are *ripe* now.
ripe (rīp) *adjective,* **riper, ripest.**

royal Of or pertaining to a king or queen or their family. The *royal* family lives in the palace.
roy•al (roi′ əl) *adjective.*

rubble Rough, broken pieces of stone, rock, or other solid material. The rescue workers searched through the *rubble* of the collapsed building.
rub•ble (rub′ əl) *noun.*

ruin Harm or damage greatly. The earthquake *ruined* the town. *Verb.* —Destruction, damage, or collapse. The storekeeper faced financial *ruin. Noun.*
▲**Synonym:** destroy
ru•in (rü′ in) *verb,* **ruined, ruining;** *noun, plural* **ruins.**

Sabana Grande
(sə bän′ə grän′ dā)

scatter 1. To spread or throw about in various places. The wind *scattered* the leaves all over the yard. **2.** To separate or cause to separate and go in different directions. The loud thunder *scattered* the cattle.
▲**Synonyms:** cast, fling, sprinkle
scat•ter (skat′ ər) *verb,* **scattered, scattering.**

404

scene 1. The place where something happens. The police arrived on the *scene* just as the thieves were escaping. **2.** A part of an act in a play or movie.
▲Another word that sounds like this is **seen.**
scene (sēn) *noun, plural* **scenes.**

schedule The time at which something is supposed to happen. The train was running behind *schedule* because of the weather.
sched•ule (skej′ ül) *noun, plural* **schedules.**

score The points or a record of the points made in a game or on a test. The final *score* of the game was 5 to 4. *Noun.*—To make a point or points in a game or test. She *scored* 10 points for her basketball team. *Verb.*
score (skôr) *noun, plural* **scores;** *verb,* **scored, scoring.**

season 1. Any special part of the year. There is almost no rain during the dry *season.* **2.** One of the four parts of the year: spring, summer, fall, or winter.
sea•son (sē′ zən) *noun, plural* **seasons.**

season

Word History
The word **season** comes from a French word that originally meant, "the season of spring," or "planting time."

section 1. A part of an area or group. We visited the old *section* of the city. **2.** A part taken from a whole; portion. Please cut the apple into four *sections.*
▲**Synonym:** quarter
sec•tion (sek′ shən) *noun, plural* **sections.**

serious 1. Dangerous. Sam risked *serious* injury when he drove so fast on that icy road. **2.** Not joking; sincere. Were you *serious* about taking piano lessons?
▲**Synonyms:** grave, critical
se•ri•ous (sîr′ ē əs) *adjective.*

at; āpe; fär; câre; end; mē; it; īce; pîerce; hot; ōld; sông; fôrk; oil; out; up; ūse; rüle; půll; tûrn; chin; sing; shop; thin; <u>th</u>is; hw in white; zh in treasure. The symbol ə stands for the unstressed vowel sound in about, taken, pencil, lemon, and circus.

405

shallow Not deep. The water in the pond is *shallow.*
shallow (shal′ ō) *adjective,* **shallower, shallowest.**

shelter 1. To find or take refuge. It is not safe to take *shelter* under a tree during an electrical storm. **2.** To give shelter to. The umbrella *sheltered* us from the rain. *Verb.* —Something that covers or protects. The hikers used a cave as *shelter* during the thunderstorm. *Noun.*
shel•ter (shel′ tər) *verb,* **sheltered, sheltering;** *noun, plural* **shelters.**

skill The power or ability to do something. Swimming is an important *skill* to know when you are out on a boat.
▲**Synonym:** talent
skill (skil) *noun, plural* **skills.**

sloth A slow-moving animal that lives in the forests of South America. *Sloths* use their long arms and legs and their curved claws to hang upside down from trees.
sloth (slôth *or* slōth) *noun, plural* **sloths.**

snipping The act or sound of cutting with scissors in short, quick strokes. *Snipping* coupons from the newspaper is a way to save money on groceries.
snip•ping (snip′ ing) *noun.*

soldier A person who is a member of an army. The *soldiers* marched in a parade.
sol•dier (sōl′ jər) *noun, plural* **soldiers.**

Sosa, Sammy
(sō′ sə, sam′ mē)

souvenir Something that is kept because it reminds one of a person, place, or event. I kept my ticket as a *souvenir* of my first play.
▲**Synonym:** keepsake, memento
sou•ve•nir (sü′ və nîr′ *or* sü′ və nîr′) *noun, plural* **souvenirs.**

steamship A large ship that is powered by steam.
steam•ship (stēm′ ship) *noun, plural* **steamships.**

406

stem The main part of a plant that supports the leaves and flowers. Water and food travel through the *stem* to all parts of the plant.
▲**Synonym:** stalk
stem (stem) *noun, plural* **stems.**

straighten 1. To make or become straight. The picture on the wall slanted to the left, so I *straightened* it. **2.** To put into proper order. I asked you to *straighten* your room.
straight•en (strā′tən) *verb,* **straightened, straightening.**

struggle To make a great effort. The children *struggled* through the heavy snow.
strug•gle (strug′ əl) *verb,* **struggled, struggling.**

stumble To lose one's balance; trip. I *stumbled* over the rake.
stum•ble (stum′ bəl) *verb,* **stumbled, stumbling.**

surround To be on all sides of; form a circle around. A fence *surrounds* our yard.
▲**Synonym:** enclose
sur•round (sə round′) *verb,* **surrounded, surrounding.**

Sweden A country in northern Europe.
Swe•den (swē′ dən) *noun.*

Tt

tall tale A made-up or exaggerated story; a tale too fantastic to believe.
tall tale (tôl tāl) *noun, plural* **tall tales.**

Tanksi
(tawnk′ shē)

tarantula A hairy spider that is found in warm areas. The *tarantula* has a painful bite.
ta•ran•tu•la (tə ran′ chə lə) *noun, plural* **tarantulas.**

Tiblo
(tē′ blō)

toucan A bird that has a heavy body, a very large beak, and colorful feathers. *Toucans* are found in Central America.
tou•can (tü′ kan) *noun, plural* **toucans.**

at; āpe; fär; câre; end; mē; it; īce; pîerce; hot; ōld; sông; fôrk; oil; out; up; ūse; rüle; půll; tûrn; chin; sing; shop; thin; <u>th</u>is; hw in white; zh in treasure. The symbol ə stands for the unstressed vowel sound in about, taken, pencil, lemon, and circus.

407

towering Very tall; lofty. *Towering* palm trees lined the beach.
tow•er•ing (tou′ ər ing) *adjective.*

trade To give one thing in return for something else. I'll *trade* you two of my cards for one of yours.
▲**Synonyms:** exchange, swap
trade (trād) *verb,* **traded, trading.**

triangle **1.** A musical instrument made of a metal bar bent in the shape of a triangle. A *triangle* sounds like a bell when it is hit. **2.** A figure or object with three sides and three angles.
tri•an•gle (trī′ang′əl) *noun, plural* **triangles.**

trim To cut away or remove parts to make something neat and orderly. Please *trim* the hedge evenly.
trim (trim) *verb,* **trimmed, trimming.**

unusual Not usual, common, or ordinary. It is very *unusual* for them not to want to go to a movie.
un•u•su•al (un ū′ zhü əl) *adjective.*

vibration Rapid movement back and forth or up and down. People many miles away could feel the *vibration* of the earthquake.
▲**Synonym:** shaking
vi•bra•tion (vī brā′ shən) *noun, plural* **vibrations.**

visitor A person who visits. I have to clean my room because we're having *visitors* this afternoon.
▲**Synonym:** guest
vis•i•tor (viz′ i tər) *noun, plural* **visitors.**

wilderness A natural place where no people live. In a *wilderness* there may be a dense forest and wild animals.
wil•der•ness (wil′ dər nis) *noun, plural* **wildernesses.**

within In or into the inner part or parts of. The troops camped *within* the walls of the fort.
with•in (wi*th* in′ *or* with in′) *preposition.*

Woutilainen, Johan
(woo ti lā′ nən, yō′ han)

woven Formed or made by lacing together thread, yarn, or strips of straw or other material. Gold thread had been *woven* into the blouse.
wo•ven (wō′ vən) *past particple of* **weave.**

wrap To cover by putting something around. Please help me *wrap* these presents.
wrap (rap) *verb,* **wrapped, wrapping.**

zinnia A garden plant that has rounded, brightly colored flowers.
zin•ni•a (zin′ ē ə) *noun, plural* **zinnias.**

at; āpe; fär; câre; end; mē; it; īce; pîerce; hot; ōld; sông; fôrk; oil; out; up; ūse; rüle; pu̇ll; tûrn; chin; sing; shop; thin; *th*is; hw in white; zh in treasure. The symbol ə stands for the unstressed vowel sound in about, taken, pencil, lemon, and circus.

Cover Illustration: Lori Lohstoeter

The publisher gratefully acknowledges permission to reprint the following copyrighted material:

"The Ants" from BEAST FEAST by Douglas Florian. Copyright © 1994 by Douglas Florian. Used by permission of Harcourt Brace & Company.

"Arachne the Spinner" from GREEK MYTHS retold by Geraldine McCaughrean. Text copyright © 1992 by Geraldine McCaughrean. Illustrations copyright © 1992 by Emma Chichester Clark. Used by permission of Margaret K. McElderry Books, Macmillan Publishing Company.

"Arkansas Traveler" from GONNA SING MY HEAD OFF! Used by permission of Alfred A. Knopf.

"At the Flick of a Switch" from EARTH LINES, POEMS FOR THE GREEN AGE by Pat Moon. Copyright © 1991 by Pat Moon. Used by permission of Greenwillow Books, a division of William Morrow & Company, Inc.

"Basket" from WORLDS I KNOW AND OTHER POEMS by Myra Cohn Livingston. Copyright © 1985 by Myra Cohn Livingston. Used by permission of Marian Reiner for the author.

"Frog and Locust" from A HEART FULL OF TURQUOISE by Joe Hayes. Copyright © 1988 by Joe Hayes. Used by permission of Mariposa Publishing.

"From the Bellybutton of the Moon/Del ombligo de la luna" from FROM THE BELLYBUTTON OF THE MOON AND OTHER SUMMER POEMS by Francisco X. Alarcón. Poems copyright © 1998 by Francisco X. Alarcón. Illustrations copyright © 1998 by Maya Christina Gonzalez. Used by permission of Children's Book Press.

"A Garden" from ALWAYS WONDERING by Aileen Fisher. Text copyright © 1991 by Aileen Fisher. Illustrations copyright © 1991 by Joan Sandin. Used by permission of HarperCollins Publishers.

"The Hen and the Apple Tree" from FABLES by Arnold Lobel. Copyright © 1980 by Arnold Lobel. Used by permission of HarperCollins Publishers.

"The Hurricane" from SING TO THE SUN by Ashley Bryan. Copyright © 1992 by Ashley Bryan. Used by permission of HarperCollins.

"Ice Cycle" from ONCE UPON ICE AND OTHER FROZEN POEMS by Mary Ann Hoberman. Copyright © 1997 by Mary Ann Hoberman. Used by permission of Wordsong/Boyds Mills Press, Inc.

"If I Find a Penny" from THE BUTTERFLY JAR by Jeff Moss. Text copyright © 1988 by Jeff Moss. Illustrations copyright © 1988 by Chris Demarest. Used by permission of Bantam Doubleday Dell Publishing Group.

"In Daddy's Arms" from IN DADDY'S ARMS I AM TALL, AFRICAN AMERICANS CELEBRATING FATHERS by Folami Abiade. Text copyright © 1997 by Folami Abiade. Illustrations copyright © 1997 by Javaka Steptoe. Used by permission of Lee & Low Books, Inc.

ACKNOWLEDGMENTS

The publisher gratefully acknowledges permission to reprint the following copyrighted material:

"Abuelita's Lap" by Pat Mora from CONFETTI: POEMS FOR CHILDREN by Pat Mora. Text copyright © 1996 by Pat Mora. Reprinted by permission of Lee & Low Books Inc.

"Baseballs for Sale" from MAX MALONE MAKES A MILLION by Charlotte Herman. Text copyright © 1991 by Charlotte Herman. Illustrations copyright © 1991 by Catherine Bowman Smith. Reprinted by permission of Henry Holt and Company, Inc.

Entire text and art and cover of CITY GREEN by DyAnne DiSalvo-Ryan. Copyright © 1994 by DyAnne DiSalvo-Ryan. By permission of Morrow Junior Books, a division of William Morrow and Company, Inc.

"Closed, I am a mystery" by Myra Cohn Livingston from A PLACE TO DREAM. From My Head is Red and Other Riddle Rhymes by Myra Cohn Livingston. Copyright © 1990 by Myra Cohn Livingston (Published by Holliday House, NY) by presmission of Marian Reiner.

"Different Drum" by Joe Scruggs from ANTS by Joe Scuggs. (Produced by Gary Powell.) Copyright © 1994 by Educational Graphics Press, Inc.

"Dream Wolf" is from DREAM WOLF by Paul Goble. Copyright © 1990 by Paul Goble. Reprinted with the permission of Simon & Schuster Books For Young Readers.

"Fog" by Carl Sandburg from CHICAGO POEMS by Carl Sandburg. Copyright © 1916 by Holt Reinhart & Winston Inc.; renewed 1944 by Carl Sandburg. Reprinted by permission of Harcourt Brace Jovanovich, Inc.

Cover permission for THE GIRL WHO LOVED WILD HORSES by Paul Goble. Copyright © 1978 by Paul Goble. Reprinted by permission of Simon & Schuster Books for Young Readers.

"Grandfather's Journey" by Allen Say. Copyright © 1993 by Allen Say. Reprinted with the permission of Houghton Mifflin Company. All rights reserved.

"The Little Painter of Sabana Grande" by Patricia Maloney Markun, illustrated by Robert Casilla. Text copyright © 1993 by Patricia Maloney Markun. Illustrations copyright © 1993 by Robert Casilla. Published by Simon & Schuster Books for Young Readers. Reprinted by permission.

"Moses Goes to a Concert" by Issac Millman. Copyright © 1998 by Isaac Millman. Reprinted by permission of Frances Foster Books/Farrar, Straus and Giroux.

"My Pencil" by Shirley R. Williams from POETRY PLACE ANTHOLOGY by Instructor Publications, Inc. Text copyright © 1983 by Instructor Publications, Inc.

"Opt: An Illusionary Tale" from OPT: AN ILLUSIONARY TALE by Arline and Joseph Baum. Copyright © 1987 by Arline and Joseph Baum. Used by permission of Viking Penguin, a division of Penguin Putnam, Inc.

"The Patchwork Quilt" from THE PATCHWORK QUILT by Valerie Flournoy, illustrations by Jerry Pinkney. Text copyright © 1985 by Valerie Flournoy. Illustrations copyright © 1985 by Jerry Pinkney. Published by arrangment Dial Books for Young Readers, a division of Penguin Putnam, Inc.

"Phoebe and the Spelling Bee" by Barney Saltzberg. Text and illustrations © 1996 by Barney Saltzberg. Reprinted by permission of Hyperion Books for Children.

Cover permission for RABBIT MAKES A MONKEY OUT OF LION by Verna Aardema; pictures by Jerry Pinkney. Pictures copyright © 1989 by Jerry Pinkney. Reprinted with the permission of Dial Books for Young Readers, a division of Penguin Books USA, Inc.

"The Sun, the Wind and the Rain" from THE SUN, THE WIND AND THE RAIN by Lisa Westberg Peters. Text copyright © 1988 by Lisa Westberg Peters. Illustrations copyright © 1988 by Ted Rand. Reprinted by permission of Henry Holt and Co., Inc.

Cover permission for TURTLE IN JULY by Marilyn Singer; illustrated by Jerry Pinckney. Illustrations copyright © 1989 by Jerry Pinckney. Reprinted with the permission of Atheneum Books for Young Readers, an imprint of Simon & Schuster.

"Who Am I?" by Felice Holman. Copyright © Felice Holman from AT THE TOP OF MY VOICE AND OTHER POEMS. Published by Charles Scribner's Sons, 1970.

"My Pencil" by Shirley R. Williams in POETRY PLACE ANTHOLOGY, published by Scholastic Professional Books. Copyright © 1983 by Edgell Communications, Inc. Reprinted with premission of Scholastic Inc.

Illustration

Myron Grossman, 105; B.B. Sams, 108–123; Pat Rasch, 107; Andy Levine, 171; Pat Rasch, 224; Vilma Ortiz–Dillon, 231, 234, 236; Mike DiGiorgio, 232, 237, 242; Andy Levine, 243; Mike DiGiorgio, 288; John Kanzler, 352–371; Leonor Glynn, 374; Tom Foty, 10–11 Marni Backer, 138–139 Greg Couch, 140–141 Christopher Zacharow, 254–255 Steve Barbaria, 256–257 Peter M. Fiore, 386–387; Rodica Prato, 391, 396, 407; George Thompson, 399.

Photography

12–13: The Bridgeman Art Library International/Christopher Wood Gallery, London UK. 48–49: Jane Wooster Scott/Superstock. 78–79: Art Resource, Inc./Herscovici. 50: t.l. Courtesy of Hyperion Press/Barry E. Levine, Inc. 106–107: The Norman Rockwell Museum at Stockbridge. 128–129: The Bridgeman Art Library International/Wingfield Sporting Gallery, London, UK. 135: Duomo/William Sallaz. 142–143: The Image Works/Cameramann. 172–173: The Bridgeman Art Library International/Bonhams, London, UK. 204–205: Art Resource, Inc./K.S. Art. 226–227: Madison Press Books. 228: m.l. Courtesy of Diane Hoyt–Goldsmith/Lawrence Migdale. 228–229: DRK Photo/(c) Tom Bean 1990. 230: DRK Photo/(c) Larry Ulrich. 231: Animals Animals/(c) Bill Beatty. 233: DRK Photo/(c) Stephen J. Kraseman. 236: Photo Researchers, Inc./(c) Scott Camazine. 238: ENP Images/(c) Gerry Ellis. 239: Photo Researchers, Inc./(c) Jewel Craig. 244–245: The Bridgeman Art Library International/Kathryn Kooyahoema/Jerry Jacka Photography. 250: b. Photo Researchers, Inc.. m. Photo Researchers, Inc. 258–259: Superstock/Gil Mayers. 260: t.r. reprinted by permission of Farrar, Straus and Giroux Books for Young Readers/(c) Daniel Lee. 318–319: Photo by William C.L. Weintraub for the Georgia Quilt Project, Inc. . 350–351: Gerald Peters Gallery, Santa Fe, New Mexico. . 376–377: Superstock. 383: Peter Arnold, Inc./(c) Kim Heacox.

"Paul Bunyan, the Mightiest Logger of Them All" from AMERICAN TALL TALES by Mary Pope Osborne. Copyright © 1991 by Mary Pope Osborne. Used by permission of Alfred A. Knopf, Inc.

"Pincushion Cactus" from WHISPERS AND OTHER POEMS by Myra Cohn Livingston. Copyright © 1958, 1986 by Myra Cohn Livingston. Used by permission of Marian Reiner for the author.

"The Rabbit's Tale" from THE DRAGON'S TALE AND OTHER ANIMAL FABLES OF THE CHINESE ZODIAC by Demi. Copyright © 1996 by Demi. Used by permission of Henry Holt and Company, Inc.

"Seeing the Animals" from NATIVE AMERICAN ANIMAL STORIES by Joseph Bruchac. Copyright © 1992 by Joseph Bruchac. Used by permission of Fulcrum Publishing.

"The Song of the World's Last Whale" words and music by Pete Seeger. Copyright © 1970, 1994 by Stormking Music Inc.

"Spider on the Floor" from RAFFI'S TOP 10 SONGS TO READ. Words and music by Bill Russell. Text copyright © 1976 by Egos Anonymous (PRO). Illustrations copyright © 1993 by True Kelley. Used by permission of Crown Publishers, Inc., a Random House company.

"Take a Bite Out of Music" from TAKE A BITE OUT OF MUSIC, IT'S YUMMY by Mary Ann Hall. Copyright © 1986 by Mary Ann Hall's Music for Children.

"Take Me Out to the Ballgame" words by Jack Norworth, music by Albert von Tilzer from GONNA SING MY HEAD OFF! Used by permission of Alfred A. Knopf.

"Toad's Trick" from TO RIDE A BUTTERFLY by Verna Aardema. Text copyright © 1991 by Verna Aardema. Illustrations copyright © 1991 by Will Hillenbrand. Used by permission of Bantam Doubleday Dell Publishing Group, Inc.

"Using Your Head" from JATAKA TALES edited by Nancy DeRoin. Text copyright © 1975 by Nancy DeRoin. Drawings copyright © 1975 by Ellen Lanyon. Used by permission of Houghton Mifflin Company.

"Whale" from THE RAUCOUS AUK by Mary Ann Hoberman. Copyright © 1973 by Mary Ann Hoberman. Used by permission of The Viking Press.

"Why Bears Have Short Tails" from AND IT IS STILL THAT WAY by Byrd Baylor. Copyright © 1976 by Byrd Baylor. Used by permission of Trails West Press.

"The Wind and the Sun" told by Margaret Hughes from AESOP'S FABLES. Copyright © 1979 by Albany Books. Used by permission of Chartwell Books Inc., a division of Book Sales Inc.

"The Wolf and His Shadow" from THE BEST OF AESOP'S FABLES retold by Margaret Clark. Text copyright © 1990 by Margaret Clark. Illustrations copyright © 1990 by Charlotte Voake. Used by permission of Little, Brown and Company.

Notes

Backmatter Contents

A Garden

Aileen Fisher

We wanted a garden,
and oh, what fun
to plan a garden and dig in one.

But it was awful
the way the weeds
grew every place we planted seeds.

And it was frightful
how rain and such
was either too little or else too much.

But it was jolly
the day we spied
little green pods growing peas inside.

The Hurricane

Ashley Bryan

I cried to the wind,
"Don't blow so hard!
You've knocked down my sister
You're shaking
And tossing and tilting
The tree!"

And would the wind listen,
Listen to me?

The wind howled,
"*Whooree!*
I blow as I wish
I wish
I wish
I crush and
I splash and
I rush and
I swish."

I cried to the wind,
"Don't blow so wild!
You're chasing the clouds
You're whirling
And swishing and swirling
The sea!"

And would the wind listen,
Listen to me?

The wind howled,
"*Whooree!*
I blow as I wish
I wish
I wish
I'm bold and
I'm brash and
I'm cold and
I'm rash!"

I said to my friends,
"Please, call out with me,
Stop, wind, stop!"
"STOP, WIND, STOP!"

Ah, *now* the wind listens
It brushes my hair
Chases clouds slowly
Sings in my ear,
"*Whooree, whooree!*"
Stretches out gently
Under the tree
Soothes little sister
And quiets the sea.

Seeing the Animals

Joseph Bruchac

Their eyes are
not our eyes
yet we can see
ourselves in them.

We do not walk
the ways they walk,
yet we follow
their footprints in sand.

Sometimes they come
to us, when we
hold their silence
they understand.

When they live with us
we must give them respect,
though most stay apart
like the bird which is hidden
yet touches us with its song.

Sometimes we think
that we humans can live
without them,
but we are wrong.

Spider on the Floor

Bill Russell

There's a spider on the floor, on the floor.
There's a spider on the floor, on the floor.
Who could ask for any more than a spider on
the floor?
There's a spider on the floor, on the floor.

Now the spider's on my leg, on my leg.
Oh, the spider's on my leg, on my leg.
Oh, he's really big! This old spider on my leg.
There's a spider on my leg, on my leg.

Now the spider's on my stomach, on my stomach.
Oh, the spider's on my stomach, on my stomach.
Oh, he's just a dumb old lummock, this old spider
on my stomach.
There's a spider on my stomach, on my stomach.

Now the spider's on my neck, on my neck.
Oh, the spider's on my neck, on my neck.
Oh, I'm gonna be a wreck, I've got a spider on
my neck.
There's a spider on my neck, on my neck.

Now the spider's on my face, on my face.
Oh, the spider's on my face, on my face.
Oh, what a big disgrace, I've got a spider on
my face.
There's a spider on my face, on my face.

Now the spider's on my head, on my head.
Oh, the spider's on my head, on my head.
Oh, I wish that I were dead, I've got a spider on
my head.
There's a spider on my head, on my head.

Spoken: But he jumps off...

Repeat 1st Verse

Arachne the Spinner

retold by Geraldine McCaughrean

Once, when all cloths and clothes were woven by hand, there was a weaver called Arachne more skillful than all the rest. Her tapestries were so lovely that people paid a fortune to buy them. Tailors and weavers came from miles around just to watch Arachne at work on her loom. Her shuttle flew to and fro, and her fingers plucked the strands as if she were making music rather than cloth.

"The gods certainly gave you an amazing talent," said her friends.

"Gods? There's nothing the gods could teach me about weaving. I can weave better than any god or goddess."

Her friends turned rather pale. "Better not let the goddess Athene hear you say that."

"I don't care who hears it. I'm the best there is," said Arachne.

An old lady sitting behind her examined the yarns Arachne had spun that morning, feeling their delightful texture between finger and thumb. "So if there were a competition between you and the goddess Athene, you think you would win?" she said.

"She wouldn't stand a chance," said Arachne. "Not against me."

All of a sudden the old lady's gray hair began to float like smoke about her head and turn to golden light. A swish of wind blew her old coat into shreds and revealed a robe of dazzling white. She grew taller and taller until she stood head and shoulders above the crowd. There was no mistaking the beautiful gray-eyed goddess, Athene.

"Let it be so!" declared Athene. "A contest between you and me."

Arachne's friends fell on their faces in awe. But Arachne simply threaded another shuttle. And although her face was rather pale and her hands did tremble a little, she smiled and said, "A contest then. To see who is the best weaver in the world."

To and fro went the shuttles, faster than birds building a nest.

Athene wove a picture of Mount Olympus. All the gods were there: heroic, handsome, generous, clever, and kind. She wove all the creatures of creation on to her loom. And when she wove a kitten, the crowd sighed, "Aaaah!" When she wove a horse, they wanted to reach out and stroke it.

Alongside her sat Arachne, also weaving a picture of the gods.

But it was a comical picture. It showed all the silly things the gods had ever done: dressing up, squabbling, lazing about, and bragging. In fact she made them look just as foolish as ordinary folk.

But oh! When she pictured a butterfly sitting on a blade of grass, it looked as if it would fly away at any moment. When she wove a lion, the crowd shrieked and ran away in fright. Her sea shimmered and her corn waved, and her finished tapestry was more beautiful than nature itself.

Athene laid down her shuttle and came to look at Arachne's weaving. The crowd held its breath.

"You *are* the better weaver," said the goddess. "Your skill is matchless. Even I don't have your magic."

Arachne preened herself and grinned with smug satisfaction. "Didn't I tell you as much?"

"But your pride is even greater than your skill," said Athene. "And your irreverence is past all forgiving." She pointed at Arachne's tapestry. "Make fun of the gods, would you? Well, for that I'll make such an example of you that no one will ever make the same mistake again!"

She took the shuttle out of Arachne's hands and pushed it into her mouth. Then, just as Athene had changed from an old woman into her true shape, she transformed Arachne.

Arachne's arms stuck to her sides, and left only her long, clever fingers straining and scrabbling. Her body shrank down to a black blob no bigger than an ink blot: an end of thread still curled out of its mouth. Athene used the thread to hang Arachne up on a tree, and left her dangling there.

"Weave your tapestries forever!" said the goddess. "And however wonderful they are, people will only shudder at the sight of them and pull them to shreds."

It all came true. For Arachne had been turned into the first spider, doomed forever to spin webs in the corners of rooms, in bushes, in dark, unswept places. And though cobwebs are as lovely a piece of weaving as you'll ever see, just look how people hurry to sweep them away.

City Green • PRACTICE

Name_____________ Date_________ **Practice 38**

Cause and Effect

The person, thing or event that makes something happen is called the **cause**. The **effect** is what happens, or the result of that cause.

Read each cause. Then choose the correct effect from the box and write it on the line.

Effects

The cake got burned.
She decided to call the garage for help.
The plow trucks were busy.
She ran out of food for her guests.
The students went outside to play.

1. **Cause:** The school bell rang.
   Effect: **The students went outside to play.**
2. **Cause:** Anna's car made a lot of strange noises.
   Effect: **She decided to call the garage for help.**
3. **Cause:** Jay fell asleep while his cake was in the oven.
   Effect: **The cake got burned.**
4. **Cause:** More people came to Amanda's party than she expected.
   Effect: **She ran out of food for her guests.**
5. **Cause:** It snowed for twelve hours.
   Effect: **The plow trucks were busy.**

At Home: Have students tell you some of the effects that could be caused by a rainy day.

Name_____________ Date_________ **Practice 39**

Vocabulary

Decide whether each statement is **true** or **false**. Explain the false statements.

1. There is still room left in a bucket that is filled *halfway*.
   True
2. *Excitement* usually causes people to fall asleep.
   False; it usually stirs people up.
3. A big pile of things is called a *heap*.
   True
4. *Stems* are the part of a flower that grow out of the ground.
   True
5. When a train is running on *schedule*, it is going to arrive at the station very late.
   False; the train will arrive on time.
6. A picnic *area* is a space set aside where people can eat.
   True

At Home: Have students read the dictionary definition for each of the italicized words.

Andrew's Award

The school awards show was *halfway* over. So far the program had perfectly followed the printed *schedule*. Andrew felt so much *excitement* that he paced back and forth. He was in the *area* where all the award winners waited.

Early in the school year, Andrew had collected used cans. He brought them to a place where a city worker counted them. Then the worker threw them into a big *heap* of other used cans.

Andrew received twenty dollars for the used cans. With the money, he bought flowers to plant in front of the school. By the day of the awards, the *stems* were just beginning to pop up from the ground.

1. Where did the city worker throw Andrew's cans?
   into a heap
2. What did Andrew feel at the awards show?
   excitement
3. Where did Andrew pace back and forth?
   in the area where the award winners waited
4. What part of the flowers were beginning to pop up?
   the stems
5. Why was Andrew winning an award?
   He spent the money he made on planting flowers for his school.

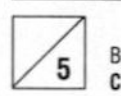

At Home: Invite students to talk about what they would do to help their school look nice.

Name_____________ Date_________ **Practice 40**

Story Comprehension

Think about "City Green." Then complete the chart below.
Answers may vary.

1. **Setting of the Story:** **a city neighborhood**
2. **Main Characters:** **Marcy, Old Man Hammer, Miss Rosa, Marcy's mother and brother**

Beginning of the Story

3. **An old building was torn down, leaving behind an empty city lot.**
4. **The empty lot became filled with trash and litter.**
5. **Old Man Hammer said nothing good will ever come of the empty lot.**

Middle of the Story

6. **Marcy and Miss Rosa passed around a petition to lease the lot from the city.**
7. **Everyone in the neighborhood helped to clean up the lot and plant a garden.**
8. **One night, Marcy saw Old Man Hammer planting seeds in the garden.**

End of the Story

9. **Marcy begged Old Man Hammer to come see his seedlings in the garden.**
10. **When summer came, Marcy and Old Man Hammer enjoyed sitting in the garden near the sunflowers.**

At Home: Have students identify and discuss problems on their street or in their own community.

City Green • PRACTICE

Name______________________ Date__________ **Practice 41**

Use a Telephone Directory

102 **Garage Doors—Gas**

Garage Doors
Clegg Brothers
45 Simpson St 555-3423
T.J.'s Garage Supplies
523 Maple Ln 555-6520
Garbage Removal
See Rubbish and Garbage Removal
Garden Centers—plants, supplies
Chestnut Hill Farms
456 Harrison Blvd 555-0456
Harry's Garden World
Route 5 + Gray Way 555-4589
Montclair Mall 555-1111
Garden Furniture
Chestnut Hill Farms
456 Harrison Blvd 555-0456
Moon River Junction
626 Good Hope Rd 555-8734

Pretend you're building a garden. Use the section of the Yellow Pages shown here to help you.

1. Which two stores sell plants? Chestnut Hill Farms, Harry's Garden World
2. Which store sells both both plants and garden furniture? Chestnut Hill Farms
3. What's the phone number of Moon River Junction? 555-8734
4. Pretend you need to remove garbage from your garden. Where would you look in these Yellow Pages? Rubbish and Garbage Removal
5. Which two stores sell garage doors? Clegg Brothers and T.J.'s Garage Supplies

At Home: Ask students to explain why they would not find listings of stores that sell fans on this page.

Name______________________ Date__________ **Practice 42**

Cause and Effect

Events in a story can often be organized by **cause** and **effect**. One event causes another to happen. Write the cause or effect of each event in the chart below. **Answers may vary.**

Story Event (Cause)	Story Event (Effect)
Marcy asked Old Man Hammer about the building that used to be on the lot.	1. Old Man Hammer told her to "Scram!"
Spring came.	2. Miss Rosa started cleaning coffee cans.
3. Old Man Hammer told Marcy and Miss Rosa that the lot had plenty of dirt.	Marcy and Miss Rosa dug for dirt in the empty lot. They got the idea to turn the lot into a garden.
Marcy, Miss Rosa, and other people from the block passed around a petition.	4. They got enough signatures to rent the lot from the city for one dollar.
5. Neighbors saw that the group was cleaning up the lot.	Everyone pitched in to help clean the lot.
6. Marcy saw Old Man Hammer plant seeds in the garden.	Marcy patted the neat and tidy garden row for good luck.
Marcy saw the tiny green shoots of Old Man Hammer's seeds sprouting in the garden.	7. Marcy brought Old Man Hammer to see the seedlings.
Summer came, and in the back of the garden grew a tall patch of sunflowers.	8. Marcy and Old Man Hammer sat in the garden and enjoyed the sunflowers that he planted.

At Home: Have students write a paragraph explaining the possible effect that the garden had on Old Man Hammer's life.

Name______________________ Date__________ **Practice 43**

Draw Conclusions

To draw a **conclusion** about a character or an event in a story, you use facts from the story. You also use your own knowledge and experience. Drawing conclusions as you read can help you better understand a story.

Answer each question below. Base your conclusion on your own experience and on information from "City Green." **Answers may vary.**

1. What kind of person is Marcy? She is friendly, thoughtful, concerned, and involved with her neighborhood.
2. What details from the selection helped you to draw that conclusion? She knew everyone and kept trying to be friends with Old Man Hammer.
3. What kind of relationship did Old Man Hammer and his neighbors have? Not very friendly.
4. What details from the selection helped you to draw your conclusion? Old Man Hammer hollered "scram" to Marcy when she asked him a question. He yelled to the neighbors that they were all wasting their time working to build the community garden.
5. Why did Old Man Hammer secretly plant seeds? The old building meant a lot to him. Deep down inside, he was really a nice man.
6. What details from the selection helped you draw that conclusion? He used to live there; he sat with Rosa in the finished garden.

At Home: Have students draw a conclusion about the effect the community garden had on the neighborhood.

Name______________________ Date__________ **Practice 44**

Context Clues

When you read an unfamiliar word you can use **context clues**, or the words or sentences before or after the word, to help you determine the word's meaning.

Read the sentence or sentences. Use context clues to figure out the meaning of the underlined words. Write the meaning of each word. **Answers will vary.**

1. The mother whale takes good care of its <u>calf</u> after it is born.
   calf means baby whale or animal
2. People joined together to <u>rescue</u> the whale when it was in trouble.
   rescue means save
3. The whales <u>migrate</u> from the north each winter and swim to the warm waters in the south. They return to the north again each summer.
   migrate means travel, travel each season
4. Many save-the-whale groups are working to protect these big <u>creatures</u> of the sea.
   creatures means animals
5. Blue whales are <u>mammoth</u> and can grow to one hundred feet.
   mammoth means huge

At Home: Have students point out the context clues in each sentence that helped them to determine the meaning of each word.

City Green • RETEACH

Name______________________ Date__________ **Reteach 38**

Cause and Effect

The **cause** is what makes something happen. The **effect** is the thing that happens.

Cause: The dog barked so loudly.

Effect: We brought him inside.

Knowing about cause and effect can also help you make **predictions**. For example:

Perhaps the dog will stop barking when he is inside.

Read each sentence. Underline the cause. Circle the effect. Then use the cause and effect to write a prediction. **Predictions may vary.**

1. It hadn't rained all week, and the flowers started to wilt.
2. Predict what might happen if it rains tonight: **The flowers will get water and they won't wilt.**
3. The playground was dirty and children didn't like to play there.
4. Predict what might happen if the playground was cleaned up. **The children would play there.**
5. Jane felt so hot that she ran to the lake and jumped in.
6. Predict how Jane feels after jumping into the lake. **She feels cooler.**

At Home: Have students identify a cause-and-effect relationship that occurred during school.

Name______________________ Date__________ **Reteach 39**

Vocabulary

area	excitement	halfway	heap	schedule	stems

Choose a word from the box to finish each sentence. Write it on the line.

1. She looked at a **schedule** to see what she should do first.
2. The flower **stems** are growing strong and straight.
3. We will plant a garden in the **area** inside the fence.
4. Going to the zoo, the happy children were filled with **excitement**.
5. We stopped to rest **halfway** up the hill.
6. We found a **heap** of rocks.

6

Story Comprehension — Reteach 40

Think about the story "City Green." Then underline the correct answer to each question.

1. What happens to the building at the beginning of the story?
   a. People move into the building. b. The building is knocked down.
2. What do Marcy and Rosa want to do in the empty lot?
   a. plant a garden b. make an area for animals
3. Who do Rosa and Marcy rent the empty lot from?
   a. the city b. Old Man Hammer
4. What secret do Rosa and Old Man Hammer share?
   a. He planted flowers. b. He paid for the empty lot.

At Home: Have students tell what they would plant if they had their own garden. Then have them draw a picture of their garden.

Name______________________ Date__________ **Reteach 41**

Use a Telephone Directory

A **telephone directory** is a collection of names listed in alphabetical order. Both business and residential listings are included. Addresses and phone numbers are listed after the names.

Use this page from a telephone directory to answer the questions that follow.

658 LEWIS — LITTLE

LEWIS
Daniel 2 Woodchuck St 545-6785
Harold 34 Juniper Ave 677-9898
LEYDON
Thea 55 Krandle Blvd 432-4567
LI
Fung 637 23rd St 990-3212
Ping Wa 22 Sea View 877-3465
LIBERMAN SEE ALSO LIEBERMAN
LIBERMAN
Mario 321 Broadway 451-3234
LIDLE
Leonard 345 Tiger Rd 677-3458
Phyllis 441 Pond Trail 993-7575

1. What is Thea Leydon's phone number? **432-4567**
2. What is Harold Lewis's address? **34 Juniper Ave.**
3. Write the two ways the name Liberman is spelled in this directory. **Liberman, Lieberman**
4. How many different people have the last name Li? **two: Fung and Ping Wa**
5. What is the phone number of the person named Lidle who lives on Pond Trail? **993-7575**

At Home: Have students write two more questions using the telephone directory. Ask them to answer the questions.

Name______________________ Date__________ **Reteach 42**

Cause and Effect

The **cause** is what makes something happen. The **effect** is the thing that happens.

Read each sentence under **Cause**. Then write the **Effect** next to it.

Cause	Effect
1. The building Old Man Hammer used to live in was unsafe.	**It had to be torn down.**
2. The place where the building had been left a big hole.	**The city workers filled the hole with dirt.**
3. Old Man Hammer used to live in the building the city tore down.	**He thinks the city could have saved the old building but didn't.**
4. Old Man Hammer tells Marcy and Miss Rosa they could fill their cans with dirt from the new lot.	**Marcy gets the idea for using the whole lot for a garden.**
5. Mr. Bennett tells Marcy and Miss Rosa about a program that lets people rent lots.	**Marcy and Miss Rosa put together a petition to use the lot.**
6. People in the neighborhood help clean up the lot.	**The community members are able to turn the empty lot into something beautiful.**
7. Old Man Hammer misses his old building.	**He is cranky about the neighbors working on the lot where the building had stood.**
8. No one except Marcy and Old Man Hammer knows who planted the sunflower seeds.	**Marcy and Old Man Hammer become friends.**

At Home: Have students think of another cause and effect from "City Green."

Name____________ Date________ **Reteach 43**

Draw Conclusions

A **conclusion** is an answer based on information. You can **draw conclusions** based on information in a story or information you know from your own life.

Read the story. Then use information in the story and from your own life to draw conclusions. **Answers will vary.**

Keri was very excited as she got ready for Earth Day. This year she was in charge of games for little children.

She drew trees and flowers on brown lunch bags for a game she made up called "Little Trash Hunt." Keri bought enough balloons for all the children. Then she packed flower seeds and craft sticks so that everyone could plant a little garden. They could mark the places they planted with sticks. Then they would blow up their balloons and tie the balloon strings to the sticks.

"For the time being, it will be a balloon garden," Keri laughed.

1. About how old is Keri? **older than the little children**
2. Has Keri ever celebrated Earth Day before? Explain. **Yes. It says "This year," so she was probably involved last year too.**
3. In the story, how long is it until Earth Day? **It is probably very soon since Keri is getting ready for it.**
4. Why does Keri say, "For the time being, it will be a balloon garden"? **It will take a while for the flowers to grow.**

At Home: Have students draw some conclusions based on the statement, "I am getting up early tomorrow."

Name____________ Date________ **Reteach 44**

Context Clues

Context clues are the words or sentences that come before or after an unfamiliar new word. All these clues can help you figure out the meaning of the new word.

Read each sentence. Underline the parts of the sentence that give clues to the meaning of the word in dark type. Write the meaning of each word. **Answers will vary.**

1. We used a brush to spread paste on the whole wall and then we hung up the **wallpaper**.

Wallpaper means **paper you put on a wall to cover it**

2. The man **linked** the dog to the fence with a rope that was tied to the dog's collar.

Linked means **connected**

3. She thought that Alice was trying to **pry** information from her by asking lots of questions that weren't her business.

Pry means **force**

4. The freezing wind makes the boy start to **shiver** and his teeth begin to chatter.

Shiver means **shake with cold**.

At Home: Have students explain how the context clues helped them determine the meaning of each word.

Name________________________ Date__________ Extend 38

Cause and Effect

Invent a wacky machine. Use it to show several examples of cause and effect. For example, you could show a marble rolling through your machine and knocking over a block which then lands in a bowl of water and splashes—what?

Draw a picture of your machine. Then explain each cause and effect on the lines below.

At Home: Have students write about a game they have played. Tell them to write about what happened during the game and who won the game. Ask them to write the cause and the effect.

Name________________________ Date__________ Extend 39

Vocabulary

area	excitement	halfway	heap	schedule	stems

Use words from the box to write a story about planting a garden. Exchange stories with a partner. Read the story. Then provide an illustration for your partner's story.

Extend 40

Story Comprehension

Select a part of the story "City Green" to write as a play. Describe the plot of your play below.

Decide on the characters you will need and who will play them. Write a script telling what the characters will say. Rehearse the play. Then act it out for your class.

At Home: Have students tell what they learned from "City Green."

Name________________________ Date__________ Extend 41

Use a Telephone Directory

Bennet & Co. 10 3rd Street	555.8835	Hammar O. M. 11 3rd Street	555-1323
Bennett Sam 101 Broad Street	555-3497	Hammer's Supplies 29 3rd Street	555-6574
Bennett's Cakes 32 3rd Street	555-1483	Hammor's Pet Shop 2 3rd Street	555-9032

Suppose you live on 3rd Street. You want to get a group of 3rd Street business owners together to sponsor clean-up of the local park. You know the last names of the business owners. You don't have their telephone numbers. Here are the names of the business people you want to call. List the correct telephone numbers for these people. Then, tell how you found the correct number.

1. Mr. Hammer **555-6574**

How did you decide his telephone number?

He is the Hammer spelled with an -er on 3rd Street.

2. Mr. Bennett **555-1483**

How did you decide his telephone number?

He is the Bennett spelled with two t's on 3rd Street.

Describe what you will do to clean up the park.

At Home: Have students use the local telephone directory to look up three businesses. Have them list the businesses' names in alphabetical order followed by their numbers.

Name________________________ Date__________ Extend 42

Cause and Effect

Answers will vary. Sample answers shown.

It is important to understand why events happen and what effect, or action, each event caused. The following are some events. Write what might have caused the event on the lines at the left. Write what might happen as a result of the event on the lines at the right.

	Cause	Event	Effect
1.	**Jo was born on this day 11 years ago.**	Jo had an 11th birthday party.	**Jo receives presents.**
2.	**Jo asked Chloe and Moira to come to the party.**	Moira and Chloe arrived at the party together.	**Moira and Chloe have fun at the party.**

Write a story about what you think happened at Jo's party.

At Home: Have students write what else might have happened at Jo's party. Ask them to write a cause and effect for each event.

City Green • EXTEND

Name________________________ Date__________ **Extend 43**

Draw Conclusions

You should draw a conclusion based on information you know from your own experience or from information you research. Read each problem below. Then find out more about the problem. Ask a teacher or family member, look in library books, or use a computer to search for more information. Then write your conclusion. Give reasons for your conclusion.

1. Many buildings are getting very old. Should they be torn down? Should they be fixed up? Why do you think as you do?
   Answers will vary, but should give valid reasons for the conclusion drawn.

2. Many areas are covered with litter and garbage. Should we help clean those areas up? Is that someone else's problem? Why do you think as you do?
   Answers will vary, but should give valid reasons for the conclusion drawn.

At Home: Have students discuss what they think should be done to solve one of the problems.

Name________________________ Date__________ **Extend 44**

Context Clues

It's not always easy to figure out what a word means. But if you look at all the other words and the pictures around them, sometimes you can figure it out. Read the sentence below each picture. Then, figure out what the underlined word means. Tell how you figured it out.

Why is that bird making such a hullabaloo?

Don't you think that horse is exquisite?

Look at that infinitesimal insect.

Yes, but the shoe looks colossal next to the ant.

Circle the correct meaning. Then tell how you learned the meaning.

1. Hullabaloo means (loud noise) or nest.
2. Exquisite means running fast or (pretty).
3. Infinitesimal means very large or (very tiny).
4. Colossal means very tiny or (very large).

At Home: Have students use each of the new words to write a sentence.

Name________________ Date________ LEARN Grammar 33

Common and Proper Nouns

- A **noun** names a person, place, or thing.
- A **common noun** names any person, place, or thing.
- A **proper noun** names a special person, place, or thing.
- A proper noun begins with a capital letter.

Write **common** or **proper** under each underlined noun.

1. Marcy and Miss Rosa are neighbors.
   proper; proper; common
2. Old Man Hammer does not sign the petition.
   proper; common
3. A woman in the city checks her files.
   common; common; common
4. Mr. Bennett brings wood and tools.
   proper; common; common
5. Mr. Rocco brings cans of paint.
   proper; common; common
6. Old Man Hammer plants some seeds.
   proper; common
7. Flowers and vegetables begin to grow.
   common; common
8. Soon the lot becomes a garden.
   common; common

Extension: Ask students to write three proper nouns that name their neighbors and three common nouns that name vegetables.

Name________________ Date________ LEARN AND PRACTICE Grammar 34

Proper Nouns: Days, Months, Holidays

- The name of a day, month, or holiday begins with a capital letter.

Complete the sentences by writing the name of the day, month, or holiday correctly.

1. Marcy gets up early on Saturday. saturday
2. On Sunday, the city drops off tools. sunday
3. A good time to plant seeds is April. april
4. Many flowers bloom in May. may
5. The garden is filled with plants by July. july
6. Pumpkins grow in October. october
7. People like pumpkins for Halloween. halloween
8. I like pumpkin pie for Thanksgiving. thanksgiving

Extension: Invite students to make up riddles about days, months, and holidays. Have students take turns writing the answers on the board.

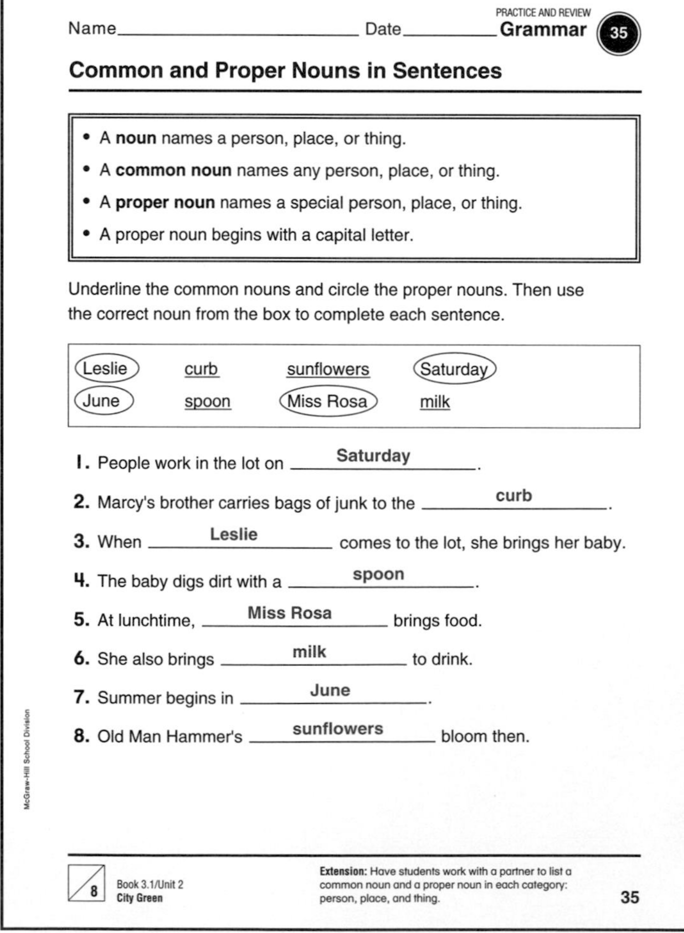

Name________________ Date________ PRACTICE AND REVIEW Grammar 35

Common and Proper Nouns in Sentences

- A **noun** names a person, place, or thing.
- A **common noun** names any person, place, or thing.
- A **proper noun** names a special person, place, or thing.
- A proper noun begins with a capital letter.

Underline the common nouns and circle the proper nouns. Then use the correct noun from the box to complete each sentence.

Leslie	curb	sunflowers	Saturday
June	spoon	Miss Rosa	milk

1. People work in the lot on Saturday.
2. Marcy's brother carries bags of junk to the curb.
3. When Leslie comes to the lot, she brings her baby.
4. The baby digs dirt with a spoon.
5. At lunchtime, Miss Rosa brings food.
6. She also brings milk to drink.
7. Summer begins in June.
8. Old Man Hammer's sunflowers bloom then.

Extension: Have students work with a partner to list a common noun and a proper noun in each category: person, place, and thing.

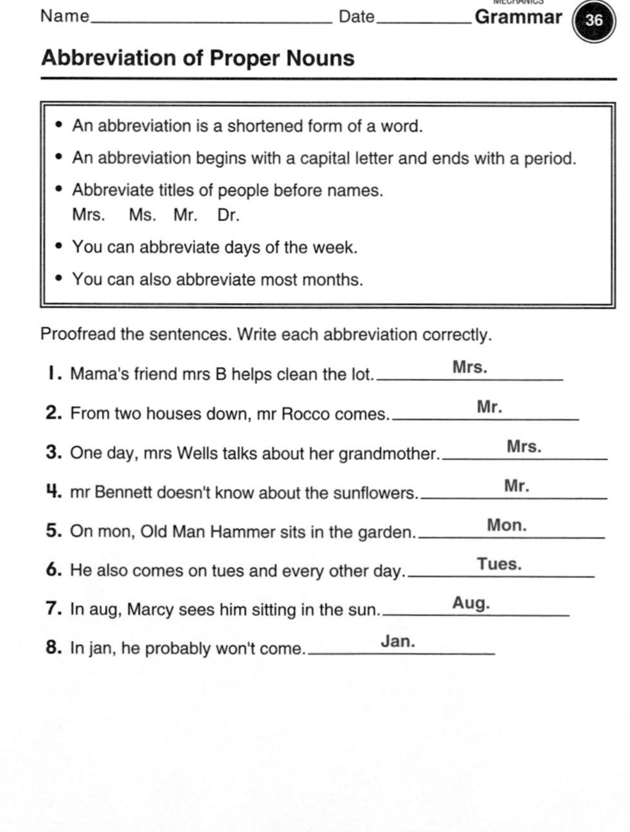

Name________________ Date________ MECHANICS Grammar 36

Abbreviation of Proper Nouns

- An abbreviation is a shortened form of a word.
- An abbreviation begins with a capital letter and ends with a period.
- Abbreviate titles of people before names.
  Mrs. Ms. Mr. Dr.
- You can abbreviate days of the week.
- You can also abbreviate most months.

Proofread the sentences. Write each abbreviation correctly.

1. Mama's friend mrs B helps clean the lot. Mrs.
2. From two houses down, mr Rocco comes. Mr.
3. One day, mrs Wells talks about her grandmother. Mrs.
4. mr Bennett doesn't know about the sunflowers. Mr.
5. On mon, Old Man Hammer sits in the garden. Mon.
6. He also comes on tues and every other day. Tues.
7. In aug, Marcy sees him sitting in the sun. Aug.
8. In jan, he probably won't come. Jan.

Extension: Have partners look through newspapers and magazines for abbreviations and underline them.

City Green • GRAMMAR

Name______________ Date__________ TEST Grammar 37

Common and Proper Nouns

A. If the underlined noun is a common noun, write **common**. If the underlined noun is a proper noun, write **proper**.

1. The building was unsafe. **common**

2. Old Man Hammer used to live in it. **proper**

3. A crane parked on the street. **common**

4. Workers knocked down the building. **common**

5. Miss Rosa took dirt from the lot. **proper**

B. Find the abbreviation of a proper noun in each sentence. Write it on the line.

6. One of the neighbors was Mr. Rocco. **Mr.**

7. Mrs. Wells was another neighbor. **Mrs.**

8. Apr. is a good month for gardens. **Apr.**

9. Dec. is not a good month for gardens. **Dec.**

10. Mr. Bennett is a neighbor also. **Mr.**

Name______________ Date__________ MORE PRACTICE Grammar 38

Common and Proper Nouns

- A **noun** names a person, place, or thing.
- A **common noun** names any person, place, or thing.
- A **proper noun** names a special person, place, or thing.

Mechanics:

- Begin a proper noun with a capital letter.
- Begin the name of a day, month, or holiday with a capital letter.

Write each sentence correctly. Then use the sentences to draw a picture.

1. marcy went to the lot on saturday.
Marcy went to the lot on Saturday.

2. mr rocco brought paint.
Mr. Rocco brought paint.

3. leslie brought her baby.
Leslie brought her baby.

4. miss rosa brought bread and jelly.
Miss Rosa brought bread and jelly.

City Green • SPELLING

Name________________________ Date__________ PRETEST SPELLING **33**

Syllable Patterns

Pretest Directions
Fold back the paper along the dotted line. Use the blanks to write each word as it is read aloud. When you finish the test, unfold the paper. Use the list at the right to correct any spelling mistakes. Practice the words you missed for the Posttest.

To Parents
Here are the results of your child's weekly spelling Pretest. You can help your child study for the Posttest by following these simple steps for each word on the word list:

1. Read the word to your child.
2. Have your child write the word, saying each letter as it is written.
3. Say each letter of the word as your child checks the spelling.
4. If a mistake has been made, have your child read each letter of the correctly spelled word aloud, and then repeat steps 1-3.

Parent/Child Activity:
Play a rhyming game with your child by taking turns saying as many rhyming words as you both can think of for each spelling word.

1. ________	1. open
2. ________	2. battle
3. ________	3. even
4. ________	4. candle
5. ________	5. frozen
6. ________	6. carrots
7. ________	7. silent
8. ________	8. bottle
9. ________	9. lazy
10. ________	10. lettuce
11. ________	11. maple
12. ________	12. fellow
13. ________	13. fifty
14. ________	14. flavor
15. ________	15. floppy

Challenge Words

________	area
________	excitement
________	halfway
________	heap
________	schedule

Name________________________ Date__________ AT-HOME WORD STUDY SPELLING **34**

Syllable Patterns

Using the Word Study Steps

1. LOOK at the word.
2. SAY the word aloud.
3. STUDY the letters in the word.
4. WRITE the word.
5. CHECK the word.
   Did you spell the word right?
   If not, go back to step 1.

Spelling Tip
If a 2-syllable word has a short vowel sound in the first syllable, it is often followed by two consonants or a double consonant.

Word Scramble
Unscramble each set of letters to make a spelling word.

1. npoe ___open___
2. yalz ___lazy___
3. ettabl ___tablet___
4. cuetetl ___lettuce___
5. veen ___even___
6. pleam ___maple___
7. elacnd ___candle___
8. welofl ___fellow___
9. nrzoef ___frozen___
10. ytffi ___fifty___
11. roratcs ___carrots___
12. foravl ___flavor___
13. telnis ___silent___
14. pyplfo ___floppy___
15. lettbo ___bottle___

To Parents or Helpers:
Using the Word Study Steps above as your child comes across any new words will help him or her spell well. Review the steps as you both go over this week's spelling words.
Go over the Spelling Tip with your child. Ask if he or she knows other 2-syllable words with a short vowel sound in the first syllable followed by two consonants or a double consonant.
Help your child unscramble the spelling words in the puzzle.

Name________________________ Date__________ EXPLORE THE PATTERN SPELLING **35**

Syllable Patterns

open	candle	silent	lettuce	fifty
battle	frozen	bottle	maple	flavor
even	carrots	lazy	fellow	floppy

Syllable Practice
Write the spelling words that contain a long-vowel sound in the first syllable.

1. ___open___ 2. ___even___ 3. ___frozen___
4. ___silent___ 5. ___lazy___ 6. ___maple___
7. ___flavor___

Write the spelling words that contain a short-vowel sound in the first syllable.

8. ___battle___ 9. ___candle___ 10. ___carrots___
11. ___bottle___ 12. ___lettuce___ 13. ___fellow___
14. ___fifty___ 15. ___floppy___

Pattern Power!
Write the spelling words with each of these patterns.

fl
16. ___flavor___
17. ___floppy___

le
21. ___maple___
22. ___battle___
23. ___candle___
24. ___bottle___

en
18. ___frozen___
19. ___open___
20. ___even___

y
25. ___lazy___
26. ___fifty___
27. ___floppy___

Name________________________ Date__________ PRACTICE AND EXTEND SPELLING **36**

Syllable Patterns

open	candle	silent	lettuce	fifty
battle	frozen	bottle	maple	flavor
even	carrots	lazy	fellow	floppy

A Fine Definition
Fill in the word from your spelling list that matches the definition.

1. Cooled to a very low temperature ___frozen___
2. A number written as 50 ___fifty___
3. Not willing to work ___lazy___
4. Making no sound ___silent___
5. A leafy, green plant, eaten as salad ___lettuce___
6. A fight between two armies ___battle___
7. A taste of something ___flavor___
8. Vegetables with long yellow-orange roots ___carrots___
9. Not closed ___open___
10. A glass container ___bottle___

Word Journal
Copy six words from "A Fine Definition" onto a separate piece of paper. Look at the meanings again. Then write a sentence using each word.

Challenge Extension: Have students write a synonym for each Challenge Word, and then use that word in a sentence.

Name________________________ Date__________ PROOFREAD AND WRITE SPELLING 37

Syllable Patterns

Proofreading Activity

There are seven spelling mistakes in this paragraph. Circle the misspelled words. Write the words correctly on the lines below.

It was a (laysy) sunny day. The gate by the garden was (opun). Jean Marie saw a rabbit with (flopee) ears hop away. The girl knew there was trouble, because she and the rabbit were having an ongoing (battel) all summer long. She quickly checked her plants. Jean Marie found three were missing. All the leaves of the (lettus) plants were chewed. Then she spotted a (bottul) on the ground. Some (mapil) syrup had spilled from it. "There's nothing this rabbit won't eat!" she thought to herself.

1. lazy
2. open
3. floppy
4. battle
5. lettuce
6. bottle
7. maple

Writing Activity

Write a description of a vegetable garden. Use at least three list words in your description.

____

____

____

____

____

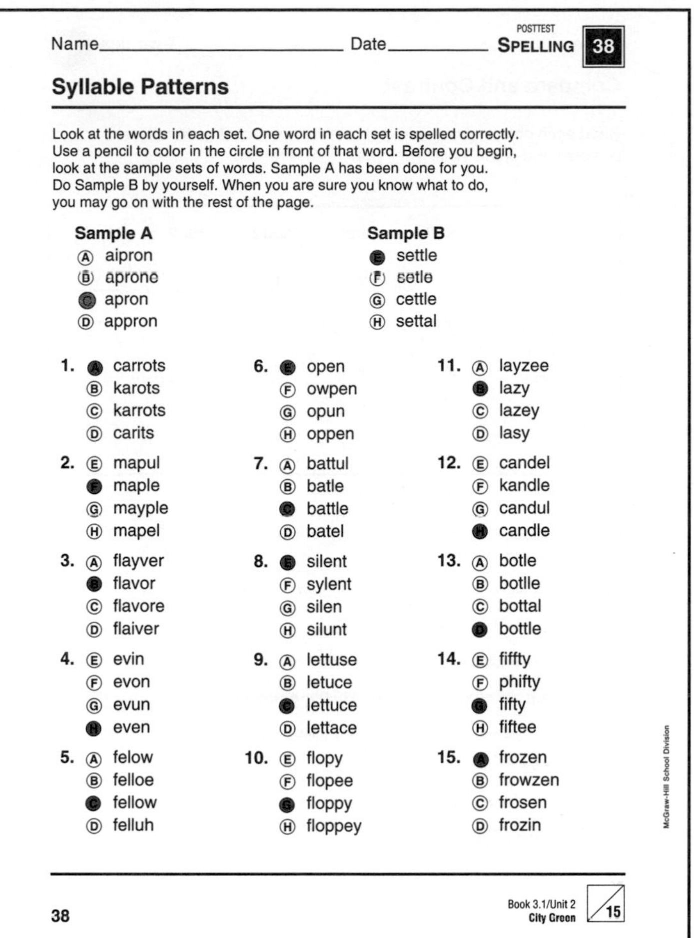

Name________________________ Date__________ POSTTEST SPELLING 38

Syllable Patterns

Look at the words in each set. One word in each set is spelled correctly. Use a pencil to color in the circle in front of that word. Before you begin, look at the sample sets of words. Sample A has been done for you. Do Sample B by yourself. When you are sure you know what to do, you may go on with the rest of the page.

Sample A
- (A) aipron
- (B) aprono
- ● apron
- (D) appron

Sample B
- ● settle
- (F) setle
- (G) cettle
- (H) settal

1. ● carrots (B) karots (C) karrots (D) carits
2. (E) mapul ● maple (G) mayple (H) mapel
3. (A) flayver ● flavor (C) flavore (D) flaiver
4. (E) evin (F) evon (G) evun ● even
5. (A) felow (B) felloe ● fellow (D) felluh
6. ● open (F) owpen (G) opun (H) oppen
7. (A) battul (B) batle ● battle (D) batel
8. ● silent (F) sylent (G) silen (H) silunt
9. (A) lettuse (B) letuce ● lettuce (D) lettace
10. (E) flopy (F) flopee ● floppy (H) floppey
11. (A) layzee ● lazy (C) lazey (D) lasy
12. (E) candel (F) kandle (G) candul ● candle
13. (A) botle (B) botlle (C) bottal ● bottle
14. (E) fiffty (F) phifty ● fifty (H) fiftee
15. ● frozen (B) frowzen (C) frosen (D) frozin

Name________________________ Date____________ Practice 45

Compare and Contrast

Read each object name. Answer the questions about each object to complete the chart. Write **Y** for **yes**. Write **N** for **no**.

A.

Is it	white?	round?	food?	fun?	hard?
baseball	Y	Y	N	Y	Y
onion	Y	Y	Y	N	Y
snowball	Y	Y	N	Y	Y
soap bubble	N	Y	N	Y	N

B. Use the completed chart to think about how the objects are alike and how they are different.

1. In what ways is the soap bubble different from the other objects?
   It is not white, and it is not hard.
2. How are snowballs and onions different?
   You eat onions, but not snowballs; snowballs melt.
3. How are baseballs and snowballs alike?
   You can throw both of them.
4. In what way are all 5 objects alike?
   They are all round.

At Home: Have students add one more question to the chart. How do the objects compare using this new trait?

Name________________________ Date____________ Practice 46

Vocabulary

Write the letter of the word that best matches each definition.

1. When you have exchanged one thing for another, you have __c__ it.
2. When the water in a stream has moved smoothly, it has __f__.
3. Hard, tiny pieces of things like rock or sand are known as __e__.
4. The amount you can hold in one hand is a __b__.
5. The pointed tops of mountains are called __a__.
6. Deep valleys with steep sides are known as __d__.

a. peaks
b. handful
c. traded
d. canyons
e. grains
f. flowed

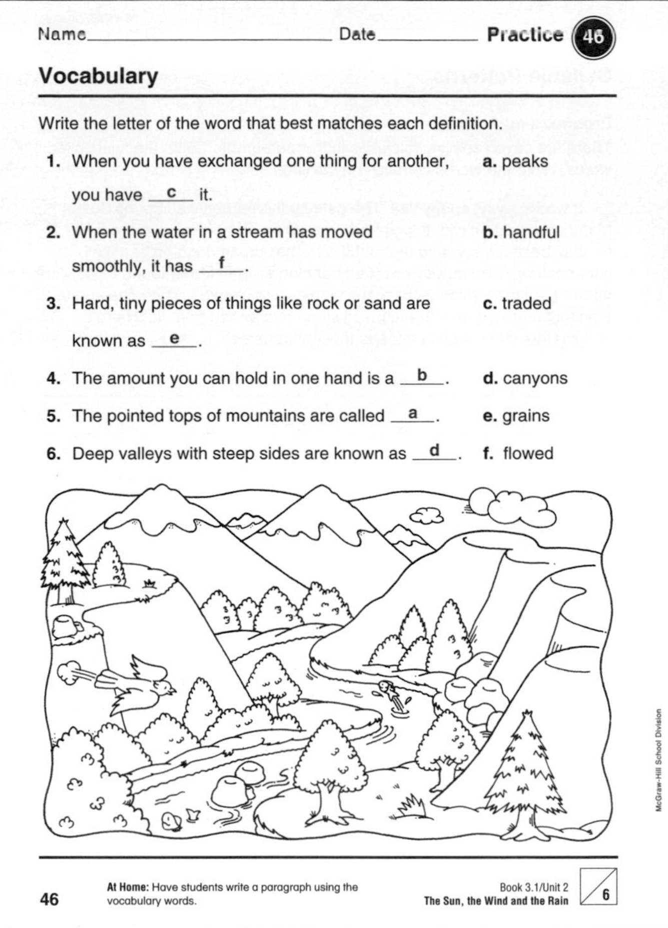

At Home: Have students write a paragraph using the vocabulary words.

A Mountain of Fun

Molly mixed paper, paste, and water. She wanted to use the material to make something. "I will make two mountains with tall *peaks*," she said. When the mountains were finished, Cliff placed sand in the *canyons* between the mountains. It took a large *handful* of sand to completely cover the canyon floor. "The *grains* will stick to the sticky surface and look like the dirt of a canyon," Cliff told Molly.

Next, Molly painted the mountain gray and Cliff painted the canyon brown. Then they *traded* places and added on another layer of paint.

Molly and Cliff stepped back to look at their finished model. There was just one thing missing. Molly knew what it was. Slowly she painted a strip of blue through the canyon. The water looked like it *flowed*.

1. What is another word for the top of a mountain?
   the peak
2. Where did Cliff place sand?
   in the canyons
3. How much sand did Cliff use?
   a handful
4. What did the blue that Molly painted onto the model look like?
   flowing water
5. What did Molly do to help make the model?
   She made the mountains and painted on the water.

At Home: Encourage students to name any famous mountains or canyons they know about. Where are they? Have they ever been to them?

Name________________________ Date____________ Practice 47

Story Comprehension

Answer the following questions about "The Sun, the Wind and the Rain."

1. Where does this story take place? **The story takes place by the ocean and on the beach.**
2. What two mountains are looked at in the story? **The mountains are the earth mountain and Elizabeth's sand mountain.**
3. What kind of information does the story tell about the real mountain? **The story tells about the way that the mountain is built and the way it breaks apart.**
4. What happens when rivers rush down the earth mountain? **The rivers cut valleys into the mountain and grind the rocks into pebbles.**
5. What makes Elizabeth cry? **Elizabeth cries when rain begins to destroy her sand mountain.**
6. Why don't either of the mountains stay the same? **The sun, the wind, and the rain break them apart.**

At Home: Have students draw a picture of one of the scenes described in "The Sun, the Wind, and the Rain."

Name________________ Date__________ **Practice 48**

Use a Dictionary

Place each of the dictionary parts below in its proper place.

sizzle
adjective
sidewalk
to make music with your voice
SIDE
(siz)

1. SIDE —SIZZLE
2. sidewalk 1. a path by the side of a street (sid′wôk) *noun*
3. **silly** 1. lacking common sense, foolish (sil′ē) *adjective*
4. **sing** 1. to make music with your voice (sing) *verb*
5. **size** 1. the amount of space an object takes up (sīz) *noun*
6. sizzle 1. to make a hissing sound (siz′əl) *verb*

At Home: Ask students to look up the word silt and to put it in its proper place in the above dictionary page, writing in the definition, pronunciation, and part of speech.

Name________________ Date__________ **Practice 49**

Compare and Contrast

Think about "The Sun, the Wind and the Rain." In what ways are the earth mountain and Elizabeth's mountain alike? How are they different? Complete the chart to compare the two mountains.

	earth mountain	Elizabeth's mountain
Formed when?	long ago	built today
Made of what?	rock and sandstone	wet sand
How big?	reaching up into the sky	as tall as a child
Rain does what?	destroys it and carries it to sea	destroys it and carries it to sea

Why do you think the author wrote about the two kinds of mountains? Circle your answer.

- to show how big they are
- to show mountain canyons
- (circled) to show how mountains change over time

At Home: Have students share experiences they have had at the beach or the mountains. Encourage them to focus on the sights and sounds.

Name________________ Date__________ **Practice 50**

Draw Conclusions

A conclusion is what you decide after you have read a story. You can also use your own experience to help you **draw conclusions**.

Draw your conclusions about the story by answering each question. **Answers may vary.**

Annie took a lot of pictures. There was one rock that looked like a bridge and another that looked like a wise old owl.

Annie wondered out loud if people had ever lived in this wonderful place.

"I'll show you something and you can decide for yourself," her father said.

It was already getting dark when they parked the car next to an enormous rock. Annie was astonished to see drawings of the horses and people.

"Native Americans made these pictures hundreds of years ago. Aren't they beautiful?" Annie's father said.

"Can we come back tomorrow when it's light enough for me to take a picture?"

1. Do you think Annie enjoyed her trip? yes
2. What information from the story helped you to draw your conclusion? She took pictures of the rocks; she liked the pictures on the rock; she said it was a wonderful place.
3. Where might Annie and her father be? Definitely in America, because "Native Americans" made the pictures on the wall, maybe in the West.
4. Had people ever lived in the place Annie visited? Explain. Yes, people made pictures on the wall hundreds of years ago.

At Home: Have students draw conclusions about whether or not Annie's father had ever visited this place before.

Name________________ Date__________ **Practice 51**

Antonyms and Synonyms

Antonyms are words that have the opposite, or nearly opposite, meaning.

Synonyms are words that have the same, or nearly the same, meaning.

Antonyms	**Synonyms**
hot, cold	large, big

Choose a word from the list on the right that is a synonym or antonym for the word on the left. Write the word on the first line. On the second line, write **S** if the word pairs are synonyms. Write **A** if the word pairs are antonyms.

1. shout	yell	S	different
2. like	dislike	A	won
3. help	aid	S	distrust
4. less	more	A	dislike
5. noisy	quiet	A	yell
6. unusual	different	S	quiet
7. believe	distrust	A	down
8. lost	won	A	aid
9. angry	mad	S	more
10. up	down	A	mad

At Home: Have students name a synonym and an antonym for **chilly**.

Name________________ Date__________ **Reteach 45**

Compare and Contrast

When you **compare**, you discover how things are alike. When you **contrast**, you discover how things are different.

Read the sentences below. Then write down the two things that are being compared or contrasted.

Sentence	What Is Being Compared/Contrasted
1. It is colder on the mountain than in the valley.	how cold it is on the mountain and in the valley
2. In summer, the days are long. In winter, the days are short.	how long the days are in summer and in winter
3. The sun comes up in the East and goes down in the West.	where the sun comes up and goes down
4. The moon moves around the Earth, and the Earth moves around the sun.	the paths of the moon and Earth
5. The Earth spins around once a day. It travels around the sun once a year.	how long Earth takes to spin around, and how long it takes to travel around the sun

At Home: Ask students to compare their height with the height of someone they know.

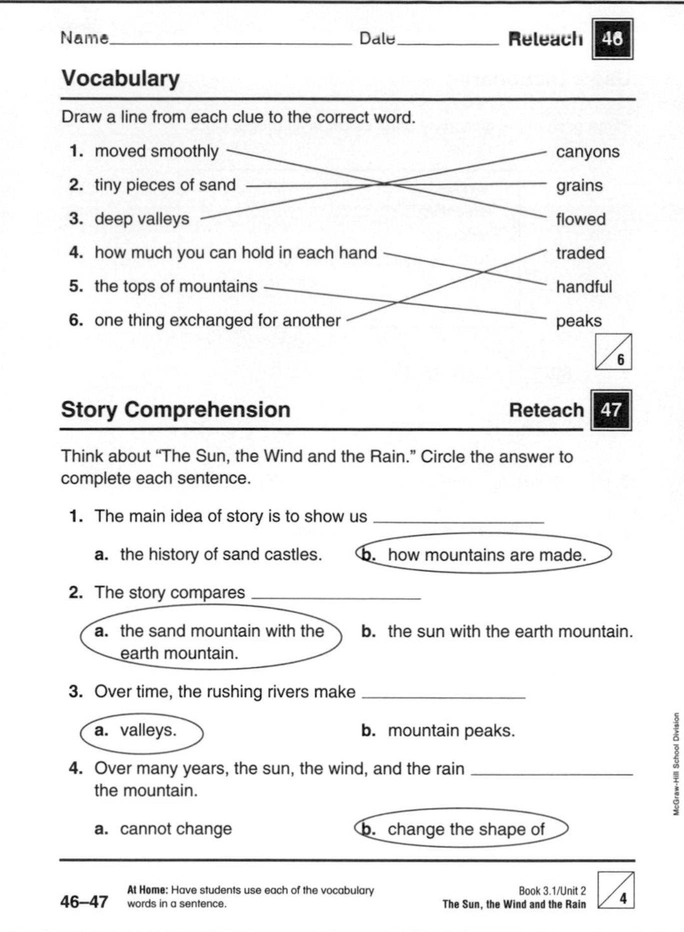

Name________________ Date__________ **Reteach 46**

Vocabulary

Draw a line from each clue to the correct word.

1. moved smoothly — flowed
2. tiny pieces of sand — grains
3. deep valleys — canyons
4. how much you can hold in each hand — handful
5. the tops of mountains — peaks
6. one thing exchanged for another — traded

(Words: canyons, grains, flowed, traded, handful, peaks)

6

Story Comprehension

Reteach 47

Think about "The Sun, the Wind and the Rain." Circle the answer to complete each sentence.

1. The main idea of story is to show us ____________
   a. the history of sand castles. **(b.) how mountains are made.**
2. The story compares ____________
   (a.) the sand mountain with the earth mountain. b. the sun with the earth mountain.
3. Over time, the rushing rivers make ____________
   (a.) valleys. b. mountain peaks.
4. Over many years, the sun, the wind, and the rain ____________ the mountain.
   a. cannot change **(b.) change the shape of**

At Home: Have students use each of the vocabulary words in a sentence.

Name________________ Date__________ **Reteach 48**

Use a Dictionary

A **dictionary** tells you what a word means. It also shows you how to say it, spell it, and divide it.

CRAYON—CUTE

crayon (krā′on) 1. a colored wax stick for drawing **noun**
2. to draw or write with a crayon **verb**
cream (krēm) 1. the part of milk with the most fat **noun**
2. the best part of something **noun**
crocodile (krok′ə dīl′) an animal with short legs, a long tail, and thick scaly skin **noun**
cry (krī) 1. to have tears come out of the eyes
2. to call loudly, shout **verb**
cup (kup) 1. a small bowl with a handle **noun**
cupboard (kub′ərd) a cabinet with shelves **noun**
cupcake (kup′cāk′) a small cake **noun**
cute (kūt) charming, delightful, pretty **adjective**

Study the dictionary page. Use it to answer the questions.

1. What is the first definition of *cry*? **to have tears come out of the eyes**
2. Is *crocodile* a noun or a verb? **noun**
3. How do you pronounce *cream*? **krēm**
4. Write the word that is an adjective. **cute**
5. Which of the three words with *cup* in them means something to eat? **cupcake**

At Home: Have students list all the nouns in the dictionary page above in alphabetical order. Then have them find the one word that is a verb.

Name________________ Date__________ **Reteach 49**

Compare and Contrast

When you **compare** and **contrast**, you point out how things are alike and how they are different. Authors often use comparison and contrast to describe things.

Think about the story "The Sun, the Wind and the Rain." Show how Elizabeth's mountain and the earth mountain are alike and different. Then answer the questions that follow.

	Earth's Mountain	Elizabeth's Mountain
What are they made of?	1. rock	2. wet sand
How long did they take to make?	3. many years	4. one day
How did they grow?	5. It rose higher as it cracked and shifted.	6. Elizabeth piled the sand higher.
What did the sun, wind, and rain do to each one over time?	7. broke it apart	8. broke it apart

9. In what ways are the two mountains alike? **They were both broken apart by the sun, the wind, and the rain.**
10. Name two ways in which the mountains are different. **Answers will vary but should reflect answers 1–6.**

At Home: Show students two objects such as a fork and a spoon, and have students describe how they are alike and how they are different.

Name________________________ Date__________ **Reteach 50**

Draw Conclusions

When you **draw conclusions**, you make a decision based on the facts. You can draw conclusions about story characters based on what they say and do.

Read the story. Then circle the correct conclusion.

All summer, Andy had been hard at work fixing up an old boat. At last it was ready. Andy went to find Mr. Ray to see if he could have a sailing lesson that afternoon.

Mr. Ray looked up at the sky. "Not today, it's too windy."

"Don't we need wind?" asked Andy.

"Not this much. I think a big storm is blowing up."

As Andy watched the clouds rolling over the ocean, he realized he hadn't noticed the changing weather. Tall waves crashed onto shore. The wind started to blow hard and Andy dug his chin into the collar of his jacket.

"Why don't you help me put the covers on these boats," said Mr. Ray. "Then we'll go inside and have something hot to drink and watch the storm. It should be a pretty good show."

1. Where do Andy and Mr. Ray live?

   (by the sea) — in the mountains

2. What information helped you draw your conclusion?

   There was a storm. — (Andy had a boat and wanted to learn to sail.)

3. Does Andy know Mr. Ray very well?

   (yes) — no

4. What information helped you draw your conclusion?

   They lived nearby. — (Andy asked him to teach him to sail.)

At Home: Discuss with students what conclusion they might draw if the weather forecast was for rain.

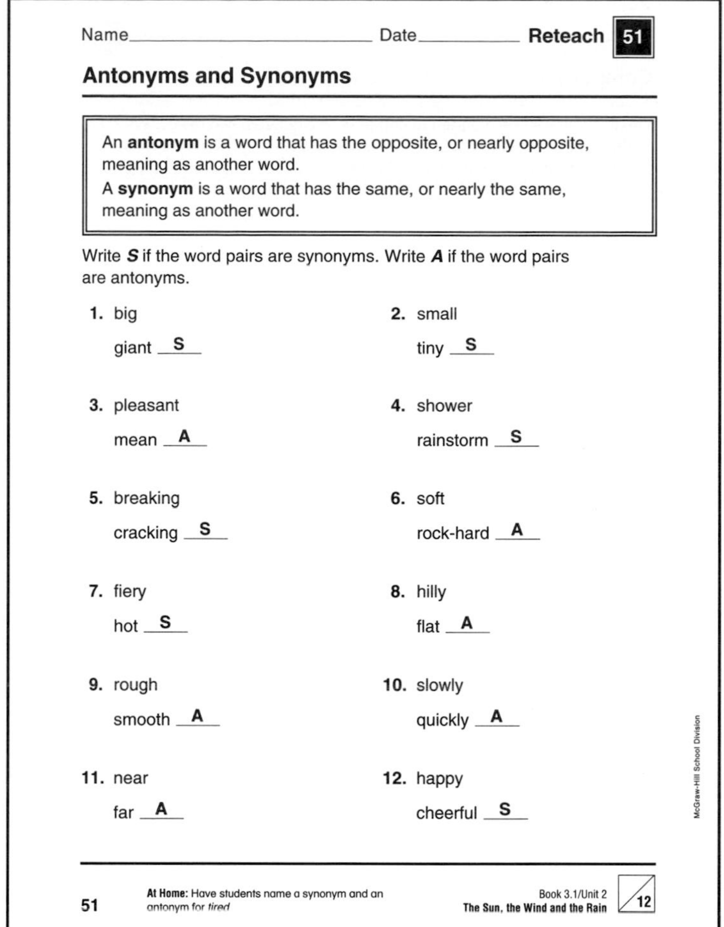

Name________________________ Date__________ **Reteach 51**

Antonyms and Synonyms

An **antonym** is a word that has the opposite, or nearly opposite, meaning as another word.
A **synonym** is a word that has the same, or nearly the same, meaning as another word.

Write ***S*** if the word pairs are synonyms. Write ***A*** if the word pairs are antonyms.

1. big — giant __S__
2. small — tiny __S__
3. pleasant — mean __A__
4. shower — rainstorm __S__
5. breaking — cracking __S__
6. soft — rock-hard __A__
7. fiery — hot __S__
8. hilly — flat __A__
9. rough — smooth __A__
10. slowly — quickly __A__
11. near — far __A__
12. happy — cheerful __S__

At Home: Have students name a synonym and an antonym for *tired*.

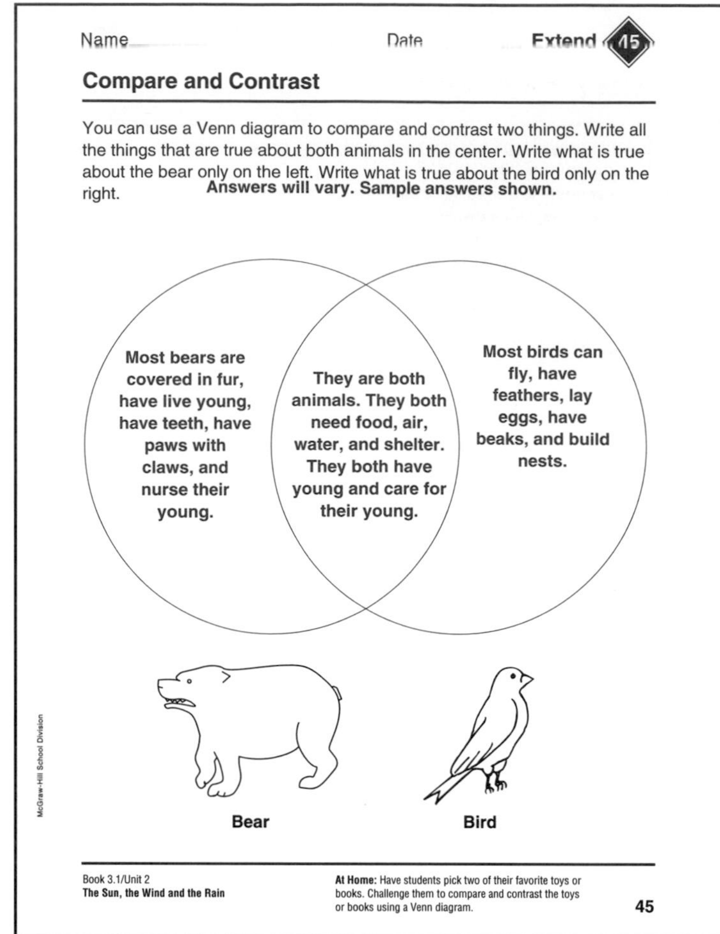

Name Date Extend 45

Compare and Contrast

You can use a Venn diagram to compare and contrast two things. Write all the things that are true about both animals in the center. Write what is true about the bear only on the left. Write what is true about the bird only on the right.

Answers will vary. Sample answers shown.

Most bears are covered in fur, have live young, have teeth, have paws with claws, and nurse their young.

They are both animals. They both need food, air, water, and shelter. They both have young and care for their young.

Most birds can fly, have feathers, lay eggs, have beaks, and build nests.

Bear **Bird**

McGraw-Hill School Division

Book 3.1/Unit 2
The Sun, the Wind and the Rain

At Home: Have students pick two of their favorite toys or books. Challenge them to compare and contrast the toys or books using a Venn diagram.

45

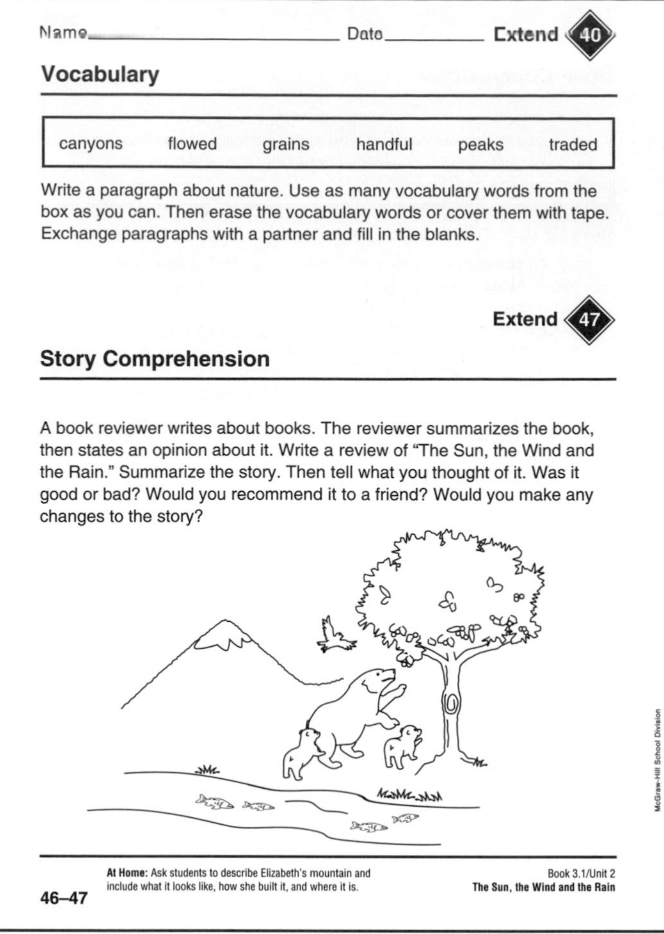

Name Date Extend 46

Vocabulary

canyons	flowed	grains	handful	peaks	traded

Write a paragraph about nature. Use as many vocabulary words from the box as you can. Then erase the vocabulary words or cover them with tape. Exchange paragraphs with a partner and fill in the blanks.

Extend 47

Story Comprehension

A book reviewer writes about books. The reviewer summarizes the book, then states an opinion about it. Write a review of "The Sun, the Wind and the Rain." Summarize the story. Then tell what you thought of it. Was it good or bad? Would you recommend it to a friend? Would you make any changes to the story?

At Home: Ask students to describe Elizabeth's mountain and include what it looks like, how she built it, and where it is.

46–47

Book 3.1/Unit 2
The Sun, the Wind and the Rain

McGraw-Hill School Division

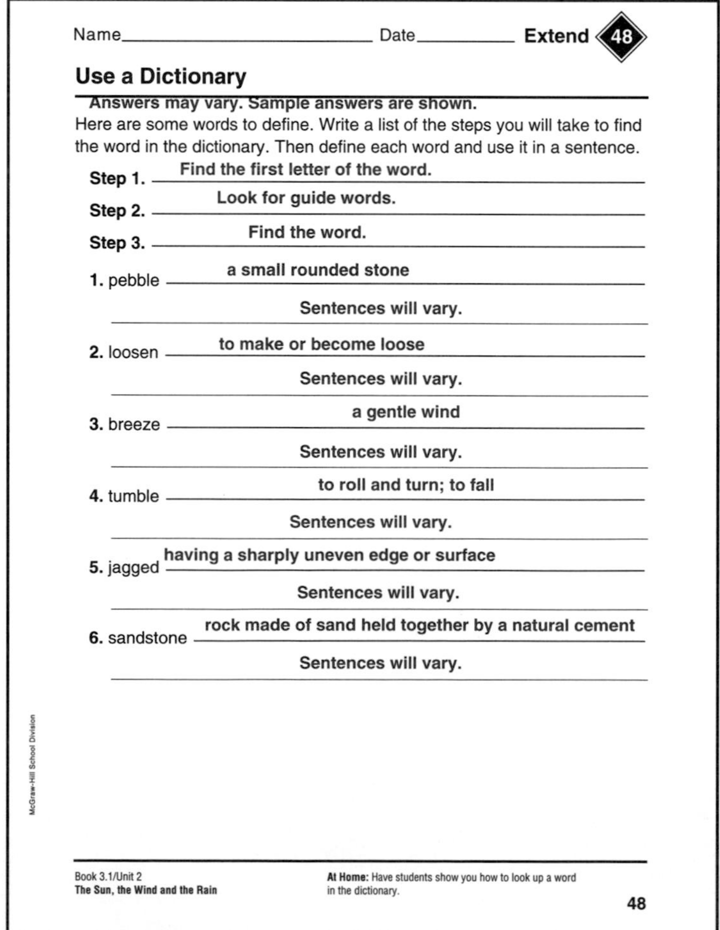

Name Date Extend 48

Use a Dictionary

Answers may vary. Sample answers are shown.

Here are some words to define. Write a list of the steps you will take to find the word in the dictionary. Then define each word and use it in a sentence.

Step 1. **Find the first letter of the word.**

Step 2. **Look for guide words.**

Step 3. **Find the word.**

1. pebble **a small rounded stone**
   Sentences will vary.
2. loosen **to make or become loose**
   Sentences will vary.
3. breeze **a gentle wind**
   Sentences will vary.
4. tumble **to roll and turn; to fall**
   Sentences will vary.
5. jagged **having a sharply uneven edge or surface**
   Sentences will vary.
6. sandstone **rock made of sand held together by a natural cement**
   Sentences will vary.

McGraw-Hill School Division

Book 3.1/Unit 2
The Sun, the Wind and the Rain

At Home: Have students show you how to look up a word in the dictionary.

48

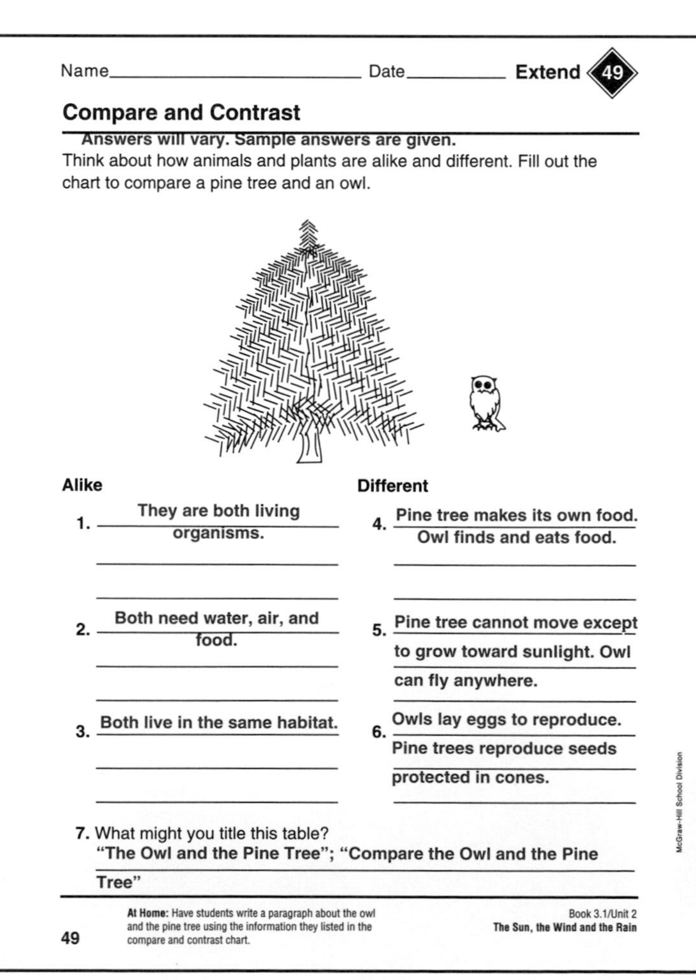

Name Date Extend 49

Compare and Contrast

Answers will vary. Sample answers are given.

Think about how animals and plants are alike and different. Fill out the chart to compare a pine tree and an owl.

Alike	Different
1. **They are both living organisms.**	4. **Pine tree makes its own food. Owl finds and eats food.**
2. **Both need water, air, and food.**	5. **Pine tree cannot move except to grow toward sunlight. Owl can fly anywhere.**
3. **Both live in the same habitat.**	6. **Owls lay eggs to reproduce. Pine trees reproduce seeds protected in cones.**

7. What might you title this table?
   "The Owl and the Pine Tree"; "Compare the Owl and the Pine Tree"

At Home: Have students write a paragraph about the owl and the pine tree using the information they listed in the compare and contrast chart.

49

Book 3.1/Unit 2
The Sun, the Wind and the Rain

McGraw-Hill School Division

Name_____________________ Date__________ **Extend 50**

Draw Conclusions

Telephone Tale

Sometimes when people pass information from person to person, the information can change. See what will happen with a story you start.

Get together with a group of your classmates. You are the story starter. Make up a story about an animal. It may be a story about a pet monkey that gets loose and into trouble. Write your story on paper so that you can compare it to the story the group ends up with.

Have your group sit together. Tell your story quietly to the person next to you. When you are done, ask him or her to pass the story on to the next person. Ask the last person who hears the story to write it down on a piece of paper.

As a group, compare the two stories. Under the columns below, list how the stories were the same. List how the stories were different.

Answers will vary.

Similarities	Differences
____________	____________
____________	____________
____________	____________
____________	____________

What conclusions can you draw from this "telephone tale"?

____

____

At Home: Have students continue the telephone tale they started in their group.

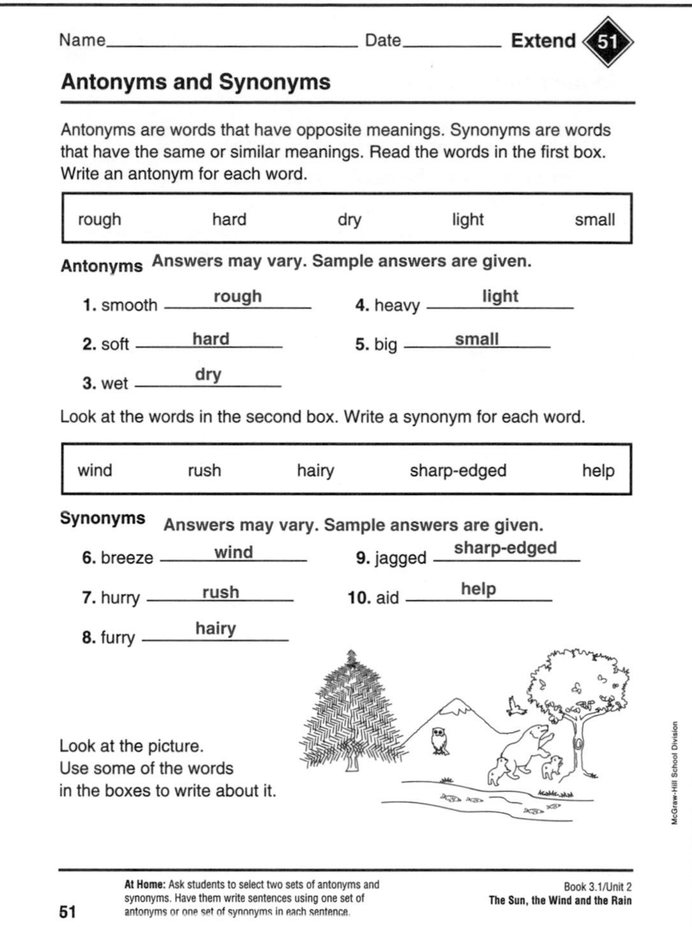

Name_____________________ Date__________ **Extend 51**

Antonyms and Synonyms

Antonyms are words that have opposite meanings. Synonyms are words that have the same or similar meanings. Read the words in the first box. Write an antonym for each word.

rough	hard	dry	light	small

Antonyms **Answers may vary. Sample answers are given.**

1. smooth **rough**

2. soft **hard**

3. wet **dry**

4. heavy **light**

5. big **small**

Look at the words in the second box. Write a synonym for each word.

wind	rush	hairy	sharp-edged	help

Synonyms **Answers may vary. Sample answers are given.**

6. breeze **wind**

7. hurry **rush**

8. furry **hairy**

9. jagged **sharp-edged**

10. aid **help**

Look at the picture.
Use some of the words
in the boxes to write about it.

At Home: Ask students to select two sets of antonyms and synonyms. Have them write sentences using one set of antonyms or one set of synonyms in each sentence.

Name __________ Date __________ LEARN Grammar 39

Singular and Plural Nouns

> A **singular noun** names one person, place, or thing.
> A **plural noun** names more than one person, place, or thing.
> Add *-s* to form the plural of most singular nouns.

Write the plural form of each noun.

1. year **years**
2. twig **twigs**
3. tree **trees**
4. pebble **pebbles**
5. eye **eyes**
6. animal **animals**
7. valley **valleys**
8. canyon **canyons**
9. grain **grains**
10. bucket **buckets**

Write the plural form of the noun in parentheses to complete each sentence.

11. The story is about two (mountain) **mountains**.
12. Small (stream) **streams** become a raging river.
13. The river grinds rough (rock) **rocks**.
14. Heavy (layer) **layers** of sand sink down into the earth.
15. Elizabeth sees sand spread into small (fan) **fans**.

McGraw-Hill School Division

15 Book 3.1/Unit 2 The Sun, the Wind and the Rain

Extension: Have students write four sentences using each of the following words in plural form: million, minute, hand, peak.

39

Name __________ Date __________ LEARN AND PRACTICE Grammar 40

Forming Plural Nouns

> - Add *-es* to form the plural of singular nouns that end in *s, sh, ch,* or *x.*
> - To form the plural of nouns ending in a consonant and *y,* change the *y* to *i* and add *-es.*

Change each word to a plural noun.

1. story **stories**
2. beach **beaches**
3. pass **passes**
4. crack **cracks**
5. wish **wishes**
6. day **days**
7. sky **skies**
8. path **paths**
9. box **boxes**
10. bunch **bunches**

Write the plural form of each noun in parentheses.

11. My family takes (journey) **journeys** to the mountains.
12. I look for birds in the (branch) **branches** of trees.
13. I also look for birds in (bush) **bushes**.
14. I see birds eating (berry) **berries**.
15. Sometimes at night we see (fox) **foxes**.

McGraw-Hill School Division

40

Extension: Have students take turns writing singular nouns that end in s, x, ch, sh, and y. Have other students write the plurals of these words.

Book 3.1/Unit 2 The Sun, the Wind and the Rain 15

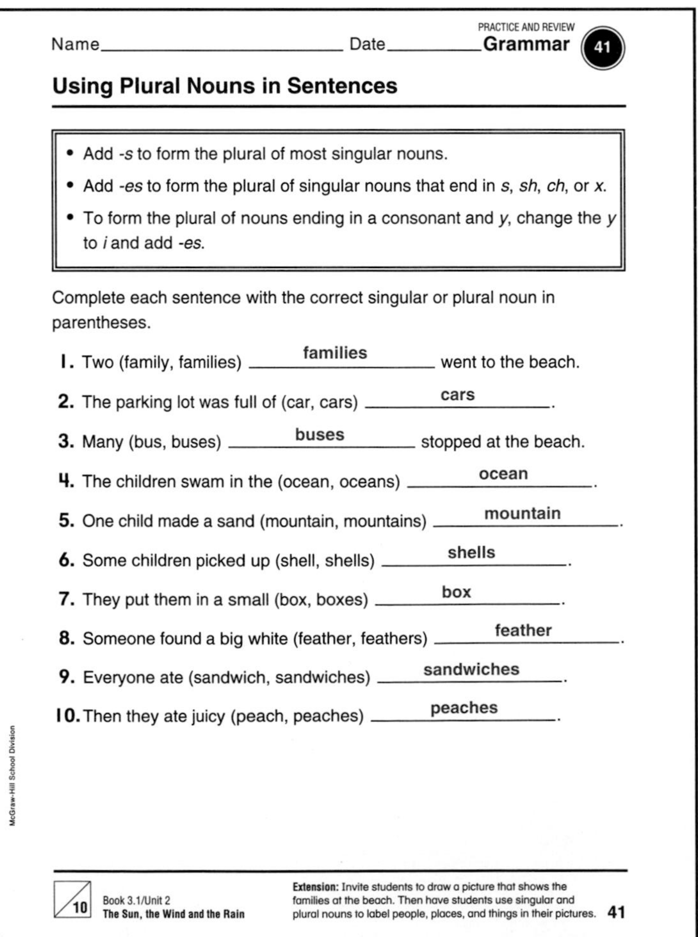

Name __________ Date __________ PRACTICE AND REVIEW Grammar 41

Using Plural Nouns in Sentences

> - Add *-s* to form the plural of most singular nouns.
> - Add *-es* to form the plural of singular nouns that end in *s, sh, ch,* or *x.*
> - To form the plural of nouns ending in a consonant and *y,* change the *y* to *i* and add *-es.*

Complete each sentence with the correct singular or plural noun in parentheses.

1. Two (family, families) **families** went to the beach.
2. The parking lot was full of (car, cars) **cars**.
3. Many (bus, buses) **buses** stopped at the beach.
4. The children swam in the (ocean, oceans) **ocean**.
5. One child made a sand (mountain, mountains) **mountain**.
6. Some children picked up (shell, shells) **shells**.
7. They put them in a small (box, boxes) **box**.
8. Someone found a big white (feather, feathers) **feather**.
9. Everyone ate (sandwich, sandwiches) **sandwiches**.
10. Then they ate juicy (peach, peaches) **peaches**.

McGraw-Hill School Division

10 Book 3.1/Unit 2 The Sun, the Wind and the Rain

Extension: Invite students to draw a picture that shows the families at the beach. Then have students use singular and plural nouns to label people, places, and things in their pictures.

41

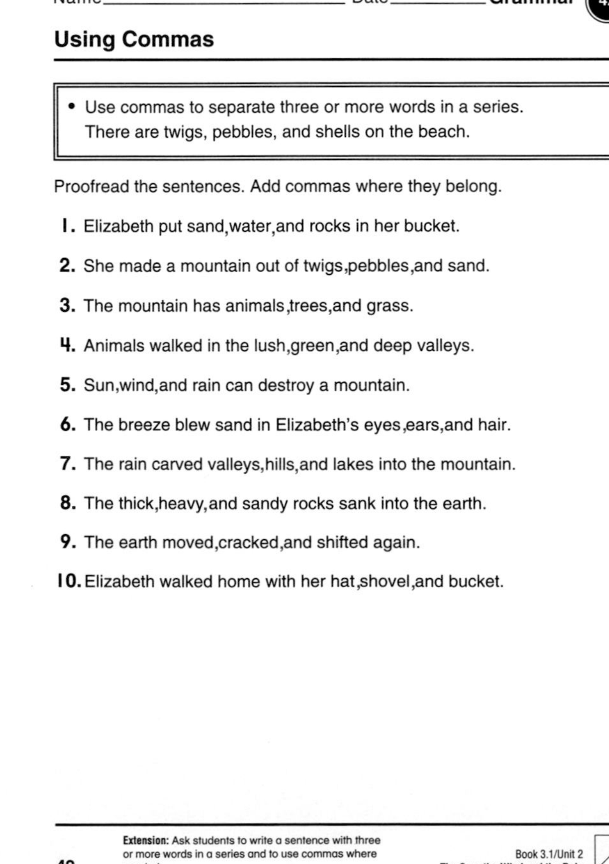

Name __________ Date __________ MECHANICS Grammar 42

Using Commas

> - Use commas to separate three or more words in a series.
> There are twigs, pebbles, and shells on the beach.

Proofread the sentences. Add commas where they belong.

1. Elizabeth put sand,water,and rocks in her bucket.
2. She made a mountain out of twigs,pebbles,and sand.
3. The mountain has animals,trees,and grass.
4. Animals walked in the lush,green,and deep valleys.
5. Sun,wind,and rain can destroy a mountain.
6. The breeze blew sand in Elizabeth's eyes,ears,and hair.
7. The rain carved valleys,hills,and lakes into the mountain.
8. The thick,heavy,and sandy rocks sank into the earth.
9. The earth moved,cracked,and shifted again.
10. Elizabeth walked home with her hat,shovel,and bucket.

McGraw-Hill School Division

42

Extension: Ask students to write a sentence with three or more words in a series and to use commas where needed.

Book 3.1/Unit 2 The Sun, the Wind and the Rain 10

Name_______________ Date__________ TEST Grammar 43

Singular and Plural Nouns

A. Read the nouns. Find the noun that is singular. Mark your answer.

1. ⓐ rocks ⓑ trees ● pool ⓓ pebbles

2. ⓐ breezes ● twig ⓒ grains ⓓ mountains

3. ● pass ⓑ canyons ⓒ layers ⓓ cracks

4. ⓐ steps ⓑ cars ● bus ⓓ eons

B. Read each sentence. Find the correct plural form for the noun in parentheses.

5. The (peak) were sharp. ⓐ peakes ⓑ peakies ● peaks ⓓ peak

6. The (beach) were sandy. ⓐ beachs ● beaches ⓒ beach ⓓ beachies

7. The (sky) were blue. ● skies ⓑ skys ⓒ skis ⓓ skyes

8. The (pebble) were wet. ● pebbles ⓑ pebblees ⓒ pebblies ⓓ pebble

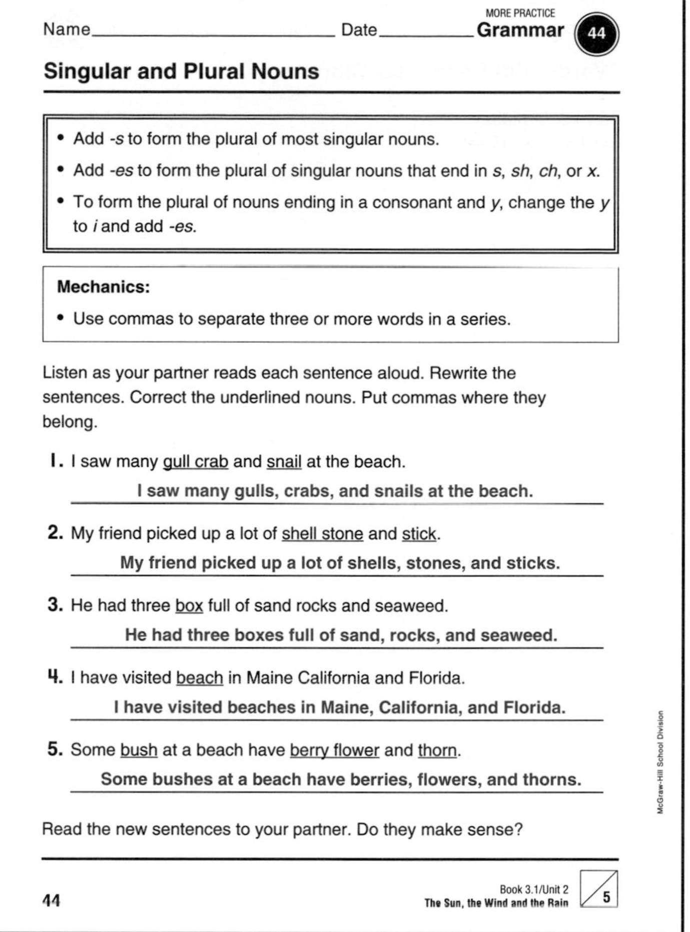

Name_______________ Date__________ MORE PRACTICE Grammar 44

Singular and Plural Nouns

- Add *-s* to form the plural of most singular nouns.
- Add *-es* to form the plural of singular nouns that end in *s, sh, ch,* or *x*.
- To form the plural of nouns ending in a consonant and *y*, change the *y* to *i* and add *-es*.

Mechanics:

- Use commas to separate three or more words in a series.

Listen as your partner reads each sentence aloud. Rewrite the sentences. Correct the underlined nouns. Put commas where they belong.

1. I saw many <u>gull crab</u> and <u>snail</u> at the beach.
I saw many gulls, crabs, and snails at the beach.

2. My friend picked up a lot of <u>shell stone</u> and <u>stick</u>.
My friend picked up a lot of shells, stones, and sticks.

3. He had three <u>box</u> full of sand rocks and seaweed.
He had three boxes full of sand, rocks, and seaweed.

4. I have visited <u>beach</u> in Maine California and Florida.
I have visited beaches in Maine, California, and Florida.

5. Some <u>bush</u> at a beach have <u>berry flower</u> and <u>thorn</u>.
Some bushes at a beach have berries, flowers, and thorns.

Read the new sentences to your partner. Do they make sense?

Name________ Date PRETEST SPELLING **39**

Words with Consonant Clusters

Pretest Directions
Fold back the paper along the dotted line. Use the blanks to write each word as it is read aloud. When you finish the test, unfold the paper. Use the list at the right to correct any spelling mistakes. Practice the words you missed for the Posttest.

1. ____________	1. block
2. ____________	2. brake
3. ____________	3. crazy
4. ____________	4. flash
5. ____________	5. grab
6. ____________	6. plate
7. ____________	7. blink
8. ____________	8. broad
9. ____________	9. crumble
10. ____________	10. flood
11. ____________	11. grand
12. ____________	12. blind
13. ____________	13. brisk
14. ____________	14. flame
15. ____________	15. plenty
Challenge Words	
____________	canyons
____________	flowed
____________	grains
____________	handful
____________	peaks

To Parents
Here are the results of your child's weekly spelling Pretest. You can help your child study for the Posttest by following these simple steps for each word on the word list:

1. Read the word to your child.
2. Have your child write the word, saying each letter as it is written.
3. Say each letter of the word as your child checks the spelling.
4. If a mistake has been made, have your child read each letter of the correctly spelled word aloud, and then repeat steps 1-3.

Name________ Date________ AT-HOME WORD STUDY SPELLING **40**

Words with Consonant Clusters

Using the Word Study Steps

1. LOOK at the word.
2. SAY the word aloud.
3. STUDY the letters in the word.
4. WRITE the word.
5. CHECK the word.
   Did you spell the word right?
   If not, go back to step 1.

Spelling Tip
Use words that you know how to spell to help you spell new words:
black + rock = block

Make Complete Words
Use the letters in the boxes to begin words.
Circle the word endings that will correctly form spelling words.

bl		br		cr		fl		gr		pl	
ock	ink	ake	isk	azy	ode	isk	ame	ash	ick	ame	enty
isk	ash	ish	ock	ope	ame	ink	ash	osh	and	ock	ate
	ind		oad	umble		ood			ab		ind

To Parents or Helpers:
Using the Word Study Steps above as your child comes across any new words will help him or her spell well. Review the steps as you both go over this week's spelling words.
Go over the Spelling Tip with your child. Ask your child to think of other words he or she knows how to spell. Help him or her spell new words with the help of other words your child already knows.
Help your child find and circle the spelling words in the puzzle.

Name________ Date________ EXPLORE THE PATTERN SPELLING **41**

Words with Consonant Clusters

block	flash	blink	flood	brisk
brake	grab	broad	grand	flame
crazy	plate	crumble	blind	plenty

Pattern Power!
Write the spelling words that have these spelling patterns.

bl
1. block
2. blink
3. blind

br
4. brake
5. broad
6. brisk

cr
7. crazy
8. crumble

fl
9. flash
10. flood
11. flame

gr
12. grab
13. grand

pl
14. plate
15. plenty

Words Within Words
Write the spelling word that contains the small word.

16. risk brisk
17. and grand
18. lock block
19. ate plate
20. ash flash
21. ink blink
22. rake brake
23. lent plenty
24. am flame
25. road broad

Name________ Date________ PRACTICE AND EXTEND SPELLING **42**

Words with Consonant Clusters

block	flash	blink	flood	brisk
brake	grab	broad	grand	flame
crazy	plate	crumble	blind	plenty

Fill in the Blanks
Complete each sentence with a word from the spelling list.

1. I washed the plate in the sink.
2. Because of the flood, the basement had two feet of water.
3. The driver pulled the emergency brake to stop the train.
4. A crispy cookie will crumble into tiny bits.
5. The flame from the oil lamp glowed yellow and red.
6. The prince and princess had a grand time at the ball.
7. Watch the thief grab the wallet and run!
8. In total darkness, a person is blind.
9. Did the prisoner have a sound mind or was he crazy?
10. The flash of lightning was followed by thunder.

"B" Matches
Write a spelling word that begins with the letter b to match each word clue.

11. moving quickly brisk
12. wide broad
13. stop block
14. without the sense of sight blind
15. a quick wink of an eye blink

Challenge Extension: Write the Challenge Words on the board in scrambled order and ask students to write them in ABC order.

Name____________________ Date__________ PROOFREAD AND WRITE **SPELLING 43**

Words with Consonant Clusters

Proofreading Activity

There are six spelling mistakes in these directions. Circle the misspelled words. Write the words correctly on the lines below.

If you plan to travel by foot:

1. Go one blauk west.
2. Walk at a brissk pace.
3. Then skip across the brawd avenue.
4. Never mind, grabb a taxi instead!

If you plan to travel by car:

5. Slam on the emergency brak when you reach the driveway.
6. Then flasch your headlights three times.

1. block 2. brisk 3. broad

4. grab 5. brake 6. flash

Writing Activity

Write a set of directions telling how to get to a certain place. You could explain, for example, how to get to your school or to your nearest library. Number each step. Use at least four spelling words.

____

____

____

____

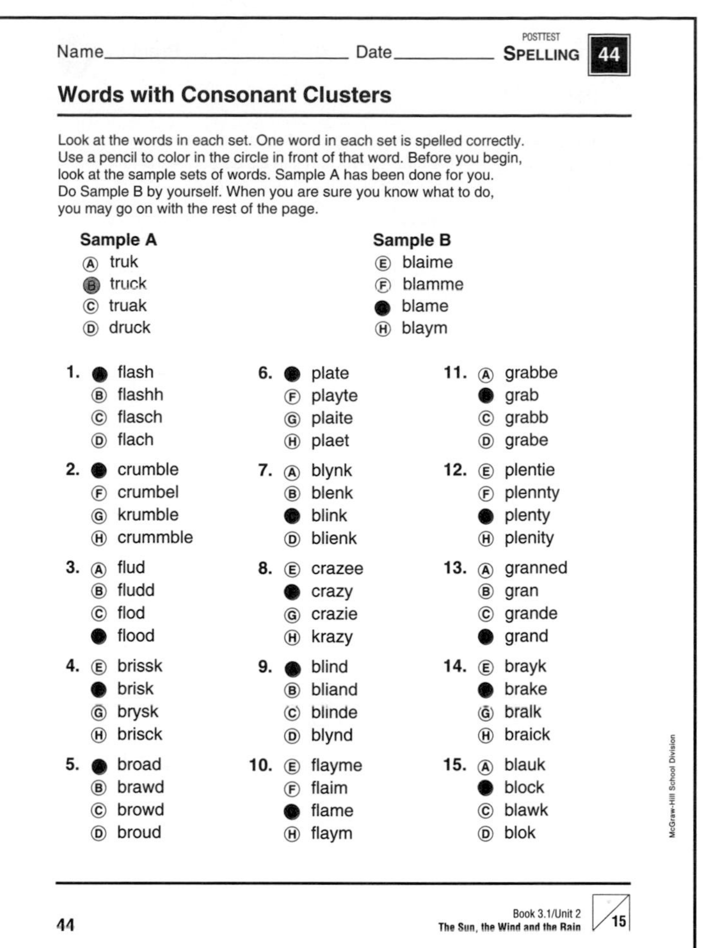

Name____________________ Date__________ POSTTEST **SPELLING 44**

Words with Consonant Clusters

Look at the words in each set. One word in each set is spelled correctly. Use a pencil to color in the circle in front of that word. Before you begin, look at the sample sets of words. Sample A has been done for you. Do Sample B by yourself. When you are sure you know what to do, you may go on with the rest of the page.

Sample A
- Ⓐ truk
- ● truck
- Ⓒ truak
- Ⓓ druck

Sample B
- Ⓔ blaime
- Ⓕ blamme
- ● blame
- Ⓗ blaym

1. ● flash, Ⓑ flashh, Ⓒ flasch, Ⓓ flach
2. ● crumble, Ⓕ crumbel, Ⓖ krumble, Ⓗ crummble
3. Ⓐ flud, Ⓑ fludd, Ⓒ flod, ● flood
4. Ⓔ brissk, ● brisk, Ⓖ brysk, Ⓗ brisck
5. ● broad, Ⓑ brawd, Ⓒ browd, Ⓓ broud
6. ● plate, Ⓕ playte, Ⓖ plaite, Ⓗ plaet
7. Ⓐ blynk, Ⓑ blenk, ● blink, Ⓓ blienk
8. Ⓔ crazee, ● crazy, Ⓖ crazie, Ⓗ krazy
9. ● blind, Ⓑ bliand, Ⓒ blinde, Ⓓ blynd
10. Ⓔ flayme, Ⓕ flaim, ● flame, Ⓗ flaym
11. Ⓐ grabbe, ● grab, Ⓒ grabb, Ⓓ grabe
12. Ⓔ plentie, Ⓕ plennty, ● plenty, Ⓗ plenity
13. Ⓐ granned, Ⓑ gran, Ⓒ grande, ● grand
14. Ⓔ brayk, ● brake, Ⓖ bralk, Ⓗ braick
15. Ⓐ blauk, ● block, Ⓒ blawk, Ⓓ blok

Dream Wolf • PRACTICE

Name______ Date______ **Practice 52**

Cause and Effect

A **cause** is what makes something happen. The **effect** is what happens as a result of the cause. You can use cause and effect to help you make predictions about what might happen next.

Read each paragraph. Write the cause that made the effect happen. Then write a sentence to make a prediction. **Predictions may vary.**

Jack grew apples to sell at the market. This year the apples were perfect. They had not been eaten by worms. Jack had found a new way to keep the worms away.

1. **Cause:** **Jack had used a new way to keep the worms away.**
2. **Effect:** The apples were perfect and hadn't been filled with worms.
3. **Predict** what Jack will do next year: **He may sell his idea for keeping worms away to other apple farmers.**

Anna decided to eat her lunch outside. She sat on a bench and took out her sandwich. Suddenly she heard a buzzing sound. There was a bee flying around Anna. The bee wanted a bite of her sandwich.

4. **Cause:** **Anna takes out her sandwich.**
5. **Effect:** A bee is buzzing around Anna.
6. **Predict** what Anna will do for lunch tomorrow: **She may eat her sandwich inside.**

At Home: Have students predict what they would do if they were ten feet tall.

Name______ Date______ **Practice 53**

Vocabulary

Identify and write down clues to the meaning of the underlined word in each question.

1. The buffalo, a large, furry animal with a hump on its back, is in danger of becoming extinct. **large, furry animal with a hump on its back**
2. The darkness of night was all around us, and there was no light to be seen. **night, no light**
3. Did the way the echoes of my voice bounced off the mountain make me seem far away? **bounced off the mountain**
4. As groups of animals traveled together across the plains, the noise the herd made was like thunder. **groups of animals traveled together**
5. The berries were ripe and juicy now that they were ready to eat. **juicy, ready to eat**
6. To protect themselves from the sun, the two girls decided to shelter under a beach umbrella. **to protect themselves from the sun, under a beach umbrella**

At Home: Have students make up a crossword puzzle using the vocabulary words. Have them write a clue for each word.

A Return to Home

Long ago, a young *buffalo* walked across the Great Plains. As *darkness* came, she began to look for *shelter.* The buffalo called out for someone to help her find a place to sleep. But all she could hear were the *echoes* of her own voice.

The buffalo grew hungry. She ate some sweet, *ripe* berries. She also ate some small plants.

Suddenly, she saw another buffalo. She followed the other buffalo. The buffalo led her to a place where several *herds* rested together.

When some of the herd saw the newcomer, they gave her food. They also made a space where she could sleep.

1. What did the *buffalo* begin to look for? **shelter**
2. What did the *buffalo* hear when she called out? **the echoes of her own voice**
3. Why were the berries the *buffalo* ate sweet? **They were ripe.**
4. In what kind of groups do *buffalo* live? **herds**
5. Why did the young *buffalo* follow the other *buffalo*? **She hoped he would lead her to shelter.**

At Home: Invite students to talk about a story they like that has animals as characters.

Name______ Date______ **Practice 54**

Story Comprehension

Think about the story of Tiblo and Tanksi in "Dream Wolf." Then answer each question below. **Answers will vary.**

QUESTIONS	ANSWERS
SETTINGS Where does the story take place?	1. the hills 2. the wolf's den 3. camp
CHARACTERS Who are the main characters?	4. Tiblo 5. Tanksi 6. the wolf
PLOT What problem do Tiblo and Tanksi face?	7. When they climb into the hills, they become lost.
EVENTS Where do Tiblo and Tanksi spend the night? What happens there?	8. They spend the night in a wolf's cave. Tiblo dreams about a wolf, who really does sleep with them and keeps them warm.
What happens when Tiblo wakes up and sees the wolf?	9. Tiblo asks the wolf to help them find the way back to camp.
CONCLUSION How does the story end?	10. The wolf leads them back to camp, where everyone is happy to see them.

At Home: Have students illustrate a scene from "Dream Wolf."

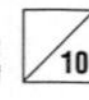

Name________________ Date__________ Practice 55

Use an Encyclopedia

Natural Bridge—Navigation

Natural Bridge is a bridge made from stone by nature. Wind or rain or rivers carved away the stone over many years. Usually softer stone is removed from under harder stone. A bridge of harder stone is all that remains.

Nauru is a small island country in the Pacific Ocean. It is the third smallest nation in the world. Monaco and Vatican City are smaller. It's greatest resource is phosphate, a substance used to make fertilizer.

Navajo, a Native American group who have lived in the southwestern United States since around 1000 A.D. They are the largest Native American group in the United States. Many members still live in houses called hogans, made of earth and logs. See also Indian, American

Naval Reserve. See Navy, United States

Fill in the blank spaces below based on the encyclopedia page.

Entry Words:

Natural bridge

Nauru

Navajo

Naval Reserve

Cross-References:

See also Indian, American

See Navy, United States

Guide Words:

Natural bridge

navigation

At Home: Ask students if they would look on this page for information about narwhal whales. Why or why not?

Name________________ Date__________ Practice 56

Cause and Effect

In "Dream Wolf," things happen that cause other events to occur. Answer the following questions about **cause** and **effect**.

1. Why do the people move from the plains to the hills and valleys? The berry bushes are ripe in the valleys.
2. What did Tiblo do when he became tired of picking berries? He decided to sneak off into the hills with Tanksi.
3. What effect did the sun going down have on the two children? They got lost.
4. While the children slept, a wolf came into the cave and kept them warm. What effect did this have on Tiblo's dreams? It caused Tiblo to have a dream about a wolf.
5. The wolf led the children back to their camp. What did the children then ask the wolf? They asked the wolf to live with them.
6. What did the people in the camp do when they saw the children coming down the hill? They galloped out on horses to bring the children home.
7. What has caused wolves to disappear from the hills where they used to live? Hunters have killed the wolves and driven them away.
8. When do the people say the wolves will return? When we have the wolves in our hearts and dreams again.

At Home: Have students draw a picture of a wolf.

Name________________ Date__________ Practice 57

Compare and Contrast

When you **compare** and **contrast** two things, you point out how they are the same and how they are different.

Look at the picture. Then answer the questions. **Answers may vary.**

1. Name two ways that Sam and Frankie look alike. They are both dogs; they both have four legs and shaggy hair.
2. Name two ways that Sam and Frankie look different. Sam is taller than Frankie; Sam has spots while Frankie is one color; Sam has small pointed ears while Frankie's ears are long and droopy.
3. What is the same about what the two dogs are doing? They are both chewing on something.
4. What is different about what the two dogs are doing? Sam is chewing a bone while Frankie is chewing a ball.

At Home: Have students organize their observations of Sam and Frankie into a two-column chart. Label the columns "Alike" and "Different."

Name________________ Date__________ Practice 58

Context Clues

Context clues are words or sentences that can help you find the meaning of an unfamiliar word. You may find context clues in the text before or after the unfamiliar word.

Read the selection. Write a definition for each word or term.

There are more kinds of plants and animals living in the warm, wet rain forests than anywhere else on Earth. It is interesting to know how a rain forest works and why it is always so moist. The leaves of the trees catch rain. The rain then travels down the stems to the ground. The ground absorbs most of the water and the rest goes into rivers and streams. Under the ground, the roots of the trees absorb the water in the soil. Then the roots send the water up the trunk of each tree, out into its branches, and into its leaves. If you stand on the ground in a rain forest and look up, all you can see is leaves. The trees' leaves collect so much water that clouds form above them. The clouds fall again as rain. When it rains, the pattern begins all over again, with the leaves catching the rain.

1. **rain forest** — a warm, wet forest where many different kinds of plants and animals live
2. **moist** — damp, wet
3. **absorbs** — soak up, take in
4. **soil** — earth
5. **pattern** — something that happens over and over again

At Home: Ask students to use some of the new words in sentences.

Dream Wolf • RETEACH

Name____________________ Date__________ **Reteach 52**

Cause and Effect

The **cause** is what makes something happen. The **effect** is what happens as a result of that cause.

Place an **X** next to the effect that best fits the cause. To help you find the effect, add the word "so" after the cause and see if the effect makes sense.

Cause	Effect
1. Jack trained the dogs well.	X The dogs do what Jack tells them to do. ___ The dogs have thick fur coats.
2. The dogs have to be strong enough to pull a sled.	___ Each sled is pulled by eight dogs. X The dogs eat a lot of food.
3. The dogs have thick fur coats.	___ Each group of dogs has a leader. X The dogs are able to live in the coldest places.
4. Jack and his dogs won the sled race.	___ Jack's friends have a sled race every year. X They all received blue ribbons.

At Home: Ask each student to write a paragraph about an animal that includes a cause-and-effect relationship.

Name____________________ Date__________ **Reteach 53**

Vocabulary

buffalo	darkness	echoes	herds	ripe	shelter

Write the word from the box that best completes the sentences.

Little Moon found __shelter__ from the rain under a tree. Big black clouds covered the land in __darkness__. To pass the time, Little Moon ate some __ripe__ corn she carried in her pocket. She listened to the __echoes__ the thunder made in the canyons. Little Moon watched __herds__ of __buffalo__ that were so far away they looked like little brown horses.

6

Story Comprehension

Reteach 54

Answer the following questions about "Dream Wolf."

1. How do Tiblo and Tanski get lost? __They climb the hills, and when it gets dark, they can't find their way home.__
2. Why isn't the boy afraid of the wolf beside the stream? __He had dreamed of a wolf the night before. The wolf kept Tiblo and Tanski warm.__
3. How does the wolf help the lost children? __He leads them home.__
4. How do the people treat the wolf after the children return? __They bring him a blanket and give him necklaces and other gifts.__

At Home: Ask the students to draw a picture illustrating something that happened to Tiblo and Tanski in "Dream Wolf."

Name____________________ Date__________ **Reteach 55**

Use an Encyclopedia

An **encyclopedia** gives you information on different subjects. Bigger encyclopedias are divided into separate books. The topics inside each book are listed in alphabetical order.

1	2	3	4	5	6	7	8	9	10	11	12	13	14	15	16	17	18	19	20	21	22	23	24
A	B	C	D	E	F	G	H	I	J	K	L	M	N	O	P	Q/R	S–Sn	So–Sz	T	U	V	W/X Y/Z	Index

Use the letters on the encyclopedias to help you answer these questions.

1. What is the number of the book where a word beginning with the letter **B** could be found? __2__
2. Which book has topics that begin with the letters **Q** and **R**? __17 or Q/R__
3. What book would tell you about Native Americans? __14 or N__
4. Would South Dakota and Squirrels be in the **S–Sn** or the **So–Sz** book? __the So–Sz book__
5. Which book contains a listing of all the topics found in the other books? __the index__

At Home: Have students list five subjects and then write the number and letter of the book where each could be found.

Name____________________ Date__________ **Reteach 56**

Cause and Effect

In a story, events cause other events to happen. Events also affect how characters respond. The following example shows a **cause** and its **effect.**

Cause	Effect
People drive away the wolves.	People don't hear the wolf call in summer anymore.

Think about what happened in "Dream Wolf." Then read each cause before writing down the effect it had.

1. **Cause:** The berries in the valleys get ripe at the end of each summer. What effect does this have on the people living on the plains?
   Effect: __The people leave the plains to camp near the berry bushes.__
2. **Cause:** The boy and girl are tired of picking fruit with their mother. What do they do?
   Effect: __They climb into the hills.__
3. **Cause:** The sun went down while the children were up in the hills. How does the darkness affect the children?
   Effect: __The darkness causes the children to get lost.__
4. **Cause:** The boy has a good dream about a wolf. How does this dream affect how the boy feels when he sees a wolf?
   Effect: __When the boy sees a wolf the next day, he is not afraid to ask for help.__

At Home: Ask students to tell you what might cause the wolves to come back to the land described in "Dream Wolf."

Name________________ Date__________ **Reteach 57**

Compare and Contrast

To **compare** and **contrast** means to point out how things are the same and how they are different.

Read the story. Then use the information to write how things are alike and different.

Dogs and cats make good pets. One reason people like them is that they like to pet them. People care for dogs and cats by washing and brushing them, feeding them, and helping them when they are sick.

People who live in small places might like having a cat instead of a dog. Cats are smaller and you don't need to take them out for walks. Their "meow" can be very funny. Some people like dogs because they bark when strangers come near. Having a dog makes them feel safe.

Cats and dogs like to play as much as children do. Dogs chase sticks and balls and like to dig. People can even teach them tricks. Cats chase mice and climb up trees. Sometimes cats seem to pretend to chase things just for fun.

1. What sizes are dogs and cats? **Dogs are bigger than cats.**
2. What sounds do dogs and cats make? **Dogs bark, and cats meow.**
3. How do dogs and cats play? **Dogs chase sticks and balls. Cats chase mice and climb.**
4. How do people take care of dogs and cats? **People feed, brush, clean, and play with them.**

At Home: Ask the students to compare and contrast two animals that they know about.

Name________________ Date__________ **Reteach 58**

Context Clues

Context clues are the words or sentences before or after an unfamiliar word that can help explain what the word means. Sometimes a writer uses synonyms for a word. Synonyms can help you figure out what the new word means.

Read each sentence. Find a word or words in the sentence that helps explain the meaning of the new word. Write the meaning on the line.

	Sentence	New Word	Meaning
1.	The girl was lazy and was not willing to walk fast.	lazy	not willing to walk fast
2.	The parents and other adults came to watch the children's play.	adults	grown-up people
3.	Jack wiggled and squirmed when his mother tried to dress him.	squirmed	wiggled
4.	The street was full of old tires and other trash and rubbish.	rubbish	trash
5.	They used the machine to make bread and produce bakery goods.	produce	make
6.	He dragged and shuffled his feet all the way home.	shuffled	dragged

At Home: Ask students to use each of the new words in a sentence.

Dream Wolf • EXTEND

Name________________________ Date__________ **Extend 52**

Cause and Effect

Answers will vary. Sample answers are given.

Look at the pictures below. Each one shows a cause. Write a story about each picture that gives a possible effect.

The snow will pile high and children will go sledding.

The baby bird will learn to fly and leave the nest.

The soccer player will make a goal and his or her team will win.

McGraw-Hill School Division

Book 3.1/Unit 2
Dream Wolf

At Home: Have students read their stories. Ask them to think of another way each story could end. Have them write a new ending showing the new effect.

52

Name________________________ Date__________ **Extend 53**

Vocabulary

Answers will vary. Sample answers are given.

Write clues for the words in the crossword puzzle.

Across

1. **No light.**
3. **Protection.**
5. **Groups of animals.**
6. **North American bison.**

Down

2. **Ready to eat.**
4. **Repeats**

Crossword answers: 1 Across DARKNESS; 2 Down RIPE; 3 Across SHELTER; 4 Down ECHOES; 5 Across HERDS; 6 Across BUFFALO

Extend 54

Story Comprehension

Decide if Tiblo and Tanksi ever meet the wolf again. Write and illustrate a story about what you think happened after the wolf left. Tell about the next adventure that you think Tiblo and Tanksi had.

McGraw-Hill School Division

53–54

At Home: Ask students if they have heard other stories about animals who have helped people. What were they about?

Book 3.1/Unit 2
Dream Wolf

Name________________________ Date__________ **Extend 55**

Use an Encyclopedia

You and your family are on the way to pick berries to make pies and cakes. You want to make sure you get berries that will be sweet and tasty. You also want to make sure that any berries you pick can be used in food.

Here are some different kinds of berries you could pick. Describe how you would find out about each one in an encyclopedia. Then pick one of these berries to research in your school library's encyclopedia. Write what you find out on another piece of paper.

- boysenberry
- elderberry
- strawberry
- blackberry
- raspberry

Let's Go Berry-Picking

Answers will vary, but should demonstrate understanding of how to look up a subject in an encyclopedia.

McGraw-Hill School Division

Book 3.1/Unit 2
Dream Wolf

At Home: Have students research information about wolves.

55

Name________________________ Date__________ **Extend 56**

Cause and Effect

Many things happen in the fall as the temperature changes. No matter where you live, the change in temperature and amount of sun cause things to happen. Describe some of the effects that fall causes where you live.

1. About what time does the sun set at the beginning of August where you live? **Answers will vary. Sample answers are shown.**

   About what time does the sun set at the beginning of October?

2. Describe some effects that the change in temperature and the amount of sunlight has on plants where you live.

   The leaves fall.
   The flowers stop blooming.
   Fruit ripens.

3. Describe some effects that fall has on animals where you live.

   Birds fly south.
   Animals hibernate.
   Squirrels hide nuts.

4. Write a paragraph that tells what happens in the fall to plants, animals, and you.

McGraw-Hill School Division

56

At Home: Have students describe what happens to the plants where they live between October and January.

Book 3.1/Unit 2
Dream Wolf

Dream Wolf • EXTEND

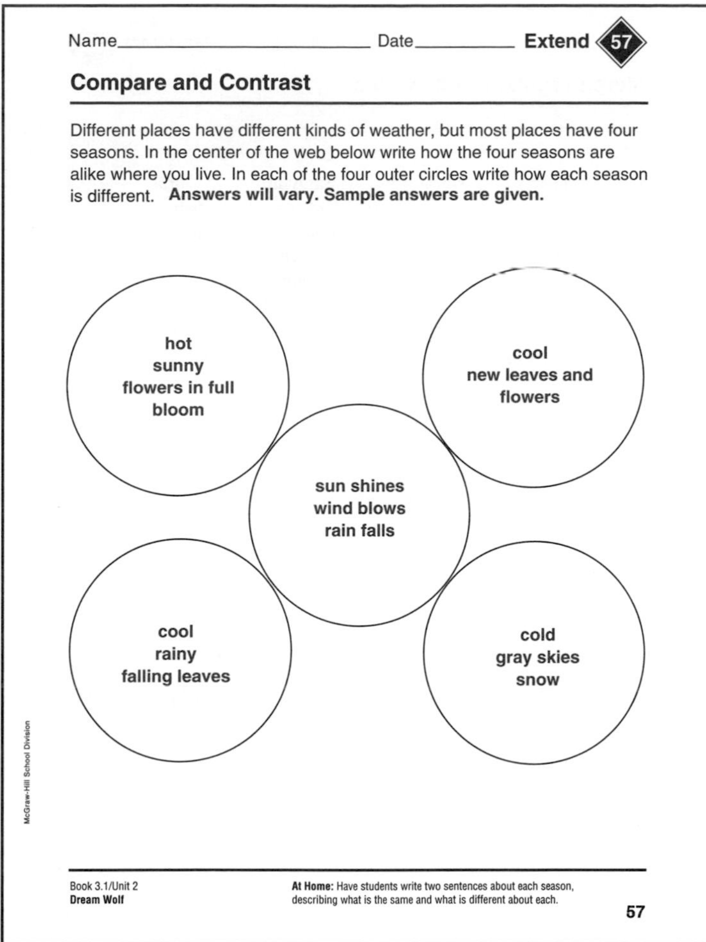

Name________________________ Date__________ Extend 57

Compare and Contrast

Different places have different kinds of weather, but most places have four seasons. In the center of the web below write how the four seasons are alike where you live. In each of the four outer circles write how each season is different. **Answers will vary. Sample answers are given.**

hot
sunny
flowers in full bloom

cool
new leaves and flowers

sun shines
wind blows
rain falls

cool
rainy
falling leaves

cold
gray skies
snow

At Home: Have students write two sentences about each season, describing what is the same and what is different about each.

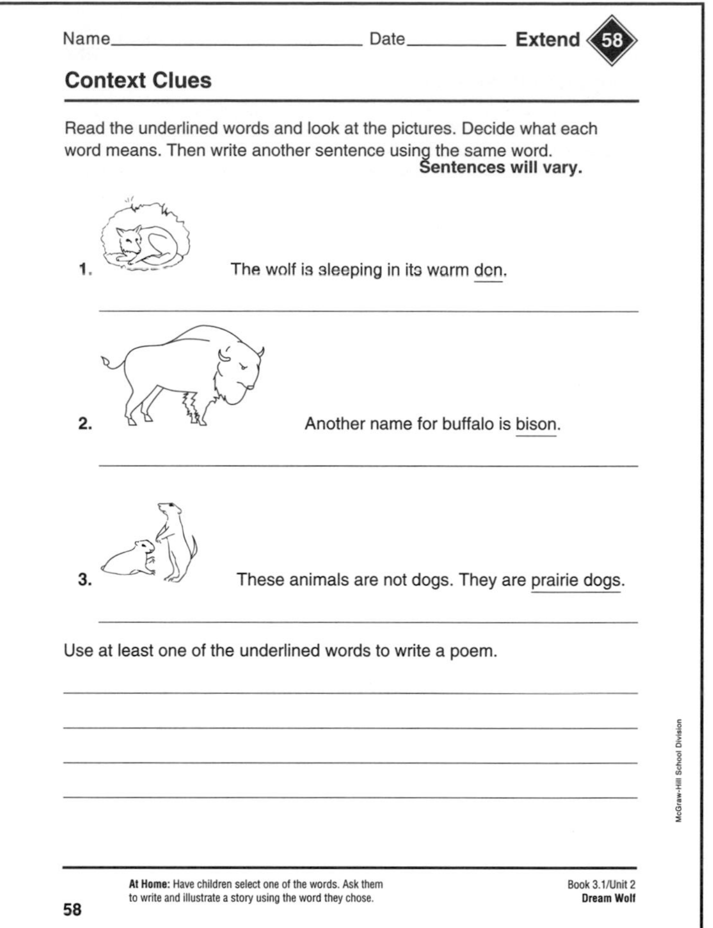

Name________________________ Date__________ Extend 58

Context Clues

Read the underlined words and look at the pictures. Decide what each word means. Then write another sentence using the same word. **Sentences will vary.**

1. The wolf is sleeping in its warm den.

2. Another name for buffalo is bison.

3. These animals are not dogs. They are prairie dogs.

Use at least one of the underlined words to write a poem.

At Home: Have children select one of the words. Ask them to write and illustrate a story using the word they chose.

Name______________ Date__________ LEARN Grammar 45

Irregular Plural Nouns

- Some nouns have special plural forms.

Draw a line from each noun to its plural form.

1. wolf	men
2. life	lives
3. man	women
4. woman	wolves
5. child	mice
6. foot	children
7. tooth	feet
8. mouse	calves
9. goose	teeth
10. calf	geese

10 Book 3.1/Unit 2 **Dream Wolf**

Extension: Have the class use the plurals on this page to tell a progressive story. Encourage each student to add a sentence to the story.

Name______________ Date__________ LEARN AND PRACTICE Grammar 46

More Irregular Plural Nouns

- A few nouns are the same in both singular and plural forms.

Singular	Plural	Singular	Plural
sheep	sheep	fish	fish
deer	deer	trout	trout
buffalo	buffalo	salmon	salmon
moose	moose	scissors	scissors

Complete each sentence with the correct plural form of the noun in parentheses.

1. The children saw bighorn (sheep) **sheep** in the hills.
2. I have seen (deer) **deer** in a forest.
3. The Wolf People followed a herd of (buffalo) **buffalo**.
4. I once saw two (moose) **moose**.
5. Some forests have streams with (fish) **fish**.
6. Rainbow (trout) **trout** live in streams.
7. I drew a picture of (salmon) **salmon** jumping in a stream.
8. When I find (scissors) **scissors**, I will cut it out.

Extension: Have pairs of students pantomime the animals on this page. Invite classmates to guess the animals, using the correct plural forms.

Book 3.1/Unit 2 **Dream Wolf** 8

Name______________ Date__________ PRACTICE AND REVIEW Grammar 47

Using Irregular Plural Nouns in Sentences

- Some nouns have special plural forms.
- A few nouns have the same singular and plural forms.

Rewrite the sentences. Change the underlined word to a plural noun.

1. The child left the berry-pickers.
   The children left the berry-pickers.
2. The woman made little cakes.
   The women made little cakes.
3. Bighorn sheep lived among the rocks.
   Bighorn sheep lived among the rocks.
4. These animals have foot made for climbing.
   These animals have feet made for climbing.
5. They can run faster than deer.
   They can run faster than deer.
6. The smiling wolf showed his tooth.
   The smiling wolf showed his teeth.
7. The man jumped on their horses.
   The men jumped on their horses.
8. People hope that wolf will return.
   People hope that wolves will return.

8 Book 3.1/Unit 2 **Dream Wolf**

Extension: Have students work cooperatively to draw a mural. Explain that the mural should show the sentences they wrote using plural nouns.

Name______________ Date__________ MECHANICS Grammar 48

Proofreading Sentences

- Every sentence begins with a capital letter.
- A statement ends with a period.
- A command ends with a period.
- An exclamation ends with an exclamation point.
- A question ends with a question mark.

Proofread the paragraph. Rewrite it correctly.

tiblo and his sister left the other children do you know what happened they got lost how scared they must have been a kind wolf helped them get home tell this story to your family

Tiblo and his sister left the other children. Do you know what happened? They got lost. How scared they must have been! A kind wolf helped them get home. Tell this story to your family.

Extension: Have students work in pairs. Ask each student to write a statement, command, exclamation, or question without a capital letter or end mark. Then have partners write each other's sentence correctly.

Book 3.1/Unit 2 **Dream Wolf** 12

Name________________________ Date__________ TEST Grammar 49

Irregular Plural Nouns

A. Decide if the underlined noun is singular or plural. Write your answer on the line.

1. The children came to a stream. plural
2. Trout live in some streams. plural
3. A trout is a kind of salmon. singular
4. Deer are quiet animals. plural
5. A wolf has sharp teeth. singular

B. Write **yes** if the plural form of the underlined noun is correct. Write **no** if it is not correct.

6. Tiblo stayed with the womans. No
7. He and his sister saw sheep. Yes
8. They did not see any mooses. No
9. The Wolf People heard wolves call. Yes
10. The cattle ate the grass. Yes

Name________________________ Date__________ MORE PRACTICE Grammar 50

Irregular Plural Nouns

- Some nouns have special plural forms.
- A few nouns have the same singular and plural forms.

Mechanics:
- Every sentence begins with a capital letter.
- A statement ends with a period.
- A command ends with a period.
- An exclamation ends with an exclamation point.
- A question ends with a question mark.

Look at the picture. Find the plural nouns in the paragraph that are wrong. Use the "take out" proofreading mark (ꝭ). Then write the correct forms. Draw three lines under each letter that should be a capital letter. Put in the missing end marks.

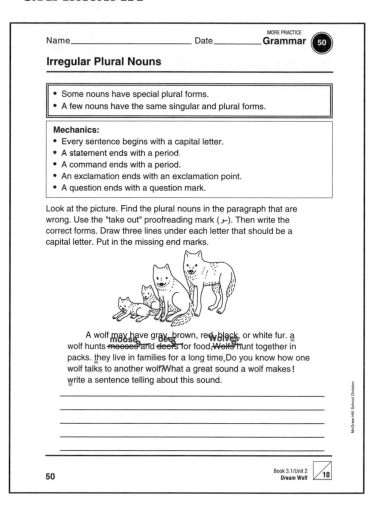

A wolf may have gray, brown, red, black, or white fur. a wolf hunts ~~mooses~~ moose and ~~deers~~ deer for food. ~~Wolfs~~ Wolves hunt together in packs. they live in families for a long time. Do you know how one wolf talks to another wolf? What a great sound a wolf makes! write a sentence telling about this sound.

____

____

____

____

____

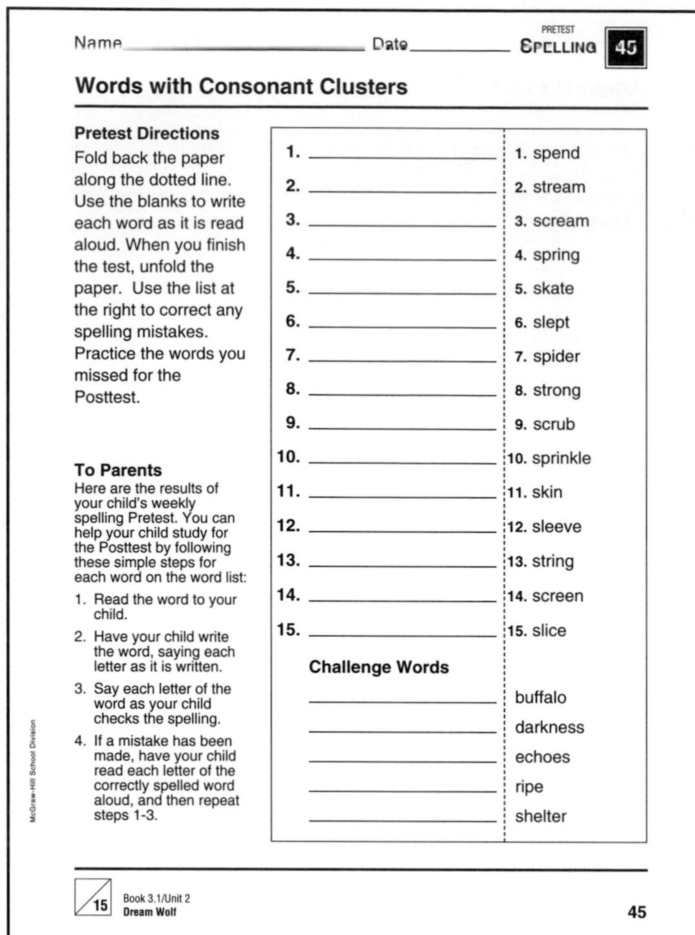

Name________________ Date__________ PRETEST SPELLING 45

Words with Consonant Clusters

Pretest Directions
Fold back the paper along the dotted line. Use the blanks to write each word as it is read aloud. When you finish the test, unfold the paper. Use the list at the right to correct any spelling mistakes. Practice the words you missed for the Posttest.

To Parents
Here are the results of your child's weekly spelling Pretest. You can help your child study for the Posttest by following these simple steps for each word on the word list:
1. Read the word to your child.
2. Have your child write the word, saying each letter as it is written.
3. Say each letter of the word as your child checks the spelling.
4. If a mistake has been made, have your child read each letter of the correctly spelled word aloud, and then repeat steps 1-3.

1.–15. ______

1. spend
2. stream
3. scream
4. spring
5. skate
6. slept
7. spider
8. strong
9. scrub
10. sprinkle
11. skin
12. sleeve
13. string
14. screen
15. slice

Challenge Words
buffalo
darkness
echoes
ripe
shelter

Name________________ Date__________ AT-HOME WORD STUDY SPELLING 46

Words with Consonant Clusters

Using the Word Study Steps
1. LOOK at the word.
2. SAY the word aloud.
3. STUDY the letters in the word.
4. WRITE the word.
5. CHECK the word.
Did you spell the word right?
If not, go back to step 1.

Spelling Tip
Become familiar with the dictionary and use it often.

Find and Circle
Where are the spelling words?

s	t	r	e	a	m	x	s	p	r	i	n	k	l	e	s	s	x
p	s	c	r	e	a	m	k	s	l	e	e	v	e	x	l	c	s
e	s	p	r	i	n	g	a	s	t	r	i	n	g	y	e	r	k
n	s	p	i	d	e	r	t	s	c	r	e	e	n	p	p	u	i
d	s	t	r	o	n	g	e	x	s	l	i	c	e	z	t	b	n

To Parents or Helpers:
Using the Word Study Steps above as your child comes across any new words will help him or her spell well.
Review the steps as you both go over this week's spelling words.
Go over the Spelling Tip with your child. Help your child learn to use the dictionary when he or she needs help with a word.
Help your child find and circle the spelling words in the puzzle.

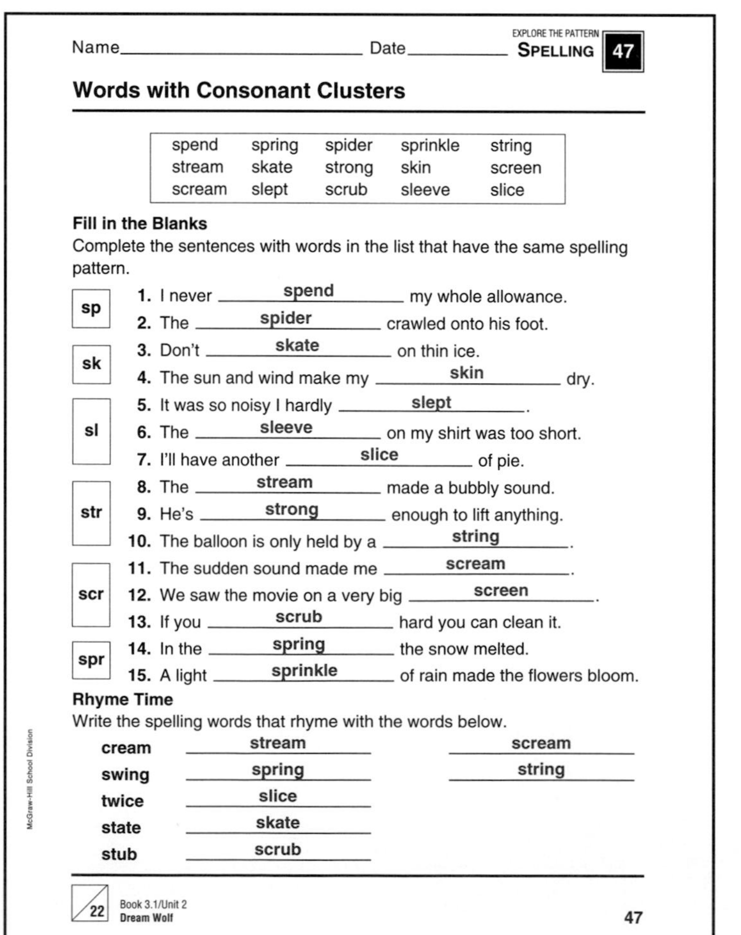

Name________________ Date__________ EXPLORE THE PATTERN SPELLING 47

Words with Consonant Clusters

spend	spring	spider	sprinkle	string
stream	skate	strong	skin	screen
scream	slept	scrub	sleeve	slice

Fill in the Blanks
Complete the sentences with words in the list that have the same spelling pattern.

sp
1. I never **spend** my whole allowance.
2. The **spider** crawled onto his foot.

sk
3. Don't **skate** on thin ice.
4. The sun and wind make my **skin** dry.

sl
5. It was so noisy I hardly **slept**.
6. The **sleeve** on my shirt was too short.
7. I'll have another **slice** of pie.

str
8. The **stream** made a bubbly sound.
9. He's **strong** enough to lift anything.
10. The balloon is only held by a **string**.

scr
11. The sudden sound made me **scream**.
12. We saw the movie on a very big **screen**.
13. If you **scrub** hard you can clean it.

spr
14. In the **spring** the snow melted.
15. A light **sprinkle** of rain made the flowers bloom.

Rhyme Time
Write the spelling words that rhyme with the words below.

cream **stream** **scream**
swing **spring** **string**
twice **slice**
state **skate**
stub **scrub**

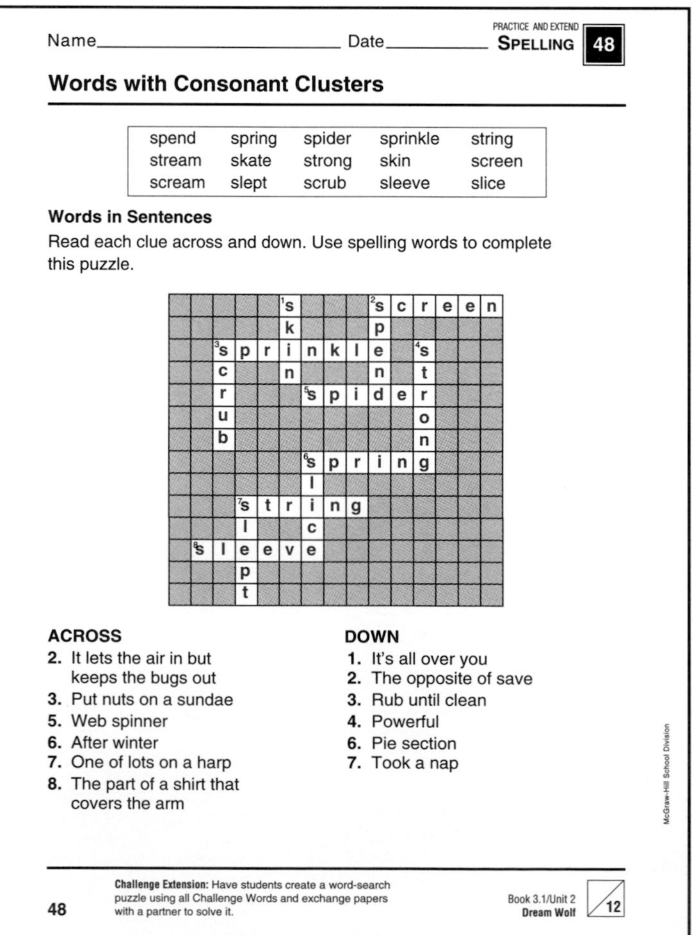

Name________________ Date__________ PRACTICE AND EXTEND SPELLING 48

Words with Consonant Clusters

spend	spring	spider	sprinkle	string
stream	skate	strong	skin	screen
scream	slept	scrub	sleeve	slice

Words in Sentences
Read each clue across and down. Use spelling words to complete this puzzle.

Across: 2 screen, 3 sprinkle, 5 spider, 6 spring, 7 string, 8 sleeve
Down: 1 skin, 2 spend, 3 scrub, 4 strong, 6 slice, 7 slept

ACROSS
2. It lets the air in but keeps the bugs out
3. Put nuts on a sundae
5. Web spinner
6. After winter
7. One of lots on a harp
8. The part of a shirt that covers the arm

DOWN
1. It's all over you
2. The opposite of save
3. Rub until clean
4. Powerful
6. Pie section
7. Took a nap

Challenge Extension: Have students create a word-search puzzle using all Challenge Words and exchange papers with a partner to solve it.

Name______________________ Date__________ PROOFREAD AND WRITE SPELLING **49**

Words with Consonant Clusters

Proofreading Activity

There are 6 spelling mistakes in this paragraph. Circle the misspelled words. Write the words correctly on the lines below.

Spring is a great time of year for Roger. He likes to spen time at the park. The trees have turned green with new leaves. Plants have started to bloom. Roger can scate along a special trail that takes him by the water. The streem looks inviting, but Roger knows it's too dangerous to play there. He'll just sprinckal some water on his face. The water feels cool on his scin and Roger wipes his face on his sleve Maybe later Roger will fly his kite.

1. spend 2. skate 3. stream

4. sprinkle 5. skin 6. sleeve

Writing Activity

What season of the year do you like best? Write about it. Explain what you like most about your favorite season. Use four words from your spelling list. Circle any words you use that have consonant clusters.

/10 Book 3.1/Unit 2 Dream Wolf

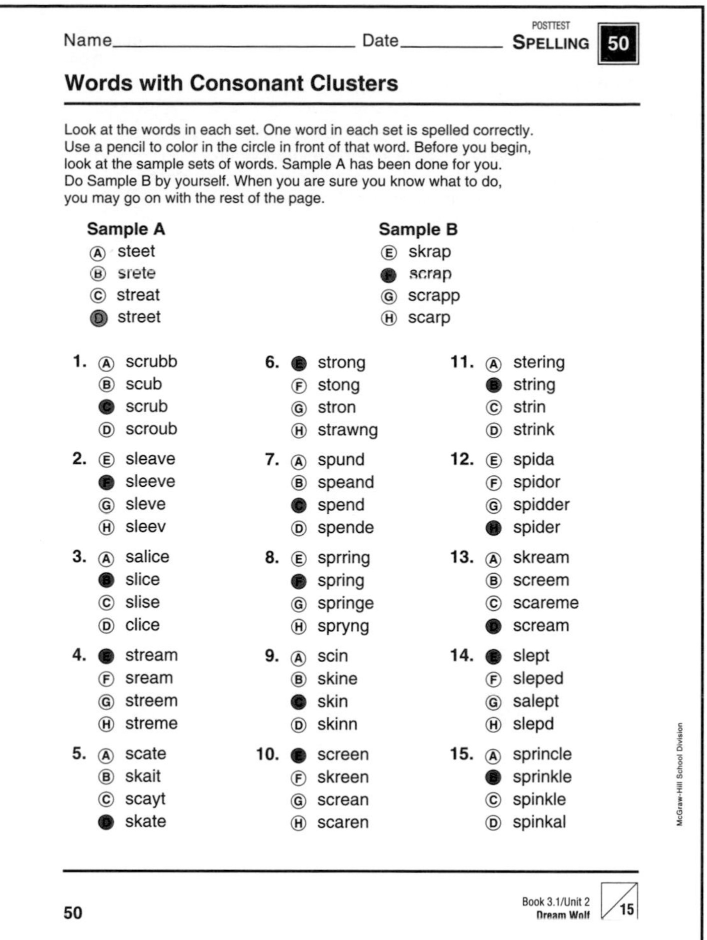

Name______________________ Date__________ POSTTEST SPELLING **50**

Words with Consonant Clusters

Look at the words in each set. One word in each set is spelled correctly. Use a pencil to color in the circle in front of that word. Before you begin, look at the sample sets of words. Sample A has been done for you. Do Sample B by yourself. When you are sure you know what to do, you may go on with the rest of the page.

Sample A
- Ⓐ steet
- Ⓑ srete
- Ⓒ streat
- ● street

Sample B
- Ⓔ skrap
- ● scrap
- Ⓖ scrapp
- Ⓗ scarp

1. Ⓐ scrubb Ⓑ scub ● scrub Ⓓ scroub
2. Ⓔ sleave ● sleeve Ⓖ sleve Ⓗ sleev
3. Ⓐ salice ● slice Ⓒ slise Ⓓ clice
4. ● stream Ⓕ sream Ⓖ streem Ⓗ streme
5. Ⓐ scate Ⓑ skait Ⓒ scayt ● skate
6. ● strong Ⓕ stong Ⓖ stron Ⓗ strawng
7. Ⓐ spund Ⓑ speand ● spend Ⓓ spende
8. Ⓔ sprring ● spring Ⓖ springe Ⓗ spryng
9. Ⓐ scin Ⓑ skine ● skin Ⓓ skinn
10. ● screen Ⓕ skreen Ⓖ screan Ⓗ scaren
11. Ⓐ stering ● string Ⓒ strin Ⓓ strink
12. Ⓔ spida Ⓕ spidor Ⓖ spidder ● spider
13. Ⓐ skream Ⓑ screem Ⓒ scareme ● scream
14. ● slept Ⓕ sleped Ⓖ salept Ⓗ slepd
15. Ⓐ sprincle ● sprinkle Ⓒ spinkle Ⓓ spinkal

 Book 3.1/Unit 2 Dream Wolf /15

Spiders at Work • PRACTICE

Name__________ Date__________ **Practice 59**

Important and Unimportant Information

When you read nonfiction, you need to be able to tell the difference between passages that include **important information**, or facts, about the main idea and passages that give **unimportant information**. Unimportant information does not add details about the main idea, although it may include interesting observations.

Read the following story. Draw a line under each sentence that contains important information about sea horses.

Sea Horses

"What kind of horse has no hair?" A sea horse, of course. Sea horses live in warm water that is not very deep. They eat tiny things in the water that people cannot even see, as well as small fish. Not many fish like to eat sea horses though. They have too many bones.

Sea horses are clever artists. They turn into the colors of the plants around them so that they can hide from fish that hunt them. It would be wonderful to see a sea horse change from brown to yellow!

Copy a sentence that includes **unimportant** information. Then explain why the sentence does not add important information about sea horses.

Possible answer: "What kind of horse has no hair?" This sentence does not give any factual information.

At Home: Have students explain how they determined which information was important to learning about sea horses.

Name__________ Date__________ **Practice 60**

Vocabulary

Supply the correct word from the list to complete each sentence.

ruin liquid capture serious skills struggles

1. A spider builds a web because it wants to catch, or **capture**, insects.
2. If you roll around on the grass in your best clothes, you might **ruin** them.
3. A **serious** problem needs to be thought about deeply and carefully.
4. When a fly **struggles** to escape from a spider's web, it makes a great effort to try and get free.
5. Water is a **liquid**, but ice is not.
6. Playing the piano and drawing are two **skills** that I have mastered.

At Home: Have students write a short story using three or more of the vocabulary words.

Brave Little Spider

Little May was very *serious* about becoming a web spinner. There was one problem, though. She just didn't have the *skills*. Every time May tried to build a web, she would *ruin* it one way or another. "My poor little girl *struggles* so much," said her mother.

One day, a little boy tried to *capture* May's mother by putting her into a jar. May didn't know what to do. Then she had an idea! Quickly she began to spin a web over a small puddle of *liquid*.

As the boy walked through the web he lost his balance and fell. May and her mother were able to escape. May's mother was proud of her daughter. "Your webs might not be strong enough to catch bugs," May's mother said. "But they sure are strong enough to save me!"

1. How did May feel about wanting to be a web spinner?
   serious
2. What does May need to have to become a web spinner?
   skills
3. What does the little boy try to do?
   He tries to capture May's mother.
4. Where did May spin her web to help her mother?
   over a puddle of liquid
5. How did May's mother feel about May at the end of the story?
   She was proud of May for being brave enough to save her.

At Home: Have students use the italicized words from the story in sentences.

Name__________ Date__________ **Practice 61**

Story Comprehension

Use the story "Spiders at Work" to help you answer these questions.

1. How many legs does a spider have? **eight legs**
2. What is a bridge line? **A bridge line is the first line in a spider's web.**
3. How can you tell if a spider is a black widow? **Black widows have shiny black bodies with a red or yellow mark on the bottom.**
4. Why do people need to look out for black widow spiders? **Black widows have a poisonous bite.**
5. What kind of spiders do some people keep as pets? **tarantulas**
6. How did the daddy-longlegs get its name? **It has very long legs.**
7. Name some places that spiders can be found. **They can be found all over the world, including jungles, mountains, up in the sky, and even out at sea.**
8. According to a Navaho folk tale, what did Spider Woman teach the Navaho people to do? **She taught them how to spin wool into thread and weave it into blankets.**

At Home: Ask students to imagine what it would be like to be a spider. Have them write a short story about a day as a spider.

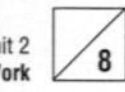

Spiders at Work • PRACTICE

Name______________________ Date__________ **Practice 62**

Use a Dictionary

The word-history section of a dictionary entry tells how the word entered our language. *ME* stands for Middle English, an older form of English. *OE* stands for Old English, an even older form of English. *Fr* stands for French, and *OFr* stands for old French. Latin is also an old language.

leg the part of the body that is used for standing or walking *noun* (leg) ME *leggr*.

capture to grab or hold *verb* (kap′ chər) OFr< Latin *captura*

insect a small animal without a backbone *noun* (in sekt′) Latin *insectum*

spin to turn around and around *verb* (spin) ME *spinnen*

weave to spin a web or cocoon *verb* (wēv) OE *wefan*

Fill in the blanks in the chart below.

WORD	PRONUNCIATION	DEFINITION	PART OF SPEECH	ORIGIN
leg	(leg)	**the part of the body that is used for standing or walking**	noun	ME *leggr*
spin	(spin)	to turn around and around	**verb**	ME *spinnen*
weave	(wēv)	to spin a web or cocoon	verb	OE *wefan*
insect	(in′sekt)	a type of small animal without a backbone	**noun**	**Latin *insectum***
capture	**(kap′ cher)**	to grab or hold	verb	OFr< Latin *captura*

6 Book 3.1/Unit 2 Spiders at Work

At Home: Ask students to look in an dictionary and find another word that comes from Middle English, Old English, French, Old French, or Latin.

62

Name______________________ Date__________ **Practice 63**

Important and Unimportant Information

People often read stories like "Spiders at Work" in order to answer questions that they have. Keeping such purposes in mind can help you sort out **important information** from **unimportant information**.

Decide whether or not each statement below is important to the given purpose. Write an **X** next to the information that is important.

Purpose: To find out which spiders can hurt people

____ **1.** The web looks pretty, but it is a trap for flies and other bugs.

_X_ **2.** Black widow spiders do not bite people very often.

_X_ **3.** The tarantula's bite is about as strong as a bee sting.

____ **4.** Spiders belong to a family of their own.

Purpose: To find out how a spider builds its web

_X_ **5.** The air helps the spider by blowing the bridge line from one plant to another.

____ **6.** Daddy-longlegs eat flies and mosquitoes.

_X_ **7.** The spider keeps building by going back and forth, and up and down.

_X_ **8.** The spider spins a sticky thread in a circle.

Purpose: To find out where spiders live

____ **9.** Some spiders are as small as the head of a pin.

_X_ **10.** Water spiders have their homes under water.

____ **11.** Ants have six legs, and spiders have eight legs.

_X_ **12.** One spider in South America lives in trees and eats small birds.

63

At Home: Ask students to illustrate one of the sentences on the page.

Book 3.1/Unit 2 **Spiders at Work** 12

Name______________________ Date__________ **Practice 64**

Draw Conclusions

You can **draw conclusions** based on information from a story or from your own life. You can often draw conclusions from just a few clues.

Draw a conclusion from each passage below.

1. Sometimes, Jeff and Bill would fight over their toys. When this happened, their grandmother played games with them so they would forget why they were fighting.

   Conclusion: What can you tell about the boys' grandmother?
   She is patient and knows how to keep children from fighting.

2. The flowers had just started to peek out from beneath the ground. The park was full of people wearing jackets and hats that they didn't need.

   Conclusion: What time of year is it? How do you know? **Spring; the flowers are coming up and the weather is warm.**

3. Kim decided to try out for the baseball team. Her brother said she was better than he had been at her age.

   Conclusion: Is Kim's brother older or younger? **older**

4. "It is too bad that so many people are afraid of spiders. Most spiders don't bite! Many are even helpful. They eat bugs that might bite you," said Jack.

   Conclusion: How does Jack feel about spiders? **He likes spiders.**

5. May spilled her milk. Her teacher still had something kind to say about May. May's teacher was good when things went wrong.

   Conclusion: What is May's teacher like? **She is kind.**

5 Book 3.1/Unit 2 **Spiders at Work**

At Home: Have students draw another conclusion about each of the passages.

64

Name______________________ Date__________ **Practice 65**

Antonyms and Synonyms

Antonyms are words with opposite meanings.
Synonyms are words with the same or similar meanings.

Replace the underlined word with a synonym. Write the answer on the line. **Answers may vary.**

1. The class was excited about going on the trip. **outing**
2. They asked their relatives for help. **families**
3. It is silent in the park at night. **quiet**
4. They were curious to learn about the animals. **interested**

Write an antonym for each underlined word. **Answers may vary.**

5. The campers were unprepared when the storm appeared.
   ready
6. They did not want to spend all night in their tents.
   day
7. After a brief shower, the ground was soaked.
   long
8. Everyone wondered if the rain would continue.
   stop

65

At Home: Ask students to form antonyms for **usual, happy,** and **pleased** by adding the prefix **un-** or **dis-** to each word.

Book 3.1/Unit 2 Spiders at Work 8

Spiders at Work • RETEACH

Name______ Date______ **Reteach 59**

Important and Unimportant Information

> **Important information** helps you understand a selection and gives you useful facts. **Unimportant information** may be interesting, but it doesn't give useful facts about the main idea.

Read each sentence from an article about grasshoppers. Write an **I** next to each sentence that tells important information about grasshoppers. Write a **U** next to each sentence that tells unimportant information about grasshoppers.

U **1.** We are used to seeing flies and grasshoppers fly through the air.

I **2.** A grasshopper gets its name from the fact that it hops on the grass.

I **3.** A grasshopper has long, strong back legs which let it jump from one place to another.

I **4.** Some grasshoppers can jump distances up to 20 times the length of their bodies.

U **5.** If people could jump distances up to 20 times the length of their bodies, we could jump about one hundred feet!

I **6.** Grasshoppers also use their back legs to make sounds.

I **7.** When grasshoppers rub their legs against their wings, they make a "song."

U **8.** It would be fun to know what grasshoppers were singing about.

I **9.** Most grasshoppers are brown, gray, or green.

I **10.** Many animals eat grasshoppers.

At Home: Ask students to explain why the sentences they marked with a U are unimportant information.

Name______ Date______ **Reteach 60**

Vocabulary

captures liquid ruin serious skills struggles

Write the word from the list that best completes each sentence.

Spiders are ___serious___ about their work. They use all their ___skills___ to build a trap to catch their food. First, they make a ___liquid___ that turns into a hard thread. Then they use the thread to spin a web that ___captures___ flies. No matter how much it ___struggles___ a fly can't get out of the web. However, sometimes the stuck insect can tear and ___ruin___ the carefully made web.

6

Story Comprehension

Reteach 61

Write the letter of the word or phrase that correctly completes each sentence about "Spiders at Work."

1. This story was mainly written to ___a___.
   a. teach about spiders **b.** to tell funny stories about spiders **c.** make people like spiders
2. The spider could not build a web without ___b___.
   a. another spider's help **b.** thread **c.** plants
3. Black widows can hurt people with their ___c___.
   a. barbed hairs **b.** pointed legs **c.** poison bites
4. Daddy-longlegs walk with the help of ___a___.
   a. small hooks **b.** shoes **c.** a kind of glue

At Home: Ask students to tell you what they recall about daddy-longlegs, black widows, and tarantulas.

Name______ Date______ **Reteach 62**

Use a Dictionary

> **Dictionaries** can give you more than definitions. Hard-to-pronounce words can be sounded out with a pronunciation key. You can also learn how to spell the plural of a word. A dictionary also tells you which part of speech a word can be.

meet to come together with someone (mēt) **verb**
merry cheerful and jolly (mer′ē) **adjective**
mitten a warm covering for the hand (mit′ən) **noun**
mosquito a small insect with two wings (mə skē′ tō) **noun**
muscle a body tissue made of strong fibers (mus′əl) **noun**

Complete the blanks in the dictionary entries below.

WORD	DEFINITION	PRONUNCIATION	PART OF SPEECH
mitten	1. a warm covering for the hand	(mit′ ən)	*noun*
merry	1. cheerful and jolly	(mer′ē)	***adjective***
mosquito	**1. a small insect with two wings**	(mə skē′tō)	*noun*
meet	1. to come together with someone	(mēt)	***verb***
muscle	1. a body tissue made of strong fibers	**(mus′əl)**	*noun*

At Home: Have students write the nouns from the list above and use each in a sentence.

Name______ Date______ **Reteach 63**

Important and Unimportant Information

> When you read nonfiction, you need to be able to tell the difference between important information and unimportant information. **Important information** gives information about the main ideas. **Unimportant information** may be interesting, but not useful for understanding the main idea.

What information would be useful if you were going to write a report on spiders? Read each pair of sentences about spiders. Write an **X** next to the sentence in each pair that contains important information that you could use in your factual report.

1. X The fastest spider in the world can run 330 times the length of its own body in ten seconds.
   ___ A person can only run 50 times his or her length in that time.
2. ___ Tarantulas look like monsters.
   X Tarantulas have eight eyes, but they still don't see very well.
3. ___ Most children know the song about the spider and the rain.
   X Most spiders live only for a year or so.
4. X The spider makes a bridge line by spinning out a long thread.
   ___ All builders should study the garden spider.
5. ___ Can you guess how the daddy-longlegs got its name?
   X Dark spots on the spider's legs help the spider to smell and taste.

At Home: Ask students how they decided which information would be useful in writing a report about spiders.

Spiders at Work • RETEACH

Name________________________ Date___________ **Reteach 64**

Draw Conclusions

A conclusion is always based on information. To **draw conclusions** about a story or a character, use the information the author gives you as well as what you know from your own life.

Read the story. Then answer each question.

Alix wasn't very excited when she woke up on Saturday. Because she had promised to help her parents clean out the barn, she would miss going ice skating with her friends. Instead, she guessed, she would spend the day brushing spiders out of her hair.

Kicking the snow off her boots, Alix went inside the old barn. Her mother was cleaning the floor. Each time her father washed another window, more light streamed into the room. As she explored the corners with her dust cloth, Alix discovered a doll's crib and a child's rocking chair.

"Look at these beautiful old things," Alix said, "I wonder who they belonged to."

1. What is Alix going to do today? **clean out a barn with her parents**
2. What information from the story lets you know what she will do? **She has to help her parents, she goes to the barn, her mother cleans, her father washes windows, Alix dusts with a dust cloth.**
3. What time of year is it? **winter**
4. What clues tell you the time of year? **Alix will not be able to go ice skating; she kicks the snow off her boots.**
5. What did Alix want to do today? **go ice skating**

At Home: Ask students to draw conclusions about whether Alix is a person who keeps her word.

Name________________________ Date___________ **Reteach 65**

Antonyms and Synonyms

Antonyms are words with opposite meanings. **Synonyms** are words with the same or almost the same meanings.

A. Read each sentence. Write the synonym that can replace the underlined word.

cry **trap** **raced** **help**

1. The cat tried to <u>catch</u> the mouse again and again. **trap**
2. Bill tried to <u>aid</u> the mouse by putting the cat outside. **help**
3. The cat started to <u>howl</u> so loudly that Bill's father couldn't stand it. **cry**
4. Bill <u>ran</u> out to get the cat and took it upstairs. **raced**

B. Write the antonym for each underlined word.

enjoyed **make** **thick** **finish**

5. Mai began to <u>undo</u> a new striped rug. **make**
6. First she made a <u>thin</u> black stripe, and then a red stripe. **thick**
7. She hoped to <u>start</u> the rug by the baby's first birthday. **finish**
8. Mai <u>disliked</u> the time she spent working on her loom. **enjoyed**

At Home: Ask students to think of another synonym for *ran* and another antonym for *undo*.

Name ____________ Date ________ **Extend 60**

Important and Unimportant Information

When you look for information, ask yourself: What questions do I want to answer? Knowing what your questions are will tell you which information is important.

Read the list of subjects below. Underline the question you might want to ask about each one.

Subject	**Questions**
1. lizards	What are different kinds of lizards?
2. the year 2050	What is an endangered plant?
3. endangered	How old will I be in the year 2050?
4. horses	What happened in 1923?
	How can I help endangered animals?
	How fast can horses run?
	Do lizards eat lettuce?

Think of two subjects. Write questions you would like answered about each one.

My subjects	**My questions**
5. ________	________
6. ________	________
	________
	________

At Home: Have students choose a subject from the list and research it.

Name ____________ Date ________ **Extend** 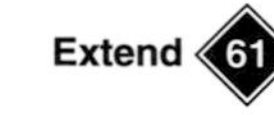

Vocabulary

capture	liquid	ruin	serious	skills	struggles

Concentration Game

Write each vocabulary word on a different card. Write the definitions on other cards. Place the cards face down. Play a matching game with a partner. Turn over two cards at a time. If the word matches the definition, keep both cards and play again. If the cards don't match, turn them both over and let your partner have a turn.

Extend 61

Story Comprehension

What did you find out about spiders? Write and illustrate a booklet about spiders. Include the most interesting facts from "Spiders at Work." Then share the booklet with your class.

At Home: Have students use some of the words in the box to write some facts about spiders.

Name ____________ Date ________ **Extend 62**

Use a Dictionary

Answers will vary. Sample answers are shown.

A. Use a dictionary. Find out what each word means.

1. dangerous **full of danger**

2. allergy **a condition in which a person is made sick by something that is harmless to most people**

3. sting **to prick painfully, usually with a sharp or poisonous stinger**

4. tarantula **a large hairy spider mistakenly believed to be dangerous**

B. Use the words to write a story about Ned the tarantula.

Stories will vary.

At Home: Have students write as many sentences as they can using the word **sting** in different ways.

Name ____________ Date ________ **Extend 63**

Important and Unimportant Information

We draw. We write. We talk. Sometimes we sign. We do these activities to communicate. When you communicate directions or instructions, you need to make sure you communicate what is most important.

Write how to make a peanut butter and jelly sandwich. Make sure you write exactly what to do. Keep it simple.

Answers will vary, but should list exact steps in making the sandwich. For example: Get two pieces of bread. Get peanut butter and open the jar. Get jelly and open the jar. With a knife, carefully spread the peanut butter on one side of one piece of bread. Use the knife to spread the jelly on one side of the other piece of bread. Put the bread together with the jelly side and the peanut butter side facing each other.

Ask a friend or family member to follow your instructions and make a peanut butter and jelly sandwich.

Now tell someone how to make a peanut butter and jelly sandwich by speaking. You can use gestures. Compare the two sandwiches. Explain why one looks better than the other.

Write down any of the information in your directions that was unimportant.

Answers will vary.

Explain how you could do a better job of telling or writing how to make the sandwich.

Answers will vary.

At Home: Have students tell how to make another kind of sandwich they like to eat. Remind them to include only the important steps.

Spiders at Work • EXTEND

Name__________ Date______ **Extend 64**

Draw Conclusions

A conclusion is what you decide to think about something based on what you see, what you already know, and on any other information you have. Look at each of the pictures below. Draw a conclusion about what is happening in each one. **Answers will vary. Sample answers are shown.**

1. **The rabbit and the turtle are having a tea party.**

2. **The rabbit fell off his bike.**

3. **The rabbit and turtle are running a race.**

Choose one picture. Write a story about it on another piece of paper.

At Home: Have students write another scenario for what might be happening in each picture.

Name__________ Date______ **Extend 65**

Antonyms and Synonyms

Antonyms are words that have opposite meanings. Synonyms are words that have the same or similar meanings. Read the story.

The helpful spider took a fly to her ill friend. The friend was grateful for a chance to eat. She took the fly and ate it quickly.
"Thank you," she said. "You are a true friend."

Possible answers given.

A. Rewrite the story using **synonyms** for the underlined words.

The **useful** spider took a fly to her **sick** friend. The friend was **thankful** for a chance to **dine**. She took the fly and ate it **fast**.
"Thank you," she said. "You are a true **companion**."

B. Rewrite the story using **antonyms** for the underlined words.

The **unhelpful** spider took a fly to her **well** friend. The friend was **ungrateful** for a chance to **go hungry**. She took the fly and ate it **slowly**.
"Thank you," she said. "You are a true **enemy**."

C. How did using synonyms affect the story? What happened when you used antonyms?

Synonyms gave the story the same meaning. Antonyms changed the story, giving it the opposite meaning.

At Home: Have students use antonyms to write pairs of sentences with opposite meanings.

Name______________________ Date__________ LEARN **Grammar** 51

Singular Possessive Nouns

- A **possessive noun** is a noun that shows who or what owns or has something.
- Add an **apostrophe** (') and an *-s* to a singular noun to make it possessive.

Write the possessive form of each underlined noun. The first one is done for you.

1. the spokes of the web — the web's spokes
2. the bite of the spider — the **spider's** bite
3. the shape of the mark — the **mark's** shape
4. the age of the tarantula — the **tarantula's** age
5. the crops of the farmer — the **farmer's** crops

Read the lists of things that tell about a spider and an ant. Write out each thing as a singular possessive noun. Example: a spider's web.

a spider	an ant
6. thread **a spider's thread**	11. feelers **an ant's feelers**
7. food **a spider's food**	12. body **an ant's body**
8. mate **a spider's mate**	13. legs **an ant's legs**
9. eyes **a spider's eyes**	14. color **an ant's color**
10. speed **a spider's speed**	15. size **an ant's size**

McGraw-Hill School Division

14 Book 3.1/Unit 2 **Spiders at Work**

Extension: Have students use three of the possessive nouns on this page in oral sentences.

51

Name______________________ Date__________ LEARN AND PRACTICE **Grammar** 52

Plural Possessive Nouns

- Add an apostrophe (') to make most plural nouns possessive. Example: spiders' webs
- Add an apostrophe (') and an *s* to form the possessive of plural nouns that do not end in *s*. Example: men's strength

Write the possessive form of each underlined noun.

1. the victims of the spiders — the **spiders'** victims
2. the threads of the webs — the **webs'** threads
3. the hairs of the tarantulas — the **tarantulas'** hairs
4. the pets of some children — some **children's** pets
5. the builders of nature — **nature's** builders
6. the patterns of the blankets — the **blankets'** patterns
7. the skills of the people — the **people's** skills
8. the feelers of an insect — an **insect's** feelers
9. the bodies of the insects — the **insects'** bodies
10. the legs of the arachnid — the **arachnid's** legs

McGraw-Hill School Division

52

Extension: Have each student use the possessive form of a noun in a sentence.

Book 3.1/Unit 2 **Spiders at Work** 10

Name______________________ Date__________ PRACTICE AND REVIEW **Grammar** 53

Possessive Nouns in Sentences

- A **possessive noun** is a noun that shows who or what owns or has something.
- Add an **apostrophe** (') and an *s* to a singular noun to make it possessive.
- Add an apostrophe (') to make most plural nouns possessive.
- Add an apostrophe (') and an *s* to form the possessive of plural nouns that do not end in *s*.

Complete each sentence with the possessive form of the noun in parentheses.

1. It was both (classes) **classes'** idea to walk in the woods.
2. We looked for (spiders) **spiders'** webs.
3. We saw a (spider) **spider's** bridge line.
4. We also saw lots of (deer) **deer's** hoofprints.
5. The (trees) **trees'** seeds were scattered on the ground.
6. The (bushes) **bushes'** berries were red.
7. On our walk, we found five kinds of (birds) **birds'** nests.
8. We heard a (bluebird) **bluebird's** song.
9. Some children found a (hawk) **hawk's** feathers.
10. The teachers answered the (children) **children's** questions.

McGraw-Hill School Division

10 Book 3.1/Unit 2 **Spiders at Work**

Extension: Have students find examples of ads that include plural possessive nouns.

53

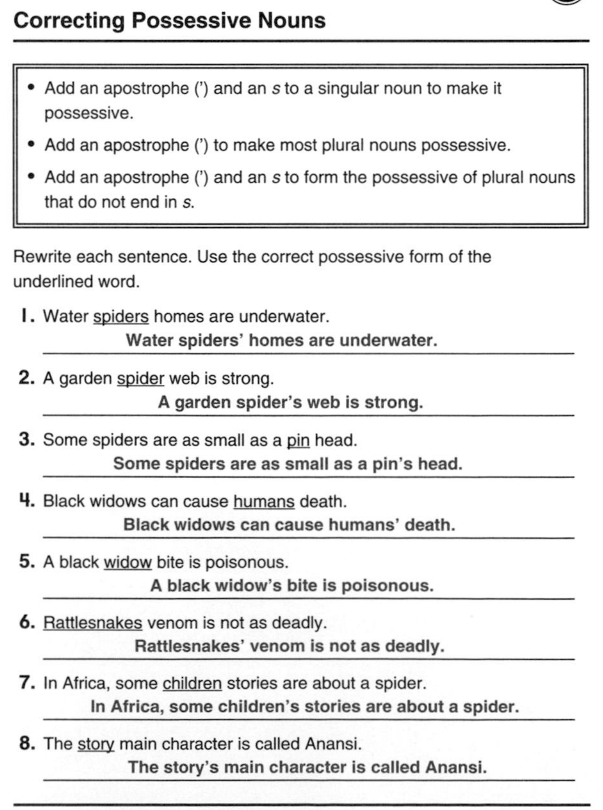

Name______________________ Date__________ MECHANICS **Grammar** 54

Correcting Possessive Nouns

- Add an apostrophe (') and an *s* to a singular noun to make it possessive.
- Add an apostrophe (') to make most plural nouns possessive.
- Add an apostrophe (') and an *s* to form the possessive of plural nouns that do not end in *s*.

Rewrite each sentence. Use the correct possessive form of the underlined word.

1. Water spiders homes are underwater.
   Water spiders' homes are underwater.
2. A garden spider web is strong.
   A garden spider's web is strong.
3. Some spiders are as small as a pin head.
   Some spiders are as small as a pin's head.
4. Black widows can cause humans death.
   Black widows can cause humans' death.
5. A black widow bite is poisonous.
   A black widow's bite is poisonous.
6. Rattlesnakes venom is not as deadly.
   Rattlesnakes' venom is not as deadly.
7. In Africa, some children stories are about a spider.
   In Africa, some children's stories are about a spider.
8. The story main character is called Anansi.
   The story's main character is called Anansi.

McGraw-Hill School Division

54

Extension: Have students use the possessive nouns *spider's, spiders', bush's, bushes'* in sentences of their own and draw pictures to illustrate each sentence.

Book 3.1/Unit 2 **Spiders at Work** 8

Name________________________ Date__________ TEST Grammar 55

Possessive Nouns

A. Read each sentence. Find the correct possessive form for the singular noun in parentheses.

1. A (spider) web looks like a wheel.
- ⓐ spiders
- ● spider's
- ⓒ spiders'
- ⓓ spiders's

2. The (web) spokes are dry.
- ⓐ webs
- ⓑ web
- ● web's
- ⓓ webs'

B. Read each sentence. Find the correct possessive form for the plural noun in parentheses.

3. Water (spiders) webs are balloon-shaped.
- ● spiders'
- ⓑ spider's
- ⓒ spider'
- ⓓ spiders's

4. (Flies) bodies have two parts.
- ⓐ Flie's
- ⓑ Flys'
- ⓒ Fly's
- ● Flies'

5. Some (people) pets are tarantulas.
- ⓐ peoples'
- ⓑ people'
- ● people's
- ⓓ peoples

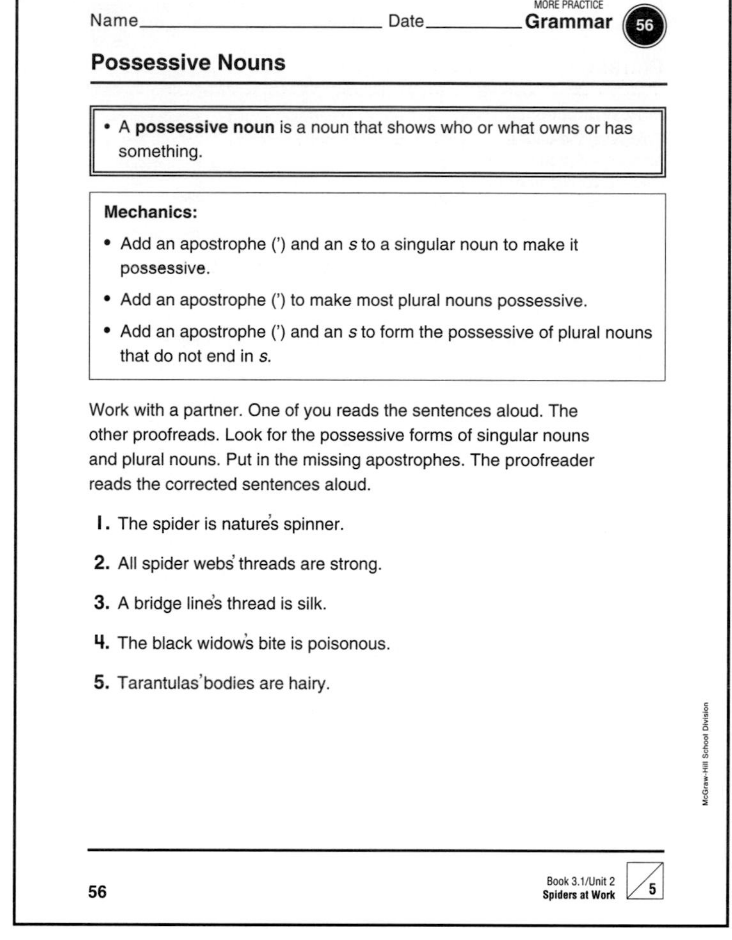

Name________________________ Date__________ MORE PRACTICE Grammar 56

Possessive Nouns

- A **possessive noun** is a noun that shows who or what owns or has something.

Mechanics:
- Add an apostrophe (') and an *s* to a singular noun to make it possessive.
- Add an apostrophe (') to make most plural nouns possessive.
- Add an apostrophe (') and an *s* to form the possessive of plural nouns that do not end in *s*.

Work with a partner. One of you reads the sentences aloud. The other proofreads. Look for the possessive forms of singular nouns and plural nouns. Put in the missing apostrophes. The proofreader reads the corrected sentences aloud.

1. The spider is nature's spinner.

2. All spider webs' threads are strong.

3. A bridge line's thread is silk.

4. The black widow's bite is poisonous.

5. Tarantulas' bodies are hairy.

Spiders at Work • SPELLING

Name__________ Date______ PRETEST SPELLING 51

Plurals

Pretest Directions

Fold back the paper along the dotted line. Use the blanks to write each word as it is read aloud. When you finish the test, unfold the paper. Use the list at the right to correct any spelling mistakes. Practice the words you missed for the Posttest.

1. ______ 1. blankets
2. ______ 2. branches
3. ______ 3. flies
4. ______ 4. mountains
5. ______ 5. states
6. ______ 6. libraries
7. ______ 7. pairs
8. ______ 8. bunches
9. ______ 9. enemies
10. ______ 10. pockets
11. ______ 11. jungles
12. ______ 12. daisies
13. ______ 13. inches
14. ______ 14. companies
15. ______ 15. addresses

Challenge Words

______ capture
______ liquid
______ ruin
______ skills
______ struggles

To Parents

Here are the results of your child's weekly spelling Pretest. You can help your child study for the Posttest by following these simple steps for each word on the word list:

1. Read the word to your child.
2. Have your child write the word, saying each letter as it is written.
3. Say each letter of the word as your child checks the spelling.
4. If a mistake has been made, have your child read each letter of the correctly spelled word aloud, and then repeat steps 1-3.

Name__________ Date______ AT-HOME WORD STUDY SPELLING 52

Plurals

Using the Word Study Steps

1. LOOK at the word.
2. SAY the word aloud.
3. STUDY the letters in the word.
4. WRITE the word.
5. CHECK the word. Did you spell the word right? If not, go back to step 1.

Spelling Tip

Add **-s** to most words to form plurals or to change the tense of verbs. Add **-es** to words ending in **x**, **z**, **s**, **sh**, or **ch**.

pair + s = pairs
buzz + es = buzzes

When a word ends with a consonant followed by **y**, change the **y** to **i** and add **-es**.

library + es = libraries

X the Words

Put an X on the word in each row that does not fit the pattern.

1.	pairs	pockets	inch (X)	bunches
2.	flies	enemy (X)	daisies	libraries
3.	company	blankets (X)	state	jungle
4.	mountain (X)	addresses	branches	pairs
5.	jungles	mountains	addresses	company (X)
6.	fly (X)	blankets	libraries	enemies
7.	pocket	inch	jungles (X)	library
8.	addresses	bunches	pair (X)	branches
9.	companies	states	mountains	enemy (X)
10.	daisy	jungle	branches (X)	fly

To Parents or Helpers:

Using the Word Study Steps above as your child comes across any new words will help him or her spell well. Review the steps as you both go over this week's spelling words.

Go over each Spelling Tip with your child. Ask him or her to add -s or -es to other words to form plurals. Ask if he or she knows other words that end with a consonant followed by y. Help him or her add endings to the words, using the rule.

Help your child find and cross out the word that doesn't fit the pattern in the puzzle.

Name__________ Date______ EXPLORE THE PATTERN SPELLING 53

Plurals

blankets	mountains	pairs	pockets	inches
branches	states	bunches	jungles	companies
flies	libraries	enemies	daisies	addresses

This week's spelling list contains plural words. **Plurals** are words that name more than one thing.

Write the spelling words for each of these plural endings.

s

1. blankets
2. mountains
3. pairs
4. pockets
5. states
6. jungles

es

7. branches
8. bunches
9. inches
10. addresses

y to i + es

11. flies
12. libraries
13. enemies
14. daisies
15. companies

Find the Base Word

Write the base word of each plural noun.

16. blankets blanket
17. flies fly
18. branches branch

Name__________ Date______ PRACTICE AND EXTEND SPELLING 54

Plurals

blankets	mountains	pairs	pockets	inches
branches	states	bunches	jungles	companies
flies	libraries	enemies	daisies	addresses

Part of the Group

Add the spelling word that belongs in each group, below.

Flowers
1. roses, lilies, daisies

Measurements
2. yards, feet, inches

Tree Parts
3. leaves, bark, branches

Insects
4. ants, bugs, flies

Two of a Kind
5. twins, doubles, pairs

Governments
6. countries, cities, states

A Clue for You

Read each clue. Then write the spelling word that fits the clue.

7. These mean the opposite of friends. enemies
8. They are taller than hills. mountains
9. Bananas grow in these groups. So do grapes. bunches
10. These are placed on top of sheets for warmth. blankets
11. You'll find plenty of books in these places. libraries
12. You can find spare change in these. pockets
13. These are often hot and sticky places. jungles
14. These are also called businesses. companies
15. Many people keep these in a little book. addresses

Challenge Extension: Have students write a "fill in the blank word" for each Challenge Word, then work with a partner to complete each other's sentences.

Name________________________ Date__________ PROOFREAD AND WRITE SPELLING **55**

Plurals

Proofreading Activity

There are 6 spelling mistakes in this fact book outline. Circle the misspelled words. Write the words correctly on the lines below.

Facts About Hawaii

I. Geography and climate
   A. Mountins and volcanoes
   B. Rain forests and jungeles
   C. Natural enemes of weather
   D. Average rainfall measured in inchez
II. Government and Education
   A. Branches of government
   B. Schools and special libarees
III. Other State Facts
   A. Transportation and Tourism
   B. State symbols
   C. Top 10 companyes

1. Mountains 2. jungles 3. enemies
4. inches 5. libraries 6. companies

Writing Activity

Use four spelling words. Describe an insect or bird that most expresses to you the beauty of flying. Write about how it looks and acts while it is in flight. Circle any plural words you use.

____

____

____

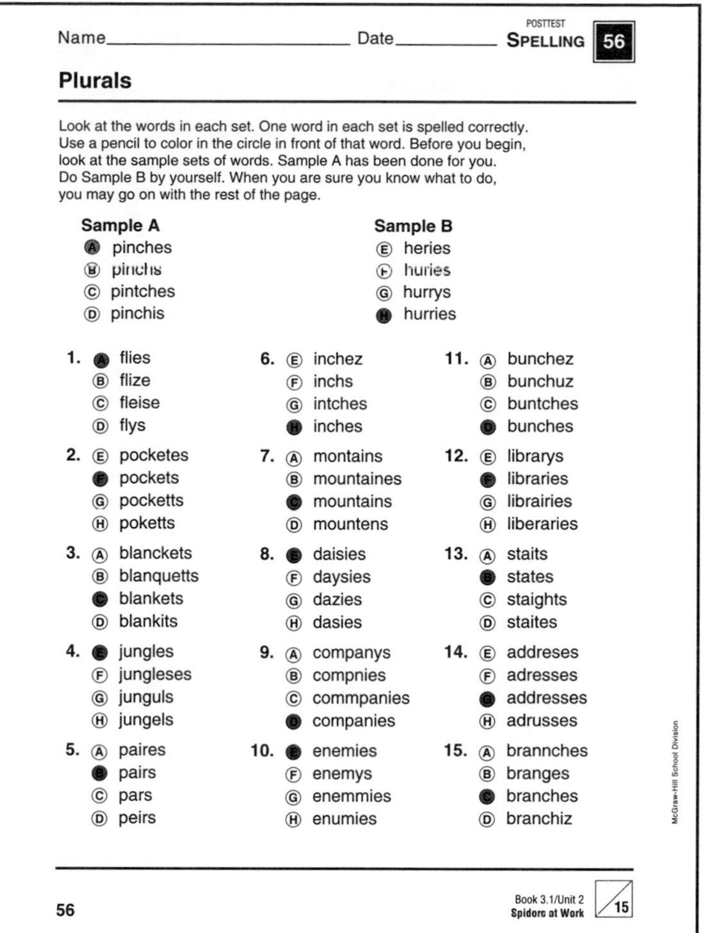

Name________________________ Date__________ POSTTEST SPELLING **56**

Plurals

Look at the words in each set. One word in each set is spelled correctly. Use a pencil to color in the circle in front of that word. Before you begin, look at the sample sets of words. Sample A has been done for you. Do Sample B by yourself. When you are sure you know what to do, you may go on with the rest of the page.

Sample A
● pinches
Ⓑ pinchs
Ⓒ pintches
Ⓓ pinchis

Sample B
Ⓔ heries
Ⓕ huries
Ⓖ hurrys
● hurries

1. ● flies Ⓑ flize Ⓒ fleise Ⓓ flys
2. Ⓔ pocketes ● pockets Ⓖ pocketts Ⓗ poketts
3. Ⓐ blanckets Ⓑ blanquetts ● blankets Ⓓ blankits
4. ● jungles Ⓕ jungleses Ⓖ junguls Ⓗ jungels
5. Ⓐ paires ● pairs Ⓒ pars Ⓓ peirs
6. Ⓔ inchez Ⓕ inchs Ⓖ intches ● inches
7. Ⓐ montains Ⓑ mountaines ● mountains Ⓓ mountens
8. ● daisies Ⓕ daysies Ⓖ dazies Ⓗ dasies
9. Ⓐ companys Ⓑ compnies Ⓒ commpanies ● companies
10. ● enemies Ⓕ enemys Ⓖ enemmies Ⓗ enumies
11. Ⓐ bunchez Ⓑ bunchuz Ⓒ buntches ● bunches
12. Ⓔ librarys ● libraries Ⓖ librairies Ⓗ liberaries
13. Ⓐ staits ● states Ⓒ staights Ⓓ staites
14. Ⓔ addreses Ⓕ adresses ● addresses Ⓗ adrusses
15. Ⓐ brannches Ⓑ branges ● branches Ⓓ branchiz

Web Wonders • PRACTICE

Name______________________ Date__________ **Practice 66**

Compare and Contrast

Read the list of animals. Use what you know to fill in the chart.
Answers may vary.

hamsters dogs goats frogs geese parrots rabbits
goldfish cats ducks sheep horses lizards canaries

Favorite Animals

May Live on Farms	May Live in Homes	Can Swim	Can Fly
goats	hamsters	ducks	geese
geese	parrots	goldfish	ducks
ducks	rabbits	frogs	parrots
sheep	lizards		canaries
horses	dogs		
rabbits	cats		

Choose two animals from the chart. Write how they are alike and how they are different.

Possible answer: Goats and geese may live on farms. Geese can fly, but goats cannot.

At Home: Have students compare and contrast two of the animals on the chart. Have them look at such topics as size, weight, and temperament.

Name______________________ Date__________ **Practice 67**

Vocabulary

Supply the correct words from the list to complete each sentence. The same vocabulary word is used twice in each example.

crops earthquake hatch respect soldiers woven

1. **Crops** are plants we grow for food. Wheat and corn are two kinds of **crops** farmers grow in the United States.
2. When the ground started to shake, I knew we were having an **earthquake**. Luckily, no one was hurt during the **earthquake**, but some buildings were damaged.
3. The hen sits on her eggs to keep them warm until they **hatch**. Watch the eggs **hatch** to see the little chicks!
4. I really admire and **respect** Mrs. Jackson. As one of the best teachers at school, she has earned everyone's **respect**.
5. My cousins joined the army because they wanted to be **soldiers**. Besides fighting in wars, **soldiers** also help to protect and rebuild cities and countries.
6. Some of the most beautiful blankets in the world are **woven** by Native Americans. Yarn is carefully **woven** together in different colored strips to make lovely patterns.

At Home: Have students use each vocabulary word in another sentence.

Two Birds in the Hand

Two *soldiers* were marching through a field. The men were returning to their families. They had been helping people recover from an *earthquake.*

Suddenly the soldiers heard a sound. On the edge of a row of *crops* they found a bird's nest. One little bird was about to *hatch.* Another was already out. There was no mother bird. For several minutes the men waited for the mother bird. Finally, they realized that the baby birds were alone.

"Poor little birds," said one soldier. He placed the nest inside his big *woven* coat. "I will take them home."

"You are a great man," said the other soldier. "You *respect* all life, no matter how big or small!"

1. Where did the soldiers find the bird's nest?
   on the edge of a row of crops
2. What in the story was *woven*?
   the soldier's coat
3. What was one little bird about to do?
   hatch
4. What had the soldiers been doing at the beginning of the story?
   helping people recover from an earthquake
5. Why did the soldier feel sorry for the birds?
   They did not have a mother.

At Home: Help students think about and discuss why baby animals might need help to survive.

Name______________________ Date__________ **Practice 68**

Story Comprehension

Answer the following questions about "Web Wonders."

1. Stories may be written to give information, to entertain, or both. Why do you think this story was written? **Answers may vary: both to inform and to entertain**
2. In the story, why did enemy arrows bounce off Genghis Khan's soldiers? **because spider silk was woven into their clothes**
3. Do you think this story is true? Why or why not? **Answers may vary: It may be true since spider silk is known to be very strong.**
4. How can baby spiders travel so far? **They spin a long silk line, and the wind carries them.**
5. Why can't farmers raise spiders for their silk? **because spiders eat each other**
6. If scientists could make something as strong as spider's silk, what would they use it for?
   car bumpers, jeans, in bridges

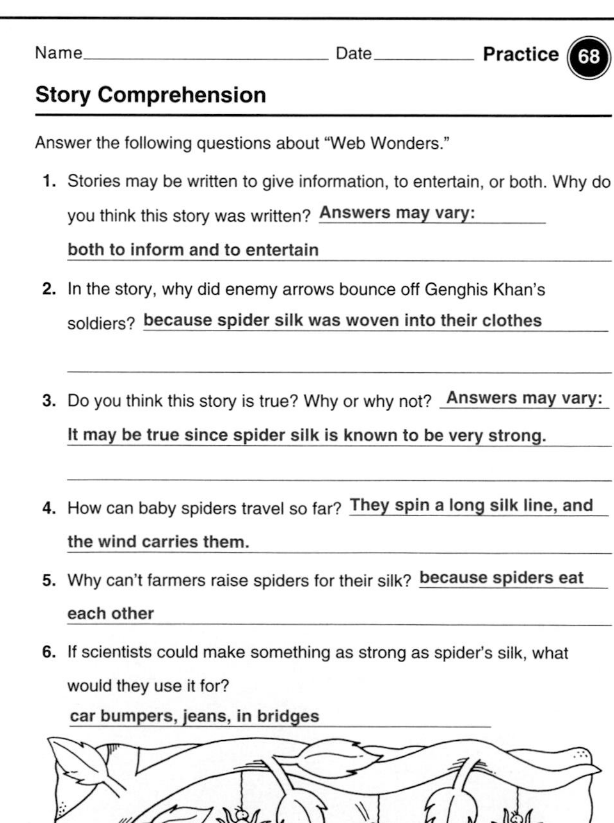

At Home: Ask students to explain why scientists are interested in making humanmade spider silk. Have students suggest some other possible uses for it.

Name________________ Date________ **Practice 69**

Use a Resource

Study the sample dictionary entry. Then take a careful look at the encyclopedia entry that is below it.

nylon a strong fabric manufactured from chemicals. Nylon is used to make thread, clothes, stockings, tires for automobiles, tents for camping, and many other things. **ny-lon** (nī'lon) *noun.*

nylon is the family name for a group of materials made from chemicals. Coal, water, and chemicals are blended to make a wide variety of products. Nylon can be both strong and flexible. In 1937, it was first used to replace silk in stockings. Wallace Carothers developed special ways to make nylon for the Dupont Company. The first nylon he produced melted at low temperatures. If you made a dress out of this early nylon, a hot iron would melt it. By adding other chemicals, the nylon we know today was created. Qiana is a type of nylon that is commonly used in modern clothes. It has many of the qualities of silk.

Now read the selections below. Decide if they might have come from a dictionary entry or an encyclopedia entry. Write *dictionary* or *encyclopedia* to answer the questions below.

1. Which resource tells the history of *nylon*?
   encyclopedia
2. Which resource defines *nylon* as a strong fabric manufactured from chemicals? dictionary
3. Which resource tells you how to pronounce *nylon*?
   dictionary
4. Which resource tells you about a type of *nylon* called Qiana?
   encyclopedia
5. Which resource tells you that *nylon* is a noun?
   dictionary

At Home: Ask students where they might look to find predictions about how nylon will be used in the future.

Name________________ Date________ **Practice 70**

Important and Unimportant Information

When you have specific questions or purposes for reading, you should look for **important information** to answer your questions. **Unimportant information** will not suit your specific purpose.

Read the story. Then write the letters of the sentences that are important to each purpose. Each sentence may be used more than once. **Answers may vary.**

(a) Scientists hope to make a cloth one day that will be as strong as spider silk. **(b)**They may have gotten the idea from an old story. **(c)** The story says that arrows bounced off some soldiers because spider silk was woven into their clothes.
(d) Spiders make spider silk from their bodies. **(e)** Baby spiders hatch from eggs and then spin a line of silk and wait for the wind to carry them to a new home. **(f)** Tarantulas, who live in holes in the ground, do not make silk.
(g) People have respect for spiders because of the spiders' skills at building. **(h)** Farmers like them because they eat bugs.
(i) Spiders spin webs to catch the bugs that they eat. **(j)** Scientists think a giant silk web could capture a plane. **(k)** It could also be used to help hold a bridge in place during an earthquake.

1. **Purpose:** To find out why scientists are interested in spider silk
   a, g, j, k
2. **Purpose:** To find out facts about spiders d, e, f, h, i
3. **Purpose:** To find out other uses for spiders besides for their silk h
4. **Purpose:** To find out how spiders have helped people c, h
5. **Purpose:** To find a story about the use of spider silk c

At Home: Ask students to underline the important facts in the story.

Name________________ Date________ **Practice 71**

Antonyms and Synonyms

A **synonym** is a word that has the same, or almost the same, meaning as another word. An **antonym** is a word that has the opposite, or almost opposite, meaning of another word.
Synonyms: *beautiful, pretty* **Antonyms**: *quiet, noisy*

Choose the word from the box that is a synonym for the underlined word in each sentence. Write the word.

turned	covered	gripe	heap	wave

1. May watched the trees sway in the wind. wave
2. All the garden tools were in a pile in the corner. heap
3. Suddenly the rain changed into hail. turned
4. Clouds hid the mountain's peaks. covered
5. It didn't do any good to complain about the cold. gripe

In each group of four words, circle the two words that are either synonyms or antonyms. Write **synonym** if the words are synonyms and **antonym** if the words are antonyms.

6.	(rough)	(smooth)	take	hide	antonym
7.	sing	(walk)	(stride)	branch	synonym
8.	(look)	chase	eat	(stare)	synonym
9.	(pull)	rush	(push)	sift	antonym
10.	gray	(clean)	(dirty)	proud	antonym

At Home: Have students tell if the following word pairs are synonyms or antonyms: **throw/catch; small/little; soft/hard; rest/nap.**

Name________________ Date________ **Practice 72**

Context Clues

The words and sentences around a word can help you discover its meaning. **Context clues** can be synonyms, antonyms, or examples. Some sentences even provide an exact definition for a word.

Write a definition for each boldfaced word. **Answers may vary.**

1. It was an **error.** Luckily, we could fix the incorrect word.
   incorrect
2. They will **admit** everyone to the play. They will let in children first.
   let in
3. Many planets move in wide circles. For example, the earth **revolves** around the sun.
   move in wide circles
4. Erin wants to **adopt** a dog and take care of it at her home.
   take care of it
5. The afternoon seemed **endless.** The children thought it would go on forever.
   on forever
6. The soldier played the **bugle,** a small instrument like a trumpet, every morning and evening.
   a small instrument like a trumpet

At Home: Ask students to think of some context clues that could be used for the word **shelter.**

Name______________________ Date__________ **Reteach 66**

Compare and Contrast

When you **compare** and **contrast,** you tell how things are alike and how they are different.

Read each passage. Then tell how things are alike and how they are different. Be sure to tell what is being compared or contrasted.

Bears are not the only animals that sleep during the winter. Turtles also like to take long winter naps. Bears sleep in caves, while turtles dig down deep into the mud to sleep.

1. How are bears and turtles alike? **Bears and turtles sleep in the winter.**
2. How are they different? **Bears sleep in caves; turtles sleep in the mud.**

Some farmers grow many different crops. If one crop doesn't grow well, there is still a good chance that another one will. Other farmers grow only one or two crops.

3. How are all farmers alike? **Farmers grow crops.**
4. How are farmers different? **Some grow many crops; some grow one or two crops.**

After the morning rain, the river rushed along. By afternoon, the river had begun to flow more slowly.

5. How is the river the same in the morning and the afternoon? **The river flowed all the time.**
6. What is different? **In the morning, the river rushed; in the afternoon, the river flowed more slowly.**

6 Book 3.1/Unit 2 Web Wonders

At Home: Ask students to tell you what is the same about summer and winter. Help students to write down their ideas.

66

Name______________________ Date__________ **Reteach 67**

Vocabulary

crops earthquake hatch respect soldiers woven

Write the word from the list that best completes the sentences.

The children were well-behaved and showed **respect** for the speakers. A farmer talked about the **crops** he grew and the animals he raised. He mentioned that his shirt was **woven** from wool from his own sheep. He told a funny story about how baby chickens **hatch** from eggs.

Next, two **soldiers** from the army told about their jobs. They spoke about how they helped save people after the ground shook in a terrible **earthquake**.

6

Story Comprehension

Reteach 68

Answer the following questions about "Web Wonders."

1. What is the strongest thread in the world? **spider silk**
2. How do baby spiders travel? **The wind carries them from place to place.**
3. Why are scientists trying to make a thread like spider silk? **It is very strong and can be used for car bumpers, to build bridges, and in clothing.**
4. Why can't spiders be raised on farms? **They eat each other.**

67–68

At Home: Ask students to use each vocabulary word in a sentence.

Book 3.1/Unit 2 Web Wonders 4

Name______________________ Date__________ **Reteach 69**

Use a Resource

Dictionaries list information about words. **Encyclopedias** list information about different topics.

Read the questions below. Then decide which reference source you would use to answer them. Write **dictionary** or **encyclopedia** in the space at the right. (Some of the questions could be answered by either reference source.)

1. Where could I find out how to pronounce *silk*? **dictionary**
2. Where could I find out about the history of silk-making? **encyclopedia**
3. Where could I find out how a silkworm spins a cocoon? **encyclopedia**
4. Where could I find out what part of speech *silk* is? **dictionary**
5. Where could I learn about changes in silk production? **encyclopedia**
6. Where could I learn the origin of the word *insect*? **dictionary or encyclopedia**
7. Where could I learn how many kinds of spiders there are? **encyclopedia**
8. Where could I find the definition of the word *tarantula*? **dictionary**

8 Book 3.1/Unit 2 Web Wonders

At Home: Have students choose a word and decide where they would look to find out about it. Ask them to explain their answer.

69

Name______________________ Date__________ **Reteach 70**

Important and Unimportant Information

Important information gives details about the main idea. **Unimportant information** can be interesting to read, but it does not tell about the main idea. Sometimes deciding which information is important will depend on your purpose for reading.

Read each purpose for reading. Then underline the sentence that has information that is important to that purpose.

Purpose: Find information for a story about scientist John O'Brien.

1. <u>John O'Brien says, "I never step on spiders. I have too much respect for them.</u>
2. Scientists think that a giant spider web could stop a jet plane!

Purpose: Find information for a report on farming.

3. The wind sometimes carries baby spiders 200 miles away.
4. <u>Spiders eat bugs that can hurt farm crops.</u>

Purpose: Find information about different kinds of spiders.

5. All spiders have eight legs.
6. <u>Tarantulas live in holes in the ground.</u>

Purpose: Find information about new kinds of cloth.

7. <u>One day, we may wear clothes made of spider silk.</u>
8. Baby spiders hatch from eggs.

70

At Home: Ask students to explain why each sentence they underlined was important to the stated purpose.

Book 3.1/Unit 2 Web Wonders 8

Web Wonders • RETEACH

Name__________ Date________ **Reteach 71**

Antonyms and Synonyms

A **synonym** is a word that has the same, or almost the same, meaning as another word. The words *happy* and *cheerful* are synonyms. An **antonym** is a word that has the opposite meaning of another word. The words *happy* and *sad* are antonyms.

Write the letter of the word that has almost the same meaning as the first word.

1. lift _b_ **a.** get up **b.** raise **c.** add
2. trail _c_ **a.** peaks **b.** globe **c.** path

Write the letter of the word that has the opposite meaning of the first word.

3. up _b_ **a.** pick **b.** down **c.** spend
4. dark _a_ **a.** light **b.** early **c.** night

Choose a word from the list below that could complete each sentence. Choose a synonym for sentences with **S**. Choose an antonym for sentences with **A**.

stopped **big** **slowly** **below**

5. The mountain peaks were tall and white. **(S)** big
6. The man ran quickly up the hill. **(A)** slowly
7. The cups are above the sink. **(A)** below
8. The road ended and soon we were lost. **(S)** stopped

8 Book 3.1/Unit 2 **Web Wonders**

At Home: Have students think of some synonyms and antonyms for the following words: *sad, bright,* and *quick.*

Name__________ Date________ **Reteach 72**

Context Clues

Context clues can help you decide if a new word is a noun or verb and help you understand its meaning. Sometimes the context may give a definition of a word or give examples.

Read each sentence. Write the meaning of the underlined word.

1. On holidays such as Thanksgiving, people like to get together with their friends and families.

   special days such as Thanksgiving

2. They make foods such as milk, butter, and cheese in their dairy.

   a place where people make milk, butter, and cheese

3. We saw a freight train, a train that carries goods and supplies rather than people.

   goods and supplies

4. The plane was soaring in the sky like a flying bird.

   moving through the air

5. He neglected his dog. For example, he sometimes forgot to feed him.

   not to give attention or care to something

At Home: Have students find a new word in a book they are reading and then try to use context clues to figure out the meaning of the word.

Book 3.1/Unit 2 **Web Wonders** 5

Name________________ Date________ **Extend 66**

Compare and Contrast

Knowing what is true and what is not true helps you compare correctly. Read the statements about plants and animals below. Write **Yes** beside the ones that are true. Write **No** beside the ones that are not true. Then use the Venn diagram to compare and contrast plants and animals.

1. Both plants and animals are living things. **Yes**
2. Some animals eat plants, but most plants make their own food. **Yes**
3. Plants can move from place to place. **No**
4. Animals can fly, walk, or swim. **Yes**
5. There are many different kinds of plants and animals. **Yes**
6. Plants do not need water, but animals do. **No**

make own food; cannot move from place to place

living things; many different kinds; need water

eat plants; can move from place to place

At Home: Have students use the information listed in the diagram to write a paragraph comparing plants and animals.

Name________________ Date________ **Extend 67**

Vocabulary

crops	earthquake	hatch	respect	soldiers	woven

Make up a tall tale with a partner. First list five things that will happen in your make-believe story. Use as many of the words in the box as you can to write your tale. Invite younger students to a story hour. Before they arrive, practice reading your story aloud. Change you voice to fit the characters in the story.

Extend 68

Story Comprehension

Write a story about how spiders spin their webs. Then use your story to create a play. Include characters, a script, and scenery. Select classmates to be in your play. Practice the play. Then, perform your play for another class.

At Home: Have students discuss other famous fairy tales they know well. List the characters together and the important details in the stories.

Name________________ Date________ **Extend 69**

Use a Resource

There are many different places you can find information. When you need a definition of a word you can look in a dictionary. When you need to know where a country is, you can look on a map. When you want to learn about a topic, you can use an encyclopedia or search the Internet on a computer.

Read the questions below. Write the resource or resources that could give you the information you need to answer the question. It may be a dictionary, a map, an encyclopedia, or the Internet.

1. What does *hatch* mean? **dictionary**
2. Is a tarantula an arachnid that spins a web? **encyclopedia, Internet**
3. Where is South America? **map, encyclopedia, Internet**
4. How do spiders spin strong webs? **encyclopedia, Internet**
5. How far can the wind carry baby spiders? **encyclopedia, Internet**

Choose two questions to answer. Use a resource. Write the answers below.

Answers will vary.

At Home: Have students use a resource to find out more about a topic of their own choice.

Name________________ Date________ **Extend 70**

Important and Unimportant Information

A. Suppose you are planning a hike in the mountains. There is some important information you will need to know. Read the questions below. Decide which information is important for your hike. Write the word **important** beside the three questions you need to find the answers to.

1. What equipment should you take on a hike? **important**
2. What should you do if you see a bear in the mountains? **important**
3. What shoes work best for running? ________
4. What snacks and drinks should you take on a hike? **important**
5. What equipment do skiers use? ________

B. Find out the answer to each important question. Write a paragraph that explains what is important for going on a hike.

Planning a Hike

Paragraph should discuss hiking equipment, snacks, water, and strategies for avoiding danger.

At Home: Have students use the important information to draw a picture of someone who is hiking safely.

Web Wonders • EXTEND

Name________________________ Date__________ **Extend 71**

Antonyms and Synonyms

A. Synonyms are words that have similar meanings. Read about some inventions that never made it. Then find a synonym in the box that you can use for the underlined words in the paragraphs.

destroyed	live	hoped	earth	sail	person

Inventions That Never Got Off the Ground

In 1869, Leopold Trouvvelot tried to get caterpillars and silkworms to reproduce. He wished **hoped** to produce caterpillars that could reside **live** in American trees and spin silk. His experiment didn't work, but his caterpillars got loose and killed **destroyed** a lot of trees.

In 1961, a "Rocket Belt" was invented. A human **person** wearing it could fly **sail** 80 feet off the ground **earth** at 6 miles an hour. The problem was that there was only enough fuel for 21 minutes.

B. Antonyms are words with opposite meanings. Choose four words from the paragraphs above. Write an antonym for each word.

1. **loose: caged**
2. **fly: walk**
3. **ground: air**
4. **problem: solution**

Answers will vary. Possible answers are shown.

At Home: Challenge students to find as many other synonyms for the words in the box as they can.

Name________________________ Date__________ **Extend 72**

Context Clues

A. The underlined words in the sentences below are scrambled. Look at the picture and read the sentences to figure out what the words should be. Write the correct word next to the scrambled word.

This spider is spinning a silk ewb **web**.
The silk web is trsgno **strong** enough to capture a grasshopper. The strong web might even capture a ribd **bird**!

B. Draw your own picture. Write sentences about it. Include three scrambled words. Give your picture and sentences to a partner. Ask your partner to unscramble the words.

Scrambled words and sentences will vary.

At Home: Invite students to read a passage in a story. Encourage them to use context clues to figure out the meaning of any unfamiliar words.

Name________________________ Date__________ LEARN Grammar 57

Sentence Combining with Nouns

- Two sentences can be combined by joining two nouns with *and*.
  Separate: "Web Wonders" tells about spiders.
  "Web Wonders" tells about scientists.
  Combined: "Web Wonders" tells about spiders and scientists.

Combine the sentences. Use *and* to join the two underlined nouns. Write the new sentence.

1. Spiders may live in holes. Spiders may live in water.
   Spiders may live in holes and water.
2. A spider's web can trap insects. A spider's web can trap birds.
   A spider's web can trap insects and birds.
3. Tarantulas have eight legs. Tarantulas have eight eyes.
   Tarantulas have eight legs and eight eyes.
4. Tarantulas eat beetles. Tarantulas eat caterpillars.
   Tarantulas eat beetles and caterpillars.
5. Strong spider silk may stop arrows. Strong spider silk may stop jet planes.
   Strong spider silk may stop arrows and jet planes.

5 Book 3.1/Unit 2 Web Wonders

Extension: Have students copy this story starter two times: I would use spider silk to make ____. Ask students to complete each sentence with a noun and then combine the sentences by joining the nouns with *and*.

Name________________________ Date__________ LEARN AND PRACTICE Grammar 58

Combining Subjects

- Some nouns are the subjects of sentences. Sometimes two subjects can be joined with *and*.
  Separate: Adult spiders travel on threads in the wind.
  Spiderlings travel on threads in the wind.
  Combined: Adult spiders and spiderlings travel on threads in the wind.

Combine the subjects of the sentences. Write the new sentence.

1. Flies are meals for spiders. Dragonflies are meals for spiders.
   Flies and dragonflies are meals for spiders.
2. Tarantulas eat grasshoppers. Daddy-longlegs eat grasshoppers.
   Tarantulas and daddy-longlegs eat grasshoppers.
3. Bird spider tarantulas eat birds. Golden silk spiders eat birds.
   Bird spider tarantulas and golden silk spiders eat birds.
4. Farmers like spiders. Scientists like spiders.
   Farmers and scientists like spiders.
5. Spiders are making spider silk. Scientists are making spider silk.
   Spiders and scientists are making spider silk.

Extension: Arrange students in pairs. Have partners take turns generating and extending sentences. One partner thinks of a sentence with one noun in the subject. The other student extends the sentence by adding *and* and another noun.

Book 3.1/Unit 2 Web Wonders 5

Name________________________ Date__________ PRACTICE AND REVIEW Grammar 59

Combining Subjects and Objects

- Two sentences can be combined by joining two nouns with *and*.
  Separate: "Web Wonders" tells about spiders.
  "Web Wonders" tells about scientists.
  Combined: "Web Wonders" tells about spiders and scientists.
- Some nouns are the objects of sentences. Sometimes two objects can be joined with *and*.

Join each pair of sentences. Use *and* to join the nouns. Write the new sentence.

1. Elena read about spiders. Elena read about butterflies.
   Elena read about spiders and butterflies.
2. She learned about spider silk. She learned about human-made silk.
   She learned about spider and human-made silk.
3. Pang looked for spider webs. Elena looked for spider webs.
   Pang and Elena looked for spider webs.
4. Garden spiders spin webs. Golden silk spiders spin webs.
   Garden and golden silk spiders spin webs.
5. Pang drew pictures of webs. Pang drew pictures of spiders.
   Pang drew pictures of webs and spiders.
6. He drew a tarantula. He drew a black widow spider.
   He drew a tarantula and a black widow spider.
7. Tarantulas live in holes. Wolf spiders live in holes.
   Tarantulas and wolf spiders live in holes.
8. Spiders are living things. Plants are living things.
   Spiders and plants are living things.

8 Book 3.1/Unit 2 Web Wonders

Extension: Have students write a pair of sentences with similar ideas and then join the sentences by combining the nouns.

Name________________________ Date__________ MECHANICS Grammar 60

Using Commas and Capital Letters in a Letter

- Begin the greeting and closing in a letter with a capital letter.
- Use a comma after the greeting in a letter.
- Use a comma after the closing in a letter.

Proofread this letter. Correct the capitalization and punctuation mistakes. Combine the underlined sentences. Rewrite the letter correctly on the lines.

dear uncle jack

we learned a lot about spiders today do you know how amazing spider webs are spider webs can trap birds. spider webs can trap flies

your niece
jan

(Greeting)
Dear Uncle Jack,

We learned a lot about spiders today.
Do you know how amazing spider webs are?
Spider webs can trap birds and flies.

(Closing)
Your niece,

(Your name)
Jan

Extension: Have students proofread their letters and use proofreading marks to show corrections. Then have students rewrite their letters correctly.

Book 3.1/Unit 2 Web Wonders 14

Web Wonders • GRAMMAR

Name________________________ Date__________ TEST **Grammar** 61

Sentence Combining with Nouns

A. Write **yes** if the sentences can be combined by joining two nouns. Write **no** if they cannot be combined.

1. Webs catch flies. Webs catch bees. **Yes**

2. Spiders spin circles. Spiders spin triangles. **Yes**

3. Spiderlings are baby spiders. Spiderlings spin a silk line. **No**

4. Spider silk may be in jeans. Spider silk may be in coats. **Yes**

B. Each pair of sentences can be combined. Write the two nouns that can be joined with the word *and.* Use capital letters correctly.

5. Flies have six legs. Ants have six legs.

Flies and **ants**

6. Ants do not spin webs. Tarantulas do not spin webs.

Ants and **tarantulas**

7. Ants have feelers. Beetles have feelers.

Ants and **beetles**

8. Tarantulas have no feelers. Daddy-longlegs have no feelers.

Tarantulas and **daddy-longlegs**

Name________________________ Date__________ MORE PRACTICE **Grammar** 62

Sentence Combining with Nouns

- Two sentences can be combined by joining two nouns with *and.*
- Some nouns are the subjects of sentences.
- Sometimes two subjects can be joined with *and.*

Read the sentences about the picture. Combine the sentences by joining the underlined nouns with *and.*

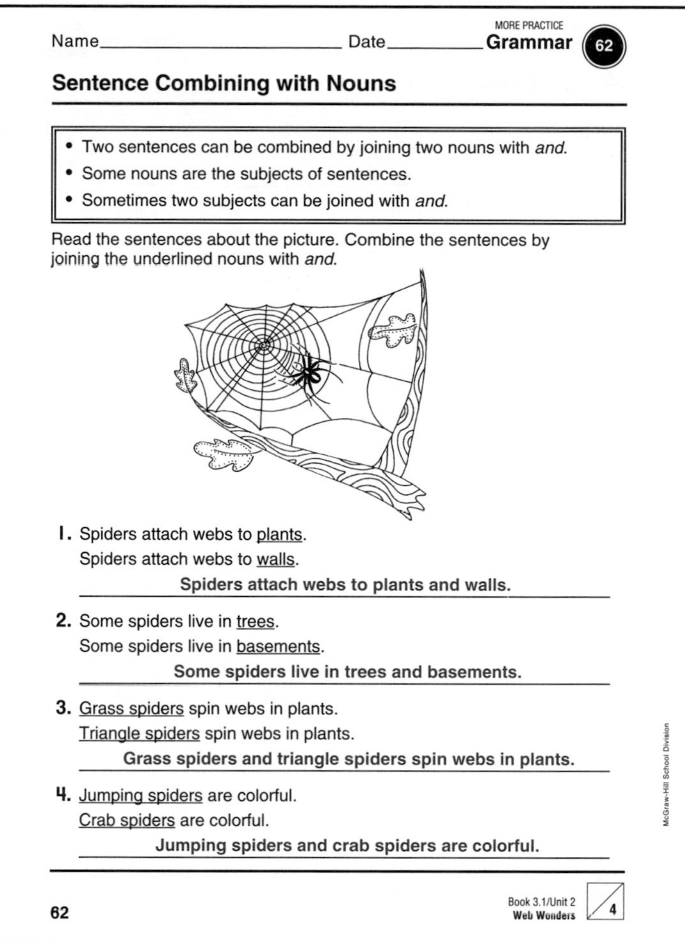

1. Spiders attach webs to plants.
Spiders attach webs to walls.
Spiders attach webs to plants and walls.

2. Some spiders live in trees.
Some spiders live in basements.
Some spiders live in trees and basements.

3. Grass spiders spin webs in plants.
Triangle spiders spin webs in plants.
Grass spiders and triangle spiders spin webs in plants.

4. Jumping spiders are colorful.
Crab spiders are colorful.
Jumping spiders and crab spiders are colorful.

Name __________ Date __________ PRETEST SPELLING 57

Words from Science

Pretest Directions

Fold back the paper along the dotted line. Use the blanks to write each word as it is read aloud. When you finish the test, unfold the paper. Use the list at the right to correct any spelling mistakes. Practice the words you missed for the Posttest.

1. ______	1. web
2. ______	2. sticky
3. ______	3. bait
4. ______	4. cell
5. ______	5. silk
6. ______	6. weave
7. ______	7. fiber
8. ______	8. strands
9. ______	9. beetle
10. ______	10. thread
11. ______	11. science
12. ______	12. fang
13. ______	13. breathe
14. ______	14. taste
15. ______	15. prey

Challenge Words

______	earthquake
______	hatch
______	respect
______	soldiers
______	woven

To Parents

Here are the results of your child's weekly spelling Pretest. You can help your child study for the Posttest by following these simple steps for each word on the word list:

1. Read the word to your child.
2. Have your child write the word, saying each letter as it is written.
3. Say each letter of the word as your child checks the spelling.
4. If a mistake has been made, have your child read each letter of the correctly spelled word aloud, and then repeat steps 1-3.

Name __________ Date __________ AT-HOME WORD STUDY SPELLING 58

Words from Science

Using the Word Study Steps

1. LOOK at the word.
2. SAY the word aloud.
3. STUDY the letters in the word.
4. WRITE the word.
5. CHECK the word. Did you spell the word right? If not, go back to step 1.

Spelling Tip

When the **/s/** sound is spelled **c**, **c** is always followed by **e**, **i**, or **y**.

Example: cells

Think of a related word to help you spell a word with a silent letter or a hard-to-hear sound.

Example: breath breathe

Word Scramble

Unscramble each set of letters to make a spelling word.

1. bew web
2. tiab bait
3. trssdna strands
4. yerp prey
5. gnaf fang
6. ksli silk
7. rfbei fiber
8. ettsa taste
9. hretabe breathe
10. stcyik sticky
11. lbteee beetle
12. vaewe weave
13. llce cell
14. dretah thread
15. nseicec science

To Parents or Helpers:

Using the Word Study Steps above as your child comes across any new words will help him or her spell well. Review the steps as you both go over this week's spelling words.

Go over each Spelling Tip with your child. Ask him or her to write and study other words with the /s/ sound spelled c. Help your child think of other related words that help him or her spell a word with a silent letter or a hard-to-hear sound.

Help your child find and unscramble the spelling words in the puzzle.

Name __________ Date __________ EXPLORE THE PATTERN SPELLING 59

Words from Science

web	cell	fiber	thread	breathe
sticky	silk	strands	science	taste
bait	weave	beetle	fang	prey

Pattern Power

Write the spelling words with the short **e** sound.

1. web 2. cell 3. thread

Write the spelling words with the long **e** sound.

4. beetle 5. weave 6. breathe

Write the spelling words with the long **i** sound.

7. science 8. fiber

Write the spelling words with the short **i** sound.

9. silk 10. sticky

Write the spelling words with the long **a** sound.

11. bait 12. taste 13. prey

Write the spelling words with the short **a** sound.

14. strands 15. fang

Name __________ Date __________ PRACTICE AND EXTEND SPELLING 60

Words from Science

web	cell	fiber	thread	breathe
sticky	silk	strands	science	taste
bait	weave	beetle	fang	prey

It Takes Three

Write a spelling word that goes with the other two words.

1. cotton, wool, silk
2. gooey, icky, sticky
3. net, trap, web
4. bee, fly, beetle
5. eat, munch, taste
6. cage, prison, cell

What Do You Mean?

Read each dictionary definition below. Then write the spelling word that matches the definition.

7. To form strands into a web weave
8. The study and explanation of knowledge science
9. An animal that is hunted prey
10. A long, pointed tooth fang
11. To take air into and out of the lungs breathe
12. Food placed on a hook to catch fish bait

Word Journal

Use the spelling words *fiber*, *strand* and *thread* each in a sentence.

13. ______
14. ______
15. ______

Challenge Extension: Have students write dictionary definitions of the Challenge Words. Then exchange papers with a partner and write the Challenge Word that matches each definition.

Name____________________ Date__________ PROOFREAD AND WRITE SPELLING 61

Words from Science

Proofreading Activity

There are 6 spelling mistakes in this poem. Circle the misspelled words. Write the words correctly on the lines below.

Web Nonsense

This spider's name is Nicky.
Its web is gooey and stickey.
Its strandes are smooth as silck
Or very rich buttermilk.
You may well not believe
How gently Nicky can weeve
Each fine thread into a net.
That's when the trap is set!
For every fibur is a way
To trap some poor insect preay.

1. sticky 2. strands 3. silk
4. weave 5. fiber 6. prey

Writing Activity

Write four words that rhyme with the spelling words. Then write a nonsense poem using pairs of rhyming words. Use the poem above as a model.

	Words That Rhyme	Your Nonsense Poem
7.		
8.		
9.		
10.		

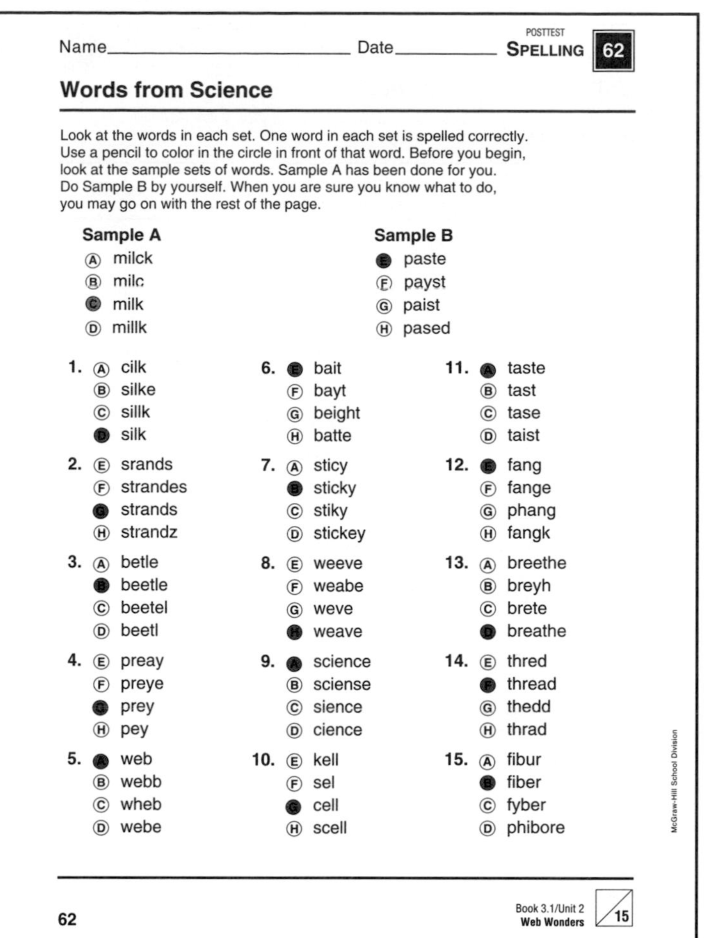

Name____________________ Date__________ POSTTEST SPELLING 62

Words from Science

Look at the words in each set. One word in each set is spelled correctly. Use a pencil to color in the circle in front of that word. Before you begin, look at the sample sets of words. Sample A has been done for you. Do Sample B by yourself. When you are sure you know what to do, you may go on with the rest of the page.

Sample A
Ⓐ milck
Ⓑ milc
● milk
Ⓓ millk

Sample B
● paste
Ⓕ payst
Ⓖ paist
Ⓗ pased

1. Ⓐ cilk Ⓑ silke Ⓒ sillk ● silk
2. Ⓔ srands Ⓕ strandes ● strands Ⓗ strandz
3. Ⓐ betle ● beetle Ⓒ beetel Ⓓ beetl
4. Ⓔ preay Ⓕ preye ● prey Ⓗ pey
5. ● web Ⓑ webb Ⓒ wheb Ⓓ webe
6. ● bait Ⓕ bayt Ⓖ beight Ⓗ batte
7. Ⓐ sticy ● sticky Ⓒ stiky Ⓓ stickey
8. Ⓔ weeve Ⓕ weabe Ⓖ weve ● weave
9. ● science Ⓑ sciense Ⓒ sience Ⓓ cience
10. Ⓔ kell Ⓕ sel ● cell Ⓗ scell
11. ● taste Ⓑ tast Ⓒ tase Ⓓ taist
12. ● fang Ⓕ fange Ⓖ phang Ⓗ fangk
13. Ⓐ breethe Ⓑ breyh Ⓒ brete ● breathe
14. Ⓔ thred ● thread Ⓖ thedd Ⓗ thrad
15. Ⓐ fibur ● fiber Ⓒ fyber Ⓓ phibore

Name_____________ Date_______ **Practice 73**

Unit 2 Vocabulary Review

A. Supply the correct word from the box.

capture	soldiers	darkness	peaks	shelter	halfway

The ___soldiers___ climbed up the mountain. There were many high ___peaks___. They needed to ___capture___ the tower on top of the highest peak. About ___halfway___ up, they heard a loud bang. They ran for ___shelter___ behind a rock. They waited for night to fall. Then they climbed the rest of the way in ___darkness___. They took the army in the tower by surprise.

B. Label each statement **true** or **false**. If false, explain why.

1. You can pour a liquid. **true**
2. Birds hatch eggs. **true**
3. You'll get sick if you eat a ripe tomato. **False; when tomatoes are ripe, they are ready to eat.**
4. Echoes don't make any noise. **False; an echo is a kind of sound.**

At Home: Have students draw a picture to illustrate a vocabulary word. They can then write a sentence telling what the picture shows.

Name_____________ Date_______ **Practice 74**

Unit 2 Vocabulary Review

A. Choose the correct word to write on each line. You need two words for each item.

grains	handful	buffalo	herds	earthquake	area

1. Damon took a ___handful___ of sand. Then he let the ___grains___ fall through his fingers.
2. ___Buffalo___ travel together in ___herds___.
3. An ___earthquake___ is rare in this ___area___ of the country.

B. Supply the correct word from the box.

serious	respect	struggles	schedule

1. Everybody should ___respect___ the judge.
2. Tanya made a ___serious___ mistake.
3. Martha ___struggles___ to stay awake until the end of the show.
4. We need to keep on ___schedule___, or we won't finish at noon.

At Home: Have students write a journal entry about something that is important to them. They should use a vocabulary word in each sentence.

Name_____________ Date_______ **Reteach 73**

Unit 2 Vocabulary Review

A. Write each vocabulary word in the correct column.

peaks	buffalos	spiders	stems	canyons	crops

Animal or insect words	Plant words	Place words
buffalos	stems	canyons
spiders	crops	peaks

B. Match each word with its definition. Write the letter of the definition on the line.

1. excitement ___c___
2. heap ___b___
3. traded ___e___
4. ruin ___a___
5. woven ___d___
6. flowed ___f___

a. harm something so much it can't be fixed
b. a collection of things piled together
c. feeling stirred up
d. laced together
e. gave something to get something else
f. moved along in a stream

At Home: Have students draw pictures to illustrate an animal or insect word, a plant word, and a place word from Part A.

Name_____________ Date_______ **Reteach 74**

Unit 2 Vocabulary Review

A. One sentence in each pair makes sense. The other is silly. Put **S** next to each sentence that makes sense. Put **X** next to each sentence that does not make sense.

1. If you're on schedule, you know all the answers. ___X___
   If you're on schedule, you are keeping track of time. ___S___
2. The river flowed to the sea. ___S___
   Trees flowed their leaves in the fall. ___X___
3. You can play a handful of music. ___X___
   You can eat a handful of grapes. ___S___
4. Students learn skills in school. ___S___
   Babies are born with ten skills. ___X___

B. Supply the correct word from the list.

ripe	area	herds	hatch

1. Do you have a good library in your ___area___?
2. When will the egg ___hatch___?
3. I think the bananas are ___ripe___.
4. Paula saw two ___herds___ of cattle when she was at the farm.

At Home: Have students read the dictionary definitions of the words in Part A. Then have them write a sentence for each word.

Name______________________ Date__________ **Extend 73**

Vocabulary Review

Read each word. Use the word to write a sentence about the picture. Or draw a picture to illustrate the sentence. **Answers will vary.**

1. **buffalo**
   Buffalo are running in the field.
2. Tom poured **liquid** into a glass to drink.
3. **flowed**
   The water flowed over the cliff.
4. The **ripe** peaches were perfect to pick and eat.
5. **canyons**
   Canyons can be too deep to cross.
6. The marching **soldier** is very proud and brave.

At Home: Have students make a picture dictionary. On each page they can write a sentence for **darkness, peaks, stems, heap** and the bold words above. Then have them illustrate some of the words in their dictionaries.

Name______________________ Date__________ **Extend 74**

Vocabulary Review

Use the words in the puzzle.

area, excitement, echoes, earthquake, darkness, shelter, heap, skills, peaks, respect

Across

1. We were filled with excitement as the party began.
3. Jan turned off the light so she could sleep in darkness.
5. We raked the leaves in a big heap and jumped in it.
6. We learned addition skills in first grade.
7. It was a large area in which to pitch our tent.
8. I have much respect for my teacher and her knowledge.
9. The mountain peaks were covered in snow.

Down

1. We heard echoes when we shouted down into the canyon.
2. The earthquake made the land shake and crack.
4. It began to rain so we ran into a cave for shelter.

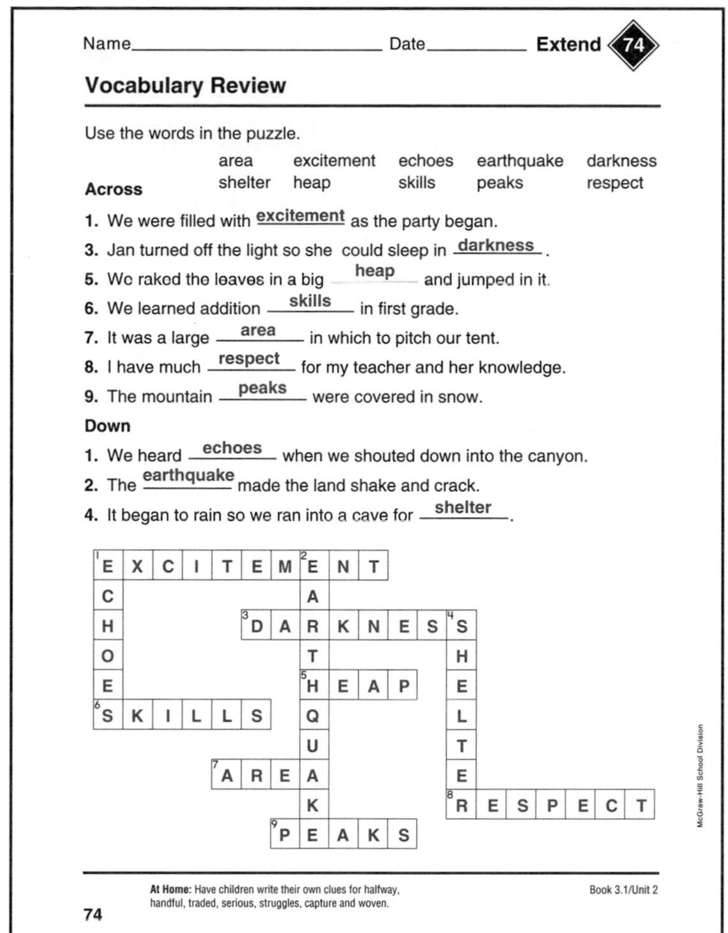

At Home: Have children write their own clues for halfway, handful, traded, serious, struggles, capture and woven.

Name______________________ Date__________ REVIEW **Grammar 63**

Nouns

Read each passage. Choose a word or group of words that belong in each space. Mark your answer.

My sister went on a trip to the Arizona desert. She saw beautiful patterns on the (1). She saw colorful rocks. The sun changed from yellow to orange. The sky turned from blue to pink. She told me, "The (2) is like a painting."

1. ⓐ fine ● sand ⓒ blow ⓓ brown
2. ● desert ⓕ see ⓖ hot ⓗ dry

Dad goes to work at Wooly's Store in (3). He went yesterday. Today (4) is home. There was an accident at the store. A toy display caught fire. People were scared. They forgot to call the Newtown Fire Department.

3. ● Newtown ⓑ country ⓒ ride ⓓ morning
4. ⓔ scare ⓕ tall ⓖ men ● Dad

From my window I watch the doves fly above the rooftops. The (5) wings flap as they soar up the sky. They can swoop down to the ground. Sometimes, they look like (6).

5. ⓐ doves ⓑ dove's ● doves' ⓓ dove
6. ● airplanes ⓕ airplane's ⓖ airplane ⓗ airplanes'

Name______________________ Date__________ REVIEW **Grammar 64**

Grandfather flew home to Canada. We brought him to the airport. There were many men, (7), and children waiting for the plane. The (8) bags were lost. Grandfather helped to find them.

7. ⓐ woman's ⓑ womans ● women ⓓ women's
8. ⓔ children ● children's ⓖ childrens' ⓗ childrens

Last night, the snow fell and covered our yard. My brother and I ran outside. We threw snowballs at each other (9) made a snowman. I forgot my cap (10). I was freezing!

9. ⓐ do ⓑ snow ⓒ white ● and
10. ● and my mittens ⓕ my mittens ⓖ mittens ⓗ cap's mittens

Spiders can spin circles (11) to make webs. Some spiders make their webs in trees. Some make their webs in houses. Webs catch (12) and bees.

11. ● and triangles ⓑ triangles ⓒ and ⓓ not
12. ⓔ fly ● flies ⓖ flys ⓗ flie's

Unit 2 Review • SPELLING

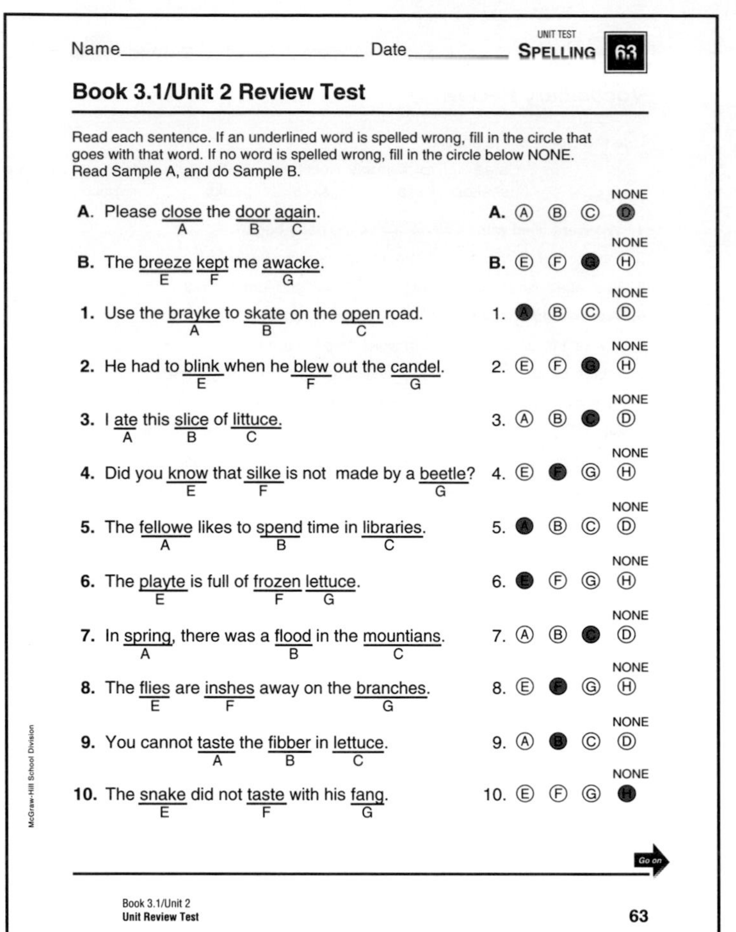

Name________________ Date________ UNIT TEST SPELLING 63

Book 3.1/Unit 2 Review Test

Read each sentence. If an underlined word is spelled wrong, fill in the circle that goes with that word. If no word is spelled wrong, fill in the circle below NONE. Read Sample A, and do Sample B.

A. Please close (A) the door (B) again (C). — A. Ⓐ Ⓑ Ⓒ ● (NONE)

B. The breeze (E) kept (F) me awacke (G). — B. Ⓔ Ⓕ ● Ⓗ (NONE)

1. Use the brayke (A) to skate (B) on the open (C) road. — 1. ● Ⓑ Ⓒ Ⓓ (NONE)
2. He had to blink (E) when he blew (F) out the candel (G). — 2. Ⓔ Ⓕ ● Ⓗ (NONE)
3. I ate (A) this slice (B) of littuce (C). — 3. Ⓐ Ⓑ ● Ⓓ (NONE)
4. Did you know (E) that silke (F) is not made by a beetle (G)? — 4. Ⓔ ● Ⓖ Ⓗ (NONE)
5. The fellowe (A) likes to spend (B) time in libraries (C). — 5. ● Ⓑ Ⓒ Ⓓ (NONE)
6. The playte (E) is full of frozen (F) lettuce (G). — 6. ● Ⓕ Ⓖ Ⓗ (NONE)
7. In spring (A), there was a flood (B) in the mountians (C). — 7. Ⓐ Ⓑ ● Ⓓ (NONE)
8. The flies (E) are inshes (F) away on the branches (G). — 8. Ⓔ ● Ⓖ Ⓗ (NONE)
9. You cannot taste (A) the fibber (B) in lettuce (C). — 9. Ⓐ ● Ⓒ Ⓓ (NONE)
10. The snake (E) did not taste (F) with his fang (G). — 10. Ⓔ Ⓕ Ⓖ ● (NONE)

Go on

Book 3.1/Unit 2
Unit Review Test 63

Name________________ Date________ UNIT TEST SPELLING 64

11. I need to blinke (A) in a strong (B) wind (C). — 11. ● Ⓑ Ⓒ Ⓓ (NONE)
12. I won't skayt (E) on the frozen (F) branches (G). — 12. ● Ⓕ Ⓖ Ⓗ (NONE)
13. She flies (A) into the mountains (B) in a floode (C). — 13. Ⓐ Ⓑ ● Ⓓ (NONE)
14. The betle (E) will taste (F) that plant (G). — 14. ● Ⓕ Ⓖ Ⓗ (NONE)
15. The libraries (A) are open (B) in the springe (C). — 15. Ⓐ Ⓑ ● Ⓓ (NONE)
16. The silk (E) worm crawls (F) on the branchis (G). — 16. Ⓔ Ⓕ ● Ⓗ (NONE)
17. I need to brake (A) on the frozin (B) mountains (C). — 17. Ⓐ ● Ⓒ Ⓓ (NONE)
18. You can find books (E) in liberries (F) that are open (G). — 18. Ⓔ ● Ⓖ Ⓗ (NONE)
19. The fiber (A) rope is stronge (B) and made of silk (C). — 19. Ⓐ ● Ⓒ Ⓓ (NONE)
20. I do not like to spende (E) the spring (F) in a flood (G). — 20. ● Ⓕ Ⓖ Ⓗ (NONE)
21. Would (A) you like to taste (B) a slyse (C) of cake? — 21. Ⓐ Ⓑ ● Ⓓ (NONE)
22. The beetle (E) only flys (F) inches (G). — 22. Ⓔ ● Ⓖ Ⓗ (NONE)
23. The snake (A) had a strong (B) fayng (C). — 23. Ⓐ Ⓑ ● Ⓓ (NONE)
24. You can crumbel (E) the candle (F) on the plate (G). — 24. ● Ⓕ Ⓖ Ⓗ (NONE)
25. Please opin (A) the window (B) only inches (C). — 25. ● Ⓑ Ⓒ Ⓓ (NONE)

64 Book 3.1/Unit 2
Unit Review Test 25

Notes

Cause and Effect

TESTED OBJECTIVES Students will dramatize cause-and-effect relationships from stories. Students will draw pictures and write captions about cause-and-effect relationships. Students will write short personal narratives.

Alternate Activities

Kinesthetic

DRAMATIZE A CAUSE-AND-EFFECT RELATIONSHIP

GROUP

Materials: student textbook, classroom props, index cards

Use the following activity to help students gain a greater understanding of cause-and-effect relationships.

- On the index cards, write one effect that can be dramatized, such as "everyone was frozen in blocks of ice."
- Distribute the "effect" cards to each group. Have the group create a tableau which depicts the effect.
- Have volunteers identify the effect. The first group that identifies the effect should suggest a cause for the performing group to create in a new tableau. ▶**Bodily/Kinesthetic**

Visual

CAUSE-AND-EFFECT ILLUSTRATION

ONE

Materials: paper, crayons or colored pencils

- Have students consider possible effects that could be caused by situations you present.
- List the following situations on the chalkboard:

  Twenty inches of snow fell in two days.

  Anita wakes up with a stomachache on the day of the school picnic.

  The school bus breaks down on the way to school.

  Dad loses his car keys.

  Sandy finds an injured bird.

- Ask each student to choose a situation and illustrate a cause-and-effect relationship that could develop from it.
- Have students write captions for their illustrations and work together to create a classroom exhibit about cause-and-effect relationships. ▶**Spatial**

Auditory

PERSONAL NARRATIVE

GROUP

Materials: paper and pencil

Encourage students to draw on personal experience to examine cause-and-effect relationships.

WRITING

Have students write short personal narratives about experiences that evoked strong feelings or caused a chain of events.

- When students finish writing, have them read their personal narratives to a small discussion group.
- Have group members talk about each experience and discuss how they would have reacted. ▶**Linguistic/Interpersonal**

See Reteach 38, 42, 52, 56

Reference Sources

TESTED OBJECTIVES **Students will use a telephone directory to look up the telephone numbers of businesses, a dictionary to look up definitions, and an encyclopedia to locate information.**

Alternate Activities

Kinesthetic

WHAT'S THE NUMBER?

GROUP **Materials:** telephone directories

Use the following activity to provide practice with a telephone directory.

- Give Yellow Pages and Business White Pages telephone directories to small groups.
- Have each group use a Yellow Pages directory to locate telephone numbers for a veterinarian, a toy store, a florist, and a movie theater or chain of movie theaters in the community. Tell students to write the names and telephone numbers.
- Then have group members look up the same names in the Business White Pages directory and compare the telephone numbers. ▶**Bodily/Kinesthetic**

Auditory

NAME THAT WORD!

PARTNERS **Materials:** dictionaries

Have students practice their dictionary skills through this activity.

- Give students a list of vocabulary words from selections in Unit 2.
- Supply a dictionary to each pair of students, and have partners take turns looking up words on the list. As one partner reads a definition, have the other partner guess which word on the list it matches.
- Afterward, have partners use their words in complete oral sentences. ▶**Linguistic**

Visual

ENCYCLOPEDIA TIME!

Materials: classroom set of encyclopedias, paper, pencil, crayons or colored pencils

Use the following activity to give students practice with an encyclopedia.

- Ask students to think of an animal that interests them and look up information about the animal in the encyclopedia.

Have students take notes about the animal's appearance, size, and natural habitat.

- Ask students to draw a picture of the animal and use their notes to write several sentences that give information about the animal.
- Have students arrange the pages in alphabetical order to create a class animal book. ▶**Spatial**

See Reteach 41, 48, 55, 62, 69

Draw Conclusions

TESTED OBJECTIVES **Students will design and draw inventions without revealing their purpose, present dramatic sketches, and give descriptions, one clue at a time.**

Alternate Activities

Visual

WHAT'S MY PURPOSE?

ONE **Materials:** paper, crayons or colored pencils

In this activity, students work to draw conclusions based on classmates' invention designs.

- Ask students to think of an invention, either serious or silly, they would like to design.
- Have students draw a picture of the invention and include visual clues to help the viewer draw conclusions about its purpose.
- Ask students to take turns presenting their inventions to the class. Remind them to study details that will lead them to a conclusion about the invention's purpose. ▶**Logical/Mathematical**

Kinesthetic

A DRAMATIC SKETCH

PARTNERS **Materials:** classroom props

Use the following activity to give students practice in drawing conclusions.

- Invite partners to think of a story situation they could dramatize for the class. Situations might involve: playing a game, preparing a meal, fixing a bike, discussing plans.
- Have partners prepare a dramatic sketch that presents clear-cut actions and dialogue the audience can analyze to draw conclusions. Tell students to include a conflict—or problem—in the scene.
- Ask partners to present their scenes but to stop before the end. Invite the class to guess the conclusion and support their guess with details they gathered from the scene. Have the partners show the class the conclusion of their scene. ▶**Bodily/Kinesthetic**

Auditory

WHAT IS IT?

GROUP **Materials:** paper and pencil

Use the following activity to guide students in using detail clues to draw conclusions.

- Divide the class into small groups, and have each group agree on a place, an object, a sport, or an animal to describe.
- When groups present their descriptions to the rest of the class, tell them to reveal only one clue at a time about a subject.
- Have students take notes and put the clues together to determine the correct conclusions. ▶**Logical/Mathematical**

See Reteach 43, 50, 64

Context Clues

OBJECTIVES Students will write and illustrate context sentences for unfamiliar words, play a game of "Context Charades," and challenge classmates in a game of "Context Clues/Twenty Questions."

Alternate Activities

Visual

ILLUSTRATED CONTEXT SENTENCES

PARTNERS

Materials: paper, pencil, crayons or colored pencils

Invite students to work in pairs to identify unfamiliar words in a story they have recently read. Tell them to list the words.

WRITING

Have partners write new sentences, underline the words from their lists, and illustrate the sentences.

- Ask partners to present their illustrated sentences to the class.
- Have volunteers explain how the context clues hint at the meaning of the underlined words. ▶**Linguistic**

Kinesthetic

CONTEXT CHARADES

GROUP

Materials: index cards

Use the following activity to stress the importance of using context to determine word meanings.

- Select vocabulary words from selections in Unit 2, and write each word on an index card. Place the cards face down on a table or desk.
- Have each student, in turn, pick a card and pantomime visual clues to its meaning until the word is guessed. ▶**Bodily/Kinesthetic**

Auditory

CONTEXT CLUES/TWENTY QUESTIONS

GROUP

Materials: paper and pencil

Provide students with practice in using context clues to determine word meanings. Have students in groups of four or five each think of a word and write it on a piece of paper.

- Students should present context clues by saying, "I'm thinking of a word that (describes, names, shows an action of) something."
- Have the other group members guess the word. Encourage them to take notes.
- For each incorrect guess, the presenter adds another clue until twenty clues have been reached. ▶**Linguistic**

See Reteach 44, 58, 72

Compare and Contrast

TESTED OBJECTIVES **Students will compare and contrast two photographs, two pieces of music, and two sports.**

Alternate Activities

Visual

COMPARE AND CONTRAST PHOTOGRAPHS

ONE **Materials:** paper and pencil

Use the following activity to give students practice in analyzing similarities and differences.

- Display two photographs that are similar in theme or subject.
- Have students study the photographs to determine ways in which they are alike and ways in which they are different.
- Ask students to create a chart in which they compare and contrast the photographs.
- After students finish writing, have pairs of students compare their observations and conclusions about how the photographs are alike and different. ▶**Logical/Mathematical**

Auditory

COMPARE AND CONTRAST TWO PIECES OF MUSIC

PARTNERS **Materials:** tape or CD player, paper and pencil

Select two pieces of music (songs with a similar subject, instrumental ballads, short classical or jazz pieces) to play for students.

- Play one piece of music, and have students record their impressions and observations. Then play the other piece, and again have students take notes.
- Give students a few minutes to review their notes.
- Then ask them to discuss with their partners how the two pieces of music are alike and how they are different. ▶**Musical**

Kinesthetic

COMPARE AND CONTRAST TWO SPORTS

GROUP **Materials:** classroom props

Explain to students that the ability to observe similarities and differences in all aspects of life and culture is a valuable skill.

- Have pairs of students select two sports, such as basketball and hockey or soccer and football, to compare and contrast.
- Ask partners to take turns demonstrating for the class how the two sports they chose are alike and how they are different. As students present their demonstrations, have the class take notes.
- Afterward, hold a class discussion about the similarities and differences between each pair of sports. ▶**Bodily/Kinesthetic**

See Reteach 45, 49, 57, 66

Antonyms and Synonyms

TESTED OBJECTIVES **Students will participate in an antonym bee, play a game of *Antonym Fish*, and draw a synonym picture.**

Alternate Activities

Auditory

ANTONYM BEE

Materials: paper and pencil

Remind students that antonyms are words that are opposite in meaning.

- Divide the class into two teams. Use a spelling bee approach, and have students respond with the appropriate antonym for the word you say. Record the antonyms on the chalkboard throughout the Antonym Bee.

After everyone has had a turn, have students work in pairs. Tell them to use five of the words from the list on the chalkboard in original sentences and to underline the list words they use.

- When students have finished writing their sentences, have partners trade papers and rewrite each sentence, writing an antonym for the word in the blank. ▶**Linguistic**

Kinesthetic

ANTONYM FISH

Materials: index cards

Use the following activity to offer students practice with identifying antonyms.

- Generate a group list of eight antonym pairs by skimming the selections in Unit 2. Write the pairs on the chalkboard.
- Have students make two cards for each antonym pair, one word per card.
- Then have students pair up to play *Antonym Fish*. Each player starts out with four cards.
- Player 1 places any antonym pairs face up, asks Player 2 for an antonym to any word still in hand, and either receives it or "fishes" in the pile.
- Player 2 takes a turn after Player 1 is unable to place a pair face up. The player with more matches wins. ▶**Bodily/Kinesthetic**

Visual

SYNONYM PICTURE

Materials: semantic word web, paper, crayons or colored pencils

Remind students that synonyms are words that have similar meanings.

- Give each student a semantic word web. Tell students to think of an overused word, such as *kind* or *happy,* and use the word web to brainstorm synonyms.
- Then have each student draw a picture that illustrates the synonyms in some way. For example, for the word *happy* and its synonyms, the picture could show a child playing with a dog in a meadow on a beautiful spring day.
- When students finish their pictures, have them design a picture border made up of the synonyms. ▶**Spatial**

See Reteach 51, 65, 71

Important and Unimportant Information

TESTED OBJECTIVES **Students will draw category pictures, listen to a passage and identify unimportant information, and act out the behavior of animals.**

Alternate Activities

Visual

CATEGORY PICTURE

ONE **Materials:** paper, crayons or colored pencils

Use the following activity to focus on important and unimportant information.

- Have students think of categories, such as tools, fruit, flowers, vehicles, or toys.
- Ask students to select a category and, on a piece of paper, draw pictures of items that belong in that category.
- Tell students to draw a picture of an item that does not belong in the category. For example, a bicycle would not belong in the category of vehicles that run on gas engines.
- Have students select titles for their category pictures.
- Display the students' work in the classroom, and challenge the class to identify the item that is out of place in each category picture. ▶**Spatial**

Auditory

STRIKE IT!

GROUP **Materials:** excerpt from a science article

Explain to students that, when they are reading for information and taking notes, they should focus only on information that suits their purpose for reading. They should disregard unimportant information.

- Select an excerpt from a science article written for children. Insert an unrelated fact or unimportant detail into the article.
- Tell students to take notes and to listen carefully as you read the excerpt so they can distinguish between important and unimportant information.
- Afterward, have students review their notes and discuss the information from the excerpt. Ask them to identify any fact or detail that seemed unimportant or unrelated to the topic. ▶**Linguistic**

Kinesthetic

ACT LIKE AN ANIMAL

PARTNERS **Materials:** paper and pencil

Remind the class of the importance of distinguishing between important and unimportant information.

- Have pairs of students select an animal whose behavior they would like to act out. Tell students to brainstorm a list of movements and sounds associated with the animal they've chosen. Have them include in their scripts a movement or sound associated with a different animal.
- Have partners take turns presenting their animal acts to the class. After each act, have a volunteer identify the movement or sound that is not associated with the animal represented in the presentation. ▶**Bodily/Kinesthetic**

See Reteach 59, 63, 70

Notes

Handwriting

A Communication Tool

Although typewriters and computers are readily available, many situations continue to require handwriting. Tasks such as keeping journals, completing forms, taking notes, making shopping or organizational lists, and the ability to read hand-written manuscript or cursive writing are a few examples of practical application of this skill.

BEFORE YOU BEGIN

Before children begin to write, certain fine motor skills need to be developed. Examples of activities that can be used as warm-up activities are:

- **Simon Says** Play a game of Simon Says using just finger positions.
- **Finger Plays and Songs** Sing songs that use Signed English, American Sign Language or finger spelling.
- **Mazes** Mazes are available in a wide range of difficulty. You can also create mazes that allow children to move their writing instruments from left to right.

Determining Handedness

Keys to determining handedness in a child:

- Which hand does the child eat with? This is the hand that is likely to become the dominant hand.
- Does the child start coloring with one hand and then switch to the other? This may be due to fatigue rather than lack of hand preference.
- Does the child cross midline to pick things up or use the closest hand? Place items directly in front of the child to see if one hand is preferred.
- Does the child do better with one hand or the other?

The Mechanics of Writing

DESK AND CHAIR

- Chair height should allow for the feet to rest flat on the floor.
- Desk height should be two inches above the level of the elbows when the child is sitting.
- The chair should be pulled in allowing for an inch of space between the child's abdomen and the desk.
- Children sit erect with the elbows resting on the desk.
- Children should have models of letters on the desk or at eye level, not above their heads.

PAPER POSITION

- **Right-handed children** should turn the paper so that the lower left-hand corner of the paper points to the abdomen.

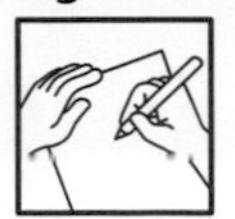

- **Left-handed children** should turn the paper so that the lower right-hand corner of the paper points to the abdomen.

- The nondominant hand should anchor the paper near the top so that the paper doesn't slide.
- The paper should be moved up as the child nears the bottom of the paper. Many children won't think of this and may let their arms hang off the desk when they reach the bottom of a page.

The Writing Instrument Grasp

For handwriting to be functional, the writing instrument must be held in a way that allows for fluid dynamic movement.

FUNCTIONAL GRASP PATTERNS

- **Tripod Grasp** With open web space, the writing instrument is held with the tip of the thumb and the index finger and rests against the side of the third finger. The thumb and index finger form a circle.
- **Quadrupod Grasp** With open web space, the writing instrument is held with the tip of the thumb and index finger and rests against the fourth finger. The thumb and index finger form a circle.

INCORRECT GRASP PATTERNS

- **Fisted Grasp** The writing instrument is held in a fisted hand.

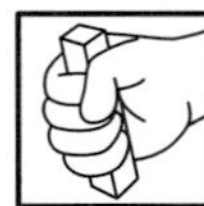

- **Pronated Grasp** The writing instrument is held diagonally within the hand with the tips of the thumb and index finger on the writing instrument but with no support from other fingers.

- **Five-Finger Grasp** The writing instrument is held with the tips of all five fingers.

TO CORRECT WRITING INSTRUMENT GRASPS

- Have children play counting games with an eye dropper and water.
- Have children pick up small objects with a tweezer.
- Do counting games with children picking up small coins using just the thumb and index finger.

FLEXED OR HOOKED WRIST

- The writing instrument can be held in a variety of grasps with the wrist flexed or bent. This is typically seen with left-handed writers but is also present in some right-handed writers. To correct wrist position, have children check their writing posture and paper placement.

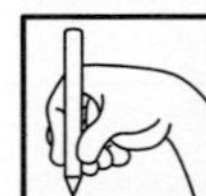

Evaluation Checklist

Functional writing is made up of two elements, legibility and functional speed.

LEGIBILITY

MANUSCRIPT

Formation and Strokes

☑ Does the child begin letters at the top?
☑ Do circles close?
☑ Are the horizontal lines straight?
☑ Do circular shapes and extender and descender lines touch?
☑ Are the heights of all upper-case letters equal?
☑ Are the heights of all lower-case letters equal?
☑ Are the lengths of the extenders and descenders the same for all letters?

Directionality

☑ Are letters and words formed from left to right?
☑ Are letters and words formed from top to bottom?

Spacing

☑ Are the spaces between letters equidistant?
☑ Are the spaces between words equidistant?
☑ Do the letters rest on the line?
☑ Are the top, bottom and side margins even?

CURSIVE

Formation and Strokes

☑ Do circular shapes close?
☑ Are the downstrokes parallel?
☑ Do circular shapes and downstroke lines touch?
☑ Are the heights of all upper-case letters equal?
☑ Are the heights of all lower-case letters equal?
☑ Are the lengths of the extenders and descenders the same for all letters?
☑ Do the letters which finish at the top join the next letter?
(*b, o, v, w*)
☑ Do the letters which finish at the bottom join the next letter? (*a, c, d, h, i, k, l, m, n, r, s, t, u, x*)
☑ Do letters with descenders join the next letter?
(*f, g, j, p, q, y, z*)
☑ Do all letters touch the line?
☑ Is the vertical slant of all letters consistent?

Directionality

☑ Are letters and words formed from left to right?
☑ Are letters and words formed from top to bottom?

Spacing

☑ Are the spaces between letters equidistant?
☑ Are the spaces between words equidistant?
☑ Do the letters rest on the line?
☑ Are the top, bottom and side margins even?

SPEED

The prettiest handwriting is not functional for classroom work if it takes the child three times longer than the rest of the class to complete work assignments. After the children have been introduced to writing individual letters, begin to add time limitations to the completion of copying or writing assignments. Then check the child's work for legibility.

Handwriting Models—Manuscript

A B C D E F G H

I J K L M N O P

Q R S T U V W

X Y Z

a b c d e f g h

i j k l m n o p

q r s t u v w

x y z

Handwriting Models—Cursive

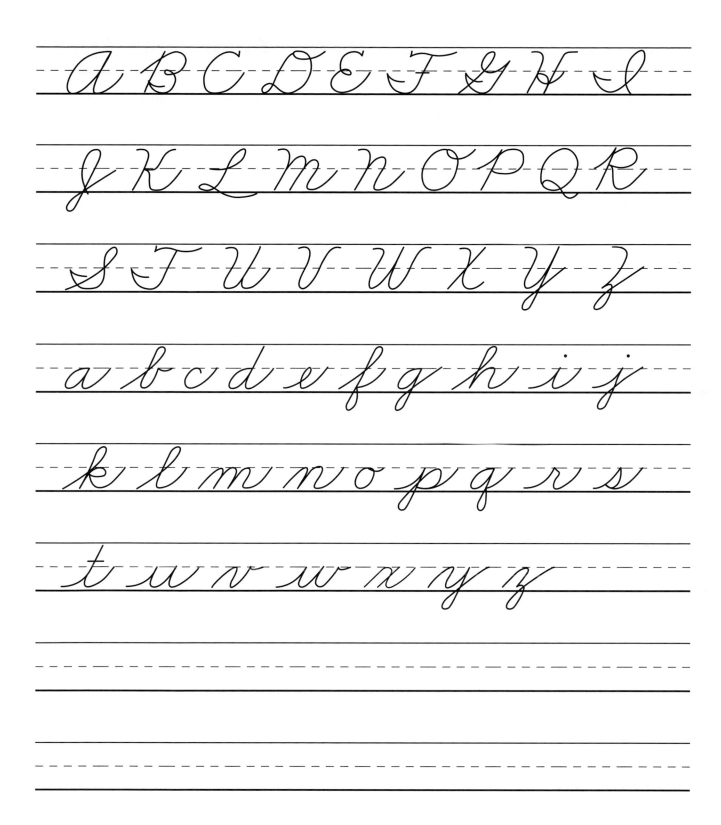

A B C D E F G H I

J K L M N O P Q R

S T U V W X Y Z

a b c d e f g h i j

k l m n o p q r s

t u v w x y z

Selection Titles	Honors, Prizes, and Awards
CLOSED, I AM A MYSTERY Book 1, p.10 by ***Myra Cohn Livingston***	**Poet:** ***Myra Cohn Livingston,*** winner of National Council of Teachers of English Award for Excellence in Poetry for Children (1980); ALA Notable (1984) for *Christmas Poems;* ALA Notable (1987) for *Cat Poems;* ALA Notable (1992) for *Poem-Making: Ways to Learn Writing Poetry*
GRANDFATHER'S JOURNEY Book 1, p.14 by ***Allen Say***	**Caldecott Medal, Boston Globe-Horn Book Award, ALA Notable, Booklist Editor's Choice, Blue Ribbon, *New York Times* Best Illustrated, School Library Journal Best Books of the Year (1994)** **Author/Illustrator:** ***Allen Say,*** winner of Caldecott Honor, ALA Notable (1989), Boston Globe-Horn Book Award (1988) for *The Boy of the Three-Year Nap;* Christopher Award (1985) for *How My Parents Learned to Eat*
OPT: AN ILLUSIONARY TALE Book 1, p.80 by ***Arline and Joseph Baum***	**IRA-CBC Children's Choice (1988), National Science Teachers' Association Outstanding Science Trade Book for Children (1987)**
ABUELITA'S LAP Book 1, p.138 by ***Pat Mora***	**Author:** ***Pat Mora,*** winner of National Association for Chicano Studies Creative Writing Award (1983); New America: Women Artists and Writers of the Southwest Award (1984)
FOG Book 1, p.140 by ***Carl Sandburg***	**Poet:** ***Carl Sandburg,*** winner of Pulitzer Prize for history (1940); ALA Notable (1993) for *More Rootabagas*
CITY GREEN Book 1, p.144 by ***DyAnne DiSalvo***	**Author/Illustrator:** ***DyAnne DiSalvo,*** winner ALA Notable (1996) for *You Want to Vote, Lizzie Stanton?*
THE SUN, THE WIND AND THE RAIN Book 1, p.174 by ***Lisa Westberg Peters*** Illustrated by ***Ted Rand***	**Illustrator:** ***Ted Rand,*** winner of Christopher Award (1991) for *Paul Revere's Ride;* ALA Notable, National Council for Social Studies Notable Children's Book Award (1998) for *Mailing May;* National Council for Social Studies Notable Children's Book Award (1998) for *Storm in the Desert*

Selection Titles	Honors, Prizes, and Awards
DREAM WOLF Book 1, p.206 by ***Paul Goble***	**Author/Illustrator: *Paul Goble,*** winner of ALA Notable, Caldecott Medal (1979) for *The Girl Who Loved Wild Horses;* ALA Notable (1985) for *Buffalo Woman;* ALA Notable (1989), Aesop Accolade (1994) for *Iktomi and the Boulder: A Plains Indian Story;* ALA Notable (1993) for *Love Flute*
WHO AM I? Book 1, p.254 by ***Felice Holman***	**Poet: *Felice Holman,*** winner of Lewis Carroll Shelf Award, ALA Notable (1978) for *Slake's Limbo;* ALA Best Book for Young Adults (1985) for *The Wild Children;* Flora Steiglitz Straus Award (1990) for *Secret City, USA*
THE LITTLE PAINTER OF SABANA GRANDE Book 1, p.292 by ***Patricia Markun Maloney*** Illustrated by ***Robert Casilla***	**National Council for Social Studies Notable Children's Book Award (1994)**
THE PATCHWORK QUILT Book 1, p.320 by ***Valerie Flournoy*** Illustrated by ***Jerry Pinkney***	**Coretta Scott King Award, ALA Notable, Christopher Award, Reading Rainbow Book (1986)** **Illustrator: *Jerry Pinkney,*** winner of Newbery Medal, Boston Globe-Horn Book Honor (1977) for *Roll of Thunder, Hear My Cry;* Coretta Scott King Award (1987) for *Half a Moon and One Whole Star;* ALA Notable (1988) for *Tales of Uncle Remus;* ALA Notable, Caldecott Honor, Coretta Scott King Award (1989) for *Mirandy and Brother Wind;* ALA Notable, Caldecott Honor, Coretta Scott King Honor (1990) for *Talking Eggs;* Golden Kite Award Book (1990) for *Home Place;* ALA Notable (1991) for *Further Tales of Uncle Remus;* ALA Notable (1993) for *Back Home;* ALA Notable, Boston Globe-Horn Book Award, Caldecott Honor (1995) for *John Henry;* ALA Notable, Blue Ribbon (1997) for *Sam and the Tigers;* ALA Notable, Christopher Award, Coretta Scott King Award, Golden Kite Honor Book (1997) for *Minty;* Aesop Prize (1997) for *The Hired Hand;* NCSS Notable Children's Book Award (1998) for *The Hired Hand,* and *Rikki-Tikki-Tavi;* Rip Van Winkle Award (1998); 1998 Hans Christian Andersen nominee
PECOS BILL Book 1, p.352 by ***Angela Shelf Medearis***	**Author: *Angela Shelf Medearis,*** winner of IRA-Teacher's Choice Award Winner Primary Grades (1995) for *Our People*

Selection Titles	Honors, Prizes, and Awards
 **IN MY FAMILY** Book 2, p.40 by ***Carmen Lomas Garza***	**Texas Bluebonnet Master List (1998–99), Pura Belpré Illustration Honor Book (1998)** **Author/Illustrator: *Carmen Lomas Garza,*** winner of Pura Belpré Illustrator Honor (1996); ALA Notable, Pura Belpré Honor Book for Illustrations (1996) for *Family Pictures*
 **CACTUS HOTEL** Book 2, p.58 by ***Brenda Z. Guiberson*** Illustrated by ***Megan Lloyd***	**Parents' Choice Award, ALA Notable, NSTA Award for Outstanding Science Trade Book for Children (1991)** **Illustrator: *Megan Lloyd,*** winner of IRA-CBC Children's Choice (1997) for *Too Many Pumpkins;* ALA Notable (1985) for *Surprises*
 **BIG BLUE WHALE** Book 2, p.86 by ***Nicola Davies*** Illustrated by ***Nick Maland***	**IRA-Teacher's Choice (1998), Blue Ribbon (1997)**
 **DO OYSTERS SNEEZE?** Book 2, p.122 by ***Jack Prelutsky***	**Poet: *Jack Prelutsky,*** winner of SLJ Best Book (1979) for *Nightmares: Poems to Trouble Your Sleep; New York Times* Notable Book (1980) for *The Headless Horseman Rides Tonight;* ALA Notable (1993) for *Random House Book of Poetry for Young Children;* ALA Notable (1985) for *New Kid on the Block;* ALA Notable (1990) for *Poems of A. Nonny Mouse;* ALA Notable (1991) for *Something Big Has Been Here;* ALA Notable (1993) for *Talking Like the Rain*
 **LON PO PO** Book 2, p.128 by ***Ed Young***	**Caldecott Medal, Boston Globe-Horn Book Award, ALA Notable (1990), NCSS Notable Children's Book Award (1989)** **Author/Illustrator: *Ed Young,*** winner of Caldecott Honor (1968) for *The Emperor and the Kite;* Boston Globe-Horn Book Honor (1983) for *Yeh Shen;* ALA Notable, Boston Globe-Horn Book Honor (1984) for *The Double Life of Pocohontas;* ALA Notable (1986) for *Foolish Rabbit's Big Mistake;* ALA Notable (1989) for *Cats Are Cats;* ALA Notable (1989) for *China's Long March;* ALA Notable (1991) for *Mice Are Nice;* ALA Notable (1992) for *All Of You Was Singing;* ALA Notable, Boston Globe-Horn Book Award, Caldecott Honor (1993) for *Seven Blind Mice;* ALA Notable (1994) for *Sadako;* ALA Notable (1995) for *Ibis;* Aesop Accolade (1996) for *The Turkey Girl;* National Council for Social Studies Notable Children's Book Award (1998) for *Genesis* and *Voices of the Heart*

Selection Titles	Honors, Prizes, and Awards
ANIMAL FACT/ANIMAL FABLE Book 2, p.160 by ***Seymour Simon*** Illustrated by ***Diane de Groat***	**A Child Study Association Book of the Year (1979), Texas Blue Bonnet Master List (1982-83)** **Author: *Seymour Simon,*** winner of Texas Blue Bonnet Master List (1996–7) *Sharks;* NSTA Outstanding Science Tradebook for Children (1997) *The Heart;* ALA Notable (1985) *Moon,* (1986) *Saturn,* (1987) *Sun,* (1988) *Mars,* (1993) *Our Solar System* and *Snakes*
THE MANY LIVES OF BENJAMIN FRANKLIN Book 2, p.180 by ***Aliki***	**Author: *Aliki (Brandenberg),*** winner of NSTA Outstanding Science Tradebook for Children (1990) and Library of Congress Children's Book Award (1972) for *Fossils Tell of Long Ago*
CLOUDY WITH A CHANCE OF MEATBALLS Book 2, p.208 by ***Judi Barrett*** Illustrated by ***Ron Barrett***	***New York Times* Best Illustrated, IRA-CBC Children's Choice (1978)**
DREAMS Book 2, p.250 by ***Langston Hughes***	**Poet: *Langston Hughes,*** winner of ALA Notable (1995) for *Sweet and Sour Book*
THE BAT BOY AND HIS VIOLIN Book 2, p.254 by ***Gavin Curtis*** Illustrated by ***E. B. Lewis***	**The New York Public Library 100 Best Books for Reading and Sharing (1998); Coretta Scott King Honor for Illustration (1999)**
TWO BAD ANTS Book 2, p.284 by ***Chris Van Allsburg***	**NSTA Outstanding Science Trade Book for Children (1988), IRA-CBC Children's Choice (1989)** **Author/Illustrator: *Chris Van Allsburg,*** winner of ALA Notable, Caldecott Medal (1982), Boston Globe-Horn Book Honor, for *Jumanji;* ALA Notable (1984), for *The Wreck of the Zephyr;* ALA Notable, Boston Globe-Horn Book Honor (1985), for *The Mysteries of Harris Burdick;* ALA Notable, Boston Globe-Horn Book Honor, Caldecott Medal (1986) for *The Polar Express;* ALA Notable (1988) for *The Z Was Zapped,* (1993) for *Widow's Broom,* (1994) for *The Sweetest Fig*
CHARLOTTE'S WEB Book 2, p.332 by ***E. B. White*** Illustrated by ***Garth Williams***	***Newbery Honor (1953)*** ***Illustrator:* Garth Williams**, winner of Newbery Honor (1959) for *The Golden Name Day*; (1959) for *The Family Under the Bridge*; and (1961) for *The Cricket in Times Square*

Trade Books

Additional fiction and nonfiction trade books related to each selection can be shared with children throughout the unit.

City Green

Wanda's Roses
Pat Brisson, illustrated by Maryann Cocca-Leffler (Boyds Mills Press, 1994)

Wanda's friends and neighbors help her realize her dream to grow a beautiful rose garden.

Squirrel Park
Lisa Campbell Ernst (Bradbury Press, 1993)

A young boy and his friend, Chuck the Squirrel, combine efforts to save the neighborhood park.

Come Back Salmon: How a Group of Dedicated Kids Adopted Pigeon Creek and Brought It Back to Life
Molly Cone, Photographs by Sidnea Wheelwright (Sierra Juvenile Club, 1994)

How a group of schoolchildren from Everett, Washington, clean up a nearby stream.

The Sun, the Wind and the Rain

Where Once There Was a Wood
Denise Fleming (Henry Holt and Company, 1996)

A look at what happens to wildlife if their environment is destroyed.

A Ruined House
Mick Manning (Candlewick Press, 1994)

An old abandoned house becomes a haven for wild plants and animals.

Spring Across America
Seymour Simon (Hyperion Books, 1996)

A journey across America observing the changes that occur in the spring, in both descriptive text and colorful photos.

Technology

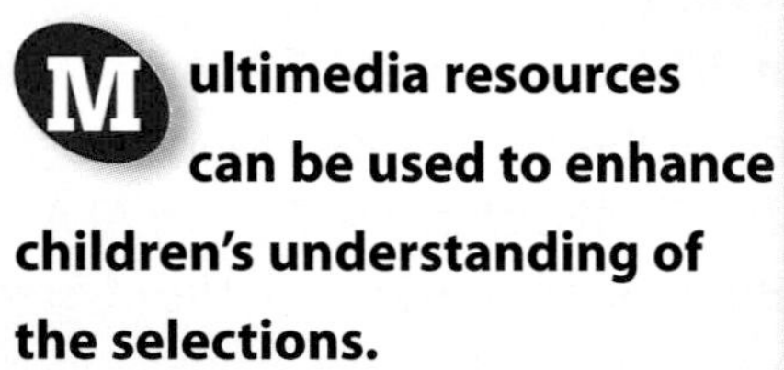

Multimedia resources can be used to enhance children's understanding of the selections.

City Green

Urban Renewal, The Green Earth Series (AIMS Multimedia) Video, 15 min. A young boy, David Grassby, explains the project he started to save Oakbank Pond.

The Spirit of St. Elmo Village (Carousel Film & Video) Video, 26 min. Two African American artists motivate inner-city children to beautify their community.

Get Activated, The Green Earth Series (AIMS Multimedia) Video, 15 min. Explores different student projects that promote environmental awareness.

The Sun, the Wind and the Rain

Wind (Pied Piper/AIMS Multimedia) Video, 12 min. A small boy learns about the wind.

Fog (Encyclopaedia Britannica Educational Corporation) Video, 12 min. Inspired by Carl Sandburg's poem, a look at the art and science of fog.

Watching the Weather (National Geographic Educational Services) Sound filmstrips, 13 min. An introduction to what makes weather and how weather is observed.

Dream Wolf

Officer Buckle and Gloria
Peggy Rathman (G. P. Putnam's Sons, 1995)

Officer Buckle gets a better reception instructing children about safety when he brings along his police dog named Gloria.

The Great Race of the Birds and Animals
Paul Goble (Aladdin Books, 1985)

A contest is held between all the two-legged and four-legged creatures. Read to find out how the birds help a team to win.

Dick Whittington and His Cat
Marcia Brown (Charles Scribner's Sons, 1950)

A retelling of the legend about a boy who made his fortune through his cat.

Clown (Coronet/MTI) Video, 15 min. A child gives his pet to a blind man.

Alejandro's Gift (AIMS Multimedia) Video, 8 min. When Alejandro digs a well to help the desert animals, his gift of water is returned in friendship.

The Lion and the Mouse (Coronet/MTI) Video, 10 min. A tiny mouse helps out a lion.

Spiders at Work

What Color Is Camouflage?
Carolyn Otto, Illustrated by Megan Lloyd (HarperCollins, 1996)

A fascinating presentation of animal disguises and how they protect each animal or insect.

Verdi
Janell Cannon (Harcourt Brace Jovanovich, 1998)

A young python, afraid of growing up, learns that he must grow and develop in order to stay safe.

What Do You Do When Something Wants to Eat You?
Steve Jenkins (Houghton Mifflin, 1997)

Discover various ways animals behave when they sense that they are in danger for their lives.

Noninsect Arthropods and Echinoderms (CLEARVUE) CD-ROM, Macintosh and Windows. An interactive exploration of the world of spiders and other creatures.

Protection (Animal Behavior Series) (Coronet/MTI) Video or videodisc, 12 min. An introduction to three means of animal protection.

Spiders and Backyard Science (BFA Educational Media) Video, 13 min. The make-up, habitat, and life cycle of the spider.

Web Wonders

Spider Watching
Vivian French, illustrated by Alison Wisenfeld (Candlewick Press, 1994)

A young girl overcomes her fear of spiders by observing spiders and their habits.

Anansi Does the Impossible
Verna Aardema, illustrated by Lisa Desimini (Atheneum, 1997)

Anansi the spider has to perform three tasks in order to buy stories from Sky God.

Like Jake and Me
Mavis Jukes, illustrated by Lloyd Bloom (Alfred A. Knopf, 1987)

Alex feels that he has little in common with his stepfather until a fuzzy spider brings them together.

Animal Architecture (BFA Educational Media) Video, 9 min. An introduction to the intricate structures that animals build for shelter and food gathering.

Spiders and How They Live (AIMS Multimedia) Video, 15 min. A young boy and his mother explore the world of an orb spider.

Why Do Spiders Spin Webs? (Coronet/MTI) Video, 11 min. An animated look at the wonders, patterns, and intricacies of spider webs.

Publishers Directory

Abdo & Daughters
4940 Viking Drive, Suite 622
Edina, MN 55435
(800) 458-8399 • www.abdopub.com

Aladdin Paperbacks
(Imprint of Simon & Schuster Children's Publishing)

Atheneum
(Imprint of Simon & Schuster Children's Publishing)

Bantam Doubleday Dell Books for Young Readers
(Imprint of Random House)

Blackbirch Press
1 Bradley Road, Suite 205
Woodbridge, CT 06525
(203) 387-7525 • (800) 831-9183

Blue Sky Press
(Imprint of Scholastic)

Boyds Mills Press
815 Church Street
Honesdale, PA 18431
(570) 253-1164 • Fax (570) 251-0179 • (800) 949-7777

Bradbury Press
(Imprint of Simon & Schuster Children's Publishing)

BridgeWater Books
(Distributed by Penguin Putnam)

Candlewick Press
2067 Masssachusetts Avenue
Cambridge, MA 02140
(617) 661-3330 • Fax (617) 661-0565

Carolrhoda Books
(Division of Lerner Publications Co.)

Charles Scribners's Sons
(Imprint of Simon & Schuster Children's Publishing)

Children's Press (Division of Grolier, Inc.)
P.O. Box 1796
Danbury, CT 06813-1333
(800) 621-1115 • www.grolier.com

Child's World
P.O. Box 326
Chanhassen, MN 55317-0326
(612) 906-3939 • (800) 599-READ • www.childsworld.com

Chronicle Books
85 Second Street, Sixth Floor
San Francisco, CA 94105
(415) 537-3730 • (415) 537-4460 • (800) 722-6657 • www.chroniclebooks.com

Clarion Books
(Imprint of Houghton Mifflin, Inc.)
215 Park Avenue South
New York, NY 10003
(212) 420-5800 • (800) 726-0600 • www.hmco.com/trade/childrens/shelves.html

Crowell (Imprint of HarperCollins)

Crown Publishing Group
(Imprint of Random House)

Dial Books
(Imprint of Penguin Putnam Inc.)

Dorling Kindersley (DK Publishing)
95 Madison Avenue
New York, NY 10016
(212) 213-4800 • Fax (800) 774-6733 • (888) 342-5357 • www.dk.com

Doubleday (Imprint of Random House)

E. P. Dutton Children's Books
(Imprint of Penguin Putnam Inc.)

Farrar Straus & Giroux
19 Union Square West
New York, NY 10003
(212) 741-6900 • Fax (212) 633-2427 • (888) 330-8477

Four Winds Press
(Imprint of Macmillan, see Simon & Schuster Children's Publishing)

Greenwillow Books
(Imprint of William Morrow & Co, Inc.)

Grosset & Dunlap
(Imprint of Penguin Putnam, Inc.)

Harcourt Brace & Co.
525 "B" Street
San Diego, CA 92101
(619) 231-6616 • (800) 543-1918 • www.harcourtbooks.com

Harper & Row (Imprint of HarperCollins)

HarperCollins Children's Books
10 East 53rd Street
New York, NY 10022
(212) 207-7000 • Fax (212) 202-7044 • (800) 242-7737 • www.harperchildrens.com

Henry Holt and Company
115 West 18th Street
New York, NY 10011
(212) 886-9200 • (212) 633-0748 • (888) 330-8477 • www.henryholt.com/byr/

Holiday House
425 Madison Avenue
New York, NY 10017
(212) 688-0085 • Fax (212) 421-6134

Houghton Mifflin
222 Berkeley Street
Boston, MA 02116
(617) 351-5000 • Fax (617) 351-1125 • (800) 225-3362 • www.hmco.com/trade

Hyperion Books
(Imprint of Buena Vista Publishing Co.)
114 Fifth Avenue
New York, NY 10011
(212) 633-4400 • (800) 759-0190 • www.disney.com

Ideals Children's Books
(Imprint of Hambleton-Hill Publishing, Inc.)
1501 County Hospital Road
Nashville, TN 37218
(615) 254-2480 • (800) 336-6438

Joy Street Books
(Imprint of Little, Brown & Co.)

Just Us Books
356 Glenwood Avenue
E. Orange, NJ 07017
(973) 672-0304 • Fax (973) 677-7570

Alfred A. Knopf
(Imprint of Random House)

Lee & Low Books
95 Madison Avenue
New York, NY 10016
(212) 779-4400 • Fax (212) 683-1894

Lerner Publications Co.
241 First Avenue North
Minneapolis, MN 55401
(612) 332-3344 • Fax (612) 332-7615 • (800) 328-4929 • www.lernerbooks.com

Little, Brown & Co.
3 Center Plaza
Boston, MA 02108
(617) 227-0730 • Fax (617) 263-2864 • (800) 343-9204 • www.littlebrown.com

Lothrop Lee & Shepard
(Imprint of William Morrow & Co.)

Macmillan
(Imprint of Simon & Schuster Children's Publishing)

Marshall Cavendish
99 White Plains Road
Tarrytown, NY 10591
(914) 332-8888 • Fax (914) 332-1082 • (800) 821-9881 • www.marshallcavendish.com

William Morrow & Co.
1350 Avenue of the Americas
New York, NY 10019
(212) 261-6500 • Fax (212) 261-6619 • (800) 843-9389 • www.williammorrow.com

Morrow Junior Books
(Imprint of William Morrow & Co.)

Mulberry Books
(Imprint of William Morrow & Co.)

National Geographic Society
1145 17th Street, NW
Washington, DC 20036
(202) 828-5667 • (800) 368-2728 • www.nationalgeographic.com

Northland Publishing
(Division of Justin Industries)
P.O. Box 62
Flagstaff, AZ 86002
(520) 774-5251 • Fax (800) 257-9082 • (800) 346-3257 • www.northlandpub.com

North-South Books
1123 Broadway, Suite 800
New York, NY 10010
(212) 463-9736 • Fax (212) 633-1004 • (800) 722-6657 • www.northsouth.com

Orchard Books (A Grolier Company)
95 Madison Avenue
New York, NY 10016
(212) 951-2600 • Fax (212) 213-6435 • (800) 621-1115 • www.grolier.com

Owlet (Imprint of Henry Holt & Co.)

Willa Perlman Books
(Imprint of Simon & Schuster Children's Publishing)

Philomel Books
(Imprint of Putnam Penguin, Inc.)

Puffin Books
(Imprint of Penguin Putnam, Inc.)

G.P. Putnam's Sons Publishing
(Imprint of Penguin Putnam, Inc.)

Penguin Putnam, Inc.
345 Hudson Street
New York, NY 10014
(212) 366-2000 • Fax (212) 366-2666 • (800) 631-8571 • www.penguinputnam.com

Random House
201 East 50th Street
New York, NY 10022
(212) 751-2600 • Fax (212) 572-2593 • (800) 726-0600 • www.randomhouse/kids

Rourke Corporation
P.O. Box 3328
Vero Beach, FL 32964
(561) 234-6001 • (800) 394-7055 • www.rourkepublishing.com

Scholastic
555 Broadway
New York, NY 10012
(212) 343-6100 • Fax (212) 343-6930 • (800) SCHOLASTIC • www.scholastic.com

Sierra Junior Club
85 Second Street, Second Floor
San Francisco, CA 94105-3441
(415) 977-5500 • Fax (415) 977-5799 • (800) 935-1056 • www.sierraclub.org

Simon & Schuster Children's Books
1230 Avenue of the Americas
New York, NY 10020
(212) 698-7200 • (800) 223-2336 • www.simonsays.com/kidzone

Smith & Kraus
4 Lower Mill Road
N. Stratford, NH 03590
(603) 643-6431 • Fax (603) 643-1831 • (800) 895-4331 • www.smithkraus.com

Teacher Ideas Press
(Division of Libraries Unlimited)
P.O. Box 6633
Englewood, CO 80155-6633
(303) 770-1220 • Fax (303) 220-8843 • (800) 237-6124 • www.lu.com

Ticknor & Fields
(Imprint of Houghton Mifflin, Inc.)

Usborne (Imprint of EDC Publishing)
10302 E. 55th Place, Suite B
Tulsa, OK 74146-6515
(918) 622-4522 • (800) 475-4522 • www.edcpub.com

Viking Children's Books
(Imprint of Penguin Putnam Inc.)

Watts Publishing
(Imprint of Grolier Publishing; see Children's Press)

Walker & Co.
435 Hudson Street
New York, NY 10014
(212) 727-8300 • (212) 727-0984 • (800) AT-WALKER

Whispering Coyote Press
300 Crescent Court, Suite 860
Dallas, TX 75201
(800) 929-6104 • Fax (214) 319-7298

Albert Whitman
6340 Oakton Street
Morton Grove, IL 60053-2723
(847) 581-0033 • Fax (847) 581-0039 • (800) 255-7675 • www.awhitmanco.com

Workman Publishing Co., Inc.
708 Broadway
New York, NY 10003
(212) 254-5900 • Fax (800) 521-1832 • (800) 722-7202 • www.workman.com

Multimedia Resources

AGC/United Learning
6633 West Howard Street
Niles, IL 60714-3389
(800) 424-0362 • www.unitedlearning.com

AIMS Multimedia
9710 DeSoto Avenue
Chatsworth, CA 91311-4409
(800) 367-2467 •
www.AIMS-multimedia.com

BFA Educational Media
(see Phoenix Learning Group)

Broderbund
(Parsons Technology;
also see The Learning Company)
500 Redwood Blvd
Novato, CA 94997
(800) 521-6263 • Fax (800) 474-8840 •
www.broderbund.com

Carousel Film and Video
260 Fifth Avenue, Suite 705
New York, NY 10001
(212) 683-1660 • e-mail:
carousel@pipeline.com

Cloud 9 Interactive
(888) 662-5683 • www.cloud9int.com

Computer Plus (see ESI)

Coronet/MTI
(see Phoenix Learning Group)

Davidson (see Knowledge Adventure)

Direct Cinema, Ltd.
P.O. Box 10003
Santa Monica, CA 90410-1003
(800) 525-0000

Disney Interactive
(800) 900-9234 •
www.disneyinteractive.com

DK Multimedia (Dorling Kindersley)
95 Madison Avenue
New York, NY 10016
(212) 213-4800 • Fax: (800) 774-6733 •
(888) 342-5357 • www.dk.com

Edmark Corp.
P.O. Box 97021
Redmond, CA 98073-9721
(800) 362-2890 • www.edmark.com

Encyclopaedia Britannica Educational Corp.
310 South Michigan Avenue
Chicago, IL 60604
(800) 554-9862 • www.eb.com

ESI/Educational Software
4213 S. 94th Street
Omaha, NE 68127
(800) 955-5570 • www.edsoft.com

GPN/Reading Rainbow
University of Nebraska-Lincoln
P.O. Box 80669
Lincoln, NE 68501-0669
(800) 228-4630 • www.gpn.unl.edu

Hasbro Interactive
(800) 683-5847 • www.hasbro.com

Humongous
13110 NE 177th Pl., Suite B101, Box 180
Woodenville, WA 98072
(800) 499-8386 • www.humongous.com

IBM Corp.
1133 Westchester Ave.
White Plains, NY 10604
(770) 863-1234 • Fax (770) 863-3030 •
(888) 411-1932 •
www.pc.ibm.com/multimedia/crayola

ICE, Inc.
(Distributed by Arch Publishing)
12B W. Main St.
Elmsford, NY 10523
(914) 347-2464 • (800) 843-9497 •
www.educorp.com

Knowledge Adventure
19840 Pioneer Avenue
Torrence, CA 90503
(800) 542-4240 • (800) 545-7677 •
www.knowledgeadventure.com

The Learning Company
6160 Summit Drive North
Minneapolis, MN 55430
(800) 685-6322 • www.learningco.com

Listening Library
One Park Avenue
Greenwich, CT 06870-1727
(800) 243-4504 • www.listeninglib.com

Macmillan/McGraw-Hill
(see SRA/McGraw-Hill)

Maxis
2121 N. California Blvd
Walnut Creek, CA 94596-3572
(925) 933-5630 • Fax (925) 927-3736 •
(800) 245-4525 • www.maxis.com

MECC
(see the Learning Company)

Microsoft
One Microsoft Way
Redmond, WA 98052-6399
(800) 426-9400 • www.microsoft.com/kids

National Geographic Society Educational Services
P.O. Box 10597
Des Moines, IA 50340-0597
(800) 368-2728 •
www.nationalgeographic.com

National School Products
101 East Broadway
Maryville, TN 37804
(800) 251-9124 • www.ierc.com

PBS Video
1320 Braddock Place
Alexandria, VA 22314
(800) 344-3337 • www.pbs.org

Phoenix Films
(see Phoenix Learning Group)

The Phoenix Learning Group
2348 Chaffee Drive
St. Louis, MO 63146
(800) 221-1274 • e-mail:
phoenixfilms@worldnet.att.net

Pied Piper (see AIMS Multimedia)

Scholastic New Media
555 Broadway
New York, NY 10003
(800) 724-6527 • www.scholastic.com

Simon & Schuster Interactive
(see Knowledge Adventure)

SRA/McGraw-Hill
220 Daniel Dale Road
De Soto, TX 75115
(800) 843-8855 • www.sra4kids.com

SVE/Churchill Media
6677 North Northwest Highway
Chicago, IL 60631
(800) 829-1900 •www.svemedia.com

Tom Snyder Productions (also see ESI)
80 Coolidge Hill Rd.
Watertown, MA 02472
(800) 342-0236 • www.teachtsp.com

Troll Associates
100 Corporate Drive
Mahwah, NJ 07430
(800) 929-8765 • Fax (800) 979-8765 •
www.troll.com

Voyager (see ESI)

Weston Woods
12 Oakwood Avenue
Norwalk, CT 06850
(800) 243-5020 • Fax (203) 845-0498

Zenger Media
10200 Jefferson Blvd., Room 94,
P.O. Box 802
Culver City, CA 90232-0802
(800) 421-4246 • (800) 944-5432 •
www.Zengermedia.com

BOOK 1, UNIT 1

	Vocabulary	Spelling			
GRANDFATHER'S JOURNEY	**astonished** **enormous** **journey** **scattered** **surrounded** **towering**	**Words with short vowels**			
		bag **black** body buzz	ever hid **kept** leg	mix **much** **rocks** rub	thing van window
PHOEBE AND THE SPELLING BEE	**continue** **correct** **embarrass** **groaning** **legend** **unusual**	**Words with long *a* and long *e***			
		awake **breeze** carry **cream**	creek grade marry neighbor	**paper** plane **raise** sail	team thief weigh
OPT	**gift** **guard** **royal** **within** **length** **straighten**	**Words with long *i* and long *o***			
		ago bicycle **find** flight	lie life might most	**own** **rode** spoke thrown	**tie** toast wipe
MAX MALONE	**ceiling** **cents** **eager** **including** **scene** **section**	**/ū/ and /ü/**			
		broom crew dew drew	**excuse** fruit **goose** group	huge juice music pool	produce soup truth
TIME FOR KIDS: CHAMPIONS OF THE WORLD	**celebrated** **cork** **fans** **pitcher** **score** **wrap**	**Words from Physical Education**			
		action **baseball** bases batter	crowd foul glove mitt	mound outfield **parade** **player**	**record** **season** strike

Boldfaced words appear in the selection.

BOOK 1, UNIT 2

	Vocabulary	Spelling			
City Green		**Two-syllable words with accented first syllable**			
	area **excitement** **halfway** **heap** **schedule** **stems**	battle bottle candle **carrots**	even fellow fifty flavor	floppy frozen lazy **lettuce**	maple **open** silent
The Sun, the Wind and the Rain		**Words with initial *bl, br, cr, fl, gr, pl***			
	canyons **flowed** **grains** **handful** **peaks** **traded**	blind **blink** block brake	brisk **broad** crazy **crumble**	flame flash flood grab	grand plate plenty
Dream Wolf		**Words with initial *sp, str, scr, spr, sk, sl***			
	buffalo **darkness** **echoes** **herds** **ripe** **shelter**	scream screen scrub skate	skin sleeve **slept** slice	spend spider spring sprinkle	**stream** string strong
Spiders at Work		**Plurals—add *s, es,* and change *y* to *i* add *es***			
	capture **liquid** **ruin** **serious** **skills** **struggles**	addresses **blankets** branches bunches	companies daisies enemies **flies**	inches **jungles** libraries **mountains**	pairs pockets **states**
Time for Kids: Web Wonders		**Words from Science**			
	crops **earthquake** **hatch** **respect** **soldiers** **woven**	bait beetle breathe cell	fang **fiber** prey science	**silk** **sticky** **strands** taste	**thread** **weave** web

Boldfaced words appear in the selection.

BOOK 1, UNIT 3

	Vocabulary	Spelling			
Moses Goes to a Concert		**Words with final *nk, mp, ng, nd, nt***			
	concert **conductor** **ill** **instrument** **musician** **orchestra**	behind belong faint friend	husband ink paint parent	stamp student swing **thank**	**thump** trunk young
The Little Painter of Sabana Grande		**Words with *tt, ll, bb, dd, pp, ss***			
	blossoms **dawn** **faded** **imaginary** **miserable** **shallow**	butter **grass** happen hobby	ladder lesson **little** **middle**	possible ribbon rubber silly	**small** supper **unhappy**
The Patchwork Quilt		**/ou/ spelled *ow, ou*; /oi/ spelled *oi, oy***			
	anxious **attic** **costume** **examined** **gazed** **pattern**	allow choice **cloudy** clown	count **enjoy** foil **found**	loyal noisy poison power	shout **spoil** voyage
Pecos Bill		**adding *ed* and *ing***			
	combine **invented** **located** **prairie** **stumbled** **wilderness**	beginning blamed buried divided	escaping fried hurried moving	robbed **saving** shaking spied	splitting stirred supplied
Time for Kids: A Very Cool Place to Visit		**Words from Science**			
	beauty **creeps** **furniture** **palace** **pure** **visitors**	arctic chill degree dense	**freezes** frost heat **ice**	igloo matter **melt** **northern**	snowflake solid thaw

Boldfaced words appear in the selection.

BOOK 2, UNIT 1

	Vocabulary	Spelling			
The Terrible Eek	**completely** **humans** **meal** **motion** **reply** **weight**	**Words with initial *ch, sh, th, wh***			
		chain cheese cherry **chicken**	shadow shelf shock **shone**	thick **thirsty** thirty thousand	whether whip whisker
In My Family	**comforting** **designed** **dozens** **encouraging** **members** **relatives**	**Words with final *ch, sh, tch, th***			
		approach coach crash fetch	finish fourth itch peach	sketch splash **squash** stitch	teach tooth **underneath**
Cactus Hotel	**discovered** **insects** **remains** **ribs** **tough** **treat**	**/ô/ spelled *a, o, au, ough;* /ů/ spelled *oo, u, o***			
		across **always** bought cause	cookie footprint fought often	**pulls** saucer song sugar	**tall** wolf woman
Big Blue Whale	**adult** **calm** **feast** **mammal** **swallow** **vast**	**Compound Words**			
		afternoon anything barnyard basketball	cardboard everything **fingernails** newspaper	notebook outside playground sidewalk	someone **sometimes** without
Time for Kids: J.J.'s Big Day	**clams** **compared** **experts** **gain** **powdered** **switched**	**Words from Math**			
		data gallon gram **hour**	mass measure meter month	ounce pint **pounds** **problems**	scale second week

Boldfaced words appear in the selection.

BOOK 2, UNIT 2

	Vocabulary	Spelling			
Lon Po Po		**Soft *c* /s/ spelled *ss, ce, c, s* Soft *g* /j/ spelled *j, g, dge, ge***			
	claws **delighted** **disguised** **furious** **paced** **route**	circle city giant gym	**jewels** jolly judge ledge	message once rage **sisters**	stage **sunset** twice
Animal Fact/ Animal Fable		**/är/ spelled *ar;* /ûr/ spelled *ur, or, ir, er, ear***			
	attack **bother** **expects** **label** **rapidly** **temperature**	alarm curtain firm learn	market merchant **person** search	**sharp** skirt startle **turtle**	**words** world worth
The Many Lives of Benjamin Franklin		**/âr/ spelled *are, air;* /ôr/ spelled *or, ore;* /îr/ spelled *ear, eer***			
	advice **curious** **discuss** **experiment** **hero** **scientific**	beard dare deer engineer	fair **force** glare hair	**important** **near** sore stare	store storm **weary**
Cloudy with a Chance of Meatballs		**Contractions**			
	avoid **brief** **frequently** **gradual** **periods** **report**	**didn't** doesn't don't he's	I'll I'm it's she'll	shouldn't they've we're we've	won't you'll you're
Time for Kids: Pure Power		**Words from Social Studies**			
	energy **entire** **future** **model** **pollution** **produce**	climate **coal** **fossil** **fuels**	**gas** globe lumber **millions**	natural **planet** recycle save	**solar** **sunlight** windmills

Boldfaced words appear in the selection.

BOOK 2, UNIT 3

	Vocabulary	Spelling			
The Bat Boy and His Violin		***/ər/ er, ar, or; /əl/ le, el, al***			
	accept **equipment** **invisible** **mistake** **perform** **talented**	barrel cellar **center** collar	**dinner** favor **fiddle** **handle**	**metal** motor sailor signal	**stumble** **summer** travel
Two Bad Ants		**Silent letters *k, w, l, b, gh***			
	bitter **crystal** **gripped** **kingdom** **vanished** **whirling**	calf comb crumb **daylight**	folk **frightening** **height** knife	knock **known** limb palm	whole wrinkle wrong
Do Animals Think?		**Homophones**			
	brain **communicate** **crafty** **social** **solve** **subject**	**ant** ate aunt **do**	due eight meat meet	**one** sew **so** **to**	**too** two won
"Wilbur's Boast" from Charlotte's Web		**Suffixes *-ly, -ful, -able, -tion, -sion***			
	boasting **considering** **conversation** **hesitated** **interrupted** **seized**	**busily** collection **comfort-able** direction	discussion expression invention possession	powerful **quietly** **sadly** unbelievable	useful valuable **wonderful**
Time for Kids: Koala Catchers		**Words from Social Studies**			
	crate **loops** **rescuers** **snug** **starve** **strip**	bay coast continent country	**forests** gulf **harmed** **island**	mainland **migrate** outdoors port	**safe** valley **wildlife**

Boldfaced words appear in the selection.

Scope and Sequence

Listening, Speaking, Viewing, Representing

☑ Tested Skill

Tinted panels show skills, strategies, and other teaching opportunities

LISTENING	K	1	2	3	4	5	6
Learn the vocabulary of school (numbers, shapes, colors, directions, and categories)							
Identify the musical elements of literary language, such as rhymes, repeated sounds, onomatopoeia							
Determine purposes for listening (get information, solve problems, enjoy and appreciate)							
Listen critically and responsively							
Ask and answer relevant questions							
Listen critically to interpret and evaluate							
Listen responsively to stories and other texts read aloud, including selections from classic and contemporary works							
Connect and compare own experiences, ideas, and traditions with those of others							
Apply comprehension strategies in listening activities							
Understand the major ideas and supporting evidence in spoken messages							
Participate in listening activities related to reading and writing (such as discussions, group activities, conferences)							
Listen to learn by taking notes, organizing, and summarizing spoken ideas							
SPEAKING							
Learn the vocabulary of school (numbers, shapes, colors, directions, and categories)							
Use appropriate language and vocabulary learned to describe ideas, feelings, and experiences							
Ask and answer relevant questions							
Communicate effectively in everyday situations (such as discussions, group activities, conferences)							
Demonstrate speaking skills (audience, purpose, occasion, volume, pitch, tone, rate, fluency)							
Clarify and support spoken messages and ideas with objects, charts, evidence, elaboration, examples							
Use verbal and nonverbal communication in effective ways when, for example, making announcements, giving directions, or making introductions							
Retell a spoken message by summarizing or clarifying							
Connect and compare own experiences, ideas, and traditions with those of others							
Determine purposes for speaking (inform, entertain, give directions, persuade, express personal feelings and opinions)							
Demonstrate skills of reporting and providing information							
Demonstrate skills of interviewing, requesting and providing information							
Apply composition strategies in speaking activities							
Monitor own understanding of spoken message and seek clarification as needed							
VIEWING							
Demonstrate viewing skills (focus attention, organize information)							
Respond to audiovisual media in a variety of ways							
Participate in viewing activities related to reading and writing							
Apply comprehension strategies in viewing activities							
Recognize artists' craft and techniques for conveying meaning							
Interpret information from various formats such as maps, charts, graphics, video segments, technology							
Evaluate purposes of various media (information, appreciation, entertainment, directions, persuasion)							
Use media to compare ideas and points of view							
REPRESENTING							
Select, organize, or produce visuals to complement or extend meanings							
Produce communication using appropriate media to develop a class paper, multimedia or video reports							
Show how language, medium, and presentation contribute to the message							

Reading: Alphabetic Principle, Sounds/Symbols

✓ Tested Skill

Tinted panels show skills, strategies, and other teaching opportunities

PRINT AWARENESS	K	1	2	3	4	5	6
Know the order of the alphabet							
Recognize that print represents spoken language and conveys meaning							
Understand directionality (tracking print from left to right; return sweep)							
Understand that written words are separated by spaces							
Know the difference between individual letters and printed words							
Understand that spoken words are represented in written language by specific sequence of letters							
Recognize that there are correct spellings for words							
Know the difference between capital and lowercase letters							
Recognize how readers use capitalization and punctuation to comprehend							
Recognize the distinguishing features of a paragraph							
Recognize that parts of a book (such as cover/title page and table of contents) offer information							
PHONOLOGICAL AWARENESS							
Identify letters, words, sentences							
Divide spoken sentence into individual words							
Produce rhyming words and distinguish rhyming words from nonrhyming words							
Identify, segment, and combine syllables within spoken words							
Identify and isolate the initial and final sound of a spoken word							
Add, delete, or change sounds to change words (such as *cow* to *how*, *pan* to *fan*)							
Blend sounds to make spoken words							
Segment one-syllable spoken words into individual phonemes							
PHONICS AND DECODING							
Alphabetic principle: Letter/sound correspondence	✓	✓	✓				
Blending CVC words	✓	✓					
Segmenting CVC words	✓						
Blending CVC, CVCe, CCVC, CVCC, CVVC words	✓	✓	✓				
Segmenting CVC, CVCe, CCVC, CVCC, CVVC words	✓	✓	✓				
Initial and final consonants: /n/n, /d/d, /s/s, /m/m, /t/t, /k/c, /f/f, /r/r, /p/p, /l/l, /k/k, /g/g, /b/b, /h/h, /w/w, /v/v, /ks/x, /kw/qu, /j/j, /y/y, /z/z	✓	✓					
Initial and medial short vowels: *a, i, u, o, e*	✓	✓	✓				
Long vowels: *a-e, i-e, o-e, u-e* (vowel-consonant-e)		✓	✓				
Long vowels, including *ay, ai; e, ee, ie, ea; o, oa, oe, ow; i, y, igh*		✓	✓				
Consonant Digraphs: *sh, th, ch, wh*		✓					
Consonant Blends: continuant/continuant, including *sl, sm, sn, fl, fr, ll, ss, ff*		✓					
Consonant Blends: continuant/stop, including *st, sk, sp, ng, nt, nd, mp, ft*		✓					
Consonant Blends: stop/continuant, including *tr, pr, pl, cr, tw*		✓					
Variant vowels: including /ü/*oo*; /ô/*a, aw, au*; /ü/*ue, ew*		✓	✓				
Diphthongs, including /ou/*ou, ow*; /oi/*oi, oy*		✓	✓				
r-controlled vowels, including /âr/*are*; /ôr/*or, ore*; /îr/*ear*			✓				
Soft *c* and soft *g*			✓				
nk		✓	✓				
Consonant Digraphs: *ck*	✓	✓					
Consonant Digraphs: *ph, tch, ch*			✓				
Short *e*: *ea*			✓				
Long *e*: *y, ey*			✓				
/ü/*oo*		✓	✓				
/är/*ar*; /ûr/*ir, ur, er*		✓	✓				
Silent letters: including *l, b, k, w, g, h, gh*			✓				
Schwa: /ər/*er*; /ən/*en*; /əl/*le*;			✓				
Reading/identifying multisyllabic words		✓	✓				

✓ Tested Skill

Tinted panels show skills, strategies, and other teaching opportunities

Reading: Vocabulary/Word Identification

WORD STRUCTURE	K	1	2	3	4	5	6
Common spelling patterns							
Syllable patterns							
Plurals		✓					
Possessives		✓					
Contractions		✓					
Root, or base, words and inflectional endings (*-s, -es, -ed, -ing*)		✓	✓	✓		✓	
Compound words			✓	✓	✓	✓	✓
Prefixes and suffixes (such as *un-, re-, dis-, non-; -ly, -y, -ful, -able, -tion*)				✓	✓	✓	✓
Root words and derivational endings				✓	✓	✓	✓
WORD MEANING							
Develop vocabulary through concrete experiences							
Develop vocabulary through selections read aloud							
Develop vocabulary through reading							
Cueing systems: syntactic, semantic, phonetic							
Context clues, including semantic clues (word meaning), syntactical clues (word order), and phonetic clues	✓	✓	✓	✓	✓	✓	✓
High-frequency words (such as *the, a, an, and, said, was, where, is*)							
Identify words that name persons, places, things, and actions							
Automatic reading of regular and irregular words							
Use resources and references (dictionary, glossary, thesaurus, synonym finder, technology and software, and context)							
Synonyms and antonyms			✓	✓	✓	✓	✓
Multiple-meaning words			✓	✓	✓	✓	✓
Figurative language			✓	✓	✓	✓	✓
Decode derivatives (root words, such as *like, pay, happy* with affixes, such as *dis-, pre-, un-*)							
Systematic study of words across content areas and in current events							
Locate meanings, pronunciations, and derivations (including dictionaries, glossaries, and other sources)							
Denotation and connotation							✓
Word origins as aid to understanding historical influences on English word meanings							
Homophones, homographs							
Analogies							✓
Idioms							

Reading: Comprehension

PREREADING STRATEGIES	K	1	2	3	4	5	6
Preview and predict							
Use prior knowledge							
Establish and adjust purposes for reading							
Build background							
MONITORING STRATEGIES							
Adjust reading rate							
Reread, search for clues, ask questions, ask for help							
Visualize							
Read a portion aloud, use reference aids							
Use decoding and vocabulary strategies							
Paraphrase							
Create story maps, diagrams, charts, story props to help comprehend, analyze, synthesize and evaluate texts							

(continued on next page)

✓ Tested Skill

Tinted panels show skills, strategies, and other teaching opportunities

(Reading: Comprehension continued)

SKILLS AND STRATEGIES	K	1	2	3	4	5	6
Recall story details	✓						
Use illustrations	✓	✓					
Distinguish reality and fantasy	✓	✓	✓				
Classify and categorize	✓						
Make predictions	✓	✓	✓	✓	✓	✓	✓
Recognize sequence of events (tell or act out)	✓	✓	✓	✓	✓	✓	✓
Recognize cause and effect		✓	✓	✓	✓	✓	✓
Compare and contrast	✓	✓	✓	✓	✓	✓	✓
Summarize	✓	✓	✓	✓	✓	✓	✓
Make and explain inferences		✓	✓	✓	✓	✓	✓
Draw conclusions		✓	✓	✓	✓	✓	✓
Distinguish important and unimportant information				✓	✓	✓	✓
Recognize main idea and supporting details	✓	✓	✓	✓	✓	✓	✓
Form conclusions or generalizations and support with evidence from text			✓	✓	✓	✓	✓
Distinguish fact and opinion (including news stories and advertisements)				✓	✓	✓	✓
Recognize problem and solution			✓	✓	✓	✓	✓
Recognize steps in a process		✓	✓	✓	✓	✓	✓
Make judgments and decisions				✓	✓	✓	✓
Distinguish fact and nonfact				✓	✓	✓	✓
Recognize techniques of persuasion and propaganda							✓
Evaluate evidence and sources of information							✓
Identify similarities and differences across texts (including topics, characters, problems, themes, treatment, scope, or organization)							
Practice various questions and tasks (test-like comprehension questions)							
Paraphrase and summarize to recall, inform, and organize							
Answer various types of questions (open-ended, literal, interpretative, test-like such as true-false, multiple choice, short-answer)							
Use study strategies to learn and recall (preview, question, reread, and record)							

LITERARY RESPONSE	K	1	2	3	4	5	6
Listen to stories being read aloud							
React, speculate, join in, read along when predictable and patterned selections are read aloud							
Respond through talk, movement, music, art, drama, and writing to a variety of stories and poems							
Show understanding through writing, illustrating, developing demonstrations, and using technology							
Connect ideas and themes across texts							
Support responses by referring to relevant aspects of text and own experiences							
Offer observations, make connections, speculate, interpret, and raise questions in response to texts							
Interpret text ideas through journal writing, discussion, enactment, and media							

TEXT STRUCTURE/LITERARY CONCEPTS	K	1	2	3	4	5	6
Distinguish forms of texts and the functions they serve (lists, newsletters, signs)							
Understand story structure							
Identify narrative (for entertainment) and expository (for information)							
Distinguish fiction from nonfiction, including fact and fantasy							
Understand literary forms (stories, poems, plays, and informational books)							
Understand literary terms by distinguishing between roles of author and illustrator							
Understand title, author, and illustrator across a variety of texts							
Analyze character, character's point of view, plot, setting, style, tone, mood		✓	✓	✓	✓	✓	✓
Compare communication in different forms							
Understand terms such as *title, author, illustrator, playwright, theater, stage, act, dialogue,* and *scene*							
Recognize stories, poems, myths, folktales, fables, tall tales, limericks, plays, biographies, and autobiographies							
Judge internal logic of story text							
Recognize that authors organize information in specific ways							
Identify texts to inform, influence, express, or entertain							
Describe how author's point of view affects text				✓	✓	✓	✓
Recognize biography, historical fiction, realistic fiction, modern fantasy, informational texts, and poetry							
Analyze ways authors present ideas (cause/effect, compare/contrast, inductively, deductively, chronologically)							
Recognize flashback, foreshadowing, symbolism							

(continued on next page)

☑ Tested Skill

▢ Tinted panels show skills, strategies, and other teaching opportunities

(Reading: Comprehension continued)

VARIETY OF TEXT	K	1	2	3	4	5	6
Read a variety of genres							
Use informational texts to acquire information							
Read for a variety of purposes							
Select varied sources when reading for information or pleasure							
FLUENCY							
Read regularly in independent-level and instructional-level materials							
Read orally with fluency from familiar texts							
Self-select independent-level reading							
Read silently for increasing periods of time							
Demonstrate characteristics of fluent and effective reading							
Adjust reading rate to purpose							
Read aloud in selected texts, showing understanding of text and engaging the listener							
CULTURES							
Connect own experience with culture of others							
Compare experiences of characters across cultures							
Articulate and discuss themes and connections that cross cultures							
CRITICAL THINKING							
Experiences (comprehend, apply, analyze, synthesize, evaluate)							
Make connections (comprehend, apply, analyze, synthesize, evaluate)							
Expression (comprehend, apply, analyze, synthesize, evaluate)							
Inquiry (comprehend, apply, analyze, synthesize, evaluate)							
Problem solving (comprehend, apply, analyze, synthesize, evaluate)							
Making decisions (comprehend, apply, analyze, synthesize, evaluate)							

Study Skills

INQUIRY/RESEARCH	K	1	2	3	4	5	6
Follow directions							
Use alphabetical order							
Identify/frame questions for research							
Obtain, organize, and summarize information: classify, take notes, outline							
Evaluate research and raise new questions							
Use technology to present information in various formats							
Follow accepted formats for writing research, including documenting sources							
Use test-taking strategies							
Use text organizers (book cover; title page—title, author, illustrator; contents; headings; glossary; index)		✓	✓	✓	✓	✓	✓
Use graphic aids, including maps, diagrams, charts, graphs		✓	✓	✓	✓	✓	✓
Read and interpret varied texts including environmental print, signs, lists, encyclopedia, dictionary, glossary, newspaper, advertisement, magazine, calendar, directions, floor plans		✓	✓	✓	✓	✓	✓
Use reference sources, such as glossary, dictionary, encyclopedia, telephone directory, technology resources		✓	✓	✓	✓	✓	✓
Recognize Library/Media center resources, such as computerized references; catalog search—subject, author, title; encyclopedia index		✓	✓	✓	✓	✓	✓

Writing

☑ Tested Skill

Tinted panels show skills, strategies, and other teaching opportunities

MODES AND FORMS	K	1	2	3	4	5	6
Interactive writing							
Personal narrative (Expressive narrative)			✓	✓	✓	✓	✓
Writing that compares (Informative classificatory)			✓	✓	✓	✓	✓
Explanatory writing (Informative narrative)		✓	✓	✓	✓	✓	✓
Persuasive writing (Persuasive descriptive)			✓	✓	✓	✓	✓
Writing a story		✓	✓	✓	✓	✓	✓
Expository writing		✓	✓	✓	✓	✓	✓
Write using a variety of formats, such as advertisement, autobiography, biography, book report/report, comparison-contrast, critique/review/editorial, description, essay, how-to, interview, invitation, journal/log/notes, message/list, paragraph/multi-paragraph composition, picture book, play (scene), poem/rhyme, story, summary, note, letter							
PURPOSES/AUDIENCES							
Dictate messages such as news and stories for others to write							
Write labels, notes, and captions for illustrations, possessions, charts, and centers							
Write to record, to discover and develop ideas, to inform, to influence, to entertain							
Exhibit an identifiable voice in personal narratives and stories							
Use literary devices (suspense, dialogue, and figurative language)							
Produce written texts by organizing ideas, using effective transitions, and choosing precise wording							
PROCESSES							
Generate ideas for self-selected and assigned topics using prewriting strategies							
Develop drafts							
Revise drafts for varied purposes, elaborate ideas							
Edit for appropriate grammar, spelling, punctuation, and features of polished writings							
Proofread own writing and that of others							
Bring pieces to final form and "publish" them for audiences							
Use technology to compose text							
Select and use reference materials and resources for writing, revising, and editing final drafts							
SPELLING							
Spell own name and write high-frequency words							
Words with short vowels (including CVC and one-syllable words with blends CCVC, CVCC, CCVCC)							
Words with long vowels (including CVCe)							
Words with digraphs, blends, consonant clusters, double consonants							
Words with diphthongs							
Words with variant vowels							
Words with r-controlled vowels							
Words with /ər/, /əl/, and /ən/							
Words with silent letters							
Words with soft *c* and soft *g*							
Inflectional endings (including plurals and past tense and words that drop the final *e* when adding *-ing*, *-ed*)							
Compound words							
Contractions							
Homonyms							
Suffixes including *-able, -ly,* or *-less,* and prefixes including *dis-, re-, pre-,* or *un-*							
Spell words ending in *-tion* and *-sion,* such as *station* and *procession*							
Accurate spelling of root or base words							
Orthographic patterns and rules such as *keep/can; sack/book; out/now; oil/toy; match/speech; ledge/cage;* consonant doubling, dropping *e,* changing *y* to *i*							
Multisyllabic words using regularly spelled phonogram patterns							
Syllable patterns (including closed, open, syllable boundary patterns)							
Synonyms and antonyms							
Words from Social Studies, Science, Math, and Physical Education							
Words derived from other languages and cultures							
Use resources to find correct spellings, synonyms, and replacement words							
Use conventional spelling of familiar words in writing assignments							
Spell accurately in final drafts							

(continued on next page)

☑ Tested Skill

Tinted panels show skills, strategies, and other teaching opportunities

(Writing continued)

GRAMMAR AND USAGE	K	1	2	3	4	5	6
Understand sentence concepts (word order, statements, questions, exclamations, commands)							
Recognize complete and incomplete sentences							
Nouns (common; proper; singular; plural; irregular plural; possessives)							
Verbs (action; helping; linking; irregular)							
Verb tense (present, past, future, perfect, and progressive)							
Pronouns (possessive, subject and object, pronoun-verb agreement)							
Use objective case pronouns accurately							
Adjectives							
Adverbs that tell how, when, where							
Subjects, predicates							
Subject-verb agreement							
Sentence combining							
Recognize sentence structure (simple, compound, complex)							
Synonyms and antonyms							
Contractions							
Conjunctions							
Prepositions and prepositional phrases							
PENMANSHIP							
Write each letter of alphabet (capital and lowercase) using correct formation, appropriate size and spacing							
Write own name and other important words							
Use phonological knowledge to map sounds to letters to write messages							
Write messages that move left to right, top to bottom							
Gain increasing control of penmanship, pencil grip, paper position, beginning stroke							
Use word and letter spacing and margins to make messages readable							
Write legibly by selecting cursive or manuscript as appropriate							
MECHANICS							
Use capitalization in sentences, proper nouns, titles, abbreviations and the pronoun *I*							
Use end marks correctly (period, question mark, exclamation point)							
Use commas (in dates, in addresses, in a series, in letters, in direct address)							
Use apostrophes in contractions and possessives							
Use quotation marks							
Use hyphens, semicolons, colons							
EVALUATION							
Identify the most effective features of a piece of writing using class/teacher generated criteria							
Respond constructively to others' writing							
Determine how his/her own writing achieves its purpose							
Use published pieces as models for writing							
Review own written work to monitor growth as writer							

For more detailed scope and sequence including page numbers and additional phonics information, see McGraw-Hill Reading Program scope and sequence (K-6)

Index

Scoring Chart

The Scoring Chart is provided for your convenience in grading your students' work.

- Find the column that shows the total number of items.
- Find the row that matches the number of items answered correctly.
- The intersection of the two rows provides the percentage score.

TOTAL NUMBER OF ITEMS

NUMBER CORRECT	1	2	3	4	5	6	7	8	9	10	11	12	13	14	15	16	17	18	19	20	21	22	23	24	25	26	27	28	29	30
1	100	50	33	25	20	17	14	13	11	10	9	8	8	7	7	6	6	6	5	5	5	5	4	4	4	4	4	4	3	3
2		100	66	50	40	33	29	25	22	20	18	17	15	14	13	13	12	11	11	10	10	9	9	8	8	8	7	7	7	7
3			100	75	60	50	43	38	33	30	27	25	23	21	20	19	18	17	16	15	14	14	13	13	12	12	11	11	10	10
4				100	80	67	57	50	44	40	36	33	31	29	27	25	24	22	21	20	19	18	17	17	16	15	15	14	14	13
5					100	83	71	63	56	50	45	42	38	36	33	31	29	28	26	25	24	23	22	21	20	19	19	18	17	17
6						100	86	75	67	60	55	50	46	43	40	38	35	33	32	30	29	27	26	25	24	23	22	21	21	20
7							100	88	78	70	64	58	54	50	47	44	41	39	37	35	33	32	30	29	28	27	26	25	24	23
8								100	89	80	73	67	62	57	53	50	47	44	42	40	38	36	35	33	32	31	30	29	28	27
9									100	90	82	75	69	64	60	56	53	50	47	45	43	41	39	38	36	35	33	32	31	30
10										100	91	83	77	71	67	63	59	56	53	50	48	45	43	42	40	38	37	36	34	33
11											100	92	85	79	73	69	65	61	58	55	52	50	48	46	44	42	41	39	38	37
12												100	92	86	80	75	71	67	63	60	57	55	52	50	48	46	44	43	41	40
13													100	93	87	81	76	72	68	65	62	59	57	54	52	50	48	46	45	43
14														100	93	88	82	78	74	70	67	64	61	58	56	54	52	50	48	47
15															100	94	88	83	79	75	71	68	65	63	60	58	56	54	52	50
16																100	94	89	84	80	76	73	70	67	64	62	59	57	55	53
17																	100	94	89	85	81	77	74	71	68	65	63	61	59	57
18																		100	95	90	86	82	78	75	72	69	67	64	62	60
19																			100	95	90	86	83	79	76	73	70	68	66	63
20																				100	95	91	87	83	80	77	74	71	69	67
21																					100	95	91	88	84	81	78	75	72	70
22																						100	96	92	88	85	81	79	76	73
23																							100	96	92	88	85	82	79	77
24																								100	96	92	89	86	83	80
25																									100	96	93	89	86	83
26																										100	96	93	90	87
27																											100	96	93	90
28																												100	97	93
29																													100	97
30																														100

Explanatory Writing: Writing a How-to Piece

Scoring Rubric: 6-Trait Writing

6. Exceptional	5. Excellent	4. Good	3. Fair	2. Poor	1. Unsatisfactory
• **Ideas & Content** crafts an elaborately-detailed how-to process that enables a reader to carry out a project. • **Organization** gives clear instructions, in a well-planned logical time sequence that moves a reader easily through the steps. • **Voice** shows originality, and deep involvement with the topic; matches a distinct personal style to the writing purpose and audience. • **Word Choice** makes thoughtful, imaginative use of challenging and everyday language in a natural way; advanced words create a striking picture of a how-to process. • **Sentence Fluency** crafts varied simple and complex sentences that flow in a smooth rhythm; may experiment effectively with fragments or other devices. • **Conventions** is skilled in most writing conventions; proper use of the rules of English enhances clarity and style; editing is largely unnecessary.	• **Ideas & Content** crafts a cohesive, focused how-to process that shows a reader how to carry out a project. • **Organization** well-planned process strategy in a time sequence that moves a reader logically through the steps from beginning to ending. • **Voice** shows originality and strong involvement with the topic; skillfully matches personal style to the purpose and audience. • **Word Choice** makes imaginative use of accurate, specific language; experiments with new words, or uses everyday words in a new way. • **Sentence Fluency** crafts effective simple and complex sentences that flow naturally; a variety of lengths, beginnings, and patterns fit together. • **Conventions** is skilled in a wide range of writing conventions; proper use of the rules of English enhances clarity and style; editing is largely unnecessary.	• **Ideas & Content** presents a solid, clear explanation of a project, with details that help convey a step-by-step process to the reader. • **Organization** gives process instructions in a logical sequence; has a clear beginning and ending; steps and details are tied together. • **Voice** attempts to convey an authentic personal touch to the reader; shows an involvement with the topic. • **Word Choice** communicates the main idea, and may experiment with both new and everyday words to make the process clear. • **Sentence Fluency** crafts careful, easy-to-follow sentences; sentences vary in length, beginnings, and patterns. • **Conventions** may make some errors in spelling, capitalization, punctuation, or usage which do not interfere with understanding the text; some editing is needed.	• **Ideas & Content** attempts to explain a project; incorporates some details to elaborate on a step-by-step process. • **Organization** attempts to give instructions, but may have trouble keeping steps in order; has a beginning and ending, but may use few time-order words and transitions. • **Voice** may not show consistent involvement with the topic; message comes across in a predictable way. • **Word Choice** does not experiment with new words or explore everyday words in a fresh way; may use words that do not fit the process. • **Sentence Fluency** constructs readable sentences, but may show limited variety in lengths and patterns; some rereading may be required to follow the meaning; may run on or use fragments that don't work. • **Conventions** makes enough noticeable errors to interfere with a consistently smooth reading of the text; significant editing is needed.	• **Ideas & Content** may have little control of explaining a how-to project; details may be few, repeated, or inaccurate. • **Organization** lacks a clear structure; steps may be vague or disorganized; few explicit connections are made between steps or details. • **Voice** is not very involved in sharing ideas with a reader; writing may be lifeless, with no sense of who is behind the words. • **Word Choice** does not use colorful words that convey a clear picture of a process; some words may detract from the meaning or impact of the text. • **Sentence Fluency** sentences may be rambling, awkward, or choppy; patterns are similar or monotonous; text may be hard to follow or read aloud. • **Conventions** makes frequent errors in spelling, word choice, punctuation, and usage; sentence structures may be confused; the piece is difficult to read, and requires extensive editing.	• **Ideas & Content** does not explain a how-to process; writing may go off in several directions, without a sense of purpose. • **Organization** extreme lack of organization interferes with comprehension of the process; steps, if presented, are incomplete, irrelevant, or unfocused. • **Voice** does not address an audience at all; does not have a grasp of conveying a personal voice or style. • **Word Choice** uses words that do not fit the process, or are confusing to the reader. • **Sentence Fluency** constructs incomplete, rambling, or confusing sentences; writer may not grasp how words and sentences fit together; text is hard to follow and read aloud. • **Conventions** makes severe errors in most or all conventions; spelling errors may make it hard to guess what words are meant; some parts of the text are impossible to follow or understand.

0: This piece is either blank, or fails to respond to the writing task. The topic is not addressed, or the student simply paraphrases the prompt. The response may be illegible or incoherent.

Explanatory Writing: Writing a How-to Piece

8-Point Writing Rubric

8	7	6	5	4	3	2	1
The writer • has crafted an outstanding informational piece that would enable a reader to accurately reproduce a project. • thoroughly details step-by-step instructions for the project described. • consistently uses time-order words to represent a logical progression in the process or project. • introduces the project or process in an engaging, innovative way. • develops a unique personal voice to add originality and unique flavor to the process.	The writer • has presented an exceptional piece of informational writing that would help a reader reproduce the project. • has arranged steps in logical sequence. • uses many time-order words to help the reader follow the process. • introduces the project clearly and concisely. • communicates a strong personal voice to add interest to the process.	The writer • has presented a strong piece of informational writing that could enable the reader to reproduce most of the project. • has arranged most steps in logical sequence. • often uses time-order words to help the reader follow the process. • presents a good opening statement. • communicates a clear personal voice throughout most of the piece.	The writer • has clearly presented a how-to piece. • includes most of the important steps in the process described, though some information may be missing or not thoroughly elaborated. • uses an adequate number of time-order words to move the process forward. • makes some attempt to capture the reader's interest in the opening sentence. • may use humor or other narrative devices to add a personal touch to the writing.	The writer • has attempted to craft a how-to piece. • includes many of the important steps in the process, but omits others. Some of the steps may be out of order. • uses some time-order words to sequence the process. There may be a few digressions or irrelevant details included in the process. • may not develop an adequate opening sentence. • may not articulate a clear, unique personal voice.	The writer • attempts to craft a project explanation, but chooses a focus that is either too narrow or too broad. • demonstrates difficulty in keeping process steps in order. • uses few time-order words and transitions between steps. • may not develop an opening sentence that clearly explains the process to be shared. • exhibits some problems with language conventions that may somewhat detract from the reader's understanding.	The writer • has inadequately crafted a how-to process. • may have developed some steps in the project process, but they are markedly disorganized or lacking in detail. • uses few, if any, time-order words, and communicates an insufficient sense of process sequence. • exhibits overall problems with grammar, usage, and mechanics.	The writer • has failed to present a how-to process. • presents few, if any, distinct steps in the process. • uses no time-order words or transitions. • does not present an introduction stating the intention of the piece. • exhibits difficulties with language conventions severe enough to seriously impair readability of the document.

0: This piece is either blank, or fails to respond to the writing task. The topic is not addressed, or the student simply paraphrases the prompt. The response may be illegible or incoherent.

Notes

Notes

Notes

Notes

Notes

Notes

Notes

Notes

Notes

Notes